SUN SIGN, MOON SIGN

To our parents, Cordelia, John, Jack and Joyce
To our children Natasha, Giles and Alexander
To Grant Lewi who lit the way

SUN SIGN, MOON SIGN

Discover the Key to Your Unique Personality through
the 144 Sun, Moon Combinations

CHARLES HARVEY & SUZI HARVEY

Thorsons
An Imprint of HarperCollins*Publishers*

Thorsons
An Imprint of HarperCollins*Publishers*
77–85 Fulham Palace Road,
Hammersmith, London W6 8JB
1160 Battery Street,
San Francisco, California 94111–1213

Published by Aquarian 1994
5 7 9 10 8 6

© Charles & Suzi Harvey 1994

Charles & Suzi Harvey assert the moral right to
be identified as the authors of this work

A catalogue record for this book is
available from the British Library

ISBN 0 85538 159 1

Typeset by Harper Phototypesetters Limited
Northampton, England
Printed in Great Britain by
Clays Ltd, St Ives plc

CONTENTS

ACKNOWLEDGEMENTS

This book could not have been written without the help of a large number of people. We are especially grateful to the following:

Michael Erlewine of Matrix software for his unstinting generosity in supplying us with copies of his superb Compact Data program and data collections without which much of the research on this book would have been rendered impossible or at least impossibly tedious; likewise to Tom Bridges and Matrix Software for supplying the Tables of Sun and Moon ingresses on pages 474–561; to Tom Shanks for permission to reproduce the Tables of Summer Time in Britain on pages 562–3 from his definitive *The International Atlas*; to Maurice Charvet of CEDRA for help and advice with data on disc; to Michael Harding for supplying us with print-out of Sun–Moon combinations from Lee Lehman's data base collection; to Lee Lehman and Margaret Meister of NCGR for supplying hard-to-find data; to the authors of the many and various collections of data now available, and especially to the late Michel Gauquelin and Françoise Gauquelin for their incomparable volumes; to Jacques Lescaut for his 16-volume *Encyclopaedia of Birth Data*; to Lois Rodden for her five pioneering volumes of *Astro-Data*; to Hans Hinrich Taeger for his magnificent three-volume *Horoskope Lexicon*; and to the Astrological Association for use of their fine data collection; to our father, Dr John Harvey, for keeping us supplied with the obituaries from the *Daily Telegraph*; to the editors of the *Independent* Gazette page for the sustained excellence of their obituary columns which are a gold mine of contemporary biography; to Jane Lee for drawing attention to the relationship between the elements and time; to the individuals who have read through their own particular combinations and made comments; to all our friends, colleagues, students and acquaintances who have indulged both our Moon in Aquarius 'people watching' propensities by supplying their own data;

to Erica Smith of Thorsons for all her help, encouragement, patience and persistent cajoling which have so much helped this book into the sunlight and moonlight and to Michele Turney for her superb editorial skills and thorough questioning which helped make the book more understandable; to Rosemary Fost for all her sustained support and encouragement; to Giles and Alexander for understanding that we sometimes could not go to the park but 'had to work on the book'.

Our grateful thanks to readers who have pointed out various errata and most especially to David Fisher, past Data Section Officer of the Astrological Association, for his detailed checking of all the data and for clearing up doubts and anomalies.

AUTHORS' NOTE

For convenience sake, and to make for easier reading, we have used the masculine gender pronoun throughout the text (most of the time). Astrology emphasizes through the Sun and Moon that we all contain both male and female attitudes and approaches to life.

Part One

INTRODUCTION

Chapter One

GETTING THE
MOST FROM THIS BOOK

———— • ————

To thine own self be true
WILLIAM SHAKESPEARE

Resolve to be thyself; and know,
that he who finds himself, loses his misery
MATTHEW ARNOLD

MAKING A FILM OF YOUR LIFE

Imagine a cinema centre. It is showing two films of your life. On one screen *Triumph* is being shown; on another screen, *Tragedy*. Each of us has the possibilities for both scenarios within us. Most of us will experience something of each.

The difference between success and failure in life ultimately comes down to self-understanding. Within you are many different gifts, conflicting wishes and pressures, obligations and ambitions. The more you are able to recognize and work with your different sides and tendencies, the more you are likely to turn tragedy into triumph, rather than snatch defeat from the jaws of victory.

We feel that the first step in recognizing and reconciling these different 'selves' inside you is getting to know *intimately* not only your Sun sign but your Moon sign as well – and how they create a lively, sometimes problematic, but always interesting dialogue within you. And what we offer you in these pages is a series of 'film clips' showing some of the main features of the 144 most important Sun–Moon story lines. One of these is *yours*. It describes the essential personality of two of the most important and central characters in the drama of your life.

3

These characters, as represented by the sign positions of the Sun and Moon at your birth, are the heart and soul of your story. The better you can get to know them the more will you be able to understand, and even consciously collaborate on, the script of your life. Once you can comprehend the innate contradictions, you can turn them to good use – a bit like adjusting the seasoning in a soufflé. You will discover it is a good recipe, a fine script – do not fight it; enjoy it!

We have tried to give you a taste of the contrasting pressures and inner dilemmas that each combination is most likely to experience, and to show how these different aspects of you can work positively together. You will not agree with everything you find here (unless you are the most watery of Water types), but if these profiles encourage you to reflect more on the full-length film of your life and how you can give it the best performance and production you can, we will be more than happy.

FINDING OUT YOUR SUN–MOON COMBINATION

If you have not had your personal birth chart drawn up, and do not know your Sun–Moon combination, Part 3 gives instructions and tables for finding the sign position of your Sun and Moon.

If you do not know your time of birth and there is uncertainty as to which sign your Sun and/or Moon is in, you will need to read the two different possible combinations. This should help you to decide which is the more likely position and so narrow down the likely time of your birth. Care is needed with this method, however, as other chart factors may be involved of which you are unaware. If your decision is between a Cancer and Leo Moon, for example, you may decide your Moon is in Cancer, yet this could be because your Rising Sign is in Cancer.

THE LAYOUT OF EACH COMBINATION

We have given our findings and interpretations for each Sun–Moon combination under the following main sections:
• quotations
• themes
• main text

- relationships
- your greatest strengths
- your greatest weaknesses
- images for integration
- famous people with this combination

Some details about the contents of each of these sections follows.

The Quotations – In Their Own Words

Each one of us views the world from a different place and in a different way. What we notice and what interests us is very much conditioned by our birth chart, and not least by our Sun and Moon positions. So if we want to understand a combination more fully we cannot do better than to listen to the ideas and observations of those who have lived a lifetime with that particular Sun–Moon combination.

In consequence, we have started each Sun–Moon entry with quotations from individuals who were born with that particular combination. These have been chosen to illustrate, directly or indirectly, some of the essential qualities of that particular type in their own words.

We regret the fact that, despite our best efforts, there are many more quotes from men than women in this book. This is a direct reflection of the ratio of eminent men to women in our society over the centuries, which has inevitably resulted in a very strong bias towards quotes from men being available in the many collections and dictionaries of quotations. For somewhat different reasons, certain categories of people, for example writers and philosophers, tend to be a more fruiful source of telling quotes than, say, sportspeople or those working in business or the helping professions. This is not surprising. Writers and thinkers spend their time reflecting on the nature of the human condition and our relationship to the world, whilst, with obvious exceptions, people engaged in sport, commerce and caring for others tend to be less immediately engaged in such reflections.

In doing our research for this book we usually found far more quotes than we could possibly use for certain of the combinations, whilst it was often difficult to find suitable, pithy observations from other soli-lunar types. This is not surprising. Certain combinations – such as the Sun in Gemini, Moon in Aquarius – were alive with wit and wisdom, whilst quotes were relatively thinner on the ground for other combinations. Even though some of these combinations are deeply reflective – such as those with both Sun and Moon in Scorpio – they seem to be less naturally verbally articulate.

Themes

This paragraph gives a very brief summary of some of the main issues of the combination, starting with the element combination of the Sun and Moon. The first element given is the Sun's; the second element that of the Moon. To avoid constant repetition and to save space, we have given further details about each of the 10 element combinations, including some observations about compatibility with other types, in Chapter 3.

The Main Text

This main essay identifies and discusses what we have found to be the main issues for the combination. We have resisted the temptation to break this text up into formal sections. Each combination is usually presented in a somewhat different way as dictated by the combination itself and by the material we have available. We have usually given suggestions about the types of work which are likely to be especially congenial to the combination, though, as we have noted elsewhere, we do not see these combinations as a clear indication to vocation, but much more as indications of the approach and attitudes that the type will bring to what they do. The one area we have separated out is *Relationships*, as these are so central to what the Sun and Moon combination in the chart is all about.

Your Greatest Strengths

This is a summary of what seem from our research to be some of the more creative possibilities of the combination. Other factors in your full birth chart will suggest other strengths and creative potential, so you should not be dismayed if your favourite virtue is not mentioned!

Your Greatest Weaknesses

Here we pull no punches. This section attempts to identify some of the greatest defects and life problems the combination can produce. We are not saying you are like this (though others may agree!), but these are issues that you would do well to note. As with your virtues, your chart as a whole may suggest more obvious blemishes to your otherwise perfect self!

Images for Integration

These may not obviously hit you between the eyes the first time you read them. They are intended to be reflected upon. Sometimes we have given just one image, more often two, and sometimes more when the very different possibilities of a particular combination seem to require it. These images are intended to evoke what we see to be some of the essential issues of the combination in question, and to get you thinking. If an image does not speak to you, put it to the back of your mind. One day when you are wrestling with some problem or theme that repeats itself in your life, the penny could drop.

Since this is a book rather than a video we have usually given these images as 'word pictures'. But we could equally well have used pictures, cartoons, sculptures, music, landscapes and other symbolic expressions of these ideas. Occasionally, where works of art and music are very well known or especially appropriate, we have used these. Under Sagittarius–Cancer, for example, you will find Jimi Hendrix's legendary Woodstock version of *The Star Spangled Banner*. Its mixture of emotional patriotism (Cancer) and raw, fiery, exuberant energy and brilliance (Sagittarius) as he imitates the 'rockets' red glare, the bombs bursting in air' on his guitar, speak volumes about this combination. In a different vein, under Gemini–Libra you will find Elgar's *Enigma Variations*. The composer dedicated it 'to my friends within'. Not only does Elgar's very concept evoke the synthesis of these signs, but if you listen to the sheer range of musical experience Elgar derives from his one simple theme you will arrive at a deeper, inner, understanding of this combination. Likewise under Scorpio–Sagittarius we have Picasso's painting *Guernica*. To view its tortured images conveys to us a moral statement (Sagittarius) about the destruction and iniquities of war (negative Scorpio) which goes to the heart of the preoccupations of this Sun–Moon combination.

The Famous People

This book grew from our study of peoples' lives. You will find that one of the most fruitful ways of finding out more about the subtleties, dilemmas and creative possibilities of a specific Sun–Moon combination is to study the biographies and autobiographies of famous individuals who have that combination. The list of celebrities that are given at the end of each entry is a selection of some of the better-known contemporary and historical individuals whom we have recorded as being born with that particular Sun–Moon pairing.

We have made every effort to check on the accuracy of the charts we have used for these individuals, but inevitably some errors may have crept in. If you have reason to suppose that any of the people given under a combination are there under false pretences, we would be pleased to hear from you.

While the Sun–Moon combination can give some clues and indications as to career choice, it will be found more useful to consider the famous people listed in terms of the *kind of approach* they had to their particular work, the *ideas and themes* which have engaged them, and the *general flavour* of their lives. So, for example, to understand the acute paradox of the combination of clinical detachment and intense passion of those born with Sun in Aquarius and Moon in Scorpio, one can learn volumes by looking at the output of the writer Alex Comfort. The very titles of Comfort's best sellers – *Sex in Society* and *The Joy of Sex: A Gourmet's Guide to Love Making* – encapsulate a creative synthesis of these very different approaches to life. His many other books, plays, poetry, essays and novels draw upon similar themes, with the clash between freedom and possessiveness, between intellect and emotions, between personal liberty and social obligations. His work is often expressed in a pungent blend of Aquarian–Scorpio humour as in *Come out to Play*, his satirical fantasy about a biologist deeply learned in the knowledge of human mating habits.

It would be wrong to conclude from this example that all Aquarius–Scorpios will be writers, or that they will all be preoccupied with understanding their relationship to sex (though many will be!). But what we can conclude from Comfort's life, and many other cases, it that the creative pivot around which this Sun–Moon combination revolves is the conflict between mind and emotion. By attempting to reconcile the fundamental tension between a need to see the world through a strongly developed rational intellect and the irrational intensity of their emotional life, this type finds their own unique creativity.

If you take some time out to study the lives, accomplishments and aspirations of those people we have listed, you can gradually build up a picture of how other people have used your own particular combination creatively, how they have reconciled conflicting pressures, and indeed where their dilemmas have tripped them up. To illustrate this further, let us take a brief look at the different lives of all the people listed under Sun Scorpio–Moon Pisces (see page 329).

Scorpio and Pisces are both Water signs. Water is the element (see Chapter 3) that emphasizes the feelings and emotions and a general sensitivity to, and understanding of, other people's needs and experience. Hence such types often have a strong attraction towards the caring professions and other occupations that demand emotional sensitivity, such as the theatre and creative writing. Even though all Water signs are theoretically highly compatible, the intense, self-controlled, purposeful and ambitious Scorpio is a very different kettle of crustaceans from the free-flowing, adaptable, often self-sacrificing and addictive sign of the fishes, and this combination of signs can experience as much inner conflict as any other. A consideration of our list reveals the wide variations of expression possible from this one combination, yet the common themes they tend to share.

Hilary Clinton

A lawyer by training and one of the US's most influential First Ladies. But forget her profession – what is she like? She has been described alternately as a Lady Macbeth and a Florence Nightingale. The astrological truth is that she is both. Sun Scorpios are naturally forceful and ambitious, but Moon in Pisces gives a softer, caring concern for the world, and especially the underdog. So it is that her solar public image can be typically Scorpionic – stiff, icy, aloof – whilst in private she can be warm and funny, with the classic Piscean flair for mimicry.

In her work in the White House, as in her earlier legal practice, it is clear that Hilary Clinton really cares (Pisces) passionately (Scorpio) about what she does. She is not only concerned with personal power (Scorpio), but is guided by a natural concern and compassion (Moon Pisces) for the sick, addicted, unemployed, underprivileged and the underclass – all groups traditionally symbolized by the Moon in Pisces. With characteristic Scorpio concern for regeneration, Clinton's purpose is to help these people help themselves with hand-ups rather than hand-outs. Also typical is her determination and intense commitment to get to grips with and to purge the Scorpio abuses of the drugs industry, ruled by Pisces.

Gene Tierney

This actress was famous for her silky, feline femininity, which she used in portraying classically Scorpionic indefatigable scheming heroines and seductresses in *film noir* thrillers. Indeed mystery thrillers themselves are of the essence of this combination.

Tierney's life was marked by a deep struggle to get to grips with (Scorpio) her chaotic emotional life, which was constantly running away with her (Pisces). As so often seems to be the case with this type, her emotional life went in waves of collapse into self-abandonment (Pisces), and self-motivated dramatic recovery and regeneration (Scorpio).

Grace Kelly

Another actress, Kelly is remembered particularly for her elegant, coolly self-possessed (Scorpio) yet intensely vulnerable (Pisces) roles in Hitchcock suspense thrillers such as *Dial M for Murder* and *Rear Window*. Her marriage to Prince Ranier is a classic combination of the romance (Pisces) and purposeful ambition (Scorpio) that this type needs to marry within themselves.

In her very private, private life as Princess of Monaco she was famous for her dedicated work (Scorpio) for numerous charities and good causes (Pisces). Details of her closely guarded emotional life are only now beginning to emerge, but these suggest that this was vastly more complex and tangled than her outward, almost chilly Scorpio self-assurance would have suggested, and that she had an intermittent drink problem.

Bela Lugosi

Lugosi is one of the many actors that this combination seems to produce, but more significant is the kind of parts he played. Like Grace Kelly he is associated with suspense thrillers in particular and with menacing, Dracula-type roles which appeal to, and evoke, the darker (Scorpio) aspects of the imagination (Pisces).

Like others of this combination, Lugosi was tempted by the enchanting Piscean world of drugs and the sense of self-transcendence and emotional release they can bring. Equally typical of this type, however, he successfully fought his addiction and, with typical Scorpionic powers of regeneration, regained his creative equilibrium.

Martin Scorsese

The films of this highly imaginative (Pisces) cinema director focus upon the darkest aspects of male aggression and violence (Scorpio) and a preoccupation with sexual inequality. Typical of his work is *Taxi Driver* with its nightmarish Scorpio–Pisces vision of New York as an open sewer spewing forth pimps, whores, addicts and criminals.

Equally expressive of the mixture of social concern (Pisces) and personal struggles (Scorpio) is Scorsese's melodramatic *Alice Doesn't Live Here Anymore*, in which a newly-widowed woman tries to cope with economic survival and create a new life for herself and her 12-year-old son. The very title of Scorsese's *The Last Temptation of Christ* combines Scorpio, which rules temptation, and Christ, whose symbol was the fish, into one image. Indeed, on the highest level, one could say that the Crucifixion and Resurrection of Christ is the ultimate symbolic image for this combination which can plumb the depths and heights of human experience.

Robert Louis Stevenson

The themes and characters in Stevenson's writings constantly reflect the contrasting dark, passionate approach of Scorpio with its fascination with the problem of evil, and the gentle, imaginative, lyrical qualities of Pisces. This contrast is most explicit in the split personality who is both the dedicated Dr Jekyll and the murderous Mr Hyde. People who are strong Water types are very much in touch with their dream life, so it is fascinating to note that the story of *Dr Jekyll and Mr Hyde* came to Stevenson in a nightmare. He spent the next three days in a state of feverish creativity, writing down this 30,000-word story that so captures the essence of the Scorpio–Pisces split between passion and compassion, and between savagery and civilization. This incident is also a classic expression of the creative power of the inner connection of Sun and Moon, which can come about between sleeping and waking.

This same splitting and marrying of tough and tender is present in Stevenson's kindly, caring, yet utterly villainous Long John Silver in the romantic thriller *Treasure Island*. For all his wickedness (Scorpio), he still evokes our compassion (Pisces). Likewise we can contrast Stevenson's wild Scorpionic study in evil of *The Master of Ballantrae* with his superbly Piscean recollections of childhood of his *Child's Garden of Verse*.

William Cullen Bryant

The majestic writings of this poet and lawyer speak volumes of the power of Scorpio combined with the lyric sensitivity of Pisces. His dedicated anti-slavery campaigning is typical of the resolute commitment and compassion of this type.

Alexander Alekhine

Chess is a classic Scorpio–Pisces war game. It involves Pisces strategy and Scorpio plotting, Pisces subterfuge and Scorpio unexpected attack. Alekhine was not only one of the greatest of all chess players, he was passionately addicted to the game and its strategies, just as he also became passionately addicted to alcohol. When his drinking lost him his world title he, like Bela Lugosi, picked himself up from his addiction and made an astonishing comeback from his self-destructive drinking (Pisces) through his sheer determination and applied willpower (Scorpio).

Marie Curie

In the area of science, few life stories appeal to the imagination as much as that of Nobel Prize-winning Marie Curie. Her research against fearful odds into the secrets of radioactivity and its application in radiology, carried out with her husband Pierre, was typically Scorpionic in its intensity and dedication. At the same time her classic Pisces concern for the suffering of others led her, during the first world war, to equip ambulances with X-ray equipment and then personally drive them to the front so that she could help diagnose and care for wounded soldiers. So it was that one of the world's great scientists also became head of the radiology services for the Red Cross, a superb creative synthesis of these two different impulses.

Summary

From the above you can see how these lives illustrate the range of expression of this combination which, whilst often very different in terms of their occupation and detail, still reflect the underlying principles of these signs. If you want to obtain further pointers to your own inner dynamic, we would encourage you to study the lives of those born with your own combination.

If you come up with additional observations and insights about any of the types, we would be happy to hear from you. All material used will be acknowledged in future editions of this book and/or our further publications.

OTHER ASTROLOGICAL FACTORS

The sign position of your Sun and Moon are of great importance in understanding your central psychology. When it comes to refining your understanding of your Sun and Moon, your Ascendant sign and the position of your Sun and Moon in the 12 'houses' of the chart are also very significant. Interpretation of these is outside the scope of this book. The Ascendant and the houses are determined by the *time* of birth. Each house focuses on a different area of life and has qualities not unlike the signs. Regardless of your Sun sign, if you were born at sunrise, with Sun in the first house, you will have some of the self-centred qualities of Aries. On the other hand, if you were born in the hour or so after sunset, your Sun will have some of the Virgo qualities of the desire to be of service and to develop special skills.

The other important factors that will modify the basic interpretations given in these pages are the aspects made to the Sun and Moon by the planets. If you have your Sun or Moon in close aspect to Saturn, it adds a Capricorn overtone. Likewise, if one of the lights aspects Jupiter it will add jovial qualities, and so on.

For your further exploration of these and other factors, a short list of recommended astrology books is given on page 567. Of these, Grant Lewi's *Heaven Knows What* contains the classic pioneering texts on Sun–Moon combinations, whilst Liz Greene and Howard Sasportas' *The Luminaries* is an invaluable study of the deeper psychologies of the Sun and Moon, and is especially recommended for those who want to obtain an in-depth understanding of these life principles.

Chapter Two

SUN AND MOON: THE LIGHTS OF OUR LIFE

———————

As different as night and day.

The greater your understanding of what the Sun and Moon represent within you, the more valuable and interesting you will find the Sun–Moon profiles given in this book. This chapter looks in more detail at the significance of each of these 'lights' or luminaries, as astrologers call them.

We all have different sides to our personality. These different aspects of ourselves are not always in agreement with one another. The two most central and important parts of our nature are represented astrologically by the Sun and the Moon. We can think of these as rather like our masculine and feminine approaches to life that we learned from our father and mother (or those who acted as our parents). For to an astrologer, regardless of our sex, we all have both male and female dimensions to our nature. The central purpose of this book is to show something of the main issues involved with each of the different types of Sun and Moon zodiacal combinations. Equally, it is to show what can happen when we *really* become aware of these two sides and begin to work – and live – more wholeheartedly with them.

BUT WHY SUN AND MOON?

When we talk about the Sun we are essentially referring to our conscious, focused, 'thinking' level which we use to make decisions and move about purposefully in the world. By contrast, when we talk about the Moon we refer to our spontaneous, natural, receptive, 'feeling' level, and the way we seek and give nourishment and comfort to ourselves and to others. So far so good. But what, we may ask, have the Sun and Moon *out there* got to do with what is going on within us *down here*?

The ancient wisdom, of which astrology is an important part, had no problem with this question. The ancients saw no real separation between man and the cosmos. Their central dictum was 'As Above, So Below'. In other words, they saw that all things are the product and reflection of the same Creator, that 'all things are made in the image of the One'. This idea may at first sound very strange to modern ears, but, as those who have seen the film *Jurassic Park* will know, this idea is still central to contemporary scientific thought. For we now know that the instructions for making the whole body are given in the DNA of every body cell.

Just as one cell can tell us about the whole body, so likewise the ancients argued that what we see Above, in the heavens, will be reflected down here, Below, on Earth. Or, put another way, what we see in the macrocosm, the larger whole, will be reflected in the microcosm, the smaller whole. Science is increasingly corroborating this premise through discoveries about the 'inter-connectedness of all life', which has given rise to the now universally accepted idea that the ecological balance in nature, when disturbed by man's greedy interferences, threatens our survival.

The Sun and Moon are certainly the most prominent features of the heavens; they illuminate our distinctive but complementary worlds of day and night. This being the case, we can argue that all things will contain an equivalent Sun and Moon within them. So this means that the *ideas* of the Sun and Moon are to be found at work within all organisms. And, just as the DNA we see under a microscope looks nothing like the cells, tissues and organs that it can become, so the Sun and Moon take on different forms in different entities. In other words, no-one would mistake a chicken for an egg, or an acorn for an oak. They look totally different. Yet we know in fact that chicken and egg, acorn and oak are rather intimately related to each other.

Astrology is a larger expression of this same chicken and egg metaphor. The ancients saw that if Above and Below are reflections of each other, then all things must contain the same essential ingredients. (But as to the perennial question – what came first, the chicken or the egg? – that discusson belongs in another book!)

To the ancients the Sun and Moon were the gods who illuminated and ruled over the starkly contrasting worlds of day and night. So by analogy the same gods are seen to dwell within us, illuminating our own days and nights, our own minds and hearts. The Sun, which lights our days, represents the state within us of being wide awake. This 'noonday' level of consciousness enables us to be deliberately conscious, focused and attentive. In this state we know ourselves as separate, alert individuals, attempting to make our way heroically in the world, even though we may wonder why we sometimes bungle it so badly. Nevertheless, we *consciously* keep trying.

In terms of recent research on the brain, the Sun relates to that level of consciousness which is traditionally associated with a *masculine* approach to life: the left brain's activities of reasoning, manipulating objects and numbers; the ability to think in three dimensions, to orient oneself, to plan, organize and pursue specific goals.

The Moon, by contrast, represents the *feminine* level of our personality. The ancients knew that the Moon ruled the world of night and the mystery of the unconscious, of dreams, imagination and the ebb and flow of our emotional needs, responses and sympathies. At this level we are in the realm of the feminine and all matters related to the right hemisphere of the brain, such as sensitivity to sights, sounds, smells; verbal fluency; and interest in people and relationships. The Moon is our connection with the larger world of what some would call Soul, that principle by which we are connected through body and feeling to all life. The Moon is our ability to respond to our own needs and to the needs of others for nourishment, protection and affection.

To put it on a postcard, we could say that the Sun shows our more individual side and what we are like when we make wide-awake, conscious decisions about our life, what interests us and where we are going. Whereas the Moon shows our natural, gut-level, instinctive response to life, our emotional needs and our approach to looking after ourselves and the needs of others. And the vital thing to remember is that, whether we are male or female, we each have *both* Sun and Moon sides to our nature. To clarify further what these two different sides actually *mean* for us in real life, let us look at some real-life situations.

The Sun and Moon in Everyday Life

Imagine you are at a party. At most parties the aim is to make everyone feel at ease and sociable and, without realizing it, more in touch with their Moon level. Hence, parties are usually held in the evening, as the

Sun is setting or has set, and the time of carousing begins. Nourishment is provided – plenty of food, drink, music and probably soft, muted lighting. These are all lunar things which encourage us to feel relaxed, more intimate, and in touch with our spontaneous feelings, or in other words our Moon side.

Now, imagine that you have had a bit too much to drink and you are drifting along with the mood, and are generally a bit 'out of your head'. Suddenly someone behind you drops a glass which smashes on the floor. As this happens you find yourself 'pulling yourself together' and 'getting back into your head'. You may shake yourself and blink your eyes so as to 'wake up' and be able to size up the situation and take appropriate action, such as stopping people stepping on the broken glass, or helping mop up the spilt drink. If the situation is potentially dangerous you may actually turn up the lights to 'shed more light on things'.

This scene illustrates a shift of consciousness from the relaxed, cosy, soft-lit Moon level, to the more purposeful, bright-lit, focused, decision-making level of the Sun. Indeed, whenever you hear someone saying 'pull yourself together', you are hearing the instruction 'move from your Moon level (where you have become over-identified with your feelings and emotional responses) into your Sun level (where you can have more conscious, decisive control of what is happening to you)'. If, while you are reading this, you take a moment out to say 'pull yourself together', you will probably find that as you do this you will pull your shoulders back and straighten up your spine. You are, as it were, taking possession of your body or, as we say, 'becoming more self-possessed'. It is interesting to note that, astrologically, your back and spine are ruled by Leo, the Sun's natural sign. So when we say of someone who is weak-willed that they are 'spineless' or 'lacking backbone' we are suggesting that they are lacking solar qualities.

To give another example of the way we switch levels in daily life – imagine you have just had a serious talk with your bank manager about your overdraft. With good Sun-level conviction you have assured him or her that you are working hard to get your debts paid off. Outside the bank you meet an old friend. You start talking and soon you are deep in the lunar world of your mutual memories and shared experiences. Then out of the corner of your eye you see the bank manager coming down the street. Immediately you recognize that you are 'wasting time'. You straighten your back, 'pull yourself together'

17

and briskly 'go about your business', back into your Sun level again. For most people such shifts of consciousness occur repeatedly throughout the day. With a bit of deliberate self-awareness you can catch yourself shifting between these levels.

We most obviously experience this shift when we wake in the morning from the lunar world of dreams. We gradually become conscious that it is time to get up and that there are things that have to be done. The more important the things are that have to be done, the more quickly we are likely to wake up and get going. (Indeed when there is a 'big day' ahead some people find it very difficult to surrender to the Moon level and her healing sleep.) This shift of consciousness represented by waking up is, for most people, normally around dawn as the Sun is beginning to rise in the sky. With sunrise, our own consciousness begins to rise, and we gradually leave the world of lunar unconsciousness behind.

Each of these cases illustrates the very normal process of moving our *centre of consciousness* from a responsive, reactive Moon mode to a purposeful, decision-making Sun mode, or vice versa. Each level serves an important purpose in our natures; each has its own strengths and weaknesses, its own desires and aspirations, and each will tend to pursue its own interests irrespective of the other. This is why so many people find that they are in conflict with themselves. One side pulls us one way, the other side pulls another. When this happens, we feel inclined to ask 'Which is the real me?'

The answer, of course, is *both*. Ideally we need to be more aware of both, and to be more adept at recognizing when one is dominating to the detriment of the other. Indeed, as we shall see, the more we can accept, understand, and work with both these Sun and Moon levels, the more we will move towards that 'inner marriage' of the lord and lady within us, of which the great alchemists and philosophers have always spoken. We *are* this inner marriage all the time; there is no hard and fast separation of these modes in the way we actually live our lives. But is it a *good* marriage, or does one side feel like divorcing the other all too often?

You will find some of the ideas associated with Sun and Moon listed on the next page.

Some Ideas Associated with the Sun and Moon

SUN	MOON
Day	Night
Male	Female
Yang	Yin
Dry	Moist
Gold	Silver
Illumination	Reflection
Father	Mother
King	Queen
Prince	Princess
Mind	Heart
Thinking	Feeling
Science	Art
Left Brain	Right Brain
Right Hand	Left Hand
Logic and Structure	Imagination
Clear facts	Symbols
Focuses attention	Reflects the moment
Interested in things	Interested in people
Guided by reason	Guided by experience
Purposeful, goal-oriented	Responds to needs
Takes action	Receptive
Makes decisions	Feels what is needed
Present and Future	Past and Present
Progress	Tradition and Habit

Table 1. The Sun and Moon can be seen to correspond to two very different ways of relating to the world. We each use both. When either is overemphasized, there is an imbalance. When both are used together (see Table 2), we can become increasingly vital and creative.

GETTING IT TOGETHER – THE KEY TO CREATIVITY

When our conscious, masculine side is at war with our feeling, feminine side, our life can become an endless struggle between what

19

we feel we *need* to do and what we think we *ought* to do – like a child living with constantly arguing parents. This can lead to a perplexing sort of self-sabotage which trips us up at the crucial moment. Indeed, we say of some people that 'their left hand does not know what their right hand is doing'. As we have seen above, this is just another way of saying that our left-brain, conscious, Sun side does not know what our right-brain, unconscious, Moon side is on about.

But experience shows that the more these two sides can be brought into contact with each other to form an inner dialogue, the more whole, fulfilled and creative our life becomes. In fact, there are times when these two aspects of ourselves *do* come together. As we wake we may remember a dream we have had. Dreams speak from our lunar side. By training our solar side deliberately to remember our dreams, we can learn to *listen consciously* to our *unconscious*. Working with dreams in this way gradually brings the conscious and unconscious mind first into a recognition of, and eventually into a dialogue with, each other.

FALLING IN LOVE – WITH YOURSELF

The experience of falling in love is a good metaphor for what happens when the masculine and feminine, the Sun and the Moon, begin to work more harmoniously within us. As anyone who has ever been in love will know, when we are in love everything seems possible. The world is beautiful and life is good. The bliss of being released to life's magic through falling in love can even become addictive. It makes us feel alive and, even more important, it makes us feel *creative*.

It is a notable fact that, even in puritanical periods of history, the affairs and infidelities of the creative artist tend to be accepted. In some way, we admit that strongly creative people, be they artists, musicians, poets, politicians, entrepreneurs, indeed philosophers, are in the business of finding their *inner wholeness*. As such, it is recognized by society, albeit unconsciously, that deep emotional experience and experimentation is for such people the essence of their life.

Everyone loves a lover. This is because their love reawakens our own capacity for love, and we are reminded that we, too, are alive and *potentially creative*. A loving relationship can be an immensely powerful outer trigger to our own inner creativity. This is because falling in love connects us with both our Sun and Moon energies and, at least temporarily, creates a state of inner 'alchemical marriage'.

This inner fusion and creativity can, however, take place at any time if we encourage it and give both sides enough space to develop in conjunction with each other. It is probably no coincidence that Leonardo da Vinci, who was a great scientist as well as a great artist, was ambidextrous and could actually write different messages with each hand simultaneously. In other words, Leonardo had equal access to his conscious, purposeful, scientific-orientated left brain (through his right hand), and to his poetic, artistic right brain (through his left hand). Although very few of us are ambidextrous, this inner marriage is something that can happen to all of us. Having tasted it once, it gets easier and easier.

We hope the profiles in this book will help you to recognize some of the main qualities of the central Sun–Moon polarity within you, something of its conflicts and something of its creative magic. The more conscious you can become of the issues in your own Sun–Moon polarity, the more will your left hand be able to shake your right hand, and the more you will be able to *get your act together* and move towards a greater level of vital wholeness and harmony.

Table 2 offers some images for the resolution of the Sun and Moon, which show how much more valuable it is when we have the Sun and Moon working together. As the old saying goes, it takes two to tango, and this is also true for the individual personality. Happy dancing!

The Middle Way – Working with Both Sun and Moon

SUN	MOON	SUN+MOON
Day	Night	Dawn, Dusk
Sunlight	Rain	Growth
Father	Mother	Child
Male	Female	Androgyne
King	Queen	Alchemical marriage
Active	Passive	Aware
Mind	Heart	Wisdom
Thinking	Feeling	Intelligent kindness
Self-Conscious	Spontaneous	Conscious spontaneity
Right hand	Left hand	Ambidexterous
Logic	Imagination	Creative thought
Science	Art	Inspired invention

SUN	MOON	SUN+MOON
Progress	Tradition	Living tradition
Interest in things	Interest in people	Practical help
Awake	Asleep	Creative dreaming
Words	Music	Opera, song, poetry
Purposeful	Responsive	Attentive

Table 2. The often opposing priorities and methods of the Sun and Moon can find a creative resolution in the ways shown in the third column.

Chapter Three

ELEMENTARY, DEAR READERS

Walk groundly, talk profoundly, drink roundly, sleep soundly.
WILLIAM HAZLITT

The zodiac divides people into 12 different types. Underlying the signs, however, is an even more basic division into what the ancients called the four elements: Fire, Earth, Air and Water. These were seen as the basic building blocks of all life. In this chapter, we will look at this four-fold division in detail.

PEOPLE AS 'TYPES'

The 19th-century English critic William Hazlitt may not have known much about astrology, but his off-the-cuff summing-up rhyme of how a person should behave (quoted above) actually touches closely upon the four element types and the thing they each tend to do best. But before we look at these four types and why they are good at certain things, it is helpful first to think about categories and why we categorize people at all.

People are different, and yet the same. Sameness and difference are what make the world go round. The sameness and difference about human beings has been argued about since the dawn of human life on Earth, but the differences are in fact what attract us to one another and bind us together in the tension of *creative conflict*. We say tension because if we can be attracted, we can also be repelled, but we are still bound by that repulsion – the repulsion of difference – and remain in some kind of dynamic relationship because of it.

Something which is very different from us tends to fascinate us, and often we are compulsively attracted to it in order to develop and nurture something which is deficient in ourselves. An example, and a very common occurrence: the well-organized, logical 'thinking' type of man is often found in relationship with the romantic, somewhat dreamy and chaotic, emotional woman. Both irritate and yet fascinate each other. Communication is often difficult; each thinks the other quite odd at times; and their own particular realities are so different. They each develop typical defences which become more pronounced if they cannot recognize their mutual dependence on each other's strengths. They may become accustomed to a habitual sort of tension and conflict and yet they *need* each other. They live in different universes but each affords the other more than a glimpse into another universe that enriches and expands their own. If they want more than a superficial understanding of the differences between them, they would be well advised to look into their own astrological strengths and weaknesses – and differences.

So categorizing difference is just a natural way of trying to make sense of what we experience in life in all kinds of ways. People are different, need and want different things, see and value different things, and understanding just how 'we' are different from 'them' makes us feel better about ourselves. It gives us a starting point, a handle with which to negotiate with the 'unknown'. Categorizing is also about defining, and defining is about affirming and respecting uniqueness.

Harking back to Hazlitt's rhyme, an astrologer can see the four element types poetically evoked by this ditty. The earthy individual tends to 'walk groundly' and seems rooted in the world like a 200-year-old oak. In fact, we rely on him to be that way: solid, immovable, absolutely dependable. The airy individual can usually 'talk profoundly', and we envy that gift of the gab and dexterity with ideas and people which make the air type the socializer *par excellence*. When we say the fiery individual 'drinks roundly', we are alluding to the intensely dramatic *joie de vivre* of this type which fuels his childlike faith in life, his romantic visions and his celebratory, dare-devil approach to most endeavours. And what do we mean by asserting that the watery individual 'sleeps soundly'? A bit of poetic licence perhaps, but nevertheless, in human terms, water rules the realm of feelings and the instinctual, unconscious process of making evaluations. Water seeks union, safety and relatedness, and responds irrationally, always from the sleeping depths, from the heart, and from a need to safeguard his or her precious emotional possessions.

No, William Hazlitt may not have known much about astrology, but as a good Sun-Aries he must have sown a few wild oats and learned a thing or two. It is said of Hazlitt that he 'was possessed of a peculiar temper, which led to his quarrelling with most of his friends'. Maybe if they had known that he was a fiery Sun in Aries, for whom being assertive and argumentative is as natural as birds taking to flight, they would have chuckled and taken no offence. Indeed, understanding what makes others tick can help us get beyond stereotyping, which tends to make us dismiss people before we have a clue about where they are coming from – and what they might have to offer.

THE FOUR ELEMENTS

The four element types are of special interest to astrologers and psychologists. Ever since the Greek philosopher Empedocles offered his thoughts on the subject in the 5th century BC, there has been the idea that all things in the Universe are composed of a mixture of these four elements: Fire, Earth, Air, and Water. An ancient Eastern myth describes the Great Mother Kali as apportioning the elements to create life, with water giving blood, earth forming the physical body, air providing breath, and fire producing vital heat.

The elements can be seen to represent four different types of energy, four distinct states of consciousness or approaches to the world. They have their counterpart in the four states of matter identified by modern physics: plasma (Fire), solids (Earth), gas (Air) and liquid (Water). Equally, the elements can be seen to correlate with the Great Swiss psychologist Carl Jung's four main psychological types: Intuition (Fire), Sensation (Earth), Thinking (Air) and Feeling (Water). These correspond to the medieval personality classifications of choleric, melancholic, sanguine, and phlegmatic. Early on, the Greeks allocated these elements in an orderly sequence around the zodiac, starting with Fire for Aries and repeating the sequence Fire, Earth, Air, Water, three times, as shown overleaf.

As you can see, three signs are allocated to each of the elements. The fire signs are Aries, Leo and Sagittarius; to Earth belong Taurus, Virgo and Capricorn; Air governs Gemini, Libra and Aquarius; and the Water signs are Cancer, Scorpio and Pisces. You can begin to understand the dominant characteristics of each element type by thinking of the imagery each element evokes.

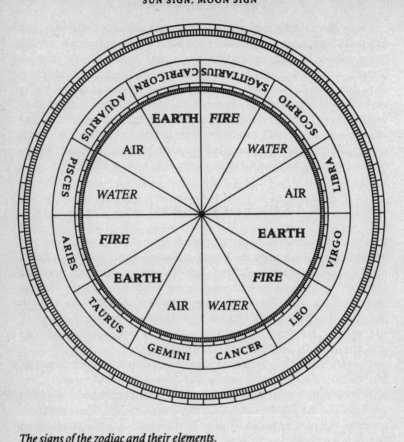

The signs of the zodiac and their elements.

Fire

The most obvious characteristic of this positive, 'yang' element is its power to transform (whether we like it or not!) When we speak of a fiery temperament, we are referring to a quality of behaviour that pushes ahead into life. It is unpredictable, even unstable, active and forceful, and usually extremely noticeable! Fire types need to make things happen, and to be in the absolute centre of their lives. They can sense the potential of a situation and make that crucial leap into the unknown either to fall on their face or to create a 'roaring success'.

Likewise, we can imagine how people living with a Fire type can be

26

inspired and encouraged by their partner's enthusiasm, but also how easily they might get 'burned' by the flames of fire's passionate ego and outrageous escapades. Fire evokes descriptive phrases such as 'burning with zeal', 'hot-blooded', 'can't stand still', 'hot stuff', 'energizing', 'stimulating', 'inspiring', 'ego-centric' and 'visionary'.

Earth

The Earth is usually referred to as a feminine, 'yin' element – Mother Earth, the ever-dependable source of all life. In the realm of Earth all material forms stand out and are distinct: we receive our ultimate material definition as well as our material limitation from Earth. No matter how fiery and wonderful our visions of what could be, the final test of their reality resides in the world of matter. How does it act, taste, feel, measure up in the 'real' world?

The predominantly earthy individual tends, therefore, to be matter-of-fact, solid, reliable, sensual, productive, grounded in the practical everyday world, and preoccupied with the here and now. The virtues of this type are obvious: they know how to get things done, run a household and a business, balance the books and make flowers grow. But Earth types go for security, not risk; order rather than chaos; and, as a result, often have a problem expanding beyond their known, quantifiable and controllable universe.

Air

Like Fire, Air is a positive 'yang' element, but has a more impersonal quality. Just like the wind, it is all-pervasive and constantly moving, and connects and relates everything it touches in the outer world. Hence the need for airy individuals to socialize and share ideas with many different people. Unlike the intensity of Fire, Air is more detached, abstract and non-intimate in its mode of operation. To find the rational principle at work behind the operations of nature and human behaviour is what the airy individual seeks. And so we usually find that the airy temperament is breezy, intellectual, communicative, curious, co-operative, sometimes 'airy-fairy' but always interested in cause-and-effect, in the past-present-future relationship of things, and in understanding people and situations with their minds.

Air types handle ideas well, they are logical, cool, civilized, witty and usually the life of the party where they can indulge themselves in the sheer variety of people. In the realm of feelings, however, the airy individual is often insecure and naive, as feelings do not lend themselves easily to the logical measurement of the rational mind.

Water

When we think about the 'yin' element of Water, we immediately enter the realm of the mysterious Feminine. Images arise such as the refreshing, nurturing, cleansing, cooling qualities of spring rain and also the power, enchantment and mystery of the deep, blue sea. Water flows, dissolves and unifies, and indeed the watery temperament desires to be intimate, to merge and to experience the bliss of emotional security and containment. Containment is an important clue to understanding this type, as water will be contained by its boundaries, or else, as with the terror of a flood, it overwhelms, engulfs, saturates and drowns.

The watery individual is moved by feelings, by the irrational realm of romance and imagination, and seeks meaning through relating at a deeply personal and unexplainable level. Unconcerned with whether or not someone or something makes 'logical sense', they ask instead 'does it feel right?' The emotional, watery individual is concerned with feelings, values, rapport, belonging and memories.

THE ELEMENTS AND TIME

The subjective experience of time is one of those perennial mysteries of the human condition. Our state of mind – our temperament – seems largely to determine whether we constantly look at the clock or sail through the day as if it consisted of a few interesting moments. Some people are constantly harping back to the 'good old days', whilst some are focused on the immense possibilities of the future. Others are ploddingly preoccupied with the here-and-now, and other types are happy to scan the past, present, and future and how they relate in a cause-and-effect way.

Fire is preoccupied with the future, with the hidden meaning and potential of things and what can be made of them. Earth is interested in the here-and-now, in facts and figures, concrete accomplishments, and getting things done in a practical way. Water is concerned with personal feelings and emotions, with safety, security, and connectedness, and is especially concerned with the past. Air is concerned with the abstract reasons behind things and their cause and effect; air scans past, present, and future in an attempt to get the broad picture and the abstract principle.

INTERPRETING THE ELEMENTS

The elements can at times be taken literally. Thus those with a strong Earth element in their charts will be strongly physical in some way – they will like and feel at home with the earth, gardening, farming, pottery, building and working with their hands to make things. Water types will often thrive beside the sea or next to a lake or a stream. Fire types can quite literally enjoy piling up a roaring open fire and even being the blacksmith. Air types often love the open air, walking in the wind, bird-watching, flying, gliding, or simply flying a kite or listening to their wind chimes.

It is not quite that simple, however. A person may be strongly Water, yet be an airline pilot, or strongly air and be deeply attached to farming or become a master builder. Strength in an element or elements shows us an approach to the world. This can be illustrated by considering the chart of Gertrude Ederle. One of the great pioneer women swimmers of early this century, she became, in 1926, the first woman to swim the English Channel. Surely someone who spent so much time in the water would have to have her Sun, the focus of her life, in a Water sign? In fact, Ederle had Sun in Libra and Moon in Capricorn, making her an Air–Earth type. So what is an Air–Earth type doing spending their days immersed in the salty deeps?

First of all, it should be said that her birth chart *does* have a great deal of Water in it, not least a conjunction of Jupiter and Neptune in Cancer trine Saturn in Pisces, indicating watery ideals and ambitions, and Mercury in Scorpio, indicating a mind attracted by oceanic depths. But what is her approach to swimming? Listen to what she has to say on the subject:

> *To me the sea is like a person – like a child that I've known a long time. It sounds crazy, I know, but when I swim in the sea I talk to it. I never feel alone when I'm out there.*

So although she spent much of her life immersed in water, her approach and attitude to swimming was utterly airy.

THE ELEMENT COMBINATIONS

Each Sun–Moon type is a combination of elements. In the following descriptions of the element combinations, please remember that the pairing can be *either way around*. For example, a Fire–Earth combination refers equally to Sun Fire–Moon Earth as it does to Sun Earth–Moon Fire. There *will* be subtle differences, but the dynamic is generally the same. The diagram on page 26 will tell you which elements your Sun and Moon are in. See the table of Sun–Moon combinations (below) to find your Sun–Moon type.

The Sun-Moon Combinations

SUN/MOON:

	AR	TA	GE	CA	LE	VI	LI	SC	SA	CP	AQ	PI
AR	1	2	3	4	5	6	7	8	9	10	11	12
TA	13	14	15	16	17	18	19	20	21	22	23	24
GE	25	26	27	28	29	30	31	32	33	34	35	36
CA	37	38	39	40	41	42	43	44	45	46	47	48
LE	49	50	51	52	53	54	55	56	57	58	59	60
VI	61	62	63	64	65	66	67	68	69	70	71	72
LI	73	74	75	76	77	78	79	80	81	82	83	84
SC	85	86	87	88	89	90	91	92	93	94	95	96
SA	97	98	99	100	101	102	103	104	105	106	107	108
CP	109	110	111	112	113	114	115	116	117	118	119	120
AQ	121	122	123	124	125	126	127	128	129	130	131	132
PI	133	134	135	136	137	138	139	140	141	142	143	144

The four pure types, with both Sun and Moon in the same element, most vividly express the element involved. Such an emphasis on one element also represents an imbalance, so such types are liable to swing into their complementary or opposite element.

Fire–Fire Combinations
(See nos. 1, 5, 9, 49, 53, 57, 97, 101, 105)

Fire is the most primary of elements – hot, volatile, creative, dramatic. The double-fire type is intensely passionate and lives from a very self-centred perspective. That is, he approaches life according to his keenly-felt beliefs and visions of what could be and what is truth for him. The double-fire type may be so in tune with his inner reality that he becomes insensitive to others. Frequently his relationships suffer from his lack of awareness that others might not have such a strong sense of destiny. Whatever his interests might be, this individual throws himself into life with enormous enthusiasm, often bumping into and scattering others in the process.

When Aneurin Bevan described Winston Churchill – a double-Fire type (Sun Sagittarius, Moon Leo) – he summed up the problems of the pure-Fire combination:

> *The seven league boot tempo of his imagination hastens him on to the sunny uplands of the future, but he is apt to forget that the slow steps of humanity must travel every inch of the weary road that leads there.*

There is about the double-fire type all that one associates with the imagery of fire – it burns, it roars, and it waits for nothing. This type can be brash, arrogant and impatient, but also inspiring and childlike with an immense capacity for enjoying life and persuading others to believe in themselves and to 'have a go'. This type will often sense the hidden opportunity in a situation, and his belief that anything is possible is the magic ingredient behind his natural leadership qualities. Never mind the fact that he needs plenty of lackeys to make it all happen in the concrete world, *he* has the vision – the rest is incidental!

Shadow

Because of his very enthusiastic flight towards glory, the strongly fire type may paradoxically develop a compensating pessimism when he comes down to earth. Indeed, coming down to earth is generally what he tries to avoid, for the mundane necessities of life seem like obstacles thwarting the pursuit of important things. Churchill's oppressive periods of what he called 'black dog' and Mark Twain's, (Sagittarius–Aries) bouts of dark depression are classic examples of what can happen when there is a loss of meaning for the fiery individual. This type's tendency to rebel angrily against the confines of the mortal condition, such as seeing to the needs of the body and the bank account, will severely restrict his potency. He needs to develop patience, moderation, practical skills, sensitivity to others, and respect for the simple, inarticulate material world.

Relationships

The pure-Fire type may gravitate towards other Fire types, but this can be too much of an exhausting good thing. The airy individual is intellectually provocative and challenging for the double-fire type, and together they can make a very creative team. A relationship with the watery individual can be quite exciting and romantic but also volatile and unstable. The most compelling relationships tend to be with the Earth type, people who are comfortable and adept at dealing with the everyday world – making breakfast, mowing the lawn, getting the tax returns in on time. There is a strong mutual fascination between these two types which can help to build a strong relationship although inevitably there will be some difficulties in understanding each other's basic values.

Male v. Female

Men in Western society are undoubtedly more inclined to feel at home with the strongly extrovert qualities that Fire normally bestows. Whilst 'spirit' and energy are admired in women, there is no question that the Western woman who overtly uses her Fire energies is likely to be rather disparagingly labelled as 'pushy, forceful, quick-tempered and bossy'. This is slowly changing, however. The double-Fire woman is not inclined to care too much about what others think, and is very able to stand up for herself in a man's world.

Earth–Earth Combinations
(See nos. 14, 18, 22, 62, 66, 70, 110, 114, 118)

The double-Earth type is down-to-earth and matter-of-fact. His pragmatic philsophy and concern for material well-being was expressed well by Karl Marx, a double Taurus, in his famous dictum:

from each according to their abilities, to each according to their needs.

This type is usually well grounded in economic and physical reality. He is very much in tune with his senses and instincts through which he feels connected to, and in control of, his world. There is often an innate understanding of the natural, organic processes of growth which gives this individual persistence, patience and self-discipline in the pursuit of his goals. Stable, realistic, practical, dependable and down-to-earth, this individual is the 'pillar of society' type on whom others rely for sound judgments and solid, traditional wisdom.

Usually very much at home in their bodies and appreciative of sensual pleasures, the earthy individual knows that the body and all the material realm sustain us and supply us with evidence that we do indeed exist – and that we have a creative existence, too. This type readily learns how to manipulate the material world to his own delight and advantage, and usually with the awareness that the Earth and the laws of nature deserve respect. However, an overly earthy consciousness eventually becomes sceptical and fearful of what may lie beyond the physical realm. He risks losing his vision and sense of meaning through over-concern with concrete facts and trusting only what he can touch, taste, see, hear and, most of all, measure.

Shadow

The double-Earth type's deepest, darkest fear is chaos and the loss of control. The unconventional and deviant are seen as threatening, or even evil. The intangible, unseen realm of spiritual meaning and purpose tends to elude him or only peeps into his life via the classic superstition and the odd psychic apparition. A strongly traditional and too-rigid adherence to concrete reality can create an increasingly hollow treadmill and enslavement to the physical – which the earthy type with dread has to admit only ends in death. What then?

The double-Earth type often needs to develop his imagination, his trust in new possibilities, and to accept that his need for spiritual sustenance need not threaten his physical security and his need to be in control, as far as possible, of his life and circumstances. To entertain the idea that there may be a realm in which quantitative measurement does not apply – the realm of meaning and spiritual purpose – can only release him from the risk of stagnant imprisonment in the fleshly cage.

Relationships

The double-Earth person is one of the best marriage partners of all, for he is an able provider and a loyal, dependable mate. He may gravitate towards other earthy types with whom he will share many values and feel secure and validated. But he is likely to have a more tantalizing attraction to the fiery type whose enigmatic and unpredictable ways stimulate and challenge.

The airy individual and the double-Earth person make a compatible pairing due to their mutual impersonal, practical, logical approach to problem-solving. The watery individual finds the double-Earth person a perfect container for his emotions, and these two can build a cosy nest and a strong, binding attachment that wears well.

Male v. Female

The qualities of the practical double-Earth type fit comfortably with both male and female in Western society. Both will have a strong sense of duty and commitment, and in the case of the female, a strong inclination to serve human needs.

Double-Earth women are enormously capable, able to sustain demanding long-term professional projects as well as order and well-being. They tend to be protective, resourceful, patient, and hard-working, capable of showing their loyalty and love through action but remaining somewhat restrained in the expression of feelings. The male of this type may not fit into the stereotype of the 'macho' western man with all his extrovert courage and Indiana Jones-like panache, but his groundedness and quiet determination, plus his strongly rational bias, make him a practical and effective leader who can map out his territory with polished organization, and work steadfastly towards the mastering of whatever medium he chooses.

Air–Air Combinations
(See nos. 27, 31, 35, 75, 79, 83, 123, 127, 131)

Intelligent, gracious ladies and thoughtful gentlemen, double-Air types are the most reasonable, civilized, clear-headed of combinations. They are probably the most cultured and elegant as well, never at a loss for a word or comment, always ready for discussion and reasoned argument and debate. Being told this will not go to their head for they are not normally prone to self-importance – that would be far too illogical for their poised and intelligent approach to life.

The double-Air type assumes independence as his birthright. To be able to move and connect with ideas and people is the stuff of life for him. Witty, cerebral, urbane and polite, the double-Air type is a natural communicator and thinker who prefers to soar in the ideal realm where he can build social, political or philosophical schemes that help improve humankind's lot.

A thinker *par excellence*, the double-Air type finds security in taking the broad intelligent viewpoint, in stepping back in order to see the patterns and principles at work in the whirlwind of life's activities. He is an observer and theorizer of life, and his faith in the power of ideas is well exhibited by the British economist John Maynard Keynes (Sun Gemini, Moon Gemini) who said:

The ideas of economists and political philosophers, both when they are right and when they are wrong, are more powerful than is commonly understood. Indeed, the world is ruled by little else.

This detached, observant mode is useful but it often earns this type the accusation of being cold and unfeeling. Although others may experience double Air in this way, the strongly airy individual insists, often at considerable length, that he is only doing what comes naturally – questioning, examining and remaining open, fair-minded, friendly and harmonious, and above all communicating with whoever will listen and discuss.

Shadow

The double-Air type labours under the illusion that there is such a thing as complete objectivity and perfect impartiality. He is utterly honourable and, alas, childlike, in his attempt to understand, analyse and name everything. Childlike in that his feeling for life, because it is such a conundrum to him, tends to remain immature, undeveloped and very often unconscious. The whole range of human feelings – hurt, angry, jealous, dependent, fearful, in love, hateful – tends to be avoided, repressed or played down with great agility. The only possible exception is cheerfulness, which Air is particularly good at.

The rejection of the feeling dimension makes this type curiously sensitive and vulnerable to the waywardness of human behaviour. The strongly airy individual can therefore be a real challenge in a relationship. It is not easy being the only one admitting to all those unpleasant and uncontrollable feelings whilst your airy mate looks on with a cool, nonchalant and maddeningly debonair gaze. The double-airy individual weaves clever arguments so you have to be subtle and careful when you try to bring his feelings to his attention.

Relationships

The double-Air person is an adventurer and a traveller, if not geographically then intellectually in some way. He will usually meet a wide variety of people throughout his life and be attracted to adventuresome souls. Communication is paramount for this type, and he needs mental rapport and mutual respect in a relationship for it to be satisfying and long-lasting.

Air is compatible with Earth and they make a good team, for they both approach life logically and practically. Fire and Air stimulate each other in the realm of ideas and possibilities, but this relationship could lack stability and burn itself out. Air is fascinated by the watery individual whose predominant feeling mode will help the airy person to get in touch with his mysterious emotions and to develop his imagination. Airy thinking and watery feeling are opposites, and yet because of that very fact they are intensely drawn to one another.

Male v. Female

Traditionally we expect to see the objective, witty, thinking characteristics of the double-Air type in men whose intellects make them leaders of thought and action. Women of this type are just as independent, inquisitive and extroverted, and rebel when others try to peg them into more traditional female roles. Adaptability, ingenuity and handling people with cunning insight and skill are double-Air virtues, and the female of this type can employ these qualities in both the home and the marketplace. Both sexes are often drawn towards learning and communication, as well as professional activities that allow for maximum freedom of movement and travel.

Water–Water Combinations
(See nos. 40, 44, 48, 88, 92, 96, 136, 140, 144)

Water is the element of feelings and imagination, and the English language is full of Water imagery which is descriptive of this type. The strongly Water type is able to get into the mainstream and go with the flow. They drink in life's experiences, and nothing washes over them. They can gush with feelings, quickly go misty with emotions and dissolve into tears. Sentimental and nostalgic about the past, this type can wax lyrical about his longings for times gone by, as does the Anglo-

Irish dramatist Oliver Goldsmith (Sun Scorpio, Moon Cancer):

> *I love everything old: old friends, old times, old manners, old books, old wine.*

This type can also at times be a wet blanket, especially to more boisterous Fire types and restless Air types. In politics their compassionate natures incline them to be the caring and compassionate 'wets', rather than the airy 'dries' with their doctrinal purity. Heartier types may consider Water individuals to be 'drips' and 'still wet behind the ears'. But 'still waters run deep', and the feeling strengths of the double-Water type give the capacity to empathize with others and to show caring concern for everyone in need.

This individual also has a rich imagination and often the ability to 'get inside the skin' of another; hence the poetic, artistic and theatrical talents often come easily. A confusion of personal boundaries is, however, an occupational hazard of the strongly watery type. They can be so sensitive that they become psychic sponges, picking up moods and emotional undercurrents in the environment, and unable to differentiate their own feelings and needs from those of others.

This type wants emotional security and emotional food, and because the two do not always come together in equal doses, they easily get hurt. If wounded he can withdraw into an icy silence, but once his feelings are recognized and addressed, his heart quickly melts and thaws out and he is soon back in the flow of things.

Shadow

Swimming in the seas of subjectivity does not make it easy for double-Water types to engage in clearly reasoned arguments and objective judgements. They know how they personally feel about people or situations, and that is their reality – rather than a collection of objective facts which lead indubitably to a logical conclusion. Hence the strongly watery individual tends to remain irrational when he thinks he is being rational. This type needs to learn how to think things through with more detachment. Yes, he may have had a bad experience with a Malaysian taxi driver, but does that really make all the Malaysian race bad?

The double-Water type is also prone to cling in relationships, because they provide the arena for the emotional exchange, containment and security that is so vital for this individual's wellbeing. This type often needs to learn that letting go just a little, and allowing loved ones more room for manoeuvre, usually strengthens rather than jeopardizes a relationship.

Male v. Female

Water is undoubtedly a feminine-oriented element, and hence generally much easier in our society for females to handle than males. Whilst men can be sympathetic, caring and compassionate, it is still not easy for men in the West to show their feelings or to allow themselves to be seen dissolving into tears. In consequence, strongly watery men may actually swing into the opposite pole and become ultra-rational, detached, and unemotional to a degree that some would see as almost pathological. This can lead to men of this type, and some women, taking pride in showing no emotions and acting only through reason.

When this does happen, however, this type of polarized individual will almost always be found surrounded with highly emotional people and situations that 'act out' the inner emotional life they find themselves unable to handle. This can be seen in the super-rational husband with the hysterical wife, and the calm, reasonable psychologist who is deeply concerned in a supremely rational way to help those who have become 'confused' and 'emotionally disturbed'.

Fire–Earth Combinations
(See nos. 2, 6, 10, 13, 17, 21, 50, 54, 58, 61, 65, 69, 98, 102, 106, 109, 113, 117)

The Fire Sun–Earth Moon type is a strong, compelling personality. We can see this as the volcano pouring forth lava which will eventually become new, fertile lands. This individual can deal with molten metal like the blacksmith or the engineer shaping raw material into serviceable tools. Here is the practical enthusiast, the doer who can also enthuse others to action.

This combination has been called the bull-dozer, for he has tremendous weight and drive to push ahead in exactly the direction he wants. J. Pierrpoint Morgan (Sun Aries, Moon Virgo), the American industrialist, typified this combination well when he said:

I don't want a lawyer to tell me what I cannot do; I hire him to tell me how to do what I want to do.

Likewise, the Earth Sun–Fire Moon combination is also the practical visionary who consciously keeps his feet on the ground but has the instinct to go for the main chance, to know when to risk, and to pull rabbits out of hats when least expected. This individual could be the hard-headed pragmatic entrepreneur who sees future opportunities and can seize them with confidence and know-how, turning them into solid and often lucrative realities in the present.

Earth–Fire types may possess a raucous sense of humour, a pronounced sensuality and a real penchant for the good life, as can be seen in the life of Alexander Woollcott (Sun Capricorn, Moon Sagittarius), the American drama critic and wit, who said, whilst surveying an elegant country estate:

Just what God would have done if he had the money.

Either way, with this Fire–Earth combination there is a strong practical, rational bias coupled with a powerful intuition and a compelling need for freedom and power. When the positive interaction between Fire and Earth is not working, this person can become very tense, swinging between a burning, intuitive faith and a down-in-the-dumps inertia and Doubting Thomas scepticism.

Shadow

People with Fire–Earth combinations tend to have enormous conviction and certitude about themselves and their beliefs. As a result, they can suffer from the defects of their virtues and become fixed, dictatorial and insensitive to others and to the subtler nuances of human relationships.

Whether it is Fire Sun–Earth Moon or Earth Sun–Fire Moon, this combination produces a powerful ego which can easily run the show in any relationship. When the urge to dominate meets with resistance, they can become baffled and frustrated until they begin to respect the rights and needs of others.

Relationships

Fire–Earth may find his own type atttractive, but can enter into very creative and complementary relationships with Air–Water types who can both fan the flames and water the garden! Often a benevolent dictator in relationships and in the home, this type nevertheless is usually a very committed mate, tending to show his romantic feelings through actions. His stubbornness can, however, sometimes block domestic harmony and get in the way of intimacy.

Male v. Female

This is a good combination for people in politics and managerial positions who must make high-powered decisions and push through policies and procedures. Indeed, these individuals can be quite pushy and competitive, qualities the Western world feels are more acceptable in males.

The female of this type is authoritative and pragmatic and is unlikely to waste time over failures or adverse reactions to her independence. Both males and females tend to have substantial ambition and terrific stamina.

Fire–Air Combinations
(See nos. 3, 7, 11, 25, 29, 33, 51, 55, 59, 73, 77, 81, 99, 103, 107, 121, 125, 129)

The Fire–Air type is a real 'live-wire', full of exciting ideas and able to communicate them with tremendous zeal which impresses and persuades everyone around them. If taken to the extreme, this makes this individual full of bluster and bombast, long-winded and prone to be carried away by his own rhetoric and eloquence. Others may also be carried away as he tends to have lots of *joie de vivre*, cleverness and charisma. Noel Coward (Sun Sagittarius, Moon Gemini) expresses the wit and impatience of this combination well:

I write at high speed because boredom is bad for my health.

Indeed, boredom is something this type shuns and can usually avoid because they think and live at such a fast pace.

If the Sun is in Air and the Moon in Fire, the effect is rather like that of a hot-air balloon – a beautiful way to travel that takes you way up into the giddy heights. So likewise this type tends to be a Utopian idealist, seeing ever more distant sunny shores to which the human race may travel, loftier vistas and wider horizons. Alternatively, if this type gets on a high horse, they can be very moralistic, 'knowing exactly what is good for us'.

Shadow

This type is a potential visionary, but visionaries need earthiness in order to bring ideas to fruition. The Fire–Air individual can be impractical and may exhaust himself with his intense sociability and the generation of stimulating ideas and new risks. If he remains in the realm of impersonal possibilities, he becomes cut off from body and the more mundane but essential needs of human life. And without emotional vulnerability, he misses out on real intimacy.

Relationships

Fire–Air types are so mentally active and gregarious, so keen to understand and to share their understanding, that they rarely play the role of the loner in the crowd. Their interests drive them on, and when they get to their destination they meet and strike up conversations and relationships with other interesting mavericks. In a relationship they need intellectual rapport and plenty of freedom to pursue their own interests.

They may often be out of touch with their feelings and emotional needs, and an Earth–Water type can help remind them that they *are* in fact human. There is a kind of restless, eternal youthfulness about the Fire–Air type which is very appealing, but without the challenges of a serious relationship they can remain somewhat emotionally immature and superficial.

Male v. Female

The extroverted, enthusiastic and argumentative qualities of this type are applauded in males, whilst females of this type tend to be seen as 'masculine' and intimidating. Female Fire–Air types tend not to settle for traditional roles that limit their potential, and are therefore often at the cutting edge of social change. Both males and females of this type lead pacey lives to some extent, and can often live by their wits and land themselves at opportunity's doorstep with the greatest of ease.

41

Fire–Water Combinations
(See nos. 4, 8, 12, 37, 41, 45, 52, 56, 60, 85, 89, 93, 100, 104, 108, 133, 137, 141)

Take fire power and water power and put them together and you get steam, the power which drove the great trains. Steam is used to cleanse and sterilize and can also scald. Emotionally, this combination has a reputation for being especially given to passionate emotional involvement. Volatile, romantic, moody, the Fire–Water person has the artistic temperament which can fluctuate wildly. It is a poetic, ardent temperament, courageous in its visions yet vulnerable in its need for love and inspiration.

The poet Shelley (Sun Leo, Moon Pisces) exemplified this passionate, artistic nature very well and could equally be describing himself when he rejoices in the Skylark:

Pourest thy full heart in profuse strains of unpremeditated art.

When the Sun is in Water and the Moon is in Fire, the result is a passionate crusader whose feelings fuel his purpose and art. But fire can make water evaporate, and water may extinguish fire. When this happens, this type can feel unstable, depressed, and disoriented.

Shadow

The Fire–Water individual often lacks the ability to take the impersonal view; that is, to step back and reason impartially about things. Their approach is intensely personal, urgent, passionate, and for them life lacks meaning and colour if that vital personal ingredient is taken away.

Often a slave to the intense fluctuation of moods, this type's volatility can reach fanatical proportions, especially if a cool, reasoned argument is called for. Instability and impracticality can play havoc with the smooth running of their lives.

Relationships

The Fire–Water type is a highly romantic, warm and emotional person, and to a large degree thrives on love and satisfying relationships. Whilst one part of the nature may want to merge and gain absolute

42

security, however, another part wants excitement and challenge: one part may feel an infinite capacity to give whilst another part is impelled to devour. This mixture can be demanding to live with, but also exciting and rewarding in the way that it might stretch other, less emotional types.

People with this combination tend to feel contained and grounded by Earth–Air types. Their moodiness and changeability is less problematic as they learn to direct some of their emotional energy into their own creative pursuits.

Male v. Female

This combination blends the most feminine and the most masculine of the elements. An extreme 'yang' and an extreme 'yin' quality together produces a very creative but also a very volatile and often difficult combination for either sex to handle. Both males and females can experience huge mood swings as they contact first their powerful independence and pride, and then their sensitivity and vulnerability. In general, both males and females will seek highly personal professional avenues. Conforming to convention is not their strong point!

Under the label of the 'artist', both the male and female Fire–Water type will find more compassionate acceptance as well as intense admiration from others. In other words, their artistic inspiration and highly theatrical style usually more than compensates for their lack of emotional stability.

Earth–Air Combinations
(See nos. 15, 19, 23, 26, 30, 34, 63, 67, 71, 74, 78, 82, 111, 115, 119, 122, 126, 130)

This combination produces a productive, rational personality which can be both innovative and efficient. The challenge of being up-in-the-air and down-to-earth at the same time is that of bringing together abstract thought with the nitty-gritty issues of getting on in the world. These two elements combine easily and make for a clear-headed, objective and scientific approach. This is the temperament of the practical idealist who observes, thinks, plans a course of action and then acts. American president John F. Kennedy (Sun Gemini, Moon Virgo) is an example of this combination, and expresses the lunar instinct to give service to a rational, well-considered ideal in his famous injunction:

> *Ask not what your country can do for you—ask what you can do for your country.*

When the Sun is in Earth and the Moon is in Air, the conscious, rational impulse is to get to grips with reality, to build, consolidate and organize with the logical instinct to make one's efforts as humane and far-reaching as possible. There is often a dry sense of humour and capacity to use language with adroit accuracy. The late American poet Carl Sandburg (Sun Capricorn, Moon Aquarius) had a talent for using colloquialisms, which is characteristic of this combination, and his view of slang expresses this down-to-earth communicative ability:

> *Slang is a language that rolls up its sleeves, spits on its hands and goes to work.*

Shadow

The Earth–Air individual is adept at mastering the mundane world, learning how things work and then applying his knowledge in many different and normally useful ways. He can, however, easily lose touch with the less quantifiable things of life such as emotions. When this happens he risks the danger of becoming 'dry as dust' and stuck in the pragmatic, cost-effective, scientific approach.

Relationships

This type enjoys communicating and being helpful, and tends to get on well with most people at a practical, social level. They will find predominantly Fire and Water types either alien or fascinating, but either way the latter would enable the Earth–Air person to contact the more mysterious and emotional, irrational parts of his personality. The Earth–Air individual seeks rational rapport in a relationship and is very supportive and adaptable, but he needs help in learning how to discover and share his feelings.

Male v. Female

This is a very androgynous combination, encouraging both the supportive skills associated with natural female roles and the intellectual skills of the male.

Earth–Water Combinations
(See nos. 16, 20, 24, 38, 42, 46, 64, 68, 72, 86, 90, 94, 112, 116, 120, 134, 138, 142)

Flanders and Swan sing 'Mud, mud, glorious mud', and you do not have to be a hippopotamus to appreciate the qualities of mud. Think of the rich fertility of well-irrigated fields, the potter's clay on the wheel ready to be formed, the clay of bricks and tiles, or the malleable concrete which forms the basis of so much construction. This is one of the most practical, supportive and nourishing of combinations. It combines the capacity to feel sympathy for others with a devotional determination and enterprising ability to do what needs to be done to meet others' needs. American churchman Reinhold Niebuhr (Sun Cancer, Moon Taurus) gives eloquent expression to this type's orientation:

> *God grant me the serenity to accept the things I cannot change, courage to change the things I can, and wisdom to know the difference.*

When the Sun is in Earth and the Moon in Water, the individual can readily develop a practical understanding of day-to-day life, and seems to have the innate wisdom to know what is important and what is not in a situation. For this type, both practical and emotional needs 'make sense' and should intertwine in a balanced, normal life. Consider this view of the 18th-century wit Samuel Johnson (Sun Virgo, Moon Pisces):

> *A man is in general better pleased when he has a good dinner upon his table, than when his wife talks Greek.*

A bit dated yes, chauvinistic indeed, but nevertheless Johnson expresses that practical wisdom and measured sensuality of the Earth–Water combination.

Shadow

The Earth–Water individual wants both material and emotional security, and therefore usually views change and challenge as threatening. As a result, there is with this type a propensity to get stuck in the mud, and a danger of getting swamped by duty and slowed down by the inertia of possessiveness and limited viewpoint.

Life is highly personal for this individual; what he can see, taste, hear, smell and feel, and how it might affect his world, is all important to him. The larger, detached viewpoint is usually lost on him. He may need to learn how to move just a little out of his well-defined groove so that life does not become too stagnant.

Relationships

The Earth–Water person normally finds immense satisfaction in a relationship that brings out the innate dependable, resourceful, gentle, devotional qualities of this combination. This individual feels affirmed and valued when he knows he is needed and valued for his useful accomplishments.

People with this combination are particularly good at serving and caring for others, and once they find their romantic niche they get on with nurturing and nest-building. Hence they make excellent partners, and tend to prefer sitting around the fire drinking hot cocoa to lots of razzle-dazzle on the town. This type helps to ground and contain the more unstable, exciting Fire–Air type, and there is likely to be a mutual attraction due to the striking differences.

Male v. Female

This is a primarily receptive, feminine combination and has all the hallmarks of the female stereotype – caring, domestic, loyal, quiet, persevering. Both male and female of this type will tend to be introverts and could work well on their own in an artistic medium, but they could also develop a shrewd business sense and do well in the marketplace. They can employ their pragmatism and sensitivity in quiet but purposeful ways, 'sussing out' the climate of the times and the integrity of would-be business partners.

Air–Water Combinations
(See nos. 28, 32, 36, 39, 43, 47, 76, 80, 84, 87, 91, 95, 124, 128, 132, 135, 139, 143)

Air and Water together produce mist which is a seemingly

insubstantial, rather ethereal mixture. In fact, this combination of mind and emotion can produce a wonderful sense of humour and an extremely creative imagination, making for an equal interest in both sciences and the humanities, in people and things, in fact and fiction. This individual is enormously sensitive and potentially insightful, but may need to exert terrific effort in handling the real world. It is potentially a romantic, poetic combination, powerfully expressive and often theatrical. The Welsh poet Dylan Thomas (Sun Scorpio, Moon Aquarius) expressed this ironic blend of mind and heart in a note about his *Collected Poems*:

> These poems, with all their crudities, doubts, and confusions, are written for the love of Man and in praise of God, and I'd be a damn' fool if they weren't.

When the Sun is in Air and the Moon in Water, the individual may be a thinking type who consciously reflects upon the mysteries of life. This person thinks he is a free spirit, but soon finds out how deeply attached he has become. The Scottish birth-control campaigner Marie Stopes (Sun Libra, Moon Pisces) was typical of the combination in her idealism, which was concerned with the realm of human values and the mysterious world of feeling and emotion. She expressed this well when she said:

> There is nothing in the world I so reverence as beauty, whether of the world, of character or in a soul.

Shadow

The Air–Water type may sometimes get confused as to whether he is thinking or feeling something. An apparently detached viewpoint may in fact be tinged with personal bias. This individual may also experience a mind–emotion split, feeling both emotionally involved and even dependent, and yet detached from the object of his affections at another level.

In general, there can be a tendency for a rich imagination to remain somewhat 'up in the air', and for procrastination and an impractical approach to limit the possibilities of successful self-expression. If Water is the stronger element, there can be intense emotionality, receptivity and self-dramatization, but with a lack of strategy about one's creative energies. If Air is the stronger element, the individual initiates well-thought-out schemes but they may lack that touch of originality which comes from the depths of an inspired heart. To find out which element is stronger, you need to know further details about the horoscope, such as whether there are several planets in Water or Air.

Relationships

The Air–Water type is interested in relating and communicating, and makes a delightful and stimulating partner. But there may be a kind of divine discontent in this individual, a sort of unconscious yearning for something more and a sense that the grass is greener somewhere else. Relationships can be problematic because there is a need for intimacy and security as well as for variety and change.

Women with the Moon in a Water sign may tend to gravitate towards men with a strong Water component, for they will help bring out their sense of femininity, which could otherwise get suppressed and intellectualized. For similar reasons, men with the Moon in an Air sign may find themselves drawn to Air-type women, with whom they will feel a spontaneous affinity. It may be possible for this combination to drift into new intimacies without realizing it is happening, and they would expect to be able to remain friends with all past lovers.

Male v. Female

This combination is probably best handled by females who can stay in touch with their feelings and also reflect on them without too much distress. The female role requires 'diffuse awareness' – the ability to be aware of many different things at once – and it also requires tremendous adaptability, which this combination provides. It is likely that males will tend to polarize towards the mental and intellectual dimension, defending themselves against the overt expression of feelings. This will especially be the case when the Moon is the water element.

Part Two

THE SUN-MOON COMBINATIONS

Chapter Four

SUN IN ARIES

———————

— 1 —

SUN ARIES ♈ MOON ARIES ♈

An actor's a guy who, if you ain't talking about him,
ain't listening.
MARLON BRANDO

Glory to Man in the highest! for Man is the master of things.
ALGERNON SWINBURNE

Themes

FIRE/FIRE Bold; quick-thinking; innovative mind; extrovert; passionate; blunt; impatient; self-centred; courageous; intuitive; adventurous; nervous energy; touchy ego; optimistic; progressive; integrity; maverick and crusading temperament.

Fools rush in where angels fear to tread – that certainly sums you up. Always ready to take up a challenge and express what is on your mind, no matter how outlandish it might be, you have a forceful, eager, hard-driving personality and a basic assumption of total independence. You are not strong on forethought or patience, but your independent spirit and unabashed self-interest is very impressive, sometimes inspiring, and always a force to be reckoned with.

Enthusiastic, quick-thinking, courageous and action-oriented, you may become restless and irritable if things do not go your way or get too quiet. Your clearly defined personal goal is never far from your mind, and your tendency is to plunge into life spontaneously and impulsively, seeking the first prize crusadingly. You are a non-conformist and enjoy challenging people if they get too set in their ways. This habit can mean that you tend to stir up controversy wherever you go, but it often spurs others on to realize more potential. Whether or not they thank you for it depends on your ability to develop diplomacy.

You are the original rugged individualist, determined to do what you want in the way *you* want to do it. Your unquestioned belief in yourself and ability to succeed is indeed enviable, especially to less confident and more emotional mortals who may get caught up in the clouds of glory that you trail around everywhere.

Your inner picture of yourself is the independent thinker, the fearless leader, the force to be reckoned with, the hero who must be about his business. But you are so absorbed with Your Business that you may fall into the trap of intolerance towards viewpoints that are different from your own. You identify with your own ideals with impassioned certainty, and in many ways they are more real to you than the mundane world.

Although you are sociable and you like people, you do not want them to take too long in explaining themselves. Your weak point is lack of sensitivity to other people and *Their* Business. If you can take more interest in other people's problems, opinions, and feelings and put yourself in the other guy's shoes more often, you will be amazed at the response and the increased level of co-operation you get from others.

Relationships

Although you are a real romantic, your tendency to be careless and domineering when it comes to human relations reflects the way you treat your hidden 'feeling' side. You are easily vexed by 'emotional needs' – your own or anyone else's – for they slow you down and get in the way of more exciting pursuits. You just want to get on with things! They may also remind you of forgotten feelings of vulnerability from the past and your own need to be nurtured and loved. To assuage your insecurity, you sometimes lay on more bravado and apparent self-sufficiency through a show of aggression and simplistic fixed attitudes. Certainly you are an independent person, but you will be more fulfilled when you can learn to recognize and then to respect your own feelings and emotional needs.

For you, the main enjoyment of love is the pursuit, and if you catch a too-submissive partner, it is unlikely that the relationship will last. You need challenge and change: a predictable routine is likely to put the fire out. Your partner needs to have his or her own life and interests so that an element of surprise always exists. If you find yourself enjoying too much harmony, you will create some conflict by playing Devil's advocate. That will get the sparks flying and, for you, sparks are the stuff of life.

Your Greatest Strengths

Honesty and courage (nothing is impossible for you); incisive intellect that cuts through non-essentials; optimism and youthful spirit. Your vitality and assertive enthusiasm can inspire others to see how simple it is to believe in themselves. You have that initiating sort of personality for which lesser mortals yearn.

Your Greatest Weaknesses

Blunt approach to life; lack of sensitivity to the spoken or unspoken needs of those around you; a tendency towards overt selfishness and bossiness; a hasty approach to work and a dislike of attending to details or finishing what you started; a one-track mind that can miss important nuances and invite antagonism rather than cooperation.

Image for Integration

An invincible Hercules, propelled by a primeval power, bursts into the dark castle, unties the fair maiden, and together they ride off into the sunset.

Famous Personalities

Marlon Brando (actor), Sue Cook (TV presenter), Anatole France (novelist), Sir John Gielgud (actor), Joan Grant (writer), Samuel Hahnemann (homoeopathic doctor), James Hillman (archetypal psychologist), David Steel (politician), Algernon Swinburne (poet and critic), Max Von Sydow (actor), Booker T. Washington (educator), Emile Zola (novelist).

—2—

SUN ARIES ♈ MOON TAURUS ♉

A tart temper never mellows with age, and a sharp tongue is the only edged tool that grows keener with constant use.
WASHINGTON IRVING

I move at a hell of a pace and I can't bear anybody who pussyfoots around.
GLORIA HUNNIFORD

Themes

FIRE/EARTH Gentle yet tough; intuitive yet pragmatic; diplomatic yet tactless; straight-from-the-shoulder charm; energetic; confident; self-assertive; sexy; staying power; bawdy sense of humour; ambitious, possessive.

You have a flair for living. You know how to enjoy yourself, how to get others to enjoy themselves, and how to get the things you want done, done. But are you a six-shooting enforcer or a softly-softly, sweet-talking charmer? Are you a slow and steady conservative or an impatient radical? Are you a sensualist or a romantic? Should you believe your mind as it leaps to intuitive truths or should you follow your instincts and not believe anything you cannot see and touch, count and measure? You are torn between the eager need to make your mark upon the world immediately as Mr or Ms Action, and your instinct for the slower but surer comforts of the inside track and doing leisurely business over a long drink. You can equally be divided between art and science, between your need for personal self-expression and economic security. You are equally divided between your instinct to mother and support others and your conviction that people must do their own thing and make their own mistakes.

When these tough and tender aspects of you come together they can produce a formidable drive, energy, endurance and determination and an irresistible charm, charisma, creative drive and, let's be frank, sex appeal. Sex and sensuality are very much at the roots of that natural, bright-eyed magnetism you give off when you are firing on all cylinders. This dynamic combination of energies with its easy-going toughness enables you to bring a freshness and hang-loose zest to whatever you do, be it in the arts, the sciences, business, sport or leisure.

Whilst you can be judicious in smoothing down ruffled feathers, you hate hypocrisy and are never afraid to speak out with a dry, pointed wit to name names, or to fight hard for what you believe to be rightfully yours. Many will be those who wish they had your healthy dose of self-respect, and equally many will be those who wish you had a stronger dose of tolerance and sensitivity. Such wishes will be tinged with both envy and truth, for yours is a personality which is impressively confident, strongly influential, and blatantly determined to get what you want. This, together with your sheer enjoyment of the material world, gives you a natural flair for financial and business matters where your mailed-fist-in-velvet-glove approach can produce powerful results.

You have a natural understanding of money and property which, combined with a competitive instinct makes you a natural entrepreneur, a ready player of the stock market and a merchant adventurer. But whilst you have an instinct to build up your wealth, you are likely to find that your hedonism and generosity can spend it even faster. For all your firm grasp of material matters, your intuitive vision of the larger realities makes you suspicious of out-and-out materialism. This means that, whatever you may be or do, there is always a space in your life where, despite yourself, an element of enchantment and the sheer dynamic mystery of life expresses itself.

Relationships

You are wonderful company. You have a real zest and appreciation for life and not least of the opposite sex. You love the rough and tumble of a good challenge, yet you love life's luxuries. One moment you can be taking on all comers in open competition, and the next you can be lounging at ease, cracking bawdy jokes.

Other people are intensely important to you and you can make them feel deeply cared for and needed. Yet on analysis you somehow seem to end up in charge and running the show. You can be deeply possessive and prone to fits of intense jealousy. Whilst your strong masculine and feminine energies make you naturally attractive and encourage your roving eye, you can be extremely loyal and romantically devoted. The problems begin if you start getting taken for granted, for you like to be centre stage in any relationship. When you are ignored you can be inclined to brood and sulk and give off vibes which will deter all approaches. Yet once you click on again you can charm those who moments before had become life-long enemies.

Your Greatest Strengths

Forceful and magnetic charm; courage, stamina and determination; practical ambition and go-for-it will to win and endure; ability to enjoy your successes and feel you deserve them!

Your Greatest Weaknesses

Self-centredness and personal ambition; stubborn resistance to anything you do not want to do; your go-stop-go approach to work; letting ego get in the way of basic co-operation and harmony.

Images for Integration

An explorer practises the violin in a jungle clearing ... Having won an arduous race, the champion sits down to a gourmet meal.

Famous Personalities

Hans Andersen (writer of fairy tales), Karen Blixen (novelist, author of *Out of Africa*), Pierre Boulez (composer), René Descartes (philosopher), Gloria Hunniford (television personality), Washington Irving (writer), Tama Janowitz (novelist), Elton John (singer, entertainer), Marcel Marceau (mime artist), Gregory Peck (actor), Diana Ross (singer), Leopold Stockowski (conductor), Wernher von Braun (space travel pioneer).

— 3 —

SUN ARIES ♈ MOON GEMINI ♊

When a man gives his opinion he's a man.
When a woman gives her opinion she's a bitch.
BETTE DAVIS

'Do you come here often?'
'Only in the mating season.'
SPIKE MILLIGAN, *The Goon Show*

Themes

FIRE/AIR Purposeful or scattered; communicative; live-wire; direct; humorous; deft; witty; persuasive; entrepreneur; young at heart; too many irons in the fire; creative; musical.

'Quick, quick, what does it say about *me*? Brilliant! A load of old cobblers!' Slow down a moment and you may learn something. Ask yourself whether you are single-minded or many-minded? A single-shot, high-velocity rifle or a shotgun, hot-metal sprayer? You will certainly be in many minds about that. So, should you try and focus your very considerable drive and ambition on one objective, or is your greatest asset the sheer diversity of your interests and aspirations?

You have immense dynamism and nervous energy and a very sharp mind, but you can lack focus and stamina. You bore easily, be it in work or relationships. Variety is the spice of your life, so whatever you do, you need to be in situations and with people that keep you on your turbo-assisted toes. Make an asset of the fact that you are a starter rather than a finisher. Simply by working with someone who can carry things through from where you left off will greatly enhance your self-esteem. Not that it needs enhancing, but there are moments when you wonder why nothing has come of yet another brilliant idea.

You are one of the great persuaders. Words are your greatest gift. As with everything else, you are a fast mover – fast-talking, witty, with a love of, indeed a veritable flair and inspiration for, slang and witticisms. (If you need to learn a foreign language, your best bet is to go to the country and focus first on the slang.) You would be tops at telephone selling, indeed selling anything to anyone at any time.

Your vital, lively, witty *joie de vivre* makes those with whom you come into contact feel more alive. Great! The problem is that you can get carried away with your own wit and eloquence and talk yourself, as well as everyone else, into shooting off after your latest enthusiasm before the last project has reached its prime. You can, and do, reach for the stars, but you can simply play the star with your ready quick quips and ease of self-expression and forget to put in the solid homework or appoint the helpers who will ensure the goods get delivered.

You enjoy yourself and want others to enjoy themselves. You can be the life and soul of the party – a bit crazy, but definitely vital, alive, light, bright and vivacious. Whether you are partying, playing or working you like to keep things bubbling along. There is something of the eternal youth about you: vivacious, outrageous, highly vocal and eternally optimistic.

You are probably naturally creative in many directions, and not least musical. Top of the pops, or top of the classics, here you come. When you focus your attention and gifts on some idea or experience that has captured your imagination, you are capable of formidable creative outpouring. But again you have to ask yourself whether you are seriously ambitious or simply doing it for the laughs and because it comes easily.

Relationships

Are you blowing hot or cold today? You are inclined to fall in and out of love mighty fast, though you expect to remain good friends. You are essentially a romantic, specializing in knights in shining armour and/or Princesses to be rescued. You are a delightful companion until you get bored, when suddenly you find that 'good old X' is really rather wet behind the ears and not all that exciting intellectually ... and you are on to the next sure-fire winner.

For fidelity you require someone who will constantly surprise you, but you may be drawn to the understanding, 'mothering' type to give you the security you need deep down – and your partner gets you to spice up his or her life. Well it could work ... for a while!

Your Greatest Strengths

Zest; enthusiasm; quick wits; gift of the gab; capacity to take an idea and run with it; eye for an opportunity and entrepreneurial skills; your sheer oomph and chutzpah.

Your Greatest Weaknesses

Brash impatience; unreliability; insensitivity to less extrovert and expressive types; naivety; unwillingness to learn from experience.

Images for Integration

A fencing master carries off the prize ... A racing driver plays the piano to relax ... Haydn's *Farewell Symphony*.

Famous Personalities

Howard Cossell (sports commentator), Bette Davis (actress), Doris Day (actress), Marilyn Ferguson (writer), Alec Guinness (actor), Joseph Haydn (composer), Helmut Kohl (German Chancellor), Spike Milligan (comedian), Modest Petrovich Mussorgsky (composer), Sergei Rachmaninov (composer, pianist and conductor), Jochen Rindt (champion racing driver), Omar Sharif (actor), Spencer Tracy (actor), Herbert von Karajan (conductor).

— **4** —

SUN ARIES ♈ MOON CANCER ♋

Americans are like a rich father who wishes he knew how to give his sons the hardships that made him rich.
ROBERT FROST

I have more memories than if I were a thousand years old.
CHARLES BAUDELAIRE

Themes

FIRE/WATER Artistic temperament; rich imagination; indirect self-assertion; volatile; sensitive; protective; temperamental; self-centred; strongly individualistic; clannish; responsible; devoted; romantic.

Independent by nature, you are self-protective and emotionally sensitive as well. Like a rugged, pioneering poet, you rush headlong into romance and adventure but often, to your great chagrin, come home with your tail very much between your legs.

Your nature is complex. Self-centredness and independence are

59

marked, as is your charismatic appeal, as others can sense your real desire to sympathize, help and understand their needs and motivations. You are also the inspirational type with a gift for imaginative work, although the impulse to create may come in fits and starts. But creative self-expression is essential for your wellbeing, as is having an appreciative audience.

You can size up a situation intuitively and, in a seductively caring way, say just the right thing at the right time. Because you readily sense what a group or an individual needs, people tend to look to you as a natural leader. You are excellent at motivating people – even to do something they may not initially want to. With deep, emotional conviction about 'what is good for humanity' (and for you), you influence people by appealing to their heads *and* their hearts. But you can just as easily invite resistance and conflict if you get too attached to your own views and come over as preciously self-preoccupied. You think of yourself as – and indeed you *are* – incredibly sensitive, and would not want to hurt anyone. But your natural self-centredness, based on your Arien need for self-assertion and your Cancerian emotional defences, means that your own concerns are dramatized and are vastly more important to you than the needs of others.

Paradoxically, one of your greatest difficulties derives from one of your most sterling qualities: sensitivity. Whilst you can be an extremely charismatic leader, you can also descend into the grips of bitterness, self-pity and depression if you and your ideas are not wholeheartedly embraced. You have a lot of pride, take yourself very seriously, and your outlook is always distinctly subjective. This means that you are capable of carrying a grudge if disagreements escalate into a win-or-lose situation.

You may be astute in business matters for you like the exhilaration of a gamble as long as you know it is a sure winner. Your challenge is to combine security and adventure – cosy cream teas and high drama – and it will produce enough creative tension to keep you going for your whole life.

Relationships

You think of yourself as daring and original, but in your heart of hearts you want your emotional and physical needs to be taken care of. You may idealize the romantic chase but end up with someone decidedly like mother. If you explore your emotional patterns you will discover just how much of your life is conditioned by your *feeling* responses. And if you look even deeper you may find that the root of emotional patterns of brooding and spiteful over-reaction is in childhood relationships.

You are independent and dependent at the same time. With too much solitude you easily get restless, depressed and your outlook can become warped. You need a close, loving relationship and domestic security in order for your talents to really flower. And when they do, your charm, wit and dramatic flair will flow seductively from your tongue, for at your best you are your own best publicity. You are a maverick, a creative artist who is more susceptible to the whims of your public than you want to be.

Your Greatest Strengths

Smooth-talking charisma; uncanny knack of catching the imagination of your audience; ability to bring your feeling for the past to bear on your visionary thrust towards the future; the immediacy and enthusiasm of your personal involvement in projects and relationships; your very individual, dramatic style and sense of the poetic.

Your Greatest Weaknesses

Difficulty handling personal criticism; a conflict between needing to belong and needing to be different; oversensitivity and tendency to be emotionally defensive, which results in moodiness and a basic instability that undermines your best talents and achievements.

Images for Integration

A child in a fit of petulant fury runs away from home ... A lightning storm at sea gives way to a peaceful, radiant dawn ... The Salvation Army.

Famous Personalities

Jeffrey Archer (politician and author), Charles Baudelaire (poet and critic), William Booth (founder of Salvation Army), Adrian Boult (composer and conductor), Jerry Brown (politician), James

Callaghan (former British prime minister), Aretha Franklin (singer), Robert Frost (poet), William Holden (actor), Erica Jong (writer), Mary Beth Whitehead (actress).

— 5 —

SUN ARIES ♈ MOON LEO ♌

The big question is whether you are going to be able to say a hearty yes to your adventure ... the adventure of the hero – the adventure of being alive.

Follow your bliss.
JOSEPH CAMPBELL

I am an optimist, unrepentant and militant. After all, in order not to be a fool an optimist must know how sad a place the world can be. It is only the pessimist who finds this out anew every day.
PETER USTINOV

Themes

FIRE/FIRE Proud; optimistic; sociable; warmly enthusiastic; playful; adventurous; stubborn; creative; imaginative; showmanship; self-centred; big thinker; honourable; romantic; intensely devoted; an impassioned idealist; big appetite for life; a leader; the hero.

You have a BIG personality – fiery, romantic, adventuresome – and you exude a warm, uplifting influence on the people in your life. There is such a deep belief within you that your rightful place is at the very centre of the universe that, by willing it, it usually happens. You know what you love and love what you securely know about; it is simply a part of you.

Mentally you are incisive, quick and immediate; emotionally you are intense, fervent and devoted. This forceful combination of fiery feeling and sharp intellect is a winner. A certain nobility of manner coupled with a deeply romantic view of life (and of yourself) tends to attract

62

admirers to you – people who are impressed by your generosity of spirit, your conviction, your social magnetism and your devil-may-care personality. You are a natural actor, a talented and self-indulgent ham who eats up attention like a kid in a sweet shop. You mythologize your life, your needs, your goals; you are the hero in search of the finest performance of self and in love with your role in life (and if you are not, then you are pretty unhappy). You make a fine leader, for you have that envious ability to inspire others just by being yourself.

It is easy, however, for you to go over-board because your need for ego-gratification is immense. Your vanity is easily wounded and a certain emotional immaturity – a tendency to throw temper tantrums when your cherished view or dignity is challenged – can be your *bête noire*. You want your own way, and you know no other way of being your real self than to play the role of Boss. Although you do this with great panache, so much so that you convince others of your specialness and importance, your behaviour can nevertheless be domineering and condescending if you rely on others too much for applause. You can be a bit like Toad of Toad Hall, who was in love with the grandiose adventure of his life, but who needed his loyal comrades to witness fully his heroism on every escapade ('I only want to give pleasure to you fellows. Live for others! That's my motto in life.'). You want to be in command of your life, but you also want to share your enjoyment of success.

You are a person of enormous courage, vitality and integrity. You can inspire others, not only by the way you dramatically live your life (mistakes and all), but also by the sheer intensity of your enjoyment of life. This makes you a wonderful teacher and communicator. Your creativity is immense and your enthusiasm contagious; you paint a big picture of yourself and others will want to catch whatever secret it is that you have.

Relationships

You are the original romantic – totally involved with the love of your life, heart, mind and soul. Love and friendship play a very important part in your life; you need passion and adoration from your partner, as well as thoughtfulness. You in turn will give the same, and you tend to throw all of yourself into the burning passion of the moment.

You can be wonderfully loyal, but your loyalty is severely tested by a relationship that loses its romantic savour. Your mate could grow tired of being the loyal dogsbody if you are too consistently uninterested in ordinary life. You also need to admire and respect your loved one. You want only the best!

Although you can be fairly demanding in an intimate relationship, sometimes impatient and temperamental and exasperatingly intolerant, you are always intensely honourable and honest when it comes down to it. You do not give up easily, and you have reserves of optimism and vitality that make you a person others will not want to give up on either.

Your Greatest Strengths

Creative imagination; ability to communicate your ideas to a wide variety of people and situations so that you easily muster support around exciting causes; ability to inspire others with your inner faith in yourself which makes you a potentially heroic figure in whatever sphere of life you work.

Your Greatest Weaknesses

A tendency to insist childishly on only seeing things your way; to go for the biggest and best before finishing and tidying up the debris from your last project; and a propensity to let your ego needs for affirmation and applause blind your true self-perception.

Image for Integration

After slaying the black dragon of sloth and greed, the young warrior is knighted by the one true king. He marries the maiden of purity and they live happily ever after.

Famous Personalities

Joseph Campbell (mythologist), Olivia Hussey (actress), Neil Kinnock (politician), Melanie Klein (psychologist), Andrew Lloyd Webber (composer), Gloria Steinem (feminist and journalist), Peter Ustinov (actor, producer and writer), Michael York (actor).

SUN ARIES ♈ MOON VIRGO ♍

Poetry is the spontaneous overflow of powerful feelings
... recollected in tranquillity

Strongest minds
Are often those of whom the noisy world
hears least
WILLIAM WORDSWORTH

I don't want a lawyer to tell me what I cannot do; I hire him
to tell me how to do what I want to do.
J. PIERPOINT MORGAN

Themes

FIRE/EARTH Selfish yet dutiful; outspoken yet timid; impulsive yet orderly; bossy yet diffident, with organizational and administrative skills; straightforward and direct; strongly analytical and critical; practical perfectionist.

Go, go – stop, stop – go. Are you boisterously outspoken or shyly reticent? Careful or careless? Conscientious or carefree? Do you lead a quiet, self-contained life or are you out in the world shouting the odds and telling everyone what to do?

Whichever way you are, and you are probably frequently torn both ways on different occasions, there will often be times when you wish you were doing the opposite. You want to throw caution to the wind and follow your creative impulses, yet habit, and your easily aroused sense of guilt, seem to demand that you live your life for others in the fulfilment of the endless duties that life seems to place in your path. This means that you can often find yourself torn between the desire to be selfish and do your own thing, and the tug of duty and the worthy cause.

Despite your natural modesty, you are in fact impatient to be where the action is, and to be in command of the show, because you usually have clear ideas of how things should be done. You can be self-effacing, disciplined and conventional yet also highly forthright, argumentative, judgmental and outspoken. Whatever your inward sense of inadequacy, you like to be the one giving the orders, and expect to be obeyed (though you may protest too loudly to be convincing that this is *not* the case). You want everything and everyone to fit into well-defined roles and are likely to have strong likes and dislikes. Whilst this may put some people's backs up, you can soon gain others' respect with your forthright, upfront manner and probably boisterous, and at times outrageous, sense of humour.

Your inner creativity can catch fire in those areas where your natural self-assertion and penchant for being in charge can marry with your reliable, realistic, conscientious, dutiful and perfectionist approach to the work in hand. You are likely to be efficient and effective in whatever you set yourself to do and could flourish in senior management and administration, though you may find the earlier rungs of the ladder frustrating. Your strong powers of analysis enable you to identify the most effective course of action in any situation, and when you get yourself together you may find that you have natural flair as an entrepreneur and organizer. Added to your strong need to make your mark and your natural qualities of leadership, this is a combination that would find itself at home in the armed services, or in any work that requires strength of character and a desire to be of real service to society.

Your master/servant dilemma is often best resolved by becoming an expert in some field, or developing a high-level craftsmanship in a specialized area. When consciously developed, this can make you an admirable teacher, both able to identify with students' problems and to goad them into trying harder. As a creative artist you are the classic craftsperson, combining passion with sheer technical skill and mastery and an eye for detail.

As you mature, your toughness and modesty can develop into a nobility of spirit inclining you to 'little, nameless, unremembered acts of kindness and of love' which help make the world a better place.

Relationships

You are inclined to find yourself torn between a dedicated loyalty to an ordinary family life and the desire for excitement and adventure. Should you play the field or settle down? If you are a woman you are likely to be torn between your wish to speak your mind and to be tough and assertive, and your natural instinct to be passive, self-effacing and adaptable. The modest virgin or the raucous whore?

Whether male or female, you can develop a charismatic quality, and bring both the 'bliss of solitude' and the joy of the chase to your relationships by combining your natural modesty with your more impetuous side.

Your Greatest Strengths

Power of analysis and criticism and your eye for quality and detail; ability to refine new skills; administrative gifts and your ability to combine duty and initiative; willingness to put your cards on the table and say what you think.

Your Greatest Weaknesses

Intolerance of others' weaknesses; bossiness and insensitivity to the feelings of others; proneness to feelings of self-doubt and guilt; tendency to stand in your own shadow and to sabotage your own initiatives through extreme self-criticism.

Images for Integration

A surgeon performs a daring operation ... A metal worker forges an intricate masterpiece ... A William Morris design ... A remembrance that the perfect is the enemy of the good.

Famous Personalities

R.A. Bloch (writer), John Harvey-Jones (business specialist), George Jessel (actor), J.P. Morgan Snr. (banker), William Morris (artist and designer), Amedee Ozanfant (artist), Bessie Smith (jazz singer), Dorothy Tutin (actress), Erich von Daniken (writer), William Wordsworth (poet).

SUN ARIES ♈ MOON LIBRA ♎

The love of liberty is the love of others; the love of power is the love of ourselves.

The art of pleasing consists in being pleased.
WILLIAM HAZLITT

No annihilation without representation.
ARNOLD TOYNBEE

Themes

FIRE/AIR Forthright; charming; ingenious; eager for life; apparently confident but inwardly indecisive; gregarious; convivial; amorous; chivalrous; idealistic; intellectually precocious; self-centred but kind-hearted; emotionally naive; vacillates between independence and dependence.

Throughout your life you may often have to ask yourself: Who has the power, me or others? Does my need for harmonious relations frustrate my basic get-up-and-go individuality?

You have a vivacious, outgoing, and aspirational personality as well as an almost childlike desire for creative self-expression and huge doses of social involvement. You may have big ideas about your potential and the success and admiration your creative efforts should bring. But although you may feel that no one deserves first prize more than you do, you become aware early on just how much you depend on a gracious, appreciative audience.

Harbouring a romantic inner picture of yourself that sometimes takes on heroic proportions, you let your vivid imagination work overtime as you plan out your route to glory. But then you find yourself amazed, and not a little hurt, when you discover that others do not (at first) see the same heroic picture, and that life does not hand you your dreams on a platter.

Although your imaginative powers are considerable, they can be a vice as well as a virtue because you indulge them when you should be getting on with things. Sometimes you are lazy and find it difficult to get going and to make your dreams come true. You have ambition but hate strife, and very often for you the former invites the latter to some degree. Most of the time you throw yourself wholeheartedly into life, wearing your heart on your sleeve and hoping for the best. When you do not receive the positive response that you crave, you can be truly thrown off beam.

This is a full-Moon position, which means that your head and your heart often work against each other. You are eager to please, to co-operate, to make peace and to be helpful, and this makes you a natural diplomat – courageous but strategic, a maverick but a lover of justice.

Sometimes your keen awareness of others and instinct for justice causes you to suppress your personal power in the interests of harmony. You may then become overly accommodating and eventually very frustrated. When this happens you can feel that you are on an emotional see-saw, going up and down but essentially nowhere. Sometimes you feel powerfully self-directed; at other times you feel your fate is sealed by others. Feeling loved and appreciated will always be a strong need within you, and when you have gained a certain amount of emotional contentment your confidence and assertiveness will blossom. Teamwork and group goals help you to come alive and to find that innate aptitude for leadership which can inspire others.

Relationships

Romantic and devoted by nature, you tend to be quite a flirt and experimental in your youth, but feel happier when you are in a good relationship. 'Good' means a relationship that is supportive, exciting, aesthetic, egalitarian but lets you at least *think* that you are in command. You enjoy lighthearted but stimulating and convivial social situations, but in relationships your lightheartedness and essential naivety could attract emotional heaviness or complexities that baffle you and from which you run. You may feel awkward when it comes to looking at 'nasty' emotions, preferring to emphasize the 'nice' and the 'heroic'. You want adventure but will be surprised to confront the emotional extremes that your Libran Moon may attract.

Your emotional nature is strongly challenged by the prospect of a mature relationship, because your Arien goal of independence and your Libran instinct for dependence and co-operation have to be worked with, balanced and affirmed in order for you to be truly happy with yourself. The more aware you are of just how much you invest in being accepted, even adored, by others, the more you will be able to minimize the roller-coaster quality of your emotional life.

Your Greatest Strengths

Ebullient sociability and charming hospitality; idealism and hopefulness; sensitivity to others; capacity to inspire optimism; artistic imagination and talents; ability to be exactly who you are in close relationships – and to make your partner love it!

Your Greatest Weaknesses

Tendency to vacillate; to think great guns and then peter out; to let frustration eat up your confidence; to permit your need for appreciation to fuel your vanity rather than your creativity; and to rest on your laurels when you should be making strides.

Image for Integration

A conductor leads an orchestra with passionate conviction and a vibrant, pulsating organism of musical perfection is created to the ecstatic uplifting of the audience.

Famous Personalities

Pearl Bailey (singer), Jean Paul Belmondo (actor), Richard Chamberlain (actor), Antal Dorati (conductor), William Hazlitt (essayist and journalist), Shirley Jones (actress), Julian Lennon (musician), Simone Signoret (actress), Gloria Swanson (actress), Arnold Toynbee (historian), Jack Webb (actor), James Dewey Watson (biologist), Wilbur Wright (pioneer aviator).

SUN ARIES ♈ MOON SCORPIO ♏

*Live all you can ... it doesn't so much matter what you do in particular, so
long as you have your life. If you haven't had that what have you had?*
HENRY JAMES

The best part of married life is the fights. The rest is merely so-so.
THORNTON WILDER

Themes

FIRE/WATER Personal integrity; witty; intense; powerful; passionate;
highly motivated; persuasive; ambitious; forceful; self-dramatizing;
charismatic.

Should you storm life by the front or back door? Is life full of fresh-
faced opportunities and bright laughter, or is it a corrupt place, worthy
of cynical humour and dark suspicions?

You are a forceful individual with drive, energy and tenacity. You
know what you want and will find ways, direct or indirect, of achieving
it. But you can become torn between an impatient, up-front, naive,
trusting approach to the world and a suspicious, distrustful doubt;
between a self-denying, intense, slow-burning determination and a
go-for-it pizzazz. When these two sides of yourself work against each
other you may find yourself becoming embroiled in bitter conflicts
which seem to be none of your making. Relationships fall apart, and
those you thought of as friends stab you in the back. When you get
your act together, however, you become unstoppable, a courageous,
humorous, charismatic, co-operative leader, prepared to push yourself
to the limit and beyond in your determination to set the world to rights,
and to leave your mark.

People may see you as cynical, brash, self-assured and pushy, or as
somewhat private and quietly purposeful, but none will doubt your
sincerity and commitment to your chosen path. Most would, however,
be surprised at how much you care about others' good opinions. For
though you want to make a real and lasting impact upon the world by
one route or another, you especially want and need the approval,

appreciation and loud applause of your peers and can even brood, get bitter and self-destructive if your path is blocked, or your plans are crossed.

Your secret weapon, when you find it at your centre, is your belief in your own abilities. This gives you a formidable will to win. Equally it gives you a great capacity to help others stand on their own two feet, and to motivate and encourage them. To bring out this creative core you need demanding projects and ambitions to occupy your energies, especially when young.

Life for you is a drama, and self-dramatization is your forte. This can draw you towards the theatre or any arena, such as sports, where there is an opportunity to shine. No matter what career you follow, however, you will make a career out of your life. You believe in yourself and make a natural leader, but at the same time you want to be thought well of, and can become withdrawn and even bitter if your enthusiastic ideas meet with resistance.

Yours is a sharp, clear-headed, penetrating approach to life. You identify what you want to achieve and you go about achieving it with a natural gift of strategy and leadership. You have many of the qualities of the natural leader: an ability to put yourself and your cause first single-mindedly; dedication; charisma; force; a talent for research, probing into hidden corners, which is excellent for military campaigning tactics and manoeuvres, but also for campaigning journalism; and a gift for psychological insights and penetrating analysis.

You are attracted to physical exercise and sport. If you do not consciously channel your physical, emotional and mental aggression in a purposeful way you can become very bitter, frustrated and self-destructive. You can take a real disliking to people, and can be arrogant, irascible, rude and bloody-minded. Yet you are a person of integrity. You are frank, honest and like to tell it as you see and feel it. This refreshing honesty keeps you young and open-minded, always ready for new ideas and experiences. Your forceful, sharp, biting wit and wry cynicism about human weaknesses makes you an excellent humorist and comedian.

Relationships

In relationships you are a full-blooded romantic. Very highly sexed, you are not one for half measures! You are a person of intense physical passions who needs to be totally involved and committed in a relationship.

Whilst you are attracted to a mate who can fight their own corner, there is also about you the romantic spirit of the gallant crusader rescuing the helpless, drawn to wounded birds who need your strength and who will give you the unquestioning devotion you need. You can be intensely faithful or intensely unfaithful, but never indifferent.

Your Greatest Strengths

Integrity; belief in your own and others' individual worth; relentless single-mindedness; ambition; courage; determination; capacity for gutsy hard work; ability to push through your ideas and plans against all obstacles.

Your Greatest Weaknesses

Narcissism; self-dramatization; insatiable hunger for applause; determination to put yourself first; impatience and self-assertion which can, unless reined in, become overbearing and ruthless.

Images for Integration

Charlie Chaplin saves a maiden in distress ... A passionate woman sells herself for her cause... *The Godfather* films.

Famous Personalities

Warren Beatty (film actor), Anita Bryant (entertainer and evangelist), James Caan (actor), Claudia Cardinale (actress), Charlie Chaplin (actor and comedian), Julie Christie (actress), Francis Ford Coppola (film director), David Frost (actor and entrepreneur), Leslie Howard (actor), Henry James (novelist), Hayley Mills (actress), Dudley Moore (actor and comedian), Wilhelm Rontgen (physicist who discovered X-rays), Arturo Toscanini (conductor), Thornton Wilder (novelist).

SUN ARIES ♈ MOON SAGITTARIUS ♐

*Man's main task is to give birth to himself, to become what he potentially is.
The most important product of his effort is his own personality.*
ERICH FROMM

*There's no reason to bring religion into it. I think we ought to have as great a
regard for religion as we can, so as to keep it out of as many things as possible.*
SEAN O'CASEY

Habit is a great deadener.
SAMUEL BECKETT

Themes

FIRE/FIRE Visionary; highly-strung; explorer; impatient; emphatic;
talkative; confident; intense moral certainty; exuberant; optimistic;
big-hearted; fun-loving; prone to exaggeration; outspoken;
competitive; friendly; an adventurer.

Your ability to radiate warmth, enjoyment of living and an effortless
resilience to the ups and downs of existence makes you one of life's
irrepressible winners. Your intense vitality and independence is hard
to keep up with, and loved ones will have to fasten their seat belts,
expect the unexpected and enjoy an adventure in order to appreciate
the whole of your BIG personality.

You are dynamic, highly enthusiastic, fabulously gregarious, and
your visionary qualities plus the sheer energy you generate make it
easy for you to rally support around any number of exciting projects
and pet causes. You are restless and require lots of movement and
space – to you, life is one big journey, one large adventure that holds
many exciting possibilities. Delightfully refreshing to meet, you
cannot help but exude a *joie de vivre* and inner commitment to life
which can inspire and motivate others to action. And this is never so
true as when you are engaged in intellectual exchanges and arousing
public interest in moral and social causes.

Outspoken, intensely honourable and deeply intuitive, you are

74

essentially more interested in the future and in making sure it will be exciting than in finding security in the humdrum routine of daily living. Your focus on large ideas could take you into law, religion or academia. It also takes you often into the realm of speculation and risk-taking; you 'sense' that a particular solution is right and will magically unlock the door to a brighter future, even though it appears flagrantly inappropriate to other, more practical souls. In other words, you often by-pass the logical, step-by-step thinking process of the left-brain because of your capacity to perceive instantly the essence of any given situation. Your hunches are more real to you than a set of mundane facts. To you, life must be a game well-played (even if not always won), a challenge to the imagination and a test of your deep, creative, innovative spirit.

This intuitive approach to life can, however, create some instability for you and your household. Being true to your visions – doing what you want to do – takes priority over completing mundane tasks, and the result in your day-to-day life can sometimes be chaos. But even in failure, your honour is likely to stay intact for 'nothing ventured, nothing gained' is what you say; 'it is the idea that counts', and things will 'all come right' in the end. You are an incurable optimist, very noble and a touch arrogant as well. One of the most important things in your life is being able to express yourself freely and without inhibition, for honesty and fair dealing are virtues that are nearly gods to your inner life.

Relationships

Emotionally you are ardent, uncomplicated, warmly spontaneous and in love with the experience of falling in love. You give yourself wholeheartedly, but at the same time you can be pretty restless and impatient, eager to jump the fence if you feel stifled with someone.

More aware of your own feelings and needs than those of others, you can get wrapped up in ideologies and hold forth about some 'ism' at inappropriate times (when all that your mate requires is a cup of tea). Practical duties weigh on your spirit, so you need to know that there is room for movement and new adventure in your relationship.

Quite frequently you need to just drop everything and go camping, get on an airplane, go to a party or take up a new hobby. You have got to enjoy yourself! The great thing about you is that you can swing from the depths of philosophical sobriety to the heights of bawdy fun in the twinkling of an eye.

Your Greatest Strengths

Contagious optimism; entrepreneurial spirit; powerful influence on others. You need challenging, stimulating work where there is scope to let your intuition play with ideas. Just remember that generalities need details, inventions need practical working out, and that remaining in the realm of limitless possibilities will not get the job done.

Your Greatest Weaknesses

Grandiose philosophizing; moving around and never landing; insensitivity to human feelings; impatience with the limitations of the material world; total self-absorption to the extent that your capacity for relating remains childlike; and a tendency to let your daredevil side sabotage your material security.

Image for Integration

A child shoots an arrow towards the enchanted castle in the distance as he follows the road less travelled.

Famous Personalities

Richard Alpert ('Ram Dass' – psychologist), Kingsley Amis (writer), Samuel Beckett (playwright), Dirk Bogarde (actor), Rory Bremner (comedian), Robert Fludd (metaphysician), Erich Fromm (psychologist), Gus Grissom (astronaut), Sterling Hayden (actor), Thomas Hobbes (philosopher), Garry Kasparov (champion chess player), Sean O'Casey (playwright), Wilhelm Reich (psychiatrist), Ravi Shankar (zitharist), Vincent Van Gogh (artist).

SUN ARIES ♈ MOON CAPRICORN ♑

When I was one-and-twenty
I heard a wise man say,
Give crowns and pounds and guineas
But not your heart away.

A.E. HOUSMAN

The great questions of our day cannot be solved by speeches and
majority votes ... but by iron and blood.

OTTO VON BISMARCK

Themes

FIRE/EARTH Unstoppable; ambitious; tough-minded; domineering; enthusiastic and forceful manner; pragmatic intellect; droll sense of humour; sensible; ardent; persistent; aggressive; good organizer; a realist; the winner; the boss.

You are a go-getting realist, a maverick traditionalist whose strident energy and ambition takes you into the struggle of life at an early age. It is not so much that your life is a struggle, but that you experience life as a series of challenges to be conquered, and you more than most need a challenge in order to feel alive.

Something of a young up-start with an eye to the main chance, you are likely to be found in the establishment but often waging war against oppressive laws or traditions. You could also be a creative entrepreneur forging some new and exciting product or enterprise. Whatever you are involved with is likely to possess both originality and longevity, flair and endurance.

Politics is a very natural habitat for you, and it is here that you can be a very persistent thorn in the flesh of the status quo, bringing a searing honesty and fresh viewpoint which shocks people out of stagnant ways of working. And despite the insults and threats that you may provoke, you do not go away. You have tremendous willpower and are thick-skinned enough to see your personal aim through to its completion. You respect the law and learn to work within its boundaries, but just by a hair's-breadth, because you have to push the system to its absolute limit to make enough room for your individuality to express itself – and leave its stamp for posterity.

You say matter-of-factly what you intend to do, then you do it. You may be fairly low-key, not obviously a colourful Aries, but you are all the more determined for the close focus of your attention. There is something of the working-class hero about you, droll, down-to-earth and unaffected, with a scathing wit and a controlled cheekiness. You often use humour and sarcasm to get your point across.

You go for sound, solid ideals, and rarely waver from your path once you have seen the way ahead. You always assume you are right until proved wrong, and it takes quite an audacious opponent to stand up to you. Although you are naturally arrogant and impatient, you are nonetheless devoted to truth and respect personal courage in anyone, and you will immediately climb down to acknowledge the soul who is strong enough and wise enough to teach you a new lesson.

Although you want to win (and usually do), your self-respect and personal integrity is more important to you than anything. This goes for personal relationships, too: they tend to play second fiddle to your career ambitions and to those personal challenges that are such powerful grist to your mill.

Relationships

Your approach to love probably has as much practical common sense about it as your approach to work. In your bold enthusiasm to drive home a point you can seem somewhat abrasive to a partner who just wants a cuddle.

You are basically very self-controlled, and constantly push for more control of your outer world. Because of this, you may frequently mistake confrontation for relating, and loved ones may easily feel bruised and learn to avoid confrontation with you. Nevertheless, you are honest and open and ready to learn what you have to in order to be a success, be it in love or in career. You have certainly got what it takes to succeed, but you need to take care that your passion for winning and for economy of effort does not compromise the quality of your personal life. Do not forget to smell the roses along the way to success. Otherwise, it can be pretty lonely at the top.

Your Greatest Strengths

The sheer magnetic force of your personality; a quick and pragmatic mind which sizes up situations accurately and astutely; the powerful mixture of risk-taking and caution in your approach to problem-solving; natural leadership abilities; the total involvement and courageous commitment you bring to each moment of life.

Your Greatest Weaknesses

The sheer magnetic force of your personality which can overwhelm weaker souls; a propensity to charge ahead with your instinct to conquer in inappropriate situations; a too blunt, businesslike manner in personal relationships; a lop-sided and overpowering need for control and to be recognized as 'tops'.

Images for Integration

A young soldier is rewarded by the King for exceptional bravery in the cause of freedom and individual human rights ... Columbus discovers America, and a new world order is born.

Famous Personalities

Kenneth Clark (politician), Al Gore (American vice-president), A.E. Housman (poet), Eric Idle (actor and comedian), David Lean (film director), John Major (British prime minister), Elizabeth Montgomery (actress), Stephen Sondheim (composer), Rod Steiger (actor), Mstislav Rostropovitch (cello virtuoso and conductor), Mies Van Der Rohe (architect), Sarah Vaughan (singer), Otto von Bismarck (statesman).

— 11 —

SUN ARIES ♈ MOON AQUARIUS ♒

I shall marry in haste and repent at leisure.
JAMES BRANCH CABELL

To be free is to have achieved your life.
TENNESSEE WILLIAMS

Themes

FIRE/AIR Selfish yet altruistic; full of bright ideas; friendly; congenial; extrovert; enthusiastic; incisive; sharp; analytical; sociable; progressive; revolutionary; social activist; dramatic; exceptionally individual.

You are where it is at, and beyond that too. But are you a self-obsessed revolutionary or a social prophet? Are you a passionate progressive or a detached onlooker? Or have you discovered how to combine both through a vocation which meets your need for constant challenge?

You may appear to be self-centred but, just when everyone thinks you are in it only for yourself, you reveal your capacity for true friendship and interest in the needs of others. You can be very civilized and very selfish. You want to make your mark upon the world but you do not want to scar it in the process, though it may not believe you at first. When firing on all cylinders, and not just spouting hot air, you are original and inventive; a natural pioneer, entrepreneur and leader of progressive causes; a great improver, able to see the big picture and inspire others with a large and distinctly different vision of things. You will take an active interest in anything that appeals to your maverick, heretic and non-conformist approach to life. New schemes and ideas may be more exciting to you than the prospect of finishing what you have already started, for orderly routine is a living death for you. Being self-employed and doing your own thing attracts you, yet you also have a strong social sense and can work well with others, provided you are in charge. You rightly have a high opinion of your own genius, and in order to be happy you need to be working and playing in areas where you feel free to take the initiative and pursue your observations and insights.

With your razor-sharp mind, you enjoy an intellectual challenge, and have an ability to look at things from a different perspective. You delight in being controversial and poking fun at the status quo. You see yourself as a go-ahead mould-breaker, an anarchist even. Be it in politics, film, fashion or the very way in which you express yourself, you are drawn to the non-conformist, original and maverick, and are never happier than when out on limb arguing for a viewpoint that others do not yet share. In this you can combine courage and imagination, for you are a natural campaigner who can pursue what you believe in with a burning conviction.

Friendships and social contacts are very important to you, and here as in so much of your life you can oscillate between self-interest and social concern. One moment you are being an elitist social climber, using your natural charisma and powers of persuasion to chat up the in-crowd with a cynical eye to the main chance; the next you are giving your time and energy to help the socially deprived and under-privileged. This dichotomy may play havoc with your philosophical and political affiliations as you veer from radical liberalism to complete free-enterprise. If you can allow room for both you will probably end up embracing an enlightened self-interest and make friends right across the fascinating spectrum of human viewpoints.

Relationships

You are a great 'people person', intrigued by individual differences and able to get on with most types. You should appreciate, though, that your combination of romantic passion and clinical detachment which can be disconcerting for you can be even more bewildering for your partner. For whilst you pursue the object of your desire with a sense of ardent adventure, your natural instinct is for personal friendship and intellectual companionship.

Sex, likewise, is something that can both obsessively absorb you and yet be something to be dismissed lightly and humorously. Your infatuations turn into friendships, and your friendships into ardent desires. Though you may be unconsciously drawn to maternal types, you need someone who will keep you guessing as well as help ground you for a long-term partnership .

Your Greatest Strengths

Gift of the gab; broad intellect; energy and enthusiasm; interest in people; large, individual vision; natural charisma; idealism.

Your Greatest Weaknesses

Selfish altruism that sacrifices others for your social vision; insensitivity to others' feelings; over-rational approach to life and people; impatience with practical details and dull routines; elitist tendencies.

Images for Integration

A gallant crusader turns his sword into a computer chip and broadcasts New Age philosophy ... A militant feminist joins a non-sectarian commune.

Famous Personalities

Béla Bartók (composer), James Branch Cabell (novelist), Peter Brook (film and theatre director), David Cassidy (singer), Joan Crawford (actress), William Harvey (physician and scientist), Violette Leduc (novelist), Jayne Mansfield (actress), Steve McQueen (actor), Debbie Reynolds (actress), Dane Rudhyar (astrologer and composer), Charlie Tuna (disc jockey), Tennessee Williams (dramatist, novelist and poet), F.W. Woolworth (businessman).

— 12 —

SUN ARIES ♈ MOON PISCES ♓

If you don't swing, don't ring.
HUGH HEFNER

I am a realist in my novels – and a trance realist at that.
ROBERT LOWRY

Themes

FIRE/WATER Romantic; moody; affectionate; restless; a worrier; enthusiastic but inwardly timid; hopeful; thoughtful; nervous but eager; non-conformist; artistic; stylish; inspirational; imaginative; expressive; temperamental.

You are a bit like the BFG – the Big Friendly Giant – forceful but diffident, single-minded but dreamy, maverick and very much your own person but kind-hearted and needy of affection and consideration from others. You have plenty of initiative and strong personal motivations, and you seem to want to be out in the forefront of human activities. Underneath your impressive exterior, however, you are often quaking with doubt and timidity and wondering how you could have made such a challenge or said such an outrageous thing.

One part of you is very independent, impulsive, eager for action and rooted in a sense of yourself as an opponent of social injustice. This part thrives on self-assertion, on making things happen and feeling at the helm of all the action-making. But another part of you shrinks from excessive exposure, risk, bright lights and noise, and prefers to slip away into the inner sanctuary of your own room, or mind, to brood and worry and often just to dream. This part of you abhors the brisk self-definition after which your other part strives. You know what you want, but do not feel right about insisting that you get it. You know what needs to be done and can rally the troops to join your crusade, but all of a sudden you can feel like a stranger in your own crowd – lost, misunderstood, convinced in self-pitying mood that no one could possibly understand the real you or your true intentions. Masculine assertion versus feminine receptivity; bold defiance versus the soft blurring of boundaries; self-interest or self-sacrifice; sticking your neck out or living it all out in fantasy – this is your dilemma.

The needs of your Arien ego versus your Piscean instinct for self-immolation can create a conflict within you. This is perhaps best resolved in a career that brings you both personal recognition as well as a sense of being emotionally involved with people and life. You are an aspiring individual who wants a unique identity and, well, just a little bit of recognition, but you also need to feel connected in a broad impersonal way with the world in which you find yourself. In some ways you are a maverick, and in other ways you very much need the support of understanding colleagues and friends.

Unusual ideas interest you, and you need a harmonious environment in which to develop your own self-expression. You feel happier when you get these ideas down on paper, canvas or photographic film – whatever the particular direction you take. When you find yourself feeling that life is too harsh and demanding, you can be sure that the gulf between the realist and the idealist within you is widening. It is time to withdraw, to get in touch with your own feelings and dreams and make sure that they *are* your own. Then you must work to master a medium of expression so that there is always a bridge of communication between the bold Arien and the elusive Piscean dreamer within you, between the daring child and the artistic visionary.

At your very best, you combine the spirit of enterprise with the human touch of care and understanding. Together they make you a powerful force for good in the world.

Relationships

You are a very romantic person and you need intimacy, but you will find it difficult getting everything you need from one person. When it comes to emotions, you are easily influenced and have a tendency to go for the tragic love story at least once in your life, where you get involved with a person or people who let you down. The sense of emotional suffering you may be left with can either eat you up – if you allow it to – or it can fuel your heroism and creative inspiration.

One minute you are all dreamy and ready to risk all for love, the next you are industriously engaged with your own personal goals and concerns, with no intentions at all of leaning on anyone. Whilst you are both passionate and caring, you may experience a conflict between running the show and giving in. Try not to martyr yourself by attracting the lame dogs to show how strong you can be: moderation in all things!

Your Greatest Strengths

Fertile imagination; off-beat but wonderfully original style and philosophy of life; vulnerability and openness to experience; commitment to the never-ending quest to find your *real* identity and to be true, intellectually and emotionally, to yourself.

Your Greatest Weaknesses

Tendency to worry too much, which can weaken your vitality; the power of your mood swings, which can undermine your relationships and darken your state of mind; emotional impressionability; tendency to drift into dreams rather than concentrating on the here and now.

Image for Integration

A world-champion boxer and an artist in Greenwich Village meet, fall in love, marry and struggle happily ever after.

Famous Personalities

Herb Alpert (bandleader and trumpet player), Jacques Brel (actor, singer and director), Roberta Cowell (transsexual), Paul Daniels (magician and showman), Dr Richard Dawkins (geneticist), Hugh Hefner (creator of *Playboy* magazine), Thomas More Johnson (Neo-Platonic philosopher), Robert Lowry (novelist), Ann Miller (actress), Mistinguette (actress).

Chapter Five

SUN IN TAURUS

------------◆------------

— 13 —

SUN TAURUS ♉ MOON ARIES ♈

Power takes as ingratitude the writhings of its victims.

The greed for fruit misses the flower.
RABINDRANATH TAGORE

All poetry is putting the infinite within the finite.

Oh, to be in England/Now that April's here.
ROBERT BROWNING

Themes

EARTH/FIRE Determined; forceful; strong desires; go for what you want; great panache; musical; artistic; energetic; enduring enthusiasm; independent; powerful; selfish; steadfastly ambitious; good at practical or technical skills; a leader.

Are you a wandering gypsy, a nature mystic or a kind of Davy Crockett figure, king of the wild frontier, who aspires to become lord of the manor? Whatever you do, you have the instincts of an artist and the mind of a businessman. You want fixity, permanence, power and security, and yet you are ever the pioneer, looking for new frontiers once your territory gets too familiar and easy.

You want action, so you make things happen, throwing yourself into life. If something feels comfortable, however, you put your foot down and it will not budge. Instinctively tuned into your own needs and desires, you have extraordinary determination and unabashed self-interest, which probably carry you into the drama of your life at an early age. You do not wait around for the approval or permission of others – you are a self-starter and usually finish what you have begun. Direct and forthright, you call a spade a spade, and are so certain of yourself and your ideas and feelings that you do not easily stop to question your actions or how they could be improved. You want what you want and usually plough full-steam ahead to get it.

You love action and enterprise but you also need security and roots, and this can create a tension within you which manifests from time to time in impatience and intense irritability. At home you can be the benevolent dictator. You possess such a strong instinct to manage and control that the co-operative spirit you *say* you believe in – it makes good sense, right? – is usually put on the shelf. You were made to be captain of your own ship, but to prevent mutiny you have to learn how to treat others with more respect, kindness and equality.

Your need for achievement, and indeed your talent for using your resources with inspiring innovation, is much stronger than your interest in human nature. Practical and hard-working, you just do not have time for people who moan or have complex emotional problems. With so much drive to conquer and establish, you will find it difficult understanding dreamier, more fragile types.

Uncontrolled passion and temper is what trips you up: you can express real infantile rage if pushed to the limit. But with more self-awareness, that same energy can go into creative endeavours and move mountains in the business world or in some artistic profession. Often you just want to sit on that mountain after you have got it where you want it, like Smaug the dragon sitting on his mound of jewels. You want to consolidate your position and use your resources to their maximum advantage – and then live off the interest. You could be an excellent entrepreneur, may be very musical or artistic, would be an efficient provider, an organized homemaker and an untiring servant of your own inner vision. That vision will include whatever you feel is your duty to family and mate.

Relationships

Sometimes you seem to be the absolute epitome of the rational, sensible person, ready to invest only in what you can taste, touch, see and add up. And yet at other times you are capable of acting from totally emotional concerns, and of expressing outlandish beliefs, fantastic ideas and irrational behaviour.

Although you are romantic and loyal, given half a chance you will dominate most relationships. You are possessive and demanding, but can be generous, fun-loving and exciting when you have found the right person to balance your big appetites. Home life is extremely important to you, and you want it to be a haven for enjoyment and creative hobbies.

In co-operative ventures you are quick to take charge, and you may develop a following of subordinates who come to trust your competence and leadership implicitly. But your raucous sense of humour and love of a party endears you to others. Quite simply, your personality stands out as vital, outrageous and funny, but you will win more friends and influence more people if, paradoxically, you attach less importance to personal conquests. If you can do this, you will be an inspiration to loved ones instead of a moody artist they have to put up with.

Your Greatest Strengths

Charisma; confidence; courage; indefatigable resilience; unswerving belief in yourself; organizational flair and practical instinct for making your dreams come true.

Your Greatest Weaknesses

Stubbornness; tendency to be quarrelsome and to ride roughshod over others; self-centredness; tendency to let emotionalism turn you into a bully.

Images for Integration

A pirate's chest full of gold is discovered, which adds to the already vast empire of Ghengis Khan ... An orgy of love on a carpet of bluebells.

Famous Personalities

Robert Browning (poet), Georges Braque (artist), Salvador Dali (artist), Susan Hampshire (actress), Immanuel Kant (philosopher), Ernst Ludwig Kirchner (artist), Kathryn Kuhlman (minister and healer), Robespierre (French revolutionary leader), Rabindranath Tagore (poet), Stevie Wonder (singer and musician), Malcolm X (American black leader).

— 14 —

SUN TAURUS ♉ MOON TAURUS ♉

From each according to his ability, to each according to his need.
KARL MARX

Doin what comes naturally.
IRVING BERLIN, *Annie Get Your Gun*

Themes

EARTH/EARTH Sensuality v. self-control; love of nature; practical; supportive; seeks certainties; slow and steady; deep calm v. explosive anger; good business sense; natural counsellor; dry, mischievous humour; dictatorial; possessive; unflappable.

Is life for you a delight and pleasure to be enjoyed, or a practical affair to be managed and organized? You can be torn between a lazy, sensual self-indulgence and a deliberate, even stoic, self-control; between an almost mystical love of nature and a matter-of-fact cost accountant's approach to life.

You are naturally a sensualist, with a keen, raw enjoyment of the tastes and scents of foods, the sounds of music and the countryside, the textures of things, the visual delights of life and art. Yet you seek to be in command of the changing material world, and that includes your own body, a tendency that can lead you to deny your own feelings and desires. For above all you seek certainty and security for yourself and your loved ones.

In all you do, you want to get down to basics, to the practical certainties and self-evident realities. You want to define things, lay foundations and simplify. You can become impatient with abstract theories and yet be as rigid and dogmatic in the way you believe things should be done as any theorist. Your criterion is: does it work? You are a hands-on teacher who believes in the power of experience and in what you can directly see for yourself.

You have a deep understanding of some of the basics that make the world go round, such as pleasure, sex, security and money. This makes you excellent at business matters and equally gives you a gift for therapeutic work and counselling. You are at your happiest and most creative when you are doing work that both expresses your loving care of others and brings pleasure, and yet also produces tangible results. Careers or pursuits that will bring out the best in you include cooking, music, painting, creating a home, nursing, counselling, teaching or indeed building up a business around your own interests.

Whilst you very much live in the here-and-now, you also like to feel that the foundations you are laying will be of permanent value. You have the rare gift of real common sense, and whether in the area of psychology, business, art or science, you can always be depended on to offer sound, well-grounded, straight-from-the-shoulder insights. You have a rather slow, steady, dependable approach to things, and a quiet, even shy, manner. This can make your dry, tell-it-as-it is, often bawdy sense of humour all the more surprising.

You are a deeply grounded individual with great reserves of practical kindness, and your sheer sanity and stability can be enormously reassuring to those who know you. In consequence you can become the proverbial rock to your friends, on whom all depend. Your tea is served in mugs not in cups, in the kitchen not the sitting room. You enjoy what is in front of you and you deal with the problems, often those of other people, with a quiet stability and directness of spirit. All this makes your occasional outbursts of seemingly uncontrollable rage all the more mystifying. Such rages, when they occur, are the consequence of your habitual calm and desire for order which demands that you keep the dark side of life at bay. Hence when your accumulated angers and irritations do break through, you have little experience of coping witn them.

Because you can be so understanding and supportive of others, the great risk for you is that you will be treated as Atlas, the support of the world, so that your own needs are constantly neglected. When this happens you may find yourself retreating into illness to attract the attention and support that you too need to receive.

Relationships

As a strongly earthy, sensual type, sex is likely to play an important part in your relationships, yet you are not inclined to play the field. On the contrary, you tend to be solidly, stolidly faithful, for what you want in relationships is security, stability and, as in all things, certainty.

You can offer total dedication and loyalty but you will expect the same in return. You expect to possess your mate and to be possessed for always. Once this is agreed, you become a living demonstration that true love and devotion is centred in the will rather than the heart. Yet for all your love of stability there is one big exception to this picture: you find yourself being drawn magnetically, and irrationally towards strongly Fire types (see page 33). The magic of Fire's unbridled imagination and intuition, and their courage to plunge into the unknown without looking at the map and checking the supplies, can irresistably attract you, as much as your effortless stability can attract them.

Your Greatest Strengths

Kind, calm, supportive approach; logical mind; endurance; realism and practical skills; ability to call a spade a spade, and to bring a sense of order, stability, certainty and security to your world.

Your Greatest Weaknesses

Lack of contact with your own anger which can erupt directly or indirectly as passionate hatred; possessiveness; lack of imagination; rigidity and stubbornness; intolerance of those with whom you disagree.

Images for Integration

A successful baker is surrounded by delighted children eating fresh bread rolls ... A loving teacher resolves an angry dispute.

Famous Personalities

Irving Berlin (composer), Carol Burnett (comedienne), Angela Carter (writer), Giovanni Falcone (anti-Mafia judge), Stewart Granger (actor), Jack Klugman (actor), Joanna Lumley (actress), Karl Marx (social scientist), Rollo May (psychologist), Florence Nightingale (pioneer nurse), Henri Poincaré (mathematician and philosopher), Tyrone Power (actor), Jane Roberts (author of *Seth* books).

— 15 —

SUN TAURUS ♉ MOON GEMINI ♊

Where id is let ego be.
SIGMUND FREUD

*The trouble is that my heart would not willingly
remain one hour without love.*
CATHERINE THE GREAT

Themes

EARTH/AIR Mind v. body; quick-slow, quick-slow; clear, practical intelligence; dogmatic yet flippant; good business sense; charming; witty; persuasive; opportunist.

Are you a quick, streetwise, light-hearted city slicker or a slow country soul tuned into the rhythms of nature and the serious business of survival? Are you a flippant, easy-come-easy-go flirt or an ardent, possessive lover, loyal to the last? Often torn between mind and body, half the time you can be a stanger to yourself. At one moment you are taking ultra-conservative decisions that restrain your light-hearted love of free-flowing freedom; and at another you are acting on spontaneous, flip, fun-loving impulses which challenge your hard-won security and desire for certainty and stability.

When you can contain these two aspects of yourself and get them talking to one another, you can realize your gift for understanding the natural world and for conveying an inner understanding of things. Yours is a combination of the earthy sensual and the breezy intellectual approaches to life. This can give you an enormous practical intelligence and a great gift for vivid, direct communication – the kind that is invaluable not only to teachers and scientists but also to writers, artists and businesspeople. Your creative genius flowers when these two sides – solid realism and light brightness – are kept in balance. Then you can become both prolific and practical in your projects, always willing to entertain a new idea and put it to work.

If you give precedence to your body and your desire for control and certainty in your life, you can end up denying the playful child in you who breathes life into your feet of clay and puts a spring in your otherwise ponderous gait. If you emphasize the mind at the expense of the body, you can end up attempting to rationalize the sensual life out of existence. Taken too far, this can divorce you from your own sensuality and appetites and cut you off from the direct experience of life as a living reality. When you work with both sides of yourself it can produce the delightful free-flowing movements of a Fred Astaire dance or the delightful zest and irreverant fun of the music of Sullivan's operettas with Gilbert.

Your gift for practical communication makes you a natural teacher, but you will flourish equally in any kind of work or business connected with the media, publishing, negotiations and sales. You have an enviable gift for both understanding the real value of things and for being able to express it. This makes you a natural fund-manager or fundraiser, with a gift for promoting your own or your company's best long-term interests.

Although you would like to be the strong, silent type and want to be able to brood on things, you are an impulsive talker, needing to communicate your experiences. In consequence, you can be an extremely witty yet penetrating conversationalist, though perhaps rather given to laying down the law and wanting the last word. You have a strong will but an ability to hide your natural determination behind a flexible exterior and your natural gift of the gab. Since your approach to life is strongly practical and you want to see results from your activities, you quickly learn that you can get your own way best through a light touch and a willingness to be flexible rather than from confronting others.

Relationships

If you do not acknowledge your tendency to blow hot and cold, your relationships can be a constant souce of perplexity to yourself and all concerned. You are not an emotional type; indeed you can seem quite dry, unflappable and detached, whilst at heart you are a passionate sensualist. This can lead you to play the field – a butterfly flitting from flower to flower, seeking ever new sensual delights – unwilling to commit yourself, yet becoming ever more deeply dissatisfied as your need for permanence and possession of your loved ones asserts itself. You bring both playfulness and common sense into a relationship. Just remember that a 'logical' emotional relationship does not exist. A perfect match would bore you anyway.

Your Greatest Strengths

Practical intelligence; fine reasoning abilities; ability to translate sensual experience into words and far-reaching ideas; sheer capacity for being effectively busy and for talking others round to your point of view.

Your Greatest Weaknesses

Tendency to become dry as dust, reducing life's pleasures to matter-of-fact ideas; inclination to argue your way through life with bullying bombast; lack of sympathy for the emotional needs of others (and yourself) and for the loftier aspirations of the human spirit.

Images for Integration

A sculptor carves the figure of a dancer ... A wealthy publisher launches another new project ... A restaurateur earns a reputation for delicious soufflés and meringues ... A scientist brilliantly discourses on the mysteries of nature.

Famous Personalities

Fred Astaire (dancer), George Carlin (stand-up comedian), Catherine the Great (Empress of Russia), Teilhard de Chardin (philosopher and mystic), Sigmund Freud (psychologist), Edward Lear (author of nonsense verse), Marie Theresa (Empress of Austria), Eric Morecombe (comedian), Robert Peary (explorer), David O. Selznik (film producer), Arthur Sullivan (composer – Cancer Moon if born after 11 a.m.), Shirley Temple (actress).

— 16 —

Sun Taurus ♉ Moon Cancer ♋

The Common Sense Book of Baby and Child Care
TITLE OF BOOK BY DR BENJAMIN SPOCK

You can't tell people they must consume less when their children are hungry. We, the fortunate people, must consume less so they can consume more.
DAVID ICKE

Themes

EARTH/WATER Sensitive and determined, or easily hurt and obstinate; caring; nourishing; resourceful; the world is my family; likes to be thought well of; fertile; creative; imaginative; sensual; romantic; enduring loyalty; tenacious.

Whether you are male or female, and whatever you do – be it in business, catering, the caring professions or indeed at home – you are undoubtedly one of the great 'mothers' of the world. You have a strongly protective, sensitive and nurturing approach to all that you do. But are you a self-sacrificing Earth Mother who lavishes endless loving care upon your offspring? Or are you a strict Scottish nanny concerned that children learn from an early age to be strong and self-sufficient? Are you an emotional, indeed sentimental, mum or are you practical and common-sensical? When you connect both these sides of you, like Dr Spock of baby-book fame, you can become the ideal parent, teacher and friend. Immensely sympathetic, understanding and supportive, you are able to encourage and bring out the best in those people and organizations you care for and with whom you come into contact.

Your strong sense of the value of things gives you an excellent business and economic sense, enabling you to spot a bargain and to conserve and build up your financial resources. This is assisted by your capacity for getting others to feel protective towards you. Whilst you tend to lack the more dynamic get-up-and-go self-confidence of the classic entrepreneur, you have nonetheless a quiet determination which gets you wherever you want to go.

Your home, and no doubt your evergreen garden, will be especially important to you and you will make your 'nest' both secure and comfortable. You are a naturally good neighbour, and although you tend to be a rather quiet, private and indeed even secretive person, you do feel a sense of responsibility for those around you. This can mean that you are the child who ends up looking after your parents when your brothers and sisters are off doing their own thing.

You are strongly sensual and tend to be rather allergic to ideas and theories. You think best in pictures and symbols and by simply doing and experiencing things, and getting the feel of how they work. You are naturally creative and artistic with a strongly lyrical, musical and poetic bent. You can get swept away on a soaring melody, or by a particular nuance of colour, scent or texture. You can use your body as a barometer, for it will tend to reflect faithfully your inner moods and emotions.

Childhood was, and probably still is, enormously important to you. In an often threatening world, you may well seek to retreat into the secure and familiar. This may lead you to seek out a steady, routine occupation which offers long-term security rather than something that can feed your rich imagination.

When these two sides of you are working in creative tandem, this is an immensely caring combination. It is an ideal mix for anyone in the caring, counselling or nursing professions or indeed in any kind of work where the care and nourishment of others is the central preoccupation, such as infant-school teaching, catering and hotel work.

Relationships

Emotional relationships and family are central to your well-being. You are strongly domestic, and your capacity for intimacy and nest-building blossoms when you have found the right person. You long for total union and, once you have taken the plunge, you will invest all your rich emotional and supportive energy into your relationships.

You need to feel sure of your ground, however, before you will commit yourself. Your romantic and possessive qualities make for stability and endurance.

Your Greatest Strengths

Nourishing, protective and diplomatic approach; reliable, sustained, supportive concern for others; capacity to translate emotional experience into works of art.

Your Greatest Weaknesses

Tendency to carry the world upon your shoulders; sensitivity to real or imagined insults; stubborn prejudices; a narrow preoccupation with your own approach to life; lack of sympathy for ideas and theories which are outside your experience.

Images for Integration

A baker undertakes to feed an orphanage ... Dr Spock teaching mothers how to bring up their children ... Tchaikovsky's *Swan Lake*

Famous Personalities

Bert Bacharach (songwriter), Sandra Dee (film actress), Gabriel Fauré (composer), David Icke (sportsman and New Age prophet), Lynn Redgrave (actress), Ted Mosel (dramatist), Robert Oppenheimer (atomic physicist), Juan Miro (painter, sculptor), Peter and Anthony Shaffer (dramatist twins), Dr Benjamin Spock (childcare specialist), Pyotr Ilyich Tchaikovsky (composer).

— **17** —

SUN TAURUS ♉ MOON LEO ♌

Whenever you accept our views, we shall be in full agreement with you.
MOSHE DAYAN

True patriotism doesn't exclude an understanding of the patriotism of others.
QUEEN ELIZABETH II

Themes

EARTH/FIRE Artistic; regal; practical imagination; substantial personality; fixed opinions; a leader; inflexible; proud; love of beauty; loyal; affectionate; vain; strong values; materialistic; snobbish; ambitious; capable; masterful.

Do you want possessions or fame? Are you a charismatic show-off or a predictable, solid property owner? Do you want to conserve or flaunt the things you love most? You have what could be called a substantial personality – the kind that builds empires and runs them for a hobby. Although you tend to be conventional in values, you are nevertheless quite outspoken and flamboyant in expression, and you leave no one in doubt about where you stand, at least on the issues that seem worthy of your attention.

You are one of the combinations that rarely suffers from an inferiority complex, and as a result you can do almost anything to which you set your mind. You do your homework too, and are secure in what you know. With fixed ideas about how to get things done, you will definitely do things your way because you want the best and the longest-lasting result.

You make a good executive or leader of some sort because you have amazing powers of concentration which take you through to the end. And you are not afraid to call a spade a spade and to stick to your guns on principle. No wavering or dilly-dallying for you. Even in the most humble of positions, you bring a dedication and nobility to your work that makes others admire and respect you.

There is a quiet introvert within you, which is happy to plod along in comfortable grooves as long as your security and plans for greater security remain intact. At one level, your needs are straightforward – you value the solid, sensible and sensual things of this world and you want a steady supply of them as well. On the other hand, however, a simple, quiet life is just not quite enough. The darkest side of you could be a bit like the fisherman's wife who always wants more – her grandiose fantasies keep mushrooming until finally it is God she wants to be! The need for tangible proof of your specialness, greatness and loveableness can make you a bit like her, and your pride can get out of hand.

If you find life is getting a little boring, you are likely to do something a bit risky. Sticking your elegant neck out, you discover that you have a real ham inside you that loves to sing, dance, and entertain. And what fun you have doing it! In other words, besides the introvert you also have a daredevil extrovert inside you that wants to throw caution to the wind and go on wild spending sprees. That side of you is also very sociable and you can be a courteous, classy host or hostess when you choose to entertain. The people you invite to your home – which is where you like to do your socializing – will be individuals and friends you truly value. You just cannot fake the way you feel so why pretend that you identify with the waifs and losers of the world?

Relationships

In close relationships you are passionate, loyal, generous and 100-percent involved, although that percentage means you can be pretty demanding as well. Arguments can be real knock-out affairs because triumph is all-important to you, so you need to be sure that what you are arguing about really merits your digging-in of heels.

You care very deeply about your roots and ancestry, about the wellbeing and comfort of your family, and you really enjoy traditional family get-togethers. In these situations you shine because your steadiness, playfulness and warmth come out and are appreciated. Whilst your ability to indulge and enjoy yourself endears you to others, you need to be aware that they may have different ways of enjoying themselves so, as in all things, you need to loosen up and develop some sensitivity. If you can do this, your powerfully magnetic and capable personality will attract loyal admirers and friends.

Your Greatest Strengths

Magnetic, sociable personality; tremendous willpower and leadership abilities; innate resourcefulness and creativity; instinctive patience and persistence which allows you to reach your goals with minimum stress.

Your Greatest Weaknesses

Arrogance and pride; stubborn refusal to see the other person's viewpoint; tendency to express your own opinions with terrific force which alienates others; the difficulty you have in relaxing, laughing at yourself and being just 'one of the guys'.

Images for Integration

On a perfect summer's evening, a performance of *A Midsummer Night's Dream* is held in the palace garden ... Keeping up with the Joneses.

Famous Personalities

Thomas Beecham (conductor), Scott Carpenter (astronaut), Moshe Dayan (Israeli general and archaeologist), Willem de Kooning (artist), Dwayne Hickman (actor), G. Marconi (physicist), Zubin Mehta (conductor), Robert Montgomery (actor), Evita Peron (actress), Queen Elizabeth II, Ida Rolf (psychologist), Barbra Streisand (actress and singer), Victoria Wood (comedienne).

— 18 —

Sun Taurus ♉ Moon Virgo ♍

The State, in choosing men to serve it, takes no notice of their opinions. If they be willing faithfully to serve it, that satisfies.
OLIVER CROMWELL

There is overnight success and there's longevity ... and my thing is longevity.
MAUREEN LIPMAN

I am probably the most successful actor in the history of movies, financially speaking. I only wish the world would listen to me more.
JACK NICHOLSON

Themes

EARTH/EARTH Responsible; ethical; poise; stability; hard-working; earthy; lucid; common sense; good teacher and student; graceful; dutiful; likes practical tasks; discriminating intellect; physical beauty; skilful; epicurean; artisan.

You are a perennial student of life, methodically adding to your skills, talents, security and enjoyment. You chart your future with a clear, rational grasp of what is necessary, and you lay foundations that are index-linked and geared to letting you enjoy the good things of life whilst never shirking your duties at work or at home.

Enormously responsible, capable and blessed with lots of earthy charm, you aim to do the right thing for yourself and for loved ones – nothing pleases you more than serving those who depend upon you. One side of you is very fixed and self-assured: you know yourself and your needs and desires well, and you are confident in what you can do. You are also clear about what you do *not* want to do. Another side of you, however, tends to question and analyse yourself, and doubts that you have really got it right. This is the side that tells you that you could always do a little bit better.

You are a sticker, a veritable workaholic and persevering perfectionist, dedicated to high standards and sterling service. But you are also quite independent, and prefer to be able to choose when, where and for whom you work. Ideally, you work for yourself, and you are a jolly hard taskmaster whose work is never done. Work and service is what you instinctively centre yourself around, and yet it can at times weigh you down if you let yourself get lost in the sea of details that you try to master.

You are the great pragmatist. At home in the world of the senses, you are able to build up realistic priorities and a good sense of reality by dealing sequentially and logically with the things of this world that you can touch, taste, see and add up. As a result, you are an excellent organizer and can manage many types of responsibilities admirably, from domestic arrangements, gardening, child-rearing and teaching to writing, dancing, painting, singing and running your own theatre company. You make it your business to know your medium inside out, and your professional approach inspires confidence in everyone.

Essentially you aspire to a life of simplicity, usefulness and rational harmony. You need to create something concrete and enduring, something that is morally sound, practical and contributes to the wellbeing of others, and something that is ultimately an expression of your own worth. When you are fully engaged in the purpose of your life, however quiet and humble it may appear to be, your love of excellence and of pleasure come together to create a warmly humorous, sharp-witted and innately wise personality whom others admire and respect.

Relationships

Emotionally your needs are straightforward: physical affection, loyalty, thoughtfulness and adherence to the domestic schedule that makes the most sense for everyone (and especially you). You take emotional commitment seriously, and can be the most devoted and kind-hearted of mates. But because you expect others to see the intelligence of organizing their lives as you do, more spontaneous individuals may find you rather demanding and strict. And yet you are often attracted to fiery, irrational types who 'need organizing.'

You can easily feel offended when others rebel at your 'oughts' and 'shoulds', for you are only trying to fulfil your obligations. You can also be quite sensitive and brood about not being appreciated or taken seriously, for you think about yourself as an alert, discerning thinker and a sane, constructive member of society. What life may teach you at some point is that there really are different ways of perceiving things, and that different individuals value different things.

Your Greatest Strengths

Earthiness and excellent common sense; practical efficiency and reliability; resourcefulness and constructive critical eye; your thorough and professional approach to work; your good sense of timing and ability to say the right thing at the right time; and your charming, gracious, humorous temperament.

Your Greatest Weaknesses

Fear or abhorrence of chaos; overdependence on rational explanations; need to control the here-and-now and to have absolute material security; tendency to rest on your laurels, get into a rut and neglect your deeper potential.

Images for Integration

In her sumptuous garden, the music teacher entertains her now accomplished past pupils ... The treasurer for the Association for Social Reform invests proceeds of a jumble sale into gilt-edged securities.

Famous Personalities

Michael Barrymore (entertainer), Candice Bergen (actress), Oliver Cromwell (statesman), Daniel Day Lewis (actor), Lonnie Donegan (folk singer), Donovan (singer), Hirohito (former emperor of Japan), Englebert Humperdinck (singer), Maureen Lipman (actress and comedienne), Shirley Maclaine (actress), Doug McClure (actor), Jack Nicholson (actor), Sir Laurence Olivier (actor), Jack Parr (golfer), Mort Sahl (comedian), Peter Townsend (singer).

— 19 —

Sun Taurus ♉ Moon Libra ♎

*A leader who doesn't hesitate before he sends his nation
into battle is not fit to be a leader.*
GOLDA MEIR

*Every time I talk to a savant I feel quite sure that happiness is no longer a
possibility. Yet when I talk with my gardener, I'm convinced of the opposite.*

What is matter, never mind; what is mind, no matter.
BERTRAND RUSSELL

Themes

EARTH/AIR Rational; charming; love of harmony; aesthetic sense; romantic; devoted; sentimental; sociable; pleasantly persuasive; a realist; common sense; sensual; attractive personality; search for justice; need for companionship; practical idealist; social theorist.

Are you an idealistic artist or an artistic philosopher? Are you an incurable romantic who is searching for permanent love, but who keeps finding beautiful human beings less than ideal? Whatever your walk of life, the principles of justice and harmony will feature strongly in all you do. You want to get to grips with ideas and translate your vision of Utopia into a realistic proposition, but will probably discover the necessity for compromise. This may disillusion you at first, but later will become central to the way you operate.

Innately sociable and convivial, you are genuinely interested in other people and indeed need large amounts of kindness and affection. You want the best for everyone but you make sure that you do not skimp on yourself. You thrive in beautiful surroundings and in the company of elegant minds. An innately aesthetic person, and probably quite romantic as well, you bring a genuine warmth and lively concern to all social gatherings, which makes you downright flirtatious sometimes. If you are an artist, you will probably create works of art that are good enough to eat; if you are a chef, dishes that are works of art. Whatever you do, your creations will express your innate sense of harmony, beauty and style.

A lively social conscience is another aspect of this combination, as well as an awareness of the importance of education in the healthy development of the individual and of society. You are attracted to progressive ideas that assert the inalienable rights of every human being, and you can accept the paradoxical fact that everyone is different and yet the same. Everyone has different talents and preferences, and yet everyone has the same fundamental needs: a full stomach, a roof over their heads and lots of love. You believe in a society that respects both material needs and high moral values, and your social instinct and pragmatic perseverence may take you into social-welfare work or the political arena where you can express your power and idealism.

You learn how to make others see the intelligence of your thinking by first listening to and valuing *their* thinking on the subject. But you probably have a diplomatic knack of making sure the substance of *your* view prevails. And you can really impress with the practicality of your approach: you can economize with flair and use the resources to hand. Waste not, want not, you always say. You also know that a happy, convivial, relaxed atmosphere is the most conducive to constructive communication and compromise. Conflict is anathema to your being and you employ your natural diplomatic skills to overcome antagonism in any setting – with the sheer force of your magnetic personality.

Relationships

Relationships are of central importance to you, from the platonic and professional to the sensual and amorous. You are deeply romantic and will crave the ideal love relationship, both physical and spiritual. A meeting of minds and a meeting of bodies is what you are after!

You tend to invest an enormous amount in your loved one, and you may remain unaware of how dependent you are on him or her because you think of yourself as independent. Although in some ways you are fairly self-sufficient, independence is not really one of your traits. Sometimes you can be fussy and fastidious, even a touch cantankerous when things are not going harmoniously, and you will always be happier in tandem, with tea for two on the menu.

You like security and creature comforts, and put a lot into serious relationships – you like to have someone whom you can devote yourself to and share candle-lit dinners with. As you are always open to suggestions and better ideas, you are keen to discuss inspirations with your friends and lover.

Your Greatest Strengths

A flair for persuasive diplomacy; practical idealism; gentle wit; impeccable artistic sensibility; strong social sense; ability to enjoy people and life to the hilt.

Your Greatest Weaknesses

Over-reliance on popularity and social acceptance; reluctance to engage in conflict; over-emphasizing rational solutions to every kind of problem.

Images for Integration

A loaf of fresh bread in an art exhibition ... A computer produces a beautiful painting ... Cream tea for two.

Famous Personalities

William Ball (theatre director and producer), Judy Collins (singer and songwriter), Joseph Cotton (actor), Fernandel (actor), Ella Fitzgerald

105

(jazz singer), Henry Fonda (actor), Steve Ford (actor), Ernst Karl Kraft (astrologer), Golda Meir (Israeli politician), James Mitchum (actor), Sergei Sergeyevich Prokofiev (composer), Bertrand Russell (philosopher), Gary Snider (poet), Rudolph Valentino (actor).

— 20 —

SUN TAURUS ♉ MOON SCORPIO ♏

There are three ingredients in the good life: learning, earning, and yearning.
CHRISTOPHER DARLINGTON MORLEY

If you can't stand the heat, get out of the kitchen.
HARRY S. TRUMAN

Themes

EARTH/WATER Stubborn; confident; passionate; protective; sensual; possessive; strong appetites; magnetic; staying power; resourceful; persevering; wilful; shrewd mind; intensely creative; egotistic; forceful self-expression; subjective views; protective; independent; perceptive; strategic.

You believe in yourself so deeply that the concept of an inferiority complex is probably alien to you. Your instincts of self-preservation and self-defence work powerfully to claim your territory and just desserts, and only you will decide with whom you will share them. Your 'territory' can include material possessions, your home, ideas, professional power and people.

You have deep, almost obsessive convictions about what you do, and you bring such conscientious commitment to your activities, loves and hates that you can exhaust yourself without realizing it. You possess both an unflappable, earthy, maternal temperament as well as a powerful fighting spirit. When working well together, they could be described as the immoveable object and the irrisistible force in an earth-moving *pas de deux*.

Your tremendous magnetism and self-confidence make an

unforgettable impression on others. People sense they need you as an ally because they would really fear you as an adversary! Saying you are wrong or sorry is *not* one of your strong points, and your sheer perversity and entrenched stubbornness may lead you to over-estimate yourself at times.

Passionate sensuality and appetite make you a *bon viveur* and, potentially, a very talented artist as well. You live life fully, relishing both domestic security and emotional intensity. You can taste the beauty of a rose and feel the strength of the diving roots of a massive oak. Your character is a kind of personification of the primeval life force itself, and there is very little you cannot do when motivated. The one thing that can sabotage your best interests is *inertia*. This can be a problem because you can attract what you want and then get into a rut, mistaking ownership for contentment. You can dominate others easily and assume their respect and good opinion too readily, turning some into weaklings and others into enemies.

You cannot understand it when people call you bossy; you just happen to know best and are most comfortable running the show. In fact, you can be quite a showman and are a natural self-dramatist, putting tremendous energy into any kind of performance, be it a college debate, a party political broadcast or a Broadway opening night. You need to watch out for negative emotions: they can have a destructive hold over you, especially anger, jealousy and resentment.

When you have become more self-aware and in control of your temperament and energies, however, you are capable of immense amounts of work and commitment. You can be a devoted teacher or doctor, or a perceptive counsellor, a solid, dependable home-maker, a shrewd businessperson, an impassioned social leader, a dedicated artist or musician. If you take to the pen, you could be a merciless satirist of man's incongruous habits and morals. Luckily, your compelling charm makes the deadly accuracy of your criticism more palatable for others.

Relationships

There is a paradoxical side to your personality. On the one hand you aim for material security and are loathe to change your ways, your opinions, or (heaven forbid) move house. On the other hand, something in you seeks risk and challenge where you can test your strength and feel the adrenalin coursing through your veins. This side of you is likely to express itself in your emotional life.

Passionate and demanding to live with, you may drive your partner crazy at times because of the complex mixture of independence and possessiveness which colours your affectionate nature. Sometimes you are outrageously demanding, but at other times you are equally generous and devoted. You exude the sunny, peaceful warmth of spring, but once caught in your emotional web you are a dark enigma who dares the other to figure you out. Your willpower is tremendous and your potential for success great, as long as you can harness and direct your energies along rational, rather than purely emotional, lines. Aim to control yourself, rather than others!

Your Greatest Strengths

Enormous confidence and persistence; administrative power and organizational abilities; a heightened aesthetic and artistic sense; creative drive; loyalty and commitment to others; a dramatic and charismatic presence.

Your Greatest Weaknesses

Terrific stubbornness; strongly subjective responses and fixed prejudices; ruthless desire for power; a difficult temper.

Images for Integration

The mating Season. Persephone and Pluto. *The Phantom of the Opera.* Dennis Potter's *The Singing Detective.*

Famous Personalities

Janet Blair (actress), Alana Ladd (actress), Gaston Leroux (dramatist and mystery writer), Christopher Darlington Morley (writer and journalist), Baba Muktananda (guru), Dennis Potter (TV playwright), Roberto Rossellini (movie director), Dame Margaret Rutherford (actress), Warren Spahn (baseball pitcher), Anthony Trollope (novelist), Harry S. Truman (former American president), Fred Zinneman (film director).

SUN TAURUS ♉ MOON SAGITTARIUS ♐

*Agnosticism simply means that a man shall not say he knows or believes that
for which he has no grounds for professing to believe.*
THOMAS HENRY HUXLEY

There is no such thing as a great talent without a great will-power.
BALZAC

Themes

EARTH/FIRE Magnetic instability; grounded yet high flying;
adventurous yet conventional; practical; persuasive; inspired; sees
possibilities and seizes them; dedicated; hard-working; sense of the
absurd and paradoxical.

Are you Speedy Gonzalez or the Slow and Steady Plodder? Are you a
brilliant wit or a dull, straw-chewing fool? A slothful, fleshy materialist
or a wide-eyed, soaring-spirited gypsy wanderer? Are you gambler or
banker? Conservative or radical?

You are torn between an instinct to roam free and a determination
to find security and make a solid, lasting contribution to the world. As
you repeatedly change horses in search of both ultimate certainties and
high-spirited adventure at the same time, you can find yourself deeply
divided and uncertain. You seek to earth the Fire from heaven and put
it to work, but you find all too often that it will not let you rest.

In your search for stability and security, you become a farmer and
are immediately confronted with the changing seasons. You embrace
the solid certainties of geology and are hit by an earthquake. Feel the
solid Earth move! You seek certitude and permanence, yet your
endless enquiries constantly confound yesterday's certainties. When
you get your own uncertainties together (by accepting you want the
best of both the changing and the unchanging worlds), you can be a
brilliant teacher, conversationalist, counsellor, entertainer, wit,
creative artist or entrepreneur – in fact you can be anything you want.
Once focused, you can be a human dynamo, and wonderfully
humorous, witty and entertaining with it.

109

As you will have discovered, your quest for solid material certainties does not make a happy bedfellow for your yearning for excitement and larger religious and spiritual understanding. In one way or another, be it through philosophy and the spiritual quest or through writing, music or art, you will need to put together and formulate a total vision of the universe which is based on unassailable facts yet satisfying to your idealism. Constantly seeking, you are a natural agnostic, applying the criteria of science to counter woolly speculations, yet at the same time highly sceptical of the limited and statistical pronouncements of unthinking science.

The danger, if you do not marry these elements within you, is that you will swing from one to the other and undermine the virtues of both. A restless changing of jobs, careers, partners, visions or aspirations can leave you drunk with your own spinning. When you deliberately try to remain sober and commonsensical, it seems to make matters worse for there is something of the gambler in you. This all-or-nothing streak can temporarily overcome your natural caution and enable you to burn your bridges (though you will usually ensure there is something tucked away for a rainy day). You feel an impulsive need to do things on a grand scale, to live with commitment, to feast on the world, and to understand what it is to be alive in all possible ways.

You seem called both to explore the reaches of the imagination and to build secure foundations. You can bring far-reaching visions into manifestation, and these visions can inject your conservative desire for stability and security with flair and colour. Your vision of tomorrow and the larger world can give spice to any project you undertake. You see endless possibilities and want to make them real. In this you can be the natural entrepreneur who can see economic opportunities at every turn, an inspiring counsellor and teacher, and a stimulating companion whatever you do.

Relationships

You need strong relationships and you are an excellent, warm, supportive and generous friend. No sooner have you settled down, however, than you find yourself restless. You can flit and flirt from one delightful partner to another, yet casual relationships leave you feeling hollow. Your ideal partner will be both warmly supportive and traditional, yet unafraid of new adventures and unusual ideas. You are a live wire yet a home body, and any relationship must somehow contain both elements if it is to succeed.

Your Greatest Strengths

Down-to-earth capacity to marry common sense and inventive imagination, inspired flair and a matter-of-fact realism; enthusiasm with practical politics; a good, if at times wild, business sense.

Your Greatest Weaknesses

Restless instability and craving for excitement; reluctance to be tied down; infuriating unreliability just when you seemed to have mended your restless ways.

Images for Integration

A monk builds a cathedral whilst contemplating the infinite reaches of the universe ... The prodigal son returns to the home farm ... Balzac's *La Comédie humaine* ... Brahms' *Violin Concerto*.

Famous Personalities

Philip Armour (entrepreneur), John James Audubon (naturalist and painter), Johannes Brahms (composer), Honoré de Balzac (novelist and playwright), Sandy Dennis (actress), Albert Finney (actor), Thomas Huxley (scientist), Edwin Land (inventor of instant camera), Liberace (pianist and entertainer), Ferdinand Magellan (explorer), Glenda Jackson (actress), Hedda Hopper (gossip columnist).

— 22 —

SUN TAURUS ♉ MOON CAPRICORN ♑

You've forgotten the grandest moral attribute of a Scotsman, Maggie, that he'll do nothing which might damage his career.
JAMES BARRIE

A considerable number of persons are able to protect themselves against the outbreak of serious neurotic phenomena only through intense work.
KARL ABRAHAM

Themes

EARTH/EARTH Shrewd pragmatist; dignified; authoritarian; dependable; down-to-earth; ambitious; logical; sensual; loyal; loving; protective; realistic; determined; resourceful; need for security; traditional; formal; staunch friend; the boss.

Are you a sensible, home-loving, slow-paced, solid Earth Mother (or Father), or are you an ambitious go-getter? You like to put down roots, grow, bloom and become a solid member of the community; and yet you also want to remain upwardly mobile, carving out your own career.

You are a traditionalist through and through, and definitely not one of life's gamblers. You were born with your feet planted firmly on the ground. Realistic, capable, hard-working and even somewhat stoic, you work with what you can taste, touch and see. Your values are of the earth and you have a deep need to produce something tangible, permanent and useful. You also want to shine as a responsible leader and to be recognized as a creative, powerful individual in your own right.

Your ambitions are a mixture of wanting the security of a home and clean socks in the drawer, and the desire for wordly success, authority and recognition. And your unflappable common sense, innate self-confidence and excellent organizing ability usually help you to achieve both. Some days you may just want to stretch out and breathe in the fresh air, or curl up in a cosy corner in the comfort of your own home with a cup of tea (or a gin and tonic) and the melodic strains of Elgar. Despite this, your instinct for competition and conquest never really goes away. Your mind is ever active and needs something tangible with which to get to grips, to manage and to influence.

Your image of yourself is of a responsible, serious professional, and it is into your profession that you will pour your substantial drive. You carefully and patiently follow your professional goals, later consolidating all increments of personal power and position with foresight and shrewd acceptance of responsibility. Social work, politics and academia are areas which would appeal to your need for

112

challenge, although you may be quite artistic as well.

You are an honourable, gracious, conscientious person with a solid sense of self and an almost ducal presence that commands respect. A shrewd judge of character, you can size up a person readily, keeping your mental judgements quietly on the backburner for future reference. Despite a self-restrained manner, you are very approachable, sentimental and caring, and you show your concern in concrete ways. People therefore place confidence in you and feel safe in your tremendously capable hands.

You have incredible control over yourself, especially your emotions, but when you are with close friends whom you respect and trust you can relax and enjoy convivial gatherings. There is a very sensual, artistic, and musical side to your nature. You may surprise others with quite an earthy, bawdy sense of humour when your guards are down, but you would hate to say or do anything in bad taste. As a provider you are consistent and generous; as a friend faithful and long-suffering; and as a critic severe and utterly honest.

Relationships

You really bloom in a happy, secure, devoted relationship. Somewhat possessive and stubborn, you know what you want and can be pretty demanding. Once committed to a person, however, you are very loving and affectionate and the staunchest of mates. Your needs are straightforward: lots of physical affection, absolute faithfulness, and mutual respect.

You do not enjoy emotional complexities although, whatever the problem, you do not give up easily on relationships. You may get tired, cross and discouraged, but still you doggedly pursue happiness and security and may cling to a rather old-fashioned sense of honour.

Family life is extremely important to you and you take your responsibilities seriously. Sometimes the demands of career interests may conflict with the needs of family, but you somehow learn to handle this. You do not easily forget wrongs, but kindnesses you always remember. And you always try to live up to the best in yourself – morally, artistically and financially.

Your Greatest Strengths

Practical, earthy instincts; a high sense of integrity and dependability; shrewd business sense and organizational savvy; affectionate loyalty and paternal concern for those in need.

Your Greatest Weaknesses

A tendency to be overmaterialistic and rational, pig-headed and dictatorial; an over-emphasis on security and fixed routines; a tendency to see and honour only what you know.

Image for Integration

A royal banquet honours the longest-serving headmistress of the oldest and most prestigous school in the land.

Famous Personalities

Karl Abraham (psychoanalyst), James Barrie (writer), Yogi Berra (baseball player), David Byrne (rock musician), Cher (singer and actress), Sheena Easton (singer), Joe Louis (champion boxer), Willie Mays (baseball player), Yehudi Menuhin (concert violinist), James Monroe (former American president), Maureen O'Sullivan (actress), Chris Patten (politician), James Stewart (actor), Jeremy Thorpe (politician), Tammy Wynette (country singer).

— 23 —

SUN TAURUS ♉ MOON AQUARIUS ♒

When you're down and out, something always turns up – and it's usually the noses of your friends.
ORSON WELLES

May the Force be with you.
GEORGE LUCAS, *Star Wars*

Themes

EARTH/AIR Confident; independent; honest; morally sound; capable intellect; proud; friendly; helpful; gracious; resourceful; sensible; hard-working; shrewd; tenacious; artistic; trustworthy; faithful; holds fast to ideals; an innovative pragmatist.

Are you a nuts-and-bolts pragmatist who wants cash on the nail, or a far-seeing idealist whose philanthropic outlook opens doors for others? No matter which side is strongest within you, this is a winning combination because you can back up your high ideals and broad vision with hard work and perseverence.

You do not lose touch with reality; rather, you bring humanitarian values down to earth and put them to use in a productive way, for yourself and for others. People respect you because you are utterly honest and they know you employ the same scrutiny to yourself as you do to them. You were born with a strong sense of self which is very hard to dent. This is not because you are defensive; rather it is due to your staunch humane conservatism and your tenacious loyalty to sound ideals.

You respect yourself, feel you deserve what you want, and are willing to work hard to get it. Your creations express your uniqueness and your strong sense of identity in a very tangible way. The freedom to be yourself, to work patiently towards the marriage of your ideals and your bank account, and to enjoy with loved ones the fruits of your hard-headed genius, is to a large extent what makes you tick.

One of your strongest points is your clear-headed, frank and forthright manner of communication. You have a sound intellect, grasp essential facts and figures readily, and tend to tell it like it is. You enjoy imparting knowledge to others which makes their lives more rational, productive and ecological in every sense of the word. You therefore make a good instructor – helpful, friendly and egalitarian, although you know in the end everyone has to be their own teacher and live according to their own principles. And certainly you never abandon yours; they are the central hub around which your life revolves, and you have a natural way of persuading others of the soundness of your views.

You do not like conflict and feel, really, that it is beneath you. You will find 'civilized' ways of circumventing obstacles, for which your amiable, pleasant personality is a great asset.

You are drawn towards areas of work which can express both your natural love of freedom and your sound sense of material values. Because of your strong independence, you are well-suited to self-employment. Because you are gregarious as well, however, you are a natural for working with the public. You often go for progressive ideas which serve your fundamental well-being – and that means the body. Indeed, it is quite likely that you are very in tune with the needs and rhythms of the body, and you could be attracted to practices that highlight the mind–body relationship, such as t'ai chi or yoga.

You love good food and intelligent company, although you may swing between gourmet indulgence and religious fasting. Essentially you want to be in *control* of yourself. For you, this is all part of being a competent maverick – and you know that means being in control of your considerable sensual appetites as well.

Relationships

In relationships your instinct is for mental rapport and independence, but at heart you may find yourself a real romantic, wanting emotional security and full possession of your partner. Usually, however, you can look at these opposite sides of yourself with total honesty, and with loved ones you will earn full marks for your candid self-assessment. You do not need to fool people; it is simply not your way.

Because you are utterly fair and always respect others' needs and views, you have the capacity to be a friend as well as a devoted lover. You are only attracted to people you respect. You are an ecologist of the heart and mind, designed to create wealth and then dispense it with humanitarian noblesse oblige.

Your Greatest Strengths

A sound sense of values; an ability to be totally objective and realistic; integrity and natural rapport with people; an ability to inspire confidence; commitment to principles; warm, friendly helpfulness which can make a tangible difference in others' lives.

Your Greatest Weaknesses

Stubbornness and proneness to inertia when things are not going your way; reluctance simply to flow with the moment and let things happen; an overconfidence that can come across as conceit.

Image for Integration

A country squire holds the summer fête in his garden; all monies raised are divided equally between the three charities in the village – the Friendly Farmer's Trust, the Local Artists' Guild, and the Quakers' Orphanage.

Famous Personalities

Anouk Aimée (actress), Pietro Aretino (satirist and writer), Burt Bacharach (songwriter), Anne Baxter (actress), Charlotte Brontë (writer and poetess), Loraine Hansberry (playwright), Jean Houston (psychologist), Peter Hurkos (psychic), George Lucas (film director), Ryan O'Neal (actor), Michelle Pfeiffer (actress), Alessandro Scarlatti (composer), Orson Welles (actor).

— 24 —

SUN TAURUS ♉ MOON PISCES ♓

I pity those poor critics who might try to disentangle the Gordian Knot of my obsessive symbols and images.
FREDERIC PROKOSCH

...all the business of life is to endeavour to find out what you don't know by what you do ...
DUKE OF WELLINGTON

Themes

EARTH/WATER Imagination and realism; creative; musical; poetic; easy-going yet determined; responsive yet reserved; the practical dreamer; caring sensitivity; love of beauty; the nature mystic; resourceful.

Are you a feet-on-the-ground steady achiever or are you constantly being swept away on the wings of poetic imagination? Are you the policeman or the poet, the songwriter or the estate agent, the banker or the mystic, the capitalist or the socialist?

Your idealistic instincts give you a compassionate concern for the needs of others, but your common-sense head tells you that you must look after yourself and ensure your own stability. At heart you are a dreamer, but in practice you are indeed practical and know you must earn what your imagination spends with such ease.

Ideally, and you are at heart an idealist, you need to be involved in work that both gives you security yet enables you to follow your inner vision. You can drift and dream, but when put up against it you have an enviable ability to bring in the cash. Money is never likely to stick to you for long, however, for you know that it is only a means to an end, and you always have new ends and visions you feel inspired to pursue. When you get these two sides of yourself together you can become the turned-on businessman, with a superb sense of strategy, or the practical poet, musician or artist who can manage your affairs better than any agent.

You can be very responsive to the needs of others yet you are at heart a private person, inclined to be withdrawn and given to periods of inner brooding as well as dreaming. Indeed when things are down you can get very despondent, and your imagination begins to conjure up the worst. At such times you can readily eat and drink for comfort as much as pleasure. Yet just when everyone thinks you have taken a vow of silence, there you are pouring forth flashes of insight and revealing your need to communicate your inner experience.

Central to all your work, in whatever sphere, is a strongly lyrical, feminine, caring sensibility, and a natural understanding of the relationship between feelings and the body. Whether or not you are in the helping or healing professions, you understand that illness is often an expression of mixed-up emotions, and you have a gift for reconnecting people with themselves and their feelings. Likewise you feel yourself connected to the Earth and to Mother Nature, and are likely to have special places to which you go, either in reality or in your imagination, in order to centre yourself. This is one expression of your flair for giving symbolic expression to your feelings through some form of art, be it music or accountancy (even this can become a fine art when in your hands!).

You are a hands-on person who learns best by doing and

experiencing and working things out for yourself. Whilst you may have an intuitive flair for science, you can find abstract ideas and theories as such dull and uninviting. This can make you feel academically inadequate. To learn a subject you need to feel yourself emotionally engaged by it.

You directly experience the power of the imagination to give form to dead matter. Thus you will flourish best in any kind of work which can draw upon both your practical skills and your rich imagination. Whatever type of work you undertake – across the spectrum from business and banking to music or mysticism – you have an instinctive understanding of the creative, healing power of poetic imagery and imagination. You believe in making dreams come true.

Relationships

You are solid and dependable, and when you make friends it is for life. You deeply need a partner, and seek to recreate through him or her the certainties and securities of the womb. You can be torn between the romantic idealist and the simple sensualist. Any sign of sympathy and inner understanding from others is a real turn-on, for warmth and physical affection are food and drink to you.

Though you fall in love easily, once committed you are a loyal, and indeed possessive soul and will not readily relinquish your prize. Falling in love brings out the magic and poetry in your heart. Even if you are the very dullest bureaucrat, Cupid's dart transforms you into a starry-eyed lover. Your feet may still be on the ground but your heart is dancing with the stars. If, however, you fail to keep in touch with the magic of your true love, he or she can readily become your brother or sister, and you can find yourself 'just good friends' after all.

Your Greatest Strengths

Quiet, self-contained strength; capacity for practical sympathy and understanding; resourcefulness and willingness to work hard and long to make your seemingly idle dreams come true; social conscience.

Your Greatest Weaknesses

Naivety; deep stubbornness, which you cover with an apparent flexibility; sudden despondent moods, which can sink into self-pity;

resistance to logical argument when it does not suit you.

Images for Integration

Through the power of the imagination a man is healed. A poet prepares his accounts in verse ... The *Mona Lisa*.

Famous Personalities

Anna Maria Aberghetti (musician and songwriter), Anne Boleyn (second wife of Henry VIII), Leonardo da Vinci (artist, scientist and polymath), Ellen Glasgow (writer and novelist), Audrey Hepburn (actress), Norman Lamont (British politician, former Chancellor of the Exchequer), Norman Luboff (musician, choral conductor and composer), Charles Mingus (jazz musician), Samuel Morse (inventor of Morse Code and portrait painter), John Muir (naturalist, explorer and conservationist), Ryan O'Neil (actor), Frederic Prokosch (novelist), Duke of Wellington (soldier and politician).

Chapter Six

SUN IN GEMINI

———•———

— 25 —

SUN GEMINI ♊ MOON ARIES ♈

*Show me a man who enjoyed his schooldays and I will show you
a bully and a bore.*
ROBERT MORLEY

Where is My Wandering Boy Tonight?
NOVEL BY DAVID WAGONER

Themes

AIR/FIRE Freshness and clarity; enthusiasm; quick; alert; energetic;
forceful; decisive; impatient; restless; versatile; witty; dextrous;
communicative; argumentative; persuasive.

Hate motorcars or love them, there is something of the racing
champion in you. You have speed, flair and a self-assertive pugnacity
which is constantly jockeying for position. In you, nerves and
adrenaline combine or conflict. Are you all restless talk, or are you
Action Man or Woman? Are you passionately impulsive or endlessly
curious? Do you think and then act, or act and then think? Are you a
knight errant or a quick, beguiling trickster? Are you a rough-tongued
toughie or a smooth-talking persuader?

   When you combine your intense willpower and convictions with
your strong communicative ability and intelligent curiosity, you can

become a great persuader and salesperson with a touch of poetry and a clear, inspired vision. Indeed you can become a purposeful, ambitious intellectual. You expect to have your own way and are a natural leader and spokesperson in your chosen field. Your quick, intuitive mind leaps to conclusions and always has a plausible reason for your every impulsive utterance and action. Indeed you are a whizz with words, wit, satire and pointed jokes, and can be a veritable escape-artist and rationalizer when it comes to talking your way out of situations and arguing that black is white.

You like to travel, to be up-to-the-minute, on the move and on your toes. Twenty-four-hour rolling news and current-affairs programmes were dreamed up for and by the likes of you. With your quick intelligence and enthusiasm you make a vivid speaker and inspiring teacher, though you get impatient with those less nimble-witted than yourself. You have the gifts of a formidable lawyer, a natural writer, broadcaster, politician or debater. In short, this is an ideal combination for any job where you have to think on your feet. Nonetheless you are probably at your best when you develop an area of expertise in which you can be an authority, for you need to be your own person, to be able to say what you think and not pull your punches.

Your eternal youth, explosive energy and exuberance will be the envy of many. When it comes to putting over your ideas on something in which you believe, your power-assisted words can hit the world like sustained gunfire. Yet for all your quickness, curiosity and with-it, street-wise dexterity, you have about you a certain naive, bright freshness and spontaneity, which no amount of negative experience can dull.

You say what you see, hear and think, though seldom what you feel, for feelings are not your strong suit. Although you 'feel strongly', even passionately, about things, you do not empathize well with other people. You consider their problems and pains to be something they need to sort out themselves, unless you happen to share their problems, in which case you could soon be mounting a one-man crusade with the assistance of your clear, incisive wit, passionate rhetoric and scathing indignation. Your forthright, pugnacious approach and strongly held views make you a formidable adversary but can also make you, to your indignant surprise, some bitter enemies. Yet at the end of the day you can shrug this off with a witticism, for often humour and a good belly laugh are your best medicine.

Relationships

For you, relationships are either intellectual or passionate impulses that you do not really understand, even though you can play the troubadour and spin a love lyric to try and express them. You are essentially self-centred, so can be insensitive to the needs of others and impatient with the complexities of human needs. You may find it difficult to grow up.

The men among you, after playing the field, may settle for a good mother figure who will give you the stability you need. You ladies may find yourselves having little patience with conventional feminine roles and morality, and can take to supporting feminist issues. Man or woman, you are likely to find yourself repeatedly falling headlong into love, only to wake to a sense of impatience once things get into a routine. Variety is the spice of your life, and if you are after long-term stability, you must seek out a partner as spicey and quick-witted as yourself. Then the both of you will never be bored, even if you never really understand each other.

Your Greatest Strengths

Fresh, alert mind; enthusiasm and spontaneity; zest and vitality; moral and intellectual courage; gift for language; powers of persuasion.

Your Greatest Weaknesses

Egotism; monopolizing conversation; impatience with lesser minds; insensitivity to feelings of others; partiality; tendency to ride roughshod over others.

Images for Integration

A nimble-footed streetfighter dodges his way to victory over all comers ...The eternal freshness of a Constable landscape.

Famous Personalities

Albert II (King of Belgium), Sir John Cockcroft (nuclear physicist), John Constable (painter), Christiana Crawford (writer), Gerald Kaufman (politician), Robert Morley (actor), Bill Moyers (journalist), Albert Neuhuys (painter), Geoffrey Rippon (politician), Jackie Stewart (World Champion racing driver), David Wagoner (novelist).

SUN GEMINI Ⅱ MOON TAURUS ♉

If I had learned education I would not have had time to learn anything else.

What do I care about the law? Hain't I got the power?
CORNELIUS VANDERBILT

Let me say ...that the true revolutionary is guided by a great feeling of love.
CHE GUEVARA

Themes

AIR/EARTH Sensual yet intellectual; flirtatious yet faithful; practical, applied intelligence; reasonably unreasonable; practical communicator; artist; business and entrepreneurial flair; determined and loyal.

Are you a fixed point or the turning world? You love to be on the move, yet you love to be still. You are really with-it, yet deeply conservative. You have the bright-eyed vitality of fresh-sprung spring, but do you belong in the town or the country? Do you want to sit and savour the wine and stroll across the fields and hills, or must you be nipping off, late again, for your next engagement? Do you want to build up your material security or are you really interested in pursuing bright ideas, talking and developing your mind? Although you can be impatient with your need for tranquillity, you can also rebel against your nervous haste and restless quest for fresh stimulation by slipping into low gear. You are often an enigma to yourself.

When you can allow your natural understanding of the material world and your appreciation of the value of things to work together with your clever mind and your need to communicate, you have all the makings of a successful scientist, businessperson or indeed writer, poet, musician or painter. The important thing for you is to be able to talk about and communicate your feelings and experiences, and to translate them into permanent form. There is a need to be in touch with your sense perceptions and also to question and explain them. You are at your most creative, and most content, when you are combining your natural understanding of the sensual world with your quick-witted ingenuity. Things really come together for you when you are planning, shopping for and cooking a meal, or when you are translating perceptions into poems or paintings or music.

You have a natural understanding both of the laws of nature and of finance, and you know how money can be effectively accumulated and put to work. You enjoy the operations of your five senses – they tell you about the world you find so beautiful and interesting. Like a child in a toy shop, you experiment with what you find, and your ingenuity always helps you put your understanding to good use. You have a shrewd sense of the value of things and of people, and a strong capacity for highly practical, factual evaluation of situations, and for coming to objective judgments.

Relationships

Your relationships are vital to your wellbeing. Friends and partners are your source of stability, security and feedback. Despite your occasional wanderings, you can be deeply loyal and utterly dependable to those who have earned your respect. Since you thrive on mental stimulation and live-wire dialogue, however, you are quickly bored by overly stable, secure, reliable types.

You have a high level of sensuality and are constantly tempted by the idea of new relationships. This, combined with your need for stability, means that you find it difficult to be either faithful or unfaithful. At one and the same time you can be deeply possessive yet thoughtlessly fickle, wildly flirtatious yet lovingly loyal.

As a stable, thinking type you tend to be out of touch with your deeper feelings and intuitions. Consequently, you may find wild, hysterical and unstable types fascinatingly attractive, and become involved with partners who disturb you rather than comfort you, who are a challenge rather than the touchstone you so much want.

Your Greatest Strengths

Deep common sense; capacity to turn ideas into realities and to translate experience into words; practical flexibility; stability; intelligent support and generosity.

Your Greatest Weaknesses

Tendency to get overly absorbed in your experiences; lack of sympathy for the feelings of others; talking over and over the same ground; scepticism about and resistance to matters spiritual.

Images for Integration

A country boy lives it up among the city bustle but goes back to the farm at night ... A master chef gives a dinner party for her intellectual friends ... The cancan from Offenbach's *Orpheus in the Underworld*.

Famous Personalities

Elias Ashmole (antiquarian), Björn Borg (tennis champion), Charles II (the 'merry monarch'), Joan Collins (actress), Gerard de Nerval (poet), Ian Fleming (author, creator of James Bond), Michael J. Fox (actor, *Back to the Future*), Stephen Frears (director), Che Guevara (guerilla leader and revolutionary), Burl Ives (folk singer), Jacques Offenbach (composer), Vance Packard (author, *The Hidden Persuaders*), Isabella Rossellini (model and actress), Marshall Tito (Yugoslav president), Cornelius Vanderbilt (railway entrepreneur).

— 27 —

Sun Gemini Ⅱ Moon Gemini Ⅱ

One of my chief regrets during my years in the theatre is that I couldn't sit in the audience and watch me.
JOHN BARRYMORE

Ideas shape the course of history.
JOHN MAYNARD KEYNES

As I grow older and older
And totter towards the tomb,
I find that I care less and less
Who goes to bed with whom.
DOROTHY SAYERS

Themes

AIR/AIR A thinker; expressive; vivacious; *joie de vivre*; childlike; lively; inventive; flirtatious; cerebral; self-analysing; moody; translator; mimic; juggler; fidgety; nervous; contradictory; critical; fast-talker; lots of contacts; sociable; on-the-go.

You are a thinker and a talker, a restless collector of facts and people, driven by a thirst for knowledge and novelty which takes you in to and out of many relationships. Variety is the veritable stuff of your life – mentally, emotionally and socially. You love to meet new people and to find out what makes them tick; to you, almost everyone and everything is interesting in some way. In finding out about others, you discover more about yourself because, essentially, you are many people all rolled into one.

You cover a lot of ground very rapidly and your particular gift is your ability to communicate cleverly an impression of your whole experience with a few vivid images. As a quick-silver lateral thinker, you observe, register and express – and then you are off again. For this reason you make an excellent neighbourhood or professional roving reporter: you promptly cull the essentials of a situation, pick out the distinguising feature or gesture and then communicate it. The media and writing of any kind will employ your talents well. You are also a good middle-man: something is always reminding you of something, and you can make fruitful links between friends and acquaintances of completely different worlds in an utterly natural, effortless manner.

Because you are such a Mercurial mimic and can use words so effectively, your reports can feel a bit brisk and cutting to more emotional types, but you never mean to hurt anyone's feelings. You are like a child discovering the world and then unselfconsciously reporting back. You love games and anything that challenges your mind, but you may often find that you are too mentally aware and clever for your own good because your constant mental activity exhausts your nervous system.

You can also be very clever with your hands. Making things – whether cupboards and cabinets, paintings and etchings, model trains and airplanes, or knitting sweaters – will help you to ground your nervous energy and balance your up-and-down temperament.

Relationships

The realm of feelings is difficult for you, not because you have none, but because you have very little patience with anything that pulls you down into the murky, watery realms. And also, quite simply, because you do not like things you cannot rationally control.

Your suave, charming, sophisticated nature may suddenly show its immature, naive side when faced with the complexities of feelings and close relationships. You can appear cold and turned off when your partner feels too emotionally demanding, as though you are going to suffocate with boredom. Interestingly enough, however, you tend to end up with emotional types who perhaps provide a nurturing, supportive environment in which you can safely explore your multi-faceted, fascinating self.

You will either let your mate do all the feeling for the relationship or, in time, and given plenty of space, you will eventually learn to recognize and respect your own feelings, and to discover that they are not as dark and threatening as you had feared. In fact, you discover that they provide more interesting fodder for self-reflection, and that, rather than trapping you, they give you the key to understanding and enriching your life in a deeply satisfying way.

Your Greatest Strengths

Quick, agile mind; lively sociability; openness to experience; ability to learn, teach, communicate and bring different people and ideas together in a fruitful way; friendliness and outrageous sense of fun.

Your Greatest Weaknesses

A tendency to live in your head, with the result that nervousness depletes your energy; childlike self-absorption; proneness to live a double standard and to find plausible excuses for not looking at deeper motives.

Images for Integration

A butterfly in a garden tires of the bright-blue delphinium and suddenly discovers the most exquisite red rose ... A young child entertains his friends by standing on his head whilst eating an ice cream cone and playing marbles ... A circus trapeze artist writes his autobiography.

Famous Personalities

John Addey (astrologer), John Barrymore (actor), C.C. Beck (cartoonist), M.C. Escher (artist), Steffi Graf (tennis champion), Stan Laurel (comedian), Christopher Lee (actor), John Masefield (poet), John Maynard Keynes (economist), Kylie Minogue (singer and actress), Salman Rushdie (author), Dorothy Sayers (writer), Brooke Shields (actress), Queen Victoria.

— 28 —

Sun Gemini ♊ Moon Cancer ♋

If I have to lay an egg for my country, I'll do it.
Bob Hope

My music is best understood by children and animals.
Igor Stravinsky

If Galileo had said in verse that the world moved, the Inquisition might have let him alone.
Thomas Hardy

Themes

AIR/WATER Intimate communication; friendly; chatty; kind; quick learner; nervously charming; sensitive; family life important; sibling relationships; poetic; artistic; communicating a feeling; clannishness; acute perception; private and cautious but great interest in people.

Do you think things over carefully and then make up your mind with your heart? Are you often unsure as to whether it is your thoughts or your feelings that are in charge? They work in a closely intertwined way, illuminating and reinforcing each other, so that your personality functions like a finely tuned radar/response system, reflecting back to the world what it receives.

You are expressive, nervous, never settling for long, as though your whole manner of living were an ebbing and flowing 'stream of consciousness'. Insatiably curious, quick-witted and charmingly sympathetic, you are the first in the neighbourhood welcoming party to greet the newcomers with a bag of home-grown tomatoes and an invitation to your barbecue. You are warm and ultra-sociable, and could be quite gifted at working with people in social welfare or mental-health organizations where your light-hearted human touch can do so much good. Equally, you can work with children in early education. Your insight into people is certainly one of your greatest gifts.

So versatile and sensitive is your personality that, without clear direction or emotional stability, you rapidly lose confidence and waste creative energy by muddling through nervously. The minutiae of personal life can distract you too readily for your own good so that you easily become the town gossip. Like a wide-eyed child, you are interested in many things and have an innate restlessness which can make you feel uncertain about what you should be doing.

You are not quite content with where you are and whom you are with until you can settle your mind and truly focus on something that absorbs you utterly. You want to be stimulated, forever learning, always needing to express your impressions and intuitions. If you can discipline yourself, your artistic and/or literary talents will surely develop. This is the only way you will transform that divine discontent into a creative momentum.

You have a well-developed sixth sense about many things, and your uncanny intuition makes you a good psychologist or fiction writer, for you have a deep understanding of emotional needs and of the way the human mind works. Although you are generally a conventional sort of person who cherishes traditional values, you are in your own quiet way a non-conformist and will insist on being true to yourself and protecting your best interests. You can be quite shrewd in doing so for you do not wish to rock the boat, but you will always find ways of uncovering the important facts and assessing their significance in a flash.

Relationships

Essentially you are a romantic who falls in love easily but apprehensively. You are sensitive, impressionable and need lots of affection and intimacy. Your moodiness could drive your partner wild, and you too, because you do not always understand where your feelings come from.

One of your greatest emotional dilemmas is the speed with which you can shift from being content on your own in your private world, to needing to share your experiences with your loved one. You want to know that you are safe in your own familiar niche, and domestic stability is very important for your best development. You are both a private *and* a people person, for you need interaction with others to inspire your creativity. You have a unique sense of irony and fondness for the foibles of human nature, and when you feel secure in your private world you can contribute your view of things through writing or through one of the arts.

Your Greatest Strengths

Receptive mind and sympathetic ear; capacity for 'diffuse awareness' – being aware of many things at once; clever self-expression and gentle manner with others; genuine interest in people and devotion to family life; romantic imagination.

Your Greatest Weaknesses

Oversensitivity to external stimuli, especially criticism; tendency to spread yourself too thin and to question and doubt yourself too much; defensive reactions and proneness to nervousness – especially in the absence of domestic tranquillity; a fear of leaving the family domain and thus a tendency to remain attached to old emotional biases and myths.

Images for Integration

A brother and sister and other neighbourhood friends play rounders in the garden until mother calls them in for Sunday lunch ... A university student comes home for the summer.

Famous Personalities

Don Ameche (actor), Boy George (singer), Thomas Hardy (novelist and poet), Bob Hope (actor-comedian), Grant Lewi (astrologer and writer), Paul Lynde (actor-comedian), Thomas Mann (novelist), Enoch Powell (politician), Beryl Reid (actress), Henri Rousseau (painter and writer), Nancy Sinatra (singer), Igor Stravinsky (composer).

— 29 —

Sun Gemini ♊ Moon Leo ♌

I celebrate myself; I sing myself.
WALT WHITMAN

Whoso would be a man must be a non-conformist.
RALPH WALDO EMERSON

In spite of everything, I still believe that people are really good at heart.
ANNE FRANK

Themes

AIR/FIRE Colourful conversationalist; warmly convivial; childlike sense of fun; positive; graceful; intellectual; good dramatist and storyteller; regal bearing but unstuffy; love of beauty; good at improvisation; rebellious; generous.

You are the eternal child whose fantasies of royal blood ensure that your confident social performance rarely sags. An amusing raconteur and possibly a talented weaver of magical images, you love being the centre of attention and the complete master of your listeners' emotions. You embellish your life, your loves and your stories with imaginative skill. Timing and exaggeration are your God-given gifts and you use them to great effect – to entertain others and to impress for your own advantage.

You assume your natural right to be exactly who you are. When young you are intellectually precocious; later on you are astute, but always full of enthusiasm, fun and probably mischief. In a sense you are a born performer, and your flair for self-dramatization is one of the things that makes you popular. People find you approachable, broad-minded and usually irresistibly charming, although when you feel insecure or unloved you can get pretty infantile and haughty. Likewise, your charm and diplomacy can disintegrate around bores, and maybe this is because there is nothing you would hate more than to be considered one yourself. Undoubtedly, you have a biggish need to be loved, adored and appreciated, and when you are, you turn on like a gorgeous wind-up doll – except that your passion and romance is hot-blooded and very real!

You are an 'ideas' person, a natural salesperson with an eye to the main chance – witty and quick off the mark. A cheerful, laid-back, insouciant manner may actually hide a very determined, ambitious side of you which has strong principles and knows exactly what you want. Thus you are a natural in a position of power – such as in teaching or social organizations – where both your creative expertise and your ability to deal confidently with people can combine.

Although you can be flexible and tolerant and interested in a wide variety of human perspectives, you will not compromise yourself on important issues, and you will argue with a sense of impassioned authority when it comes to standards of excellence and morality. Impatient of shoddiness in thought, language and personal decorum, you strive always for grace and clarity in your personal expression, and thus can be a real inspiration to others.

You are a person of strong but not overbearing personality, and by temperament always an individualist. You do not like to be pigeon-holed, for you instinctively know that the longer you live the more your abilities surprise you. But your honesty and sense of integrity are unshakeable, as is your dignity, warm courtesy and innate generosity.

Relationships

You are just as fussy about your love life as you are about your intellectual and artistic achievements. You want the best, and when you find him or her you bestow upon your lover your devoted heart. Like the romantic troubadours, you give yourself to your beloved body, mind and soul.

Love and affection are very important to you. When it comes to matters of the heart, you may have an innocently radiant charisma, opening yourself with all the vulnerability and tenderness of a child. You need to admire your loved one and will be happiest when an intellectual rapport keeps the interest going on many levels. And yet you have so much energy and such a lively social side that your mate will have to be resigned to sharing you with your other creative pursuits and with your many friends. You are the mobile, youthful artist, the creative communicator, the friend and mentor of all those who wish to create and enjoy the best.

Your Greatest Strengths

Quick mind and fertile imagination; flair for creative self-expression; optimistic and enthusiastic disposition; ability to stand up for the best without oppressing inferiors; friendly and spirited sense of fun and adventure which inspires others and keeps you ever popular.

Your Greatest Weaknesses

Your need for flattery and to hold centre-stage; childlike haughtiness and stubbornness which surfaces when you feel unappreciated; extrovert tendency to spend so much energy socializing that you fail to develop your abilities to their fullest.

Image for Integration

A king holds court and surprises his audience by joining the mandolin player in a duet of song and story.

Famous Personalities

Zola Budd (runner), Ralph Bellamy (actor), Helena Bonham Carter (actress), Mary Cassatt (artist), Jacques-Yves Cousteau (oceanographer), Clint Eastwood (actor), Anne Frank (diarist), Joe Montana (quarterback), Paul McCartney (musician), Ralph Waldo Emerson (philosopher and essayist), Walt Whitman (poet).

Sun Gemini ♊ Moon Virgo ♍

*Ask not what your country can do for you —
ask what you can do for your country.*

*If we cannot now end our differences, at least we can help
make the world safe for diversity.*
JOHN F. KENNEDY

Whence do We Come, What are We, Where are We Going?
PAINTING BY PAUL GAUGUIN

Themes

AIR/EARTH Analytical; nervous; mental energy; sense of service; clarity of expression; conscientious; practical expertise; communication skills; restless worrier; divine discontent; intellectual and artistic aspirations.

You are probably thinking, 'This astrology business is all very interesting, but why should I believe any of it?', for you combine a restless curiosity with a strong critical sense. You want to know about everything, to have, as it were, *superior knowledge*. Since time is precious, however, you become a speed reader rather than a profound scholar, and your priorities focus on what makes sense and is useful, and will be of service to yourself and other people.

You enjoy posing questions, even though you know the agony of never being satisfied by the answer that will follow. Are you flippant or serious, a communicator or an organizer, a theorist or a pragmatist? Do you prefer the lively city centre or the quiet garden suburb, a comedy show or a socially concerned documentary? If you are honest (and half of you can be as strictly honest as the other half can bend any facts to fit your case), you will have to answer 'Yes' to both sides of those questions and admit that you really are a paradox. You are unlikely to admit this, however, because you do not really like being told anything, preferring to work out and follow your own views.

Your natural critical bent can make it difficult for you to feel happy for very long in any of your projects or relationships. When unsatisfied, you start to overanalyse yourself and everyone else. This leaves you depleted, restless, and drifting from one great idea to the next, but constantly feeling discontented and needing to try one more thing, one more relationship. But when you finally *do* get your need to communicate together with your desire to be of practical service, you can be immensely effective in helping to make your community a better place.

Your worst enemy is perfectionism and elitism, and when you overcome that and realize that what you create is 'good enough', your cleverness, agility and good business sense will be a recipe for success. Versatile, objective and realistic, you need to be working in those areas where your gifts for analysis and communication can be given free rein, and where you can help find the answer to your endless childhood and adulthood questions of 'Why? Where? Who? How?'

Busy, busy, constantly active with lots of nervous energy, executive skill, wit and dry humour, you like to keep on the go but have a way of exhausting yourself with good intentions. Your best environment is the 'nervous system' of society, be it in transport, communications, the media or teaching, and you will hanker to be the queen bee rather than the worker. You can be a great gatherer and purveyor of information, and you belong among the intellectuals and artists of this world – or so you believe. You will flourish in any area where facts need to be accurately processed and evaluated in the shortest possible time. You can work with zest, for example, in such areas as journalism or on the news desk of a radio or television station, or on a City trading floor.

Yours is also a strongly logical, scientific combination with a natural talent for questioning and discovering the causes of things, and for sorting information into order. Working with computers, or in accountancy or economics would suit this aspect of your character. In artistic endeavours you have a gift for translating your immediate living experiences of the world into words, images, songs, carvings or canvas.

Relationships

Although you can be shy, you love to flirt and enjoy the fun of the chase. In any long-term relationship, mutual interests and plenty of intellectual stimulation are important for you. Others may accuse you of lacking warmth and romantic sympathy, but this is untrue. You often feel awkward about showing your feelings, but in fact you have plenty of feeling and can be very generous and devoted when you feel loved, respected and understood. You love to be of help and to feel needed, but can easily feel taken advantage of and swing into a self-pitying mood.

Emotional relationships will always be a challenge because you need space to pursue your own varied interests as well as just the right amount of tender, loving care. You need a partner who is neither too cloying nor too distant, and very good looking! You are a perfectionist in love and life.

Your Greatest Strengths

Fine, analytical mind; wit and sense of fun; flair with technical skills and precise communication; heightened aesthetic sense; practical commitment to helping others.

Your Greatest Weaknesses

Permitting anxieties to arrest your creative talents; a rather clinical insensitivity to the emotional needs of others; tendency to find fault and criticize negatively, and to jump discontentedly from one thing to the next.

Images for Integration

A specialist in nervous diseases gives a lecture in aid of local charities ... An art critic gives a brilliant master class ... Gauguin's *Arearea*.

Famous Personalities

Francis Crick (molecular biologist), Dennis Gabor (physicist who invented holography), Paul Gaugin (painter), John F. Kennedy (former American president), Rockwell Kent (artist and writer), Robert McNamera (politician, financial analyst and banker), Eddy Merckx (cycling champion), Alain Resnais (film director), Rosalind Russell (actress), Rise Stevens (opera singer), Richard Strauss (composer), Sir Alan Walters (economist).

SUN GEMINI ♊ MOON LIBRA ♎

I wasn't really naked. I simply didn't have any clothes on.
JOSEPHINE BAKER

Henceforth the adequacy of any military establishment will be judged by its ability to keep the peace.
HENRY KISSINGER

Read my lips.
GEORGE BUSH

Themes

AIR/AIR A wandering spirit; charming; diplomatic; bright; clear-headed; persuasive; graceful wit; intelligent; flexible; the gift of friendship; sociable; entertaining; spontaneous but tactful; clever; deft communication.

Highly civilized, charming and persuasive with a deep desire for justice, you seem to be one of those enviably suave and confidently easy-going people who breezes through life without a care. And yet, if you look underneath the surface polish, you often grapple with some awkward questions. Do you want to spend your life cultivating yourself, the beauty of your home and your career, or do you want to be off, restlessly travelling and enjoying the world and, at least theoretically, solving its problems? Should you tell the truth as you see it, or diplomatically smooth over the cracks? Are your relationships for life or do you seem to get bored with people quicker than most? Do you want to celebrate life or do you want life to celebrate you and your talents? None of these questions are impossible to reconcile, and especially for you, for when you get your act together you can be a master of diplomacy and the 'middle way'.

Just as you can usually solve your own inner conflicts with insight and clever thinking, so your breezy charm and humour, your gift for the soothing phrase and your obvious impartiality and integrity can disarm most opponents and bring understanding between bitter enemies.

Although you are strongly idealistic and deeply concerned with furthering individual and social justice, you are not as altruistic as you may appear. You are likely to be well aware of your own worth, and will demand the respect and loyalty you feel you deserve. In fact, you are quite shrewd and can figure out complex situations quicker than others can, which enables you to adjust to people and events, and to place yourself advantageously.

Your ambition is an adaptable and unobtrusive kind. If you are honest with yourself, however, you would like a little bit of spotlight and challenge, and you use your considerable charms to further your career. In the end, this self-interest is a valuable counterbalance to your ever-obliging tendency to say 'Yes' and to want to see the other person's viewpoint, which can, if left unchecked, leave you without a life of your own.

Your appreciation of beauty and justice can attract you to work in areas such as the law and politics, but also to conciliation, arbitration and counselling. You are, in fact, suited to any area in which you can deploy your objectivity and your desire to connect with people and learn from many views. You also need to use your mercurial skills for analysis, quick thinking, writing and communicating. This makes you a natural negotiator and go-between. You will especially enjoy anything that involves travel, for you love the stimulation of new faces, new landscapes and other perspectives. But you are also an explorer of ideas, and may gravitate towards scientific enquiry and information, and communication science. On the other hand, your deep appreciation of beauty will draw you to the arts. Whatever the field of your work, you have a natural gift for teaching and inspiring others. You readily express your enthusiasm for your chosen subject.

Quick to see the possibilities in things, you can be good in any business that depends upon keeping alert to changing tastes and fashions. Your verbal gifts make you a natural salesperson, and you will especially flourish in any area that brings you into touch with people and keeps you stimulated with new ideas.

Relationships

These are of immediate importance in your life, and you are likely to draw a large circle of friends around you, and make a loyal and understanding partner. When it comes to *the* relationship, however, you may hesitate to commit yourself, as you can easily get bored. You can find yourself divided between settling into the one real relationship that you feel you need to make your life complete, and your restless quest for variety and mental stimulation.

The world is your oyster and offers so many possibilities. No sooner have you found Mr or Ms Right than, well, another even more interesing and socially desirable candidate sails into view. In personal relationships you may find that the beautiful romance you crave is somehow devoid of the passion you read about. This can give you an irrational attraction to the dark and deeply emotional types whom you do not understand yet waken you to your hidden side.

Your Greatest Strengths

An immense capacity for friendship; appreciation of beauty and grace; natural tact and diplomacy; ability to see and argue the other person's viewpoint; colourful imagination and eternal sense of fun.

Your Greatest Weaknesses

A restless desire for change and ever-new vistas; reluctance to face the darker side of life; eagerness to smooth over difficulties and differences rather than confront them; childlike insistence on skimming the surface and living by your wits.

Images for Integration

An elegant hostess puts on a party and exhibition to help a worthy cause ... A shuttle diplomat brings together warring factions ... Elgar's *Enigma Variations* – 'to my friends depicted within'.

Famous Personalities

James Arness (actor), Alice Bailey (occultist), Josephine Baker (singer-entertainer), George Bush (former American president), Edward Elgar (composer), Sir James Guthrie (painter), Henry Kissinger (American statesman and diplomat), Norman Vincent Peale (author of *The Power of Positive Thinking*), Martha Washington (hostess, wife of George Washington), Duchess of Windsor (wife of Edward VIII).

Sun Gemini ♊ Moon Scorpio ♏

The Bible tells us to love our neighbours, and also to love our enemies; probably because they are generally the same people.
G.K.CHESTERTON

You can be the best athlete in the world but if you aren't in control of your emotions, you won't achieve anything.
LIZ McCOLGAN

Themes

AIR/WATER Extrovert yet introvert; passionate yet superficial; vitality and sensuality; breezy but intense; communicative yet secretive; quick-witted and deep-hearted; colourful and paradoxical.

Are you jokingly serious or seriously joking, or somewhere in between? Your life seems to be a breeze until you start noticing the monsters from the deep coming up for air. Then life begins to seem more like an expedition across hostile territory than a jaunt to visit friends.

You are a provocative and paradoxical individual who can be determinedly trivial and passionately eloquent. Your core issues can be expressed in the following questions: are you ruled by your head or your passions? Are you an amusing lightweight or a penetrating intellectual? Are you passionately committed to what you do, or do you change your allegiances with your shirts? There is a mixture of intensity and dexterity about the way in which you move, talk and communicate that has everyone guessing. Which will you be next – flip and comic or the passionate protester? You have an ease of expression and intensity of concern which can either contradict or complement each other. You can be loftily remote and detached from your feelings and yet entirely consumed by them.

When you are in work and situations that allow you to draw upon both your passionate intensity and your versatility and communicative skills, you can be an ebullient, quick-witted, provocative operator with a tart, sharp wit and colourful, if sometimes

141

cynical, view of the world. Then you are able to get your own way in whatever you decide to do, from creating a masterpiece to selling sausages.

You have a particular gift for selling, be it as a dedicated teacher, educationalist or politician putting over bright ideas; an artist communicating your complex soul vision; or as an actual salesperson of anything from zip fasteners to aardvarks. Add a dash of challenge and intrigue and this combination will sing whilst it works as a penetrating research scientist, psychotherapist, financial or other journalist, a detective, a spy or a special agent or investigator of any kind. Alternatively, you have many of the skills of a top barrister, able to argue your case with a wit, persuasion, intelligence and purposeful drive which can devastate lesser minds. Who can blame you if such versatility leads you on occasion to scatter your energies and close attentions?

Finding a deep happiness is not always easy, as you can be restlessly torn by the conflicting messages of your head and heart. Your instincts tell you that life is a private, painful and messy place where dog eats dog, and the devil takes the hindermost. Meanwhile, your mind tells you that the world is, or should be, an entirely reasonable, logical and rather fun and enjoyable place.

Wrestling with, and communicating, your insights and the paradoxes of your deep inner experience is essential to your larger health and contentment. The more you are driven to highlight, clarify and express the uncertainties and obscurities, and can wrestle with a single phrase or concept, the happier you will be.

Relationships

These bring out the best and worst in you, highlighting as they do your capacity for passion and pretence. You have considerable magnestism, but gadfly gifts make you both a persecutor and victim of the flames of the sex war.

Your paradoxical nature, which veers so readily between depths and superficiality, is particularly tantalizing and infuriating in partnerships. One moment you are passionately involved and totally committed; the next you are playing the field. When someone captures both your heart and mind, however, you can rejoice in delighting them with your multifaceted approach and the sheer poetic power of your whole soul.

Your Greatest Strengths

Forthright devotion and dedication to your convictions; investigative gifts; robust humour and penetrating satirical wit; colourful language and verbal skills; ability to communicate great depth of feeling with flair and passion; stoicism.

Your Greatest Weaknesses

Your often ferocious temper and scathing tongue; restless and erratic approach to life; self-doubt; manipulation of others by words and sexual innuendo; resistance to requests for change despite your own changeableness and inconsistencies.

Images for Integration

A long-distance runner ... A string quartet plays with lightness and dark intensity ... Father Brown solves a murder ... A kaleidoscope reveals ever-changing images of people and passions.

Famous Personalities

Paul Ableman (novelist), Lady Barbara Castlemaine (mistress to Charles II), G.K. Chesterton (critic, novelist and poet), Miles Davis (the 'Evil Genius' of jazz), Barbara McClintock (Nobel prize-winning genetics researcher), Liz McColgan (Olympic track athlete), Michael Portillo (politician), Terry Waite (special envoy), John Wayne (actor), Patrick White (novelist, poet and dramatist).

SUN GEMINI ♊ MOON SAGITTARIUS ♐

As a child I became a confirmed believer in the ancient gods simply because as between the reality of fact and the reality of myth, I chose myth ...myth is the truth of fact, not fact the truth of myth.
KATHLEEN RAINE

I was born at the age of twelve on a Metro-Goldwyn-Mayer lot.
JUDY GARLAND

Themes

AIR/FIRE Inquisitive; intellectual; independent; flamboyant communicator; outspoken; impatient; friendly; reverence for ancient learning; love of journeys; seeking; open to experience; emotionally immature but spontaneous; the eternal student; the scholar.

Are you just along for a nice ride or are you going somewhere important ? Do you want information or a profound education? In this pairing, the eternal child combines with the moral teacher to create an exceptionally alert, ever-questing, precocious and friendly personality.

You possess tremendous mental agility, ingenuity and perception, and can make lateral leaps of understanding that leave others far behind. You use logic combined with intuitive understanding with such swift ability that you can win debates and talk others – and yourself – into almost anything. This is the combination of the wily spiv or the impassioned professor, the used-car salesman or the leader of the Peace Corps. It all depends on the discipline and mental training you receive, for you have great potential and just need to harness and direct that intellectual curiosity and gregariousness so your best talents can develop.

Being warm, enthusiastic and always ready to have a go, you attract many friends and enjoy getting to know a wide variety of interesting people. But you will most admire and want to identify with real thinkers, poets and great idealists, people who soar beyond mortal limitations and make their mark through vision and understanding.

144

You are restless and probably love travel, and if you do not actually take off around the world, you will travel in your mind and explore ideas, possibilities and people. Sports, dance and outdoor activities are also likely to take up much of your time. You love to be with people, observe them, learn from them, entertain them, fall in love with them, but *not* be tied down by them. Freedom of movement is absolutely essential to you, for both your solar and lunar natures give you the urge to 'be where it's happening' and to experience life to the full. You want to understand ideas and then re-express them, even perform them in your own individual and dramatic way.

Relationships

You are generous and open, romantic and resilient, and eager for love, adventure and friendship. The latter will always be an important ingredient of any serious relationship, and intellectual rapport will be crucial.

Your eternally seeking nature is likely to take you into more than one serious relationship (not necessarily all at the same time). You thrive on stimulation and 'feeling good', and so may tire of people when the dust settles onto the nitty-gritty dynamics of relating. If things begin to feel like too much of a treadmill, you might be off to look for greener pastures. Likewise, if a relationship gets too emotionally swamping, you may react by stepping back and preaching with high-minded rationalization about 'positive thinking' and your need 'to be true to yourself'.

You wriggle out of tight corners and near misses like Peter Pan, with a cloud of innocent misdemeanours and harmless indiscretions trailing behind you. This is in part due to your eternal youthfulness which can get in the way of mature and committed relating. Your vivid imagination, your gift of the gab and your insatiable curiosity may also have something to do with it. Without mental discipline you can be too credulous and reckless, and end up wasting much of your creative potential on adventure and good stories.

Nevertheless, you really are a natural communicator, and in your heart of hearts want to discuss Important Issues rather than mere chit-chat. When you learn that freedom of intellectual movement is always there for the taking, and that it is enhanced rather than limited by rigorous self-discipline, then you will be able to enjoy the journey of a committed relationship without chafing so much at the restrictions.

Your Greatest Strengths

Vivid imagination; mental dexterity; intuitive leaps; voracious appetite for people and experiences; optimism; good ideas; insight into people; flair for communication and enthusing others.

Your Greatest Weaknesses

Tendency to talk too much and somewhat indiscreetly; impatience with feelings and taking responsibility for yourself; tendency to breeze through life using your quick wit rather than your higher intellectual faculties; your need to know it all.

Images for Integration

The Pied Piper leads his merry band of youths to the amphitheatre on the hill for an afternoon of music lessons, philosophical teachings and baseball ... A young man goes abroad to attend university and becomes a foreign correspondent.

Famous Personalities

Gemma Craven (actress), Rennie Davis (American political activist), Bruce Dern (actor), Douglas Fairbanks (actor), Judy Garland (actress and singer), Guy Lombardo (big-band leader), Barry Manilow (singer), Kathleen Raine (philosopher and poet), Prince Rainier (of Monaco), Beverly Sills (opera singer), F. Weingartner (composer).

— 34 —

SUN GEMINI ♊ MOON CAPRICORN ♑

Try to arrange your life in such a way that you can afford to be disinterested. It is the most expensive of all luxuries, and the one best worth having.
DEAN INGE

My own experience of myself is that I write quite slowly, and painstakingly ...I
guess what may be different about me is that I work every day, for long hours.
I stay with it.
JOYCE CAROL OATES

Themes

AIR/EARTH Serious yet carefree; sociable yet solitary; a cynical
optimist; clarity of thought; quick-witted; humorous; devoted friend;
practical helpfulness; intelligent; clever; good business mind; teaching
skills.

Are you a high-spirited socializer or a solemn loner? Do you come alive
on breezy, flower-strewn summer days or is your season the bare, crisp
clarity of mid-winter? By choice you are a light-hearted,
communicative extrovert, yet your natural instinct is to take a more
serious and 'responsible' view of life. You start out with amusement
and intention to enjoy, but your observations soon move you into
pragmatic mode for you are a born organizer with a big need to run the
show, even if the show feels like a burden after a while.

The tug between these very different sides to you can be a difficult
one, and you may spend a lot of effort hiding your more pessimistic and
anxious side through a conscious brightness and flip laughter. Your
up-beat Pollyanna side insists that there is always a silver lining when
actually you are feeling perfectly dreadful. You can talk with real
interest about almost anything, yet you find it almost impossible to talk
about your own pain, doubts and fears. But when the gad-about and
the sceptic within you shake hands, you come alive with *creative
intelligence*. Your shrewdness and quickness of mind make you a great
problem-solver. You can apply yourself to any challenge with a deep
sense of concern yet with a sparkle in your eye, a gift for
understatement and a witty word to wash away any tears.

When you work equally with both your light and heavy sides, your
dry, clear-headed mental precision helps you become a successful
professional and invaluable friend. You can get to grips with basic facts
and principles and then work hard to apply them. A dab hand at any
kind of routine, you can be relied upon to find all the short cuts to make
for maximum efficiency. You can be extremely methodical and may
well have a special aptitude for subjects like maths, accounting and
science, and also for business and administrative work.

Your mind is focused but speedy, which enables you to observe others with a pungent wit and objective clarity. Your gift for simple explanations of complex issues makes you an excellent teacher. And, when coupled with your interest in people, your social conscience gives you a special gift for bringing out the best in the underprivileged and handicapped.

Whilst you know how to enjoy yourself, there is a solid strand of ambition in you which wants to get on and improve your lot in life. This leads you to place more emphasis on your career and promotion prospects than on personal fulfilment. You are the type who pursues higher education and self-improvement even into old age. Any role that offers both movement and a *soupçon* of power will attract you, but in the longer run you are likely to be too critical and cynical to take the stuff of politics over-seriously.

On the artistic side, your combination of lightness and seriousness can make anything you create both immediately enjoyable and yet real food for thought. Visually you enjoy both light, bright colours and earthy browns and blacks, and the more these combine and contrast, the better. But it is with fine-tuned words of every shade that you are most likely to excel and find a voice to speak your own clear truth.

Relationships

These are an area of ambiguity for you. You have a roving eye but a love of solitude. You can be shy and yet saucy. Your elegant self-restraint can attract mysterious, emotional types who find your mischievous self-control equally mysterious. Emotionally you seek serious commitment, yet intellectually you need variety, stimulation and challenge. You need mental rapport with your partner but, at the same time, you prefer it if he or she is no slouch on the dance floor.

You have a strong family sense and will be devoted to loved ones in a sensible, practical way. But you may sometimes mask emotional insecurity with an overly paternal approach to loved ones. They will not always want to be organized as expertly as you are capable!

Your Greatest Strengths

A quick, clear, factual mind; conscientiousness and reliability; gift for working with people and assessing their needs; speed at picking up practical organizational skills that you can use in all areas of your life.

Your Greatest Weaknesses

A tendency to hide your needs from yourself, and to replace real sympathy for others with 'common sense'; impatience with the emotional realm, which you either cannot fathom or gracefully sidestep.

Images for Integration

A scientist captures, examines and names a new species of exotic butterfly ... A philosopher points to the deeper realities behind the transient world ... A socialite becomes mayor of the town.

Famous Personalities

Luis Alvarez (experimental physicist), Joseph Brodsky (poet), Ninette de Valois (dancer), William Douglas-Home (playwright), Rainer Fassbinder (film director), George III, William Ralph Inge (clergyman and philosopher), Dean Martin (actor), Elsa Maxwell (actress, pianist and journalist), Stevie Nicks (lead singer with Fleetwood Mac), Joyce Carol Oates (novelist and playwright), Jane Russell (actress, comedian and dancer), James 'Jim' Thorpe (athlete).

— 35 —

SUN GEMINI ♊ MOON AQUARIUS ♒

The age of chivalry is never past, so long as there is a wrong left unredressed on earth.
CHARLES KINGSLEY

Though leaves are many, the root is one;
Through all the lying days of my youth
I swayed my leaves and flowers in the sun;
Now I may wither into the truth.
W.B. YEATS

Childhood decides.
JEAN-PAUL SARTRE

Themes

AIR/AIR Bright and light yet sober and serious; clear-headed; intelligent; witty; the eternal youth and the wise old man or woman; the outsider; the reformer; a restless energy and curiosity; prophetic gifts.

Is your game Trivial Pursuit or chess? Do you want to go dancing or to study philosophy? Are you a skittish, quick-witted, ever curious, talkative livewire, or are you an impartial observer, scientist and poet, determined to follow your vision of the larger Truth wherever it may lead?

Whatever your actual age, you are possessed by a restless, bright bird of youth which constantly vies for your attention with a serious, wise old owl in you. Thus on the one hand you have a need for endless variety and stimulation; on the other your instinct is to look for the one root Truth which encompasses all others, and which will help you make the world a better place. In short you have the light, breezy, adventurous and flirtatious qualities of spring combined with the reflective, cool mood of dark mid-winter.

Your Middle Way, through which these approaches can be resolved, is an equable autumnal observation post. From here you can relish the fruits of spring and plan forward, with a spectator's wisdom, for the demands of winter, and in this you can at times be uncannily prophetic. This gives you an enviably broad view of life, which combines your deft, childlike lightness of touch with your deeper, serious sense of purpose.

As one of life's Great Spectators, you can display a deep understanding of your chosen career, enabling you to achieve almost anything you want. Thus you are a great talker and theorizer and you can do remarkably well at whatever you give yourself to wholeheartedly. You especially like people, or at least their minds, and are fascinated by what makes them tick. This can attract you to psychology and sociology, and yet also towards the creative arts, especially music. You are likely to have the natural sense of words and rhythm of the writer, poet and musician. You respond to life with a freshness and vitality. Above all, you aspire to know the truth, the

Whole Truth, and you love talking about it and trying to give it expression.

If you are drawn to business, your objectivity and cleverness enable you to spot opportunities. Needing plenty of interaction with people and lots of movement, you are best as an organizer, go-between and negotiator, leaving the practical work to others. Whilst you can turn your hand to anything, the important thing as far as work is concerned is to make a virtue out of your flexibility and to ensure that, one way or another, you have several screens to your computer.

Philosophically, and this is a philosophical combination, you are likely to identify with the view that, as human beings, we are naturally free, and that it is only our false assumptions that prevent us from doing or becoming whatever we want. What you may fail to recognize is that it is in fact your ultra-reasonable approach to things that limits your potential freedom. Your very reasonableness cuts you off from your own unreasonable emotions, yet understanding such emotions enables you to cross the last frontier in your potential growth. Indeed, you may deny that you are plagued by any such feelings. But you, more than most, have a way of romanticizing the idea of personal growth. You take readily to paths of self-improvement, as long as they are *intellectually sound*.

Relationships

In your mind you may long for passionate intensity and total self-surrender, yet in practice you are more likely to find yourself drawn by friendship and mutual understanding. You need intelligence in your loved ones, and talking and communicating are essential. You also need plenty of space and a sense of personal freedom if you are not to feel stifled and claustraphobic. This can attract you to seemingly well-thought-out 'open' relationships, yet you should beware of such overly intellectual human arrangements. Although they may make perfect logic, they can be a way of avoiding emotional vulnerability. Ultimately such cerebral solutions can only leave you feeling empty, cheated and removed from that mysterious inner marriage you so long to consummate.

Your Greatest Strengths

Quick, alert, objective mind; the sheer breadth of your intelligence;

ability to see the large view; versatility and adaptability; humanitarian feeling; friendly, open tolerance.

Your Greatest Weaknesses

Getting 'all up in your head' and talking far too much; allowing your mind to run too fast and neglecting the realities of your life; lack of connection with the painful, dark aspects of yourself.

Images for Integration

Sherlock Holmes ... A scientist suddenly sees the caterpillar, chrysalis and butterfly as one single being ... Wagner's *Der Ring des Nibelungen*.

Famous Personalities

Pat Boone (singer), Sir Arthur Conan Doyle (writer), Edvard Grieg (composer), Charles Kingsley (writer), Donald Maclean (spy), Anton Mesmer (pioneering medical hypnotist), Marilyn Monroe (actress), Sally Ride (first American woman astronaut), Jean-Paul Sartre (philosopher and novelist), Oswald Spengler (philosopher and historian), Richard Wagner (composer), W.B. Yeats (poet).

— 36 —

SUN GEMINI ♊ MOON PISCES ♓

Well, my deliberate opinion is – it's a jolly strange world.

Journalists say a thing that they know isn't true, in the hope that if they keep on saying it long enough it will be true.
ARNOLD BENNETT

I like men to behave like men – strong and childish.
FRANÇOISE SAGAN

Themes

AIR/WATER Sentimental; versatile; chameleon; moody; rich imagination; poetic; vacillating; sociable; adaptable; talkative; nervous; casual; blow with the wind; dreamy; sympathetic; literary ability and artistic sensitivity; submissive but cunning.

Do you try to make logical sense out of Beethoven's 9th? Do you chatter away eloquently and suddenly find yourself overcome with worry about something you remember you said the day before yesterday? You think on your feet, wear your heart on your sleeve, explain your inner mental workings to the world, and then wonder why you feel so exposed, depleted, and even betrayed.

You are a sociable seeker of knowledge and wisdom but have trouble in sorting it all out and expressing exactly what you mean. How can you assimilate all those ideas? Sometimes you just do not know, and so you decide to sleep on it and have a dream. Your intellectual curiosity has a way of going to sleep on you, and you need to recharge your batteries frequently with peace and quiet.

You are an introvert in extroverted disguise, and yet it is not a disguise – it is really you. You are a master of improvisation and imitation, and your subtle perception of people's idiosyncracies can make you a good actor. But because you so easily understand and identify with passing feelings and ideas, often you are not sure in the end what you feel and who, exactly, you are.

You are ultra-sensitive, highly aware of your world, and keen to interact and communicate with people. The problem is that you are so impressionable that you tend to try out many different ideas and attitudes, some of them contradictory, because each has its own inner logic that deserves a hearing. Logic versus sympathy is your struggle. Left brain versus right. There is great literary or artistic potential inherent in this attitude but only if you can establish an interior dialogue between your head and your heart which forms the essential core of yourself. This will enable you to develop the one thing you badly need: *concentration*. Without this you are prone to breeze along on the surface of a pleasant life with the sense that a potentially profound life is just around the corner, but somehow always eludes you.

You would make a fine counsellor or group co-ordinator, as you have lots of compassion and want to understand and express the intangibles about people and what makes them tick. You are a natural student of the non-rational and do not have to be convinced that 'there are more things in heaven and earth, Horatio, than are dreamt of in your philosophy'. You have plenty of empathy, an ability to work with symbols and images, and a strong need to communicate. But you will find that your communication with others is more effective if you communicate with yourself in private more often. Stress and nerve problems may calm down miraculously if you develop a musical or artistic talent. Words are not the only way to communicate, and your desire to express the inexpressible requires an art form, not a chat.

Relationships

What you lack in concentration you certainly make up for in affection, imagination and sociability. You feel deeply for others and will eloquently defend the underdog. A strong need for tenderness and love makes you vulnerable to others, and open and eager for emotional experience. Somewhat fickle and hard to pin down emotionally, you may tend to get going when the going gets rough. You may lean on your loved one for support, yet be quite fault-finding and hard to please at the same time.

Idealistically romantic and mentally critical, you have many ups and downs in relationships until you find something solid to occupy your active mind. There is something eternally youthful about you, fanciful and fun-loving, effervescent and brimming over with expectations. As a result you may be good with children, for you are a child yourself with fantasies, hopes and dreams that feed your soul.

Your Greatest Strengths

Vivacious empathy; quick, versatile imagination; sensitivity to art and all forms of beauty; compassionate, gentle and charismatic sociability; originality in communication; eternally youthful readiness for adventure.

Your Greatest Weaknesses

Lack of boundaries, which can lead to a superficial emotional life; tendency towards mental confusion when overstimulated; jack-of-all-trades attitude which can result in a lack of confidence in yourself;

tendency to withdraw in self-pity when you feel misunderstood.

Images for Integration

A weather vane on a church spire sparkles in the sunshine as the wind twirls it around, turning it into a mysterious sky gem ... Peter Pan marries Tinkerbell and they live happily ever after in Never Never Land.

Famous Personalities

Richard Benjamin (actor), Arnold Bennett (novelist), Cilla Black (singer and television personality), Raoul Dufy (artist), Allen Ginsberg (poet and writer), Mikhail Glinka (composer), Sally Kellerman (actress), Jerry Kozinski (writer), Prince (pop singer), Françoise Sagan (writer).

Chapter Seven

SUN IN CANCER

— 37 —

SUN CANCER ♋ MOON ARIES ♈

*One is happy as a result of one's own efforts, once one knows the necessary
ingredients of happiness – simple tastes, a certain degree of courage, self denial
to a point, love of work, and, above all, a clear conscience. Happiness is no
vague dream, of that I now feel certain.*
GEORGE SAND

*We flatter those we scarcely know,
We please the fleeting guest,
And deal full many a thoughtless blow
To those who love us best.*
EDNA WHEELER WILCOX

Themes

WATER/FIRE Sociable; sensitive; restless; impatient; a tenacious
survivor; moody; shrewd; insightful; active imagination;
individualistic; creative and heroic spirit; poetic; feminine but feisty;
defensive but forthright.

Are you vivaciously gregarious one day and the next intensely
agoraphobic? Do you come out fighting or do you protect those who
need your care? In fact, you do both very well. Sensitive, romantic and
insightful, you have a colourful, artistic and somewhat volatile

temperament which exudes charisma and mischief as well as tremendous capability. You are moody and can easily develop a chip on your shoulder if you imagine you are ill-treated or if you do not get the affection and attention you crave. But you are just as likely to direct any militancy towards defending family and loved ones as you are to staging a campaign for yourself.

You feel passionately about individual rights, about the need for everyone to contribute something unique, and about your own right to self-expression. The fact is that you may often feel a conflict between your devotion to home and family responsibilities, and your need for blowing your own trumpet; between your need for security and intimacy, and your need for freedom and excitement. One side of you is reflective, intuitive, always feeling out the emotional climate of environments with uncanny accuracy. This side of you wants security and oodles of tender loving care. The other side of you is gregarious, impulsive, almost pugnacious in its demand for self-expression. You both fear and thrive on disagreement, and this complexity – a kindly, compliant feeling for others hiding an agressive, competitive interior – can result in stress and nervous ailments if you are not careful.

Your combination is potentially extremely powerful, as it contains not only the epitome of feminine intuition, but also masculine assertion and individualism, as well as equal components of tenderness and bravado, selfless caring and 'me-first' courage. You want to nurture others and to engage with them dynamically, and that can be both exciting and unnerving for all concerned, including yourself. You want to be made a fuss of, and to be your own person. You want to protect and establish security, but to be first as well.

Your love of home life is marked, as is your need to spend time in your private creative world. You guard your privacy jealously; but you also want to get out into the world. Domesticity is not enough for you, and always seems to present a thorny issue which weighs heavily on your freedom.

Rather than getting all the family support you would like, you often end up supporting parents or family yourself in some way. Your creative strengths seek a challenge, and if you want that challenge to be all your own, you may need to stay far away from old family matters that so easily tug at your patriotic heart. Nevertheless, your recipe for contentment is to integrate your drive for independence with your need for roots. It may not always be easy, but with your enthusiasm and ingenuity there is little you cannot achieve.

Relationships

You have a lot of love to give, but you can be demanding, temperamental and quite jealous if you suspect your loved one is not 100-per-cent devoted. You are afraid of getting hurt, but still you thrive on risk – at least a little. Passionate and romantic, you instinctively adore the challenge and excitement of love, but you consciously need commitment and continuity.

This soft–tough dilemma within you may also cause you to 'swap roles' at times: sometimes you feel masculine and assertive, other times feminine and submissive. Sometimes you want peace and intimacy, and other times you want a fight – and even then you are not sure if you want to win or lose! Your emotional life can be a bit of a roller coaster; just try to make sure that you are behind the steering wheel.

Your Greatest Strengths

Quick, shrewd mind; ability to use both receptivity and self-assertion to good effect; individualistic approach to life; emotional commitment to personal values and relationships; sensitivity to people's needs; social flair; original, magnetic style.

Your Greatest Weaknesses

Self-absorption and oversensitivity to criticism; impatience and sharp tongue when you reach the end of your tether; tendency to hide behind a brisk, authoritative manner when at your most vulnerable; a sort of divine discontent that makes you stir up trouble when there is none.

Images for Integration

A suffragette takes to the barricades in aid of her cause ... A quiet home-body becomes a sports champion.

Famous Personalities

Bernard Buffet (artist), Barbara Cartland (romantic novelist), Arlo Guthie (folk songwriter and singer), Sir Edmund Hillary (mountaineer), Don Knotts (actor), Regine (discotheque proprietor), Diana Rigg (actress), George Sand (novelist), Edna Wheeler Wilcox (poet).

— 38 —

SUN CANCER ♋ MOON TAURUS ♉

God grant me the Serenity to accept the things I cannot change, Courage to change the things I can, and Wisdom to know the difference.
REINHOLD NIEBUHR

Skill without imagination is craftsmanship and gives us many useful objects such as wickerwork picnic baskets. Imagination without skill gives us modern art.
TOM STOPPARD

Maturation is a continuous process of transcending environmental support and developing self-support, which means an increasing reduction of dependencies.
FRITZ PERLS

Themes

WATER /EARTH Down-to-earth yet imaginative; emotional but realistic; affectionate and supportive; love of friends and family; intuitive and instinctive wisdom; mothering or smothering; traditional; sensitive to the needs of others; artistic sensibility; musical; responsible; dependable; tenacious; practical idealist.

Are you a cosy, intimate, family person who can suddenly become quite stubborn, even tyrannical and autocratic about how domestic life should be organized? Do you treasure the people in your life but sometimes find that they do not want to be treated like treasure? Do you tune in easily to others' needs but then find you wish they were more self-reliant and able to clean up their own mess?

You feel deeply about your relationships, especially your family, and you tend to be a good role model because you are caring *and* responsible, romantic without being silly. You can be vulnerable, but no matter how much you have depended on others, you will find self-respect and contentment from developing and relying on your own abilities. Nevertheless, you are loving, caring, ready with kind words and helpful deeds. You thrive on being needed, but you are also able to claim time to nourish your own artistic and intellectual gifts. You love what you do and do what you love, and you make sure you enjoy it all as well. 'Make the world one happy, prosperous family', could be your motto. To you this means loving and working well and stopping to smell the roses, too – a simple philosophy which you believe would, if practised, make the world a saner place.

Although your values are rooted in the past, you are usually absorbed in the here-and-now, attending to feelings, practical problems and needs, developing and nurturing talents and opportunities. All your senses are extremely sharp, and powerful memories are evoked by their stimulation. You have a lot of basic common sense and can be quite shrewd and strategic. Indeed, material security is important to you, and you have luxurious taste – if you want something, you will find a way of getting it. You tend to be well-organized and methodical but not in a fanatical way – you are too emotional by nature to turn your back on the moods that fill out the canvas of your daily life.

You have a natural understanding of people and their needs, and would make a good psychologist or counsellor. And you are such a naturally helpful, supportive individual that it is suprising how quickly you can sink into sullen moods and passive resistance when things are not going your way. But you come to know yourself well, find your own best therapies (music, drama), and are not without an ironic sense of humour.

If you are in business, you will have a flair for providing the public with what it wants (you could make an excellent hotelier or restaurateur). As a creative artist, your sensitive response to the world usually appeals, and so you tend to be popular and successful. You are too realistic to be oversentimental and too sentimental to be a total realist. In other words, you are *very human*, and whether you are a full-time mother, manager, musician, nurse, doctor, gardener, actor or in business, you are always encouraging healthy growth and development.

You make an ideal teacher because you instinctively understand that maturation is a slow, organic process, and that everyone must first learn that he or she should grow according to the inner blueprint rather than to society's ideal. You have a strong sense of both the past and the present, and this enables you to translate experience into practical understanding.

Relationships

Your relationships are pretty central to your life, and you need lots of physical affection and devotion. Romantic, deeply caring and wonderfully responsive, you naturally seek permanence in a relationship, and will happily create a sense of home and security for those you love. But relationships for you may have a decidedly maternal 'feel' to them, and it may be important for you to remember that there is a very thin line between mothering and smothering. You get comfortable in relationships and do not like things to change – intimacy and dependability are what you want. But just a *frisson* of excitement keeps your imagination heightened and your interest engaged.

Your Greatest Strengths

Powers of dedication and perseverance; shrewd perception; artistic imagination; practical idealism; belief in the worth of every individual; capacity to listen to others' needs.

Your Greatest Weaknesses

Fussy, overprotective concern for your nearest and dearest; tendency to be lazy and stubborn; subjective prejudices; your expectations about how others should look after you.

Images for Integration

A family photo album ... A flourishing family business ... A painter captures the taste and smell of a landscape.

161

Famous Personalities

Bill Blass (fashion designer, businessman), Ernst Bloch (philosopher), Donald Carl Johanson (anthropologist), Frida Kahlo (symbolic-realist artist), Reinhold Niebuhr (theologian), Fritz Perls (founder of Gestalt psychotherapy), Marcel Proust (novelist), Jean Jacques Rousseau (social philosopher), Tom Stoppard (playwright), Meryl Streep (actress), Lord Woodrow Wyatt (socialist politician).

— 39 —

SUN CANCER ♋ MOON GEMINI ♊

I never met the companion that was so companionable as solitude.
HENRY DAVID THOREAU

Happiness is as a butterfly, which, when pursued, is always beyond our grasp, but which if you will sit down quietly, may alight upon you.
NATHANIEL HAWTHORNE

Themes

WATER/AIR Strong family sense; emotionally expressive; restless; good storyteller; vivacious; clever; musical; good memory for personal detail; self-reflective; moody; childlike sense of fun; devoted; shrewd thinker; friendly; eternal student; good teacher; sympathetic; sociable; sensitive conversationalist.

Are you ruled by your heart and emotional needs or by your mind and your need for freedom? Whether you are ruled by one or the other, one thing is for sure: you are a particularly talented individual with a warm, sensitive, almost elf-like nature who can tune into people like a bee in a field of tulips.

In this combination, the defensive, emotional negotiating skills of Cancer blend with the quick-witted, imitative opportunism of Gemini to produce an extremely sensitive, emotionally responsive and colourfully expressive personality. You are genuinely interested in people, and your perception of them – their needs, their differences, their fascinating quirks and funny habits – is often disquietingly accurate. This talent makes you either a natural counsellor or stand-up comic.

You are good at sensing where a person is at intellectually, and zeroing in with Cancerian compassion and deft skill, striking up a conversation and offering the necessary insight – all to the delight of the recipient. Then, like Tinkerbell, you are off again, but not for long, as you carry your concern for others with you, and the prospect of enjoying the pleasures of friendship will prompt your return.

You get to know a remarkable number of people and you take great interest in all of them – and if you do not it is only because you find them too boorish and unnecessarily rude. Sensitivity and nuance count a lot for you. You seek to understand people and have a way of affirming them and adapting to their needs, which makes you popular and loved. People generally find you both witty and kind-hearted, both comical and caring, both fun and comfortable to be around.

You make a wonderful teacher, mainly because you love to learn yourself, and your curiosity combined with your excellent memory and imagination mean that you can do well in the academic world. You may have a facility with music, mimicry, languages, writing or painting, but whatever it is, you have a strong need for creative self-expression. Like a child who delights in the discovery of his abilities, you relish the creative process and can make the hardest things seem simple and fun. You may be very well tuned into children because the child in you is such a dominant force.

Inwardly you are less sure of yourself than you seem. This is partly due to your openness and sensitivity to others, which can sometimes deplete your energies and make you feel indecisive. You need peaceful time alone when you can cultivate intimacy with yourself, keep a journal, observe both life and your thoughts about life, and express yourself artistically. In some ways you are just a kid at heart, and you may remain somewhat emotionally immature all your life. You shrink from heavy, ponderous entanglements; you lighten everyone's load by launching into song, poetry or hilarious imitations.

Relationships

You may chat away and give the impression that you breeze easily through life, side-stepping difficult situations by turning things into a joke (sometimes at your own expense). Yet you do, in fact, have very deep feelings, which you may hide from the dangers of the world. Your feelings can be imposed upon and you have probably been hurt by this. As a result, your naivety soon transforms into shrewdness, even though you still remain vulnerable and warm-hearted, ready to give and to help friends and family as much as you can.

Romance feeds your soul, so you may deduce that the more romance the better! You need mental affinity with your partner; without that you get bored and may think of something and someone else. In a close relationship you will sometimes be the carer – maternal and understanding; other times you will need to be the child – to run around, play the field, meet up with your friends and generally enjoy the more light-hearted side of life.

Your Greatest Strengths

Whimsical charm; understanding heart; accurate perceptions of others; quick wit and poetic mind, which together enable you to teach and communicate with others with warm enthusiasm and intuitive versatility.

Your Greatest Weaknesses

A tendency to scatter your energies by becoming overstimulated; to be emotionally indecisive and immature; to let nervousness eat away at your confidence; your knack of making a joke when things get difficult, which although temporarily helpful, just sidesteps the issue you need to examine.

Images for Integration

A performance of a puppet show at an infant school Christmas play ... A family plays a game of charades ... Young children enacting a play wedding in the garden.

Famous Personalities

Ned Beatty (actor), Dianne Feinstein (politician), Nathaniel Hawthorne (novelist), Cheryl Ladd (actress), Lord Mountbatten (Supreme Allied Commander), Clifford Odets (playwright), Sally

Priesand (first American woman rabbi), John D. Rockefeller (industrialist and philanthropist), Henry David Thoreau (essayist and poet).

40

SUN CANCER ♋ MOON CANCER ♋

But I want first of all to be at peace with myself ... I want to live an inner harmony, essentially spiritual, which can be translated to outward harmony.
ANNE MORROW LINDBERGH

We deprive the dying by shutting them out, by isolating them from the activities of life. The dying are grateful for the chance to talk, to share and explore their experience, and to be liberated from the conspiracy of silence.
ELISABETH KÜBLER-ROSS

My Old Kentucky Home
SONG BY STEPHEN FOSTER

Themes

WATER/WATER Emotional; kind-hearted; romantic; helpful; perceptive; timid; defensive; secretive; clannish; imaginative; artistic; attached to the past; shrewd; protective; sympathetic; love of security; mother complex.

You are ultra-sensitive – and how! Your inner world is your inner sanctum and you protect it religiously. It in turn provides you with an almost religious vitality which, at its best, pours nourishing energy into all your creations and relationships.

Profoundly emotional, you can feel, and make others feel, the whole rainbow of emotions – elation, despair, compassion, loneliness, inner peace – and thus one of your potential gifts is your mastery of many moods and your capacity to inspire others through art, poetry, music or, more importantly, loving. But if you do not master the moods, they master you, which means that you are often at the mercy of huge mood swings.

You crave sympathy, affection and understanding, and you give the same generously in return, provided you feel safe and secure. Being extremely sensitive, your tendency is to over-react to real or imagined rebuffs or callousness. Quite simply, you are afraid of being hurt and no one in the world can completely protect you from the perils of life. Thus, like your mascot the crab, you will use your innate shell of self-protection for all its worth, poking out your toe to test the water before you enter into the fray.

But even though you are defensive and even cagey, you are by no means weak; in fact, you are extremely shrewd in business matters with, possibly, a serious interest in collecting valuables – stamps, coins, antique furniture, art – on the side, which will reinforce your sense of material security (a very important consideration). If you are typical of this combination, you will rarely go around with an empty wallet. Even if you are quite wealthy, you are pound wise, rarely foolish, and have an eye for value rather than an urge for spending sprees.

You have a retentive memory and an interest in all things old – and you often have an especial interest in your own ancestry and following up interesting family links. You are therefore a natural historian, and even if you eschew book-learning and dusty academics, you will be interested in those aspects of culture that knit people together.

You love your home and all things associated with it. A safe, private place is absolutely central to your creative development. Your roots go deep, whether you like it or not. This is why at some point you will benefit from carefully examining their psychological hold over you. You may need to open up a bit, and not let your clannish consciousness limit your experiences. Like a chain in the ancestral succession, you will pass on the family imprint, the funny complexes, the intuitive wisdom and strength to your own family and students, as the case may be, in your uniquely personal way.

Relationships

An extremely subjective person, you assess and evaluate things emotionally all the time. You brood about things and then you overflow with the feelings that have been welling up inside. You seek security, affection and nourishment, and emotional exchange with your loved one is the life-blood of your soul. You nurture and protect and need nurturance and protection in return. But you have to be careful that possessiveness does not choke your cherished intimacy to death, for no one wants to be loved by a Jewish mother forever.

Emotionally, the waters ebb and flow between you; your feeling antennae are always at work, picking up undercurrents of meaning, possible danger signals or tantalizing promises of delicious satisfaction (food, money or love!). But, once committed in a relationship, you are there for richer or poorer. Your partner will just have to put up with your mysterious moods. You are not to be fathomed by logic; you know it – and the sooner he or she learns it, the better for your domestic harmony.

Your Greatest Strengths

Emotional perception and tenacity; poetic imagination and expressiveness; excellent memory and intuitive economic sense; warm concern and devotion to family and friends.

Your Greatest Weaknesses

Oversensitivity and moodiness; shyness and tendency to worry and sulk inside your shell; strong desire to be needed and appreciated; deep attachment to the way things were.

Images for Integration

A gosling peeks out of its shell as mother goose chases away the farm cat ... A theatrical family performs *A Midsummer Night's Dream* in their own garden.

Famous Personalities

Giorgio Armani (fashion designer), Bella Abzug (politician), Henry Cabot Lodge (politician), Tom Cruise (actor), Phyllis Diller (comedienne), Jacques Delors (politician), Harrison Ford (actor), Stephen Foster (songwriter), Woody Guthrie (songwriter), Elisabeth Kübler-Ross (psychologist), Anne Morrow Lindbergh (writer and poet), George Orwell (writer).

Sun Cancer ♋ Moon Leo ♌

It was morning, and the new sun sparkled gold across the ripples of a gentle sea.
RICHARD D. BACH

Love does not consist in gazing at each other but in looking outward together in the same direction.
ANTOINE DE SAINT-EXUPÉRY

Themes

WATER/FIRE Dramatic sensitivity; compassionate; devoted; clannish; artistic; magnetic; imaginative; proud; aristocratic; trustworthy; affectionate and adoring; love of family; deep feelings; private but radiant; warmly hospitable; shy but with inward greatness; attractive personality.

Are you a timid, kind-hearted introvert, or a radiant, dignified extrovert with an instinct for centre-stage?

You may seem at times to be a shy, vulnerable, romantic individual who only wants to please, but underneath you have a voracious appetite for adoration and respect, and will not stop until you get it. Without a doubt, you have a very warm feeling for others, and domestic security with plenty of happy togetherness is high on your list of priorities. When it comes to cooperation with others, however, you have your limits because you are profoundly individualistic and, albeit in a charming manner, you will insist on doing things your way when it comes down to it.

Ultimately the most important thing for you is believing in yourself and being true to your standards and aspirations. Most of all, you need to fulfil your creative potential, which is like an intimate companion with whom you share your life. You nurture it, protect it, and then you show it off, and whatever walk of life you are in, you tend to be a fine performer. This gives you a lot of self-respect and a touch of vanity as well, and your emotional sensitivity combined with your underlying imperiousness tends to impress others and makes them take you seriously.

You are a devoted member of your flock, and you zealously and jealously protect and promote whomever you are devoted to. When it comes to developing your own talents, however, you seem to know that you have to pull away in order to grow into your greatest self. Others may think you are a bit of a show-off but that is not the case: you simply have a deep sense of the importance of your own creative talents, and you will feel only half alive if you do not honour them. Although you are pretty sensitive to criticism or rebuffs, you are just as committed to honesty and personal integrity; and despite your vanity, you eventually learn to laugh at yourself.

Relationships

You love to open your home to friends but you do not always like waiting on them. If you sense you are being taken advantage of, your hospitality goes sour. You need to express your creativity but you need to be protected too.

Romantically you are both passionate and compassionate, extremely loving, generous and vulnerable as well. Sometimes you want to nurture, protect and fuss over your loved one; other times you want the same in return; and still other times you want to dazzle and impress, and simply be adored. You are a bit demanding in love because at all times you want to know you are held in high esteem, but you need romantic surprises, too; it is as though you want to be continually wooed in new and wonderful ways, while feeling fundamentally secure.

Your emotionally ardent and colourful personality is both open and hidden. Your natural instinct is to test the water before jumping in, but your heart will always want to play. This may also apply in your business life where your intuition and ingenuity make you a shrewd customer – approachable and personable but sophisticated in the ways of the world. You have a keen eye for value and may be an avid collector of art and artefacts. Your strongly individualistic and traditional values will be expressed in whatever it is you buy, do or love.

Your Greatest Strengths

Grace and aristocratic charm; warm devotion to family and friends; artistic sensitivity and love of excellence; fine intuition; subtle sense of drama; business sense and organizational abilities; a personal commitment to your aspirations and faith in yourself.

Your Greatest Weaknesses

Tendency to play the primadonna and to reject criticism in a proud, self-absorbed way; to cut off from others if they do not tow the line; a voracious need to rule the roost and to have others jolly well like it.

Images for Integration

After serving a sumptuous five-course dinner, the hostess leaves the washing-up to her guests while she serenades them on the piano with *Moonlight Sonata* ... A child ventures forth from her family to seek her greatness.

Famous Personalities

Claudio Abbado (conductor), Richard D. Bach (writer), Eleanour Clark (writer), Van Cliburn (concert pianist and conductor), Antoine de Saint-Exupéry (writer), Tom Hanks (actor), Susan Hayward (actress), Kris Kristofferson (songwriter and singer), George Michael (pop singer and songwriter), Nancy Reagan (American First Lady), Ken Russell (film director), Eva Marie Saint (actress), Carlos Santana (musician), Phoebe Snow (singer), Ringo Starr (Beatles' drummer).

— 42 —

SUN CANCER ♋ MOON VIRGO ♍

It was becoming clear to my mind that men regarded women as a servant class in the community, and that women were going to remain in the servant class until they lifted themselves out of it.
EMMELINE PANKHURST

... tradesmen could always stall Mrs. Osborne while attending to more demanding clients ... and then she would be too timid, too embarrassed, to call him again ...
JOHN ANTHONY WEST, *Osborne's Army*

Themes

WATER/EARTH Imagination and analysis; reflective and attentive; caring and helpful; concerned; sympathetic; loyal; dutiful; timid; proper but forgiving; shrewd; fussy; discriminating intellect; domestic organization; protective; self-controlled; introvert; perceptive; integrity.

Are you a sensitive, sympathetic, emotional person whose razor-sharp mind tries to make logical sense out of all your moods? Do you yearn to be appreciated and understood but end up sitting back shyly and analysing others? Are you the permissive, compassionate parent or the strict Scottish nanny? Do you find yourself criticizing because you care?

You are an essentially self-contained but very responsive individual, alert and sensitive to your environment, prepared to love and embrace the world you find yourself in but tending to analyse and rationalize your needs so that they do not become overwhelming. Your sensitive antennae make you a bit nervous; you hold yourself back, and you develop ways of protecting yourself from the big, bad world. But that same sensitivity, coupled with your mental accuracy and capacity to put feelings into words, can make you an excellent teacher, counsellor, social worker, or writer – an observer and 'fixer' of the human condition. You need to understand your world in order to feel secure and good in yourself; you need to know what is expected of you; to be able to know and name your allies and your enemies; and to know the rules, because the rules will, as it were, set you free.

One moment you may feel inspired, ambitious, creative and wanting to embrace the whole world, to see the largest possible picture of the meaning of history and evolution; and the next minute you find yourself splitting hairs over who is to blame for lunch being late. You can be both wonderfully kind, helpful and carpingly critical, both genuinely sympathetic and sarcastic. But the latter trait generally surfaces as a defence during the times you feel threatened, unloved and depressed. Your moodiness can be hard to live with.

Coarseness offends you deeply, and you will learn to overcome your shyness in order to make a stand for yourself and for the principles and mores by which you live. When you have garnered enough courage to see its supportive effect, you can become positively pedantic, even puritannical at times, so you need to guard against stuffiness and a too strict adherence to the letter of the law. In fact, it does not take much for you to respond with the warmth and empathy of your Cancerian solar nature. Lucky for you and your family, you are a pushover for the soft touch.

Your gifts are imagination and analysis, emotional insight and conventional common sense, creative initiative and the desire to serve. When these work together you are one of the quietly dynamic and devoted workers of this world, combining dedication and service which would find a natural expression through the healing and caring professions. When you care about something you can become a pretty vociferous crusader and campaigner, surprising even yourself with your boldness and refusal to accept lame excuses.

Relationships

Your sympathetic, loving nature truly blossoms when you are in a happy, committed relationship, although nothing will ever be quite as perfect as you would like. Domesticity brings out the best in you because you can fuss about things and then put them right; you can design your life around yours and your family's intimate needs.

You have a real yearning to give, to love and care for someone, but also a real fear of ridicule – humiliation is almost a physical experience for you. You feel dwarfed by unkindness, and so by nature you are not a person who enters relationships lightly. When you feel you can trust someone, when you feel you can bask in their understanding and encouragement, you open up and reveal your special qualities – insight, devotion, purity of heart and humour. You want the *continuity* of an intelligent and compassionate love, and you give the same – and more – in return.

Your Greatest Strengths

Clear-headed and conscientious concern for others; refined charm; social adaptability; capacity to combine imagination and efficiency; unflagging moral integrity; ability to serve with both compassion and common sense.

Your Greatest Weaknesses

Tendency to nag and worry too much; proneness to self-criticism which results in anxiety and depleted confidence; narrow-minded and self-righteous clinging to rules and right procedure in order to establish your security and authority; a weakness towards being subservient and self-effacing.

Images for Integration

The 'perfect' mother ... A health visitor weighs an infant with tender precision ... A wine taster makes pointed comments, restrained accolades.

Famous Personalities

Alberto Ascari (champion racing driver), Bill Cosby (actor), Gina Lollobrigida (actress), Lord (David) Owen (politician), Emmeline Pankhurst (feminist activist), Peter Sissons (television presenter), Barbara Stanwyck (actress), John Anthony West (writer and novelist).

— 43 —

SUN CANCER ♋ MOON LIBRA ♎

My mission in life is to give hope, pleasure and assistance to others.
SYLVESTER STALLONE

My ideal would be to have wonderful dancers come to me and I'd make work on them and then they'd go away and perform it brilliantly forever.
TWYLA THARP

The Group
TITLE OF NOVEL BY MARY MACCARTHY

Themes

WATER/AIR Social awareness; graciousness and charm; elegant simplicity; popular appeal; oversensitivity; observant; perceptive;

keen student; tentative but eager for attention; romantic; kind-hearted; artistic style; adaptable but strong; defensive but devoted; idealistic and emotional; perfectionist; indecisive.

Do you think of yourself as a romantic, sensitive, caring soul who nevertheless balks at the first sign of emotional demand from others? Do you study your environment carefully, let chic conversation and company stimulate and educate you, but make sure you do not give too much away about yourself?

You are an interesting mixture of the quiet maverick and the outgoing artisan, the warm friend and the wily businessman. You need to be part of the world but you are reluctant to engage with it at the gut level because your instincts tell you it is dangerous – to your emotionally vulnerable side, which wounds easily. You have strong and original ideas about things, and an ambition to express yourself and to be recognized, appreciated and rewarded. In order to do this and to protect yourself as well, you tend to adopt a far more detached stance than is really the case.

You find ways of placing yourself in favourable positions, and you know how to appeal to people, for you have a lively, appealing personality with a kind of provocative, beguiling quality that invites people into your orbit. Others may at times be baffled by the contradictions in your nature – your blend of warm idealism and possessiveness, independence and protective self-interest gives out confusing signals. But in the end your conviviality, adaptability, perceptiveness and unique viewpoint make the struggle to get to know you worthwhile.

Although you need and love a stable home life, your real interest is in society. You tend to be a socially progressive thinker, intellectually precocious and interested in all manner of things to do with human culture, from art, music and history to commerce and social organizations. Whilst you appreciate old-fashioned values, you also develop a love or at least a fascination for the unusual and the exotic.

Your social conscience and patriotic conviction to ideals could take you into politics where your concern for the underdog and your desire for justice can express itself eloquently. It is in large organizations that your voice has a particularly persuasive appeal – you sense the mood, you observe and see what is required, you focus on others with unnerving accuracy, and you manoeuvre things as best you can, making sure you are in a safe, cosy place yourself.

Your powers of observation and analysis could make you an excellent writer or artist. You have refined, aesthetic taste in things as well as in people, and can even be a bit elitist, intellectually snobbish, with a kind of upper-class clannishness that puts you in the favoured family of friends. But even with your best friends, you are never quite sure how close you want to be, how much you can trust. Your emotional Cancerian side wants to belong, but your idealistic Libran side wants comfortably detached egalitarian relationships. This uneasy alliance within you may compel you to keep your own company a lot of the time, whilst all the while hankering for the stimulation of the world and the Beautiful People.

Relationships

Your relationships are your greatest challenge, for you want them, and yet they never turn out quite as you had imagined. Your mixture of heart and mind can either make for rich and rewarding relationships or for a split between what you *feel* you need and what you *think* should be happening. You can never quite decide what your role in relationships is – do you want to be adored and petted; are you the devoted, parental partner; or are you an equal looking for courtly romance and mutual respect based on intellectual affinity? This dilemma gives you a kind of divine discontent when it comes to commitment, and a proneness to nit-pick when indecision and dissatisfaction get the better of you. And if you stay too much on the surface of this dilemma you are liable to manipulate emotionally those you love and end up brooding, lonely and mistrustful.

When you can understand your different needs you can direct your analytical talents to *yourself* and see that it is okay to be both needy *and* friendly, emotional *and* intellectual, self-protective *and* outgoing. Once your caginess softens you become a compassionate, affectionate, considerate mate – but one who will always need plenty of space for other friends and opportunities.

Your Greatest Strengths

Natural sense of justice; artistic imagination; fine intellect; powers of observation and articulate self-expression; compassion and concern for the welfare of others; love of beauty and harmony; highly original style; scrupulous efforts to be fair and honest with everyone.

Your Greatest Weaknesses

Nervous defensiveness and mistrust of others; a perfectionist attitude that makes you nag and complain when things are not 'right'; tendency to unwittingly stir up trivial arguments that become storms in a tea-cup; proneness to rationalize away all your dependence on others and your idiosyncracies and self-protectiveness.

Images for Integration

Mother Goose recites a poem, surrounded by adoring fairy-tale creatures ... A family holds a lucrative sale of its artistic heirlooms to the neighbourhood.

Famous Personalities

Alexander the Great, Louis 'Satchmo' Armstrong (jazz musician), Harriette Arnow (novelist), Arthur Ashe (tennis player), St. Francesca Cabrini (founder of orphanages and hospitals), Pierre Cardin (fashion designer), Antonio Gaudi (architect), Janet Leigh (actress), Mary MacCarthy (writer), Sylvester Stallone (actor), Nikola Tesla (inventor), Twyla Tharp (dancer and choreographer).

— **44** —

SUN CANCER ♋ MOON SCORPIO ♏

If an idea cannot be expressed in terms of people, it is a sure sign it is irrelevant to the real problems of life.
COLIN WILSON

The human body is private property.
JONATHAN MILLER

Themes

WATER/WATER Intensely emotional; perceptive; self-protective;

self-centred; secretive; investigative mind; romantic; sensual; magnetic; dramatic; compelling personality; possessive; resourceful; tenacious; daring.

Do you love wolfhounds but go for cuddly lapdogs, too, or even pussycats? Are you soft and sentimental but sometimes as sharp as a surgeon's scalpel? Do you long for devotion, security and recognition but privately ward off any threat to your personal freedom?

You are brooding emotion incarnate, very subjective in your outlook, a trifle overprotective and suspicious, and fully confident that your intellect and perceptive powers will enable you to make rapid progress on the upward path. Tenacious determination to prove yourself and secure the dignity and position you feel you merit makes you often appear formidable, proud and haughty. But whilst you are capable of going great lengths not only to survive but to win, there really is not an unkind cell in your body. You genuinely care about your world and the people in it, and your humanity is strong and potent, reaching out to help and transform the darker corners of human existence.

If you are part of the establishment you will defend it to the death. If you are an outsider you will attempt to probe into every social assumption and reveal the truth behind the façade, the mysterious behind every commonplace occurrence. The secret and emotional are everything. You love suspense and mystery, and are drawn to understanding and grappling with the dark side of life, the inordinate and the ugly, in order to see the redeemable, transforming spark of life that lies behind it.

Deeply fascinated by what makes people tick, you have something of the detective and the psychoanalyst in you, which could manifest powerfully in medical or psychological work. But even if you do not have a career, a part of you will always be preoccupied with hidden realities and creatures from 'inner space'. You guard your own inner space with great vigilance, and you likewise respect other people's privacy. You truly come alive, however, when you have been entrusted with a secret or given a search warrant to look inside a troubled mind (or bank account). All your analytical powers become concentrated and uplifted by your reverential, single-minded, determined attitude to discover the truth.

You are unafraid of the dark and undaunted by the truth. If you work in a healing profession you bring a genuine caring concern and gentle intensity to those ailing in a psychotic underworld. You can contribute the love and wisdom of the tender mother together with the exacting discipline of the doctor or policeman. Under your scrutiny and guardianship all your creative projects should flourish, whatever they may be. Just remember, you have the temperament of a fanatic (as do most outstanding artists!) so try to loosen up a bit and learn to let go. Your loved ones will not run away from you – they will love you more for the trust you give them.

Relationships

Emotionally you are somewhat complex because you want both security and intrigue, and the two do not really go together. You need to feel special and adored, but you also like to live on the edge. Sometimes you are so deeply engrossed in your personal feelings that your survival instinct can suffocate the loved one you are trying to protect (or hold on to).

Your emotional control may be strong, but no matter how you try to hide and protect yourself, your feelings exude a powerful message and very tangibly affect the atmosphere. And moods are something you have in abundance. If you feel threatened or insecure, a brooding, hard-bitten mood can take over and will only be appeased by bags of affectionate reassurance (and an expensive gift might help, too). Indeed, you probably have lavish taste, and a shrewd business sense as well, but you also have an original wit and satirical sense of humour which, along with your natural dignity, has a compelling influence on others.

Your Greatest Strengths

Personal magnetism; emotional strength and courage in times of crisis; acute perception and analytical imagination; intensity of your devotional nature and commitment to others; caring, healing capacities.

Your Greatest Weaknesses

Defensiveness, moodiness, and possessiveness; proneness to react with fanatical prejudice, to cling to the past, and to live through other people if your own creative aspirations have not been developed.

Images for Integration

Under a full Moon an exorcist performs a life-giving ritual; the possession fades away and a child's life is saved ... Whilst preparing his genealogical tree, a young man discovers the lost grave of his great-great-grandmother.

Famous Personalities

Eric Ambler (writer of detective stories), A.J. Cronin (novelist and physician), Cynthia Gregory (ballerina), Lena Horne (singer), Jonathan Miller (neuropsychologist, actor and writer), Theodore Prostakoff (musical prodigy), Rembrandt (artist), Nelson Rockefeller (American politician and art patron), Colin Wilson (writer).

— 45 —

Sun Cancer ♋ Moon Sagittarius ♐

I look upon the whole world as my parish.

Beware you be not swallowed up in books!
An ounce of love is worth a pound of knowledge.
JOHN WESLEY

He had no longer any need for home, for he carried his Gormenghast within him. All that he sought was jostling within himself. He had grown up.
MERVYN PEAKE, *Titus Groan*

Themes

WATER/FIRE Traditional yet progressive; reserved yet talkative; kind; idealistic; intuitive; imaginative; colourful; restless; changeable; the romantic traveller; careful yet adventurous; dramatic; emotional volatility; an ear for music; an eye for patterns and harmony; a love of beauty.

Do you follow your cautious, conservative heart and hanker after the good old days, ways and values? Or are you a natural progressive, seeking to push back the wide frontiers and open new doors?

Change and excitement is what you love and fear. Drawn to the bonds of home and childhood, your impulse is nevertheless to risk the next horizon. Sensitive, sometimes shy, you easily come out of your shell and can be a lively, witty, provocative talker. When you communicate on topics dear to your heart, you express a kind of poignant enthusiasm and a fervent but restrained defiance: you know what you think, feel, and believe and, with courtesy and thoughtfulness, you will speak your piece.

When early childhood prejudices become married to your instinctive sense of moral certainty, you can become surprisingly conservative and set in your ways. You are an impressive and impressionable person, vulnerable but courageous, considerate but forceful, careful but wholehearted. The contrast within you is between your desire for emotional and economic security, the need to belong, and your impulse for adventure and individual self-expression.

You desire intimacy and attach yourself to your goals and your loved ones with immense loyalty. But you are also independent, outspoken and sometimes argumentative. When your extrovert and introvert qualities are combined they give you a dramatic, original flair, a wry sense of humour and a feel for the poetic and fantastic. You may be quite 'psychic', capable of spontaneously getting the *real* meaning behind words and behaviour. Your mixture of openness and sensitivity when working well gives you a remarkable capacity for getting the best out of people, whether you are an employer, teacher, preacher or healer. There is much of the traveller and explorer about you, yet intuitively you know that you always take your home with you.

Having a strong sense of family and concern for social issues and the community, you are one of life's born carers. But you want to lead more than a useful life; you want to lead a *meaningful* life. Therefore some sort of abstract ideal will inform all you do, and no aspect of your life will escape the invisible but all-embracing circle of your moral integrity. You feel strongly about things, but you do not like to waste time. You are a person of action and deed, and have the ability to grasp the big picture and then tenaciously follow up on the details and carry things through. You respect social institutions that preserve the safety of the individual, but you have little patience for the red tape that must be got through if you choose to work in the professional fields. Your spirit is independent, visionary, and you work best if you set your own limits.

Relationships

For you, these can be a source of great joy and frustration. You are a sociable person, even quietly flirtatious, and a warm, loving, generous partner. Yet you can be emotionally possessive, craving intimacy whilst expecting total personal freedom. Your charm comes from your combination of vulnerability, honesty and outspokenness. Whilst you can appear to be extremely open and up-front, there is something deeply private about your real feelings, which you may keep a secret even from yourself.

You are very emotional and prone to mood swings; despondency is very debilitating for you, and it often descends upon you when a loved one has not lived up to some romantic ideal. You want your partner to be both a parent and a playmate. As one of life's romantics, you see the immense possibilities in your loved one and your life together, and you are liable to be disproportionately disappointed when he or she turns out to be a mere mortal. Yet you are not interested in superficial relationships, and when you really get involved, you give it your best shot, and devote yourself heart, mind and soul.

You are good-humoured and philosophical about problems. You learn from any rough rides, and bounce back. As long as you are assured of love and affection, you will face the music and dance.

Your Greatest Strengths

Colourful, poetic imagination; enthusiasm and capacity for encouraging and bringing out the best in others; natural optimism and breadth of vision; wholehearted commitment to both people and your ideals.

Your Greatest Weaknesses

Impatience and carelessness with detail; alternating need for excitement and privacy which keeps people guessing about where you stand; capacity to justify your personal prejudices with detached argument; the sarcasm that hides your vulnerability and dependency.

Images for Integration

Philosophy and friendship round a large, old kitchen table ... In your home on a yacht you cruise the seven seas ... A racehorse gives a child a ride.

Famous Personalities

Josephine Beauharnais (Napoleon's first wife), Jody Brady (child actress), Jean-Baptiste Corot (painter), Lord Kitchener (soldier), Gian Carlo Menotti (composer and librettist), Milan Milisic (poet, dramatist and traveller), Eddy Nelson (singer), Peir Luigi Nervi (architect, engineer and academic), Mervyn Peake (writer of *Gormenghast* trilogy), John Wesley (preacher).

— 46 —

SUN CANCER ♋ MOON CAPRICORN ♑

Courage is grace under pressure.

What is moral is what you feel good after.
ERNEST HEMINGWAY

Every man thinks God is on his side. The rich and powerful know he is.

Saintliness is also a temptation.
JEAN ANOUILH

Themes

WATER/EARTH Gentle disciplinarian; capable and caring; tenacious; shrewd; responsible; considerate; patient; introvert; reflective; authoritative; maternal; sense of humour; dutiful; strong family person; professional; perceptive.

Intuition and precision, warm sensitivity and a sharply pragmatic mind combine to make you a very appealing and trustworthy friend and co-worker. The gentle understanding of the good mother and the shrewd resolve of the worldly father make a marvellous mix for reaching others and influencing your public.

Intensely loyal, responsible and devoted to loved ones, your idea of heaven simply never departs from the realm of work and purposeful caring, tending to your duties as professional nurturer. Your uncanny perception of others' needs and your sense of loyalty make you appear a very serious person. Being also very cautious, prudent and private means that this serious persona does indeed correspond to an inner reality. You *are* serious, you *are* ambitious and rise swiftly to the call of duty and the needs of weaker mortals, and you apply yourself with great diligence to the task of personal attainment and the establishing of your own security. Underneath that Scottish-nanny exterior of common sense and tenacity, however, you have a rich sense of humour and a great capacity for fun and tenderness.

With family and intimate friends you are a pillar of strength and an indefatigable confidant. In fact, a very big part of you needs to be needed. Deeply self-reflective and self-demanding, you know yourself well and this helps you to know others well. You are consequently a natural counsellor – compassionate, honest, articulate, as well as a shrewd, diplomatic businessman.

In the wider world of the marketplace, you are the soul of courtesy and affability. While appearing to smooth the way for others you can, however, drive a hard bargain and quietly look out for Number One. People easily respect and like you, for you sympathize with basic human needs and motivations while, at the same time, gently cultivating maturity – in yourself and others. You are also respected for your excellent sense of propriety, and because you know the wisdom of good boundaries.

Home life and family interests play an important role in your life. You need roots and may enjoy charting the intricate course of your family's geneology. Where did you come from, and where are you, personally, going? The pull between total devotion to parenting and home-making, and your need for a wider, more professional form of success and recognition, will occupy your mind a great deal at some point in your life. At times your private ambitions may seem at odds with your more popularist side. You know how to appeal to the masses, how to communicate, inspire and help; but you are also deeply concerned with standards and with fulfilling your Own Personal

Mission. Your need for affection is as great as your need for success and recognition.

Relationships

You will thrive in a secure partnership where you can share your enjoyment of intimacy, affection and home-making. Although you are romantic, you value security and continuity and you are not interested in fast-paced, highly-charged relationships. You need time and trust in order to blossom, and peace and quiet with your loved one in order to develop your best qualities as a lover, a parent or a friend. You can be over-sensitive and cautious, and if you err it is usually through over-nurturing and protecting. Whilst you require a certain amount of independence in a relationship, you are happiest when you know that someone is at home waiting for you. Besides much tenderness, you require from your mate admiration and respect – and a promise of undying loyalty.

Your Greatest Strengths

Intuitive, shrewd mind; innate sense of responsibility and concern for others; good business sense; organizational abilities; sense of economy; gentle diplomacy and patience; instinct for leadership; firm but tender parenting; hard-headed but soft-hearted benevolence.

Your Greatest Weaknesses

Your need to be needed; oversensitivity; tendency to close off from others when you feel slighted; a somewhat insatiable desire for love and recognition; your need for authority and control.

Image for Integration

An ancient water mill works away in rhythmic fashion, meting out just the required amount of fluid force to grind the corn that nourishes and sustains the village.

Famous Personalities

Jean Anouilh (writer), Karen Black (actress), John Glenn, Jr.

(astronaut), Ernest Hemingway (novelist), Robert J. Laski (political theorist), Sue Lawley (radio and television presenter), Joseph Papp (theatre director and producer), Rupert Sheldrake (biologist), Cesare Zavattini (novelist and screenwriter).

— —

47

SUN CANCER ♋ MOON AQUARIUS ♒

... to reminisce about the past and speculate about the future.
ADAM FAITH

Literature could be said to be a sort of disciplined technique for arousing certain emotions.
IRIS MURDOCH

Themes

WATER/AIR Feeling v. thinking; past and future; humanitarian; concern for public welfare; generous spirit; family of man; sociable; kind-hearted; nurturing the world; openness and honesty; mentally acute; encouraging; popular, wholehearted and direct; visionary; tolerant; protects the under-dog, shrewd; a love of symbols.

Are you sometimes a careful, cautious, old-fashioned crab with a romanticized view of the past, but at other times your quirky need for 'space' rears its funny head, upsetting the proverbial applecart? Do you like traditional Sunday lunches and family get-togethers, but end up bringing along all your stray friends and analysing the world's problems? Are you torn between the old and the new, the conservative and the radical? Are you a feeler or thinker, an artist or scientist, poet or mathematician?

If and when you can roll these into one you can become an understanding and forgiving friend of the world, a progressive traditionalist. You have a flair for reading signs and symbols, be it in interpreting dreams or reading the flight of birds. Combined with your gift for translating your feelings into words, this can find its most fulfilling expression through poetry and song.

The clannish instinct of Cancer can be widened and universalized in this pairing so that your immediate concerns are broad social issues. You are interested in people and have great insight into the workings of the human mind and heart. Although you are a strong family person with interest in your ancestors and heritage, you tend to treat your friends and colleagues as an equally important, extended family, and there is nothing you would not do for most of them. When you work at it, you can combine personal warmth and abstract thought in an admirable, effective way. Feeling deeply about other's pain, joy and aspirations, you do not go overboard with the sloppy stuff but, like a true friend, you enter into the spirit of the idea and help others to understand things more clearly.

Your personality is ideally suited to working with people, either in the caring and healing professions, or in politics or teaching. Your personal integrity and ability to communicate your vision with unselfish feeling can often work a kind of magic on your audience, making popularity almost a birthright. Although you can be a shrewd businessman and are proud enough in a noble sort of way, essentially you are a humanitarian and you match your sentiment with actions which leave no one in doubt about your values and trustworthiness.

Relationships

You are very much a people person and are inclined to collect a wide range of aquaintances, but you may not necessarily find it easy to let others get close to you. Emotionally you like continuity but also enjoy unconventionality in your partner. You are passionate but zany, devoted but equally detached, which means that it is possible for you to have a relationship that combines emotional fulfilment with stimulating friendship.

Desiring intimacy and attachment, you nevertheless have a need for a wide variety of friends and contact with people with whom you share ideals and viewpoints. Therefore you naturally respect your partner's need for the same thing. Sometimes, however, your tolerant, egalitarian outlook glosses over your emotional hurts and hang-ups, which then fester down in the cellar. Suddenly you find yourself moody, cantankerous, arrogantly going your own way. You are paradoxical – not nearly as rational as you think you are, and not half as irrational as you feel. Basically you just need to apply some of your considerate, humanitarian care to yourself. And you are a natural self-psychologist, although it will always be easier for you to explore *other* people's feelings and to help them. For all your gregariousness, you are a very private person when it comes to your own needs. Essentially, you are continually defining your individuality and integrity, and you do it best in your dealings with people.

Your Greatest Strengths

Ability to reach out to your public and communicate your ideas with force and conviction; compassion and respect for the rights of all people; fine intellect; vivid imagination; tenacious loyalty to friends and family.

Your Greatest Weaknesses

Tendency to fly into the sanctuary of your mind when you are beset by emotional problems; propensity to 'mother' the world and to take on too many burdens, and to attract eccentric people and situations that, although they bring excitement, actually mitigate against your essential peace of mind.

Images for Integration

A mother and child skip down the street, arm in arm, to attend the Vision for World Peace charity fête at the park ... The world as family ... A science museum inside a restored medieval castle ... Carl Orff's *Carmina Burana*.

Famous Personalities

Dan Aykroyd (actor and director), Mary Baker Eddy (founder of Christian Science), Vicki Carr (singer), Leslie Caron (dancer-actress), Princess Diana (Princess of Wales), Adam Faith (singer and actor), H. Rider Haggard (novelist), Leibnitz (philosopher), Carl Lewis (athlete), Iris Murdoch (novelist), Carl Orff (composer), Esther Rantzen (television personality), Linda Rondstadt (singer), Jerry Rubin (activist), Donald Sutherland (actor).

Sun Cancer ♋ Moon Pisces ✕

If you hate a person, you hate something in him that is part of yourself.
What isn't part of ourselves doesn't disturb us.
HERMAN HESSE

I require a spot that has beauty!
CAMILLE PISSARRO

Themes

WATER/WATER Affable; funny; loveable; kind-hearted; a cagey crab-fish; slippery and secretive; sensitive; whimsical; romantic imagination; charitable and compassionate; blow with the wind; popular; dreamy; intuitive; poetic; musical.

You are a remarkably intuitive, sympathetic and adaptable person. Essentially emotional and acutely receptive to the hidden messages in people's behaviour, you can easily act as an emotional barometer of your environment. This is sometimes to your own advantage and sometimes not, for you can become swamped with feelings that are not your own. You are so affable and sensitive, so kind and helpful by nature, that your own real opinion or position on anything often remains hidden or disguised. You do not really mind; in fact, you instinctively feel that it is far more advantageous not to show your cards.

You like to please but you also like to be pleased, and very often you manage to combine both needs. Kind-hearted and responsive, but shrewd and self-protective at the same time, you are able to wriggle out of unsafe situations in a quiet, invisible way. Yet your sympathies extend to all the victims of life and people sense your non-judgmental acceptance and undying spirit of camaraderie. You are often a great comedian, and your subtle powers of observation and mimicry could pay off in some way. But even if it does not bring a big financial reward, your popularity is assured because people like being around your soft-spoken, quietly humorous, sympathetic savvy. Although you are often nervous and fidgety, you are just as tenacious when you decide on something that is right for you. By stealth, intuition and shrewd manoeuvre, you usually end up exactly where you want to be.

Emotionally you are very sentimental, moody and vulnerable, prefering to fit in harmoniously rather than to create waves, although this is not to say that you do not have strong ideals. Your inner life and moral integrity is most real to you and there is no question of you transgressing personal values. But you are an expert diplomat and most times you will choose to give in to others rather than to argue points that may lead to disharmony. You are the crab-fish, silently slithering sideways out of the line of fire.

Although you are quite sociable, your need for quiet, reflective periods on your own is also very pronounced. A simple life amidst rural beauty where you can commune with nature would suit you just fine. Or better yet, right near the sea where the sparkling scintillation of light would inspire your artistic side. Balancing your vocation for people with your need to nourish your own creative imagination and self-expression is the great challenge in your life.

Relationships

You have enormous love and warmth to give but you are cautious about exposing yourself. Once you feel secure, loved and appreciated you overcome your shyness and can literally flood your loved one with devotion and affection. Terrifically romantic and idealistic, you may have to be careful about your tendency to self-deception. You thrive on intimacy, and your love of giving plus your sense of the pathos of life and love mean that you can get yourself into relationships that deplete rather than enhance your well-being. A strong, earthy partner could be very beneficial to you. Family life, which you will enjoy, should also help to make you feel more rooted in reality, and therefore more capable of realizing your own potential.

Your receptive ear will always encourage others to unburden their souls, and your talent for protecting and comforting people may take you into the counselling or caring professions. At any rate, your responsive, sympathetic way with others means many will seek you out as a confidant or sounding board for their ideas and dilemmas. You make a good muse, but you will not be possessed.

Your Greatest Strengths

Uncanny insight into people; unaffected humanity and capacity to give your time, energy and warm, encouraging words of wisdom; artistic sensitivity and appreciation for the intangible realm of emotions and images; adaptability and diplomacy in the face of almost any difficulty.

Your Greatest Weaknesses

Shyness and suspicion of others' motives; a propensity to daydream and to put people on pedestals; a tendency to wallow in self-doubt instead of kicking into gear when you have an artistic inspiration; a fear of getting hurt or being fooled, which can keep you withdrawn and keep real relating at bay.

Images for Integration

An artist teaches recuperating patients to paint the images of their dreams in soft water colours ... A lone sailboat offshore at sunset. *Ol' man river ... he keeps rollin' along*. The musicals of Rodgers and Hammerstein.

Famous Personalities

Buckminster Fuller (inventor and philosopher), Oscar Hammerstein (composer with Rodgers [below] of musicals), Deborah Harry (rock singer), Herman Hesse (novelist), Helen Keller (blind and deaf writer-lecturer), Gustav Mahler (composer), Camille Pissarro (impressionist painter), Della Reese (singer), Richard Rodgers (composer with Hammerstein [above] of musicals), Ginger Rogers (dancer and actress), Robin Williams (actor and comedian), Richard Wilson (actor).

Chapter Eight

SUN IN LEO

———

— **49** —

SUN LEO ♌ MOON ARIES ♈

*There are two things that will be believed of any man, and one of them
is that he has taken to drink.*
BOOTH TARKINGTON

*When a woman has twinkles in her eyes, no man notices if she has
wrinkles under them.*
DOLORES DEL RIO

Themes

FIRE/FIRE Self-confident; intuitive; abundance of ideas; passionate
and adventurous; courageous; dictatorial; reckless nobility; social
conscience yet self-centred; ambitious; hero-worship; vanity; great
integrity; whole-hearted; idealistic dedication; satirical;
unconventional.

Do you want to shine as part of the group or dazzle the world in your
own right? Are you a knight in shining armour or a bit of a Don
Quixote, looking for conquests that will define you but often ending
up a victim of your need for appreciation?

You have a large, warm-hearted, extroverted personality that is
always eager to embrace life, love and success – in big doses. There is
something about you that assumes the divine right to live life to the

191

full, and your intensity and impatience, along with your personal ambitions, will pull you ever onwards into new projects, fresh relationships and greater challenges.

You are something of a gambler and have a daring and dramatic spirit which propels you forward to make your mark, a sense of personal destiny which can only be exciting and noble. And you are prepared to fight for that glorious destiny if you have to, although you would rather simply steal the show and convince everyone with your intelligence, originality, courage and fabulous style.

One of your most beguiling qualities is that you are totally lacking in guile and pretence. Although your own personal destiny is what interests you, paradoxically you at first look for people you can admire and make into personal heroes. Strongly influenced by a favourite teacher, friend, poet, sports champion or movie star, you can then emulate them and learn through experience how to *be great*. You love the process of creating, as well as the applause that comes at the end. Indeed, you rely on those adoring strokes and affirmative responses more than you like to admit. Life without people would be colourless and boring for you. Social interaction is your life-blood – you can be the life of the party, a real ham and an eccentric, ready to take up the most outrageous dare. But when your extrovert escapades dry up, so do you. You may, in fact, drive yourself to exhaustion and then collapse like a child, home from an all-night rave-up.

Yet despite your headlong rush into the experience of life, you are not necessarily irresponsible. Daring and highly idealistic dreams work away inside you and make you want to improve things, to show people the way, and you may simply take charge – for a while. Intensely self-motivated, you do not respond well to orders from others, even though you can be quite bossy yourself. There is a touch of the preacher inside you, and you approach your work with great enthusiasm and commitment. You need space to do your own thing, to learn from your own mistakes, and to learn how to impose your own brand of self-discipline. Your innate self-dramatizing tendencies make you a natural for the theatre, business, lecturing, the media – areas that involve group interaction and provide scope for your original and iconoclastic ideas.

Relationships

These are of intense importance for you, as you seek to experience life and be consumed by it. Romantic, kind-hearted and intensely devoted to your sweetheart, you will show your love in charming, even chivalrous, dramatic ways when you have found *the one*. But you can be brusque and demanding without realizing it, for your high standards and varied interests are never far from your mind and often cause you to talk too much and listen too little.

That high-powered energy never stops long enough to focus sensitively on your partner's needs, or on the boring household tasks that have to be done. An earthy partner will help you to slow down and pay the bills; a watery partner will fascinate you with their mysterious depths – and you will find, if you give it time, that you also have those same depths and emotional needs.

Your Greatest Strengths

Personal courage; raw ambition; leadership abilities; intuitive imagination; powers of persuasion; optimism; integrity; honourable ideals; an uncomplicated desire to make your mark upon the world – and leave the world a better place.

Your Greatest Weaknesses

Overestimating your abilities; lack of objectivity and therefore a proneness to let grandiosity trip you up; rashness with others; recklessness and lack of self-criticism; tendency to let your ordinary human, emotional needs get lost in the heat of your noble endeavours.

Images for Integration

A knight errant dedicates his next grand adventure to the mistress of his heart, and then rides off into the sunset in a cloud of dust ... A young child wakes in the morning with wide eyes and great excitement, as a whole day of play lies ahead.

Famous Personalities

Melvin Belli (attorney), Richard Belasco (actor), Claud Bragdon (architect), Dash Crofts (rock musician), Dolores Del Rio (actress), Ludwig Feuerbach (philosopher), Jerry Garcia (rock musician), Anna Heidelberg (nurse), Whitney Houston (singer and actress), Jackie

Kennedy Onassis (widow, socialite and publisher), Alan Leo (pioneer astrologer), Jean Shepherd (humorist), Roger Sperry (Nobel prize-winning neurologist), Booth Tarkington (novelist).

— 50 —

Sun Leo ♌ Moon Taurus ♉

Whether you think Jesus was God or not, you must admit that he was a first-rate political economist.
GEORGE BERNARD SHAW

For most people the fantasy is driving around in a big car, having all the chicks you want and being able to pay for it.
MICK JAGGER

Themes

FIRE/EARTH Love of grandeur; generous; magnetic; stubborn; traditional; sensual; dictatorial; egocentric; administrator; regal; seeks a powerful position; pragmatic; dependable; capable; productive; materialistic; artistic flair; the showman; loyal; self-seeking.

Does your need for permanence inhibit your love of risk? Does your fiery individualism get pulled into traditional grooves that make you reluctant to try new things?

You have a powerful and confident, splashy sort of personality, which combines the heights of extravagance with the pragmatism of financial common sense. Your life is shaped by large ideals and you make sure that you are the physical embodiment of your motivating fantasy – and it is usually a lucrative one which shows your best profile. You can be vain and uncooperative, but also courageous, dynamic, completely sincere and honourable. Sometimes your flair for self-dramatization works against your painstakingly cautious side which needs security and a full stomach. When the two sides of you are working well together, you combine creative talent and shrewd

194

commercialism, and when you really get going you can create great things in the artistic field or in the business world.

You are generous and fiercely loyal to those you love. In the main, however, life starts and finishes with your needs, desires and goals. Due to your unabashed and forthright honesty, people usually feel comfortable around you. There is no doubting your position – it is as plain as day. People will also know that you rarely budge. As a result, they will most likely find other ways of working around you, as arguments can be unpleasant.

Intensely stubborn and sure of yourself, you are not especially easy to deal with if things are not going exactly the way you want them to. And if your pride really gets out of hand you can fall into negative moods and sullen inertia, and waste creative energy moaning about unimportant things. More than anyone, you need to make sure you have got your priorities right, and your view of life, love and money in proportion. Your powers of attraction are formidable and you will get what you value, sure as night follows day.

Relationships

Emotionally you are intense but not overwhelmingly romantic or vulnerable. You look for reliability in a mate, as well as someone who is beautiful or handsome and interesting enough to enhance your own self-image. You are a bit elitist, wanting the best in people, paintings, poetry and provisions, but when these essentials are secure and you feel you can be familiar with comrades, you can really let your hair down and win the hedonist of the year award if you want to.

In intimate relationships you can be demanding and your vanity may drive your sweetheart crazy at times. And yet you are constant and diligent with your affections, and can surprise your partner with sudden displays of devotion – such as spur-of-the-moment tickets to the opera or a candlelight dinner at *the* most expensive French restaurant in town. Your appetites are large and fixed, and it takes a fairly strong individual to influence you at all, let alone curb your habits into more human proportions.

Everything you do is a result of your own values and free will. But you are such an essentially positive and dependable person that you more than make up for your proud grandiosity with your unwavering integrity and capability. You have a great capacity for either enjoying life or getting stuck in the mud – or rather in molten lava, which interestingly enough repels all life at first but later gives rise to lush rebirth in nature. You can be just as creative in a deeply permanent sense when your Leo Sun and your Taurus Moon work cooperatively within you.

Your Greatest Strengths

Moral and emotional commitment to yourself and your goals; personal charisma; staying power; ability to think big; capacity for hard work and also to enjoy the good things of life; strong sense of responsibility and unflappableness in times of crisis.

Your Greatest Weaknesses

Tendency to be intensely subjective and biased, proud and inflexible with inferiors; to be overtly selfish and withholding if offended; and to speak out scathingly without thinking when a little diplomacy would win people over and magically move the obstacles that seem to stand in your way.

Image for Integration

Old King Cole was a merry old soul, and a merry old soul was he; he called for his wife and he called for his pipe and he called for his fiddlers three. Pygmalion, *My Fair Lady*. Eliza Doo Little is transformed into a Duchess. A master potter turns dull clay into an exquisite vase.

Famous Personalities

Bill Clinton (American President), John Dryden (poet and dramatist), Alexandre Dumas (dramatist and novelist), Ted Hughes (poet laureate), Mick Jagger (rock musician), Arthur Janov (psychologist), C.G. Jung (psychologist), E.F. Schumacher (philosopher and economist), George Bernard Shaw (playwright and critic).

SUN LEO ♌ MOON GEMINI ♊

For I dipt into the future, far as human eye could see
Saw the Vision of the world, and all the wonder that would be.
ALFRED, LORD TENNYSON

Love is at the core of my poems. I try to incarnate spiritual reality and
spiritualise or humanize material reality ... A poet is, after all, an
animal with the sun in his belly.
RAYMOND ROSELEIP

Women must try to do things as men have tried. When they fail, their
failures must be but a challenge to others.
AMELIA EARHART

Themes

FIRE/AIR Creative mind; warm spontaneity; humorous; both intuitive and analytical; friendly; restless and sociable; clever and resourceful; high aspirations; imagination; organizing ability; youthful spirit; proud and independent; romantic; honourable but playful.

Are you the cool-headed charmer who can pull out the right phrase and the perfect smile to impress your new friend, colleague or boss? Do you sense that you will have to take your ambitions seriously but find you rebel against getting *too* serious and purposeful?

Even though you want to be active and live an important and eventful life, you are essentially a big-hearted kid who looks for the new, the amusing or the sensational in whatever environment you find yourself. This keeps you on the hop, looking for purpose and play at the same time. But you figure things out quickly, make new ideas your own with astonishing facility, and instinctively move into interesting and influential positions where you can express your social and communicative talents, as well as handle responsibility with casual aplomb.

You are adaptable as well as ambitious, and this makes you a perennial student, always mentally geared up to apply the usefulness of an idea and to try out a new method. And if you have been strictly forbidden to do so, you will enjoy it even more.

You certainly find people interesting and have a nose for gossip and the analytical discussion of a wide variety of things – from children and preferred educational approaches to love and literature. But a clear eye for the things that really matter, plus a talent for expressing what you mean persuasively and with real feeling, make you an excellent manager or teacher – you will shine in any area where the challenging energy flow of group dynamics must be handled intelligently and firmly.

You quite like being in charge – for a while – but it is quite likely that eventually you will find hierarchical relationships too rigid and stultifying for your taste. You also like being admired and being popular. That always helps to silence that self-deprecating little voice inside you that is never quite sure what you are thinking, feeling, and if the right choice has been made.

You have an intelligent certainty about you when you explain yourself and your views and goals, but your noble integrity always falls short of pomposity as you would simply get bored with being right all the time. You enjoy travel and change and know that you can learn a lot from others. This makes you ideally suited for work that involves variety, quick-thinking and communicating.

You are an opportunist in the most positive sense, as your optimism, intuition and mental/verbal speed usually come together just in time to save you from disaster, and put you in exactly the right place. Indeed, you can be extraordinarily well organized and do exceptionally well at anything that presents a challenge and grabs your imagination.

Essentially you are a *thinking activist* who combines a philosophical social conscience with an irreverent, light-hearted disdain for anyone who takes life too seriously. Faced with life's problems, you shrug your shoulders with a perceptive wisecrack, and then determine to do your bit to make the sun shine again upon the darkling world.

Relationships

'In the Spring a young man's fancy lightly turns to thoughts of love' – or so says Lord Tennyson, a fellow Leo–Gemini. This describes something essential about your romantic style – you love that new feeling of falling in love, and your penchant for variety can make you a difficult person to catch and keep. You are deeply affectionate and, in your unique way, very loyal to loved ones. If a new person embodies a familiar or favourite ideal, however, you will want to add this individual to your wide circle of loved ones.

You have a childlike innocence which does not wear well in relationships. As your lively, inquisitive mind never stops for long, you may need to take care that you do not deplete yourself emotionally. Unbeknown to you, your constant busyness could be a ploy to avoid the more subtle levels of relating with others.

When you have nothing left to analyse, and have to face your feelings, you can slip into quite a despondent mood, like a young child who discovers she is lost. When you remain out of touch with your feelings, a kind of cynicism creeps into your bright personality, so that you seem to veer from having a trusting confidence in the goodwill of others to a disdain for those who have broken faith. Intimate relationships will challenge your assumption of supreme independence.

Your Greatest Strengths

A fine mind; quick wit; open-hearted friendliness; organizational abilities; optimism and resilience; the original way in which you combine high ideals with a love of adventure and an instinct for opportunity.

Your Greatest Weaknesses

A tendency to rationalize; general restlessness and fickleness in emotional affairs; proneness to manifest all the undesirable qualities of the rebellious child when it pleases you to do so.

Images for Integration

On a bright summer's day a butterfly turns into a radiant being ... Children singing 'Happy Birthday to you' at a celebrity birthday party.

Famous Personalities

Amelia Earhart (pioneer aviator), Norris and Ross McWhirter (twin authors of *Guinness Book of Records*), Benito Mussolini (Italian dictator),

Raymond Roseleip (poet), Clive Sinclair (inventor and entrepreneur), Alfred, Lord Tennyson (poet).

— 52 —

SUN LEO ♌ MOON CANCER ♋

Child! do not throw this book about;
Refrain from the unholy pleasure
Of cutting all the pictures out!
Preserve it as your chiefest treasure.
HILAIRE BELLOC

The secret is to be true to yourself.
BERNICE RUBENS

I don't want to live – I want to love first, and live incidentally.
ZELDA FITZGERALD

Themes

FIRE/WATER Emotional; vulnerable; ardent; self-dramatizing; funny; poetic; intuitive; individualistic; big-hearted; love of family life; sociable; sensitive; understanding; maternal/paternal; proud; colourful and receptive personality.

Are you the loveable, radiant star of the show or are you too busy in the kitchen making pâté de foie gras to play elegant host or hostess? Are you domineering and self-assured, or impressionable, moody and shy?

You may sometimes want a safe, simple life where you feel emotionally contained and able to pursue your own creative interests. Then, however, the compulsion to strive for a more central, leading role rears its challenging head, and you know you have it in you – so out into the spotlight you go. So immense is your creative energy as well as your warm feeling for others that you can become both the artistic home-maker and the home-loving artist/writer/entrepreneur.

Your personality is large and welcoming, colourful and theatrical because you have such an uncanny knack of dramatizing your vivid impressions and selling yourself in the most genuine, heartfelt way.

Both the paternal and the maternal urge is strong in you. You need to use your will to project and establish your identity in the world, and to use your instincts to nurture and protect your emotional and material security. The Sun and the Moon are in their 'home' signs here, so that potentially you have the creative vision of Apollo and the lunar wisdom of Diana all rolled into one. This can make you pretty overpowering at times, and indeed you need a partner and a family on whom you can lavish your emotions.

Your bearing is often aristocratic, sometimes haughty, oversensitive and self-absorbed, but you always seem to have enough affection to go around so that no one feels left out. You also manage to remain approachable and compassionate because you are so aware of your own vulnerability and need to be loved. Thus you make a warm and understanding friend, and you enjoy expressing your feelings with original flair and thoughtfulness. You are protective, possessive and clannish, a stalwart member of your family, group and nation, and utterly devoted to your ideals. Deeply honourable and dependable, you bring an attitude of devotion and romantic style to all you do.

You may have a good head for business because you possess an instinctive knowledge of security needs as well as a shrewd understanding of people, their desires, fears and foibles. Your refined taste for comfort and beauty is part of the impetus for success – you know your own mind and do not easily budge from your preferences and high standards. Aesthetic sensitivity is strong, and combined with your innate tenacity and quiet ambition means that you could be quite successful in the arts.

You are a true romantic with a deep need for love and belonging. Your vanity makes you fairly sensitive in emotional matters and your moods could drive your partner crazy at times. You can sometimes play the dominant role, sometimes the passive role. Whether or not you apply this versatility very much depends on how you are feeling when you get up in the morning.

Even though you readily turn a bright face to the world, you do not always feel confident and strong. You have a lively sense of individuality, but your potency is sometimes too dependent on emotional familiarity, and the range of your self-expression too circumscribed within repetitive emotional patterns. Inwardly you shy away from encounters with the big, bad world, and early in life you may need to find ways of handling challenges that normally push the panic button. This will not be hard for you because your creative drive is tremendous and your individuality needs recognition.

You may sometimes play a game with yourself in order to get going, but ultimately you learn that you take your security with you wherever you go. Intuitively you discover how to master the wide range of life's funny situations by trusting your gut reactions and developing a superb sense of humour.

Your Greatest Strengths

Vulnerability; openness to other's experiences; deep sense of integrity and personal loyalty to standards and to loved ones; rich imagination and colourful expressiveness; hugely creative spirit.

Your Greatest Weaknesses

Engulfing emotionalism; tendency to be so self-absorbed that you drown out or distort all signals from the environment; proneness to sulk when you do not get your way.

Images for Integration

A young child sits on a throne, and with great dignity and tenderness, crowns his father and mother king and queen ... A man and a woman walk hand in hand along the edge of the sea at high noon on a summer's day.

Famous Personalities

Ethel Barrymore (actress), Hilaire Belloc (writer), Clara Bow (actress), Claude Debussy (composer), Guy de Maupassant (writer), Zelda Fitzgerald (writer and wife of F. Scott Fitzgerald), Llewellyn George (politician), Evonne Cawley (tennis player), Robert Horton (actor), Omar Khayyam (poet), Princess Margaret, Annie Oakley (markswoman), Ira Progoff (psychologist), Kenny Rogers (country singer), Bernice Rubens (novelist).

SUN LEO ♌ MOON LEO ♌

Was this then how youth, how life should truly be? No endless poring over books and dusty manuscripts, but acting out the glory of the word made flesh? Such tenderness! Such breathless apprehension of the mystery in things! And afterwards, such peace!
LINDSAY CLARKE, author of *The Chymical Wedding*

To be a poet is a condition rather than a profession.
ROBERT GRAVES

Children are our most valuable natural resource.
HERBERT HOOVER

Themes

FIRE/FIRE Warm; enthusiastic; magnetic; authoritative presence; demonstrative; generous; arrogant; single-minded; visionary; poetic; intensely creative; dramatic; vain; open; playful; proud; flair for showing your best side; magnanimous.

You are larger than life. Into the Big Time, you simply dazzle yourself and others with the magnitude and charisma of your bearing. You tend to forget details, however, believing this to be someone else's job. Everyone has a place and a purpose, and yours is centre-stage. And when you have finally found the centre of your own true, magnanimous, creative self you really will get to the core of your life and be able to inspire a lot of other people on the way.

To discover and nurture your vision of yourself may require a certain amount of introversion, and so you may be a rather moody person a lot of the time. You can be fiercely happy and full of vitality or you can be stern and tyrannical, compelled by the absolute inner certitude of your perceptions. Your tremendous magnetism dominates your environment, and it will do so either beneficently or despotically, depending upon whether or not your ego dominates you.

The Leonine ego is not easy to satisfy, as it gives you a need for very tangible expressions of your creative power, and to feel that you are in control. This could take you onto the stage where you can command absolute attention, or into an executive position in the business world where both your creative intellect and your personal magnetism will have a potent influence. If your life is centred in the family, you will make a wonderful parent who takes pride in your children and delights in watching them grow into unique individuals, although there may be times when you are unsure as to who is the child and who is the parent.

Your sense of self, the self you aspire to become, is mythological in its proportions. Either consciously or unconsciously, you are always on a journey towards self-recognition. In the process you are likely both to alienate and stir many people. Although you have a strong social conscience, you are an individualist and need to stand out from the group in some way. You appear and desperately want to believe that you are completely confident and the authority on whatever it is that occupies your attention. Underneath, however, you tend to be always keenly aware of others' response to you, and your reliance on your audience's reactions is the key to your essential vulnerability.

You tend to be so absorbed in your own ideals and activities that you forget that the outside world does not revolve around you in the same way as your inner one does. Nothing is quite so important to you as your own world, and it is this intense subjectivity and inability to detach from your own committed view of things that gives you problems in relationships. A childlike naivety attaches to your warm, radiant personality, and you genuinely feel hurt when accused of wilful self-importance. Your life feels meaningless if everything about it is not an extension of yourself.

Relationships

Emotionally you are generous, passionate, fiercely loyal, trusting, chivalrous and romantic. You offer deep devotion to your loved ones, but in return require equally massive doses of love, tenderness and admiration – and an understanding from your mate that you have Important Things to think about. You can also be jealous and demanding, difficult to please, and strangely cold and imperious if you do not receive the kind of attention and gratitude you feel you deserve.

Although you are a warm and affectionate person for whom love is a very important part of life, you are not always easy to live with. But when you can add some earthy wisdom and a sense of humour to your noble integrity and high standards, you are an exciting and uplifting individual to be around. You generate optimism and hope for others, and they love you for that and much, much more.

Your Greatest Strengths

Generosity; creative intuitions; powerful intellect; dignity and nobility and insistence on seeing the same in others; courageous moral sense; ability to uplift magically the spirits of all those with whom you come in contact.

Your Greatest Weaknesses

Vanity and arrogance; self-centredness and inflexibility; tendency to be gullible and to let flattery impair your judgment; temperamental tantrums when things do not go your way.

Images for Integration

A child in an Edenic paradise builds a beautiful sandcastle in the sunshine with all the creatures of nature in joyous attendance ... In full pageantry, the new king is crowned before his kingdom.

Famous Personalities

Brian Aldiss (science-fiction writer), Dame Janet Baker (mezzo-soprano), Lindsay Clarke (author), Robert Graves (writer and poet), Max Heindel (metaphysician), Herbert Hoover (former American president), Peter O'Toole (actor), Martin Sheen (actor), Patrick Swayze (actor), Barbara Windsor (actress).

54

SUN LEO ♌ MOON VIRGO ♍

I was not made for group activity, I just wasn't.
ROBERT REDFORD

A good review from the critics is just another stay of execution.
DUSTIN HOFFMAN

Themes

FIRE/EARTH Dedicated; ethical; intellectual; kind-hearted and purposeful; highly moral; capable; striving for excellence; noblesse oblige; choosy; critical; temperamental; restrained charm; articulate; discriminating taste; the artisan.

Are you the imperious king or the humble servant? There is a lot of both in you, and sometimes you struggle with that fact. You have a radiant, regal, strong spirit and a self-effacing, timid, over-critical inner voice that keeps you looking and working for perfection.

You are the actor's actor, the introverted orator, the mystical scholar, the devoted housewife, the magical trainer of young minds. You have an independent, idealistic nature and will do exactly what you believe is right, but underneath you are not quite as sure of yourself as you seem, and you rely on others' good opinion more than you care to admit.

Your desire for excellence can make you a bit prudish, high-minded, aloof, self-contained and nervous. If only you could relax more you would be able to influence others strongly with your dedication and talents, and with your aesthetic sensitivity and controlled charm which is just waiting to get out. When you feel nervous, your efforts to delegate may come across as officious and schoolmarmish. Nevertheless, your tremendous integrity, kindness, consideration and thoroughness in all you do usually inspires respect and admiration in others.

You know you have something important to contribute, but as you hate pretension you tend to analyse and re-analyse yourself until your confidence ends up severely dented. When, however, you get your Virgoan precision channelling your Leonine vision, you really know what you want and go straight for it. It is then that what you produce in a practical sense will define you in a spiritual sense, as you aim to put your best self into all your labours with great attention to detail.

A certain chastity of mood and inner tenacity gives you moral force, and this makes you a good teacher, counsellor – and friend. You always try to live up to an inner ideal, and through patience and doggedness you show others that true fulfilment lies in selfless service to this ideal.

For you, the root of dignity *must* lie in humility, although it may take some time to realize that this is the answer to your inner self-contradictions.

You need a creative outlet, some kind of a stage. This can be either grand or humble – the smooth running of a household or a theatre company – but it must give you the opportunity to pour your whole self into the challenge. And a sort of old-fashioned sense of noblesse oblige does not let you rest until you have ploughed some of your intense, individualistic energy into altruistic ventures, like the Boy Scout leader who inspires virtue and courage in others by just being himself. You aim for excellence but you instinctively know that practice makes perfect and that perfection takes a lifetime.

Relationships

In matters of the heart, too, chronic nit-picking can undermine your creative energy, and being too exacting with others can cause friction in close relationships. You can be warm and demonstrative, caring and protective, and yet incredibly fussy and touchy about some of the most minute domestic details.

Requiring lots of attention and very particular care from your loved one, you also need room to run things your own way, and can feel easily wounded if others do not bow to your superior knowledge. Your innate diplomacy and courtesy can freeze into huffiness if this happens, and you can suddenly withdraw your warmth under a fastidious, fault-finding defence.

When you get lots of devotion and emotional pampering, you are happy and trusting, and your Leonine confidence radiates its benevolence. You are something of a recluse, even though your social manners are of the Emily Post variety when you do mix with society. But still, your private life and personal career are more important to you than group movements. Your devotion is to personal goals and standards, but when you are appreciated for the person you have become through stamina and talent, you radiate largess and deep contentment.

Your Greatest Strengths

A sound, analytical mind and articulate expression; devotion to duty and aspiration to personal excellence; ability to inspire others with the results of your practice-makes-perfect creed.

Your Greatest Weaknesses

A tendency to be too pedantic, high-minded and critical; to hide your insecurities under a pushy and defiant exterior; and to sulk in a self-pitying way when you feel slighted.

Image for Integration

After the ball, Cinderella polishes the floor until its shiny surface perfectly reflects her happy, contented face.

Famous Personalities

Princess Anne, Vida Blue (baseball player), Ann Blyth (singer and actress), Emperor Claudius, Rajiv Gandhi (politician), Dustin Hoffman (actor), Myrna Loy (actress), Madonna (singer), Ricardo Muti (conductor), Frederic Raphael (writer), Robert Redford (actor and director).

— 55 —

Sun Leo ♌ Moon Libra ♎

He passed a cottage with a double coach-house
A cottage of gentility!
And he owned with a grin
That his favourite sin
Is pride that apes humility.
ROBERT SOUTHEY

Only a fool would assert that there is no more on Rembrandt's canvas
than paint, nothing on Mozart's music-paper but notes.
BERNARD LEVIN

Themes

FIRE/AIR Gracious; charming and expressive; out-going; intellectual curiosity; authoritative but cooperative; diplomatic nobility; artistic; powerful imagination; love of luxury; romantic idealism; regal friendliness; polished individualism; imperious but tolerant; animated communicator; refined sociability.

Are you an independent, confident, even imperious sort of person who gets caught out by just how much you care about other people's view of you? Do you think of yourself as very individualistic, even a maverick, and then find yourself conforming to custom with seeming conviction and finesse?

You have a prestigious, compelling presence, even when you are just clowning around, and a natural ability to command both respect and affection from your friends and colleagues. In the nicest possible way you assume the position of the leader because you have a strong independent streak and believe in your lofty, worthy ideals, but you also gravitate towards collaboration and an impartial examination of the facts.

You can be bossy and yet your bossiness is so diplomatic that it is convincing, even impressive. Although you want esteem and tend to identify with honourable goals and people, you can work alongside others you respect and you really want the best for everyone. You have style, and you instinctively know that 'manners maketh man' and that, if for some reason they don't, they go a long way in making life worth living.

When you come into your own, you develop a strongly aesthetic approach to life and are naturally creative. You need a very positive, active medium through which to express yourself, such as drama, teaching or running your own business. Anything to do with beauty and harmony will interest you, such as decorating, design and painting. Your interest in social equality may take you into politics or the law.

You have a strong sense of yourself and will stubbornly follow your own personal code of ethics, yet you also enjoy being part of a group that has a common purpose or bond. You cherish ideals of liberty and equality, but if there are some distasteful tasks to perform you can move very smoothly into the role of delegating – well, you think, someone has to give the orders around here or we would have no harmony at all!

Although you seem to enjoy an easy, breezy approach to life, there is quite a serious side to your personality, and you can be suprisingly controversial and provocative. You are willing to stand up and be counted, and perhaps make it look easy. You have a natural appreciation and enjoyment of the good things of life; you will assume that they should be yours by birthright. And through cunning charm, calculated boldness, and intelligent manoeuvre you manage to have plenty.

Relationships

You are a very social being – warm-hearted, romantic, eager to engage with another and to create 'magic' together. In your imagination you give your all for love, but in practice you are often more rational, very pragmatic, reasonable and helpful. You have bags of charm and can give and receive affection easily. But you need *more* than affection; you also need verbal love games and the sharing of ideas and ideals.

You want to share an elegant domestic life with your loved one, and your home needs to be stimulating, full of books, music, conversation and interesting people. But you need to beware that an unconscious preciousness does not blind you to the fact that others do not always agree with you. You have a sensitive ego and you will be challenged in a close relationship to express yourself wholeheartedly and vulnerably whilst acknowledging how much you depend on your loved one's response.

When you can tame your wilful, rebellious, independent side, or at least get it into a manageable size, emotional relationships will go more smoothly and you will discover how easy it is for you to make things work. A bit of flattery and tenderness goes a long way for you. If you are absolutely convinced that he or she feels honoured and 'over the Moon' to have you, you will gladly do the washing up.

Your Greatest Strengths

Integrity and love of justice and honour; appreciation of beauty and excellence and the good things of life; diplomatic charm and organizational skills; idealism and desire to give people the benefit of the doubt; the unique artistic style you bring to all you do.

Your Greatest Weaknesses

Vanity and unconscious snobbery; self-righteousness when it comes to social behaviour and morality; proneness to develop lazy habits; tendency to lean on others without always acknowledging their support.

Images for Integration

Jeeves the butler welcomes Bertie home with a jolly party of artists, important personages and eccentric friends ... A monarch discusses poetry with a visiting diplomat ... The Actors' Guild stages a political rally.

Famous Personalities

Helena Blavatsky (occultist), Fidel Castro (Cuban statesman and communist prime minister), Wilt Chamberlain (champion basketball player), Julia Child (television chef and cookery writer), John Derek (actor), Paul Dirac (physicist and mathematician), Knut Hamsun (Nobel prize-winning Norwegian novelist), Bernard Levin (writer, satirist and music critic), Robert Southey (poet), Esther Williams (actress).

— 56 —

SUN LEO ♌ MOON SCORPIO ♏

I love a lassie.

Keep right on to the end of the road.
SONGS OF SIR HARRY LAUDER

I do believe in the evolution of consciousness as the only thing which we can embark on, or in fact, willy-nilly, are embarked on.
CONRAD AIKEN

Themes

FIRE/WATER Imperious; extraordinarily magnetic personality; fiercely loyal; hard-working; arrogant; self-dramatizing; strong appetites; stubborn and possessive; defiant; powerful instincts; fanatic when motivated; star quality; deep integrity; shrewd; ambitious.

Are you a classy show-off who wants the best and is ready to believe everyone loves you, or are you a complex and intensely guarded soul who hides a tangled inner world of doubt, longing and emotional strategies? Do you have a noble, sunny identity and aspirations to excellence which, however, seem to be undermined by a more brooding, suspicious, emotional nature?

You are a magnetic, fascinating and powerful individual, and your bark *is* just about as bad as your bite. Likewise, however, your power to create, to spread beneficence and to reap substantial reward for yourself is equally great. It is all a matter of mastering your powerful desires and fears, which have a way of taking over and running the show, as well as your innate talents and your instinct for conquest and control.

You are not a good loser. You aim to win and, by hook or by crook, you will. But by becoming more aware of what is going on inside you – your motives, fears and suspicions – you will be able to find a more workable balance between your powerful, extrovert tendencies and your cautious, introverted side. This is easier said than done, however, because you are the sort of person who naturally goes to extremes, and there are times when this extremist quality, coupled with your innate stubbornness, creates not a little havoc in your personal life.

Nevertheless, you are a survivor, incredibly persistent in pursuit of your goals, and often very ingenious and imaginative in the way you get around problems. People may be fascinated by the mystique that surrounds your personality, and sometimes taken aback by the sheer force of your 'want'-power.

You appear, at first, to be completely out-going and up-front, but you have ways of letting it be known that there is a world of secrets within, that one cannot read *this* book by its cover. This secret dimension can be a great source of power to you, especially when you are assessing the environment for important facts and favourable trends, and quietly organizing your plan of action. But it can also burden you unnecessarily if you harbour fears, resentment, anger and jealousy for too long. Your creative powers are truly considerable, and you more than anyone therefore need to develop the power of positive thinking, as well as a more detached awareness of your voracious and vulnerable ego.

Powerful emotions will either help or hinder your path to self-expression. The more you can honestly confront what is eating you, without feeling that you are losing face, the more you are likely to end up the hero of your own story. You simply will not be rushed – you will work at your own pace and must be your own boss, even if you are in the employ of someone else.

You have a lot of pride and feel you know how you want things done. Interference from others, even though it may be well-intended, usually gets a negative response from you – how dare anyone rain on your parade? You will over-react even if you actually *do* want some help, or at least support, because you do not feel comfortable in any kind of dependent position. You were made for leadership, autonomy and the lap of luxury!

Relationships

You are a person of enormous passion and emotional complexity, and whoever loves you has their work cut out. Although you need security and can be undyingly loyal (and obsessively possessive), you may be unaware that you tend to have a double standard when it comes to relationships. You bitterly resent any encroachment on your own freedom, but at the same time demand absolute fidelity and, if possible, obedience, from your loved one.

You enjoy drama, even a touch of danger, and you need to be aware of your tendency to throw tantrums and create unhealthy scenes just to stir things up. You need a partner who is just as interested in sexual passion as yourself, and who does not mind being tested from time to time. On the whole, you are likely to find more happiness in love if you learn to relax and trust more, keep fewer secrets and admit that you feel pretty vulnerable and out of control at times. It will make you, paradoxically, a stronger person and a more sensitive lover.

Your Greatest Strengths

Creative talents; inscrutable belief in yourself; willpower; indefatigueable determination to succeed; deep personal loyalties to principles and loved ones; personal charisma and astuteness which makes you a natural leader – if you ever choose to lead anyone other than yourself!

Your Greatest Weaknesses

Arrogance and tendency to over-extend yourself; lack of detachment; fanatical desire for personal success and survival; temper tantrums and stubborn resentment when things do not go your way; proneness to let phobias and a cynical attitude to life limit your potential for happiness.

Images for Integration

The conception of a divine child takes place during a total eclipse of the Sun ... A fateful, passionate love affair between the queen and a mysterious, wandering peasant.

Famous Personalities

Conrad Aiken (poet), Francesco Cossiga (president of Italy), Alex Haley (author), Alfred Hitchcock (film director), Stanley Kubrick (film director and writer), Sir Harry Lauder (music-hall artist), John Logie Baird (inventor of television), The Queen Mother, Karlheinz Stockhausen (composer), Terry Wogan (television personality).

— 57 —

'SUN LEO ♌ MOON SAGITTARIUS ♐

Be prepared to accept such good fortunes as the Gods offer.
SIR ALEXANDER FLEMING

Two antagonistic influences ... one to mount direct to heaven, the other to drive yawingly to some horizontal goal.
HERMAN MELVILLE

Themes

FIRE/FIRE Hero-worship; honourable; adventurous; passionate; outspoken; intuitive; independent; loyal; proud; generous; warm sincerity; romantic visionary; restless; sociable; imperious; impractical; impatient.

Are you the self-confident leader attached to home and empire, who sometimes feels like shirking all responsibilities, throwing caution to the wind and hitting the road for some new adventure? You are a combination of fixed, self-centred creativity and the restless striving for novelty and knowledge. You may be the kingly nomadic, the travelling entertainer, the daredevil extrovert, the lucky artist, the regal philosopher, the captain of the team. You are self-assured, proud and resilient, and you have so much enthusiasm and imagination you sometimes may not know what to do with it.

A nobility of spirit coupled with the savvy of a gambling gypsy combines to make you a creative adventurer wherever you turn up, and usually you play the hero. Essentially a restless explorer, either geographically or in the mental realms, you react rebelliously against being trapped in any one place, job, philosophy or relationship. Your instinct is to go, go, go, and to exploit personal potential in the most immediate and exciting way.

You are autocratic in style but egalitarian in spirit. Friendly, ready to get involved with others, full of innovative ideas and original ways of viewing things, you easily see the 'big picture', and find it challenging to see how many ways there are for fitting the various pieces of the whole together. Your inner ideals constitute the 'real' world for you and always serve as a guide to action and behaviour.

Because you are intensely honourable, you can seem somewhat high-minded at times, even though you are one of the most kind-hearted souls in the zodiac. Enthusiasm and eagerness for adventure makes it hard for you to say no, but the result of your intense, speedy and risk-taking ways can be instability. You may have enormous financial swings, as well as a lot of domestic disarray. This is because 'doing your own thing' – which means being allowed to dream up and pursue possibilities with the minimum of accountability – will almost always take precedence over completing yesterday's tasks.

This is not to say that you are anything other than utterly honest and moral. Integrity is your middle name; you detest human hypocrisy and will feel personally called upon to expose it where you find it. Indeed you can be very contemptuous of those whose moral standards fall too low to qualify, in your view, as human. But life for you is essentially about exploring, creating and giving free rein to your imagination, and creating in the here and now.

Relationships

Emotionally you are pretty challenging, too. Naturally generous with your affections as well as with any material goods you have, you may need more than one person on whom you can bestow your fun-loving beneficence. You can, in fact, be quite exhausting. One famous owner of this combination once said, 'I find myself interesting – but tiring.'

Restless, passionate and somewhat nervous, you do not like things getting too heavy, and you avoid like the plague being given a verbal list of your childish faults. You need intellectual rapport with your partner, and to share your romantic vision of life – to live out your myth of the adventurous hero – with someone who will not interfere with your independent escapades of body, mind, and spirit. Just make sure, however, that you learn how to share taking out the rubbish and doing the washing-up, as well.

A kind of manic 'upness' and constant pursuit of excitement may mask a hidden fear of being ordinary and bound by mortal limits, and you may be prone to unexplainable bouts of depression. The more you can pause for self-reflection, appreciate what your senses are reporting and tune into the more tender moments of intimacy, the less will you experience imbalance in your life. This will also enable you to bring to fruition more of your creative ideas – and to enjoy the rewards of your labours with less impatience.

Your Greatest Strengths

High personal standards; broad and far-ranging intuitive mind; enthusiasm for learning and for personal development; and your open, resilient and positive friendliness towards others.

Your Greatest Weaknesses

Restlessness and inability to tie yourself down for long to relationships or projects; tendency to jump before thinking things through; and to dismiss ideas or others arrogantly with brusque, sarcastic pronouncements that wound far more than you intend.

Images for Integration

Merlin the Magician teaches young Arthur the mysteries of algebra, alchemy and archery ... The knight in shining armour wins a game of poker and the drinks are on the house.

Famous Personalities

Sri Aurobindo (guru), Ray Bradbury (writer), Sir Alexander Fleming (scientist), Lawrence of Arabia (soldier and writer), Herman Melville (author), Sally Struthers (actress), Ellen Yoakum (healer).

— 58 —

SUN LEO ♌ MOON CAPRICORN ♑

We must laugh at man to avoid crying for him.

Religion is excellent stuff for keeping common people quiet.
NAPOLEON BONAPARTE

The world is charged with the grandeur of God.
GERARD MANLEY HOPKINS

Themes

FIRE/EARTH Ambitious; proud of achievements; workaholic; practical visionary; the self-centred child and the wise old man; laughter and sadness; sprightly and sombre; self-demanding; domineering; organized and purposeful; stubborn and temperamental; the authoritative leader; the ardent chief; the sombre star.

Do you imagine yourself in a position of power and acclaim, but then quietly quake when you realize how much depends on you? Do you naturally put your best foot forward and easily impress the world, but hide an inner world of loneliness and hunger for love? Are you supremely self-assured or deeply self-doubting?

You have immense vitality and purposeful ambition. Quite simply, you want to get on with the job and achieve your aims. So determined are you that your gaze rarely deviates from the road most likely to succeed. But you may not realize how much your ego is depending on those glorious achievements. Worldly recognition, in the form of rewards, university degrees, badges of honour, positions of authority, applause from those who matter most and fat cheques to put in the bank, is what you want. You have the disposition of the megastar who will not rest until she is convinced that she has arrived and can call the shots.

Although you wish to shine and be well thought of, you often gravitate towards solitude, preferring your own company. Despite a spontaneous, childlike creativity, you need to be in charge and to formalize all that you do. In your path upwards, however, you tend to take yourself too seriously and forget to take other people's lives – and feelings – into consideration. Arrogance is your downfall, and passionate perseverence your strength. If you can develop *compassion* as well, you will gain the affection as well as the respect of your comrades.

There is about you a great vitality, sense of adventure and *joie de vivre*, and yet also a guarded, serious, self-protective side which has experienced, and almost expects, setbacks. Your punch and vigour contrast with your matter-of-fact formality and desire to get things finished and under control. In this guarded side there is considerable tension, a kind of defensive anxiety which keeps you ready for life's attack.

Early in life your shyness may hold you back, but later you mould your vulnerability into self-controlled polish so you can deal with the outer world effectively. Authority figures may have crushed your confidence at one point, and as a result you want to become strong, even impervious to criticism. You are the type who can pull yourself up by your bootstraps, determined to make good in the world and rarely letting anything prevent you from reaching your aim.

You have a need to shine, to be seen and appreciated for your unique individuality, and your Capricorn Moon will help you stick to the work at hand so that your success as a *professional* will be assured. You will be made aware of the power of the media and, if you are in a profession that puts you in front of the public, you will rapidly learn how to use publicity to put forward your best profile. Your biggest challenge may be learning how to relax and let go of your defences when you are not in front of the camera, which, of course, is a lot of the time!

Relationships

You are not sure whether you are a hermit or a socialite. You can be either, and will probably go through phases of putting work first and then, when you feel acceptably secure, jumping into romance with lusty enthusiasm. You are romantic, devoted and love being extravagant towards your loved ones.

You have a deep respect for traditional values and you are as loyal as the day is long. At times, however, you can be demanding, stubborn and vain, letting your touchy ego rear with wounded dignity if you are not 'handled' in just the right way. You are paradoxical because you would like someone who could devote themselves to your needs, but you also want your partner to be someone you can show off, someone of whom you are proud.

Your independence, toughness and self-preoccupation will soften with experience, when you have learned to laugh at yourself more easily, and when personal successes let you feel more secure.

Your Greatest Strengths

Ambition; diligence; ability to carry plans through; practical intellect, which can assess facts accurately and organize accordingly; courage and powers of leadership; and the enthusiasm and personal commitment you bring to all your responsibilites and pleasures.

Your Greatest Weaknesses

A need to dominate and be in control; impatience with imperfection; the way in which you hide insecurities behind an impermeable arrogance and a false intellectual stance; an insensitive sweeping aside of other people's needs, views and feelings; arrogant ruthlessness.

Images for Integration

An orphan rummages in the attic and finds an old geneaology book which maps out the family tree of her long-lost, forgotten royal ancestors ... A prince organizes his father the King's weekly schedule.

Famous Personalities

Lucille Ball (actress), Napoleon Bonaparte (French soldier and emperor), Ernst Cassirer (philosopher), Joe Chambers (rock musician), Teng Hsiao-Ping (Chinese politician), Gerard Manley Hopkins (poet), Yves Saint Laurent (fashion designer), Arnold Schwarzenegger (actor), Norman Schwarzkopf (army general), Joe Weber (satirical comedian).

— 59 —

SUN LEO ♌ MOON AQUARIUS ♒

Idealism increases in direct proportion to one's distance from the problem.
JOHN GALSWORTHY

'Who in the world is this?' inquired Johnny Townmouse. But after the first exclamation of surprise he instantly recovered his manners.
BEATRIX POTTER, FROM THE *The Tale of Johnny Townmouse*

If I should die think only this of me
That there's some corner of a foreign field
That is for ever England ...
RUPERT BROOKE

Themes

FIRE/AIR Aristocratic; vivid imagination; idealistic; truthful; friendly; proud; theatrical; broad-minded; loyal; strong social force; love of friendship; standing out within the group; extreme individualist; deep convictions; spiritual strength; noble bearing.

Do you want passion and stardom or freedom and friendship? Do you want to woo the audience or to help and befriend them? Sometimes you want both, but always you are the individual who stands out in a crowd.

Fiery, proud, romantic and inspirational, you feel great concern for other people's troubles and will want to do something about them – but only after you have sown your wild oats and discovered who you are. Your need to be special can find its outlet in large enterprises that further the welfare of the many. You also need, however, to be a leader in some way, to be recognized for your integrity, intellect, individuality and laudable ideals.

You love a challenge and will flamboyantly cross accepted social boundaries to make your point. You are the soul of honesty, a bit rebellious, elegantly outspoken and completely unable to be anything but yourself in all situations. That self is enthusiastic about social ideals but also chivalrous, wanting to see only the best in your fellow man. Broad-minded with a noble bearing, you are kind-hearted and have a touching naivety when it comes to human relations, for you expect to find people as pure and good as the inner figures of your imagination. One of your deepest needs is to cultivate mutually beneficial relationships and to promote a lenient and altruistic understanding of human needs. But you also possess innate self-dramatizing abilities which may be put to good use on the stage, directing or portraying the greatest human stories. Alternatively you may choose other creative forms such as writing, music, teaching and 'storytelling'.

Your need for love and adulation, and for egalitarian friendship may sometimes create a conflict within you. Highly individualistic, you need to feel special, but also to belong to a group of like-minded souls where you can sometimes sublimate your ego in philanthropic service. You are often brimming over with generous affection, outrageous plans, noble intentions and a preponderance to lecture others on how to run their lives. What you may need to develop is more practicality, for your head is often in the clouds. You need to look at things more objectively, and come to more comprehensive solutions.

Reason and imagination work creatively within you, but you can be so autocratically certain of your perceptions as 'right' that you become inflexible, almost intolerant of others – something you would hate to admit. But, in general, so well meaning are you that any hint of arrogance or condescension towards others is usually dismissed as one of your endearing, idiosyncratic ways.

Relationships

You have strong beliefs and principles, and you readily share your dreams, visions and values with your friends, colleagues and lovers. In emotional relationships you are romantic, loyal and magnanimous, and you also have a real need to be friends. One of the creative dilemmas you will need to face is how to combine passionate romance and platonic friendship.

You will learn that true loyalty in love inspires the spirit of largess and compassion, so that you want for your loved one exactly what he or she requires to thrive. Your faithfulness, your sense of justice and your uniquely imaginative flair can work together to influence your world in an uplifting and personally satisfying way.

Your Greatest Strengths

Warm, sympathetic nature; excellent powers of observation and fine mind; commitment to personal ideals; inventiveness; courageous and independent spirit of leadership.

Your Greatest Weaknesses

A tendency to be a bit of an impractical dreamer; proneness to fixed views and arrogance; tendency to be restless and rebellious and a self-appointed law unto yourself – which causes you to squander your creative resources.

Images for Integration

The chairman of the board raises his glass to his able colleagues ... The king of a large, prosperous empire invites everyone to his wedding.

Famous Personalities

Menachim Begin (Israeli politician), Louise Bogan (poet), Rupert Brooke (poet), Kate Bush (singer), Rory Calhoun (actor), Henry Ford (industrialist), John Galsworthy (novelist and dramatist), Melanie Griffith (actress), Keir Hardie (socialist politician), Linda Martel (child healer), André Maurois (novelist and essayist), Beatrix Potter (writer and artist), Jacqueline Susann (writer), Ambroise Thomas (composer).

— 60 —

Sun Leo ♌ Moon Pisces ♓

Poetry is the record of the best and happiest moments of the happiest and best minds.
Percy Bysshe Shelley

Then I thought of the whole world. Who cares for its travail and seeks to encompass it in like lovingkindness and peace?
Hugh MacDiarmid

Themes

FIRE/WATER Modest yet proud; great integrity; compassionate and concerned; poetic imagination; one who can feel poetry and understand philosophy; eccentric; warm friendliness; highly emotional; strongly devotional and idealistic; enthusiastic; extravagant; creative inner world.

Do you love the warmth of the social and artistic limelight, and yet often shun it because you sense it is fickle and will ultimately hurt you? Are you a stunning show-off or a modest help-mate? A lion or a lamb? A plutocrat or pleb?

You have star quality but privately prefer to be a wallflower. You have a strong need for excellence and social approval, yet you honour your own private, individual values more – and perhaps even come to expect there to be a conflict between your moral integrity and the demands of your audience.

Very impressionable and easily moved by suffering, you are a mixture of self-assured certainty and oversensitive, confused

223

uncertainty. Sometimes self-denying and withdrawn, other times autocratic and wilful, you have a great longing to belong as well as a strong need to be actively useful. When you can combine these two sides, you are one of the most poetic and creative of all combinations with a spontaneous and childlike delight in the world, an immense sense of fun and a capacity to translate experience into words and colourful images.

You can sometimes feel torn between your desire for plenty of peace and privacy, and your need for worldly success and the affection and approval of people you love and respect. You have an essentially artistic temperament and need to learn how to be your own best friend – how to look after your own best interests – as you are so easily drawn towards looking after *others*.

Whether or not you are overtly religious, there is a strongly reflective and devotional side to your nature. You may even feel that it is nothing less than every human being's duty to realize his or her immense spiritual potential. At the same time, you never lose your compassion for people and their problems and failures. You know yourself how you go through phases of striving and then retreat, successful self-expression and then, perhaps, a refusal to play the game if the cost to your integrity is too high. You can be severely shaken by the ways of the world, and yet it would be unhealthy for you to relinquish your active role altogether.

Full of ardour and deep feeling for life, you are the lion-hearted mystic, the gentle king, the gullible sweetheart who would not harm a fly, the flamboyant, fiercely loyal friend who will share others' sorrows and successes with equal intensity. You are courageous in the face of difficulties, ever true to your word through thick and thin, and dignified and hopeful even when pain absorbs you utterly as it is wont to do quite often.

Changes of mood are your way of life, and if you can make them fodder for your creative imagination, they will serve you well. As a writer, a poet, an actor or any kind of artist, you can indulge in your feelings dramatically, and readily transpose your inner life out into the world.

Relationships

Compassionate love is central to your way of being. Intensely charismatic and emotionally available, you literally pour yourself heart and soul into your personal interests, your career and your relationships.

At heart you are a total romantic and also a dreamer, and you may give your all for someone who turns out to be not what you think. Your desire both to dominate and be dominated can make for some tension. You may also find the more humdrum aspects of human relationships a bit of a treadmill, and if you do, you can withdraw into your own world or wander off to greener pastures.

You can never feign what you really feel, and that can cause you some anguish as you hate the idea of hurting anyone. As well as needing lots of affection, you also need to be understood, but this is unlikely to happen. Once you accept this, your emotional life will become more satisfying.

Your Greatest Strengths

Rich, artistic imagination; theatrical sense of both the beauty and tragedy of life; emotional sensitivity and generous, caring qualities; commitment to your individual ideals and morals; openness to life, whatever it may bring.

Your Greatest Weaknesses

Subjectivity; moodiness; proneness to dejection; tendency to over-dramatize your life with you playing the victim; a kind of divine discontent in romantic affairs which keeps you emotionally unsettled, wondering if you will ever be *really* happy.

Image for Integration

The Wizard of Oz gives the Lion a heart and he becomes King of Oz.

Famous Personalities

Coco Chanel (designer), Robert De Niro (actor), Gaston Doumergue (former French president), Dorothy Hamill (champion ice skater), Mata Hari (spy), Carrie Jacobs Bond (songwriter), P.D. James (thriller writer), Philip Larkin (poet), Hugh MacDiamid (poet), Petrarch (poet, humanist), Susan St James (actress), Jill St John (actress), Norma Shearer (actress), Percy Bysshe Shelley (poet).

Chapter Nine

SUN IN VIRGO

———————

— 61 —

SUN VIRGO ♍ MOON ARIES ♈

Heed well the precepts of the saints, who have all warned those who would become holy to speak little of themselves and their own affairs.
ST. FRANÇOIS DE SALES

A thought is often original, though you have uttered it a hundred times.
OLIVER WENDELL HOLMES

Themes

EARTH/FIRE Intellectual precision; enthusiasm for excellence; self-motivated; skilful and pragmatic; diligent; caustic wit; practical joker; scholarly; detached; dedicated to ideals; self-centred; committed; workaholic; bossy.

Are you the willing servant who gets rebellious when given your orders? You feel yourself to be a leader but really only want to be in charge of yourself. You have a diligent but crusading temperament, and whether you are an artist, a trade-union representative or a well-disciplined athlete, you know that victory comes to those who do their homework.

Your personality has a decidedly impersonal cast to it. This is because you have a practical, no-nonsense approach to life which over-rides the finer, more sensitive human feelings that may want to get out. You

226

are a born professional, and you work best under your own steam because you combine both a meticulous eye for detail with an exuberant, wholehearted approach to all your projects. But work you must, for whatever you do your work is your *raison d'être*, and to be happy, your work must employ your quick mentality and forcefulness.

You have a clever mind, a sharp tongue, and do not, as a rule, suffer fools gladly. Full of good advice and well-intentioned criticism, your manner of delivery is often cutting and blunt, revealing that the more refined shades of feeling and communication do not always compute with you. Ideas and facts are more important to you than feelings, especially when they are *your* ideas and facts. You respond rapidly to situations, and verbal repartee is one of your strong points. You are a great debater.

But whilst you can be forthright, honest and downright impatient with people who do not speak their mind, you are not quite as courageous and confident as you sometimes seem. Although you are capable of making a lot of noise and mustering up a lot of bravado when the occasion calls for it, you are also aware of your own doubts and niggling imperfections. One side of you is the humble servant – simple, innocent, dutiful, trying to be a devoted, useful, healthy member of society. But then your restless hair-trigger reactions take over, revealing the intensity of your self-absorption and personal ambition. You cogitate, analyse and synthesize your environment, and then you hold forth with great impetuosity.

Whatever your age, there is in you both a young, brash extrovert and a staid, conscientious introvert. Sometimes you are prone to quick flashes of anger, whilst another side of you tends to be overly apologetic and self-effacing. You are a person of great pizzazz yet you can also be extremely practical and content with routine. You may not always feel very comfortable with yourself as these two sides alternate.

Relationships

All the factors mentioned above can make you edgy in emotional relationships. You are sociable but very much your own person, and very self-driven and self-contained. You are not particularly flexible, and naturally assume that you will get on and run things more efficiently your own way. A marriage of minds is more important to you than true love, and you have to really work on relationships because the more subtle shades of feeling usually pass you by.

227

Emotionally you can blow hot and cold. You may sometimes act the virgin but there is a lot of you that wants to play the bawdy ram. Your main problem with emotions is your hastiness and, quite simply, your lack of interest in your partner's needs. You may hurt others without meaning to because your orientation is so self-centred. You just cannot help the fact that all your main interests are always at the forefront of your mind. This trait, however, serves you well in hobbies and professional pursuits. And when you are happy in the latter, you are, in general, easier to please in relationships.

In many ways, you are a real character. Your purposefulness, your intellectual curiosity and your zany sense of humour more than make up for your lack of romantic empathy.

Your Greatest Strengths

Ability to get on and do things with skill and energy; quick, analytical mind that gets to the point with utmost precision; capacity to bring original flair and enthusiasm into the commonplace and mundane realms of life.

Your Greatest Weaknesses

A tendency to be scathingly critical, over-cerebral in emotional relationships, a bit too self-sufficient for your own good, and excessively verbose and know-it-all towards those dependent on you.

Image for Integration

A jolly, rotund monk enjoying his food and wine while excelling in well-worn Latin sayings, witty responses and kindly good humour.

Famous Personalities

Leonard Bernstein (composer and conductor), Ingrid Bergman (actress), Henry Ford II (industrialist), Donald A. Glaser (physicist), Ellic Howe (historian and writer), Max Reinhardt (theatrical producer), St. François de Sales (scholar and mystic), Lily Tomlin (actress and comedienne), Oliver Wendell Holmes (poet and essayist).

SUN VIRGO ♍ MOON TAURUS ♉

There are some satisfactions you can only find in work.
PETER SELLERS

I want to be alone.
GRETA GARBO

Themes

EARTH/EARTH Dependable; kind-hearted; self-restrained; earthy and practical; common sense; love of routine; affinity with nature; artistic; craftsperson; diligent worker; financial savvy; instinctive wisdom.

Are you a practical perfectionist, discriminating and systematic in almost all you do, or are you content to smell the roses and plod along making the best of things? Invariably the latter comes easy to you because you are resourceful and take life as it comes, even if another part of you gets flustered when you see things being done in an unintelligent and wasteful manner.

You are at home with the earthy reality of life, and take part in the daily, weekly, yearly round with ease and enjoyment. In other words, you possess the farmer's instinct to cultivate and nurture. All things concerned with physical wellbeing may interest you, either at the 'Earth Mother' end of the spectrum (gardening, food preparation and home-making) to practical craftsmanship (carpentry, sculpture, decorating, designing), to the shrewd management of financial resources (banking, insurance, accountancy). All you really want is to live a full, useful life in which your talents are productively engaged, helping you carve out a solid, secure and well-ordered niche for you and yours. In whatever sphere you work, your vocation is to serve and provide.

You are not just a 'farmer', however, as it is very likely that you have exquisite taste and a deep appreciation for beauty in many forms – the fine arts, music, drama, opera, literature and people. Tangible beauty and the cornucopia of artistic life delights you and you want to be near it, participate in it, patronize it, and perhaps possess some of it, too. Indeed, you can be quite possessive about your valued belongings, including people and children, but you know how to look after them, how to honour and respect their integrity, and how to enjoy and take responsibility for treasured assets. As a result, others sense your trustworthiness, feel safe and comfortable in your presence, and respect you implicitly.

Your penchant for duty, order and security can sometimes blind you to the more subtle realms of fantasy, feeling and imagination, and to the more individualistic and eccentric outlook on life which is typical of a fiery individual. You are simply not interested in what you cannot see and understand logically. You study the facts; you get to know your world; you use your experience and acquired knowledge to function efficiently and successfully in the 'real' world, and often wonder why everyone else cannot do the same thing.

You make a wonderful parent and provider, instinctively knowing how to live on a budget, to help others cope with busy schedules and get their homework done, to plan for house redecoration and the annual holiday, and still be able to end your day unruffled, enjoying that glass of wine or cup of tea by the fire. However, you have a relative inability to nurture anything which is not practical and valuable to your life in a tangible way. It is not that you do not have the patience to nurture creativity; it is just that you would rather nurture that which you can touch, taste and measure and which will yield a good harvest in time.

Relationships

When it comes to love you have an attractive modesty and inner contentment as well as an affectionate and thoughtful nature. You do not express yourself with lots of fireworks, but you are very sensual, loyal, reliable and willing to go the extra mile to bring home the goods.

You are caring, and enjoy helping and being useful to your loved ones. You know that actions speak louder than words, and you express your love in quiet, tangible ways. But you may lack romantic idealism, and habitually dismiss the more elusive and non-material values of a mate or friend. However sensible you may be, you may have a hidden fascination with the intangible, which has a way of attracting you to emotional, enigmatic people. You are earthy, dependable, always there to clean up the mess, but you might find it is fun once in a while to actually make the mess instead of cleaning it up!

Your Greatest Strengths

Excellent reasoning ability; dependability; common sense; capacity for organization and hard work; quiet reserve and resourcefulness which makes everyone feel that everything is under control; commitment to serving others and making them happy.

Your Greatest Weaknesses

Tendency to be too rational, materialistic and black-and-white in your thinking; stubbornness which comes out when hierarchical relationships are ignored; addiction to routine.

Images for Integration

A nun finishes washing up in the refectory, and then takes the keys to her Bentley and drives off to see the new art exhibition ... A sculpture of still life.

Famous Personalities

Yasser Arafat (leader of the Palestine Liberation Organization), Greta Garbo (actress), John Houseman (actor and director), Raymond Massey (actor and director), Mother Teresa (living saint), Captain Mark Phillips (ex-husband of Princess Anne), Peter Sellers (actor and comedian), John Smith (former leader of the Labour Party).

— 63 —

Sun Virgo ♍ Moon Gemini ♊

Our motto: Life is too short to stuff a mushroom.
SHIRLEY CONRAN

An atheist is a man who has no invisible means of support.
JOHN BUCHAN

Take what you can use and let the rest go by.
KEN KESEY

Themes

EARTH/AIR Mental ingenuity; love of words; refined tastes; perennial student; chop logician; pragmatic and playful; youthful; moody; analyser of minutiae; a worrier and a worker; reasonable; detached observer; quick-witted; cool and debonair; the gourmet jack-of-all-trades.

Are you the quick, chatty salesman or the thoughtful, conscientious craftsman? Do you diligently get stuck into something and then notice your attention wanders ... and suddenly you are seduced by an alternative agenda? Do you have bits of expert knowledge and fancy yourself as a specialist, but get despondent over your own lack of patience and ability to stick-to-it? In this combination there is a mixture of the light-hearted and the seriously dedicated which can leave you strung out half-way between.

You are seriously interested in a variety of things but your eager interest can fool you into thinking you are an authority by just imagining yourself to be one. You always mean well and love to talk about the things you are learning, and for your quick, active mind a little education goes a long way. You are a thinker and a doer, an intellectual and a general dogsbody, a kind-hearted Peter Pan prankster who always pulls through when family or friends need your help.

You are a logical person with a cool, reasonable approach to life. Your analytical and critical mind grasps the details and slots everything into place, and you try to organize your life with streamlined efficiency, making sure everything makes sense. But you also delight in the spontaneous visit, the unknown quantity, the exception to the rule which makes life more interesting, more fun.

Although you are a conscientious worker, you are not really a workaholic, for you take play just as seriously as you do work. If it is sport you take up for relaxation – which is a good antidote to your nervous, busy mind – you will approach it like a pro with a dedicated, critical eye. Music, art and cooking are soothing, too.

You tend to have sophisticated tastes and a refined aesthetic appreciation. Variety, interesting connections and links, opportunities for shrewd advancement – these things your Gemini side relishes. Your Virgoan side, however, which tends to get into a rut, does not like its finely tuned system to be disturbed. This clash in your nature can be upsetting, and can even cause debilitating worry.

If you collect more information and experience than you can usefully digest, you become plagued by 'indigestion', discontent and a sense of futility. A bit like the experimental rodent going round and round its wheel and getting nowhere in particular. But when you find a direction and sufficient enthusiasm for a goal, the strengths of your combination make you an excellent communicator, analyst, journalist, linguist, teacher, guide or writer. Having a settled domestic life and pursuing artistic hobbies which engage your nimble hands will help you to be less self-critical and enjoy life more.

Relationships

Being so strong on the mental side, your deficit turns up in the area of emotions. You like people and are congenial, hospitable and friendly, although you tend always to sit in judgement of others – no malice intended, it is just your observant, classifying nature registering the types and differences in people. You do not mean to be a snob, but you can easily appear superior and aloof. You may fancy yourself as a romantic, and indeed you are in an idealistic sense; but you may not be aware that you do not get as emotionally involved as you think you do.

Emotionally you are fitful, restless and superficial; insecurity and discomfort with passion and emotional demands make you fickle and somewhat erratic in relationships. A warm fiery type or a dreamy watery type could help you relax and explore the mystery of your emotional needs. Although you would feel overwhelmed by too much emotion, your curiosity is always up for a challenge – and if the challenge is the fathomless depths of yourself, then all the better!

Your Greatest Strengths

Mental dexterity and rational, analytical abilities; practical common sense and quick adaptability; shrewd, resourceful eye for organization and progress; flair for communication and presentation; clever approach to work and pragmatic approach to fun.

Your Greatest Weaknesses

Over-intellectual and critical approach to life and relationships; proneness to get side-tracked and then swamped with too much disparate information; tendency to get stuck in unproductive work patterns which give rise to dry, pessimistic, worrisome moods.

Images for Integration

A precision engineer develops new methods of communication ... A raconteur potters in his garden.

Famous Personalities

John Buchan (Lord Tweedsmuir – writer and diplomat), John Cage (composer), Shirley Conran (writer), Buddy Holly (musician), Ken Kesey (writer), Frederic Mistral (poet), Grandma Moses (painter), Cliff Robertson (actor), Oscar Sanchez (Costa Rican president; winner of Nobel prize for peace), Mario Scelba (Italian politician).

— 64 —

SUN VIRGO ♍ MOON CANCER ♋

New opinions are always suspected, and usually opposed, without any other reason but because they are not already common.

The discipline of desire is the background of character.
JOHN LOCKE

Is it altogether a Utopian dream, that once in history a ruling class might be willing to make the great surrender, and permit social change to come about without hatred, turmoil, and waste of human life?
UPTON SINCLAIR

Owls Do Cry
BOOK BY JANET FRAME

Themes

EARTH/WATER Mind v. emotions; sensitivity and practicality; shy yet sociable; self-repressed but observant; kind-hearted and supportive; intuitive and quick-thinking; nervous and defensive; conscientious; fastidious about nourishment; devoted; sentimental; principled but flexible.

Do you feel more comfortable being the devoted servant of your family, but crave time by yourself to get on with your own ideas and inspirations? Do you want to live a quiet, orderly life, but find you are happy to be drawn into lively company which brings down your barriers and takes you out of chronic introspection? Do you think of yourself as a sensible, logical fellow but admit in your heart of hearts that essentially you are as emotional as they come?

You have a fine, quick mind, but your heart has a way of running the show when you least expect it. This makes you human, warm, approachable and embarrassingly muddled at times. You can at first seem the sensitive, shy, retiring type, even something of a wallflower – overly cautious and discreet, an anxious sort of person who has a lot going on inside but has trouble getting it all out.

Yet there is also a caring, charismatic and sociable side to you, and a strong need to be involved in bettering the lot of your fellows. Your family may benefit first from this impulse, for your doting domestic streak needs a practical outlet and you are only too happy to pour out the vitamins for everyone after a gourmet breakfast. But it is likely that you will also need a professional sphere in which to express your qualities of mental discrimination, emotional sensitivity and concern for the wider environment.

You may fuss and worry about details, and can get worked up about a variety of problems. Being so sensitive and self-reflective, you tend to analyse and brood over your feelings. You can be pedantic and finicky, but when this gets translated into a profession it can become a discriminating and fine-tuned sensitivity to human problems. Essentially you are both extremely tender-hearted and conscientious, in the realm of human relations as well as in professional endeavours. You will give freely and ungrudgingly of your time and energy, but you may often find that the spirit is willing but the flesh is weak. This is because nervousness and anxiety can deplete your physical resources, leaving you exhausted and withdrawn. You need to respect your bodily rhythms and dietary needs; your mind may be logical but your body is not.

Yours is a marriage of logic and imagination, a powerful one for understanding the human condition. Your interests and talents may be in medicine, mental health and counselling, education and writing. You may enjoy following the rich tapestry of history and social development, and this could take you into academia. Whatever it is, you will have exacting professional standards but you will not want anyone else to hold you to them – you figure you are your own best taskmaster. From others you want encouragement, love, and support – as long as it is not too cloying and you have room to stir the creative brew.

Relationships

In close relationships, you are a considerate, loyal and affectionate person, strongly inclined to serve and fuss over your loved ones in a very caring, supportive way. You also expect to get the same kind of attention yourself, and can feel horribly wounded and suddenly insecure if you are somehow overlooked. Your reticence makes you appear self-sufficient when you are really dying to be petted and adored.

Misunderstandings and your oversensitivity can put you in a huffy mood; you are prone to nag and moan and then go silent. Your moods become familiar and your partner must apologize in a very particular way and then just leave you alone. You have your own inner logic and organic processes that eventually bring you back.

It is quite likely that you are a very domestic being and will therefore enjoy building a nest with someone and then bringing it to life. And when you have a partner with whom you can communicate intelligently, trust emotionally and share your vulnerability, your constancy combines with romance to make you one of the most desirable of mates.

Your Greatest Strengths

Deep concern for the welfare and needs of others; empirical turn of mind which is enriched by intuition and imagination; adaptability and pragmatic helpfulness; quiet generosity, warmth and loyalty to family and friends.

Your Greatest Weaknesses

Proneness to criticism and complaining; to rationalize away your own idiosyncracies; to cut off from others when you feel misunderstood; to get stuck in old habits, suspicious attitudes and energy-depleting self-pity.

Images for Integration

Two old Chinese women gossip about family problems as they work rhythmically in the rice paddies ... The working mother ... A nutritionist serves his family organically grown chicken soup.

Famous Personalities

Jackie Cooper (actor), Janet Frame (writer), Antonia Fraser (writer), San Martin Grau (statesman), Julio Iglesias (singer), Jesse James (outlaw), John Locke (philosopher), Alison Lurie (novelist), Walther Reuther (trade-union leader), Upton Sinclair (author), Frederick Soddy (physical chemist), Queen Wilhelmina of Holland.

— 65 —

SUN VIRGO ♍ MOON LEO ♌

Man must choose whether to be rich in things or in the freedom to use them.
IVAN ILLICH

I think the whole glory of writing lies in the fact that it forces us out of ourselves and into the lives of others.
SHERWOOD ANDERSON

I'm always cast as someone in authority ... I enjoy it because ... it's an expiation of that part of myself which wants to be grand.
STEPHEN FRY

Themes

EARTH/FIRE Elitist; noble-minded; devoted; hard-working; artistic flair; elegant; refined intellect; superiority complex; gentle and aesthetic; kind-hearted; dutiful; naive; nobility; humility; discreet but radiant; deeply honourable.

Are you a servant or a monarch? The ruler or ruled? Although you may have a mundane job, in your heart of hearts you are the indispensable star of the show and you bring this 'star' quality to everything you do. You are dutiful and devoted to your vocation, and you have a genuinely caring and conscientious attitude about all your professional activities and leisure hobbies. This attitude is fuelled by your high standards and is refined by your mindfulness and by the sense of privilege you feel in using your skills to create beauty or to repair the mess you observe around you. Although you have this deep inner sense of worth and noblesse oblige, you have a difficult time convincing the world that you deserve more respect – because you do not have as much confidence as it often appears.

You have a discerning eye for people and beauty; you give your best and prefer to possess the best but with your cleverness you are probably adept at turning sow's ears into silk purses. Standing for the best is not snobbery, you tell yourself; it is merely dedication to excellence, something you no doubt feel is sorely lacking in the world.

There is a very reticent, self-effacing side to you, and timidity sometimes holds you back. But your inner nature is fiery, courageous and proud, and so may resent the earthy part of you which is content to remain incognito, busily seeing to the details. Mentally alert and careful with the words you use, you make a fine teacher. Within you is the conviction that people are meant to be creative, intelligent and beautiful, if they could only shrug off the laziness that holds them back. In your universe hard work is rewarded by a job well done and, of course, by just a little prestige and respect. A stylish home and all the accoutrements of a highly civilized life are also on your list.

On your bad days you can become a pedantic know-it-all; a finicky fix-it man with entrenched, lordly views; a kind of good-advice machine which over-estimates itself. But although you may sometimes appear to be a snob, you actually have a heart of gold. On good days your radiant, generous spirit and competent mind work very effectively and with instinctive creativeness, and it is then that you can be an excellent role model for individual excellence.

A hard task-master, you work best when you have to answer only to yourself but still know that your efforts are influencing others practically and beneficially. When the two sides of your personality work in tandem, your imagination and robust individuality can be harnessed and directed by your rigorous intellect, and turned into something real by your need to be of service.

Relationships

With people you can be diffident but charming, and in close relationships you are both passionate and modest, adoring but needing to be adoringly petted. When you feel insecure you become haughty and untouchable, although you melt again like butter if your lover says the right thing. This is because, in the struggle between the playful child and the sensible adult within you, the playful child has the greater resilience and the greater need for love.

You want to be treated elegantly and to be appreciated for what you are, but it is as though you sometimes live in an innocent fantasy world where good people always win the reward. And if you do not get the reward you can be pretty insufferable by sulking and making your loved one feel guilty. When you begin to feel more comfortable with your inner dilemma between humility and grandiosity, between being self-effacing and self-promoting, between serving and being served, your emotional life will have fewer hiccups and indigestion!

Your Greatest Strengths

Moral integrity and high standards; intellectual strength and articulateness; ability to think in the large and work hard as well; kind-hearted devotion to others which you express in utterly intelligent and useful ways.

Your Greatest Weaknesses

Naivety and lack of confidence; over-elitist attitude which can make opportunities slip by; a kind of self-pitying vanity which is self-defeating.

Images for Integration

Cinderella works diligently to produce her wedding gown ... A medieval monk crowns his cathedral with a 300-foot spire ... A senior doctor cheerfully changes an old lady's bedpan.

Famous Personalities

Sherwood Anderson (writer), Jacqueline Bisset (actress), Karl Bohm (conductor), Eric Coates (composer), Stephen Fry (actor, comedian and writer), William Golding (writer), Ivan Illich (educational/social theorist), Jean Claude Killy (Olympic skier), Louis XIV (French monarch), Aldo Moro (Italian statesman), Twiggy (model and actress).

— 66 —

SUN VIRGO ♍ MOON VIRGO ♍

The happiness of man consists in life. And life is in labour ... The vocation of every man and woman is to serve other people.
COUNT TOLSTOY

I strive for the best and do the possible.
LYNDON B. JOHNSON

Themes

EARTH/EARTH Identifies with work; perfectionist; utilitarian; analytical; precise; desire to synthesize knowledge and use it; self-critical; shy; helpful; kind-hearted; industrious; efficient; worried; sculpted personality; concerned and conscientious; thoughtful; attention to details.

You are the soul of honesty and kindness, of systems and schedules, and of precision-like adherence to party line. But you worry too much about getting it right, and you are constantly looking within, criticizing yourself and eventually learning that real criticism is observation without judgement.

There is no one better than you at scrutinizing and analysing data. When you are at your best you sift everything through your excellent brain and then slot it all into place so as to make the best practical use of available resources. You worship the intellect, but your brain-to-hand connection is equally strong, which means that you are probably a natural craftsperson or artist of some sort.

You are a thinker *and* a doer, industriously applying your understanding to help and improve things. Whatever your milieu, you approach creativity with a scientific mind, for you want to master your art by knowing the principles by heart. This trait allows you to know when something is wrong, and no one – especially yourself – can relax until you have fixed it.

Your identification with your work can be so strong that your identity wobbles on weekends off. So you develop a useful hobby – something useful to your domestic environment and useful to you because it allows you to perfect another skill. Well, 'perfect' is a strong word; perfection is what you aim for but feel you never reach. And when you are absorbed in a job you are both the master-craftsman and the boss who does not like being interfered with.

Your critical super-ego is the toughest of all task-masters, so you do not need to answer to anyone else but yourself. Doing this constantly makes you a bit serious, nervous and burdened by your sense of imperfection. You are not ideally suited to act as superior in large enterprises because your tendency to analyse and doubt yourself impairs your conviction to go forward in a definite direction. You do not always make life easy for yourself because if you are not seeing the practical results of your efforts you feel insufficient. How can you relax and play when there is so much that needs doing?

Relationships

You are sentimental, kind-hearted and devoted to those close to you, and you hate to think you have offended anyone in the least. Tending to be conventional and discreet in the expression of love, your motto is 'actions speak louder than words', and you show your devotion through service and unfailing loyalty. You may be an exceptional cook and a home improver with exquiste taste. Good health habits are also important to you, and you can wax lyrical on the virtues of trace elements as though you had discovered a new elixir of life.

Your affectionate nature is as pure as the driven snow, but that means you get cold and overfastidious if you feel unappreciated or hurt. And you are unlikely to be attracted to someone you do not respect intellectually. You may find yourself involved in an unsatisfactory relationship for a long time. This is due to your love of moral beauty, and the fact that, as long as you are helping someone, you are vindicating yourself as the superior party and not having to address your inner feelings of inferiority; and it is also partly due to the difficulty you find in breaking an established routine.

Your Greatest Strengths

Modest and conscientious nature; dedication to service; quiet, studious attention to detail and technique; observant, analytical mind and powers of discrimination; ability to be truly impartial and to be a practical idealist.

Your Greatest Weaknesses

A tendency to let high standards turn you into a finicky fault-finder; self-conscious worrying which depletes your confidence and your capacity for enjoyment; allowing your criticisms to become too sharp and destructive – a sign that you have let your feelings go underground and become too 'old-maidish', and that you definitely need to do something frivolous once in a while!

Images for Integration

A ballerina practises alone in a room of mirrors and, sensing her potential perfection, focuses on her flaws and begins again ... A well-oiled printing machine hums away, producing perfectly bound copies of *The Layman's Guide to Essential Nutrients*.

Famous Personalities

Nadia Boulanger (composer), Lola Falana (singer and dancer), Lyndon B. Johnson (former American President), David McCallum (actor), Derek Nimmo (actor), S. Radhakrishnan (guru), Jimmy Rogers (country and western singer), Clancy Sigal (writer), Count Tolstoy (author).

SUN VIRGO ♍ MOON LIBRA ♎

The universe ought to be presumed too vast to have any character.
CHARLES PEIRCE

If one sticks too rigidly to one's principles one would hardly see anybody.
AGATHA CHRISTIE

Themes

EARTH/AIR Practical idealist; the well-organized critic; the courteous intellectual; pragmatic; love of order; the beauty of the mind; the impartial analyst; moral integrity; appreciation of the simple and natural; strong sense of community; gift for words; simplicity; charity.

Are you a humble but self-satisfied intellectual, living in a world of your own, who then finds your pursuits are disturbed by the annoying demands of others? Do you consider yourself a nice, reasonable person who minds his or her own business, and then discovers that people you love want *their* business to be yours, too?

You are an essentially humane, considerate, rational individual whose quiet charm, humour and powers of observation enable you to move in and out of society with grace and effectiveness. You like to do your own thing and are a bit of a loner, very self-composed and controlled, analytical and reflective, and endowed with a gift for social observation. But whilst you enjoy thinking and talking about social ethics and moral structures, you find the whole sphere of relating with warm-blooded human beings a bit messy, although you will admit that you do need some sort of social life to be happy.

You clean things up quickly and effectively with reasoned arguments, with the emphasis on *reasoned*. This is because you would not hurt a fly, and are a master at finding tactful, reasonable ways of saying your piece, even though you are a natural critic of current affairs. And even if you sometimes appear aloof and above the hoi poloi, you have a deep awareness of your own fallibility so that you are as ready to forgive as you are to criticize.

With your eye for detail, clear insight into what any situation calls for, and your desire to refine and improve what already exists, you would make a good organizer, social worker or quality-control specialist. You think carefully about what you do, and this care and consideration makes you highly valued as a friend, colleague and counsellor. If you are needed, you will share your ideas and energy willingly.

You listen thoughtfully to other points of view, but after sifting and analysing arguments you love to push through with your own ideas. You delight in paradox, and you get a charge from controversy which challenges your mental powers, but you do not approve of injustice in any form. In your own quiet way, you stand for everything that is decent and good (which you may find actually leaves a lot of things out). You have a profound sense of values and the importance of the rule of law. And you yearn for the day when others will see the light so that everyone can live in a more civilized way.

You live according to a personal moral code and, although you are charitable and kind-hearted, you will not go out of your way for people you deem to be inferior – or simply boring and aesthetically and intellectually offensive. It would surprise you to hear someone accusing you of being a snob, but so influenced are you by your high ideals and moral propriety that you can forget how to be *simply human*. Once reminded, however, you quickly come back to earth, for you have a critical interior monitor which filters through the bits of feedback that *do* make sense. And above all, you are honest with yourself – scathingly so – and that helps you to laugh at yourself and in the end makes you far more approachable, and loveable, to others.

Relationships

Matters of the heart may be your Achilles heel, even though in some ways you are one of the easiest of the zodiac types to be around. Whilst you are essentially independent, you will discover that you need to love and to be loved, and relationships will show you just how much you have to give.

Courteous, engaging, gentle and respectful of your loved one, you extend to others what matters most to you – respect for individual dignity. You are dependable and trustworthy and deliver what you promise. But you are so damned (whoops!) reasonable and tactful that your partner may find it almost impossible to get you involved in a passionate argument. If you feel that messy rows are beneath you, then you risk the danger of *thinking* you are in a relationship when in fact you are not. You need to tip the scales sometimes, get caught off-guard and angry, relinquish your grip on harmony, bring your passions into the centre of your life rather than keeping them under a neat lock and key. Intellectual rapport and mutual respect is essential for you in any relationship, but your emotional life will offer you more if you ease the control over your emotions.

Your Greatest Strengths

Excellent reasoning powers; civilized concern for the wellbeing of all; enlightened and diplomatic approach to helping others; aesthetic appreciation of both art and science; basic tolerance, kindness, and good will; ability to cooperate with others for a common cause.

Your Greatest Weaknesses

Being maddeningly rational in close relationships; fussy insistence on things being 'just right' before you have anything to do with them; feigning independence when you know you need the input and support of others; assuming intellectual superiority which separates you from potential friends and the enrichment of different views.

Images for Integration

A monastic husband ... A community of researchers work together in the cause of truth ... One's daily mantra: the unexamined life is not worth living.

Famous Personalities

Otto Oscar Binder (writer of science fiction), Agatha Christie (writer of detective fiction), Charles Bishop Kuralt (broadcaster and journalist), Maurice Maeterlink (poet and dramatist), Bob Newhart (deft comedian), Seigi Osawa (conductor), Charles Peirce (philosopher and logician), Alan Villiers (sailor and author), Chen Ning Yang (winner of Nobel prize for physics).

SUN VIRGO ♍ MOON SCORPIO ♏

*The greatest happiness you can have is knowing that you do not
necessarily require happiness.*
WILLIAM SAROYAN

Aren't women prudes if they don't and prostitutes if they do?
KATE MILLETT

Themes

EARTH/WATER Probing mind; critical and analytical; discriminating;
dedicated; meticulous worker; resourceful; self-sufficient;
emotionally controlled; loyal; health fanatic; opinionated; pious;
subjective; conscientious; loyal; long-suffering.

Do you just want to get on with a useful, well-defined job but find you
react perversely when ordered around? Do you have a servant's
loyalty but a tycoon's lust for power? Sometimes you function logically
and purposefully, going about life with a sense of modest dedication
and clear understanding of what you are about. But then a very proud
voice speaks up inside you and will not be satisfied until it has its say –
and its way.

Essentially you are a rational, analytical type, very focused on duty,
improving methods, and increasing the order and security in your life.
You think you are logical and indeed you are; nothing gives you greater
pleasure than solving problems and knowing how to get from A to B
(and then back to A again – you do not like to stay away from home too
long!), whether it involves reading a map, playing cards or fixing your
car. You are a clear-thinking, self-sufficient, immensely capable
person who can be just a little fanatical about 'getting it right'.

Underneath all your cleverness and practical concerns you are,
however, far more emotionally motivated than you are aware. You
feel intensely about things but may find all those powerful feelings a
little disconcerting, so it all comes out as your fighting spirit in the
name of truth. Thus you are often subjective when you think you are
being objective, and passionate when you think you are being

246

reasonable – which can make you a very difficult opponent in an argument.

You are capable of astute, careful thinking, and excel at detailed mental work where you have to scrutinize and arrange data. But you tend to be somewhat limited in your outlook, and frequently unaware of how much your emotional forcefulness colours your thinking processes. You are industrious and practical, and perhaps famous for your critical acumen, whether for proficiency in playing a winning hand at bridge, for artistic or literary skill, for making scientific breakthroughs in the lab or kitchen, or for analysing people's minds. But your Achilles heel will always be the prejudices you express and to which you hold on with an utter conviction, prejudices that ultimately limit your experiences and potential in life.

You need to work in a concentrated manner, at your own pace and according to your own understanding, rather than according to someone else's command. Neither are you particularly good at giving orders, and when you do you may assume a forced air of authority which works contrary to your desired goal. But you are the soul of dedication when you are left to get on with the work in hand, for you have a strong sense of duty and place much value on a job well done.

You are a humble soul with hidden depths, which you may not ever fathom entirely yourself. It is as though you know that there is a part of you that simply will not yield to analysis. When you get your two sides working creatively together, however, you are the dedicated healer, the intuitive critic, the passionate servant or the observant artisan, whose quiet concentration and industry is respected and emulated by many.

Relationships

You keep a tight rein on your own feelings which are often bottled up until, eventually, they have to come out. And when they do it is usually with quite a bite. You care deeply about people, especially members of your family, and take your responsibilities seriously. When you have made a commitment, you are the most constant and supportive of mates, although you are likely to be more passionate about your work than your loves.

Your stringent self-sufficiency and resistance to depending on others can make relationships a real challenge for you. Despising weakness in yourself and in others, you sometimes seem mean with your affections, and you can also be vindictive if you are pushed into an uncomfortable corner.

Your Greatest Strengths

Shrewd, discriminating intellect; capacity for enormous amounts of hard work; perceptiveness about people; dependability and practical support for loved ones; commitment to high standards and the completion of tasks.

Your Greatest Weaknesses

The way in which emotionally charged opinions limit your thinking; your defensive and over-critical bent; self-demanding independence which makes relaxation and play difficult – 'work before play' is your motto, but you can always find something that needs doing.

Images for Integration

A zealous insect lover stands quietly in the bushes observing the mating habits of the praying mantis ... An impassioned doctor contributes statistics and personal views at a forum for discussing anti-abortion laws.

Famous Personalities

Bruno Bettelheim (psychologist), John Curtis (entomologist), Charles Gates Dawes (financier and former American Vice-President), Kate Millet (feminist author), Maria Montessori (psychologist and educationalist), Donald O'Connor (actor), William Saroyan (author and playwright), Jack Valenti (film executive), Raquel Welch (actress).

— **69** —

Sun Virgo ♍ Moon Sagittarius ♐

The principal mark of genius is not perfection but originality, the opening of new frontiers.
ARTHUR KOESTLER

*Many a man has fallen in love with a girl in a light so dim he would
not have chosen a suit by it.*
MAURICE CHEVALIER

Themes

EARTH/FIRE Intellectual enthusiasm; restless but controlled; great
integrity; genuinely helpful; intelligent; quick wit; moralistic; critical;
dedicated student and teacher; urbane; a thinker and a communicator.

Do you want fact or fiction? Do you want a useful, upright, dedicated
life or freedom to roam the universe? Your independent and inquiring
mind may sometimes be at odds with your desire for neat, definite
answers. Your spirit yearns for a concrete system which addresses all
the moral, philosophical and religious dilemmas that concern
humankind. But you embrace ideas so passionately that reality could
never live up to your expectations.

One side of you is truly expansive, restless, philosophical and eager
for adventure and learning, whilst the other is utilitarian, analytical,
sensible and hard-working. Inspired by large concepts and great
achievements, open spaces and new people, you easily imagine
yourself in all kinds of exciting places and situations. This side of you is
courageous, optimistic and usually ready to have a go.

Your Virgoan side, however, brings you down to earth. Sometimes
it can make you despair at the seeming futility of attempts to 'get it
right', whether this is to do with your job, marriage or holiday, or with
the government, the Church or other broad, humanist concerns. At
such times, philosophical inspiration becomes philosophical
resignation, and you soldier on, determined to figure out and then
master the possible in order to improve your life. For understanding
and improving life is what you are all about.

To marry these two sides of yourself you need to become more
aware of how your preconceived ideas influence the way you
experience people and events, and how they can set you up for
disappointment. You have high standards, for yourself as well as for
others, and can be quite critical of people who stoop to conquer, so to
speak. If your beliefs are offended you can get high-minded and aloof,
even though inwardly you are more often quaking than
congratulating yourself.

Although you have a strong sense of propriety and duty, you love to throw out the rules and play truant more than once in a while. You love critical discussion, travel and study. Your idea of fun is an impromptu picnic or visit to the theatre, and you really come alive as the suave raconteur and the prim-and-proper eccentric in a gathering of amusing people.

Essentially you are a kind person, and sometimes very reticent about advancing your own deeply felt views. Your generous concern for others, coupled with your impeccable discretion, means that you could be adept at gestures such as quietly placing the perfect book in a friend's path, one that you guessed might assist in some important quest.

You need to nurture your vivid imagination and then anchor it with your capable, pragmatic side. Your visionary qualities and industriousness can take you far in many fields: you make an excellent teacher, counsellor, lawyer, clergyman and travel guide. Your Virgoan critical bent helps you to bring your Sagittarian dreams down to manageable proportions, and makes you realize that Earth is not such a bad place to take a journey.

Relationships

In close relationships you need mental affinity and plenty of space, and the only thumb you want to be under is your own. Sentimental and idealistic rather than romantic, you are genuinely humanitarian and seek to show your feelings in practical ways. You tend to look for paragons of perfection, and disillusionment occurs when you meet, repeatedly, the huge gap between the ideal you fall in love with and the actual flesh-and-blood, imperfect person.

You are a curious mixture of egalitarian and elitist sentiment, and tend to believe in an absolute hierarchical order of things. It makes rational sense to you, and it frustrates you when people cannot see the sense of things the way you can – it is so obvious!

Your Greatest Strengths

Fine intellect; ingenuity and perception of essentials; combined realism and optimism which makes you an excellent teacher; the way your pragmatism brings your vision down to earth; friendliness and readiness to serve, help and guide.

Your Greatest Weaknesses

Moral certitude; desire for 'reasonable' answers in the face of human suffering; lack of empathy and tendency to judge those who appear to live without guiding ideals – Socrates said 'the unreflected life is not worth living', and he may have shared this Sun–Moon combination!

Images for Integration

A bespectacled librarian locks the door at closing time and transforms into Superwoman ... An anthropology class goes on a field trip.

Famous Personalities

Maurice Chevalier (actor), Wernher Erhardt (positive-thinking guru), Arthur Godfrey (broadcaster), Karen Horney (psychoanalyst), Arthur Koestler (author), Michael Scott (mystic and scholar), Mary Shelley (writer), Margaret Trudeau (wife of former Canadian prime minister), Hank Williams (country singer).

— 70 —

SUN VIRGO ♍ MOON CAPRICORN ♑

Puritanism – the haunting fear that someone, somewhere, may be happy.
H.L. MENCKEN

Never compose anything unless the not composing of it becomes a positive nuisance to you.
GUSTAV HOLST

You can't teach an old dogma new tricks.
DOROTHY PARKER

Themes

EARTH/EARTH A rational pragmatist; streamlined efficiency; self-doubt and ambition; modest; sceptical; clear-headed; purposeful; quiet dignity; elegant simplicity; a polished professional; methodical; organizing ability; kind and helpful; diligent; a private perfectionist; frugal.

Are you a self-restrained critic or a diligent creator? Are you a self-demanding workaholic who justifies personal sacrifices through the long-lasting contributions you hope to make? Do you analyse the data, get at the truth, but then wonder despondently about the meaning of life? Do you prefer living a quiet hermit's existence, far from the madding crowd, but find that some sort of public acclaim is necessary for you to feel okay about yourself?

You are an extremely capable, kind-hearted, but serious and single-minded person who can focus exceptionally well on your vocation – and it must be a vocation, not just a job, because you have to believe in what you are doing. There is a self-contained and purposeful quality about you which enables you to pursue your chosen path with quiet determination and long-term stamina. You also hope that your efforts will help to make the world a better, more efficient and more beautiful place. Towards this end you direct your intellectual powers to question, analyse and fine-tune your medium.

You are naturally ambitious, a quick learner, discriminating and industrious, and want to give of your very best in whatever you do. Nonetheless, as one of life's natural critics, you are the first object of your own criticism. So you sometimes sink into despondency; you struggle with self-doubt, self-reproach, and feelings of inadequacy. But you are not a quitter; you learn to let go of old convictions so you can become the superlative professional you want to be.

As you are extremely good at managing resources, you could easily fall into an organizational role. You are mentally quick and practical, and if you cannot get to a teacher, you will teach yourself whatever you need to know. Very much a hands-on person, you are usually able to do-it-yourself very much more effectively and economically than almost anyone else, quite possibly to the chagrin of those around you. In your eagerness to help, take care that you do not outdo everyone else with your efficiency and superb capabilities.

You want the plain facts and the unvarnished truth; therefore you make an ideal literary critic or editor. You also require tangible proof of your achievements; you want concrete products that bear the mark of your self-expression, your blood, sweat and tears. You may enjoy working with your hands to produce exquisitely chiselled fine art or precisely executed pieces of music. It is as though you were born with an assumption that life is about work and dedication. When you win the prize, you do not gloat – you just look for more work. You may need to learn that the quality of your life can be enhanced by periods of frivolous self-indulgence.

Relationships

You are slow to enter into relationships, but when you do it is with a deep sense of commitment and duty. A certain self-restraint follows you all the days of your life, although you warm up and relax more in the second half of life. Your modesty is charming, even disarming, when people get to know you, because its source is your purity of intention in all your endeavours.

You are dependable and expect to work for your keep, and to get back what you give out to others. But until people *do* get to know you, you can appear cold and aloof, and if you get hurt you will retreat into a very tight, secure place inside yourself. A proneness to separate yourself from your loved one with sullen moods makes you not always easy to live with. But most of the time you make a delightful companion because you are thoughtful, kind, a good listener and seriously interested in making your life work. Your emotional insecurities can make you seem a little self-centred, but when you feel appreciated, understood and loved, all your caring qualities blossom. You are a bit enigmatic as well, and your depths slowly open and develop in a secure, loving relationship.

Your Greatest Strengths

Remarkable ability to organize and discipline yourself to be efficient and productive; fine critical mind and refined aesthetic taste and sense of proportion; dedication to excellence; quiet, constant devotion to friends and family – your giving is full of substance, not rhetoric.

Your Greatest Weaknesses

Nervous timidity and a proneness to hide your light under a bushel; to be over-critical of yourself and of others which leads to a sense of futility; a defensive preoccupation with rational justifications for everything you feel and do.

Images for Integration

A headline: 'Small-town boy makes good' ... A student passes entrance examination to a prestigious technical college ... Fine bone china.

Famous Personalities

Augustus (first Roman emperor), Anton Bruckner (composer), Anne Diamond (television presenter), Theodor Dreiser (writer), James Franck (Nobel prize-winning phycisist), Gustav Holst (composer), Charles B. Huggins (Nobel prize-winning biologist), H.L. Mencken (author), Dorothy Parker (writer), J. Pierpoint Morgan Jr. (business man), Jaroslav Seifert (Nobel prize-winning poet).

— 71 —

SUN VIRGO ♍ MOON AQUARIUS ♒

No woman can call herself free who does not own and control her body.
MARGARET SANGER

The real lost souls don't wear their hair long and play guitars. They have crew cuts, trained minds, sign on for research in biological warfare, and don't give their parents a moment's worry.
J.B. PRIESTLEY

If the world does not please you, you can change it.
H.G. WELLS

Themes

EARTH/AIR Reliable yet rebellious; a progressive thinker; intellectual; principled; imaginatively scientific; dispassionately critical; forward-looking; a reformer; a purist in love and work; naive eccentric; philanthropic dedication; worthy ideals; kind-hearted; wholeheartedly and pragmatically helpful.

Are you impeccably precise in your thinking but emotionally erratic and unpredictable? Do you think of yourself as a sane, law-abiding citizen but find you can suddenly go off on what others consider to be odd tangents which feel perfectly normal to you? Do you want the global vision but find you get stuck in the minutiae of logic?

You bring a conscientious dedication to both the large social concerns and the small domestic hobbies that claim your attention, and you have great capacity for hard work. There is something endearingly odd about you. Although you can be very exact and self-contained, which gives the impression that your horizons are strictly limited by personal duties, you can surprise everyone with your grasp of large ideas and your nonchalant attitude towards the whole spectrum of society, its problems and idiosyncracies.

You have the potential for vast understanding, but when it comes to emotional savvy you can be naive and a bit wooden. You are a social creature, but on your own terms – although helpful and supportive, you need freedom, sanity and space to get on with your own life.

You have a rather scientific, detached, objective approach to life, and an urge to understand and explain, rather than go with the flow. You value order and rules that organize society into one well-functioning, environmentally friendly family. But without even thinking you will make up your own rules and go your own way, for you listen first and foremost to your own conscience which tells you where your best path lies.

You have a quirky sense of humour, which alternates with a very dry, matter-of-fact presentation and quiet humility. Your unintentional mastery of 'understatement' gives you charm. And an interesting mixture of traditional and progressive thinking makes you a true egalitarian, critical in taste and judgement but essentially devoid of prejudice. Your rational powers are excellent; you are single-minded and industrious and this helps you to succeed in any career that you deem worthy of your time and energy. If you are not careful, however, your personality can become too hygienic – remember, you are a human *being* not a human *machine*.

You may be a people watcher, given to analysing motivations, dilemmas and the passional conflicts which you yourself wish to avoid, always from a once-removed position and perhaps with a view to finding practical answers to age-old human problems. Your empirical turn of mind and detached stance makes you a good psychologist or theoretician. In politics you are inclined to favour pragmatic socialism with its concern for the working man, and the practical, smooth regulation of things for the betterment of all. Be it in medicine or social work, teaching, politics or international planning, you are attracted to work which allows you to be of original and practical worth and service to the larger community.

Relationships

You are the most devoted and possibly naive of people, a friendly, kindly, yet aloof soul who can be out of touch with, or at least untouched by, your own passions. Emotions are a bit thorny for you, for they can erupt from nowhere, disconnected from your normally reasonable grip on life.

You enjoy friendship when it is based on common intellectual interests. You are thoughtful, kind and philosophically disposed to social intercourse. In intimate relationships, however, where dependency and emotional vulnerability feature strongly, you can get nervous, as though something will be demanded of you that you either do not feel you can deliver, or will cramp your style.

You never mean to hurt your loved ones, but you need to remember not to treat them as patients or as interesting but demanding objects for study. Your monk-like self-sufficiency makes you assume others should be the same way – independent and self-controlled. With a bit of practice in communicating how you feel, and a bit less reliance on logic, you make an admirable domestic companion, full of both supportiveness and surprises!

Your Greatest Strengths

Great powers of detached observation and impartial analysis; shrewd intelligence; idealistic social concerns and conscientious dedication to work; quiet dignity and respect for the dignity of all.

Your Greatest Weaknesses

Overfastidious eye and tendency to focus on black and white facts; proneness to distance yourself from others and from your own feelings; to over-invest in perfection and thus to remain pessimistic, unsatisfied, and lonely.

Images for Integration

Staring into a microscope, a scientist sees the past and future writ large ... Aliens land and embark on building a new and improved world order.

Famous Personalities

Lord George-Brown (politician), Denis Healey (politician), Ruby Keeler (dancer and actress), Ted Key (cartoonist), Sophia Loren (film actress), Jesse Owens (Olympic runner and jumper), J.B. Priestly (writer), Jimmie Rodgers (hillbilly-country music star), Margaret Sanger (pioneer of planned parenthood), Fay Weldon (writer), H.G. Wells (writer and social philosopher).

— 72 —

SUN VIRGO ♍ MOON PISCES ♓

One ought, every day at least, to hear a little song, read a good poem, see a fine picture, and, if it were possible, to speak a few reasonable words.
GOETHE

The love of life is necessary to the vigorous prosecution of any undertaking.
SAMUEL JOHNSON

Themes

EARTH/WATER Insightful; compassionate; modest; poetic; kind-hearted; refined taste; sense of humour; inspirational; helpful;

dedicated servant; natural counsellor; intuitively wise; discreetly generous.

Are you a scientist or an artist? Potentially you are both, for you possess the scientist's mind and the artist's heart. Your personality combines a fine intellect, lots of common sense and a deep feeling for the woes of humanity. You have an active inner world in which you absorb, analyse and digest knowledge, whilst at the same time your sixth sense is busy slotting everything into place according to your feelings.

Logic, compassion and practicality blend within you to make you a steadfast and devoted friend and one of the most useful members of society. At your best you are the wise sage who derives profound meaning out of the exercise of carrot-peeling or any mundane task. And through serving the needs of others you can shine as a model of humanity. But you are naturally shy, and prone to anxiety and nervous introspection. Your critical, self-effacing tendencies can eat away at your creative energies – which are considerable when you are centred and at peace with yourself. It is when you manage to shake off your timidity that you can make the most of your talents.

You possess the capacity to see things intuitively as a whole. Additionally, you are able to work systematically, one step at a time towards the completion of your goal – be it an artistic design, mastering a violin concerto, writing a book, learning to sail a boat or producing the perfect soufflé. It is as though your mind works so closely with your heart that the result of your efforts is infused with your whole being. You hold within your mind the purpose, the method and the desired end-product, so you become completely absorbed in your activities. Work is an art and an act of devotion for you. Your strivings towards excellence are aided by your rich imagination and penetrating insight into people and situations.

Emotionally, there is no one more giving and practical in the expression of affection than you. You are one of life's servers and healers. Whether in social work, medicine, teaching or art, you have a way of detecting the hidden need, and finding the best way to respond to others with the right word and deed. You can, however, be so giving and oversensitive that you easily get hurt, and wonder why people are not as considerate and conscientious as yourself. Your touchiness can make you clam up and fret, at which time your own troubles – real or imagined – assume tragic proportions in your mind. At such times you are prone to depression. Criticism is hard for you to bear, even though you tend to be a stringent self-critic with regard to your own work.

Relationships

In emotional relationships you need the tender and complete acceptance of your loved one – which is what you give in return. You have a dreamy, romantic side to you that may find life too harsh, and which may seek various avenues of escape, such as day-dreaming.

Your Piscean empathy and tendency to merge emotionally with another makes it easy for you to become a martyr. This may often be at variance with your conscious striving for self-definition and your dislike of being in anyone's debt, but it also increases your understanding of the human condition. As you can put yourself easily in the other person's shoes you have no problem in forgiving the fragilities and foibles of others.

You are not particularly self-assertive, but you possess a strong moral sense which makes itself felt in both your personal and professional life. That, plus your compassionate understanding and deep humility, make many people admire you and want your company. Your only problem may be learning how to say no!

Your Greatest Strengths

Sound mind and intuitive insight; devotional nature and reverent attitude to work and life in general; charming sense of humour; humanitarian desire to serve others and the larger good.

Your Greatest Weaknesses

Tendency to get swamped by details in your attempt to reach perfection; shyness and diffidence about expressing your views; inclination to worry too much about everything, from your own problems to the famine in Ethiopia.

Images for Integration

The scientist has a dream and then, in his sacred laboratory, puts the finishing touches on his magnum opus ... A peasant rests in the wheat field, and shares his bread, cheese, wine and wisdom with the hungry labourers.

Famous Personalities

Claudette Colbert (actress), Anselm Feuerbach (painter), Goethe (poet and dramatist), Lenny Henry (actor, comedian), Christopher Isherwood (novelist and playwright), Michael Jackson (pop singer), Maurice Jarre (composer), Samuel Johnson (lexicographer and writer), Jules Romains (writer and philosopher), Pierre de Ronsard (poet).

Chapter Ten

Sun in Libra

— 73 —

Sun Libra ♎ Moon Aries ♈

Hell hath no fury like a liberal scorned.
DICK GREGORY

A politician is an arse upon which everyone has sat except a man.
E.E. CUMMINGS

Themes

AIR/FIRE Sociable; lively; restless; wilful; entertaining; independent but needs others; self-development through relationships; diplomatic; enthusiastic sense of justice; influential; convivial and convincing; controversial; cheeky; fun-loving; romantic.

You are the peace-making crusader, the champion of your team, the feisty but cool-headed idealist who has spunk and courage. With your high energy levels and great ideas, you are good at initiating projects – and parties! – yet you rely on others to help you bring your plans into being. You need to be actively engaged in life and to be working towards something – often with an unusual or eccentric twist to it. Although you inwardly feel yourself to be strongly independent, you are easily jolted by emotional conflict and criticism from others. The latter can truly throw you off beam.

261

You can be a lively and sensitive companion, capable of bringing optimism, an exciting sense of challenge and great expectations to joint enterprises. Your gentle, diplomatic manner can, however, suddenly break down in the face of opposition as, contrary to appearances, you do not budge on issues when you have really made up your mind.

How do you balance your aspirations for social harmony with your strong, me-first, impulsive personality? You need others, but you want to be left alone. Other people's experiences and opinions stimulate and feed you intellectually, but you feel you have to do things your own way in the end anyway. You want love, respect and friendship, but you can be hard to live with at times because you chafe at the mundane constraints of everyday life. When you feel hemmed in you may get restless, argumentative and fault-finding. It is a combination of your Arien rashness and your Libran search for the ideal: you want the best but resent what you have to sacrifice to get it. You feel independent and have a strong need to define yourself, but you discover that other people help you to do just that. Love them or hate them, people must be in your life, and personal relationships will provide an important path to your growth and self-development.

There are usually gender issues with this combination. If you are a woman, you may not be satisfied with traditional female roles. You are outspoken and ambitious and will seek some creative form of expression for your fine intellect and potential artistic skills. For a man, this combination confers refinement and elegant persuasion to all your arguments, so that with strategic manoeuvres you learn to manage people beautifully and get exactly what you want.

Regardless of sex, you can be amazingly companionable, enthusiastic, influential and deeply romantic – so much so that, when your passions are spent, your romantic ideal keeps you gallivanting from one partner to the next. A stable emotional life is what you require in order to grow. You must try for a workable alliance within you between your need for dominance and your need for intimacy and partnership. Sacrificing some of your freedom for the sake of the greater good (such as your relationship) is one of the main themes that will crop up in your life.

Relationships

Relationships are central to your life, and there are probably many times when you depend on your partner more than you care to admit.

You love the ritual of love – the romance, the excitement, the courtship, the suspense – and then the fight! If the spark goes out of your relationship, you will look elsewhere for a thrill. You tend to get impatient with the idea that you might have to do a bit of growing up and create some of your own excitement yourself, but your emotional life will improve – in depth and consistency – if you do.

Too much insistence on having your own way will tend to cut you off from your ability to make sound judgements, and from your deeper needs as an individual. You require companionship, and to discover that you can still be true to yourself in a relationship of equals.

Your Greatest Strengths

Your combined personal strength and diplomacy which wins people over; desire for justice and commitment to defending the underdog; quick mind and persuasive use of argument; strong aesthetic sense; daring spirit and courage in trying new things; ability to bring warmth and adventure to all your relationships.

Your Greatest Weaknesses

Difficulty in reconciling your need for independence as well as dependence on others; awkward stubbornness when you have reached your limit; tendency to sabotage your chances for harmony (which you badly need due to your strong competitiveness); inclination to make rash judgements when you think you are being astute.

Image for Integration

A little girl and a little boy barter whilst playing on a see-saw. She wants his toy gun; he wants her cream cake. They decide to share.

Famous Personalities

Shaun Cassidy (singer and actor), John Coltrane (jazz musician), e.e. cummings (poet), Enrico Fermi (physicist), Dick Gregory (comedian), Luciano Pavarotti (opera singer), Cliff Richard (singer and actor), Giuseppe Verdi (composer), Simon Ward (actor), the Duchess of York.

SUN LIBRA ♎ MOON TAURUS ♉

I produce music as an apple-tree produces apples.
CAMILLE SAINT-SAËNS

The teacher's job is to evoke love. This he can only do by loving.
A.S. NEILL

Themes

AIR/EARTH Sensitive taste; love of music and art; cooperative; good business sense; a campaigner for social welfare; sentimental; affectionate; understanding; generous; nurturing; romantic; self-indulgent; ability to infect others with gaiety and laughter; vanity; stylish; upper class.

Are you interested in abstract theories, impartial judgements, balanced and open-minded discussions, but at the same time find that you dig in your heels at the thought of change? Your personality is paradoxical – and at the same time enormously attractive. This is because you put across your ideas with a kind of impartial passion – some would call it innocence – that surprises and convinces others.

You want to understand your world from the outside in, so you live and enjoy life with both intellectual clarity and deep, earthy conviction. You are an ethical person and want things to make moral sense, yet at the same time you simply want to 'be' – to experience and enjoy the exquisite, meaningful beauty all around you. You require harmonious, pleasant surroundings and certain basic inalienable rights – you believe that everyone has a right to health, wealth and adequate education – and without these you may feel that life is not worth living. Your conviction for these values may take you into politics or social work where you can be a persuasive and charismatic reformer.

You are either an artist or an art connoisseur, a musician or a lover of music, and a much-liked and probably sought-after member of your social circle. There is something about you that makes you very easy to have around, as indeed you often are, as people are important to you.

You often feel you know what is best for them and can argue, in the nicest possible way, until the cows come home about the ideas and causes that are important to you.

You are cooperative rather than competitive, and believe that everyone's view should be heard, yet you have an instinct to control, which can sometimes make you seem intractable. You can infect others with a sense of gaiety and laughter, and although you are devoted to your partner you are still a notorious flirt – not in order to stir up excitement but because you possess such tangible allure and sociability that you just cannot help it. A natural carer and counsellor, you know how to put people at ease, and to make them feel special and cared for, and people may fall in love with you temporarily (or permanently!) if you are not careful.

You are idealistic and hedonistic at the same time, capable of turning any mundane chore into an art form. You love the lush beauty of nature and have a keen eye and nose for all things pleasing to the senses. In a unique way you combine strong reasoning powers with good earthy instincts. Extremely friendly, helpful and optimistic, you are so attractively persuasive about the things you believe in that others will find you irresistible most of the time. You exude a sense of effortless charm which makes you seem pliable and easy-going, and then suddenly you surprise people with your purposefulness and stubbornness.

Relationships

Home and family life are central to your happiness, and just as important as vocational interests. The way to get to you is through your need for affection, harmony, understanding and love. At times your sentimental idealism sweeps you along and propels you into romantic escapades, but when you have found your mate you are a devoted and steadfast lover, both friendly and amorous, dignified and warm, conservative and sensuous.

Your capacity for being both mentally and emotionally engaged in your artistic or business interests, in your friendships and your intimate relationships, is the magic ingredient that makes those on whom your gaze falls feel so flattered.

Your Greatest Strengths

Graciousness; practical and emotional generosity; sensitivity to the needs of others; balanced and patient commitment to justice; refined aesthetic sense and perception; abiding faith in the power of love.

Your Greatest Weaknesses

Tendency to be oversentimental and gullible; to over-indulge yourself both emotionally and materially; a proneness to get stuck in black-and-white moral positions; your sometimes superficial salesmanship style.

Images for Integration

Newlyweds go on a gourmet's tour of Italy for their honeymoon ... A lecture on ancient Greek architecture and town planning.

Famous Personalities

Angie Dickinson (actress), Carrie Fisher (actress), F. Scott Fitzgerald (writer), George Peppard (actor), Harold Pinter (playwright), A.S. Neill (educationalist, founder of Summerhill), Camille Saint-Saëns (composer).

— 75 —

Sun Libra ♎ Moon Gemini ♊

Time is a dress maker specialising in alterations.
FAITH BALDWIN

There are no really ugly women. Every woman is a
Venus in her own way.
BRIGITTE BARDOT

The immature poet imitates; the mature poet plagiarizes.
T.S. ELIOT

Themes

AIR/AIR Lively intelligence; entertaining; communicative; youthful; questioning; conciliatory; diplomatic; a love of words and ideas; clever; artistic; graceful and charming; witty; neighbourly; a natural teacher; seeks justice, understanding and novelty.

You have a youthful, engaging personality and, as is characteristic of youth, you have lots of questions. Direct questions about people and the world are never far from your quick, persuasive lips, but will you *ever* be satisfied with the answers you get? And do you seriously question *yourself* and your own motives, or is that a taboo area which brings out all your most cunning diversionary tactics? Indeed, is life a serious business or is it something of a cosmic joke?

Of the many questions life poses you, some of the key ones centre around your relationships with others. You like attention and to be accepted and well-thought-of by others, but you also get bored easily and like to play devil's advocate, to have your say and let others think what they will. Like Groucho Marx, you can aspire to social elegance and propriety, yet find that you instinctively take a much more ad-lib, happy-go-lucky approach to things.

Although deep friendships and one-to-one relationships are central to your life, you can be remarkably carefree, flippant and outrageously flirtatious. You like to see yourself as a thinker who lives a reflective life, and indeed you possess real intellectual potential. In order to make the most of it, however, you need to cultivate some perseverance. You glibly agree with the maxim that the unexamined life is not worth living, yet you easily get by without examining *too* deeply.

You have definite ideas about most things, which you can put over with great charm and persuasion. What you think, and what other people think, is all important to you, and you enjoy exchanging gossip, games and good times. Ideally, however, you would like to have a mind so clear that it sees beyond opinions. Sociability and lively discussion with friends is your lifeblood. You want to live your life as smoothly and intelligently as you can, and this may lead you to espouse some particular 'ism' or collection of dependable mottos which, in general, work most of the time.

Although you prefer harmonious intercourse, you have a gift for seeking and arguing both sides of any question. In other words, you cannot help stirring up a bit of healthy controversy. This characteristic is welcome if you work in academics, politics or the theatre, but it is not as appreciated in close relationships where you use that cunning wit of yours to wriggle out of tight corners and irksome responsibilities. This you may do when your own feelings or the emotional demands of others seem threatening, for although you are romantic enough, you do not suffer emotional inquisitions gladly.

Naturally articulate, versatile, socially skilled and humane, you can readily slip into other ways of looking at things. This is because you are truly interested in ideas, and you will do almost anything for a laugh. You use your logical approach to explore and reconcile the irreconcilable; that is, the enigmatic behaviour of people and society in general. You work well with others, and your easy-going, adaptable nature, and your relaxed, jokey, yet courteous approach to human relations, make you a natural diplomat who can be guaranteed to make any collaborative effort run smoothly.

Relationships

The other person in your life is of very great importance to you, though your casual and sometimes off-hand ways can seem to deny this. Close friends and loved ones fill your life with fascination and colour – you learn from them and are genuinely interested in what makes them tick. And they reflect back to you what makes *you* tick.

You have an intelligent approach to relationships and may well take the view that any two people can get along, so you will do your best to make your partnership work. The other side of your somewhat naive and sweetly reasonable, breezy approach to relationships is the turbulent depths of emotions which you crave and yet find frightening and a bit distasteful at the same time. Your mysterious emotional depths can take you by surprise and cause an imbalance which you really dislike. You can be a fickle chatterbox and a bit exhausting to your partner if you do not slow down long enough to delve deeper than surface facts.

Your Greatest Strengths

Clarity of your mind; impartiality; willingness to consider opposite viewpoints; lively and articulate self-expression; charm and genuine friendliness that puts people at ease.

Your Greatest Weaknesses

Your tendency to skim the surface and therefore never fully develop your talents; to try to cover too much ground and spread yourself too thin; to remain emotionally immature; and to be lazy and just rely on your luck.

Images for Integration

Birds circle in perfect formation on the breeze of a bright autumn day ... Having delivered a fair judgement, the chairman of a conciliation and arbitration board chats amiably with the previously opposing factions.

Famous Personalities

Faith Baldwin (writer), Brigitte Bardot (film actress), James Chadwick (brilliant experimental physicist), Edwina Curry (politician), Helene Deutsch (pioneer psychoanalyst), T.S. Eliot (poet, dramatist and critic), Bryan Ferry (singer), Madeline Kahn (comedienne and actress), Ursula LeGuin (author of *Earthsea* books), Arthur Lovejoy (philosopher and historian of ideas), Groucho Marx (comedian), Jean F. Millet (romantic painter), Barbara Walters (TV interviewer and news presenter).

— 76 —

SUN LIBRA ♎ MOON CANCER ♋

Sentimentality – that's what we call the sentiment we don't share.
GRAHAM GREENE

Losing love is like a window in your heart, everybody sees you're blown apart, everybody sees the wind blow.
PAUL SIMON

Themes

AIR/WATER Sensitive; emotional; moody; entertaining; adaptable; sociable; love of intimacy; caring and considerate; domestic; artistic; musical; intuitive; prudent mind; talkative; nervous; devoted friend.

You are the socialite of the family, a romantic individualist, ambitious for both career success in the outer world and for the intimate kinship that keeps you going. Sensitive to the feelings and needs of others, you use your 'feminine' intuition and amazing adaptability to help others as well as to protect yourself from disharmony.

You know what you feel, but is it really true? You are frequently torn between your inner emotional, often sentimental, response and your need for reasonable understanding, and for objective, clear-headed relationships. You like to think of yourself as impartial, fair and socially concerned, but when your personal feelings are touched or your safety threatened you suddenly become a sentimentalist, subject to envy and every heart tug in the book. This makes you moody, apprehensive and a little timid, as you are aware, at some level at least, of how powerfully other people can effect you.

Sometimes you are convivial and eager for friendly discourse. On such occasions your genuine interest in people, ideas and creative possibilities comes to the fore, as does your natural diplomacy and charisma. You can easily adapt and go with the flow in social situations, and if you are shrewd (which you usually are) you can use your adaptability in a personally advantageous way.

Intimate friendships in which true affection and trust are shared are vital for your happiness. When you feel appreciated and truly 'seen' you purr like a kitten and your creative adrenaline works overtime. There is nothing you would not do for those friends. At other times you sink into a brooding, withdrawn shell, wanting to be left alone to get on with your private life, your thoughts, impressions, problems and your creative inspirations. You get hurt easily, deplore any kind of unkindness, and can carry a strong resentment around until you feel justice has been restored. Your inner equilibrium is disturbed by injustice – you do not like it intellectually and it does not feel good emotionally, either. Your innate sensitivity can work both for you and against you, and this you know only too well.

Essentially you are a family person with a real need for a harmonious home life and a steady emotional environment. But differences in outlook and values and the introduction of new cultural influences into the family will be part of your life theme. This will stretch you and ultimately bring out the best in you.

You have a good mind for art, history, mythology, music and teaching. You want to venture out into the wider world and then bring that world back into your own private one, enlivening it with romance, vitality and personal meaning. You probably learn how to put your best foot forward and to get the best out of people with the minimum disruption to yourself. You may, therefore, become a good manager of people, understanding their needs and problems as well as inspiring them with your personal convictions, honesty and integrity.

Relationships

You have a tremendous need for love. Close relationships are a big part of your life and will bring out the best in you – eventually. Psychologically speaking, childhood behaviour scripts are deeply imbedded and can turn your mate into mum or dad before you know what is happening. But you are the most sensitive of mates, wanting to comfort, amuse and encourage your loved one, and you are very receptive to the same from him or her. Your pitfall is being too accommodating and also overly possessive and manipulative. You need to honour your vulnerable feelings, to bring them out into the open and not to be ashamed of them.

Your Greatest Strengths

Sensitivity, warmth and concern for others; emotional energy; intellectual curiosity and alertness; quiet individualism and respect for others' rights; artistic imagination and powers of communication; adaptability in the face of obstacles.

Your Greatest Weaknesses

A tendency to over-romanticize people and places; sentimentality; need to please others; emotional instability and vulnerability; proneness to self-pity and carping when people do not look after you in the 'right' way.

Image for Integration

A patriot rouses the masses to seek education, and then goes home to cook dinner for his friends.

Famous Personalities

Rona Barrett (Hollywood gossip columnist), Annie Besant (theosophist), John Kenneth Galbraith (economist), Graham Greene (writer), Clive James (critic, writer and television presenter), Olivia Newton-John (singer and actress), Paul Simon (songwriter and musician), Eleanour Roosevelt (Amercian first lady).

— 77 —

SUN LIBRA ♎ MOON LEO ♌

It is absurd to divide people into good and bad. People are either charming or tedious.
OSCAR WILDE

Hate the sin and love the sinner.
MAHATMA GANDHI

Twinkle, twinkle, little star,
How I wonder what you are!
Up above the world so high,
Like a diamond in the sky!
JANE TAYLOR

Themes

AIR/FIRE Vivacious; theatrical; vain; aesthetic; love of literature; idealistic; graceful; honourable; poetic; romantic; trusting; visionary; religious; ardent; high-minded; witty; flamboyant; has 'an unconquerable gaiety of soul'.

A passionate idealist and lover of noble and beautiful ideas, you are true to your inner vision of yourself as an artist of life and love, even to the point of sometimes appearing rather high-minded and imperious. Magnetic, warm, and charming, you are a social being committed to nurturing the highest potential in people and society. Something of a visionary, you have ardently romantic goals and are unlikely to compromise yourself on any issue of importance – and nearly all your issues are important. In fact, it is your burning conviction to your ideals that gives your personality a radiance that attracts people to you.

You are often a real character – fun-loving and playful, satirical, elegant and refined. Although you are a good practical joker, you do not relish jokes being played at your own expense. You can be temperamental and huffy if your pride is wounded, although when you get argumentative and overbearing it is usually because you are feeling wobbly and insecure. Your resilience is great, however, and even in the worst of times you possess an unconquerable gaiety of soul which sustains your optimism and creative inspiration.

You idealize partnership and seek stimulating, intelligent companions, and you are likely to be found in lively, artistic or literary social circles where you will often be the life and soul of the party. A very strong need to be loved and admired makes you vulnerable and somewhat dependent, although you prefer to think of yourself as the one on whom others lean. You need to guard against your intense idealism setting you up for continued disillusionment when you find that people have fallen off the pedestals on which you have put them. No one is as pure and perfect as you would like them to be.

Although you have great faith in yourself, you need romance and beauty to keep your inspiration flowing. You have a tendency to cover up any feelings of insecurity by behaving in a snobbish, outlandishly self-important way – substituting social position for true accomplishment. Although you express yourself with great personal flair, even when lacking confidence, your over-the-top behaviour can, ironically, make your deepest insecurities more apparent.

You like to be flattered but you cannot stomach empty adulation. Your theatrical skill is matched by your natural diplomatic bent. Thus, you make a charismatic political or social leader, an adored teacher, and a respected and loved friend and lover.

Relationships

Romance is the staple of your life – you need it, in some form, to survive. When you are in love you taste the ecstasy of completion, the purity of passion, the meaning of life, but you soon find that this is all a bit heavy for your partner. Love brings out your nobility and your highest ideals, but you will have more fun if you realize you are relating to a flesh-and-blood mortal who just wants to be loved for him- or herself.

You fall in love with love and with the self that you become when you are in love. You need to come down to earth a bit, take the stars out of your eyes for a while and detach from the courtly side of the love game. As you become more honest about your own doubts and inadequacies, you will be less affronted by those you find in your partner; and instead of a role player in an exciting drama, he or she will be allowed to become an individual, a human being in a human relationship. Taking out the rubbish and balancing the cheque book then become part of the joint effort to live joyfully and fully in the real world.

Your Greatest Strengths

Great kindness, playfulness and gentility; quick wit and capacity for seeing the dramatic and comic in everyday situations; nobility and ethical conscience; the artistic flair you bring to public service; generosity of spirit.

Your Greatest Weaknesses

Vanity; reliance on others' admiration and good opinion; luxury-loving self-indulgence and laziness; a stubborn refusal to recognize your own limitations; a tendency to make poor judgements when flattery will get you everywhere.

Images for Integration

A performance of *The Importance of Being Earnest* ... The managing director throws a birthday party... A political idealist is crowned leader by adoring followers.

Famous Personalities

Catherine Deneuve (actress), Eleonora Duse (actress), Mahatma Gandhi (Indian national leader), Evel Knievel (stunt motorcyclist), Angela Rippon (television presenter), George C. Scott (actor), Jane Taylor (poet), Margaret Thatcher (former British prime minister), Rev. Desmond Tutu (archbishop of Capetown), Oscar Wilde (playwright).

— 78 —

Sun Libra ♎ Moon Virgo ♍

I would say that music is the easiest means in which to express ... but since words are my talent, I must try to express clumsily in words what pure music would have done better.
WILLIAM FAULKNER

The 'what should be' never did exist but people keep trying to live up to it. There is no 'what should be', there is only what is.
LENNY BRUCE

Themes

AIR/EARTH Eminently civilized; fine intellect; social critic; correct behaviour; refined simplicity; considered actions; particular aesthetics; kind-hearted and helpful; philosophical and judicial mind; exquisite composure; devoted artist.

Are you the stylish peacemaker who dialogues with the whole spectrum of humanity – tramps, vamps, artists and aristocracy – to get their views? Or do you find security in fastidiously adhering to a black-and-white approach that weeds out the unsanitary elements of life?

You are the socially concerned artist, the diligent craftsman or the social theoretician with a flair for people. Essentially, you are the epitome of the civilized person – rational, articulate, peace-loving, modest, graceful, socially concerned and purposeful. People interest you and you interest others because of your understated charm and wit. Nevertheless, you are very picky about the people you take into your confidence, and quite matter-of-fact about where you stand on most things.

Even though you have a diplomatic way of delivering your criticisms and opinions, it is easy for you to appear aloof and rather cool. This is because your preferred mode of operation is to bring everything, even irrational emotions, to the bar of reason. Sometimes your desire to be fair and courteous conflicts with your conviction that you are right and your annoyance with others who do not share your opinion. You never actually want to upset anyone, however, and harmony and cooperation are ultimately more important to you than standing alone on principle. You can be scathingly honest when you relate with others, but your purpose is to find the bare bones of truth and to polish and refine them so as to reveal the most intelligent way to live.

You like to observe people because you learn from them, but you analyse, compare and weigh things up because of your intense dislike of hypocrisy. Your instinct for finding the practical principle underneath all the superfluous fuss is what makes you a good teacher. You probably enjoy helping to open other people's minds to the detailed beauty of the world through cultural jaunts and visits to museums, theatres, libraries and concerts. You enjoy the best achievements of civilization and prefer to leave the ugly bits out. Possessing an independent mind that naturally observes and analyses, you enjoy actively putting your knowledge and skills to practical use. This means that an independent career of some kind where you can hone your specialized talents as close to perfection as possible is where you are most likely to flourish.

Relationships

In relationships you have a kindly, devoted, affectionate nature, and you love to be of practical help to your loved one. At the same time, you enjoy attention and being pampered, and may have a kind of repressed vanity which sulks cheerlessly if your lover does not get the message that you are feeling sensitive.

Anything coarse or ludicrous turns you off, and you may find the irrational world of emotions a bit overwhelming and bewildering at times. Wildly emotional people seem messy and unattractive to you, but also extremely fascinating. You can feel intensely, but as you dislike losing control, you find more elegant and modest ways of showing your feelings.

Love for you must contain a strong mental rapport and a sharing of hobbies, artistic interests and humour. You may also be quite domestic and love gardening and cooking, although your purist, finicky tastes may be too rarified for most of your family. Although you tend to think of yourself as pretty self-sufficient, you will blossom and develop more confidence in a secure relationship where you can relax enough to learn how to be silly and play.

Your Greatest Strengths

Self-sufficiency; reasoning abilities; social concern; practical helpfulness; intelligence; aesthetic sensibilities; fine sense of discrimination; kindness; tactfulness; devotion to your values and loved ones.

Your Greatest Weaknesses

Finicky attitudes and dislike of messiness; inclination to over-analyse, critize and intellectualize feelings; a sometimes 'holier-than-thou' attitude based on your cleverness and quick summing up of the facts.

Image for Integration

With minute precision, a sculptor chisels the finishing touches to his work of art for the 99th time, and then sweeps up before leaving for his art-therapy group.

Famous Personalities

Lenny Bruce (comedian), John Evans (politician), William Faulkner (writer), Lucien Gaudin (Olympic fencer), Dante Gherst (opera singer), Frank Herbert (writer), Alberto Giacometti (sculptor), Deborah Kerr (actress), Horatio Nelson (admiral), Max Schmeling (world heavyweight boxer).

Sun Libra ♎ Moon Libra ♎

Charming people live up to the very edge of their charm and behave as
outrageously as the world will let them.
People say life is the thing, but I prefer reading.
LOGAN PEARSALL SMITH

The opposite of a correct statement is a false statement. But the opposite
of a profound truth may well be another profound truth.
NIELS BOHR

Themes

AIR/AIR Intensely idealistic; diplomatic; fine intellect; powers of comparison; zeal for justice; courteous; deplores harshness; gracious and friendly; vacillating; seeks relationships and romance; flirtatious; vivacious; chivalrous; refined way of treating others; 'gentle parfit knight'.

Do you like people, love people, need people, feel inspired by people, but find that you inevitably become utterly disillusioned with them? Diplomatic, graceful, sociable, you are something of a 'gentle parfit knight' (Chaucer), set on a happy, even course by the love of a good woman, man or ideal. But life throws you plenty of curve balls when that good man or woman turns out to be less than ideal.

Intellectually you tend to be a perfectionist, but, ironically, you are often a master at *laissez-faire*, realizing that everyone has their own idea about what is important and that every person's truth has value. You are an idealist, but when it comes to working with people you strive for the best, most balanced option. This entails plenty of discussion in order to arrive at a truly ethical, fair, consensus decision or plan of action.

You truly hate unfairness of any kind and will complain strongly if you or those you love and respect are wronged. In fact, you can really wage war in the name of re-establishing justice. Courtesy and refined manners are important to you – you cannot imagine anyone behaving crudely or with malice and so you are often rudely awakened by the harsher realities of human nature. Discord throws you off balance.

If you lived in ancient Greece, you would be an ideal philosopher, a follower of Plato, a soul for whom the True, the Good and the Beautiful are as real as the constancy of the seasons. In the modern world you could be a diplomat, an artist, a judge, a musician, a writer or a teacher – for in all these professions there is the common aim to express eloquently the most just and beautiful ideal or form.

Chaos and crudeness are anathema to your very being. In your efforts to restore harmony and live an ideal life, you will, however, find that you have to make many adjustments and compensations, which you are well equipped to do because of your gift for strategy and negotiation. Just be careful that you do not bend too much to fit into what you *think* others want. Even though you say you want peace and harmony, you actually come alive when you have to fight for what you believe in, when you are forced to jump off the fence and take command.

But just what *do* you believe in? It takes a while and contact with many people to find out. You may seem to jump onto one side of the fence, and then to the other, but it is only in order to see the truth in all views and to try to balance things out. In fact, you can use opposition to your own advantage, and will find controversy a catalyst for your own powers of understanding and decision-making.

Relationships

Whether professional, platonic or passionate, relationships play a central role in your life. In order to feel complete and right you need someone to meet you half-way; and you need feedback from others on all your ideas. You may espouse independence, but you need above all to be loved and balanced by a partner.

Romantic relationships are almost a 'wisdom path' for you. That is, you need them in order to find out who you really are, as though another will supply the missing ingredient in your own personality. You are romantic and loving, but your idealistic, airy designs help you to manoeuvre around those irksome, raw emotions which do not fit into your perfect paradigm. When things get too 'heavy' you may fly off to another potentially 'ideal' relationship.

Your breakthrough comes when you discover that your *real* Achilles' heel is dependency – depending on others to convince you that you are loveable. Then you will feel more secure and able to get on with the real challenge of making your relationship human as well as beautiful.

Your Greatest Strengths

Devotion to truth and justice; ready kindness and companionability; capacity to see your opponent's view; artistic inspiration; a desire to uplift and encourage others with understanding and optimism.

Your Greatest Weaknesses

A tendency to be indecisive; insistence on civilized, rational discussion to avoid real emotional involvement; dependency on others for your sense of wellbeing and confidence.

Image for Integration

A prince and princess of warring tribes fall in love and marry, and 1,000 years of peace ensue.

Famous Personalities

Jack Anderson (political journalist), Niels Bohr (physicist), Michael Douglas (actor), Dwight D. Eisenhower (former American president), Heidegger (philosopher), Derek Jacobi (actor), Felicity Kendall (actress), Angela Lansbury (actress), Christopher Lloyd (actor), Logan Pearsall Smith (essayist), Arthur Rimbaud (poet), Arthur Schlesinger (historian), Romy Schneider (actress), Bruce Springsteen (singer and songwriter), Lech Walesa (trade unionist and politician).

— 80 —

SUN LIBRA ♎ MOON SCORPIO ♏

The century on which we are entering – the century which will come out of this war – can be and must be the century of the common man.
HENRY A. WALLACE

Venice is like eating an entire box of chocolate liquers in one go.
TRUMAN CAPOTE

Themes

AIR/WATER Self-possessed; restrained cordiality; good instincts; astute, analytical and judicial mind; strategic; perceptive; love of the good life; ambitious, aloof and intense; magnetic and powerful; urge for social regeneration; love of debate; desire for truth; intellectuality v. sensuality.

A diplomatic, enticing, quiet demeanour plus great fortitude and penetrating insight combine to make you a charmingly formidable person. You are the blonde bombshell whose self-possession and sanguine smile says 'don't mess with me'; the cordial, debonair businessman who surprises colleagues with his rod-of-iron willpower and astute decisions.

Underneath that conciliatory veneer, your powerful instincts work overtime sizing up people and situations – and you do not miss a trick. A strong social sense takes you into the mainstream of life where your love of learning, your need for mental challenge and critical debate over social issues, and your hefty desire for respect will find you a vital, active role in the world.

You are a charismatic mixture of social idealism, emotional intensity and judicial detachment, and your exacting but diplomatic mind offers its criticism in a way that makes others sit up and take notice rather than wince. You are interested in people, politics and power, and how these three mega-ideas can be balanced to regenerate society. You can face the mess around you with unruffled poise and get on with making your analysis and judgement about what needs to be done. This, plus your innate friendliness, makes you enormously effective and popular, though some may be disturbed by your double messages.

The theme of fairness versus personal gain is one you will meet often in your life. You are a good detective and enjoy rooting out hypocrisy, calling a spade a spade, and standing up for the underdog. Equally, however, you have an appetite for security, comfort and luxury, and you are unlikely to neglect yourself or your material needs whilst busily performing your duties and upholding the law (as you see it).

You are something of a maverick, enjoying controversy and intellectual challenge where your social ideals and survival instinct come together to create a champion debator of great integrity. You are one of the few Sun Librans for whom decisions are not such a terrifying prospect, and because of your incisive mental abilities and your capacity to face facts, you would be a natural in politics or social-reform movements. Whatever you do, your sincerity, enthusiasm and positive approach win admirers and fans with ease.

Relationships

You can be very emotionally controlled but this does not alter the fact that you are very needful of love and emotional fulfilment. High standards keep you playing the field, but suddenly you fall head over heals for someone, and raw emotion takes over. True love has to have some passionate intrigue and angst to keep you interested – and you will create it if it is not forthcoming. One part of you may think you can handle a light-hearted affair, but unless you experience emotional depth you will not feel that any relationship is worth the bother.

Your emotions are powerful and your desires profound, hence you may fear the dependency on others that you sense could develop. That might feel too much like giving up your cherished autonomy and control, yet you need intensity and you need people. As you learn to trust yourself and the depth of your feelings, you will be able to risk the thrill and pain of intimate relationships without hedging your bets so much. You have a lot of pride; love will bring you the pleasures of humility.

Your Greatest Strengths

An exacting sense of justice; courage and tenacity in the face of difficulties; subtle, clever way of delivering clear-headed judgements; devotion to ideals and to loved ones; ability to weigh evidence impartially and to make decisions.

Your Greatest Weaknesses

Moodiness; temptation to manipulate others; self-interest which can masquerade as a crusader for social justice and harmony; a tendency to be overly suspicious and paranoid of other's motives, which can damage the ideal harmony between you and a loved one you want so much.

Images for Integration

An army general becomes patron of a new museum of art. A wolf and an elegant Burmese cat become inseparable friends.

Famous Personalities

Julie Andrews (actress), Christopher Booker (journalist and author), Truman Capote (writer), Jimmy Carter (former American president), Richard Gordon (writer), Trevor Howard (actor), François Mauriac (writer), Linda McCartney (photographer and musician), Roger Moore (actor), Henry A. Wallace (politician).

— 81 —

SUN LIBRA ♎ MOON SAGITTARIUS ♐

I explained to him that I had simple tastes and didn't want anything ostentatious, no matter what it cost me.
ART BUCHWALD

I see people out there enjoying themselves and I want to join them. I like the camaraderie of the House.
BETTY BOOTHROYD, SPEAKER OF THE HOUSE OF COMMONS

Themes

AIR/FIRE Calm yet restless; idealism; foresight; spontaneously helpful; ardent but flighty; generous spirit; adventurous; witty; intelligent; enthusiastic; missionary zeal; philosophical and philanthropic interests; persuasive powers.

Are you purposefully ambitious or easy-going? Are you happiest socializing with friends or when chasing the next project and a new horizon? Do you run everywhere or stroll at your leisure? Do you listen, all-ears to others or do you tend to hold forth about your latest obsession to the nearest audience you can find?

If you are doing what you want to do and what you believe in, life for you is a constant love affair, as you delight in doing your own thing, especially if it involves helping others. You are the soul of diplomacy, capable of seeing all sides of any question and genuinely wanting to be truthful and fair, but this does not prevent you from being fabulously enthusiastic about your own convictions and viewpoints. Your obvious integrity gives emphasis to your compelling charm and may help to hide from you your very real, if almost invisible, ambition and determination to make your mark.

The person who said 'If you want something done, ask a busy person' probably had you in mind. With your immense enthusiasm, energy, charm and humour, you manage to juggle several things at once. You not only show interest in, but also actually facilitate, other people's pet projects. An excellent organizer and communicator, you enjoy cooperative ventures. You also have the qualities of a natural diplomat, with an added touch of flair, elegance and extravagance.

Naturally considerate and concerned for the welfare of others, you can harness your high moral sense and forthright approach to further their needs and do what you believe to be the right thing. Although you are not always terribly practical, you can usually get down to the essentials and cut through protocol. You are helpful and obliging, but can also see how to get your own way in most things without necessarily bending the rules, and certainly without offending anyone – the only time this *might* happen is when your sense of moral correctness gets carried away and you become a bit holier-than-thou and unable to adapt to imperfect circumstances.

Your lively, original mind is constantly tuned in to the *Zeitgeist*, so you know spontaneously where things are going and what needs to be done. This gives you an immense flair as a populist and as a formulator and mouthpiece for grand visions that take society by storm, or for establishing businesses that speak to the needs of the masses. You want others to hear what you have to say; you love spreading the message and make an inspiring teacher, lecturer and educationalist. You may also excel in advertising where your charm, wit and ability to see patterns and recognize trends can take you far. Whether drawn to science or art, you love to look ahead and explore new paths. You may have a deep appreciation for philosophy, art and literature and may be especially drawn to music, though you enjoy expressing yourself and your ideas through most media, given half a chance.

Relationships

Although you have an independent nature, you are really quite romantic. Relationships are vital to your wellbeing, yet they can also be your Achilles' heel. As a born idealist, you are a natural team player and are prepared to give your all to those you believe in and to any worthy cause that has caught your imagination. But you do expect your enthusiasm to be reciprocated. In this you can be disappointed, for few can match your dedicated zest and commitment. Thus you are likely to suffer 'downers', periods of disillusionment when you wonder why you give so much of yourself to so many, for so little return. But you are resilient and forgiving and ever an optimist.

You need love and affection and you are devoted in your own fashion. But you are fairly independent-minded and do not really like to be interfered with by a disgruntled lover when you are engaged in one of your single-minded pursuits. Your loved one will need to keep up with a fast pace, as you like to travel and go places – both physically and intellectually.

Your Greatest Strengths

Your lively spirit of cooperative enthusiasm; grace; wit; eternal optimism; good humour; ability to see the larger vision and new ways of doing things; flair for persuasion and publicity.

Your Greatest Weaknesses

Tendency to overstretch yourself and over-estimate your capacities; to hide personal problems with workaholism; appearing too proud and aloof from others; emotional naivety; a lack of introspection and blindness to your own deeper motives.

Images for Integration

Bob Geldof spins Band Aid out of the air to help famine-stricken Africa ... An educationalist creates a Palace of Discovery to feed and stimulate young minds.

Famous Personalities

Elle Abel (radio journalist), Salvatore Accardo (violinist), Pierre Bonnard (painter), Betty Boothroyd (Speaker of the House of Commons), Art Buchwald (writer, journalist and humorist), Bruce Catton (historian, editor and journalist), Sir Joseph Chamberlain (English statesman and winner of 1925 Nobel prize for peace), Bob Geldof (musician and philanthropist), Sean Taro Lennon (singer son of John Lennon), Jean Perrin (Nobel prize-winning physicist), Dory Previn (songwriter), Richard Alan Meier (modernist architect), Christopher Reeve (actor).

— 82 —

SUN LIBRA ♎ MOON CAPRICORN ♑

*The Supreme Court has handed down the Eleventh Commandment:
'Thou shalt not, in thy classrooms, read the first ten.'*
FLETCHER KNEBEL

We must start coming forth with our energies ... our intellects, and our abilities to see what is right and what must be done, so the suffering will stop, and the phrase 'life, liberty, and the pursuit of happiness' begins to make some human sense.
BOBBY SEALE

Themes

AIR/EARTH Purposeful; pragmatic; courteous; tasteful; orderly; sophisticated; strategic; the just politician; tactful; good manners; opportunistic; skilful at managing people; diplomatic; powerful; controlling; persuasive; responsible; sensitive to the moods of others.

You are the artful manager *par excellence* – the sociable patriarch, the serious socialite, the professional artist, the steadfast friend. Your great sense of diplomacy and your instinct for power work together to make you a shrewd, formidable but likeable person. You believe passionately

286

in fairness, law and order, propriety and ethical systems, but you also believe strongly in yourself and in living a life of which you (or mum and dad) would be proud.

Fairly ambitious and determined to succeed, you can translate your idealism into prudent and decisive action and land yourself exactly where you want to be. But your sensitivity to others' opinions and needs is as strong as your personal ambition, and this makes you popular, impressive, trusted and well-liked. You give personal ambition a good name; you carry others along on your own tide of success; and you make others realize that power and wealth are okay when used in the right way. At the same time you need recognition for your successes and contributions, and in this sense you rely on others and are not as independent as you think.

You have a love of both material and moral order, and this can manifest in a number of ways – in a love of art and a desire to keep your home well stocked and aesthetically harmonized; in impecable manners and a respect for hierarchical relationships as well as rules and regulations; or possibly in a lively public spirit and in the need to fulfil an important role in the world. You take your responsibilities seriously and your word is as good as gold. You tend to have a cool, controlled exterior but underneath you are sympathetic, congenial, and paternal towards your close friends.

There is a side of you that likes solitude, but in general you want to be part of a team – preferably the team-leader. The truest way you express your love is to unfailingly provide what you have promised – letting someone down would be the worst thing you could ever do. But your ambitious, professional approach to life could be a little irksome to a partner or to close family members who do not want to be organized down to the last detail of relaxation periods. You are so good at organizing people that you may not know when to stop, and taken to the extreme, your innate managerial talents can turn into compulsive behaviour.

Your standards are very high, and you may need to cultivate more tolerance – you are something of a perfectionist and can be a snob if you are not careful. Comfort, beauty and designer labels are important to you – there really isn't an ounce of gypsy blood in you.

Relationships

A close relationship is very important for your wellbeing, and when you have found the right person you can be extremely devoted. You need to be adored – and respected – and when you know you have this you can relax and enjoy yourself.

One side of you wants to do everything with your partner, whilst another knows how to enjoy being alone and answering only to yourself. Perhaps somewhere deep inside you know that the final human condition is a lonely one, so you adjust and adapt and survive. You have to be careful that this part of you does not turn cynical and wish loneliness. You like to control things and you have to learn that being in a relationship is not the same as running a business.

Your Greatest Strengths

Executive skills and organizing abilities; your fair, rational and tactful approach to problems and your logical, sharp mind; social conscience and sense of responsibility; sense of duty; determination to win; sensitivity to the mood of your environment and the needs of others.

Your Greatest Weaknesses

Subtle talent for manipulation; an inner conflict between the cooperative spirit and blatant self-interest; an over-rational approach to relationships and emotional matters; a desire to keep all areas of your life completely tidy; an over-sensitive ego which takes offence too easily.

Images for Integration

At the annual company Christmas party, the chairman dresses up as Father Christmas and hands out new gold-engraved stationery for everybody ... The Statue of Liberty.

Famous Personalities

Johnny Carson (television talk-show host), Dr David Clark (politician), Joan Fontaine (actress), Fletcher Knebel (novelist), Pope John Paul I, Mary McFaddon (fashion designer), Helen Newington

Wills (champion tennis player), Anne Robinson (television and radio presenter), Bobby Seale (Black Panthers activist), Dimitri Shostakovich (composer).

— 83 —

Sun Libra ♎ Moon Aquarius ♒

If there's anything that you want,
If there's anything I can do,
Just call on me,
And I'll send it along with love from me to you.
JOHN LENNON

Whenever I prepare for a journey I prepare as though for death. Should
I never return, all is in order. This is what life has taught me.
KATHERINE MANSFIELD

Turn Off, Tune In, Drop Out.
TIMOTHY LEARY

Themes

AIR/AIR Spirit of cooperation; independent but romantic; rational; outgoing; communicative; love of truth and beauty; gracefully anarchistic; detached but humanitarian; objective; friendly; receptive; idealistic; vivid imagination; refined artistic taste; lively sociability.

Do you want to be one of the team but stand out as the awkward individualist who does not fit in? Do you have so much faith in the essential goodness, truth and beauty of life that you occasionally put a spanner in the works just, well, to make things more interesting? Are you well-meaning and receptive to others but also maddeningly resistant to being pinned down or put into a convenient pigeon hole?

You are a reasonable and idealistic person. For you, problems and dilemmas are things that can be resolved by reason, discussion and, at the last resort, by law. Although society, elevated principles, and social institutions matter to you, perhaps even more than the individual people who go to make them up and run them, for you it is vital that you *live* the principles that you hold in such high esteem. This makes you something of a visionary and prone to set yourself up for disappointment, for nobody – including yourself – could be as ideal as you would like.

Equality, liberty, fraternity is probably your credo, and no matter how impractical you might be, your friends will always glean the good intentions that inform your actions and behaviour. Although you can be charming, magnetic and witty, you willingly bring up contentious subjects and speak your mind with a kind of serene frankness. You look at all sides of any issue, and you bring a lively interest and enviable clarity to all social interchange. Even when you have strong views, you do not really want to rock the boat *too* much, and this makes you an ideal diplomat.

Friendships are enormously important to you, yet because you hate upsetting anyone, you find it difficult to be friends with anyone with whom you cannot be totally frank and open. The challenge you face again and again is how to keep the harmony and connectedness, without sacrificing your autonomy. Because you are such an equable, rational person, you easily feel threatened by powerful emotions such as hate and jealousy. They feel like enemies of the intelligent world order you seek, and yet paradoxically you are often attracted to emotional types.

Emotions tend to play hide-and-seek with you, pulling you into a merry chase that feels both exhilarating and frustrating. Emotional intrigue actually fascinates you, and you allow it to feed your instinct for self-dramatization. Whilst all the while pretending to figure out why someone could behave so irrationally, you are really getting a buzz and, if inclined towards the literary arts, planning your next plot.

Relationships

You come alive in social settings and know how people like to be treated. You can be flirtatious and sincere at the same time, both provocative and philosophical, demure and straightforward. All kinds of relationships are important to you, but True Love takes priority. In the midst of closeness and intimacy you can, however, somehow feel detached and remote, and yet strangely yearning for more.

Despite your strongly intellectual approach to life, you tend to romanticize people and to spin imaginative ideas around them and your relationship with them. You can be passionate and devoted enough, but you may retain a sort of childlike arrogance about what should and should not happen in relationships. You may be a brilliant psychologist with a profound understanding of human emotion and motivation and what makes people tick, but in practice you may find you feel overwhelmed by any measure of emotional tension or conflict. But you do not give up easily!

Your Greatest Strengths

Your natural sense of justice; social conscience and sense of belonging to the human family; kindness and desire to be of help; openness to new ideas; relaxed, forgiving approach to other people's foibles; aspiration to impartiality and to a universal viewpoint.

Your Greatest Weaknesses

A proneness to laziness and lack of ambition; naive insistence on rationality at all costs; an over-emphasis on the *laissez faire* approach which prevents definite answers and choices being made; a tendency to be too idealistic and impractical, which makes you ineffectual; blindness to your own dependence on others; inclination to dream your life away, building castles of romance and a Utopia in your mind.

Images for Integration

A group of literary radicals stage a 'love-in' to protest against government military policy ... In an elegant opera house, a trendy jazz musician performs rag time with a symphony orchestra.

Famous Personalities

Louis Auchinloss (novelist), George Gershwin (composer), Charles Ives (composer), Aaron Judah (novelist and children's writer), Katherine Mansfield (writer), R. D. Laing (psychiatrist), John Le Carré (writer of spy novels), Timothy Leary (psychologist, psychedelics' guru), John Lennon (musician and songwriter), Susan Lucas (novelist).

— 84 —

SUN LIBRA ♎ MOON PISCES ♓

There is nothing in the world I so reverence as beauty, whether of the world, of character or in a soul.
MARIE STOPES

None of us can help the things life has done to us ... at last everything comes between you and what you'd like to be, and you have lost your true self forever.
EUGENE O'NEILL

Themes

AIR/WATER Sensitive; artistic; adaptable; wistfulness; inconstant; sociable; talkative; an idealist of the heart; a dreamy romantic; loving; insightful; dependent; vacillating moods; perceptive intellect; generous; helpful; rich imagination; lazy.

Your ethereal charm and your genteel diplomacy make you one of the easiest and nicest people to have around. Your essentially diplomatic spirit and helpfulness mean that, in a very real sense, your bliss is making others happy. Idealistic and romantic, and often gullible and impressionable, you are a Utopian dreamer who will work, in either your personal or public life, for social equality.

You observe and analyse others; you seek others' views and, with your keen intuition, you reformulate your own. Your gifts of openness and imagination ennable you truly to 'get inside the dragon's skin', to see the other viewpoint, to feel what it is like to be someone else, and to effortlessly follow the mind of your nearest companion – whether he or she is a crook or a saint.

You have the mind of a detective, a psychologist or an actor. And because you intuitively know that motives are usually inextricably mixed, your impulse is always to see and to understand rather than to judge. This uncanny ability to peer into the private feelings behind the public face lends an air of mystery to your personality. You can be sociable and outgoing, but all the while your secret heart is testing the true climate, the real message in the emotional environment.

A natural worker on behalf of others, you are capable of both initiative as well as fitting in with larger plans. You can handle controversial matters smoothly and diplomatically, because the cause of unity is always close to your heart. You work gracefully and charmingly, hearing the feelings and thoughts behind another's words, and this makes you a superb counsellor and group facilitator. Your largeness of mind and humility in the face of the variety and vagaries of human nature give the impression of massive fairness and compassion, which endears you to others.

Relationships

Close relationships are the pivotal experience in your life, for through identification with others and their best interests, you find yourself and your own. The slippery slope for you, however, is losing your balance when romance takes over. Because you are so giving and sympathetic and yearn for harmonious union with another, your emotional nature is often easy prey to the delusions of romance. You desperately want to believe in your lover, and there is a part of you that secretly yearns to capitulate, to give your partner sole ownership, so you can bask in a dreamlike abandon. This can lead to that ever-present tendency to martyr yourself and unconsciously to assume the role of doormat.

Through being unable to stand others' suffering and giving too much in relationships you will discover the deep well of emotional strength you possess. And when you pull yourself out of hopeless emotional symbiosis and despair, as you will do periodically throughout your life, you will realize how strong you in fact are. Intense emotional involvements leave you either drowning in delicious puddles of self-pity or feeling newly self-defined, enriched, empowered and more committed to allowing your own self-taught wisdom to guide your actions.

Your Greatest Strengths

An intuitive mind; non-judgemental empathy; romantic devotion to the 'great ideals' (love, brotherhood, freedom); ability to listen and understand; capacity to retain the innocence of childhood even when portraying the silky elegance of stardom.

Your Greatest Weaknesses

Lack of conviction; vacillation at crucial crossroads; tendency to drift into new intimacies when the delights of romance fade; identifying with numerous viewpoints and positions – this creates confusion and leaves you out of touch with who you really are, and you may have to withdraw into yourself to regain your confidence.

Image for Integration

The curtains come down, the actor takes off his mask and, in privacy, looks into his mirror to find himself as a child of six with his imaginary friend.

Famous Personalities

James Clavell (writer and director), Aleister Crowley (occultist), Lillie Langtry (actress), Carole Lombard (actress), Yves Montand (actor), Anthony Newley (singer), Eugene O'Neill (playwright), Marie Stopes (feminist, family planner and poet), Pierre Trudeau (former Canadian prime minister).

Chapter Eleven

SUN IN SCORPIO

— ✦ —

— 85 —

SUN SCORPIO ♏ MOON ARIES ♈

Lord give me chastity – but not yet.

None save great men have been the authors of heresies.
ST. AUGUSTINE OF HIPPO

Nothing great will ever be achieved without great men, and men are great only if they are determined to be so.
CHARLES DE GAULLE

Themes

WATER/FIRE Large appetite for life; a fighter and strategist; volatile; impatient yet circumspect; dedicated; missionary zeal; ambitious; courageous; determined; egocentric; passionate views; wilful; proud and persuasive; ruthless; a tenacious individualist.

Fight! Fight! Fight! You rally to the call of battle of any kind with unstoppable courage and determination. Yet you can also find conflicts where others see none. This can arise from an inner duel between your instinct to assert yourself and your immense desire for self-control.

With your natural pride, ambition, vigour and self-esteem, you want to be great in some way and to make your mark upon the world. But should you go about it head first, rushing in where angels fear to tread? Or do you approach the world, deeply suspicious of its perils and pitfalls, determined to conquer it by strategy and stealth? Either way, you are one of life's warriors, and when you can bring together the fighter and the strategist within you, you are well-nigh invincible.

As someone with great personal and public ambition you 'aim high and stand upright'. You may, however, find yourself caught between a smouldering, silent intensity, which you find difficult to express, and a need to get out there, guns blazing, and tell the world what you are going to do – shooting straight from the hip. Despite your volatile swings in mood you can be highly committed and deeply persuasive in your approach to life, and will flourish best when you have some kind of overriding, personal mission with which you can identify.

When you do get your two very different sides together and start firing on all cylinders, you have at your command a passionate zeal and an intense drive for action. This goes beyond your own personal needs to the desire to champion larger causes. When that happens you can become positively inspiring and able to kindle in others the fires of your own convictions.

With your incisive mind, sharp wit, penetrating vision, foresight and tenacity of purpose you are a natural problem-solver who relishes nothing better than getting your teeth into an issue that others consider unresolvable. Whether in education or science, medicine or social work, art or commerce, you flourish on challenging situations which can harness your naturally tough and determined approach to life. You can be hard on yourself, driving yourself to fulfil self-imposed goals, and equally demanding on those in your orbit. Yet those to whom you can communicate your vision will find themselves profoundly motivated and empowered. Because of your self-punishing tendency, however, you sometimes push yourself on to the point of exhaustion. You therefore need to make conscious efforts to relax, rather than only stopping when you have finally run down your formidable reserves of energy.

Deeply aware of the harsh realities of human aggression, you may find that fast, pugnacious and highly competitive sports, such as ice-hockey and squash, serve as an excellent outlet for your own forcefulness, stamina and will to win. You are never frightened to mix it with those who cross your path. Indeed both friends and enemies are probably inclined to think of you as impatient and antagonistic, yet also as someone who can be relied upon in a corner to rally to the barricades and enthuse everyone with your sheer vigour and your wild, often riotous and ribald sense of humour.

Relationships

The best of friends or the worst of enemies, you are suspicious by nature. Although you can be an excellent leader, you are not naturaliy co-operative and tend to suspect anyone who is too friendly. Once you have committed yourself, however, you give nothing less than 100 per cent, and require the same in return. You are most at home in partnerships where there is a large degree of common interests, shared sympathies and a common cause for which you can jointly do battle. Emotionally intense, indeed passionate, you know whom you want to be with and you will set your sights upon winning them with an unremitting zeal. Unless you have learned to listen to others, however, you may lack sensitivity to your partner's real needs and sensibilities, and can tend to ride roughshod over his or her feelings, assuming that your point of view is the only one that really counts. Then you may be surprised to find that you seem to live in a state of disruptive ferment, constantly engaged in an antagonistic falling out with those you most love.

Your Greatest Strengths

Ability to motivate and inspire others; astute, penetrating mind; indefatigable courage; intensity of purpose; magnetism; charisma; powers of persuasion; willingness to give your all to any cause you embrace.

Your Greatest Weaknesses

Volatility; moodiness; impatience; intolerance of those who do not agree with you; attraction towards subterfuge; reluctance to see another point of view or to compromise readily; insensitivity to the feelings of others; workaholism.

Images for Integration

A crusader fights for her vision of truth ... A dedicated scientist pioneers new frontiers of knowledge.

Famous Personalities

St Augustine (Church father), Sarah Bernhardt (actress), Benvenuto Cellini (artist and adventurer), John Cleese (actor and comedian), Alain Delon (actor), Charles H. Dow (economist), Bill Gates (CEO of Microsoft), Charles de Gaulle (statesman), Sally Field (actress), Martin Luther (religious reformer), Lise Meitner (pioneering nuclear physicist), Dame Sybil Thorndike (actress).

— 86 —

SUN SCORPIO ♏ MOON TAURUS ♉

British management doesn't seem to understand the importance of the human factor.
PRINCE CHARLES

Our country needs not heroics but healing; not nostrums but normalcy; not revolution but restoration.
WARREN HARDING

Themes

WATER/EARTH A quiet strength; determination; concern for others; order and control cover a seething inner world; sensuality and self control; the mystery of the material world.

You are a person who loves the colours, scents, tastes, sounds and light of spring, yet who is equally drawn to the dark decay and mystery of autumn. More vividly than most, you see the world as a dance between the sensual delights and pleasures of life, and the dark, inevitable threat of death and corruption of innocence. In consequence you can be torn between bright optimism and brooding pessimism, between a desire to enjoy life and a need to protect life from its darker elements. When these two sides of you are working together you will be drawn by an intense idealism to uphold and promote all that is solid, lasting and dependable in society. Equally, you are likely to develop a passionate interest in work that encourages the healing and regeneration of society and individuals.

Though you can at times appear rigid, inward-looking and withdrawn, you are by nature intensely practical and factual, and are likely to be a touchstone and a dependable rock for all your friends. Although you rarely show it to the outside world, you have a rich inner life and imagination which draws you to look beyond the bald facts to the mysterious and the challenge of the unknown. This gives you a gift and fascination for any kind of research, be it in science, the arts or the world of business and society. Whether your career is in psychology, sociology, medicine, archaeology or the marketplace, you have a real sense of the basic impulses that motivate people – love, devotion, hate, fear and greed. Whatever you do, you need to feel a sense of commitment and dedication, and once your attention is engaged it is seldom distracted. You have a good sense of values and are likely to have shrewd business acumen, with a gift for handling money and resources well, though in practice you may have a love–hate relationship with money.

You are an essentially quiet and gentle, if passionate, individual, who thrives on harmony. At times, however, you can appear quite surprisingly dogmatic, stubborn and even pig-headed, especially when your pride and self-esteem seem threatened. You would see this resistance to others' viewpoints as a determination not to be deflected from upholding those values you know to be important. This inner strength and your mixture of compassionate sensitivity and plain common sense may draw you towards work in the area of counselling and the helping and caring professions. Whatever your vocation, you have a strong need to live a useful, dedicated life, to be of solid, practical service to the world, and to make your mark.

You can work hard and play hard, and swing between self-indulgence and self-denial, between feast and famine. Good food (you are probably an excellent cook), good company and good music can be central to you, yet equally you have an opposite desire to control such delights lest they run away with you. What is important for you is to be involved in a life to which you can give yourself in wholehearted dedication and commitment.

Relationships

You care deeply about those near and dear to you, and can readily sense what is going on in any situation. You can also, however, seem somewhat removed and remote, and may find it difficult to put your inner insights into words.

Emotionally you are intense and possessive, an all-or-nothing individual, and can develop rigid ideas about relationships. You will either be very emotional, abandoning yourself to sensual pleasures wherever you find them, or strongly contained, focusing all your passions within one special partnership to the exclusion of all others. In return you need and expect the same degree of devotion from your partner.

Your Greatest Strengths

Ability to dedicate yourself totally to what you are doing; your natural understanding of basic human needs and financial and economic realities.

Your Greatest Weaknesses

Wilful inflexibility; stubbornness; possessiveness; tendency to cling to what you know; self-doubt on emotional issues; occasional blindness to the motives of others.

Images for Integration

A celebrated surgeon amasses a fortune ... A successful businessman probes the mysteries of life ... Pluto takes Persephone into the Underworld.

Famous Personalities

Prince Charles (Prince of Wales), Michael Crichton (director and writer), Michael Dukakis (politician), Nanette Fabray (musical actress), Warren Harding (former American president), Clifford Irving (author), Robin Moore (author), Daniel Nathans (Nobel prize-winning micro-biologist), Erwin Rommel (German field marshal), Roy Sheider (actor).

SUN SCORPIO ♏ MOON GEMINI ♊

It is a good morning exercise for a research scientist to discard a pet hypothesis every day before breakfast. It keeps him young.
KONRAD LORENZ

*For lust of knowing what should not be known
We take the Golden Road to Samarkand.*
JAMES ELROY FLECKER

*If the devil doesn't exist, but man has created him,
he has created him in his own image and likeness.*

*I plunge into the depths, and, while analyzing every atom,
I search out the whole.*
FYODOR DOSTOYEVSKY

Themes

WATER/AIR Quick-witted yet intense; passionate yet detached; ambitious yet easy-going; penetrating insights; the gift of psychological understanding; communication; poetry; satire.

Butterflies, sunbathers and carefree good cheer flourish in the sunlight; deeply searching astronomers, thinkers, lovers and anxieties thrive at night. You cannot decide which is your time of day. Are you a bright, cheerful, witty, sociable and, let's face it, rather superficial soul? Or are you a dark, concerned, passionate, mysterious seeker of the inner secrets of the universe? You have a tantalizing duality which can be flippantly superficial about the seven deadly sins, yet deadly serious about trivia.

When you are able to combine and work with both sides of yourself equally, you become the natural, quick-witted, clever communicator of the wisdom of life and the emotions of the soul. This can be an especially powerful gift if you train as a writer, artist or musician, as it enables you to give your audience immediate access to hidden depths of feeling. Likewise, at a personal level, you are able to help others

301

connect with and articulate their own inner issues that they may not want to face or simply cannot see. This makes you a natural psychologist, counsellor and therapist, and also a writer and teacher who can translate the hidden and the mysterious into vivid images. When it comes to communication, one side of you is the village gossip; the other will take your secrets to the grave, though not without extracting their inner essence first.

You can combine intensity and fun and are likely to have a glorious sense of the ridiculous. One moment you are seriously marching into passionate battle; the next breaking into pointed laughter. This gives you the ability to defuse awkward situations and move from the tragic to the light-hearted in one step, making light of disaster and death, yet willing to look problems in the eye and acknowledge their place in our journey into the unknown. You can use the same technique and your sense of the absurd to alleviate and defuse your own tendency to develop irrational worries, fears and anxieties, which can otherwise so undermine you.

You are endlessly curious about human emotions (your own as much as other people's), and have a writer's gift for articulating and evoking the gamut of human experience. The dark, destructive and sexual dimension particularly fascinates you, and you can be both profoundly serious and devastatingly witty on such matters.

That said, however, you can find in practice that it is difficult to let yourself go emotionally and become really involved with others. There can be something of the voyeur about you. You constantly find yourself one-step removed, detached and needing to remain in control so that reason takes the place of the living passion of life. This in turn can cut you off from the spontaneity of your own emotions and leave you feeling very insecure and vulnerable.

Relationships

You yearn for passionate, emotional security, yet you want to keep your options open, flitting across the surface of life, plunging into the depths and up again for fresh air. You can blow hot and cold, being deeply involved and flirtatiously faithless. This can introduce a love–hate element as you are torn between the desires of attraction and the need to be free.

Your emotional life is both the hub of your life and an incidental appendage. In relationships you can be fiercely loyal, and yet naively unfaithful and experimental, as you love to explore the vivid world of changing emotional colours. You simply enjoy the widest variety of people and working out what makes them tick – preferably over a cordon-bleu meal.

Your Greatest Strengths

Restless energy and curiosity; quest for understanding; ability to translate feelings into ideas and to interpret the heights and depths of human passions into words; wit and insight.

Your Greatest Weaknesses

Emotional restlessness; volatility; self-doubt and anxieties; sense of splitness and division; your on-again, off-again involvements.

Images for Integration

Trivial Pursuits goes macabre ... A virtuoso violinist touches the hearts of her audience ... The mystery of life in a strip cartoon ... Dostoyevsky's *The Brothers Karamazov* ... Rodin's *The Kiss, Hands*.

Famous Personalities

Sir Thomas Browne (doctor and author), Stephen Crane (writer), Nicholas Culpeper (herbalist), Fyodor Dostoyevsky (novelist), Keith Emerson (rock musician), James Elroy Flecker (poet), Goldie Hawn (actress), Tina Lenert (mime artist), Konrad Lorenz (specialist in animal behaviour), Auguste Rodin (sculptor), Jonathan Ross (television personality), John Sousa (the 'March King'), Sir Christopher Wren (architect and astronomer).

— 88 —

SUN SCORPIO ♏ MOON CANCER ♋

I love everything old: old friends, old times, old manners, old books, old wine ...
OLIVER GOLDSMITH

There is a homely adage which runs 'Speak softly and carry a big stick,
you will go far.'
THEODORE ROOSEVELT

So live that you would not be ashamed to sell the family parrot to the
town gossip ...
WILL ROGERS

Themes

WATER/WATER A mailed fist in a velvet glove; deeply perceptive; imaginative; emotional sensitivity; charismatic; strong sense of duty; clannish; supportive; sincere; shrewd; passionate commitments; satirical; intensely guarded; secretive; strong sense of self; deep reservoirs of emotional strength.

Are you tough or tender? Passionate or sentimental? Self-sacrificing or self-assertive? You probably have some of all these features in your personality, which is a magnetic blend of passion and impressionability, and of nostalgia and powerful desires. You can be all kindness, sweetness and light until someone tries to take advantage of you or those you love, and then, suddenly and mysteriously, you are in exterminator mode and a quiet (or not so quiet) fury breaks out.

You are a person of *very* strong feelings, and you need to make sure your feelings are for the right beliefs because feelings are what guide you to your destiny. Although you feel the needs of others intensely and want to care for them, your own survival needs come first. You are also an instinctual being, capable of acting on irrational notions and gut reactions to people and events. And you are often right, although you do not go in for explaining yourself logically – your mind works a bit like a detective's, down nooks and crannies and the byways of human weaknesses. You tend to be suspicious and protective, taking your insights and storing them in a safe place.

Feelings literally flow through you, enabling you to see and sense much about people and the world. A certain self-sufficiency and serenity makes you a person others feel they can lean on. You do not have to lord it over people in a flashy way, but your weight and power are keenly felt nevertheless. Your profound perceptiveness and deep empathy for suffering souls could make you an understanding psychologist or a capable doctor or nurse. Your love of probing could be used to find out what makes people tick, or in an attraction to science where you can dissect and analyse the very pulse of life.

Although you have a deep fondness for the 'good old days', a desire to take control of your life and an ambition to make your own mark on the world keeps you very much in the present. Both highly sensitive and self-assertive, you have a natural flair for tapping the public pulse and taking appropriate actions to give people what they want. There may be a quality of quiet concern and compassion within you which impels you to work for the improvement of the lot of the underdog. This same quality makes you look after yourself well, and helps you become a devoted parent or a committed business person. Indeed, your cunning savvy, probable physical strength, and silent stamina serve you well if you enter the shark-infested waters of the business world. Your success comes from being able to combine self-interest and ruthless decision-making with traditional family values.

Relationships

You have a deep need to give and receive emotional support, and therefore relationships are a central part of your life. Strongly sentimental, you may find yourself trying to re-create your childhood, wanting the bliss of total dependency, or the satisfaction of revenge for early disappointments. This can turn your loved one into an unwilling parent or a rebellious child, depending on how possessive you are – and you can be *very* possessive.

Sensual, affectionate and romantic, your greatest need is for emotional security. When you have this you are the most devoted and magnetic of partners. If you are *too* devoted and oversensitive, however, your attentiveness becomes claustraphobic, demanding and manipulative. You need to be aware of your fanatic tendencies; although they may be too much for your loved one to endure, they can perform miracles in a career!

Your Greatest Strengths

Intuition; resilience and emotional tenacity; courageous capacity to nurture the downtrodden; ability to 'feel where things are at' and then take appropriate action to do something about helping restore harmony.

Your Greatest Weaknesses

Tendency to let subjective hunches replace objective reasoning; inclination to sink into self-pity and let negative emotions absorb you; a kind of egocentric sensitivity that insists on making the world come to you.

Images for Integration

A mother eagle defends her babies with immense courage ... A surgeon develops life-saving methods ... A mother passionately defends her delinquent child and pleads for a compassionate verdict.

Famous Personalities

Charles Atlas (body builder), Christian Barnard (pioneering heart-transplant surgeon), Admiral Richard Byrd (explorer), Nicol Fontana (fashion designer), André Gide (novelist), Oliver Goldsmith (poet), Edith Head (Oscar-winning costume designer), Tatum O'Neill (actress), Dan Rather (television news reporter and commentator), Will Rogers (humorist), Theodore Roosevelt (former American President).

— 89 —

SUN SCORPIO ♏ MOON LEO ♌

The Sun does not set in my dominion.
FRIEDRICH VON SCHILLER

Bah, I have sung women in three cities
But it is all the same;
And I will sing the sun
EZRA POUND

The difference between a gun and a tree ... is a difference of tempo. The
tree explodes every Spring.
EZRA POUND

Themes

WATER/FIRE Public and private; extrovert and introvert; bright or brooding; light yet intense; powerful; ambitious; shrewd; whole-hearted; intense; a sense of drama and poetry; the determined pursuit of excellence.

Is your season bright, high summer or the late, darkening days of autumn? Light and dark are both strong within you. One half of you loves the brilliant world of the noonday sun; the other half of you craves the dark dreams of midnight.

You can be frank, open and upfront, yet equally you can be reserved, secretive and private. You naturally feel that you deserve a place in the limelight of society, yet having achieved centre stage you find a key part of you really prefers to remain private and hidden. This tension between your public and private sides can cause you considerable internal angst and is at the heart of your creative dilemma. Indeed it may well incline you to wear dark glasses even in winter, and to seek out isolated, unspoilt spots in summer.

When you allow the day and night sides of you to combine, you are one of the most wholehearted, persuasive, determined and inspiring of all the Sun–Moon combinations. Someone of high ideals, creative drive and intense emotional purpose, you can bring light into the darkest corners. You can be driven by a desire to save yourself and others from the ignorance, darkness, disease and corruption that at some level you fear may consume you and the world. This can attract you towards medicine and into any work where you are able to make a difference.

At the same time you are no self-effacing saint! You have a strong satirical sense and will not hesitate to attack forthrightly what you consider to be wrong, especially the inflated, the self-important and the socially ambitious. (You should be aware, however, that we often hate in others what we cannot face in ourselves!)

You are a person of powerful and intense feelings and appetites who can be driven by the most basic desires for sex, money, power and social advancement. Whatever you do, you desire to be 'someone'. You feel you deserve it too, and need to work yourself into a position of authority to be truly happy. You are an all-or-nothing person who finds it difficult to compromise. Others can see this as unscrupulous ambition. You see it as being true to yourself and your essential nobility, which in you, of course, it is.

You both feel and imagine things intensely, and you want to give them expression. This is why you have a deeply poetic and dramatic sense and are likely to be attracted by the theatre in all its forms. For you there are no half-measures. You are strongly aware of both life and death. This gives you a strongly creative drive, for you feel that in creating you can defeat the grim reaper.

You have to believe in whatever you are doing, and when you do you are fiercely loyal and will do whatever is necessary to encourage and promote your cause. You are not frightened to get your hands dirty and will take on jobs that others will not or dare not do. You are perfectly happy to stand up forcefully for unpopular decisions and see them through.

Once you set yourself upon a career you will naturally visualize yourself at the top, and will focus your passionate drive on ensuring that you get there. Personal and economic success and social esteem are very important to you. No matter what you direct your attention towards you will tend to end up at the helm, for you are hard-working, and can even be a driven workaholic. Although you can outwardly conform for the sake of your career, you have a strongly anarchistic streak, a desire to do your own thing which really requires some measure of self-employment for its larger fulfilment.

Relationships

You are an ardent, romantic individual, and relationships are of immense importance to you. Yet your very intensity and passionate loyalty makes it difficult for you to be 'just good friends'. You tend to plunge in all-or-nothing, but if this is too frightening you can cut yourself off from getting involved at all.

When you are in a relationship it consumes you and you expect it equally to consume your other half, and for them to be as dedicated as you. During your life you may go through some dramatic changes in relationships. When young, you are likely to be very much ruled by your passions. As you grow older you seek to go beyond sex and personal gratification, and may become converted to some kind of cause which offers long-term satisfaction.

Your Greatest Strengths

Natural powers of persuasion, magnestism and charisma; loyalty and passionate, creative commitment to whatever work or cause you espouse; capacity to see and encourage light in the blackest darkness.

Your Greatest Weaknesses

Ruthless pursuit of power; snobbery; intolerance of those with whom you disagree or who in any way obstruct you; willingness to ride roughshod in pursuit of your chosen goals.

Images for Integration

A Samaritan mirrors sunshine into the depth of a dark pit bringing hope to those who live there ... A sexy superstar creates a new charity.

Famous Personalities

Terry Gilliam (cartoonist and film director), Ruth Gordon (actress), Lauren Hutton (actress), Kim Hunter (actress), Veronica Lake (actress), Hedy Lamarr (actress), André Malraux (writer and politician), Ezra Pound (poet), Julia Roberts (actress), Rev. Dr Chad Varah (founder of the Samaritans), Friedrich Von Schiller (poet and dramatist).

— 90 —

SUN SCORPIO ♏ MOON VIRGO ♍

When great changes occur in history, when great principles are involved, as a rule the majority is wrong.

Intelligent discontent is the mainspring of civilization.
EUGENE DEBS

Men always fall for frigid women because they put on the best show.
FANNY BRICE

Themes

WATER/EARTH Passion and piety; Martha and Mary; constructive imagination; romantic but practical; hard-working; quiet dedication; clarity; conscientious; simplicity; biting criticism; relentless perfectionism; powers of analysis; organizing ability; intensely loyal; witty and satirical.

Are you a modest, self-effacing soul who harbours passionate ambitions to make your mark? Or are you a forceful and determined individual who is surprisingly humble and retiring beneath that formidable front? You are the kind of person who seems to be very much in control of your life – and indeed you are. You achieve this by thinking things through logically and carefully before you act, always mindful of measuring twice so that you only have to cut once, so to speak. You are sometimes surprised, however, by powerful emotions that disrupt your logic, and you find yourself doing or saying things completely out of character. Although you have a scientist's temperament, you have the passion of an artist, and actually thrive on challenge and emotional involvement.

You are good at routine but only when you love what you are doing, and when you know that it merits your dedication. You can be somewhat distant and austere, a unique cross between the purposeful research worker and the inspired genius. The divide in you is between your need to be practical and in control of things, and your desire to experience life to the full, from the heights to the depths.

When you are on top form, you can be remarkably hard-working, thorough and systematic, a veritable dynamo of well-planned and strategically executed industry. Your dedication and creative energy can win you success and respect in a wide range of endeavours – science or art, business or sport, politics or the healing professions – where your more general concern to improve the world and our understanding of it can be expressed.

You have a strong sense of duty, though it would be unwise for anyone to try to play on that fact as you will not be bullied into anything. You like things direct and up front and do not take kindly to attempts from anyone to manipulate you. You are very much your own person, a bit of a maverick who will think and feel exactly what you decide. When you get stuck into things, you expect to work hard and you expect others to do likewise.

You have a razor-sharp mind which can spot the weaknesses in others' work and arguments, and when you decide to point these out you can speak with scathing honesty and accuracy. Your strong social conscience makes you well-suited for politics, and your sharpest criticism and biting wit is usually reserved for hypocrisy. You feel the needs and concerns of others deeply and have a natural desire to be of service. When this side of your nature is uppermost, you can be drawn to social work and to helping the underprivileged.

You have a quiet, shrewd, deeply insightful approach to life and a passionate commitment to common sense and the smooth running of society. Although you want to live a useful, productive life, you do not often choose to sacrifice your own comforts and pleasures. In fact, you can be acquisitive of the good things of life and happily hedonistic, so long as it is all in good taste. Taste and style is important to you, and you observe every detail of your colleague, enemy, or lover, summing up their essence with mental acuity and swift intuition.

You may be a progressive or you may be a reactionary, and in any area of life you can develop a combination of technical skill and physical stamina which will give you the ability to come back time and again against the odds. But whatever you do, you will certainly run your life according to firmly held principles – principles that you understand clearly and believe in passionately.

Relationships

Despite your mental approach to most matters, you are quite a physical person. You have intense desires, a part of your nature which is made all the more interesting by your instinctive modesty and self-control. You have a need for both passion and security, for intrigue and for simple trust. This can make you a trifle difficult to satisfy! If you cannot find these things combined in one person you may find yourself attracted to very different types at various times in your life.

When you are happy in your relationship you are the soul of devotion and duty. You will go out of your way to provide, not only adequately but also beautifully, for your dependents. You need to be careful, however, that you do not over-organize and over-control your loved ones; your creative fanaticism should be saved for your career.

Your Greatest Strengths

Your straight-from-the-shoulder honesty; an excellent mind; strong sense of duty and commitment; capacity for systematic hard work and getting things done; sense of humour and eye for the ridiculous.

Your Greatest Weaknesses

Narrowness of outlook; conscious aggression which can emerge as biting and destructive criticism; an arrogance which assumes that, if you can think them up, you are entitled to rewrite the rules.

Images for Integration

A scientist probes into the mysteries of the cosmos ... An artist combines simplicity with intensity in a study of still life ... Britten's opera *Billy Budd*.

Famous Personalities

Patrick Blackett (Nobel prize-winning physicist), Fanny Brice (singer and comedienne), Benjamin Britten (composer), Richard Burton (actor), Judy Canova (comedienne), Eugene Debs (socialist and trade unionist), Edward VII (former King of England), John Morris QC (politician), Elizabeth Prentiss (author), Henry Winkler (television actor – 'the Fonz'), Jonathan Winters (comedian), Viscount Linley (furniture maker and craftsman).

— 91 —

SUN SCORPIO ♏ MOON LIBRA ♎

When you stop having fun, you don't win.
BILLIE JEAN KING

Dying
Is an art, like everything else.
I do it exceptionally well.
Sylvia Plath, *Lady Lazarus*

Themes

WATER/AIR Intensely interested; magnetic sociability; emotional; analytical; self-controlled gracefulness; shrewd observations; creative intellect; innate sense of justice; organizing ability; passionate honesty; pragmatic idealism; expensive taste; quietly ambitious; perceptive.

Are you charmingly cooperative or emotionally demanding? Do you seek compromise or readily take revenge when your fairness is abused? Are you tough or tender, naughty or nice? You very much want to be kind, supportive and adaptable and to work for a better and more beautiful world, yet you will learn that difficult decisions and firm tactics are needed to defend the decency you desire. However diplomatic you can be, you will never compromise your dignity.

Although you optimistically hope for the best, you can be shrewdly understanding of the mad, the bad and the ugly. Your challenge will somehow involve engaging whole-heartedly with life as you find it, whilst not allowing disappointments to tarnish your idealism significantly. Injustices shock you but, oddly enough, tend to bring out the best in you, as you need to have access to the dark and terrible to be able to put the boot in, so to speak. The admiration and respect of your colleagues means a great deal to you, and you can do wonders in getting any group to work together. But let us not kid ourselves; you are also a pretty tough cookie, and if you cannot charm your way through to the prize, you can certainly turn on the pressure!

Because you like, even *need*, to be liked, you may find it all too easy to say 'yes' when you mean to say 'no', until you swing to the other extreme and say 'no' when you mean 'yes'. You exude charisma and capability and people readily depend on you. In fact, you can charmingly agree to do almost anything, but somehow what you do not want to do does not get done.

If you allow your instinct for compromise and your desire for affection and harmony to cover up your more forceful, dictatorial side, you can end up hating yourself. Admitting you really cannot stand some people (and that perhaps some may feel the same about you) is probably as good a way as any of getting in touch with your real power.

You have a vivid imagination, a keen sense of drama and probably rhythm, too, and if you take off in an artistic direction you can develop a very subtle yet eloquent manner of self-expression. But your best skills tend to involve people and ideas, and you will feel at home teaching, preaching or organizing. You can be a charismatic showman with a dramatic, eloquent delivery.

Although you may begin life on the gullible side, your savvy soon develops and you can become a natural psychologist, able to see into other people's motives and how best to get them to cooperate. You have passionate views but will defend them with clear, rational principles. You are a thinker and an idealist, defending justice and standing for excellence. But your animal instincts do not miss a trick so that your estimation of 'correct behaviour' always has a kind of ironic mercy about it. You aspire for the good in life and in people, but you are never very surprised by the foibles of human nature.

Relationships

Close, happy relationships are essential to your wellbeing. You need to belong to someone, to give and to feel that your presence in his or her life makes a big difference. Your passion and charm combine to make for a paradoxically intense but reasonable approach to love.

You are romantic and generous, and your capacity for intense possessiveness can sometimes be disturbing to your more rational, idealistic need for harmony and equanimity. But your openness and tenderness help you to grow through love's trials and tribulations, and you tend to be open to negotiation on most things. This, coupled with your intuitive sense of what your loved one is feeling and needs, makes you a very engaging, attractive partner and very prone to get the best out of partnerships of all kinds. What you may have to come to terms with is just how dependent on others you really are, for you *think* you are independent but in reality you get well and truly hooked when your heart is involved.

Your Greatest Strengths

Shrewd intellect; steady warmth; suave adaptability; commitment to fair play and personal honour; ability to perceive feelings and think on your feet, and to pursue what you believe in with organization, commitment and artistic fervour.

Your Greatest Weaknesses

Overdependence on others; tendency to resort to manipulation when you feel insecure, and to assume you are being impartial and fair when emotional need is really dictating your behaviour.

Images for Integration

A passionate poet leads the 'Poets for Peace' mass demonstration ... A criminal lawyer auditions for the lead part in a new play about heroes of the second-world-war resistance movement.

Famous Personalities

Billie Jean King (champion tennis player), Vachal Lindsay (poet), Jayne Marie Mansfield (actress and *Playboy* model), François Mitterrand (French president), Estelle Parsons (actress), Sylvia Plath (poet), Billy Sunday (preacher), Ted Turner (business executive).

92

SUN SCORPIO ♏ MOON SCORPIO ♏

Ah, sir, you dwellers in the city cannot enter into
the feelings of the hunter.
DRACULA, BRAM STOKER

Where I was born and where and how I have lived is unimportant. It is
what I have done with where I have been that should be of interest.
GEORGIA O'KEEFE

Themes

WATER/WATER Desire v. self-control; intense; self-possessed; whole-hearted; stubborn; passionate; astute perceptions; wary; uncompromising with strong convictions; jealous; sarcastic; private;

introspective; imaginative; relentless willpower; zeal for the truth.

Are you intensely passionate and self-assertive, or do you try to keep your strong feelings under lock and key, self-contained and self-controlled? Do you enjoy a deliberate confrontational stance that makes hypocrites writhe in humiliation, or do you seek more guarded paths for expressing your views, values and aspirations?

You are a powerfully whole-hearted individual whose personality is characterized by an internal struggle between stringent self-discipline and powerful self-expression. You love and hate with intensity, and whoever's side you are on, you fight the fight of sheer survival. Not surprisingly, you make a formidable foe!

An innate mistrust of authority figures marks you out as the quiet rebel; your instinct is to dislodge any control over your life except your *own*. The irony about you is that you are quite authoritative *yourself*, with firmly entrenched opinions and ideas. Your loyalty is first and foremost to yourself, because if you let yourself down, you have no one else to blame.

You are a very determined and resolute person, passionately committed to your beliefs and purposes. You may be a powerful innovator or a deeply reticent conservative, but whatever you do, privately you are an individual who is difficult to know and understand. This is a view of yourself that, in your more brooding and inward-looking moments (and there are an abundance of those), you may share, as you try to resolve the tension between your desires and fears. You may often ask yourself why you seem to care about things much more intensely than most people you know. Sometimes this feels like a burden, but it is one you carry well.

When you can get your passion and self-control working together, you have a formidable amount of whole-hearted, driven, emotional energy to channel into whatever enterprises or ventures capture your vivid imagination. In touch with yourself at both levels, you become someone who can excel at anything upon which you set your heart. The arts, especially music, attract you because they offer a channel of expression for your strong feelings. The sciences, especially psychology and medicine, can capture your imagination and satisfy your need for challenge and your desire to get to the bottom of things. You are a potential social reformer as well, and your desire to help the suffering will be based on your intimate knowledge of pain and on your conviction that the discarded underdogs of this world have something important to contribute to human life.

In the world of business you have many of the attributes of the successful entrepreneur: you enjoy the cut and thrust of competition and 'making a killing'; you are innovative, forceful and capable of living with tension and uncertainty. Sport is another area where you can excel, though you are not likely to be a good loser. You are the child who, if he cannot win, will not play.

Like Bram Stoker, the author of *Dracula*, you are naturally drawn to all that is powerful, mysterious and hidden. You may well have a love of the macabre, a taste for horror stories and a deep fascination with sex and death. Paradoxically, however, your very interest in death and darkness can stimulate your appreciation of life. You register beauty with tremendous force, and you may find the world of nature and its soothing rhythms very attractive and healing. Whilst pruning and cutting may bring out your love of promoting growth through control, you can be especially attracted to flowers and find their scents and colours both calming and deeply satisfying.

Relationships

You have very strong desires, and you are a naturally loyal and steadfast partner. It could even be said that you tend to become addicted to your other half once you have pledged yourself. But you expect equally uncompromising loyalty and devotion from your lover, and can become extremely possessive, jealous and indeed vindictive if your relationship is threatened in any way. Your potential for emotional fulfilment is enormous, but you may have to learn how truly to trust before your powerful need for intimacy can be met.

Your Greatest Strengths

Sheer drive, energy and stamina; astute observations and analysing abilities; loyalty and dedication to whatever captures your imagination; emotional courage; creative potential.

Your Greatest Weaknesses

A tendency to let suspicions and cynicism limit your capacity for relaxed enjoyment; reluctance to share your fears; inclination to take yourself too seriously; desire for revenge; proneness to get stuck in negative emotions.

Images for Integration

A pile of manure slowly permeates the deeper soil as the November rains soak the still, dark garden ... A millionaire businessman establishes a foundation for medical research.

Famous Personalities

Howard Baker (lawyer and politician), Leif Garrett (singer and actor), Whoopi Goldberg (actress), Paul Hindemith (composer), Louis Malle (film director and writer), Cord Meyer Jr. (reformer), Georgia O'Keefe (painter), Mohammad Pahlavi (former Shah of Persia), Bram Stoker (author of *Dracula*).

— 93 —

SUN SCORPIO ♏ MOON SAGITTARIUS ♐

Millions of angels are at God's command.
BILLY GRAHAM

Artists who live and work with spiritual values cannot and should not remain indifferent to a conflict in which the highest values of humanity and civilization are at stake.

I'd like to live like a poor man with lots of money.
PABLO PICASSO

Themes

WATER/FIRE Passionate; committed; stern judge; uncompromising; philosophical; intuitive; great integrity; zeal for truth; socially concerned; loyal; forceful; persuasive; self-dramatizing; intellectually discerning; investigative turn of mind.

Are you an over-emotional, paranoid introvert, or a sporting and spontaneous extrovert? Are you concerned with the big first and last things in life, or with all the fun things in between? You are the good-humoured detective, the passionate crusader for the truth, the moralistic artist who is aware of the unfathomable gulf between human instincts and social ethics.

Ardent and outspoken about the things you believe in, you are something of an extremist who will go to great lengths to express yourself or to uphold your view of the truth. That is, to others it may seem like you go to great lengths, but to you it is the norm. You are incapable of being lukewarm about anything; something is either essential or non-essential to your life. Not that you are a closed-minded, black-and-white thinker – not at all. You are both highly focused, able to fixate on the object of your desire with intense concentration, and yet you are also wide-ranging, hating to be fettered or constrained.

You are at your best when you are in a position to give yourself a broad canvas and then to focus on it. You are fascinated by the paradoxes of life, and this makes you something of a philosopher who struggles to make sense of the world. Your instinct is to dig and explore, as you are naturally restless and questing, searching for fundamental truths and answers to complex social problems. But you are most likely to explore thoroughly something about which you are already passionate. The things you do not examine, and which seem to belong to a different value system, can truly baffle you, and perhaps you remain a bit aloof from them.

You would make a superb educator, as you are someone who sees the large view and the broad principles, and who can communicate them with deep passion and insight. Whether or not you are into sport, you have some of the essential ingredients of the sports champion: the will to win and the stamina and enthusiasm to carry the day. When you are working with both sides of yourself you can successfully bring this combination of ambition and vitality to anything you do, be it in business, politics, theatre or the healing arts. Your instinct for self-preservation is strong, and combined with your fine intellect and powers of deduction will tend to keep you on the right side of providence.

Relationships

You make a loyal friend, generous with your time and energy, and when you say you are going to do something, you do it. It does not matter if you are usually late – that does not detract from your essential trustworthiness and effectiveness.

Your mate, your friends and your family may sometimes feel frustrated with you because you do not always reveal all the depths and imaginative insight they know you have. This is especially true when you are sizing up new people and situations. Although you are forthright about your beliefs and your moral standards, you will hold back a trump or two when it comes to feelings, if you judge it wise.

In close relationships there is some conflict between your need to possess absolutely and your need for freedom and buoyant social stimulation. You can be rather demanding, for you seek emotional intensity as well as intellectual equality. But when you learn to balance these two sides, you become more trusting, less prone to paranoid grumpiness, and even more charismatic.

Instinctively aware of people's feelings as well as your own, you are good in group dynamics. Your analytical turn of mind, plus your feeling for the regenerative potential of society makes you a natural psychologist. Whatever you do, your personal flair has a sting in its tail that provokes others to think.

Your Greatest Strengths

Inner commitment to personal values; probing, questing, analytical mind which is quick to see the larger implications of facts; unique blend of idealism and realism; enduring, affirming loyalty to those you love.

Your Greatest Weaknesses

Sudden obstinacy and fanatical side, which comes out as a tendency to moralize and expect the world to conform to your view; tendency to be a bit holier-than-thou when it comes to socializing – you will not bend the rules because your integrity is more precious to you than all the gold in Aladdin's cave.

Image for Integration

A child gazes up at the night sky, captivated by the mystery of dark space. An alien appears, and reveals a glimpse of the child's future as a famous astro-physicist. Picasso's *Guernica*.

Famous Personalities

Charles Bronson (actor), Louis Daguerre (inventor and artist), Danny DeVito (actor and director), Michel Gauquelin (psychologist, astrologer and statistician), Billy Graham (evangelist preacher), Cleo Laine (singer), Lulu (singer), Pablo Picasso (artist), Carl Sagan (astronomer), Tom Seaver (top baseball pitcher), Joan Sutherland (singer).

— 94 —

SUN SCORPIO ♏ MOON CAPRICORN ♑

Puritanism ... helps us enjoy our misery while we are inflicting it on others.
MARCEL OPHULS

Take calculated risks. That is quite different from being rash.
GENERAL GEORGE PATTON

He was like a cock who thought the sun had risen to hear him crow.
GEORGE ELIOT (MARY ANN EVANS)

Themes

WATER/EARTH Purposeful; self-demanding; serious; committed; tough; tenacious; self-righteous; loyal; hard-working; ambitious; integrity; courageous; dark intensity; brooding; enigmatic; judgemental; cynical; dry wit; a natural leader.

Do you thrive on public crusading, or on personal and private ambitions? Are you an introspective and aloof individual, or do you throw your whole self into public service? Are you defiant and rash or painstakingly cautious?

There is in you a need both for social conformity and usefulness, and also for exacting personal integrity. This will demand that you think seriously about your life at quite an early age, and that you decide what you want to achieve. When you get yourself together you are one of the most intensely purposeful and ambitious combinations in the zodiac, and you can pursue any goal you set yourself with a sometimes ruthless determination which makes less single-minded types wilt.

Your hard-working, focused intensity makes you one of nature's natural leaders. Provided that your own strong sense of self did not attract harsh treatment in your childhood, you are likely to be supremely self-confident and capable of instilling a sense of deep purpose and mission to those around you. If you had a difficult or repressive childhood, however, you may first need to learn that resentments must be purged, whatever bitterness you may feel about past events, and that there is an important role for you to play in the future. If you focus your will on something you really want to attain, nothing can stop you.

You feel passionately about the 'rights and wrongs' of social interaction, and very often you feel personally called upon to step in and play first the detective and then the judge. Strong convictions and stubborn courage make you well suited for a career in social work, politics or the law. You have a natural gift for regeneration, be it of people, laws, buildings, companies or indeed countries. But whatever it is you do with your creative energies, you will not be satisfied until you know you have won the recognition, respect and admiration of your friends, colleagues and public.

There is about you a toughness and tenacity, an urge to tackle and conquer difficult issues with your fine, rational intellect, and a love of discussion and persuasion. Although you will not compromise your principles, you have an innate sense of strategy which helps you anticipate and manipulate others' perceptions of you. If you are a family person, you devote yourself to their wellbeing with the ferocity of a mother bear. If you are involved in the arts, you employ your passion and self-discipline to develop and fine-tune your skills. Once you have focused on your mission, you will carry it through with true grit.

You feel acutely the tragedy, irony and drama of life, and you need to make sure you are prepared for whatever it may bring. Material security and powerful position, you have observed, go a long way in protecting one from the sudden twists of fate that are part of life. But an even deeper wisdom tells you that sound moral fibre is the surest way to real contentment and independence – for in the end, you have to live with yourself.

Although many of your qualities are heavy, earnest and sombre, when relaxed you surprise everyone with your pungent wit and unlikely indulgence in practical jokes, your satirical flair, and your willingness to play the giddy goat.

Relationships

You readily attract others as you have a silent, sexy charisma and a certain hard-to-get mysterious magnetism which the opposite sex loves. You are essentially a true blue sort of lover – very devoted and dependable, and capable of coping with the pressures of family responsibilities. You take yourself very seriously, however, and are inclined to get suspicious, especially if you have to recover from difficult emotional experiences in youth.

You are likely to be very highly sexed. If your partner does not share this trait you can become embittered. Try to express your feelings, not simply hide them away in the dark to ferment.

Your Greatest Strengths

Integrity and loyalty to your cause; ability for unremitting hard work; tenacity of purpose; a penetrating eye for hypocrisy and humbug; illuminating dry wit; moral and physical courage.

Your Greatest Weaknesses

Inflexibility; ruthlessness; impatience with others' weaknesses; vanity and sense of self-importance; brooding cynicism; capacity for harsh, unthinking treatment of others.

Images for Integration

A general leads his troops to victory ... A film director plans each shot to maximize its emotional impact.

Famous Personalities

Florence Chadwick (long-distance swimmer), Tom Conti (actor), George Eliot (writer), Marsilio Ficino (philosopher), Robert Kennedy (politician), Sir Robert Lorimer (Scottish architect), Montgomery of Alamein (British general), Marcel Ophuls (film director), George Patton (American general), Gary Player (world-champion golfer), Helen Reddy (singer), Elke Sommer (film actress), Sun Yat-sen (Chinese revolutionary leader).

— 95 —

SUN SCORPIO ♏ MOON AQUARIUS ♒

Integrity is in no need of rules.
ALBERT CAMUS

O may my heart's truth still be sung on this
high hill in a year's turning.
DYLAN THOMAS

How much more cruel the pen is than the sword.
ROBERT BURTON

Themes

WATER/AIR Passionately dispassionate; astute observations; exacting sense of integrity; powerful intellect; proud; radically independent views; law unto oneself; wilful; loyal; love of social ironies; principled but intolerant; self-reflective; scrutinizing; magnetic effect on others.

Are you an impenetrable enigma of human emotion, or a wide-eyed and open-armed friend of the people? Do you yield to your gregarious instinct, finding both meaning and comfort in the company of like-minded souls, or do you cut yourself off from frail humanity because you cannot tolerate their flaws and corruption?

You are often torn between being the dispassionate observer of life and the intensely engaged redeemer of human suffering. Sometimes

324

you cannot help feeling isolated and cynical; other times you find your identity with being one of the gang, and your conscience sends you out into some all-consuming cause. You have a real job combining your immense pride with your lofty idealism, your blunt, piercingly astute observations with your need for congenial companionship. But when you successfully manage it, you can become a powerful force in your own circle and in the world at large if you so deem that a cause merits your total dedication.

You pursue truth with an intensity that would exhaust more laid-back, luke-warm types. When the impartial spectator within you marries the passionate experiencer of life's mysteries, you become a natural scientist, philosopher or artist, who can bring together the heights and the depths. This can satisfy your need to understand from your lofty eyrie and make sense of what can at times seem a deeply threatening world.

Life for you can seem both a tragedy and a comedy in which both the light and darkness of the human situation are mysteriously and inextricably intermingled. And your fine intellect gets lots of mileage from this awareness – you can be a master of satire and a sharp social critic. You are all too aware, however, that the paradoxes and ironies you observe in society lie within yourself as well, and you may use a well-developed sense of the absurd as a kind of defence against the pain of being alive.

You have powerful desires and feelings and a real need to achieve. Your standards are high; you know that personal achievements reflect your essence, so you make sure that your achievements are worthy of you. But your essential seriousness and emotional control often belie some very tender feelings and a deep need for friendship, for underneath that solid ego is immense concern, affection and even compassion for the suffering to which you are so sensitive. Sometimes, however, you suspect the worst of your fellow human beings, seeing them as predators and, even worse, monstrously indifferent to the plight of other living beings.

Like Dylan Thomas, you may feel that life is summed up by the fact that 'we are born in others' pain and perish in our own'. But you have enormous resilience and tenacity, a capacity for regenerating social structures, and you can take your perceptive mind and emotional commitment into the healing professions or politics and accomplish much.

You see what needs doing and get on and do it, regardless of what others think. A certain ability to plunge into experience and observe the consequences makes you an excellent trouble-shooter. Your personality combines sheer survival instinct with aspirations for nobility. You can turn despair into hope by clinging tenaciously to your uniqueness and to your common bond with all humanity.

Relationships

Emotionally you blow hot and cold, interested and then indifferent, but your instinct is to protect yourself from pain by keeping your dangerous feelings under control. You can be a real enigma to your loved one. You may share intellectual rapport (this will be important), as well as political views and acerbic humour, but there will be vast depths that you do not express, as though your silence is the best testimony to that well of feeling.

You may at times suffer from the 'freedom–closeness' dilemma, for you can be terribly possessive whilst also needing a lot of freedom yourself. Emotional and physical fidelty may be two different things in your world. At times, therefore, you can find yourself torn between a deep natural loyalty based on scrupulously developed principles, and primitive passions.

Your Greatest Strengths

Ability for detached analysis and criticism; insistence on the truth; unwillingness to accept easy answers; intense determination; clarity of expression; sharp sense of humour; exacting self-honesty.

Your Greatest Weaknesses

Proneness to allow depression and cynicism to undermine your creative talents; setting yourself impossibly high goals or standards which only invites frustration; a lack of faith in your fellow beings, which does not give them a fair chance and can keep you lonely.

Images for Integration

A hovering hawk surveys the world, at one with nature ... An exotic moth emerges from its chrysalis, in perfect form, a specimen of the sublimity of nature's intelligence.

Famous Personalities

Margaret Atwood (novelist and poet), Robert Burton (scholar and churchman), Albert Camus (novelist), Nigel Havers (actor), Vivian Leigh (film actress), Naomi Mitchison (sci-fi writer), Jean Monnet (economist, architect of the European Community), Lester Piggot (world-champion jockey), Dylan Thomas (poet), Voltaire (philosopher), Auberon Waugh (satirist).

— **96** —

Sun Scorpio ♏ Moon Pisces ♓

... our lives are part of some greater effort ... we are connected to one another ... community means that we have a place where we belong no matter who we are.
HILARY CLINTON

The saints are the sinners that keep on going.

Fifteen men on the dead man's chest –
Yo-ho-ho, and a bottle of rum!
ROBERT LOUIS STEVENSON

Themes

WATER/WATER Aloof yet warm-hearted; vivid imagination; hard-working dedication; shrewd strategist; emotional intensity; persuasive; prone to addictions; love of the mysterious; a gift for caring and healing.

Are you a Lady Macbeth or an angel of mercy? A Dracula or a Good Samaritan? You can be a real Dr Jekyll and Mr Hyde, torn between passion and compassion. At one level you are the highly sensitive, idealistic, dreaming poet; at another the shrewd, ruthless and determined go-getter who thrives on challenge. When both sides come together you can be a deeply motivated and persuasive romantic who

327

sees life as a mission to help those whose cannot help themselves. Be it in medicine, social welfare or political reform, you have a curative magnetism that few can ignore, though some may reject.

You have a fertile, often lurid, imagination. This can add an extra dimension to whatever you do, be it work or play. It can make you a wonderful spinner of yarns and creator of atmosphere, or it can allow you to become haunted by your own inner macabre imaginings, nightmares and psychic insights.

You are capable of both great self-indulgence and immense self-discipline. Your creative middle way comes through dedication to some higher ideal, for whatever captures your strongly emotional imagination captures your life, and you will find yourself swept along by a passionate dedication and intensity. Whilst your sympathies go out to the underdog, you will not hesitate to play top dog if necessary to achieve your ends.

You love a mystery, and whether you are creating or evoking a mysterious atmosphere, or probing into the secrets of nature, you will pursue the world of the unseen, unknown and arcane with an immense thirst and relish to get to the bottom of things. Your immensely rich, powerfully poetic and creative imagination, especially for the dark side of life – death, destruction, greed, fear and sexuality – gives you a deep understanding of human nature. Your capacity for seeing into and through other people and their foibles and deeper motives makes you a natural psychologist. At the same time, your insights can be totally devastating, for despite your compassion, you can be a ruthless critic and will not hesitate to put the knife in if this is what you feel is required for the greater good.

Your motto could usefully be 'Blessed are the pure in spirit', for you are at your happiest when your sensitivity to the needs and motives of others is allowed to move you to great works rather than into cynicism, bitterness and game-playing. But if you do get hooked on games you can be a superb strategist, able to sense others' moves.

Your imaginative and emotional nature makes you more than usually prone to addiction, be it to love, drugs, alcohol, films or simply food and sex. You need the fuel of constant emotional stimuli. When you do decide to quit a particular habit, however, you can make a dramatic turn-about. During your life you are therefore likely to touch the heights and the depths, and to go through a series of dramatic rebirths as you rediscover your deep sense of purpose and commitment to a larger vision.

Relationships

An intensely emotional individual, you have a highly sensitive, telepathic understanding of the unspoken subtleties in relationships. You can, however, often hide this behind a seemingly cool, aloof exterior. Close, enduring, passionate personal relationships can be everything in life to you. You see into other people's essence and deeply need to be understood in the same way.

Earth types, especially Taureans, attract you, as you need to be with someone who can contain you and give you the clear boundries that your life may otherwise lack. You find clear-headed, bright and breezy Air types infuriatingly impersonal, yet strangely attractive for that very reason. If, however, you have been hurt in a relationship, your yearning for an all-consuming union can give way to a desire to stand alone, self-contained and self-sufficient.

Your Greatest Strengths

Intense, passionate commitment and dedication to whatever you do; ability to capture the imagination and to come back fighting.

Your Greatest Weaknesses

Addiction to your emotions; lurid imagination; lack of objectivity; penchant for strategy and subterfuge.

Images for Integration

Madame Curie works for the Red Cross whilst dedicating herself to solving the mysteries of radioactivity ... Long John Silver, with ruthless charm, becomes a successful entrepreneur.

Famous Personalities

Alexander Alekhine (world-champion chess player), Hilary Clinton (lawyer and American first lady), William Cullen Bryant (poet, politician and reformer), Marie Curie (chemist and physicist), Grace Kelly (film actress), Bela Lugosi (horror-movie star), Rene Magritte (painter), Gene Tierney (film actress), Martin Scorsese (film director), Robert Louis Stevenson (writer and poet).

Chapter Twelve

SUN IN SAGITTARIUS

———— ⟋ ————

— 97 —

SUN SAGITTARIUS ♐ MOON ARIES ♈

There was things which he stretched but mainly he told the truth ...

Always do right; this will gratify some people and astonish the rest.
MARK TWAIN

Well, if I called the wrong number why did you answer the phone?
JAMES THURBER

Themes

FIRE/FIRE Frank; forthright; big talker; picaresque adventurer; intuitive certainty; irreverence for the classic and antique; impatient; energetic; blunt but sincere; habitually hopeful; emotionally demanding; courageously idealistic; passionately honourable; the entrepreneur; the kind-hearted rebel.

Are you a restless, impulsive go-getter out to further your own interests, or does that missionary inside you call the shots with theatrical moral fervour? Do you look for patterns of meaning in the chaotic dance of life, or are you too busy dancing and enjoying the spotlight to notice?

You are a big-hearted person with a vivid, far-seeing imagination and a very strong desire to succeed. Your driving instinct is to explore, to create and to act. Running large enterprises – whether it is a multi-million business or a large and noisy family – is probably your cup of tea. You relish anything that offers challenge, adventure and scope for originality.

Basically, you are a plain-speaking, independent-minded, warm-hearted extrovert. You can talk up a storm and brew up a lot of enthusiasm – in yourself and in others – for your exciting ideas. But you will often give the impression of possessing great knowledge about something when, in fact, you have not even covered the most basic details – yet. In other words, you are quite capable of delivering the goods, but you may have to fall apart a few times before you realize that what is missing is patience and sticking to a practical plan of action – and all the boring details therein.

Champion of the underdog but first in line when it comes to receiving prizes, you may not always be sure whether you are in it for yourself or for the good of the cause. In fact, you have a healthy and, if anything, over-sized ego which finds little conflict between morally sound altruism and blatant self-interest. Whatever your field of enterprise, however, you put in enormous energy, and you can keep up quite a pace with your planning and organizing and wheeling and dealing.

Although you may seem to be competitive, what actually keeps you going is a kind of intense, childlike faith in yourself and your ideals. This enables you to express yourself like a firebrand, a bright star shining amidst the humdrum routine of earthly existence. And if you do compete with others, you will always respect anyone who beats you fair and square. In fact, you will thrive on a certain amount of challenge and creative conflict.

You need a lot of freedom to do your own thing, yet you also have a deep-rooted commitment to helping make the world a better place. You are a natural egotist, but you do not like to acknowledge facts that are unflattering. This will be accentuated if you do not gain a modicum of personal success in your career as you do need to achieve something and to feel appreciated as an authority in your particular sphere.

Your weak spots are your temper, irritability, insensitivity to more vulnerable, emotional individuals, and your tendency to exaggerate. When things go wrong, you either wail like a misunderstood artist or you fall into real dejection. Your over-riding zeal never wanes for long, however, and you can continue knocking on closed doors a lot longer than others when you have decided on the best way forward.

A person of exemplary moral integrity and philanthropic propensities, you are a believer in principles. No matter how often your bubble might burst, you will never give up your conviction to lead a life based on your own inner truth. People therefore trust you, and have good reason to do so. Your own purposes are never far from your mind, and your earnestness and honesty make you a person people respect and admire, no matter how impractical you might be.

Relationships

Intimate liaisons are not your strong suit. Although you are certainly romantic enough, you tend to lack the patience or willingness to listen that is so important where understanding other people's needs are concerned.

You need someone you can respect and who stimulates you, but you need to be careful that you see the *real* person instead of the royal consort of your romantic imagination. You may be attracted to watery or earthy types who help you to slow down and feel more comfortable with your ordinariness and emotional needs. Life with you, however, will always contain some surprises, so your partner will have to understand your gregarious instinct and need for creative space.

Your Greatest Strengths

Infectious enthusiasm; absolute honesty; courage and leadership abilities; intuitive mental gifts; exceptional moral integrity.

Your Greatest Weaknesses

Impatience; disliking of details; insensitivity to the more subtle nuances of human relationships; neurotic need to be affirmed as the biggest and best; black moods when things go wrong.

Images for Integration

He who would be King postpones the coronation for a trek through the Himalayas ... A mature student discovers her political convictions and debating talents through confronting the corruption of academia.

Famous Personalities

Heinrich Boll (novelist), Ellen Burstyn (actress), Ada Byron (inventor and mathmatician; daughter of Lord Byron), Robert Goulet (actor), Margaret Hamilton (actress; the 'Wicked Witch of the West' in *The Wizard of Oz*), Nellie Sax (poet), James Thurber (writer and humorist), Mark Twain (writer and humorist).

— 98 —

SUN SAGITTARIUS ⚹ MOON TAURUS ♉

A mind not to be changed by place or time.
The mind is its own place, and in itself
Can make a Heaven of Hell, a Hell of Heaven.
JOHN MILTON

What Price Glory?
MAXWELL ANDERSON

Themes

FIRE/EARTH Friendly and romantic; steady aspirations; generous nature; measured optimism; extravagant taste; entrenched beliefs; devotion to progress; self-confidence; a gentle authoritarian; social conscience; love of beauty; musical sensitivity; a pragmatic philosopher.

Are you a natural explorer whose get-up-and-go is undermined by a love of your own home? Do you want freedom but fear that life will force you to sacrifice it all for material and emotional security? Are you a thinker who finds your greatest inspiration comes when you are cooking (or gardening, painting or playing music)?

You are a warm, open person, restrainedly idealistic, confident and enthusiastic about your activities and interests, and possessing a strong dramatic sense with a distinct satirical edge. You can be restless and impatient, robust and argumentative, but underneath it all you have a deep need for harmony and security, and it takes a lot for you to give up on anything.

Your instinct is for the slow and traditional, for the constancy of pleasant surroundings and familiar faces, but you also would like to be at the cutting edge of the creative arts or perhaps the social/political scene. Your moral strength and warm, aspirational nature make you a person that people notice and respect, and your generosity and *bon viveur* qualities make you someone who, generally, is easy to love.

You have a good imagination and bright ideas, and fortunately you can usually see how they can be put to practical use. Philosophical ideals play an important part in your life, but they are never divorced from your practical life or those unavoidable economic necessities of life. Not for you the airy-fairy ideologies of the 'New Age', which neglect the importance of creature comforts.

You want to enjoy yourself, but you *must* earn your keep – or find someone who will do it for you. Although you revere justice and want equal rights for all just as much as the next person, your common sense reminds you that getting your bills paid and having a bit of savings makes you feel good.

It is also quite likely that you have a natural understanding of ecological beliefs, the idea that nature and the perpetual round of life that sustains us all must be valued. You not only think about these things, but you also want your life to be actively involved in the preservation of the species – your species, preferably. You can be amazingly resourceful, and will know how to value and give validation to simply enjoying the scents, sights, tastes and textures of living.

You could be something of a practical educationalist, convinced of the importance of knowing the facts about all kinds of things. You believe that knowledge will suffice, that it will protect you and enable you to make better choices in all the roles you play – parent, consumer and friend. Therefore you remain an avid student all your life, and you will have a passion for your hobbies, even if they never become lucrative. Music and art may also play a big part in your life, for you know in your heart and feel in your bones that man does not live by bread alone.

Relationships

In relationships you can express your warmth and big-heartedness along with your dependability and appreciation of the simple pleasures of the daily round. You are romantic but reliable; fun-loving but common sensical. You intend to live a good life, and to do that you need to feel happy in a close relationship, and to have familiar faces around you.

You tend to feel at ease with yourself and your tastes and cravings, and as a result you put others at ease. In emotional liaisons, however, you are bound to meet the extreme paradox of your nature head on. A part of you wants variety and excitement, whilst another part wants security, closeness and absolute promises. You can, without realizing it, become addicted to the emotional nourishment you get from your partner and family. You may even become very possessive unwittingly.

Assuming your loved ones will always be there, you may go off sporadically to quench your thirst for adventure. You need a mate who shares your excitement for learning and activity, and who, with perhaps just a touch of water in their make-up, can connect you to the more mysterious realm of feelings, and help you develop your own overlooked sensitivity.

Your Greatest Strengths

The way you combine brilliant insights with practical know-how; an expansive outlook made viable by your calm and serious bearing; commitment to ideals and people; warm approachability; capacity to enjoy life to the full.

Your Greatest Weaknesses

Lack of initiative; proneness to live in your dreams and let others pick up the bill; becoming a slave to your own exotic tastes; tendency to get stuck in ideologies that clutter your life and impede your creative output.

Images for Integration

A pirate ship searches for gold ... An armchair traveller roughs out a financial plan for his next adventure.

Famous Personalities

Maxwell Anderson (journalist and playwright), Busby Berkely (Hollywood director and choreographer), Van Heflin (actor), Richard Kuhn (Nobel prize-winning chemist), Jean Marais (actor), Ricardo Montalban (actor), Jim Morrison (rock musician of *The Doors*), Oscar Niemeyer (Brazilian architect), Dalton Trumbo (writer).

— 99 —

SUN SAGITTARIUS ♐ MOON GEMINI ♊

Creative minds have always been known to survive any kind of bad training.
ANNA FREUD

I've over-educated myself in all the things I shouldn't have known at all.
NOEL COWARD

Themes

FIRE/AIR Versatile; intellectual; witty; friendly; casual; literary genius; restless; adventurous; inventive; ironic; sociable; covers a lot of ground; both profound and fun-loving; a sage and a student; the eternal youth.

Do you want knowledge or do you want wisdom? Are you a philosopher or a jokesmith? Essentially, you are a collector of information, people and experiences, an eternal child asking 'why' and 'what for?'. When you have collected sufficient answers, however, your intuition gets working and you can become an expert map-reader, seeing the underlying meaning, the 'gestalt' behind the parts.

Getting the moral of the story for you is more satisfying than just the vocal/aural experience. That is not to say, though, that you do not enjoy talking – you can play devil's advocate to the nth degree and out-talk anyone (you find the sound of your own voice intoxicating!). For you, life is one adventure after another and one stimulating

336

conversation after another. The communication of ideas, from the profound to the anecdotal, is the essence of your life. And whatever you believe in, you articulate with moralistic fervour.

You have an engaging and wickedly mischievous personality, and are interested in a huge range of ideas, projects and people. You may be gifted with language, clarity of thought and communication, and your talents may be applied in many different areas, from teaching and writing to advertising and marketing or being an inventive entrepreneur. You are friendly and hard-working but can easily exhaust yourself from over-socializing, and become short-tempered and tactless when things are not going your way. At these times your impatient and somewhat self-righteous side comes out.

Innocently irreverent and quite capable of making jokes at the vicar's expense, you see connections between seemingly unrelated things, the levity and the profundity all in the same twinkling of an eye. Thus popularity generally comes easily for you, if you can ever be pinned down long enough to fill in your diary. You have great insight and can sum up a person in a few pithy words. But you can also be quite cutting and blunt, although you never mean to be unkind or ungenerous, and you will be dismayed when someone gets offended and huffy.

Relationships

You can be amazingly logical, and are able to give practical advice when needed, but you find people's emotional problems difficult to cope with. How could they get themselves in such a mess in the first place? When it comes to your own emotional life, you may avoid commitment because you fear boredom and the end of adventure. As you are often out of touch with your own feelings, you remain naive about many things – especially emotional depths and interpersonal intrigues. To your friends and colleagues this may be an endearing quality, whereas the love of your life may find it exasperating.

You are affectionate enough and generous with whatever you have, but tend to rationalize and wriggle out of tight corners if things get too emotionally heavy. You need intellectual rapport with your mate, the sharing of ideals, travel and philosophies. You are not fond of strong displays of emotion, as you have neither the patience for nor the interest in such things. In this area of human experience, brevity is definitely the soul of wit for you. Without realizing it, however, you can end up taking the child's role in emotional relationships, and that can cheat you of adult rewards.

Essentially you are a natural teacher, spokesperson, communicator, disc jockey, trendsetter, inspirational catalyst – someone who, by hook or by crook, opens the way for others to broaden their own views. You are a sophisticated gypsy, here today and gone tomorrow, but you will be back and just pick up where you left off.

Your Greatest Strengths

Intellectual curiosity and love of learning; gift of repartee; communication skills; frank, friendly nature; openness to experience and different cultures; inventiveness and original flair, including the way you readily share your knowledge; an eternal youthfulness which makes you charming, approachable and fun-loving, no matter what age.

Your Greatest Weaknesses

Spreading yourself too thin and not finishing projects; overanalysing things as a way of hiding from your feelings; tendency towards self-absorption and never quite growing up; never fulfilling your deeper poential because it is so easy to live by your wits.

Image for Integration

Robin Hood as a young boy plays truant from school to go to his archery lesson, but ends up teaching his card tricks to his master.

Famous Personalities

Akbar the Great (ruler of Persia), Jeff Bridges (actor), Noel Coward (playwright), Billy Connolly (comedian and actor), Benjamine Creme ('New-Age' prophet), Francisco Franco (Spanish dictator), Anna Freud (psychoanalyst), Christopher Fry (writer), Petra Kelly (founder of Green Party), C. S. Lewis (writer, painter), Edith Piaf (singer), Lewis Spence (occult writer).

Sun Sagittarius ✗ Moon Cancer ♋

And did those feet in Ancient days
Walk upon England's pastures green?
WILLIAM BLAKE, *JERUSALEM*

I remember my youth and the feeling that ... I could last for ever, outlast the
sea, the earth, and all men; the deceitful feeling that lures us on to perils, to
love, to vain effort – to death.
JOSEPH CONRAD, *YOUTH*

Themes

FIRE/WATER Mind and heart; enthusiasm and sensitivity; extremes
of extroversion and introversion; emotionally charged; intuitive,
prophetic visionary; over-extended; brilliance; pizzazz; dramatic
sense.

Do you want to stay home with mum or sail the seven seas in the
swiftest boat alive? Are you the moody, sensitive, self-absorbed
outsider or the super-optimistic, partying fun-lover? Are you fiercely
assertive or gently caring?

You are a fast-track progressive caught up with the ideas of the
moment and tomorrow, yet at the same time you are moved by
nostalgia and the good old days, and can be happy to drift along in the
realms of memory until the next enthusiasm captures you. By the
same token, you can be a very private person with a need to nurse your
feelings, and yet be someone who thrives on other people, good
fellowship, new contacts and relationships.

Your creative fires are sparked by anything that can combine your
love of action with your vivid imagination and quest for the meaning
of life. Freedom to explore by land, sea, air and the imagination, and a
home fire to come back to is what you want and need. You have a great
zest for life, immense adaptability, and will throw yourself into any
experience at least once. You enjoy people and will want to know what
makes them tick.

You delight in moral paradoxes, which is just as well, for you can often find yourself torn between pity and scorn for your fellow beings, and indeed for yourself. Your own self-pity never lasts long, as your visionary sense of what is around the corner gives you a boundless faith in Providence, and a conviction that things will turn out right. They usually do, though with your trusting naivity you can be all too easily deceived by less scrupulous types, and will do well to learn to look more carefully and systematically before you leap.

Your combination of caring intimacy, vision and panache gives you a natural magnetism and talent for motivating, teaching and persuading people. This can make you a born innovator and true educationalist who can inspire others, and gives you a gift for public relations and making a splash in the world. Whether you are in business or fashion, a travelling salesman (overseas visits your speciality), a rock musician or a teacher, you have charisma and know how to use it. You can work with great loyalty and energy yet you hate to be tied down, and will tend to get yourself hopelessly over-extended. You are someone who can shrewdly squirrel away financial resources for the future; yet your faith in life's bounty can equally lead you to throw economic caution to the wind. In business matters it will therefore pay you to listen to the most feet-on-the-ground bank manager you can find. Your motto should be 'moderation in all things', but you will no doubt add to that 'and especially in moderation'.

Relationships

You are really emotional, and a romantic with it. Feelings and passions steam up in you, and the next romantic interest in your life is always Ms or Mr Right. At one moment you could be feeling a possessive and protective love that will last for ever, and swearing undying loyalty; the next moment you are off, burning your boats and waving goodbye. You do not necessarily have 'a lover in every port', but you do like to wander the world, in fact or imagination, and know that everywhere is home. When these conflicting sides are not reconciled, you can feel torn between a deep belief in human fellowship and a sense of inner loneliness and emotional isolation.

Although you seek constant emotional stimulation, and cannot tolerate boredom, you are quite capable of being loyal to your childhood sweetheart – as long as he or she sufficiently captures your wild imagination and love of variety and changing moods. Likewise, your very wildness may attract you to solid Earth types who can offer you a sober stability and common sense which you otherwise tend to lack.

Your Greatest Strengths

Undiluted optimism; intuitive ability to tune into the times and express your own and other people's thoughts and feelings with wit and insight; personal magnetism; your kind helpfulness, generosity, good fellowship and willingness to go the extra mile.

Your Greatest Weaknesses

Restlessly searching for fresh emotional and intellectual stimulation and excitement which can push you to extremes of behaviour; constantly over-extending your financial and emotional resources; leaving projects unfinished; gullibility and misplaced faith in unworthy people and causes.

Images for Integration

A homing pigeon ... An international nanny ... An evangelist offers a vision of personal salvation ... Jimi Hendrix's Woodstock rendition of *The Star Spangled Banner* ... William Blake's watercolour *Teach These Souls to Fly* (Tate Gallery, London).

Famous Personalities

William Blake (poet, artist and mystic), Joseph Conrad (novelist), Georges Feydeau (dramatist and farceur), Sonia Gandhi (wife of Indian President, Rajiv), Jimi Hendrix (legendary rock musician), Hans Helmut Kirst (novelist), Lord Frederic Leighton (painter), Isabelle Pagan (pioneer astrologer and writer).

SUN SAGITTARIUS ♐ MOON LEO ♌

Remember, happiness doesn't depend upon who you are or what you have; it depends solely upon what you think.
HOW TO WIN FRIENDS AND INFLUENCE PEOPLE, DALE CARNEGIE

The nation had the lion's heart; I had the luck to give the roar.

Personally I'm always ready to learn, although I do not always like being taught.
WINSTON CHURCHILL

Themes

FIRE/FIRE Warm-hearted; grandiose; self-dramatizing; intuitive thinker; visionary; romantic; arrogant; nobility; absent-minded; hot-tempered; devoted; extravagant; courageous; childlike enthusiasm; adventurer; gambler; love of winning.

Are you seeking the meaning of life or the glory of self? Are you a visionary philosopher or a playful child who never knows when to stop? Your active, larger-than-life imagination hastens you on to the 'sunny uplands' of the future, but you are apt to forget that the slow steps of humanity must travel every inch of the weary road that leads there.

Intensely fiery, restless and proud, you work and play with total involvement, never losing your vision of the pot of gold at the end of the rainbow – for you want nothing less. But that pot of gold – whether it is a win at the races, a first at Oxford, a bestselling novel, or a trek in the Himalayas – is part of the future that eternally fuels your ambition and beckons you on. Your inner vision of your life with you in the star role is everything.

Your enthusiasm for life and learning is overwhelming, and can be very contagious. You therefore make a natural leader, as long as others do not mind your autocratic style and your somewhat abrupt way of giving orders. Everything you do must be true to your inner vision and to the principles that underpin all your actions. And if someone objects to the way you express yourself, well it is just too bad for them. With both the Sun and the Moon in the element of Fire, your drama and volatility can literally burn more sensitive souls who will wonder what hit them.

Your intentions, however, are utterly honourable, and when people get to know you they will realize that your autocracy has a childlike quality – innocent, pure-of-heart and omnipotent. Self-expression is as necessary as breathing for you, and you refuse to be pigeon-holed by anyone. Whatever engages your talents professionally will have to be something that offers enough room for your originality and flair. Your high sense of justice would come alive in courtroom drama or on the stage.

Following your road to ever greater and fuller self-expression can, however, cause you to collapse with fatigue. So consumed are you with your inner visions and plans that you easily neglect your physical wellbeing and treat your body as one more mundane responsibility that gets in the way of your fun. If you can develop some patience and realism, and the capacity to really think about other people's views, you will have a greater chance of bringing your ideas to fruition – with longer-lasting results.

Relationships

Intensely romantic and in love with love, you are passionate and committed in a relationship, but perhaps never quite sure that this is *the* great romance. Your love of intense experience plus your considerable vanity mean that you are open-ended when it comes to relationships, and this can be disconcerting for your mate. You give your all and expect the same in return, as love is part of the big drama of your life.

You cannot hide your feelings and, if your passions change, you will change your life as well. But you are extremely honourable and true to your moral principles – to go against them would be a gross insult to yourself. You expect others to be as morally sincere as you, and are mortified when you discover otherwise. Yet you are immensely resilient, and bounce back from emotional or professional setbacks with your integrity untarnished, your wisdom enhanced and your determination to succeed increased ten-fold.

You love the good things of life: beauty, style, talent, literary genius, champions of all kinds, and social soirées where your inner child comes out to relish the sheer delight of human intercourse.

Your Greatest Strengths

Creative imagination; sense of the drama of life; playfulness and openness to new adventure; ability to see potential in people and situations; optimism; courage; leadership abilities; nobility of spirit; capacity to bring light and warmth into the lives of others.

Your Greatest Weaknesses

Impatience; temper tantrums; being bossy and opinionated; propensity to grab the limelight of others to hide insecurity; difficulty in accepting normal human limitations; lack of sensitivity to other people's needs; taking yourself too seriously; self-centredness.

Image for Integration

At an emotionally moving ceremony, the shaman of the gypsies is given an honorary university degree in herbal lore and ancient geography.

Famous Personalities

Willy Brandt (politician), Dale Carnegie (guru of positive thinking), Winston Churchill (former British prime minister), Benjamin Disraeli (politician), Arthur Fiedler (conductor), Gustave Flaubert (writer), Jane Fonda (actress), Nancy Mitford (writer), Lee Remick (actress), Charles Ringling (of Ringling Bros. Circus), Christina Rossetti (poet), Jean Sibelius (composer), Lee Trevino (golfer).

Sun Sagittarius ♐ Moon Virgo ♍

Nothing is more terrible than activity without insight.

Work is the grand cure of all the maladies and miseries that ever beset mankind.
Thomas Carlyle

Happiness is the rational understanding of life and the world.
Baruch Spinoza

Themes

FIRE/EARTH Cavalier yet careful; socially concerned; intellectually discriminating; enthusiastically precise; ability to categorize knowledge; a practical idealist; boldly dogmatic; diffident yet outspoken; loyal and helpful friend; morally sound; philosophical; charming; humorously tactful.

As an artist of life, are you a miniaturist or would you say you work in bold, slapdash images? Are you a confident extrovert who keeps an anxious inner world under tight mental grip, or an imaginative introvert who finds pleasureable release through discovering you can make a big impact on the world? Do you flourish in the privacy of your own home, or do you want to roam the world, seeking out new friends and open spaces?

When in insecure, critical mode you can be a modest but nervous, small-minded puritan who works to the letter of the law. When you are truly inspired, however, and engaged both intellectually and emotionally in your life, you become a grand visionary who can marry broad concepts to practical human need. You are inspired by large truths but you will not be happy until you get the rules down on paper – and you want to get it right only because you have such reverence for the great ideas that bring the most hope to humankind.

You are liable to shift between periods of great certitude and self-confidence, and moods of deep doubt and self-criticism. The centre stage attracts your sense of drama and self-esteem, but if placed under the spotlight for too long you can become something of a nervous shrinking violet. Your aims really are for the greatest good of the many, rather than just for yourself.

Even if you are not particularly academic, you have the mind of the perennial student and are always learning something new that will be grist to your mill. You can talk a great deal and impress others with your zeal, but then surprise everyone by working just as hard. A good education is especially helpful in bringing out your great strengths, for you are someone who knows there is a lot about you that is just waiting to be born, so to speak, if only you could find the right teacher, the right course ...

Although you need to feel of use, you also sense that your life is a journey and that, well, you ought to be going somewhere. Your fiery-earthy temperament can create a lot of nervous tension for you, and you may sometimes find it difficult to unwind. When you catch yourself becoming obsessively active and pompously intolerant, that is your signal to slow down and smell the roses, to learn to play, to find out what you *feel*. Speaking of roses, you will find that gardening and other healthy and ecologically sound outdoor activities will do wonders for your optimum mind–body balance.

When your aspirations to a universal outlook are married to your love of clarity, detail and service, you can be a superb educator. By presenting the big picture of any subject – which you can do because you are an intuitive at heart – and at the same time getting down to its practical application, you are able to enthuse your students and bring out the best in them. When you want to be, you are a great problem solver and thrive on finding precise, logical solutions to seemingly insoluble problems.

You tend to be a person of great faith – a faith based upon reason, so you probably see no conflict between science and religion. Although you are a lover of objective truth, you sense the underlying mystery of life which, quite reasonably, transcends all those quantifiable facts!

Relationships

You can be kind-hearted and utterly devoted in relationships, and you will be shocked by disloyalty. Yet you can blow hot and cold yourself – at one moment something of an uptight prude, the next wildly vivacious and flirtatious.

You are fairly gregarious and like the company of many different kinds of people, preferably stimulating and important types, but you may find it difficult to really be intimate on a one-to-one basis unless you share an intellectual rapport with your partner, as well as having some common vision, enthusiasm and dedication to a cause.

You are warm, sentimental and dependable when people have won your respect, and very willing to stop and have a good time – as long as it is done with panache and decorum.

Your Greatest Strengths

Intellectual vigour and precision; enthusiastic dedication to ideals and hard work; quiet charm and warmly helpful attitude to others; ability to convey ideas objectively and to persuade others with your clear arguments as well as your calm integrity.

Your Greatest Weaknesses

Proneness to mental obsessions and nervous anxieties which deplete your creative energies; tendency to be moralistic, overcritical and judgemental of others' imperfections; discomfort with emotional needs; desire for certitude, which can make you pedantic and narrow-minded.

Images for Integration

An athlete gives a fundraising performance for charity ... A philosopher presents a perfect mathematical vision of the nature and meaning of the universe ... The Ten Commandments.

Famous Personalities

Ursula Bloom (prolific writer and journalist), Kenneth Branagh (actor and film director), Ashleigh Brilliant (cartoonist), Thomas Carlyle (historian, essayist and philosopher), Jaye P. Morgan (singer), George Moscone (politician), Baruch Spinoza (philosopher), Francis Thompson (poet), August von Mackensen (German field marshall of first world war).

SUN SAGITTARIUS ♐ MOON LIBRA ♎

Happiness in marriage is purely a matter of chance.

Let other pens dwell on guilt and misery.
JANE AUSTEN

*There is more treasure in books than in all the pirates' loot on Treasure Island
... and best of all, you can enjoy these riches every day of your life.*
WALT DISNEY

Themes

FIRE/AIR Optimistic; warm-hearted; philosophical mind; social conscience; generous spirit; romantic; prophetic; chivalrous; graciously gregarious; an interested observer of humankind; frequenter of coffee shops and theatres; ardent communicator; fun-loving companion.

Outspoken and iconoclastic, yet considerate and warmly available to others, you are the romantic anarchist who wins people over to your view because nobody can resist your charisma and *joie de vivre*. Self-dramatizing and independent, you are a visionary with a strong need to communicate your ideas and to have them passionately received and affirmed.

Communication for you is a fiery experience, an expression of love, an experience of myth and meaning, and this driving need to get your ideas across can take you on to the stage, or it may find its outlet in the written word, especially fiction or poetry. People-watching and the intricacies of human relationships may fuel your inspirational mind. But whether attracted to more serious pursuits such as law or politics, or a more artistic milieu, you will always have a fresh, vital approach to life that makes you a wonderful teacher and companion.

Honourable and just, you nevertheless often have to compromise between your sentiment about situations and people and the detached, broad, mental view of things by which you aim to live your life. You are a person of integrity, originality and scruples. Deploring any form of injustice, you will readily and vociferously support the underdog, the innocent child and the eccentric artist – for you are a little bit of all three.

You are a natural salesperson, and could excel in public relations or marketing where your heart and mind come together in persuasive rhetoric. Whatever you do, you need scope for the expression of your artistic flair, your strong social conscience and your intense conviviality. Your sense of humour and gift for arbitration may often be useful in defusing tense or dangerous situations; hence you may be attracted to politics, where the hustle and bustle satisfies your need for mobility, and your social savvy lands you very much on your feet. Your social grace, love of beauty and mischievous sense of fun make you an extremely resilient and popular person wherever you decide to hang your hat.

You have the gift of the gab and love to wax lyrical about your latest inspiration. Getting people together to collaborate on projects is one of the things you enjoy and are especially good at, and you excel at playing the great compromiser and coordinator, oiling the wheels of joint ventures with flair and ease. Although quite amenable to others' views, you are an assertive person and can display a lively temper when challenged or unjustly thwarted.

Relationships

You thrive on social stimulation, friendship and love, and to be happy you certainly require substantial amounts of affection and admiration. But you run away from heavy displays of emotion. You are passionate and idealistic in love, but not soppy, and you try to keep your emotions under the control of your mind.

You want to share the grand journey of life with your loved one – the drama, the beauty, the elegance – and you want to keep things positive and happy-go-lucky. When it comes to changing nappies, however, you may get restless. Luckily, your love of learning and discovery should also help you in the more mundane journey of domesticity, paying bills and sticking to some sort of healthy routine. Taking care of the latter is not your strong point, but fair's fair, and when you sense that your partner needs a lift you can always come up with a 'treat' that cheers up the down-hearted. Likewise there are plenty of times when you need lots of tender, loving care, and you will happily switch roles from time to time, being able to play parent or child, daddy or mummy, teacher or student with equal panache.

Your Greatest Strengths

Outrageous, unstuffy sense of humour; warm sincerity; your love of people; fine intellect; acute observations; quick wit; honesty, which both shocks and delights your friends; openness to adventure; your strong, resilient, positive approach to all the challenges life presents.

Your Greatest Weaknesses

Over-expansiveness in both your ideas and style so that you are frequently forced to come down to earth; gullibility; reliance on luck; restlessness and need for constant activity and social advancement; an on-going conflict between independence and needing others.

Images for Integration

Amidst a whirl of gaiety, a writer sits in a coffee house taking notes, and a painter paints ... *The Dead Poets' Society*.

Famous Personalities

Gregg Allman (singer), Jane Austen (author), Maria Callas (operatic star), David Carradine (actor), Emily Dickinson (poet and author), Walt Disney (leader in film animation), Betty Grable (actress), Werner Heisenberg (physicist), Liv Ullman (actress), Saki (writer), Henri Toulouse-Lautrec (artist).

— 104 —

SUN SAGITTARIUS ♐ MOON SCORPIO ♏

Trial by jury is the lamp that shows that freedom lives.
LORD DEVLIN

I don't let her watch anything that teaches her false values or encourages this hideous materialism that is so prevalent.
BETTE MIDLER (TALKING ABOUT HER YOUNG DAUGHTER)

Everyone is psychic; it's just that the majority of people don't use their powers or even realise they have them.
URI GELLER

If you can actually count your money, you are not really a rich man.
J. PAUL GETTY

Themes

FIRE/WATER Moralistic intensity; confident; judicial and exacting mind; emotional fervour; sensual; satirical; sociable; serious; fiercely loyal; vivid imagination; powerful desires; keen instincts; the victory of optimism over despair; entrepreneurial spirit.

Innocence coupled with a splendidly dirty mind – that's you! You optimistically look to new experiences as you love to learn, to respond to challenges, to feel stimulated and alive. But you also have a shrewd sense of both your own powers and your limitations, your need for security, and the needs and motivations of other people.

You combine warmth and hopefulness with emotional reserve; an eager morality with an ever-present awareness of primitive proclivities – desires, jealousies, obsessions. A vivacious intensity exudes from every pore, although you are very capable of deliberately restraining your affections if you think it appropriate.

You are sensitive to situations and people, sizing up the atmosphere and hidden signals therein, and this makes you a good detective and an astute judge of people. It is not that you are paranoid, although you can be suspicious enough about hidden motives; it is just that you are no fool because you know well the inner struggle between triumphant faith and the downward pull of black moods. You are fairly clear about your own standards and ideals; in fact, you have a strongly judicial temperament and register people's actions and words very vigorously. No one gets away with anything in your presence.

In many ways, you are the passionate philosopher, acutely aware of the seriousness of life and the urgency of primary issues: good versus evil, freedom versus oppression, hope versus despair. And this makes you a profound and fascinating companion, never light-weight but always ready to experience the heights and the depths because you know you are going to learn something important.

You would make a good barrister as you love grappling with demanding moral issues or anything that pushes your wits to their limit. You may also be found in politics or social work, where your personal feelings about social concerns can find expression.

Whatever you do, you think and feel passionately about things, and you will approach your relationships and career with the intensity of an artist. Your controversial and exacting mind enjoys a good argument, and you are likely to stir things up if you feel bored, or if you smell complacency creeping in.

Relationships

Given the choice, you would want an intense life in which you could often drive yourself to the edge. In love, this tendency makes you volatile, unpredictable but 100-per-cent involved – and you demand the same commitment from your partner. Extremely passionate, needful of intimacy and capable of lasting loyalty, you are either a deep, dark enigma to your partner, or a jovial companion ready for adventure.

Part of your creative dilemma is your inner swing from possessiveness and dependency to a fiery, independent stance which says 'I can do it myself – I'm the world's best survivor!' This attitude is great for climbing Mount Everest but not very conducive to intimacy. And a lack of humility can wear a bit thin as well. You are always biting off a bit more than you can chew and then defiantly pushing full-steam ahead to prove to others (and to yourself) that you have heroic qualities. And you want heroic excitement in your lover, too, although a sensible, down-to-earth type will help to balance your intensity and imagination.

If you can lighten up a bit and direct some of your emotional intensity into creative hobbies, relationships will go more smoothly, and your potential as a compassionate, humorous and wise individual can be realized.

Your Greatest Strengths

Magnetic charisma; emotional commitment and dedication to life; courage and resilience in the face of pain or fear of the unknown; powerful intellect and talent for investigation; spontaneous honesty and thirst for self-knowledge.

Your Greatest Weaknesses

A rigid, overly-critical attitude to weaker souls; a tendency to become over-zealous about your loves and hates; proneness to proud retaliation and condemnation of contrary views; a rebellious tendency to create trouble when bored.

Images for Integration

A missionary sees himself as a secret agent for God ... A psychiatric nurse and a criminal cross-examine each other.

Famous Personalities

Eileen Agar (painter), Hector Berlioz (composer), Dave Brubeck (jazz musician), Lord Devlin (lawyer and High Court judge), Phil Donohue (chat-show host), Paul Eluard (surrealist poet), Douglas Fairbanks, Jr. (actor), Cesar A. Franck (composer), Uri Geller (psychic), J. Paul Getty (oil magnate and art patron), Bette Midler (actress and singer), Captain Bertram Ratcliffe (soldier and writer), Steven Spielberg (film director), Robert Welch (founder of John Birch Society).

— 105 —

Sun Sagittarius ♐ Moon Sagittarius ♐

Give happiness and joy to many other people. There is nothing better or greater than that.
LUDWIG VAN BEETHOVEN

Intellect distinguishes between the possible and the impossible.
MAX BORN

Themes

FIRE/FIRE Laughter and solemnity; certainty and anarchy; doubt and single-mindedness; intuitive; gregarious; intensely enthusiastic; resilient; funny; freedom lover and fundamentalist; sheer enjoyment and zest for life and nature.

Are you a wise-cracking comedian full of provocative witticisms and lively banter? Or are you an earnest, high-sounding preacher full of moral certainty and determined to put the world to rights?

Life for you can feel like a never-ending adventure, a major quest into the furthest reaches of a great cosmic joke for the next source of fun and enjoyment; or it can be a well of endless wonder, education and philosophical and theological speculation which you want to tell everyone about. So the trick here is to get the balance right between frolic and fiercely important morality. When you combine your sheer vitality and zest for life with your capacity for broad understanding, however, you can command an endless reservoir of intellectual enthusiasm, which can stimulate and encourage all with whom you come into contact.

You are a person of intense, vivid feelings, whose mind is at first captured by variety but then inspired by the meaning behind the various threads of your life experience. You opt for the large view and have a flair for seeing the big picture and the central issues in any situation. Legal and moral issues fascinate you, and you would enjoy making evangelical pronouncements in the courtroom, pulpit – or the pub. Doing the right thing is important to you, and you will let others know in no uncertain terms if their behaviour does not meet your standards.

You are totally wholehearted, a kind of archetypal incarnation of sincerity itself, and as a result you find insincerity, cruelty and corruption pretty unbearable. Freedom of thought and movement are central to your wellbeing, yet your heart seeks to devote itself with a sense of moral certainty to some over-arching creed or philosophy. Extreme high-mindedness could lead you to espouse a particular belief with a fanaticism that covers up your inner doubts, and protects you from asking questions about yourself which you fear may be unanswerable.

Although you hate to be pigeon-holed, you hanker after the security of a Utopian social and moral order where justice reigns and everyone has a definite place. It is quite likely that the breakdown of values in society will occupy your thoughts and motivate you towards improving the situation. You may do this through social work, teaching, writing or the ministry. Making and/or starring in comedy films will give you an even better outlet for your goals, as even when you recognize waste and despair, you rarely lose faith in the goodness and potential brilliance of your fellow human beings. And you know that a good laugh goes a long way.

You are highly independent and probably physically restless. Lots of outdoor space and opportunities for travel are what you want, and these will help you to relax. Intensely loyal in your own fashion, you keep old friends for ages, even though you will easily pick up new ones along your many journeys. You are strongly intuitive with an ear and an eye for what will catch on, and you can usually turn your hand to a wide variety of pursuits.

Although there may be a romantic, wandering gypsy inside you, you are a serious person at heart whose inner principles define exactly who you are. You may change the way you express those principles throughout your life and, as a result, evoke criticism from more conventional people. But you understand that 'the times are a-changing', and if there is anyone who can marry expediency with eternal verities and make it work – profitably – it is you!

Relationships

People in all sizes, shapes and sentiments fascinate you. Each fresh personal relationship can feel like the ultimate revelation, but can quickly become claustrophobic. This can either lead you to flit from flower to flower, treating each with equal enthusiasm whilst it lasts; or it can create a need for stability and certainty. If the latter applies, you will be drawn to a feet-on-the-ground Earth type, whose ease with the daily round and capacity for sensual enjoyment gives you a deep sense of roots and security.

Once committed to a relationship – and it must be one that is 'fun' and allows some freedom for adventure – it can be the focus and foundation of all your beliefs. But emotional maturity will demand that you do battle with your restlessness, face your childish ways, and stay put when the going gets tough.

Your Greatest Strengths

Optimism; humour; resilience; broad, questing mind; courageous devotion to principles; faith in the future and the essential benevolence of life.

Your Greatest Weaknesses

Tendency to hold forth with self-righteousness and 'good advice'; reluctance to grow up and admit to having limitations; tendency to be slapdash and sloppy with details; proneness to sudden downers when life's realities clash with your noble ideals.

Images for Integration

A top-speed crazy comedian combines sheer silliness with profound spiritual and philosophical insights ... Beethoven's ninth symphony and *Ode to Joy*.

Famous Personalities

Ludwig van Beethoven (composer), Max Born (philosopher and physicist), Willy Claes (Secretary General of NATO), Carl Ferdinand Cori (biochemist), Joan Didion (novelist and writer), Georg Kaiser (writer), Max Kester (comedian), John McCrae (poet), Randy Newman (musician), Elissa Landi (actress and novelist).

— 106 —

SUN SAGITTARIUS ♐ MOON CAPRICORN ♑

My main themes are exploration (space, sea, time), the position of Man in the hierarchy of the universe, and the effect of contact with other intelligences.
ARTHUR C. CLARKE (AUTHOR)

We only begin to awake to reality when we realise that the material world, the world of space and time ... is nothing but a sign and a symbol of a mystery which infinitely transcends it.
BEDE GRIFFITHS

Themes

FIRE/EARTH Philosophical humour; serious exploration; both facile and profound; judicial; enthusiastically loyal; imposing personality; moral courage; self-importance; eager for success; leadership; verbose; committed friendship; generous; kind; social conscience; civil rights; Peter Pan and Captain Hook.

Although you are a freedom-loving explorer who feels challenged by every new horizon, you are also a closet businessman with the potential to make an empire out of each new discovery. You are the romantic maverick and the sober traditionalist all rolled into one, and when your inner masculine and feminine work together it is a bit like Father Christmas forming a limited company to ensure success and security for all concerned.

One part of you believes in the abundance of the universe, but the other part tends to hedge its bets in the game of life. Life *is* a game for you, but a serious one – and you do not like losing. This is a major component of your inner creative tension – the need for unabashed self-expression versus your desire for self-control, respect and concrete attainment.

You are expansive, impulsive and optimistic, eager to learn, travel, discuss, socialize and proselytize. Yet you also like to feel you are getting somewhere, making an impact, holding the reins, moving forward materially and socially, carrying responsibility and authority and building up material security for yourself and your family. Should you play or should you work? Should you put on your favorite Beethoven album or should you practise your scales? You may sometimes feel like an old soul who is dying to let that crazy inner child out. You want control over the known, but are attracted to the excitement of the unknown. Ultimately you want to extend your horizons – emotionally, intellectually and spiritually – but you want to connect them with the meaningful traditions of the past as well.

Your appetite for life is big, and one person will not satisfy it – you need a career, hobbies, stimulating people and personal challenges. You have a lot of energy and make time for an active life in politics, business or teaching whilst also trying to master some art form. But no matter how much you take on – which is likely to be considerable because you love the journey as much as arriving at your destination – your devotion to your family is deep and consistent. You have the personality of the caring, patriarchal uncle who takes his responsibilities seriously and enjoys them as well.

You are happiest when you have achieved the status of the sought-after expert in some area, so that you can be your generous, positive self while basking in the limelight of recognition. And you are not averse to being rewarded with a high standard of living and plenty of creature comforts, even though you are quite capable of living rough whilst journeying onwards and upwards towards your ideal. You can be a friend and a father, a mate and a mother, and a seeker of sound principles, self-knowledge and social relief!

Relationships

Emotionally you are passionate and wholehearted, if somewhat detached and hard to satisfy at times. And you can be suprisingly touchy and imperious if you feel your dignity has been ignored or unappreciated. You are big-hearted and trustworthy, dedicated to your partner, to family and to friends, although sometimes you have to go your own way to ponder vital issues on your own.

You are naturally, if somewhat restrainedly, assertive, and you readily impress others with your offbeat, eccentric, somewhat nervous, authoritative, but always friendly and ready-to-help ways. Conservative and altruistic, you feel responsibility keenly and always try to live up to your moral obligations. In relationships, however, you need mental affinity and a fair amount of independence. Sometimes you like it hot, and sometimes you like to be alone! You may keep others guessing, but your loyalty will never be questioned.

Your Greatest Strengths

Moral integrity; enthusiastic quest for both meaning and usefulness; generosity; responsible handling of authority; honesty; expansive intellect; delightfully witty sense of humour.

Your Greatest Weaknesses

Verbosity and occasional dogmatic bluntness; tendency to take yourself too seriously; to be overly materialistic and opportunistic; your urge to run the show and assume more power than you have.

Images for Integration

In the year 2999, a courageous explorer goes on a quest for knowledge of the past which opens up for man a hopeful future on another planet ...With patient skill a rock climber scales a seemingly impossible mountain peak.

Famous Personalities

Kenneth Baker (politician), Kim Basinger (actress), Arthur C. Clarke (writer), Helen Douglas (actress turned politician), Helen Frankenthaler (artist), Bede Griffiths (monk and author), Christina Onassis (heiress), Carlo Ponti (film producer), Richard Pryor (actor and comedian), Bhagwan Shri Rajneesh (New Age guru), Lillian Russell (entertainer turned politician), Anton Webern (composer), Maurice White (musician, Earth, Wind & Fire).

— 107 —

SUN SAGITTARIUS ⚶ MOON AQUARIUS ≈

The machine threatens all achievement.
RAINER MARIA RILKE

As a people we have developed a life-style that is draining the earth of its priceless and irreplaceable resources without regard for the future of our children and people all around the world.
MARGARET MEAD

I don't want to be immortal through my work, I want to be immortal by not dying.
WOODY ALLEN

Themes

FIRE/AIR Friendly; intellectual; visionary; seeker of truth; tolerant; independent; socially concerned; breezy; outspoken; loquacious; broad-minded and philosophical; kind-hearted eccentric; high ideals; philanthropic; romantic; open and honest.

You are the benign patriarch, egalitarian in feeling and forward-looking in method. A humanitarian at heart, ready to share your knowledge and profound insight with any and all who come under your beneficent umbrella, you immediately impress your audience with your sincerity and idealism. You may also impress them with your verbosity, your deft logic in concocting arguments and your tendency to say everything that is on your mind. Thus you can be somewhat overpowering at times. Your affection is immediate, if somewhat cerebral, but your word is as good as your bond. This, plus your intense individualism and refusal to be pigeon-holed, makes you a popular person who will always stand out in a crowd.

All your interests are tackled with high intelligence and vigour, and transacted with a warm personal manner which makes long-lasting friendships. People feel your earnestness and desire to keep human relations and the world in general as ideal as possible. In a sense, you live in a world of your own, insisting on the greater reality of abstract truth and the importance of pursuing possibilities without any personal accountability. You like to work on insoluble problems, make original discoveries and contributions, and say outrageous things that make people think. Usually you can do this with such wonderful humour that you get away with your outlandish ways.

You are primarily an intuitive thinker, something of an eccentric genius, and your thinking may sometimes be so Utopian and futuristic that others find you trying to live with. Because of your originality and awkward intensity you may, in fact, often be a few steps ahead of everyone else, and feel like the odd man out. Nevertheless, you need people – you watch them, study them, communicate, play and fall in love with them. Your ideas about people en masse and how we should all best live together will play a central role in your outlook and behaviour.

You need a definite medium through which you can express your creative insights, plenty of space in which to be an authority. But you tend to spread yourself too thin, so it is best to remember that you cannot be an authority on everything. Even if you are not particularly academic, you are capable of seeing beyond cultural norms and boundaries, and have an instinctive understanding of the common aims of the nations of the world. This gives you a lofty compassion for your fellow man and a desire to do something worthwhile, to make a difference to the world. You are a natural for teaching and academia, but you may also have enough energy left for a part-time career in

politics, social work, theatre, the ministry or some wild entre-
preuneurial venture.

Relationships

Intimate relationships can be somewhat problematic for you due to
your large appetite for experience and need for independence. And yet *true*
there is no one more thoughtful and loyal than you when you have
given your heart away – as long as he or she does not start telling you
what you can and cannot do.

You need an intelligent, stimulating partner, someone with a strong
ego who can stand on their own at times, someone you respect and
who shares some of your own passionate interests. You are much more
interested in sharing a football game or an evening at the theatre,
cinema or concert hall than you are in sharing domestic
responsibilities. Your partner may at times be driven crazy by your
absent-mindedness: while your head is in the clouds thinking about
your next exciting project, he or she is getting the practical things done
and may get tired of waiting for the lecture to finish.

Although you are romantic, you have a strong need for friendship
and group enterprise, so that even the most passionate relationship *true*
will have a brotherly-sisterly quality about it.

Your Greatest Strengths

Your intellect and breadth of vision which can accomodate all types of
viewpoints; friendliness and easy-going adaptability; positive outlook
and willingness to take risks; ability to generate many creative
alternatives to a problem; love of learning and discussion, with the aim
of finding a deeper truth.

Your Greatest Weaknesses

Tendency to be too impractical and out of touch with mundane *true*
realities; high-minded, crusading zeal, which can be insensitive to
subtle details and sentimental souls; inclination to overgeneralize and
live life purely in the realm of abstract ideas, in your belief that routine
crushes creativity.

Image for Integration

On a tour of primitive lands, a university professor goes through a tribal initiation and becomes a blood brother of the chief.

Famous Personalities

Louisa May Alcott (writer), Woody Allen (actor and film director), Andrew Carnegie (industrialist and philanthropist), Philip K. Dick (writer of science-fiction), Manuel de Falla (composer), Caroline Kennedy (daughter of John F. Kennedy, former American President), John Kennedy Jnr (her brother), Richard Leakey (anthropologist), Margaret Mead (anthropologist), Rainer Maria Rilke (poet), Tommy Steele (entertainer).

— 108 —

SUN SAGITTARIUS ♐ MOON PISCES ♓

The salvation of mankind lies only in making everything the concern of all.
ALEXANDER SOLZHENITSYN

I love mankind – it's people I can't stand.
CHARLES SCHULTZ

Life can't be all bad when for ten dollars you can buy all the Beethoven sonatas and listen to them for ten years.
WILLIAM F. BUCKLEY

There is no cure for birth and death save to enjoy the interval.
GEORGE SANTAYANA

Themes

FIRE/WATER Emotional; fervent; restless; humanitarian; visionary; rich imagination; helpful; sympathetic; philosophical; spiritually sensitive; deep convictions; an irrational logician; generous; moralistic; forgiving.

Do you want to broaden the horizons of your experience, or enrich the dreams of your fantasy life? Do you want to understand more but find intellectual principles too cold for comfort? You are a thinker and a dreamer, a sentimental philosopher, a moralistic mystic whose inner eye will scan the pitiful plight of humankind, but whose heart will understand, forgive and absolve all.

No matter how tied down you may be in the mundane world, your spirit will do a lot of travelling via your imagination and emotions. A kind of divine discontent keeps you preoccupied with broad beliefs and ideals, ever concerned with the deeper spiritual needs of people, and you may indeed have a very profound intuitive understanding of universal truths. A trusting openness and a need to give endears you to many, but due to your incredible restlessness you may find it difficult to settle on one person.

Your tremendous sensitivity to the human condition and to people in general gives you an artistic temperament with a loveable and somewhat wistful humility. You would, and probably often do, give the shirt off your own back to friends and underdogs in need. Receiving impressions readily, you communicate and give back eagerly and generously of your insight and feelings. You may often need to stop and collect your thoughts and feelings, learn to hold back and assess, in order for you not to dissipate your energies and to overpower others (as well as yourself) with the unrestrained effusiveness of your emotional expression.

Likewise, you can be just as lavish with mundane expenditures. As you are not particularly practical, you will have to make an effort to not give in to that mischievous wastrel sub-personality within you which just wants to be careless, lazy and self-indulgent. It is not that you are materialistic; far from it. But you need to develop concentration and a healthy sense of boundaries, so that insead of drifting in and out of jobs and debt and 'isms', you can more purposefully cultivate enough security to allow the best development of your considerable talents.

You love to tell your personal story and give advice because you can so clearly see the folly of others' ways. In situations where you cannot decide what advice is appropriate to give, you may just tell a joke instead. Your heart and your mind are inextricably linked. This can result in profound superstition or invaluable wisdom.

You need social stimulation – you are a veritable barometer of social climate – but you also need time alone when you can commune with music, nature and silence, and imbibe that non-verbal sustenance which is so essential for your wellbeing. During these contemplative periods you can also sort out the real from the non-real, your feelings from others' opinions, outrageous behaviour from inner motives. You have the strength of the philosopher's mind and the compassion of the mystic's heart.

Relationships

You can be gushy, sentimental, romantic and totally devoted to your family and friends. Exuding a kind of woe-begotten affection for others, you make yourself irrisistible. You yearn for meaningful contact but know beforehand that no one is likely to really understand you and the deep well of love you have to give.

You may fall hopelessly in love, idealize your lover, and then despair because he or she does not live up to the mythological ideal. But not for a petty fault do you take back your love. Indeed, you value the heights and the depths of emotional experience because they teach you about yourself. Eventually, love makes you wiser and more stable. And your resilience and compassion make you a revered friend.

Your Greatest Strengths

Openness to life and adventure; expansive intellect and intuition; ability to work with people and ideas in an open, versatile manner; warm, sensitive, forgiving and humorous nature.

Your Greatest Weaknesses

Gullibility and vacillation; lack of concentration and discrimination; emotional instability; tendency to alternate between optimism and pessimism without the patience to ground your ideas.

Image for Integration

A jolly, shabbily dressed vicar tells raucous jokes to down-and-outs, children and high society at the Church garden party.

Famous Personalities

Ian Botham (cricketer), William F. Buckley (writer and television personality), Cathryn Crosby (television hostess), Adrienne Hirt (sex therapist), Raja Rao (author), George Santayana (philosopher), Charles Schultz (cartoonist), Georges Seurat (artist), Frank Sinatra (singer, actor), Alexander Solzhenitsyn (author and philosopher), Michael Tilson Thomas (conductor), Evelyn Underhill (mystic).

Chapter Thirteen

SUN IN CAPRICORN

———•———

—109—

SUN CAPRICORN ♑ MOON ARIES ♈

Man must cease attributing his problems to his environment, and learn again to exercise his will – his personal responsibility in the realm of faith and morals.
ALBERT SCHWEITZER

I haven't asked you to make me young again. All I want is to go on getting older.
KONRAD ADENAUER

Today's woman is too intelligent to be exploited by the fashion world.
DIANE VON FURSTENBERG

Themes

EARTH/FIRE Wilful; magnetic; intensely ambitious; self-interest; purposeful; quick-thinking; rational; action-oriented; restless; rides roughshod over others; takes command; successful; powerful; rebellious; impressive personality.

Are you an establishment person or a rebel determined to rewrite the rules of the game? You have the energy of a steamroller, the mental astuteness of a criminal lawyer, and enough vitality and ambition to run three parallel lives. But since you have to make it all fit into one, you frequently bulldoze your way to success and then, desirous of further conquests, start all over again.

Even if you are not in business, you have the temperament of the zealous entrepreneur, determined to make the rules work for you in a big way. If you are running a family, then you will direct your considerable energies into the system, warmly but firmly imposing values and objectives that you feel are right. Family life is important to you, and when you can contribute your special brand of wit and wisdom, playfulness and leadership, you feel affirmed and appreciated. If, however, you do not have enough challenge in your life you will tend to be irritable and bossy, difficult to live with, and you may need to branch out to feel really satisfied. Combining the competitive spirit of the athlete with the determined, well-organized consciousness of the business tycoon, you do not waste time in deciding what you want and planning exactly how to get there.

You love to organize and lead, and you usually do it with great panache which tends to inspire confidence in others. You have a good opinion of yourself and a brontosaurus-sized ego. All the same, however, you have a deep need to prove your own worth to be really happy. Such intense personal investment in your goals can make you rather ruthless and self-seeking, but you are not likely to see it that way. For you, nothing short of total self-reliance and commitment will get the job done, and you learn early on that you are the most reliable person around.

Your goals often take on a larger-than-life importance. With obsessive single-minded enthusiasm you go for broke, but may end up emotionally bankrupt. You do not like losing in any sense – intellectually, emotionally or professionally. Your temper can flare up quickly but because you do not like to be seen in an undignified light you try hard and learn to control yourself.

You respect people who stand up for what they believe, who know that you have to take risks if you want to stand even marginally above the masses. You like people who match their heroic words with heroic actions. Indeed, you admire heroes and fancy yourself as one, and so you are usually found at the cutting edge of life. Even when you fail, you will have enjoyed your bravura performance, and after singing 'I did it my way' will pick yourself up and start again.

Relationships

Emotionally you are passionate, demanding, moody and, once you have seen that your loved one really knows how wonderful you are, devoted. You can be deeply romantic, but you also want to be proud of the one you love. You can be hard to live with because you have such strong desires and such high standards for yourself, and you can get irritable when things are not going your way.

You are so self-motivated that you naturally tend to run the show in relationships. Trying for more sensitivity and equality with your loved one may be your challenge.

Your Greatest Strengths

Shrewd tenacity; clever and astute thinking; excellent organizational skills and leadership abilities; positive attitude; amazing resilience; love of a challenge, which mobilizes all your tremendous energy and personal courage; honesty and deep sense of responsibility.

Your Greatest Weaknesses

Tendency to overvalue career success and material reward – and getting your own way; brusque manner and insensitivity to other people's needs; restlessness and constant desire for excitement and challenge; tendency to be a poor loser.

Images for Integration

A Roman city-state is attacked by barbarians but its solid walls keep the marauding bandits at bay... An impetuous entrepreneur persuades a conservative banker to back an ambitious project.

Famous Personalities

Konrad Adenauer (German statesman), E.M. Forster (novelist), Vincent Gardenia (actor), Patricia Neal (actress), Johnny Ray (singer), Albert Schweitzer (medical missionary and musician), Jon Voight (actor), Diane Von Furstenberg (fashion designer), James Watt (inventor of steam engine), Richard Widmark (actor), Jane Wyman (actress), Princess Yasmin (Swiss heiress and opera singer).

SUN CAPRICORN ♑ MOON TAURUS ♉

An idealist – that implies you aren't going to achieve something.
ARTHUR SCARGILL

I'm a Catholic ... it's my duty to believe in humanity.
PAOLO BORSELLINO

A government that is big enough to give you all you want is big enough to take it all away.
BARRY GOLDWATER

Themes

EARTH/EARTH Solid and sensible; great integrity; stubborn; patient; possessive; good organizational skills; shrewd; worldly; kind and caring; loyal; resourceful; aesthetic; dependable and practical; good teacher; staunch supporter of status quo; good eye for value; a realist.

Do you want high achievement or comfortable security? Recognition and prestige or longevity? The fact is, both position and permanence are very important to you. You usually manage to succeed in obtaining both, however, because when you get to the summit you innately know when to stop pushing your luck.

Your ideals are based on a sound assessment of what is possible and what is just, and this innate sense of both moral and material organization makes people respect you, and often lean on you. You are earthy through and through, a stalwart and healthy member of society, very much at home in the world of tangibles, pounds and pence, comfortable living and beautiful artifacts.

Hard-working, diligent and frugal, yet also capable of enjoying luxury and the best in food and finery, you have a healthy inner balance of opportunistic get-up-and-go and ability to relax and smell the roses. For you there is a time and place for everything – you get down to basics when it is time to work, and you lay out lavishly (but not excessively) when it is time to party. And due to the relability of your fine-tuned inner barometer of instinctive needs, you do not have to go to extremes. Your sense of self-preservation is too wise for that.

Your virtues can, however, become your vices if your love of security turns into a fear of change – in either the domestic or emotional sense. You need to know where you are as, for you, the unknown is anathema. You are good at controlling your bank account, children, emotions, work-and-play schedule, and most things in your life, but not so good at letting go of the familiar.

If, however, you decide that change *is* a good idea, you will gradually learn to accept it. This is because, essentially, you are nature's child adhering to society's values – you are adaptable, shrewd, and you know that you can trust your instincts, as well as your excellent reasoning abilities. The fact that there is a slow, cyclic development of human needs, desires and ambitions makes good sense to you.

You value common sense even more than predictability. This quality makes you a good teacher or executive leader because you can combine both discipline with patience, scruples with understanding, and commitment with compassion.

Relationships

You have an innate sense of dignity as well as a friendly approachability. A tireless worker and a trustworthy friend, you like people and usually understand them, but perhaps expect and make allowances for what you consider to be normal human weaknesses.

Feeling a sense of duty to do the best you can for yourself and those you love, you assume others want to do the same. Since you have a way of making it all look easy, you can usually inspire others to be productive and resourceful. And if they are not, they may feel your icy, disapproving gaze, and sense the judgements you are making underneath your calm exterior.

As you are basically a conventional person who values tradition and old-fashioned security, you may settle for the predictability of a relationship long after the savour has gone. Nevertheless, you are capable of being very sensual, loving and generous, and are generally not very moody. You tend to assume things will turn out okay, and that material supply will always be forthcoming. Your positive outlook and capabilities will always have a supportive and uplifting influence in the lives of those in your care.

Your Greatest Strengths

Tenacity and sense of responsibility; your moral strength and honour; sound intellect; immense practicality; sense of proportion and justice; allegiance to sound, traditional values; down-to-earth style and enduring devotion to loved ones, colleagues and friends.

Your Greatest Weaknesses

A inflexible system of values; possessiveness of people; attachment to familiar routine; tendency to be overly materialistic and pedantic; stubbornness, which especially comes out when you work with people who will not follow the rules.

Image for Integration

A wealthy grandfather opens a savings account for his granddaughter on her day of birth; she later becomes a famous artist, inherits a fortune and makes her own.

Famous Personalities

Isaac Asimov (writer), Paolo Borsellino (lawyer and anti-Mafia magistrate), Carlos Castaneda (anthropologist and writer), Graham Chapman (member of the 'Monty Python' team), Barry Goldwater (American politician), Danny Kaye (singer and actor), Yvette Mimieux (actress), Arthur Scargill (union leader).

— 111 —

SUN CAPRICORN ♑ MOON GEMINI ♊

There are no such things as applied sciences, only applications of science.
LOUIS PASTEUR

Teach us delight in simple things,
And mirth that has no bitter springs;
Forgiveness free of evil done,
And love to all men 'neath the sun!
RUDYARD KIPLING

Themes

EARTH/AIR Erudite; talkative; clever; adaptable; resourceful; practical thinker; good teacher; seriously silly; adaptable; intellectual pursuits; shrewd; gossip; astute; love of irony.

Do you want stability or variety? Concentration or conversation? Solitude or society? For you this is a difficult question, but you would not waste time trying to answer it because you know the answer is 'yes' and 'yes'. You are about dedication and diversity, persistence and subtlety, integrity and wicked wittiness – a combination that makes you an extremely capable, articulate and popular person.

Respected for your wit and decorum, you speak your mind but with charm and diplomacy so that others are easily persuaded to see the reasonableness of your argument. You could be a superb diplomat, judge, teacher, writer, broadcaster or comedian – and there is probably a touch of all of them in you.

You are the straight man and the funny man, the traditional, conventional businessman who surprises everyone with his roguish, playful wit and pranks. At your core you are serious, obdurate and tough, but around that core there is much of the comedian and tease about you, a lightness of touch which lifts your essentially heavy demeanour out of the dangers of ponderousness and gravity.

Mentally acute and observant, you can usually translate your perceptions into delightfully expressive, crystal-clear images, and deliver them with effortless polish. Although you are not particularly ambitious or perfectionist, you have a utilitarian view of things, which makes you enormously efficient. You are economic with words, both spoken and written, as well as with your creative energies generally. You have a good eye for what needs doing and you will create original ways for accomplishing mundane tasks and have fun in the process.

You are sincere, earnest, resolute, very aware of the need to be in control and to progress in a purposeful way. Highly resourceful and mentally quick, you can, along the way to achieving your purposes, pick up a lot of fascinating information which will be grist to your mill one day. Because of your fundamentally serious nature, your jokey side never makes you appear superficial. In fact, your opinions and views carry great weight, due as much to their precision as to your blithesome delivery, and you can at times get carried away by the glibness of your own intellect.

Exceptionally good at communicating your enthusiasm to others, you make you a good teacher. You may love changing your appearance, nimbly moving from conservative grey suits to habiliments of a more exotic kind. Equally at home in courtroom drama as at an outrageous fancy-dress party, you are also good at telling stories or jokes – as long as the joke is not on you. Your inventiveness can be extremely lucrative, and you keep busy at what you are good at whilst always keeping an eye out for more opportunities.

Relationships

You are a very companionable individual. Normally self-restrained, alert and emotionally conventional, you nevertheless like to do the unexpected, and often turn rules and convention on their head. You want stability, but within the bounds of your emotional commitment you will remain as mobile as a quark eluding measurement.

If you are not careful, your mental strengths can become your emotional Achilles heel. This is due to your tendency to cleverly avoid what feels like emotional demands or conflicts by literally sneaking out of the window – at least in your mind – or to argue your 'view' of things and distance yourself from your feelings.

You thrive in a close, committed relationship and are loyal and affectionate. A part of you will, however, always remain novelty-seeking, restless and youthful.

Your Greatest Strengths

Inventive and studious intellect; the breadth of your interests and enthusiasms; essentially hard-working and serious inner core; capacity to move with grace and flair in many different circles; droll sense of humour.

373

Your Greatest Weaknesses

An over-emphasis of the rational, which deprives you of emotional maturity; tendency to be satisfied with a pragmatic but surface understanding of people and things in general; your love of playing jokes on others but hating being laughed at yourself; flippant (but innocent) pomposity.

Images for Integration

An aged philosopher wins first prize in an international crossword puzzle competition ... A travelling salesman wins an award ... A college don reads the letters section of the paper while eating breakfast.

Famous Personalities

Joan Baez (singer, songwriter and guitarist), John Delorean (businessman), Charles Goodyear (inventor), Anver Joffrey (dancer and choreographer), Johannes Kepler (astrologer and astronomer), Rudyard Kipling (writer), George MacBeth (writer and poet), Giuseppe Mazzini (Italian patriot), Sarah Miles (actress), Walter Mondale (American politician), Louis Pasteur (chemist and bacteriologist who discovered pasteurization), Robert Stack (actor).

— 112 —

SUN CAPRICORN ♑ MOON CANCER ♋

If I have been able to see further than others, it was because I stood on the shoulders of giants.
SIR ISAAC NEWTON

I want you to let me know when I'm ahead so I can quit.
JANIS JOPLIN

Themes

EARTH/WATER Tough and tender; sensitivity and self-control; ambitious; highly observant; self-absorbed yet kind and helpful; supportive; conservative yet open to new ideas; pragmatic; loves nature.

Is life essentially sweet and light or really a dark, challenging testing ground? Are you wedded to the simple, natural world of the past and traditional values or do you embrace whatever technology will help you do what you want to do better? Do you want to shout your personal beliefs from the roof tops or whisper them quietly to those who will listen?

Thinking about yourself quite a lot, as you most probably do, you are likely to be highly aware of some of your inner dilemmas. One of them is that you are both a toughie and a softie, aware both of your ambitions and your fear of risk. You are a strong, thoughtful individual who enjoys intimacy but who can use solitude productively. During your reflective moments you assess your goals and needs, and the best way of satisfying them. You are a serious, sensitive and immensely capable person with an uncanny understanding of human nature. Sometimes you wonder if you should allow your feelings to overflow, or if self-control is the name of your game.

At your most creative, you combine the qualities of a gentle mother and a firm father. This great personal sensitivity and a shrewd, practical, no-nonsense toughness where your career is concerned can make you an extremely purposeful, hard-nosed professional who is good with people. It makes you determined to achieve whatever goals you have set yourself, whilst at the same time being an extremly caring, supportive individual with a deep love of home and family.

Having said this, you do not always find your personal life and career to be two masters that are easily served, and may be tempted to sacrifice one or the other. In fact the central dilemma in your life will normally revolve around the conflict between your inner and outer worlds, between your desire for closeness, intimacy and gentleness, and your perception that much of life is harsh, challenging and unsentimental, and that you want to end up with some real achievement to your credit. Having your own business and working from home is one solution, but one way or another you flourish best when you are able to do your own thing in your own way, and in your own time.

There is something of the artist and the scientist in you, and you thrive on work that combines a sense of mission with a deep, emotional, indeed often religious, commitment. When your attention turns away from your own internal sensitivities to the affairs of other people, you are a natural psychologist with a ready insight and understanding of what motivates people; such natural insight will help you in your ability to work with others in any occupation.

When your gift for seeing the larger, long-term picture is coupled with your determination and sensitivity to other people's needs and abilities, you can become an extremely capable manager of people and projects. Able to get the best out of people, you can generate a strong sense of belonging and togetherness. Your ability to combine hard facts with a rich imagination, whether in the area of science, art, education or commerce, encourages others to face and celebrate both the challenges and richness of life.

Relationships

Relationships are central to your life, even if you can find it difficult to admit it, for you can be both deeply engaged and yet very distanced. You care for people and you deeply want to find your 'other half', yet you may at the same time find such intimacy claustrophobic. On one level you thrive on solitude, whilst on another you yearn for an all-consuming at-oneness with a soul mate.

Your own parents may have pulled you in opposite directions, and intimate personal relationships can bring out the same childhood dilemmas. On the one hand you need to be needed; on the other you feel you are strongest when you stand alone. When really centred, you are highly sensitive to the needs of others and can be one of the kindest and most considerate and thoughtful of people. This genuine concern for others, as well as your deep need for intimate companionship, makes you a very loyal and supportive partner once you have wholeheartedly committed yourself.

Your Greatest Strengths

Strong powers of observation and love of nature; practical concern for the good of others; ability to capture and express the moods and emotions of others.

376

Your Greatest Weaknesses

The conflict between your tough and tender attitudes to life; wide swings of mood and oversensitivity to other people's views; tendency to take criticism personally; self-absorbed preoccupation with your own feelings.

Images for Integration

A priest blesses his family before setting off on a pilgrimage ... A water clock ... Carol Reed's films of *The Third Man* and *Oliver* ... A politician kisses a baby without pretence.

Famous Personalities

Michael Aspel (actor, broadcaster and writer), William Blatty (author of *The Exorcist*), Pablo Casals (cellist and conductor), Jean François Champollion (Egyptologist), Claude Adrien Helvetius (philosopher), Janis Joplin (rock singer), Emile Loubert (former President of France), Isaac Newton (physicist and alchemist), Sir Carol Reed (film producer), Frank Sinatra Jr. (singer son of Frank Sinatra), Mary Tyler Moore (actress), Andreas Vesalius (pioneering anatomist).

— 113 —

SUN CAPRICORN ♑ MOON LEO ♌

Daffodils so beautiful ... some rested their heads upon these stones as pillows for weariness and the rest tossed and reeled and danced and ... verily laughed with the wind.
DOROTHY WORDSWORTH

Wherever we go, we must unite with the people, take root, and blossom among them ...
CHAIRMAN MAO

Themes

EARTH/FIRE Laughter and hard work; inferiority and superiority; forceful; vibrant; authoritative; powerful; proud; honourable; creative and capable; responsible and ambitious; dignified warmth; assertive and theatrical; a believer or a doubter.

Deeply serious yet poetically playful, you may be torn between the self-imposed responsibilities of your career and social ambitions, and your desire to make a splash and have fun. Should you wear that sober city suit or go for that dashing piece of *haute couture*? And when you so love people to enjoy themselves, why are you so tough on yourself?

Both proud and humble, at times you cannot decide whether you are the greatest or the most inadequate person you know. When you get your industrious and playful elements working together, however, the world had better watch out, for in your own steady yet compelling way you can be the embodiment of purposeful ambition. No matter what your job is, you are a born *professional*. With expertly designed flair, you want to shine for yourself and to achieve for the world. Your reputation matters a lot to you, and when you know you have earned your praise you savour it like nobody else.

You do not really *mean* to be a snob, but you have a way of nonchalantly lording it over people. This is because your belief in yourself and in what you feel you must do is so intense. Women born with this combination are particularly likely to find their way to the top of their chosen mountain, but they will also find the J. Arthur Ranks, David Bowies and Robert Blys of this world there to party with.

This is a pairing of sunny high-summer and serious mid-winter, an adventurous, gutsy mix of tough-willed, dedicated service carried out with zest and pizzazz. You have the charisma of a star yet you can work dutifully behind the scenes, laying the foundations and preparing the party. Then on the day, you make the perfect host or hostess, carrying out your duties with total self-possession and real style.

An air of authority and immense professionalism surrounds all your endeavours. You will do whatever is necessary, no matter how hard, to produce a polished performance and a superb result. With a strong social conscience, a real sense of noblesse oblige and a desire to make the world a better place, you may be drawn to politics or fund-raising; good works and charities flourish on your enthusiasm and dedication. Whatever you do, you are likely to end up being put in charge, which is just as well, for subordinate positions are not really your scene.

At times when the sun is shining you may protest at having work piled upon you, yet let anyone deprive you of your load and you will feel not only hurt but somehow lost and guilty. Not all your work is totally altruistic. There can be something of the gold-digger in you, constantly alert for opportunities, yet you do not expect any free lunches, even if you do enjoy getting the best for the least. You are someone who, to quote a fellow Capricorn–Leo, Jack London, 'will settle for good pay, good grub and hard work rather than poor pay, poor grub and easy work'. You have pride and confidence in your own achievements and, yes, you think you could try harder, but you are not doing so badly, really, are you?

Relationships

Matters of the heart are a paradox for you. One day you choose to be alone, austere, even monastic, isolating yourself from people and the world; the next day your warm heart is brimming over with love. You can be demanding and haughty, sometimes distant and inflexible, but this is often a defence against your fear of criticism. Like Ouida, you may feel that 'with women and peaches it is only the side next the sun that is tempting'.

Although appearances do count a lot for you, nonetheless you can bring to a relationship a deep, inner strength, terrific loyalty, and a desire for quiet stability. Your characteristic vanity and need for control can be a problem in close relationships. You have high standards and fairly conventional ideas about the give-and-take in love, but learning to relax and give in to your more playful side will help you enjoy life more.

Enormously passionate when you let yourself go, you will thrive with a mate who both adores and respects you and who realizes that you need space to express your creative drive. You are stubbornly devoted to your family and will go to great lengths to provide them with the *best* – which, of course, is what they deserve.

Your Greatest Strengths

Natural flair and charisma; tremendous creative drive; capacity for dedicated hard work; organizational and leadership abilities; integrity and devotion to excellence; loyalty to those you respect and love.

Your Greatest Weaknesses

Tendency towards workaholism; snobbery, social climbing and self-importance; self-centredness and dogmatism; your need for father figures; inflexibility and dislike of change; tendency to become dictatorial to compensate for your feelings of inadequacy.

Images for Integration

After a lone, silent climb up your mountain you greet the spotlights and television cameras with flair and aplomb ... In the dark of the forest a sunbeam breaks through, bringing new life.

Famous Personalities

St. Bernadette of Lourdes (visionary), Robert Bly (poet), David Bowie (singer), Marlene Dietrich (actress and singer), Faye Dunaway (actress), Gracie Fields (singer and comedienne), Jack London (writer), Mao Tse-tung (former Chinese leader), Martin Niemoller (theologian), Ouida (novelist), Dolly Parton (country singer), J. Arthur Rank (film financier), Dorothy Wordsworth (writer), Paramhansa Yogananda (mystic).

114

— —

SUN CAPRICORN ♑ MOON VIRGO ♍

He who despises himself esteems himself as a great self-despiser.
SUSAN SONTAG

The progress of the human race in understanding the universe has established a small corner of order in an increasingly disordered universe.
STEPHEN HAWKING

Themes

EARTH/EARTH Perfectionism; quality service; craftsmanship; earthy; good organizer; caring and careful; self-controlled; self-critical; worrier; modest; professional critic; precise; aesthetic; studious.

Are you the boss or the servant? Do you want reponsibility or regularity? Although you can carry the former quite well, the latter is actually more important to you, for you want to live your life according to principle, reason and enlightened self-interest. You excel in streamlining the system, and in making your empire function better and better. And most aspects of your life usually do run smoothly, coherently and productively as you are remarkably capable, and tend always to employ your talents wisely and for the production of the greatest good.

You have a cautious, thoughtful, prudent personality, and prefer to be judged by your actions – by what you actually achieve. And in turn you will tend to judge others by their actions, and you can be quite critical if you deem someone's efforts too slapdash, not well thought-out or missing the mark. You can, however, be very critical of yourself as well. But it may be that you are too serious and sensible most of the time, and tend to forget that life's mistakes and messes usually provide the spur to growth that makes it all worthwhile. You like being prepared for all eventualities, but you may cancel out many of life's pleasant surprises if you go overboard with your shield of logic.

Indeed logic is a key to understanding your nature, for your sense of self-worth derives from your ability to analyse data in a logical, methodical manner, to arrive at a clear deduction, and then to impart your findings to those who cannot, in your opinion, reason quite so well as yourself. There is not an iota of arrogance in your impulse to do this; rather, your instinct is to carry out your duty in a helpful way.

You are trustworthy and caring, and want to serve others. Nothing makes you happier than seeing the results of your individual labours being put to good, practical use for the benefit of others. But whilst you pride yourself in your intellectual efficiency and your loyalty to the letter of the law, you are by no means as confident as you seem, and find it difficult to exercise your will in stressful or crucial situations.

You do not like being corrected by others but are always inwardly correcting yourself and thinking of better solutions, so that being in command just makes you nervous. All that responsibility! You would rather be responsible just for yourself.

Relationships

You have very precise, usually aesthetic taste in most things, especially people. The paradoxical truth about you is that, despite your fundamental inner hesitancy and self-doubt, you can be somewhat condescending when it comes to choosing an appropriate partner.

Naturally reserved and private, you may seem emotionally distant and cool to many, but when you feel safe and secure you open up, and can be convivial, humourous, sentimental and devoted. You have a gentle and faithful romantic nature, and will show your love in your constancy and thoughtfulness. When you feel admired, respected and appreciated, you can literally glow; and when you are unhappy you can be cranky, gloomy and critical – although you rarely lose your decorum. You are too pragmatic for that, and you never like being out of control, even though you can be somewhat nervous and fastidious, which can invite emotional upsets and unhappiness from time to time. Although your scientific and analytical turn of mind will take you far in a career, it can prove to be too much of a good thing in relationships. Your loved ones will not enjoy being picked apart, even if you do it ever so nicely and it is for their own good. In a relationship with a water or fire type you may have the experience of mystery and spontaneity, rather than just learning about it.

Your Greatest Strengths

Dedicated and honourable nature; fine, analytical mind; refined, articulate self-expression; practical and efficient organizing abilities; desire to live a useful, productive life; love of knowledge and ability to use it for the benefit of all.

Your Greatest Weaknesses

Lack of confidence; over-serious approach to life, which does not allow for the frivolous and mysterious; insistence on black-and-white facts, which compels you to try to quantify the intangibles; tendency to be calculating and fault-finding with yourself as well as with those you love.

Images for Integration

A famous, prize-winning scientist takes up the humble position of chemistry teacher in a quiet village school ... A psychologist analyses the history of the human condition in an essay entitled 'The Origin and Purposes of Man's Self-Contempt'.

Famous Personalities

Tycho Brahe (astronomer), Jose Ferrer (actor), Mel Gibson (actor), Oliver Hardy (comedian), Stephen Hawking (astro-physicist), John Lilly (psychologist), Sal Mineo (actor), Aristotle Onassis (plutocrat), Anwar Sadat (former Egyptian president), Helmut Schmidt (former West-German chancellor), Maggie Smith (actress), Susan Sontag (author), Stephen Stills (rock musician), Alan Watts (psychologist), Gwen Verdon (actress and dancer).

— 115 —

SUN CAPRICORN ♑ MOON LIBRA ♎

We are part of the community of Europe, and we must do our duty as such.
W.E. GLADSTONE

Which requires the greater strength, letting go or restraining? It is the greatest manifestation of power to be calm.
VIVEKANANDA

Themes

EARTH/AIR Socially aware; chic; a practical intellectual; liberal yet conservative; sense of justice; elegant; professional; clear-headed; high principles; organizer; a friendly loner; determined; a fighter for causes; courageous.

You are so cunningly capable and pleasantly reasonable that you will usually seem to be totally in command of your well-regulated life. And yet, even *you* grapple with certain dilemmas: are you a social creature or a lone ranger? Do you want to *look* like a million dollars or be *worth* a million dollars? Do you seek personal advancement or the advancement of society? Do you flourish in the outdoors, enjoying lively, intelligent talk or do you blossom in the quiet, reflective solitude of your own work? Are you a person of ideas or actions? Are you a scientist or an artist? Do you want to keep things as they are, or do you want to create greater social justice?

When you can combine your cooperative, easy-going, extrovert qualities with your reliability and purposeful outlook, you are someone who can achieve whatever you set your mind to. Your dry wit and studied charm can win you valuable friends and influence those in authority. You care very much about doing things right; anything which offends your sense of justice or your aesthetic sensibilities can get you firing on all cylinders. Then your life becomes a mission and a crusade which calls forth your wholehearted commitment.

Ignorance unsettles you, and so you learn rapidly and strive to be a polished performer, in command of yourself and your world, whether it is the world of business, fashion or family. With your gift for the larger view, for organization and forward-planning, and your instinct for fair play, you can inspire the deepest confidence amongst those with whom you work. If you play your cards right, and you usually do, your rise to a position of leadership is only a matter of time. Responsibility helps you mature. A natural conservative, you cherish traditional values, although socially you are a liberal, and your desire for justice makes you a progressive, ahead of your time.

Surprisingly for one who is so essentially shrewd and peace-loving, you can be very much a fighter, willing to join battle in earnest for a cause you deem worthwhile. You do not want to offend, but neither will your healthy self-opinion put up with abuse from others. You have a dry, rather factual approach, but this gives you a gift for communication. You are polite, but your words have *punch*.

You like to follow directions, and are good at giving clear directions to others. Business and financial matters can flourish under your astute eye, as can all kinds of relationships and social affairs, for you also know when it is time to stop working and start enjoying life and the beauties of nature. Although you may have a strong aesthetic sense, you are likely to go for the chic of understated, subtle colours.

Relationships

One of your central dilemmas comes to the fore in relationships: whether you are a romantic or a pragmatist. Although relating comes naturally to you and consumes much of your energy, to be at your best you also need prime time alone in your own company at the end of the day.

Any partnership you enter into needs to be based on strong shared interests and a common sense of purpose. Teamwork is in your blood, and one side of you enjoys sharing all the mundane bits of life that add up to so much. But you will need a partner who understands and allows for your career ambitions.

There is something of the strong, silent type about you. Loyalty comes naturally to you, and you expect others to be equally loyal and sensible. You may not realize that others need more emotional input than you seem to, and that a kindly pat on the head and a stiff upper lip is not the answer to *all* their problems. In fact, there is plenty of tenderness in you. Try being less reasonable and more impulsive at times; do what you *want* to do, not just what you think is expected of you.

Your Greatest Strengths

Strong intellect; patient pursuit of truth and justice; determination to work hard for ideas you believe in; sense of social justice, duty, decency and good faith; commitment to fulfilling your responsibilities and supporting your loved ones.

Your Greatest Weaknesses

Proneness to negative thinking; inclination to be opportunistic; scepticism which can turn into outright cynicism; inclination to become pedantic in your own areas of expertise.

Images for Integration

A beautiful, formal walled garden ... In time an oyster turns irritating grit into a beautiful pearl ... A visionary statesman fights a duel to see justice done.

Famous Personalities

Alexander I (Tsar of Russia), David Bellamy (botanist, broadcaster and writer), Cyrano de Bergerac (writer and dramatist), Louis Bromfield (novelist), Dyan Cannon (actress), Joe Frazier (boxing champion), William Ewart Gladstone (former British prime minister), Jacob Grimm (collector of fairy tales), Alexander Hamilton (American politician), Joan of Arc (visionary and military leader), Tom Keating (Australian prime minister), Shari Lewis (ventriloquist), Berthe Morisot (Impressionist painter), Michael Nesmith (rock musician – The Monkees), Russ Tamblyn (actor and dancer), Vivekananda (Hindu mystic and philosopher).

— 116 —

SUN CAPRICORN ♑ MOON SCORPIO ♏

Democracy means government by discussion but it is only effective if you can stop people talking.
CLEMENT ATTLEE

Sex is one of the nine reasons for reincarnation ... the other eight are unimportant.
HENRY MILLER

Themes

EARTH/WATER Strength of character; self-possessed; dedicated; exacting moral standards; analytical; proud; resilient; tireless worker; compassionate; loyal; sensual; self-repressed; brooding; tenacious; no time for fools; ambitious.

The ambition of the mountain goat and the emotional self-mastery of the Scorpion-Eagle combine here to create a personality with heroic strength of character and passionate dedication. Your goals, beliefs and values become personal obsessions; every once in a while you should review them to make sure they are worthy of your acute intelligence and all-consuming guardianship. Your instincts tell you to be prepared for the onslaughts of life as it can attack from the rear, and you, more than anyone else, refuse to be caught with your pants down.

You possess a naturally self-controlled, shrewd, judicial temperament. Law or social reform may attract you, as in some ways you have a resonance with suffering and the darker side of human experience, and want to do something about it. Fully in command of your powers and totally engaged in your path towards success and recognition, you take yourself seriously and know exactly where you are going and where you stand on important issues.

Extremely trustworthy, loyal and conventional, you also tend to be a bit ruthless with yourself and others, demanding total vigilance, commitment and high standards. While this may be fine for you, others may find your exacting moral standards a trifle awesome, a bit like a 'Ninja Turtle' without the sense of fun. But when you *do* decide to have fun, you can be urbane and insightful, and just as dedicated to enjoyment as you can be to anything else.

Your intensity may express itself in the form of superb satire and a wicked sense of humour. Most of the time, however, you are fairly intent on the serious business of mastering your role and responsibilities. It can be that your instinctive conservatism settles into a rather limited perspective, often made worse by a suspicious attitude to anything foreign. You tend to emphatically deny the existence of what you cannot conceive or believe, and want to scrutinize things scientifically. Probably the only way you will change is through an enlightened approach to your well-developed reasoning faculty. If it makes sense, you may just take it on board. And 'sense', in fact, is an important key to your whole nature.

Relationships

You have a tremendous amount of common sense, and you cherish traditional values which sustain the emotional and material security you urgently require. You can be a wonderful home-maker and a protective parent, like the mother bird who jealously protects her babies from attack by diverting the enemy's attention or by direct assault. The fact that you do not give up easily often makes you the indefatigable mainstay and power behind the throne in a family or company.

You are also a sensualist, delighting in the fulfilment of your basic human needs. Possessive of your own pleasures and intensely private about your feelings, you do not let go very easily unless emotional events strike a nerve so deeply that you go off the deep end temporarily, only to feel much relieved when you return to sanity and self-control. The latter you definitely prefer, but catharsis is particularly healthy for you, helping you to release internal pressures and tensions which result from your constant vigilance and desire to keep out unwanted threats to your wellbeing.

When you are emotionally committed to someone you are steadfast and possessive but equally generous and passionate. 'Life is earnest and life is real' could be your motto, and you usually manage to deepen and transform – even if just a little bit – every person with whom you come in contact.

Your Greatest Strengths

Moral integrity and strength of character; perceptive and penetrating mind; quiet but fervent support of the underdog and of those you love; ability to focus on a goal and remain undeterred by obstacles; compassion and courage to undergo suffering for the sake of regeneration.

Your Greatest Weaknesses

Tendency to be too serious, rigid and austere; to be accusatory and blind to your own prejudices; to get despondent and stuck in narrow and pessimistic attitudes.

Images for Integration

A prisoner in solitary confinement undergoes a conversion and becomes an indefatigable worker for the transformation and betterment of the lives of his inmates ... A priest turns his home into a shelter for the sick and homeless.

Famous Personalities

Clement Attlee (former British prime minister), Shirley Bassey (singer), Jocelyn Delecour (Olympic athlete), Gerard Depardieu (actor), Henry Miller (author), Nostradamus (seer), Cynthia Payne (madame of Streatham), Francis Poulenc (composer), Aleksandr Scriaban (composer), Rod Stewart (singer).

Sun Capricorn ♑ Moon Sagittarius ♐

Great lords have their pleasures, but the people have fun.
MONTESQUIEU

All the things I like to do are either immoral, illegal, or fattening.
ALEXANDER WOOLLCOTT

Themes

EARTH/FIRE Self-motivated; zealous; authoritative; broad and sweeping mind; honourable; philosophical; earnest; enthusiastic; acerbic wit; proud; loyal; sincere; moral strength; idealism and practicality; faith in values; alternately austere and humorous; high standards.

Are you a hard-headed businessperson or a visionary social reformer? Do you wear the yoke of responsibility only to toss it aside from time to time in order to indulge in a crazy adventure? There is a bit of 'old man' and 'crazy teenager' in you, and you can put them to work in a very creative and usually lucrative way.

Your Sagittarian far-sightedness and your Capricorn earthiness combine to give you a classy, charismatic and extremely capable personality. Enormously persuasive and intense about ideas, philosophies and social concerns, you are also concerned about your personal wellbeing. You can talk others into almost anything because you are both persistently pragmatic and genuinely enthusiastic. You grasp the facts and hold the vision.

Your personality is forceful, powerful but sympathetic as well, or rather humanitarian in a broad, impersonal sort of way. You are a great debater with a kind of mission to explain things, especially the implications of events and policies, at both the personal and perhaps national/international level. This makes you a natural politician, professor, priest, social critic or training manager.

You care very deeply about 'getting it right' intellectually, about pursuing kosher ideas and 'isms' and about instilling your life – and others' lives as well – with sound moral principles. A natural sort of high-mindedness pervades all your central views, as well as a sense of urgency about communicating your understanding to others. In a sense you have the missionary zeal and the inner certitude of a monk or nun, and this makes people sit up and listen. All the same, you can be guilty of huge bias without being aware of it at all. And bluntness is another thing – people will not always appreciate your straightforward, no-nonsense calling-a-spade-a-spade sort of delivery.

When in relaxed mode your satirical wit excels and you can be the life of the party. You love to share ideas, compare convictions and make absolute judgements on the nature of life and the folly of men – and then laugh about the most serious of things. You enjoy many kinds of people and can adapt easily to all kinds of situations. You enjoy the intellectual challenge of unusual problems because you have an uncanny knack of seeing into the heart of a problem and appreciating the irony of life's dilemmas.

You live your life with gusto and you have a nervous intensity that can lead you into real exhaustion if you are not careful. Your mind is going all the time and it can out-work your body, although your enjoyment of sports and outdoor activities will balance this. Ambition and high ideals keep you revved up most of the time, and after that you like to party too!

Relationships

Extremely devoted in personal relationships, you nevertheless find it easier to commit yourself when you have found true intellectual rapport with someone. You are passionate and loyal, and have a strong feeling for the importance of family and community. Working hard to provide for your loved ones is something you will not begrudge, as long as there is also plenty of time for fun and doing your own thing.

You get moody and impatient if you feel your partner is being too demanding. This is because you are not particularly sensitive to the more subtle dynamics and emotional needs which come with intimate relationships. You easily 'go into your head' when difficulties arise, and this can be a defensive tactic to protect you from your own irrational needs as well. You may need to slow down and direct some of your insatiable curiosity towards your own inner depths. What are you afraid of? Nothing, you will say, and indeed your openness and love of truth will help you relax into the cosier, non-verbal aspects of love.

Your Greatest Strengths

The range of your intellectual abilities; sense of responsibility and integrity; spontaneous understanding of the larger implications of different attitudes and situations; ambition and love of exploration; ironic sense of humour.

Your Greatest Weaknesses

Verbosity and occasional pomposity; tendency to exhibit intellectual pretension when you are actually feeling insecure; to waste energy in a nervous seeking of new pastures; to get fixated on narrow views that become rigidly moralistic.

Images for Integration

In his spare time, a High Court judge takes up the serious hobby of gambling at horse races ... A bank clerk plans a world cruise.

Famous Personalities

Steve Allen (humorist and composer), Umberto Eco (novelist and semiotician), Anthony Hopkins (actor), Kenny Loggins (rock musician), Henri Matisse (artist), Montesquieu (political philosopher), Brian Redhead (radio presenter), Maurice Ultrillo (artist), Alexander Woollcott (journalist, broadcaster and critic).

—118—

SUN CAPRICORN ♑ MOON CAPRICORN ♑

The opposition to the ordination of women is just the same opposition as when we fought for the vote ... I don't mind people giving reasons, but not stupid prejudices.
VICTORIA LIDIARD

To give up pretensions is as blessed a relief as to get them gratified.
WILLIAM JAMES

Themes

EARTH/EARTH Responsible; realistic; traditional; clear-headed; earthy; steadfast; self-demanding; autocratic; pragmatic; sophisticated; self-absorbed; ambitious; serious; conscientious; professional; self-controlled; fearful; authoritative.

You get to grips with reality like no one else! Pragmatic and purposeful, with your willpower completely mobilized towards success, you naturally aspire to a position of authority and power. And as you can keep your eye exactly on the main issue without getting distracted, you usually accomplish exactly what you set out to do.

Enormously capable, professional and ambitious, you were born with an old head upon your shoulders. Underneath your diffident, serious, responsible demeanour, however, is a thoughtful, caring soul who wants to be fair, efficient, and helpful.

You have a pathological need for security and authority, and you usually find some way of making sure that you are immune to attack. Perhaps early childhood experiences left you fearful of the power that adults wield, which made you feel impotent and servile. Second to authority, it is recognition that you require – recognition for your professional status, strength, abilities, wisdom and accomplishments.

You can be terrifically protective and helpful, and friends and family love you for your dependability: when you say you are going to do something, you do it. You are not so popular, however, for your habit of not letting them be strong sometimes, too. What you hate is appearing weak and not getting the respect and just rewards you feel should be yours. Consequently you can sometimes overdo the responsibility bit and take on more than you should. Is it a sense of guilt that makes you volunteer for Atlas's job? Could be, but you can exhaust yourself and end up resenting the amount you do.

One of your struggles is with timidity and lack of confidence, and at times with melancholy and depression. Early responsibilities or burdens test you and help to form your ambitious outlook and strong defences – life somehow tells you that these are important.

You possess both the virtues and vices of having an excellent, pragmatic mind. You reason things out with exactitude; you plot your way to the top through the thicket of duty and desires, safe roads and risky byways. You can apply your indefatigable spirit and resourceful intellect successfully to a wide variety of disciplines, but you will always need a challenge of some kind.

Relationships

You are prone to placing disproportionate value on material acquisition, security and personal control of your life. You may, therefore, try to build a safe citadel, materially and psychologically, from which you can lock out the mysterious, intangible, changeable dimension of life. That part of life both terrifies and fascinates you. You insist that all things have a 'rational' explanation and it is here that you can come unstuck, especially when faced with your emotional needs.

You in fact have a very strong need for love and companionship, but you are cautious and hold back until you feel that all the necessary ingredients for a successful relationship are present. You need constancy, security and, if possible, excellence, for you very much need to respect your partner. You can be a very sensual person, and once you have relaxed and feel loved you will let down your defences and reveal your private, bawdy sense of humour. When you learn to be easier on yourself and to accept your imperfections as part of your own uniqueness, you will find that contentment and happiness are not so hard to come by after all.

Your Greatest Strengths

Thoroughness; dependability; the serious, attentive mental attitude you bring to all situations and concerns; protective, responsible attitude to others; commendable self-control; practical organizational abilities; persistent energies; shrewd common sense; indefatigable attitude to all obstacles and challenges.

Your Greatest Weaknesses

Self-centredness; lop-sided focus on self-advancement, which can ultimately make you lonely; tendency to ignore or reject the emotional and spiritual dimension of life; propensity to wear too much defensive armour and to expect the worst; tendency to judge others from a position of pious self-righteousness (try to lighten up and indulge in some purposeless fun).

Image for Integration

A hoary old grandfather sits in his chair with his grandson on his knee. He gives him a gift for his seventh birthday – a first edition of *Pilgrim's Progress*.

Famous Personalities

Clara Barton (founder of American Red Cross), Federico Fellini (film director), Roy Hattersley (British politician), William James (philosopher), Annie Lennox (singer), Victoria Lidiard (suffragette), Floyd Patterson (champion boxer), Carl Rogers (psychologist), Claude Steiner (radical psychotherapist), Donna Summer (singer), Gus Trikonis (actor and movie director), Galina Ulanova (prima ballerina), Loretta Young (actress).

—119—

SUN CAPRICORN ♑ MOON AQUARIUS ♒

I am an idealist. I don't know where I'm going but I'm on my way.
CARL SANDBURG

One of the greatest necessities ... is to discover creative solitude.
CARL SANDBURG

Service to others is the rent you pay for your room here on earth.
MUHAMMAD ALI

Themes

EARTH/AIR Sociable yet solitary; progressive yet conservative; purposeful; sceptical intelligence; clear; concise; thoughtful; organizational gifts; love of order and love of change; social responsibility and ambition; purposeful; dedicated; practical idealist.

For someone who is so friendly and up-front, you are a remarkably private, self-contained and independent soul. So, are you a people-person or are you really something of a hermit? Do you want to reform the world or to be accepted, even revered, by it? Indeed, you might ask yourself whether you are a conventional 'square', masquerading in the clothes of a rebel, or a world-shaking reformer who loves to dress the elegant high-society part? Is your true love the old, the past, the historical, or do you want to be one of the movers and shapers of the future, not least your own?

One of your challenges in life will be to figure out how you can reconcile your desire to rewrite the rules with your strong belief in the rule of law. When you bring these contradictory sides together, you are self-disciplined, self-motivated and a great forward-planner with good business sense, administrative skills and a detached, ethical purpose to all your activities.

Your clear-headed, logical approach to any enterprise you undertake, along with your willingness to learn from your mistakes, will inspire confidence and respect in friends and colleagues. You are objective and capable of confronting problems and difficulties head on, which makes you a powerful ally and a formidable opponent. There is a stylish dignity and grace about your approach which, coupled with your insightful wit, makes you a respected authority in your field and amongst your friends.

Both ambitious and modest, you seek to get to the top of whatever mountain has caught your idealistic imagination, but never at the expense of your humanitarian ideals. Whilst you are deeply egalitarian in temperament, you know to use your power effectively, and you think to yourself 'someone's got to do it' – 'it' being managing things successfully from the top. Having scaled the heights, however, you can be self-effacing about your achievements. You have a strong sense of duty and moral obligation towards your fellow human beings. You want to make the world a better place, and are likely to have fairly clear ideas as to how this can be achieved.

Your intelligence and independent mind-set does not, however, suffer fools gladly, and you resent having to work at things which curb your beliefs and freedom of expression in any way. But you are prepared to work hard with consistent dedication for your ideals. To this end, you can be drawn to those skills and professions that will make a practical difference to the world, be they in the sphere of politics, economics, academia, or in the humanities such as literature, history, psychology and counselling. In the creative arts, once you overcome your reticence about contacting and expressing your insights and emotions, you can be a profoundly poetic soul, encapsulating the essence of people and ideas in clear, elegant words, painting, dance or music.

Relationships

Your mix of outgoing, intelligent friendliness and self-contained inner reserve can be something of a tantalizing mystery to others. Although interested in a wide range of people, you are choosey about whom you spend real time with. Intelligence and some measure of personal achievement are essential in any prospective partner. But when you admire and respect someone, you are the soul of supportive friendship, a natural counsellor and totally committed colleague and partner.

Although friends and loved ones may be ready to help, you can be remarkably self-sufficient, withdrawing into your own space like a Trappist monk or nun. You want stability and emotional security, yet you need freedom and privacy. You are extremely sociable and like people, yet you find it difficult to get close. Emotionally you need 100-per-cent security before you can admit to yourself that you have any emotional needs at all. This can lead you to remain overly self-reliant and independent. 'Still waters run deep', however, and when you allow yourself to be touched by emotional experience, your own passion will astonish you. Fire–Water types are particularly adept at reaching into your aloofness and turning you on to parts of yourself you might otherwise shun.

Your Greatest Strengths

Lucid, practical intelligence; insightful and supportive interest in people; self-motivation; diligence; professionalism; ability to combine personal ambition with respect for the rights and wellbeing of others.

Your Greatest Weaknesses

Emotional insecurity and fear of rejection; your need to be in control and independent of others at all costs; pride; facility for ignoring people and matters that do not especially interest you or further your ends.

Images for Integration

A prophetic poet is awarded high honours ... An historian points the way to the future ... Having struggled unaided to the peak, a mountaineer hitches a ride on a passing helicopter.

Famous Personalities

Mohammad Ali (former World heavyweight boxing champion), Emily Balch (social reformer), James Frazer (anthropologist, author of *The Golden Bough*), Marilyn Horne (operatic soprano), Diane Keaton (actress), Richard Nixon (former American president), Juan Ramon Jimenez (poet), Carl Sandburg (poet, writer and historian), Jean Stapleton (actress), Denzel Washington (actor), Woodrow Wilson (former American president).

— 120 —

SUN CAPRICORN ♑ MOON PISCES ♓

Dost thou love life? Then do not squander time, for that's the stuff life is made of.
BENJAMIN FRANKLIN

I want to go beyond Impressionism and make it something solid and enduring, like the art of museums ...
PAUL CEZANNE

It's very hard to live up to an image.
ELVIS PRESLEY

Themes

EARTH/WATER Scientist and poet; a pragmatic dreamer; romantic but sceptical; a compassionate realist; an imaginative organizer; faithful; helpful; philosophical; humanitarian; tough and tender; long-suffering humility; dependable but private.

Are you a gullible dreamer or a stodgy bank clerk? A theoretical mathematician or an amusing mystic? Are you a lyrical poet or a hard-headed realist? Does the unknown fascinate or terrify you? Is your life tidy and totally in order, or do you feel chaos constantly threatening to engulf you?

You could be a bit like Ratty, one side of you good at biting the end of a pencil all day with your head in the clouds, and the other side good at protecting weaker souls and providing well-packed picnics at just the right moment. Although you are a softy, you are also dutiful and work out your accounts to the last penny. You are likely to experience an underlying tension between the world of your dreams and rich imagination, and your need to stay in touch with 'reality'.

Worries about being engulfed by life's problems and whether or not you have made the right choice may plague you often, even though you are blessed with a concentration that pulls all the pieces of your jigsaw together in the end. But until that happens you may fret and feel, like one Capricorn–Pisces friend, that 'civilization is only chaos taking a rest'. But this turns into a strength as you gain self-knowledge, because your ambition for order and achievement never dulls your sensitivity to human needs and values.

Whilst you have a responsive personality and a knack of getting along with all kinds of people, you are more of an introvert than most people guess. You feel deeply about things; you think carefully and penetrate into the real nature of people and ideas. Valuing the more invisible, spiritual things of life, you try to build them into the edifice of all that you do. You may not exactly repress your feelings but you tend to keep them to yourself, for you are not a flashy person; rather, you are always *available* to people, ready to share your views and help in practical ways when needed.

Your self-reflection makes you a bit grave, solemn at times, but it also allows you to understand the plight of being human, and to forgive others for the weaknesses you try to check in yourself. As a natural humanitarian with a good head on your shoulders, you would make an excellent lawyer, social worker, counsellor, doctor or psychologist. Your penchant for mystery could make you an talented detective!

You have great insight and can often see into the hidden problems and the dark, fantastic byways of the mind. Your logical brain seeks to find meaning in the chaotic, and to give structure and order to the unmanageable. But no matter how neat, logical and practical you are, there is a side of you that is instinctively drawn towards the uncontainable, boundless poetry of life.

You like to be active and may be goal-oriented, indeed ambitious, but not to the extent that you pass up a chance to spread a bit of humour and encouragement. You want to get things done, but you also want to feel your way along – a bit – and allow the fates to invade and give you your ration of mystery. Whilst a part of you will always remain private, your energies will need to be expressed in the world, making a difference that really matters.

Relationships

You have a very romantic side, but you try very hard – and usually succeed – in not letting it get the better of you. Tender, kind-hearted, devoted, loyal, almost anticipating your loved one's need before it arises, you may desperately want the security of emotional containment and end up containing *them*.

You can either be totally needy and dependent, or you can play the self-reliant loner. Perhaps you are not sure whether you are the cat's whiskers or something the cat brought in. You give the appearance of being very self-possessed, able to cope with a whole spectrum of problems, but when you feel safe in a close relationship you open up and reveal the woes that weigh heavy on your heart. *And* the joys. Indeed, there is a whimsical, light-hearted, fun-loving soul wanting to get outside and forget the serious side of life.

Your Greatest Strengths

Capacity to give form and substance to your imagination; compassion and practical helpfulness; personal courage you find from self-reflection and moral precepts; gift for quietly bringing order out of chaos.

Your Greatest Weaknesses

Fear of the unknown; pathetic tendency to carry the burdens of others; propensity to lose your confidence in negative thought patterns; willingness to bend the truth to fit your thesis.

Images for Integration

A wine collector uncorks a rare vintage to celebrate a success ... A child builds a sandcastle of reinforced concrete ... Bilbo in Tolkein's *Lord of the Rings* ... *Bathers in a Landscape* by Cezanne ... Elvis Presley's *Blue Suede Shoes*.

Famous Personalities

Lew Ayres (actor), Paul Cezanne (impressionist painter), John Denver (singer), Ava Gardner (actress), Paul Ferroud (composer), Benjamin Franklin (scientist and statesman), J. Edgar Hoover (lawyer and former director of the FBI), Sandy Koufax (baseball player), Elvis Presley (rock 'n' roll singer), Keith Thomas (historian, author of *Religion and the Decline of Magic*), J.R.R. Tolkein (writer and scholar).

Chapter Fourteen

SUN IN AQUARIUS

— 121 —

SUN AQUARIUS ≈ MOON ARIES ♈

More than anything life calls for confidence in oneself.
VIRGINIA WOOLF

Man has been endowed with reason, with the power to create, so that he can add to what he's been given.
ANTON CHEKHOV

There is in human nature generally more of the fool than of the wise.
FRANCIS BACON

I wish I could change my sex as I change my shirt.
ANDRÉ BRETON

Themes

AIR/FIRE Self and society; quick and sound intellect; observant and astute; self-interest; social conscience; prophetic; radical views; forward-looking; analytical; disdain for hypocrisy; frank; harsh critic; bright; off-the-well; outrageous sense of humour; rebellious; intelligent individualist; maverick truth-seeker.

Are you a great observer of humanity but too much of a snob to really join in? Do you speak your own mind courageously and convincingly,

401

and then wonder why others do not always warm to you and your causes? Talkative and energetic, you are often wrapped up in your own world of ideas and projects. Your excellent mind works in a no-nonsense, quick and efficient manner, and you tackle problems with great appetite, getting much satisfaction from grasping essentials and sorting everything out.

An intellectual virtuoso, hearty adventurer and spunky, well-intentioned friend, you speak your mind in no uncertain terms, with a special knack of poking fun at the absurdities and hypocrisies of human beings and the status quo. You may not, however, be aware of how distant and arrogant you appear to others. Your drive to understand the world and to champion its most urgent causes is likely to bring you success, but your naive, overbearing self-confidence often kills off the warm response you would like from your immediate listeners. You expect others to be as forthright and resilient as yourself, as eager to learn and as desirous of intellectual mastery. But you are not easy to live up to, and few people want the glaring truth and a sparring partner *all* of the time.

You are a good friend and neighbour, capable of motivating people by your optimism and your faith in yourself to improve the future. But are you more concerned about the welfare of others or of yourself? Do you speak *your* mind or do you see yourself as spokesperson for society as a whole? At times you are torn between the two, and you can experience loneliness if you do not come to terms with your need for approval and acceptance.

One of life's zany individuals, you are a real character who is unafraid of the challenge of self-education and self-improvement. You develop original style and bring a fierce moral integrity to whatever you do. You believe fervently in your ideals of a social order that protects individual rights (yours especially!), but you are reluctant to become subservient to the group. A friendly egomaniac, you want the best for everyone and are prepared to fight for it – honourably, of course. You espouse Utopian ideas, but you are sceptical of the ability of groups to make them real. 'Them *and* me' versus 'them *or* me' – this is your dilemma.

Since you love challenges and measure yourself against society's expectations, you make a wonderful social reformer or eccentric ambassador. Self-expression without the impingement of too many rules and regulations is vital for your wellbeing, making you ideally suited to self-employment. Although you need social activity and an attentive audience, you will do things your way or not at all, and you will put yourself on the line to the last.

You do not have much patience for vulnerability and emotional complexities, and like quick, practical answers that cut through the red tape of bureaucracy. Irritations can make you flare up into a temper, but it usually passes quickly, and your sense of humour helps you recover your equilibrium in most situations.

Relationships

The brotherhood of man is a reality for you, but the partnership of love with its emotional give-and-take is not quite so familiar. You live in your head most of the time, and are therefore baffled when your impetuous mental approach to solving emotional dilemmas does not work.

In a romantic relationship you need to be friends with your partner, and to share ideas and ideals. In fact, it is unlikely that you will be attracted to someone you do not respect intellectually. You need to slow down, however, and learn to savour the subtle nuances, to feel the inexpressible, to *not know* for once so you can just 'be' with a person. The warmth and romance of your fiery Moon can then come out and add the spark that your independent life is often missing.

You are fairly restless so will need plenty of space and freedom to do your thing. An earthy partner will help you establish useful routines that help you realize your goals. A watery partner could help you relax and get in touch with your feelings.

Your Greatest Strengths

Lively, intelligent intellect; absolute honesty and devotion to truth; respect for the rights and opinions of others; courage; sense of adventure; zest for life; moral integrity.

Your Greatest Weaknesses

Arrogance and overly assertive mental approach to life; self-absorbtion and lack of sensitivity to the emotional needs of others; cool and competitive temperament which keeps you a loner.

Images for Integration

A court jester mocks the social injustices of the realm ... Robin Hood and his band of merry men outwit the evil King John once again.

Famous Personalities

Anton Chekhov (playwright), Alan Alda (actor), Francis Bacon (statesman and philosopher), Barry Humphries ('Dame Edna Everidge'), Nikos Kazantzakis (author of *Zorba the Greek*), Fernand Leger (painter), Harold Macmillan (former British prime minister, Dennis Skinner (radical politician), Virginia Woolf (novelist).

— 122 —

SUN AQUARIUS ≈ MOON TAURUS ♉

A hungry man is not a free man.
ADALAI STEVENSON

Only by transcending the everyday, by seeing human life in larger terms, can the individual escape the slow strangulation of 'permanent errors'.
E.G. PRICE

Themes

AIR/EARTH Eccentric entrepreneur; level-headed; security versus independence; tenacious; pragmatic intellect; logical; kind-hearted; generous; ambitious; capable; friendly; self-indulgent; humanitarian; peace-loving but strong-willed.

You are as peaceful and sensual as Ferdinand the bull lazing on his grassy hill, but potentially as idealistic and broad-minded as the Spectator of all time and existence. You are independent, reasonable and dedicated to self-development and honourable values. Underneath, however, your habits and assumptions are firmly rooted in the status quo and in the permanence in your life of all those things that make you comfortable, happy and secure.

You may see yourself as an open-minded, progressive thinker. It is quite likely that you are a reformer, at least in temperament. If so, your *raison d'être* is the protection and enhancement of basic human needs: economic security; the maintenance of physical and mental health; an aesthetic, preferably green environment; and the simple sensual pleasures of living.

You are extremely individualistic and pretty set in your ways. A deep inner sense of contentment and self-satisfaction can make you appear a trifle smug. Even when you are feeling unconfident, your basically high opinion of yourself impresses others and sees you through rough times. Valuing peace as much as you value your own ideas makes you a natural diplomat: gracious and sympathetic, yet practical, reasonable and detached.

A happy union of emotional and intellectual natures within you lends weight to your views and inspires confidence in others. You therefore make a good leader or executive, even though you are not really interested in selling yourself or having power over others. But you are certainly not interested in anyone having power over you either. In fact, your refusal to conform may become your traditional way of preserving your position. As a result, you are one of the most indomitable and stubborn members of society, even though you are ever so nice at being just that. You like yourself just fine the way you are and, all in all, you enjoy *being* yourself.

If there is a conflict within you it is between home comforts and your future-oriented insight and thrust. Part of you is deeply nostalgic for the past; the background mood of your personality is coloured with vivid feelings and deeply imbedded experiences and values. Another part of you, however, analyses the past in order to learn from it. You feel yourself to be very deeply attached to your roots, but you know you are more than that.

You are excellent at making sense of individual human patterns and needs, which enables you to push the world gently forwards in healthier directions. You might do this by, for example, becoming more aware of green issues, spiritual growth and complementary therapies. You are also quite likely to be very involved with art in one way or another, with a social world filled with artists and eccentrics. Whatever you do, you bring a potentially powerful blend of idealism and realism to any project or relationship, be it commercial, artistic or philanthropic.

Relationships

You can be quite loving and romantic, as well as solid and dependable. Even though you have a strong sense of your self and your independence, you do enjoy life more with someone at your side, but it must be someone you can respect intellectually and aesthetically.

Although you can be very stubborn and set in your ways, you will always be open to discussing problems rationally and harmoniously. At times you may be just a little too maddeningly rational for your own good, and prone to be aloof and detached when emotional protests get too loud. But you are devoted (even possessive and maybe jealous – although you would dispute this) to your loved one, and will instigate the slow process of change and adjustment if you can see that doing otherwise would threaten your happiness and security.

Your Greatest Strengths

Infinite patience and common sense; reliability and loyalty to loved ones; courtesy and broad, philanthropic approach to people; ability to combine your distinct individuality with sensible, realistic thinking; dedication to grounding your inspirations with persistent efforts.

Your Greatest Weaknesses

Smugness and inertia; arrogance and stubbornness; a reluctance to listen to other views; being too logical and detached in emotional matters; riding roughshod over others in order to achieve your ambitions.

Images for Integration

A country girl seeks a conventional life with an unconventional young man in the big city ... The resident caretaker of a 'New Age' community sips his Beaujolais as he systematically does the year's accounts.

Famous Personalities

Bill Bixby (actor), Charles Carter (astrologer), Juliette Greco (singer and poet), Germaine Greer (feminist writer), James Hoffa (union leader), Natassia Kinski (actress), Somerset Maugham (writer), E.G. Price (novelist), Ronald Reagan (former American president), Steve Reeves (actor), Martin Shaw (actor), Adalai Stevenson (politician), Emanuel Von Swedenborg (philosopher and mystic).

— 123 —

Sun Aquarius ♒ Moon Gemini ♊

If I am to deal with life it must be in my own way for there is no escape from one's character.
Maurice Hewlett

The sublime and the ridiculous are often so nearly related, that it is difficult to class them separately.
Thomas Paine

Themes

AIR/AIR Friendly; bright and breezy; witty; iconoclastic; philosophical yet flippant; flexible yet stubborn; progressive; communicative; language skills; strong social conscience; restless; unsentimental; detached; emotionally naive.

Light, bright, cheerful and full of outrageous, deadpan quips, you are an amicable ideas person with what Charles Lamb aptly called a 'free and holiday-rejoicing spirit'. Or at least part of you is. For whilst at one level you can skim over life with all the practised whirligigs of a drunken butterfly, at another you aspire to change the world and tackle its most demanding problems.

So are you a heavyweight thinker or a lightweight mimic? Do you take life seriously, get stuck in and do your bit to make it better, or do you take the world as it comes and shrug off its problems with a carefree nonchalance? It sometimes seems that one half of you is drinking fruit juice for the good of your health, whilst the other is breaking open the champagne and puffing away at a cigarette to steady your nerves and for the sheer zany fun of it.

When your sober commitment comes together with your quick-witted curiosity, you possess a formidable capacity for communicating radical ideas and sorting out other people's problems. Your clarity, honesty, charm, patent good will and your frank, easy-going reasonableness inspire confidence. This enables you to act both as a negotatiator and as a peacemaker. Likewise your capacity for lateral thinking, your gift for words and your lightness of touch and good humour make you a natural in such areas as sales, journalism, public relations and advertising. Equally your inventive, ingenious side may draw you towards science, especially the sciences of people and ideas. But whatever you do, it is important for you to work alongside more practical types, or your ideas can simply remain ideas. This is because you tend to be quickly bored with the nuts and bolts of things, and are inclined to move on to the next bright thought if you find yourself getting too enmeshed in the nitty-gritty.

You probably love to read and to lose yourself in other people's minds, as new ways of looking at things are your very lifeblood. And when you light upon a new idea, you want to let everyone know about it. This can attract you to everything hi-tech, from portable phones to computers. You are also drawn to 'New Age' thinking, and are constantly moving on to the next message and possibility. For, as with your political ideas, you are essentially a progressive, believing in the possibilities of changing the world and improving communications and understanding between people.

Whilst naturally drawn to city life with all its bustle and busy exchange of ideas, you find that the country and contact with the soil can earth your restless soul, releasing you from your inclination to nervous tension and anxiety. Likewise music, and indeed the song of birds, can be a soothing and refreshing balm for your ever-changing spirit.

Relationships

Immensely friendly, you are a people person who has no problems getting to know whomever you want. Naturally charming, sociable and approachable, you will strike up a conversation with anyone anywhere, but best of all over the phone, in the open-air or over a communal meal.

Partnerships for you need to be based on shared interests and open dialogue. Yet even with your easy-going and co-operative nature, you find more intimate relationships less straightforward. For whilst you understand people's motives and have many insights, deeper emotions are your Achilles heel. Indeed you may find yourself drawing back from real intimacy for fear that the irrational emotions of love and hate may leave you feeling helpless and out of your depth. This can lead to you finding yourself alone in relationships yet not really knowing quite why.

You know you are safe with fellow Air types but Water types have much to teach you, so follow up on the fascination they hold for you and find out about your hidden depths.

Your Greatest Strengths

Your gift for friendship and communication; intelligence and quick-witted originality; an eye for, and openness towards, new ideas; a way with words; idealism.

Your Greatest Weaknesses

Flippancy; restlessness; tendency to squander your talents on new ideas, projects and relationships; unsentimental reluctance to face the darker aspects of life; unexpressed emotional needs which can trip you up.

Images for Integration

A child in a balloon drifts over the city reporting back by portable phone on all below ... A white blackbird charms the garden with its song.

Famous Personalities

Saul Alinksy (social activist), Joseph Alioto (American politician), Marian Anderson (contralto), Vicki Baum (novelist and dramatist), Jack Benny (comedian), Ernst Henkel (aeronautics designer), Maurice Hewlett (writer), Alan Hodgkin (neurologist), William Bill Knott (poet), Charles Lamb (essayist), John McEnroe (tennis player), Jack Nicklaus (golfer), Thomas Paine (political writer), Proclus (neo-Platonic philosopher), Elihu Root (lawyer and statesman), Georg Trakl (poet), Joseph Wambaugh (writer of detective novels).

— 124 —

Sun Aquarius ♒ Moon Cancer ♋

The best of prophets of the future is the past.
Lord Byron

What is poetry? The suggestion, by the imagination, of noble grounds for the noble emotions.
John Ruskin

I am aware of very strong gregarious tendencies in myself. My natural disposition is to be very easily influenced ... and above all by anything collective.
Simone Weil

Themes

AIR/WATER Humanitarian; vivid imagination; idealistic; compassionate and helpful; social conscience; companionable; popular; lofty emotions; progressive thinker but emotionally old-fashioned; a sensitive individualist; democratic spirit; the kind-hearted rebel; the friend of the people; the poet and the social worker.

Are you the sort of person who sets out to buy a book on home-made wine but returns with a treatise on the future of modern society? And why is it that when you feel like putting your feet up by the fire with cakes just like mother used to make, you end up spending the evening at the local charity meeting? It is something to do with your fondness for folks and the warm popularity that this brings you. You cannot help getting involved in some way because you were born with a very developed social conscience. You possess a healthy self-respect and feel that others deserve the same, no matter where they come from.

Although you may have eccentric ideas, you are blessed with the common touch; you can listen with great perception and respond with understanding and sensitivity. Your heart yearns for shared intimacy but your head pursues objective truth and collective concerns. Although you have a logical, scientific mind, you are actually drawn to things because of your great feeling for them. It is this *personal feeling* for larger causes and for the family of man that you are able to communicate to people, and therefore you are capable of truly motivating the masses.

When at peace with yourself, you possess a most pleasantly paradoxical personality, for you are a friendly, modern, future-oriented visionary whose inspiration derives from the cradle of the past. Wherever you have belonged – in terms of family, community, or nation – you will carry it with you as a *central inner drama* into your future.

Traditional values inform all you do, even if you are not consciously aware of them, and irrespective of whether you kick against them or embrace them utterly. It is easy for you to get attached to beliefs and to remain unaware of the influence of your security needs. But one of your potentially great strengths is holding and honouring the best values from the past without becoming a slave to them, for your Aquarian spirit is two steps ahead of everyone else, and must feel free to add its unique contribution.

You come into your own where the personal and impersonal meet, where your personal feelings, lofty ideals and social conscience can work fruitfully together, as in teaching, politics, social work, art, literature or drama. You will aim to justify your love of something by studying and analysing it, and finding out how it is valid for others. In this way, you often end up universalizing your personal experiences and turn them into a cause, into a mission. Your best creativity hinges on the acknowledgement that you are not only the past but also the future, not only collective but also personal, not only an observer but also a passionate participant in the panorama of life and human history.

Relationships

Your conscious Aquarian side has a charmingly naive, detached way of studying and scrutinizing others, as if each person were a fascinating

411

object d'art in a museum. Underneath the cool, friendly veneer is a very vulnerable, clannish, possessive heart which needs lots of affection and a sense of belonging. You can be moved to tears by a memory but then seemingly indifferent to the emotional needs of your nearest and dearest – if they are too cloying.

Needing space but also a cosy niche where you are the 'special one', you are not always the easiest person to live with. Basically, you suffer from the 'freedom–closeness' dilemma: you want emotional security but also freedom to do your own thing, to keep a few doors open. You think you are independent but old behaviour patterns will shape your responses to loved ones now more than you care to admit. The more you become aware of this, the more freely will you be able to give and receive love without the nagging suspicions and fear, and without the knee-jerk escapist reaction. Your romantic soul can relax, open up and enjoy the human exchange that is so vital to your wellbeing.

Your Greatest Strengths

Genuine warmth and capacity for intelligent kindness; far-reaching imagination; devotion to both truth and the uplifting of human life; ability to express universal insight through personal images.

Your Greatest Weaknesses

Unconscious prejudices; ability to rationalize irrational actions; a tendency to get absorbed in abstract causes which cuts you off from your feelings and keeps you emotionally immature.

Images for Integration

A social worker bypasses bureaucracy to save a mother and child ... A childhood memory becomes the basis of a new world order.

Famous Personalities

Humphrey Bogart (actor), Lord Byron (poet), Fritjof Capra (physicist-philosopher), Christian Dior (fashion designer), Farah Fawcett (actress), Clark Gable (actor), John Hurt (actor), Norman Mailer (novelist and playwright), Franklin D. Roosevelt (former American president), John Ruskin (critic and sociologist), Babe Ruth (champion baseball player), Simone Weil (philosopher), Boris Yeltsin (Russian president).

— 125 —

SUN AQUARIUS ♒ MOON LEO ♌

I was a triumph, Darling!
DAME GWEN FFRANGCON-DAVIES (ACTRESS)

My people and I have come to an agreement ... they are to say what they please, and I am to do what I please.
FREDERICK THE GREAT

I am the incarnation of everybody and the zones of reassurance. I am the obstetrician of good fortune, I live in the social cages of joy.
THOMAS MERTON

Themes

AIR/FIRE Great gentleness on the surface and strength within; fearless defender of principle; wise and generous in helping others; fount of wisdom; integrity; visionary; artistic; renaissance man; friendly; trustworthy; despotic; arrogant; emotionally idealistic; romantic; chivalrous; creative imagination.

Are you a democrat or a despot? An individualist or a social being? An egalitarian or a snob? Probably all of these, in your own warm and wonderful way. You have a proud, regal, magnanimous disposition, a fine intellect, bags of personal flair, and you invest much passion and fervour into all your personal relationships, of which there will be many.

A strong sense of your own individuality and ideals is what you exude to the world, and others know they are dealing with a person of deep integrity and honour. They will also be affectionately aware of your vanity and spasmodic imperiousness, but will love you nonetheless, for despite your autocratic ways, your need for affection

413

and admiration makes you vulnerable, approachable and very human.

You need friends and can make a real family of them. Generous, encouraging, able to make everyone feel they are special, you have a way of ennobling whomever and whatever you touch. Great gentleness and respect for the heights of the human spirit, coupled with enormous inner strength, make you in your best moments a veritable fount of wisdom and inspiration, full of the type of friendly charity which accepts, embraces and forgives human inconsistencies. Likewise, however, if your dignity is offended or your generosity and talents go unappreciated, you can be difficult, retreating into a sulky silence and pious dismissiveness. At these times you are be stubborn, unbending and arrogant.

You are a romantic and a visionary at heart, and a good performer too, fully aware of your effect on others. Not that anything you do is feigned, for the purity and depth of your feelings, your inner 'truth' as a human being is what motivates you and touches others. But you possess tremendous creative flair and artistic sensitivity, and quite simply, you are a ham. All this combined with your fervent self-belief and noble ideals makes you a real character in any circle. You have a broad intellectual outlook and a lively, fertile imagination. You are a natural leader, communicating from your heart in clear, honest, straightforward ways.

You could be a social reformer, radiating a powerful commitment to uplift and improve the quality of life for others, but your humanitarianism and egoism can get mixed up. Sometimes you care very much about exterior things and how you are being received, and other times you are completely uninterested in convention, manners and protocol.

You rebel with flair and style – nothing mediocre or ordinary for you. You are truly gregarious and interested in the welfare of people, but it is still *your* show and *your* myth you are living out, and your desire is to grow into and express as much of your (glorious) self as you can. You can make categorical decisions for the greatest happiness of the people in your kingdom. Your validity and meaning as a unique individual is intimately linked with the role you play in your larger network of friends and colleagues.

Relationships

Romantically you are trusting, passionate and loyal, and you thrive on warmth and affection. Love plays a big part in your life, and you tend to need a real adoring mate.

You are a tender-hearted idealist, a potential romantic poet whose predisposition is to see the best in people, wanting to believe they are as good and worthy as your ideal. But when they are not you are deeply disappointed, and you feel your personal misfortunes as monumental tragedies. Channelling some of your self-dramatizing powers into creative avenues – such as the theatre, art or music – may help to stabilize your emotional life.

Your Greatest Strengths

Radiant humanitarianism; enthusiasm for new and original ideas; integrity and trustworthiness; unique blend of rational logic and romantic imagination; openness and helpfulness to others.

Your Greatest Weaknesses

Vanity and the need to be loved; tendency to glamorize people so that you cannot always see their true colours; arrogance and stubborn need to control; inclination to get carried away by romance and adventure and forget to come down to earth.

Image for Integration

A modern actress takes a bow, then leads the audience to a political demonstration.

Famous Personalities

Evangeline Adams (astrologer), Dame Gwen Ffrangcon-Davies (actress), Frederick the Great (King of Prussia), James Joyce (poet and literary giant), Harvey Korman (actor), Edouard Lalo (composer), Thomas Merton (Trappist monk and mystic), Graham Nash (folk musician), Tom Selleck (actor), Clare Short (politician).

Sun Aquarius ♒ Moon Virgo ♍

A rose is a rose is a rose.
GERTRUDE STEIN

A novel is a mirror walking
along a main road
STENDHAL

Themes

AIR/EARTH Intellectual; puritanical; studious; devoted researcher; social worker; helpful; kind-hearted; common sense; emotionally naive; detached; clever; sense of propriety; truth-seeker; innovative mind; rebellious yet conventional; radical yet uptight.

You are a purist in heart and mind, a streamlined self-styled individual whose special eccentricities express themselves paradoxically in a worthy, utilitarian world view. Efficiency and happiness are nearly synonomous for you, and you are perhaps happiest when others agree with your cleverly reasoned arguments on 'questions of principle'. You then feel appreciated, maybe even loved.

Emotional experience baffles you somewhat as you are first and foremost an intellectual, and rely on your formidable mental powers to solve any kind of problem. Some of your greatest strengths are your objectivity and ability to carefully think things through and convince others of the utter reasonableness of your position.

Your mental outlook tends to be dispassionate, pristine, humanitarian and based on facts and practical considerations. Extended to the world of emotions and feelings, however, this approach can be hygienic, cold and aggravatingly 'goody-goody'. Your emotional detachment may create misunderstandings, for despite your seeming self-sufficiency you really need affection and intimacy much more than others realize.

Your Virgoan Moon seeks to analyse and organize your inner life, your instinctive responses and reactions to your environment, and your need for security and nurturance. You therefore do not welcome emotional chaos into your highly categorized mindset. You need method, routine and clarity to feel right, and so you become very adept at pushing out all unpleasant and unorganizable aspects of your emotional world. Your Aquarian Sun is very idealistic anyway, and so on the surface will co-exist happily with your Virgoan side which beavers away industriously, working out all the fine details of the larger ideals you espouse and on which you base your life.

Your happiness would be nearly complete if you could find a method, a kind of mathematical formula, which would allow you to be both the unconventional eccentric and the sane, sanitized, law-abiding citizen. There is something about you that cherishes the traditional recipes for happiness in the family and society. Curiously, however, you find they are not for you because *you* are different – a gregarious loner, with exquisite original flair but a hypercritical nature which can sting.

You have an excellent mind, and when you get to the nub of things your instinct is to render your superior understanding practical and beneficial to others. You may enjoy the world of computer technology where your instinct for logical systems will flourish; or you may be a zealous and capable social reformer, as the whole business of health comes naturally to you. Fascinated by the relationship between mind and body and the laws that make for efficient, harmonious living, you will tend to advocate a proper diet, regular exercise and mental fitness.

Relationships

Intimate relationships can pose a real challenge for you. Although you are devoted and kind-hearted, you do not feel comfortable with overly demonstrative shows of emotion. You show your feelings in friendly, practical ways.

In a sense, you are a bit naive when it comes to love – utterly pure and sincere in your affections but unsure as to what to do next. You are innately independent, even eccentric, but you blossom with a little emotional excitement and nourishment. Basically, you need a gentle response in order for your emotional confidence to develop, and when it does you make the most loyal and altruistic of mates.

Your Greatest Strengths

Mental dexterity; capacity for detailed research, objective reasoning and critical analysis; refined aesthetic sense; willingness to help and to do what needs to be done; genuine kindness; devotion to ideals.

Your Greatest Weaknesses

Tendency to be obsessed with sanity and order; an overcritical, nit-picking attitude to people and relationships, in an assumption that life is about 'functioning' and that emotional conundrums can be solved by a mathematical formula, and in your tendency to take yourself and what you know too seriously.

Images for Integration

A psychiatrist makes an accurate analysis of a neurotic's symptoms and then works patiently, devotedly, consistently to facilitate the patient's return to health ... Aliens extract human genes to breed and rebuild the human race on a planet of superior design ... Inspector Maigret.

Famous Personalities

Max Beckmann (painter), Frederick Delius (composer), Vanessa Redgrave (actress), Georges Simenon (writer), Boris Spassky (chess player), Gertrude Stein (writer), Stendhal (writer), Bernard Tapie (politician), John Travolta (actor), Alessandro Volta (physicist).

— 127 —

SUN AQUARIUS ≈ MOON LIBRA ♎

Do you think it pleases a man when he looks into a woman's eyes and sees a reflection of the British Museum Reading Room?
MURIEL SPARK

As for the men in power, they are so anxious to establish the myth of infallibility that they do their utmost to ignore truth.
BORIS PASTERNAK

But if a man happens to find himself ... he has a mansion which he can inhabit with dignity all the days of his life.
JAMES MICHENER

Themes

AIR/AIR The art of sociability; highly idealistic; charming; romantic; good intellect; love of truth and beauty; reasonable; broad-minded; humanitarian; independent but devoted; artistic sensitivity; tolerant; understanding; avant-garde tastes; civilized; gentle dignity.

Are you the charming, easy-going member of the gang who can suddenly get rebellious if your 'rights' and your sympathetic nature are abused or taken advantage of? Are you the broad-minded idealist who is constantly inviting disappointment when people turn out to be mere mortals?

You are a social creature, combining breezy affability with high nobility, and your humane, friendly personality knows how to go with the flow and create provocative but enjoyable social intercourse. It is important for you to know what the hoi poloi think, to be part of the 'in' group, but you are not always sure you want to *join* it. You will settle for being an associate member – keeping the faith, but in your own unique way.

You can be torn between the need to belong and your deep conviction in the sanctity of individualism and independent thought. Intellectually you see life as one inter-related whole, and you can express your ideas and convictions with feeling and a lively sincerity. You believe in revolution but in the nicest possible way, because you would hate to actually offend others. How to combine freedom and friendship, causes and courtship – that is your dilemma.

You are long on theory and ideals but not always very practical. In an ideal world you would prefer to lead your life according to clearly thought-out beliefs which leave little room for irrational passions, prejudices or presumptions. If, however, you do not come down to earth and join the mess from time to time you can appear unapproachable and fickle, cerebral and poetic, but much less effective than you could be if you got really *involved* with life.

You *are* involved, though, in a typically airy way – you are observant, talkative, socially aware and concerned to promote ideas and 'systems' that produce a better, brighter outlook for humanity.

Indeed, this is your strong point: you are an *ideas* person and will thrive in education, communication, public relations and literary pursuits. You love beauty and could be found in the world of art and fashion. You have a unique way of imbibing the aesthetic atmosphere of your surroundings and then giving your impression through conversation, painting or intellectually astute commentary.

As an extreme idealist you tend to have one foot in heaven and the other in the royal court of reason. There is not too much room in your universe for the dark, the macabre, the sinister. You will deal with all that intellectually, putting it very firmly in its place. You may enjoy philosophy and can easily get carried away with dry discussion and argument on abstract points. You have good taste in people and knowledge. A friendly, understanding person who readily sympathizes with human problems, you may well be accused, however, of making up your philosophy as you go along so as to protect yourself from the messy side of human involvement.

Relationships

You are a very charming, romantic person who is always seeking the ideal relationship, even if you are already in one. But when asked how you feel about someone you may reply that you *think* you feel such-and-such. That is, you may have to stop thinking to get in touch with your feelings.

You like a bit of stylishness and glamour in your relationships, as well as intellectual stimulation and emotional challenge. In short, you can be a bit fussy – you need a friend, you need a lover, not too close, not too distant, not too tall, not too thin, not too secure, not too way-out; the list could go on. Certainly you need someone who amuses you – humour and fun are a big part of your life – but you also need someone who brings you down to earth a bit, who helps you physically relax and become more happily resigned to the ordinary side of life. You are capable of real devotion and friendship within a love relationship, as long as there is plenty of room for manoeuvre.

Your Greatest Strengths

Lively, far-reaching intellect which works with principles easily and sees life from endlessly new vantage points; refined sociability and global interest in people, places and purposes; romantic idealism and intelligent kindness which enobles all you do and endears you to friends; integrity and colourful pursuasiveness which impels others to look again at the old beliefs they hold dear.

Your Greatest Weaknesses

Overly intellectual and abstract approach to life; romantic idealism and emotional naivety which invites infidelity and disillusionment; lack of stamina and dislike of imperfection which keeps you out of the main fray of human life and distanced from your real power.

Images for Integration

Anarchists form a committee to overthrow the tyranny of committees ... Good friends fall in love and get married.

Famous Personalities

Edwin Aldrin (astronaut), Robert Boyle (father of modern chemistry), Arcangelo Corelli (composer and virtuoso violinist), Wilhelm Furtwängler (great conductor), Valéry Giscard d'Estaing (economist and politician), Edouard Manet (impressionist painter), Joseph Mankiewicz (film director), James Michener (novelist), Boris Pasternak (novelist), Burt Reynolds (actor), Ruth Rendell (writer), Muriel Spark (novelist).

— 128 —

SUN AQUARIUS ♒ MOON SCORPIO ♏

A little theory makes sex more interesting, more comprehensible, and less scary – too much is a put-down, especially as you're likely to get it out of perspective and become a spectator of your own performance.
DR ALEX COMFORT

Politics, as a practice, whatever its professions, has always been the systematic organisation of hatreds.
HENRY BROOK ADAMS

Themes

AIR/WATER Powerful intellect; keen insight; charismatic; detached intensity; strong-willed; egotistic; stubborn; fiercely principled; dogmatic; self-judging; ambitious; reformer; proud; self-reliant; an astute observer; controlled sexuality; passionate yet dispassionate.

You have a powerful, magnetic personality which may have a hypnotic effect on many people. Your character possesses a compelling blend of broad social-intellectual concerns and passionate self-interest; detached idealism and dark cynicism, the latter based on an intimate understanding of your own appetites and emotional needs.

In general a 'people' person and an avid student of human nature, you are popular because the intensity of your personality rarely lets up. Your obsessive individualism commands recognition – you convince people of your importance and capability, inspiring some to follow you to the ends of the Earth. Indeed, you may have the magnetism of a demi-god and the confidence of a guru, but when you can conquer an unbalanced desire for power and develop a more impartial approach your achievements will have longer-lasting success. Freedom from obsessive self-interest should be your aim.

A sort of commanding haughtiness and inner conviction that you are 'It' usually draws people into your spell. But you are equally capable of detached withdrawal and even contempt, especially if your ego has been injured or unfairly treated. You may try to rise above petty feelings, but you can carry resentment around inside for a long time if injustice has been done. It is important that your conscious, rational Aquarian side, which 'knows' itself to be fully self-determined and uniquely in charge of your life, comes to understand and respect your proud, emotionally possessive, instinctively voracious Scorpio side, whose primitive needs, if unmet, can lead to manipulative behaviour that can undermine your chances for emotional fulfilment. In order for you to maintain peace between these two sides of yourself, you must dig down deep to see what buried assumptions and denied needs are at the root of a possible mind/feeling split. Like Dr Jekyll and Mr Hyde, your intellectual and creative potential is enormous as long as both sides are working harmoniously together instead of living unconnected and mutually antagonistic lives – and this can only come through profound self-knowledge.

Your Aquarian Sun is the rational scientist; your Scorpio Moon is the hungry sensualist. Being deeply rooted in both realms gives you powerful insight into the vast spectrum of human nature. You are a good investigator of the human psyche and/or body, and you have the instincts of the reformer who sees the hidden potential in the discarded souls of life and can facilitate in their transformation. Can you embrace the whole of yourself? Your brooding desires, hatreds, jealousies, cravings, as well as your iconoclastic, individualistic Self which gazes out over the pitiful human race in detached wonder?

Relationships

Emotionally you are inclined to blow hot and cold. You have an ability to marshal your passions in an almost machine-like manner, giving total and all-absorbing attention to your loved one and demanding the same in return. Your intensity guarantees that you get it, too.

You can be quite passionate when you decide to let yourself go. Never frivolous with your feelings, you are pretty much an all-or-nothing person who can become totally absorbed in a relationship. You can surprise yourself with how deeply attached you become, and you may use rational defences to protect you from your emotional vulnerability.

Your Greatest Strengths

Intense dedication to principles; loyalty to friends and family; persevering and thorough approach to work; investigative turn of mind and devotion to truth at any cost; courageous enthusiasm for reform and desire to improve the welfare of others; capacity for living life to the full.

Your Greatest Weaknesses

Egoism and self-importance; tendency sometimes to get stuck in prejudice and dogmatic opinions; a stern, exacting eye and unbending standards; potential for ruthless behaviour and manipulation.

Images for Integration

A scientist dissects a scorpion with great tenderness and absolute precision ... A researcher presents his findings to colleagues at a

'Science For Humanity' Conference ... Jules Verne's *20,000 Leagues Under the Sea*.

Famous Personalities

Henry Brook Adams (historian, writer), Princess Caroline of Monaco, Carol Channing (actress), Alex Comfort (sexologist), James Dean (actor), Guy Fawkes (English dissident), Zsa Zsa Gabor (actress), Helen Gurley Brown (editor of *Cosmopolitan*), Emily Harris (revolutionary), Mario Lanza (singer and actor), Sinclair Lewis (writer), Merle Oberon (actress), Paul Scofield (actor), Jules Verne (writer), Kaiser Wilhelm II (former German ruler).

— 129 —

SUN AQUARIUS ≈ MOON SAGITTARIUS ♐

When I am ... completely myself, entirely alone ... my ideas flow best and most abundantly. Whence and how these come I know not nor can I force them ... Nor do I hear in my imagination the parts successively, but I hear them gleich alles zusammen (at the same time all together).
WOLFGANG AMADEUS MOZART

Liberty's in every blow!
Let us do or die!
ROBERT BURNS

I am a sociable worker.
BRENDAN BEHAN

Themes

AIR/FIRE Independent; philosophical mind; gregarious; adventurous; rebellious; humanitarian; intellectual; inspirational; social concerns; urge for expansion; verbose; big-hearted; tactless; confident; good teacher; optimistic; zany humour.

424

Your character is large, open and breezy, and intensely honest, and you have a marvellous lucidity of thought and expression that allows you, in most cases, to go straight to the point. And you make your points (and plenty of them) with such impressive enthusiasm, conviction, authoritative eloquence and wit that people tend to sit up and take notice.

Your fine intellectual grasp makes you a natural leader, or at least a leading thinker, in your social circle. You easily assume this role because you are unafraid of speaking your mind, not because you want the responsibility of leadership. You believe that uncompromising courage and independence of character is the birthright and norm of all peoples, and it takes you a while to learn that more emotional, fragile souls feel differently. Timid folk admire your forthright, noble style and many will envy your easy confidence. Likewise, however, people occasionally suffer from your tactlessness as you charge full steam ahead into your next exciting and worthy project.

You will attract many admirers and friends, people who know that you do not compromise with Truth, and that what they see and hear is what they will get. Optimistic, forward-thinking, something of a visionary in many ways, your exceptional integrity makes your deductions, opinions and viewpoints all the more valuable and weighty in effect.

A natural teacher and moral authority, you thrive in areas where your intellect is stretched and where your inventiveness can express itself. Film and theatre work is also a natural place for you to express your idealism and flair for the unusual. Sometimes you appear detached and imperious, with the result that others may not challenge or enter into debate with you since you are, without realizing it or wanting to be, a little high-minded and abstract.

Something of an eccentric absent-minded professor, you have a robust, gregarious, inspirational personality with tons of magnetism, and a need for substantial variety, adventure, and intellectual challenge in your life. Physical challenge will interest you, too – anything that gets you out into the wide, open spaces.

Relationships

Emotionally you are a bit difficult to bring down to Earth. You need friendship, intellectual rapport, and have a great capacity for spontaneous play and spur-of-the-moment adventures, but you are not particularly keen on commitment. Surprisingly, there is an awkward, almost childlike, shyness about you – or perhaps it is more of an innocence and trust in the goodness of people and the sense of excitement that you bring to new relationships and activities.

Your instinct is to remain open to the possibilities that abound in people and situations, but at the same time you seek intense personal experiences. You need to remain in charge of your life, and a partner who understands this, as well as being able to help you learn to relate more sensitively, is the kind of partner with whom you will flourish. You have to know that it is *you* who is choosing to remain faithful rather than obeying some external restriction to your freedom of movement. You like sharing your interests with your partner, but by learning to pay attention to the more subtle details of relationships and others' needs, you will find your life expanding emotionally as well as intellectually.

Your Greatest Strengths

Ability to see the broad view; intellectual speed and agility; philosophical resilience; optimism; love of learning; natural ability to teach and inspire others; humanitarian heart; outrageous sense of humour.

Your Greatest Weaknesses

Tendency to rationalize and make sweeping generalizations; a rather austere moral fervour; impatience with mundane details and the restrictions of domestic life; proneness to preach when advancing your pet causes; tendency to be tactless, blunt and unaware of the subtleties of social intercourse.

Images for Integration

A distinguished sociology professor throws a fancy-dress party for her best friends ... Indiana Jones founds a new university in the heart of the jungle ... *Alice in Wonderland.*

Famous Personalities

Brendan Behan (playwright), Marisa Berenson (actress), Robert Burns (poet), Lewis Carroll (writer), Alice Cooper (singer), Charles

Dickens (writer), Hal Holbrook (actor), David Jason (actor), Charles A. Lindbergh (aviator), Wolfgang Amadeus Mozart (composer), Yoko Ono (wife of John Lennon), Barbara Seagull (actress).

— 130 —

SUN AQUARIUS ≈ MOON CAPRICORN ♑

With malice toward none, with charity for all, with firmness in the right as God give us to see the right.
ABRAHAM LINCOLN

In Genesis it says that it is not good for a man to be alone, but sometimes it's a great relief.
JOHN BARRYMORE

It can be less painful for a woman not to hear the strange, dissatisfied voice stirring within her.
BETTY FRIEDAN *The Feminine Mystique*

Themes

AIR/EARTH Steadfast; resourceful; independent; honest; common sense; dependable; shrewd; organizational talent; understanding; practical wisdom; foresight; economic; paternal; brotherly; broad-minded; practical reformer; applied technology; inventive.

You are a broad-minded, deeply thinking citizen of the world who feels the yoke of personal responsibility to those less capable than yourself. Your complete integrity and dedicated search for a truth that is practicable and helpful to the majority makes you loved and respected by friends and colleagues. Honesty, firmness of purpose, and crystal-clear foresight are your finest gifts, and make you an individual others will not forget. They feel they can depend upon you utterly because you believe in the highest and best in others, and therefore tend to bring out the best.

You are like Old Abe – honest to the core, but as shrewd as they come; the wielder of authority, supporter of the weak, the father and the brother, the equal, the neighbour and the friend. A social being, you are interested in society and its norms and needs, and you will concern yourself with people in some way – leading them, thinking and writing about them or taking care of them. You may sometimes be torn between your humanitarian idealism and your instinctive cynicism about human nature. In time and with effort, however, you will normally be able to combine these two sides of yourself as you seek to discover the good and valuable side of life and to adapt your humanitarian values to the world as you find it.

You readily identify with all types of people, but you also know how to get the best out of them and instil them with a sense of their own dignity. Like Old Abe, you think that 'God must have loved the common man; he made so many of them'. And you, like God, will love them too, more often than not in a paternalistic sort of way.

You are a rugged individualist. Directing your stern, self-demanding ambition into realizing your whole, honourable self, you create your own success. It is all the more splendid because of your utter conviction to solid principles and because of your respect for human worth and ethical conduct. All these qualities give you an enormous appeal to many different types of people – superiors, inferiors, royals, down-and-outs, strangers, next of kin. Talking to each one in their own language, you can put them at ease, for they sense that you understand them and that they are being treated as an equal in the most exalted sense of the term.

Your natural authority seldom offends because it has an egalitarian quality. You make a good manager, teacher, writer or actor – professions which require maximum self-motivation but which allow for contact with and guidance of others. You stand on your own two feet readily and happily, and very rarely do you lose sight of your aim. Ambitious, yes, but only to be yourself, to find and perform your true vocation, and hopefully to help others to do the same along the way.

Relationships

Loyal and devoted to family and loved ones, you have difficulty, however, in feeling really dependent on others. This keeps you somewhat emotionally detached. Intimacy is not your strong point, nor are you likely to go in for wild displays of emotion. You may be attracted to emotional people – fire and water types – who help you to overcome a certain austerity when it comes to enjoying yourself.

Losing control is not your style – it is messy and illogical and somewhat beneath you. But despite your very rational approach, you will always enjoy a challenge and a calculated risk – which relationships will present. 'Comport thyself with decorum' could be your unconscious watchword. Try not to dismiss emotional needs in yourself and in others as a sign of weakness.

Your Greatest Strengths

Integrity and personal honour; shrewd honesty; savvy of human character; unspoilt fearlessness and dependability; sardonic sense of humour; unique combination of common sense and humanitarian feeling; foresight and willingness to work in the present for the future good; ingenuity and problem solving.

Your Greatest Weaknesses

Overstrict adherence to principles; no-frills approach to social life which makes you a bit Spartan and uptight; logical approach to matters of the heart with a tendency to remain aloof and self-contained; the occasional proneness to pride and stubbornness.

Images for Integration

A revolutionary is elected president ... An alien civilization comes to Earth to rescue man from imminent destruction.

Famous Personalities

John Barrymore (actor), Thomas Edison (inventor), Mia Farrow (actress), Betty Friedan (grandmother of feminist movement), Abraham Lincoln (former American president), Rosa Parks (civil rights leader), Ayn Rand (writer), Mary Quant (fashion designer), Franco Zeffirelli (film director).

SUN AQUARIUS ♒ MOON AQUARIUS ♒

A religion can no more afford to degrade its Devil than to degrade its God.
HAVELOCK ELLIS

Our differences are politics. Our agreements, principles.
WILLIAM MCKINLEY

Man-Watching: A field guide to human behaviour
TITLE OF BOOK BY DESMOND MORRIS

Themes

AIR/AIR Detached friendliness; gregarious; eccentric lifestyle; independent; highly observant; clear-headed; objective; progressive thinker; scientifically oriented; helpful; well-meaning; open to the unusual; idealistic; impractical; loyal; law unto yourself.

You may be sceptical of what follows because, more than anyone else, you hate to be pigeon-holed. You are original, one-of-a-kind – aren't we all? But you do want the truth, the whole truth, and nothing but *your* truth – although your truth tends to encompass a very wide area of abstract principles.

Are you the ever helpful friend or the rebel without a cause? Are you the detached observer of society or the committed reformer? Are you in fact torn between your humanitarian concerns and a fierce love of your own independence? You are all these and an advanced thinker as well, open to new ideas and social, philosophical and scientific innovations. Your forward-looking and prophetic vision of the world helps you see what needs doing long before most people do, and as a result you are rarely shocked by the bizarre.

Although you consider yourself to be, and indeed are, an emminently reasonable person, your own eccentricities, which you may not notice yourself, can often startle others and rock the boat. You would hate to be thought of as selfish or difficult – you espouse the complete opposite in terms of values – but your maverick spirit seems to demand total acceptance. And you prefer to keep relations on an intellectual basis – surely, you think, it is possible to solve all problems by bringing them to the bar of reason. This attitude taken to the extreme can make you an unfeeling sort of person who turns everything about life into a mechanism to be rationally understood.

Your idealism may take you into politics or social work where your genuine compassion for human problems can be practically applied. Although you may not be the most socially well-adapted person, you are always there for your friends – being a generous, selfless person is your ideal. But no-one should ever take you for granted, for you are no doormat and you can say 'No' quite as strongly as you can say 'Yes' if your good nature is abused.

You value tolerance, cooperation and harmonious camaraderie, and will assume that you behave according to these ideal norms, but in practice no-one can tell you what to do! You genuinely care about the greatest good for all, but you want to do things in your *own* way. This can produce run-ins with authority figures. You abhor petty rules and regulations and imagine that everyone is as honest as you are.

Whether a friend or foe of society, it is society that makes you tick. That is, people, their beliefs, and the way they make the world turn round is what interests you. You look at the ideas that underlie human behaviour and try to think of some even better ones that will improve things for everyone. It is the fact that you identify with this 'everyone' so much that leaves you short-changed when it comes to a sense of personal self. It might be hard for you to say what that would be, divorced from the group and the ideals that give your life meaning. So whilst your idealism can be a great thing for the world, it makes you a difficult person to know intimately. You feel more comfortable working to make the world a better place than you do working on a one-to-one relationship. You need plenty of rest and respite to calm your overactive mind and to allow you to come back to Earth.

Relationships

You are a wonderful friend, loyal to the end and willing to help others realize their goals. Indeed you know no stranger, and your zany, independent personality means you make friends with all types of human beings – you find each one interesting and valuable in some way.

When it comes to close relationships and real passion, however, you can feel uncomfortable and inadequate. You may find it difficult to engage emotionally with one person. Because you dislike restraints of any kind and tend to live in your head, you may wrongly assume that you do not need the day-to-day, cosy and dependent sort of relationships which, you may feel, tie you down and rope you in. In fact, your partner does need to be adaptable and understanding to allow for the surprises and abrupt inspirations of your highly individualistic nature. But you would benefit from someone who can show you that feelings are not so frightening, and that your emotional and physical needs are just as valid as your intellectual ones. Interestingly, you may be drawn to dramatic and highly-charged relationships so that you can be opened to the passion and intimacy that you secretly crave.

Your Greatest Strengths

Gift for friendship; ability to understand objectively the principles underlying any problem you observe; humanitarian concern for the welfare of your fellow human beings; courage and commitment to your ideals; eternal sense of hope and belief in human potential.

Your Greatest Weaknesses

Emotional naivety and impersonal approach to relationships; tendency to over-identify with causes; a blunt, insensitive and overcritical approach to comparing people with your ideals; proneness to leave abruptly when the going gets too emotional and impinges on your freedom.

Images for Integration

A friend to all the world looks in the mirror and takes time out to befriend herself ... The living, breathing entity we call society ... The Jolly Green Giant.

Famous Personalities

Claire Bloom (actress), Ronald Colman (actor), Angela Davis (militant social activist), Havelock Ellis (physician and psychologist), William McKinley (former American president), Desmond Morris (anthropologist and writer), August Piccard (physicist and balloonist),

Jackie Robinson (baseball player), George Segal (actor), Belle Star (who sheltered Jesse James), Princess Stephanie of Monaco, François Truffaut (film producer), Charles Young (American footballer).

— 132 —

SUN AQUARIUS ≈ MOON PISCES ♓

Who relies on the natural currents of God's will attains freedom from all worldly cares and anxieties, and nothing can ever chain him again.
RAMAKRISHNA

I don't want to sound pious and prudish, but my responsibility is ... to proclaim something which I believe it is my duty and my calling to proclaim.
REVEREND DONALD SOPER

Themes

AIR/WATER Independent but vulnerable; thinker and poet; altruistic; loyal; universal outlook; eccentric; gullible; kind; sympathetic; kind and humorous; intuitive; social conscience; humanitarian; psychological insight; loves people; reverent; forgiving; committed to a cause.

Are you the observant, sensible, scientific type who is strangely attracted to weird phenomena? Are you open, easy-going, and friendly, available and helpful to all, but quaking inside because you fear that your soft, vulnerable little voice will not be heard? You are an enigma, as much to yourself as to others at times. At one level you are perky and independent, and at another you are a dreamy sentimentalist, happy to blend in with your surroundings. You appear to have a confident mental grasp on life and know exactly where you are, but inside you often struggle with self-doubt.

You are genuinely gregarious and intelligently concerned about people and about a mixture – perhaps an odd one – of social causes and metaphysical ideas. Your friendliness hides a sensitive and precarious inner core, however, which few people ever really get to know. You are one of the most sociable people in the zodiac – sympathetic, helpful, enjoying the fellowship of a wide range of people and eager to learn. Your inclination is to reach out to people – you want to be involved in a way that makes a difference, and you are deeply nourished and your ego is boosted when your efforts elicit a positive emotional response.

You strive to be an independent thinker and generally like to do your own thing. You will make a stand for the things you believe in, but you secretly hope you will not have to do it alone. Whether it is in science, the arts or metaphysics, the challenge of new frontiers attracts you, and it will be due as much to the romance of the role you might play as to the soundness of the principle at stake. Your insights can be very creative and fertile because you back up your thinking with real feeling – you care deeply about both the ideas and the people in your life. Your broad, almost visionary viewpoint and your disarming sympathy for other people makes you a touch eccentric but popular, too.

If your Aquarian side is dominant, you may have a view of scientists as an international brotherhood striving to uncover the truth for the benefit of humankind. If your Piscean side is stronger, you may feel that circuses and seances are as essential to a healthy life as three meals a day and eight hours of sleep.

You want to be of service to the world, to be connected in a meaningful way. No matter how busy you are you will make time for whatever philanthropic pursuit grabs your imagination. People know you are honourable, and if you ever chastise someone you do it with gentle humour – you know you have been there yourself. Your compassion for and understanding of human nature makes you well suited for work with people, either in education, the ministry or the caring/medical professions. You treat people as equals, and with great respect. You make a wonderful teacher because you are able to bring out the inner resources in others which they do not even realize they possess.

Relationships

Matters of the heart bring out the paradox of your intense romanticism and rational realism. In close relationships you have a quality of detachment yet involvement that can make you very alluring emotionally. Your mixture of spontaneous, warm sympathy and detached intelligence makes you a wonderful friend, but sometimes

434

your partner will want a lover when you feel like being friends and vice versa.

You want gentleness and intimacy but you may hide behind the nonchalance of your airy Sun when you feel too vulnerable. Often you will want to abandon yourself completely to the object of your affections, and yet you cannot help noticing his or her shortcomings. Your sensitivity makes you rebellious as well, ready to run or escape to some Utopian dream-world when you feel badly treated or fenced in.

Basically, you are both likeable and loveable and very loyal to loved ones in your own fashion. You just need to stay in the 'real world' a bit more and accept the fact that you are tough enough to survive the ups and downs of love.

Your Greatest Strengths

Rich imagination and universal outlook; devout commitment to social causes; friendly, accepting and understanding nature; ability to work and mix with all types of people.

Your Greatest Weaknesses

Tendency to be impractical and evasive; proneness to drift too much and waste energy in day-dreams, and to let your idealism turn into gullibility.

Images for Integration

A scientist sings grand opera ... A brilliant inventor takes a sabbatical on a desert island.

Famous Personalities

Queen Ann of England, George Balanchine (choreographer), Sacha Distel (singer), Eartha Kitt (singer and entertainer), Dick Martin (comedian), Paul Newman (actor), Ramakrishna (Hindu mystic), Franz Schubert (composer), Reverand Donald Soper (popular preacher), Roger Vadim (film producer), King Vidor (film director).

Chapter Fifteen

SUN IN PISCES

———————

— 133 —

SUN PISCES ♓ MOON ARIES ♈

There is nothing – absolutely nothing – half so much worth doing as simply messing about in boats.
THE WIND IN THE WILLOWS, KENNETH GRAHAME

Every day in every way, I am getting better and better.
EMILE COUE

Themes

WATER/FIRE Romantic; independent; sensitive; affectionate; adventurer; big talker; understanding; touchy; quarrelsome; humble but self-centred; fun-loving; moody; vivid imagination; artistic; wilful; nervous; quick thinker.

Are you a sensitive, introverted poet, or a confident explorer and crusader for the truth as you see it? Sometimes you feel passive, dreamy, private and emotional, preferring to observe the world around you from your inner sanctum whilst you let your keen intuition absorb data and form opinions and preferences from a position of safety. Other times you express your self-sufficiency and alert, analytical mind in no uncertain terms, and suprise people with your sudden authority and independence.

436

You exude an easygoing but gutsy sort of exterior which protects a very emotional, sensitive heart. Very much your own person, you are courageous enough to explore ideas, people and different avenues of self-expression, and you do not shrink from claiming your rights and declaring what you want. But you are also sympathetic and yielding when emotional harmony is what you want (which is most of the time), and certainly friendly comraderie and affectionate relations are essential for your wellbeing.

You are a curious mix of the meek and mild, and the militant. You can be defensive and moody, temperamental and argumentative if your fragile ego is disturbed or if you are defending a pet cause. You know what you know and demand to be heard. This trait can cause a lot of ups and downs in your close relationships, for though you thrive on intimacy and affection, you tend to rock the boat the minute you think your loved one has assumed your compliance on some issue. You feel with your ego and think with your heart, which makes your reactions a bit biased. If, instead of reacting so quickly, you could slow down and respond reflectively to friends, lovers or imagined opponents, the inner calm that you need so much would not be threatened.

In fact, your selfishness is not as gargantuan as it sometimes seems, and you are really one of the most gentle souls around. Your creative conflict is to do with the fact that you are partly a 'me first' person and partly an 'I'll do anything in the world for you' sort of person as well. The extreme paradox between romantic vulnerability and forthright assertiveness keeps you pretty restless and your imagination easily aroused.

Essentially easygoing, adaptable, readily imposed upon because of your kindness and helpfulness, you may often feel you must defend the know-it-all maverick individualist inside who wants to be recognized as the winner, the hero, the best. Ultimately you combine gentleness and spunk, imagination and energy, compassion and frankness. You are a quietly theatrical virtuoso, unselfconsciously in tune with people as well as with your own substantial talents and the joy they bring you.

Relationships

One of the most romantic of all Sun–Moon combinations, you yearn for the bliss of union and then, when you have found him or her, you throw yourself impetuously into a relationship. You can be sweet, self-sacrificing, and sympathetic, but then you suddenly pull away, pick a fight, or in some way reclaim your sense of self. You are moody and not always easy to live with, but you would not wilfully hurt your loved one, and are always ready to forgive.

You may remain something of an enigma to your loved one, but he or she can usually boast that you are a devoted friend, a lively companion and a romantic artist who can turn any adventure into a song or a poem. You may in fact find that music is your best medium, as it helps to soothe the emotional flare-ups that disturb your repose.

Your Greatest Strengths

Quiet charisma; warmth and optimism; frank spirit and jovial fellow feeling; combined sensitivity and impetuosity, which makes you fun to be with; ability to enter the race whilst at the same time encouraging the very best in your opponents; capacity to laugh at human nature and bounce back.

Your Greatest Weaknesses

Fear that your abilities and worth will not be noticed, making you go overboard in your efforts to win; tendency to be touchy and argumentative and to take yourself too seriously; inclination to be at the mercy of emotional fluctuations between selfishness and consideration for others, and an inner frustration when to do one seems to totally deny the other.

Image for Integration

In tattered rags, the small, obscure young servant named Arthur pulls the sword from the stone and becomes king of Camelot.

Famous Personalities

Virginia Bottomley (politician), Emile Coue (psychologist), Jean Harlow (actress), Holly Hunter (actress), Galileo (astronomer), Rex Harrison (actor), William Hurt (actor), Renoir (artist), Johann Strauss sr. (composer).

SUN PISCES ♓ MOON TAURUS ♉

Castles in the air – they're so easy to take refuge in. So easy to build too.
HENRIK IBSEN, *THE MASTER BUILDER*

*Does the poet create ... the thing called a poem, or is his behaviour
merely the product of his genetic and environmental histories?*
B.F. SKINNER

Themes

WATER/EARTH Caring and capable; emotionally demonstrative; a
practical romantic; sensual; sociable; charming; seductive; fair-
minded; sensitive to beauty; love of harmony; devoted; helpful; big-
hearted; artistic; musical; moody; manipulative; strives for security; a
dreamer and a realist.

Do you easily drift off into your vivid fantasy world or do you get stuck
into the practicalities of everyday life? Are you a pushover for romance
but turned off by material insecurity? Do you need lots of love and
affection but surprise yourself by your own capacity for shrewd,
independent, decisive action when it comes to your best interests?

You are a warm, idealistic, sweet-tempered person, and can make-
believe – for a while – that you are not interested in the things of this
world. Beauty, art, music, love, the intangibles of life are what matter
to you. This is true, but if you deny your material wants you become
deeply unsettled. Emotional and spiritual values inform your
behaviour and dealings with the world, but you know that a solid
material foundation will support your dedication to loftier or more
personal pursuits.

Your gentle, compassionate nature is backed up by a real stubborn
streak which serves you well. You may appear compliant and low-
profile, but you instinctively know what is right for you, and your quiet
strength lets people know that you are not to be trifled with.

You combine a vivid, rich imagination with a solid, down-to-earth
pragmatism. Once you have put down roots and feel secure, your
fertile imagination can blossom. Even if you do not develop a career in

the arts, you will need some outlet for creative self-expression in your life. Whilst you may have elegant, artistic taste and a highly developed appreciation of music and literature, you are also something of a simple nature mystic who comes alive when your senses meet the sounds, scents, sights and tactile sensations of the countryside.

You have a deep love for life and all its delights, and your capacity for enjoyment can have a beneficial effect on others, helping them to relax and enter into the convivial ambience and magic of the moment. Although in many ways you are a conventional creature of habit, you have enough common sense to know when to abandon the chores for the spontaneous picnic, party or sing-along.

In happy, harmonious atmospheres you become more of an extrovert and more confident in sharing your thoughts and feelings which are never far from the surface. When you have the harmony, beauty, love and comforts you feel you need, you can be the most contented of people. You are loyal, sensitive, and imaginatively attentive with both friends and family. You want the same treatment for yourself, and you will not stand for harsh treatment or anything less than what you feel you need and deserve. This quality, plus your innate dependability and patience, makes you ideally suited for work with people, such as in education, medicine and social work.

Relationships

You have a charming, sociable, sensual nature which comes to life when you are in love and in a satisfying relationship. In fact, a rich, happy love life is central to your sense of well-being. Romantic and yet domestic and practical, soft-hearted and sensitive yet unflappable in times of struggle, you enjoy making your nest and are an ideal mate – as long as your partner does not want to go trekking in the Himalayas.

You love the good life but it would be pretty meaningless without someone to share it all with. This makes you a very satisfying person to be with as you have a natural instinct for keeping the daily round ticking over whilst also stopping to smell the roses as often as you like. But there is a paradox within you that could cause some conflict in relationships: your Taurean side is independent, capable, and wants to get on with its own concerns, whilst your Piscean side is more vacillating, insecure, and needy of encouragement. It is best to be honest with yourself about your neediness (and your possessiveness!) so that you do not unwittingly manipulate loved ones into giving you what you need. It does not take much to win you over – lots of physical affection and the sharing of dreams will keep the romance alive no matter how much is in the bank.

Your Greatest Strengths

Sensual imagination and feeling for music and art; vivid awareness of other people's feelings; warm, accepting and affectionate nature; appreciation of beauty and the simple pleasures of life and friendship; ability to bring your romance down to earth and realize your dreams.

Your Greatest Weaknesses

A strongly subjective and emotional view of life; possessiveness; tendency to manoeuvre situations to satisfy your security needs, and to be stubborn, old-fashioned, and to cling to the past.

Images for Integration

A nature mystic bakes bread in an earth oven ... An artist decorates her home lavishly.

Famous Personalities

Andre Breton (poet), Edgar Cayce (the sleeping healer, clairvoyant), Neville Chamberlain (former British prime minister), Tirso de Molina (playwright), Pico Della Mirandola (neo-Platonist), Fats Domino (jazz musician), Bobby Fischer (chess champion), Kenneth Grahame (writer), Henrik Ibsen (writer), Jerry Lewis (actor), Pier Paolo Pasolini (poet, novelist and film director), Andres Segovia (classical guitarist), B.F. Skinner (psychologist), Julie Walters (actress).

—135—

SUN PISCES ✕ MOON GEMINI Ⅱ

*No good opera plot can be sensible, for people do
not sing when they are feeling sensible.*
W.H. AUDEN

A professor is one who talks in someone else's sleep.
W.H. AUDEN

If youth is a defect, it is one that we outgrow too soon.
ROBERT LOWELL

Themes

WATER/AIR Fanciful; eccentric; humorous; poetic; intuitive; love of language and symbolic logic; wordy; expressive; lack of confidence; intellectual versatility; alternating sociability and shyness; blow with the wind; quick thinker; temperamental; nervous; talkative; eternal youth; fun-loving.

Do you sometimes say what you feel before you have even thought it? Do you consider yourself a rational, sensible person whose willingness to look at the whole spectrum of views sabotages your confidence? You think with your heart and feel with your head. Trying to make those lines of communication hook up inside you can sometimes feel like trying to solve an unsolvable maze.

At your best you are the epitome of feminine intuition – acute perceptions and a rich imagination enable you to respond to people and situations with accuracy and subtlety. But at your worst you use perverse inflexibility to mask your indecision and lack of confidence. There is something about you which is eternally youthful, magically spontaneous and vividly expressive of the ideas and images that inspire you. You are full of hopes and wishes, plans and schemes, interests and hobbies, things you 'might do' if ... if you do not have a change of heart mid-stream. For you, the answer is always blowing in the wind, and you are the original weather-vane personality.

Extremely sensitive, sympathetic and receptive to others, you delight in congenial companionship and can be wooed into intimate confidence easily. Your natural emotional inclination is to trust, to feel at one, to relax and let down barriers. You are fascinated by people and know no strangers, although at the same time your receptivity and vulnerability at first makes you timid. You test the water before you jump in, but all the same you are like the child who just cannot wait to have a good splash.

Inwardly you have a kind of running commentary on how you are experiencing people and situations, and you tend to think on your feet and to find out what you are really feeling whilst talking out loud. You have a love of images and words, and can be seduced by the sound of your own voice. But although you may often sound impressive and clever, you are not nearly as stable and self-assured as you seem. You do not exactly make it up as you go along, but you have to keep yourself from going down blind alleys and pursuing red herrings. You easily get worried, nervous, doubtful and disoriented, and need to take care that negative thought patterns do not consume all your creative energy.

Relationships

A strong, unwavering partner is good for you, as stability is the thing you lack. Affectionate and playful, you love the romantic word-play of relationships, and will evaporate like an ephemeral undine under the dead hand of rigid, possessive love. Variety, poetry, romance and light-hearted fun is what you want. And plenty of tenderness, for you are ultra-sensitive and can get your feelings hurt easily through misunderstandings. You need intellectual rapport and emotional sensitivity, and if you begin to lose interest you can develop a roving eye.

You can unwittingly become overdependent on your partner to supply interest, stimulation and, ultimately, purpose in your life. Boredom is often a sign that you need to take yourself more seriously. You need a variety of friends, but you also need to apply your own talents in a committed way. Your strengths and talents find an excellent outlet in music, painting and acting, as well as areas that require quick-thinking, diplomacy and playing the host. You can adapt yourself well to almost any sphere of endeavour if you practise staying in tune with what *you* really think before jumping into action.

Your Greatest Strengths

Potential creativity of your intellect and imagination; ability for fun and mimicry; diplomacy and appreciation of a wide variety of people; fluency and original self-expression; forgiving nature; open, childlike attitude to life.

Your Greatest Weaknesses

A lack of confidence in who you really are; tendency to vacillate and skim the surface; to be fickle and uncommitted in relationships; proneness to wallow in daydreams, self-doubt and self-pity; and to live according to an ever-changing relative morality.

Images for Integration

A child grips his magic red balloon as it lifts him into the sky and over the sea onto an island of eternal beauty ... A schoolboy daydreams of heroic deeds during a class on the romantic poets.

Famous Personalities

Anthony Armstrong-Jones (photographer), W.H. Auden (poet), Ray Bremser (poet), Adelle Davis (nutritionist), Henry Dixon Cowell (composer), Roger Daltry (singer), Douglas Hurd (politician), Robert Lowell (poet), Stephane Mallarme (symbolist poet), Richard Burton Matheson (writer of science fiction), Bob Richards (track and field Olympic champion), Gioacchino Rossini (composer), Ann Sheridan (actress), Albert Carel Willink (neo-realist painter), Harold Wilson (politician).

— 136 —

SUN PISCES ✕ MOON CANCER ♋

Attention is religious, or it is nothing.
ALAIN EMILE CHARTIER

Many people consider the things which government does for them to be social progress, but they consider the things government does for others as socialism.
JUSTICE EARL WARREN

Themes

WATER/WATER Ultra-sensitive; emotional; romantic; thoughtful and caring; social awareness; philanthropic; nurturing; colourful imagination; introspective; vacillating moods; intuitive; timid; healer; poetic; funny; good mimic; sense of humour; versatile; retiring.

Matters of the heart rule your life utterly – you need to be in love, to be loved, and to give love (not necessarily in that order). Your emotional life is the hub of your world and you need to be in a relationship to be happy.

You instinctively give generously and unconditionally, but can easily get hurt and moody if you sense your ministrations are not appreciated and returned. Extremely protective and secretive, you nevertheless end up wearing your heart on your sleeve. Your emotional antennae are so fine-tuned that you may occasionally need to turn the volume down so that you can just get on with normal life. Unpleasant atmospheres will do you no good. You soak in the vibes, merge with the mood, and probably alternate between romantically rushing in with open arms and scampering away to hide under a rock.

You want to get involved, for being closely involved with others is your life-blood. Your sympathetic attitude, and your ability to *know* others psychically, draws people to you. They feel that their deepest secrets can be trusted with you, and this characteristic makes you ideally suited for counselling or healing work, or for a life in the ministry, or in the police force. You can identify with people's pain and fear because you have had plenty to deal with of your own. But when you are in touch with your innate strengths, you can transform fear of the world into understanding, and then can apply it with wisdom in your work.

Although you want to be close to others, you will find that the more closely you are involved with your *own* artistic impulse and self-expression, the less like an oceanic storm will your emotional life be. You do not always make it easy for people to get to know you. You are cagey, defensive, wily, even devious if you feel it is necessary. Early on you figure out ways of protecting yourself whilst obtaining what you want.

Sometimes it is difficult for you to express yourself clearly, and then you get moody and unreasonable and retreat even more. Normally quiet and unobstrusive, when you open up you can be a riotous clown and a hilarious mimic. With family and friends, you let down your guards and become a zany *bon vivant*.

There is a very theatrical side to you, and you need to honour your fantasies and imagination by expressing yourself artistically – through painting, photography, music or poetry. You feel the pathos of life and may successfully take your need to communicate your own inner drama onto the stage.

Relationships

Although you fear getting hurt, you are far more emotionally resilient than you think. You come alive in a warm, happy relationship in which you can give of yourself generously and be appreciated and adored. At times you may play the role of the parent, clucking and cooing over your loved ones whilst they bask in your maternal love. But you can just as easily slip into the role of the naughty child who periodically abandons him or herself to fantasies. You have a way of losing yourself to the drama and sweet sorrow of love, so you must be careful not to become the martyr and doormat in a relationship that has become an addiction.

Although you have an enigmatic quality to your love nature, you actually tend to be quite conventional and traditional, loving domesticity and family life. As a natural carer, you will thrive when people need you, depend on you, and give you that blissful feeling of indispensability. You give your loved ones enormous consideration and tenderness, and if you do not get the same back you worry and eventually feel resentment. You need a partner you can rely on, and you may even develop a knack of looking slightly pathetic and needy so that he or she will dissolve in sympathy for you.

Your Greatest Strengths

Genuinely compassionate and warm-hearted nature; instinctive understanding of the human mind and heart; adaptability and versatility in the face of vacillating fortunes; colourful imagination and flair for the dramatic.

Your Greatest Weaknesses

Timidity and fearfulness; oversensitivity and tendency to take offence at the slightest provocation; proneness to let other, more extrovert, personalities define or limit your creative potential.

Images for Integration

An actress plays Clara Barton and is so inspired by her life that she leaves the theatre to become a doctor ... A school of fish ... A medical missionary voyages to the east ... We'll meet again.

Famous Personalities

Desi Arnaz (actor and musician), Shelley Berman (comedian), Cyd Charisse (dancer), Alain Emile Chartier (philosopher), Meissonier (artist), Liza Minelli (actress), Arnold Dolmetsch (musicologist), Vera Lynn (singer), Villa Lobos (composer), Linus Pauling (Nobel prize-winning chemist), Vita Sackville-West (poet), Renata Scotto (operatic diva), Justice Earl Warren (American Supreme Court Judge), Nancy Wilson (singer).

— 137 —

SUN PISCES ♓ MOON LEO ♌

To be a liberated woman is to ... acknowledge that the Cinderella-Prince Charming story is a child's fairy tale.
CLARE BOOTH LUCE

The relative positions to be assumed by man and woman in the working out of our civilization were assigned long ago by a higher intelligence than ours.
GROVER CLEVELAND

These odd bits of drama are all part of the business of survival; a small price to pay for the joy of being able to see, taste, hear, feel ...
AINSLIE ROBERTS

Themes

WATER/FIRE Emotional; moody; sociable; articulate; sensitive; lively inner world; idealistic; imaginative; apparent sureness but inner insecurity; flair for the dramatic; strong moral sense; humanitarian artist; receptive; big-hearted; compassionate; the tragic romantic; hero worship; self-hood through self-immolation.

Do you have visions of great stardom and original accomplishment but find in reality you are temperamentally a servant? Do you give the impression of confidence and capability but quietly quake at the mere thought of competition?

Your essential nature is one of humility, devoted affection and service. But within you is an image of yourself which is heroic, grand and regal, wanting pride of place and position and needing huge amounts of admiration and attention. You may not always express this side of yourself in outward activities, for you are never as sure of yourself as you would like to be – or as you seem to be.

You are a good actor – effusive, demonstrative, vivacious, self-indulgent and warm. But you are also moody, and prone to spending a lot of energy brooding, worrying and feeling inadequate underneath your convivial and kind-hearted persona. It is as though a part of you feels strangely invisible to the world whilst at the same time yearns for the spotlight, admiration and respect.

You are a person of strong moral convictions and often unwordly, rarified aspirations. Extremely kind-hearted and generous, your instinct is to enliven and encourage others, to demonstrate in your behaviour and relationships the most noble way to live a life. This may seem a tall order, and indeed sometimes you dissolve under the weight of your own honour.

A strong humanitarian feeling could take you into a public-service role of some kind where you derive both a sense of usefulness and importance. On the other hand, you may eschew noble service for a more artistic way of life, on the stage or in some similar area (music, writing or painting) where you can live out your colourful fantasies and romantic longings.

Your inspirations fluctuate wildly, as does your confidence. In fact, confidence has a way of eluding you when it comes down to the real contest of life – unless you have really discovered your purpose and have realized that your individuality can shine and radiate force and magnanimity in even the most menial of positions.

Sometimes you feel invisible around people, and then you have to burst with dramatic self-expression to let others know there is a lot going on inside you – and that you are not to be taken lightly. Your personality is a blend of the most feminine understanding and tender sympathies, with the most masculine creative vitality and dignity. In your heart of hearts you are a servant and an artist, a whimsical poet and a noble autocrat, and you have to find some way of blending into the larger scheme of things whilst at the same time expressing what is deeply and personally meaningful to you.

Relationships

When it comes to love, you are up there with the top five per cent of the most romantic Sun–Moon combinations. You *need* romance and love; you *need* to be adored. And there could not be anyone more generous, loyal or kind-hearted than you. But you are often an enigma to live with. One minute you are warm, self-assured and upbeat; the next you might clam up in a mysterious mood of self-pity and huffiness.

Emotionally volatile and vulnerable, you need to be aware of just how impressionable and dependent you can be. This is because you imagine yourself, and often seem to be, very strong and independent when actually you are quaking inside. You must learn not to expect your loved one necessarily to know how you are feeling or what you are thinking. You have high standards, although you are forgiving and will put up with a lot if someone has won your respect and love. A stable, earthy partner will help you settle down and establish the secure home you so much need in order to thrive.

Your Greatest Strengths

Intuitive insight; artistic talents and flair for self-dramatization; undying service and devotion to loved ones.

Your Greatest Weaknesses

Tendency to worry and doubt your abilities; fear of competition; moodiness and instability; proneness to dramatize your weaknesses in order to manipulate others' sympathy.

Image for Integration

Cinderella sits by the fire mending her ballgown and daydreams about her romantic evening of dance, glamour and high drama.

Famous Personalities

Clare Booth Luce (politician and journalist), Tanya Boyd (model and actress), Gordon Brown (Shadow Chancellor), Jim Clark (racing driver), Grover Cleveland (former American president), Mikhail Gorbachev (former president of the Soviet Union), Tony Lema (golfer), David Mellor (politician), Ralph Nader (consumer advocate), Ainsley Robert (writer and painter), Ronald Searle (cartoonist), Jimmy Swaggert (televangelist), John Updike (novelist and critic), Antonio Vivaldi (composer), Lawrence Welk (television-show host).

—138—

SUN PISCES ✕ MOON VIRGO ♍

Without forgiveness life is governed by ... an endless cycle of resentment and retaliation.
ROBERTO ASSAGIOLI

It is well for people who think to change their minds occasionally in order to keep them clean.
LUTHER BURBANK

Every parting gives a foretaste of death; every coming together again a foretaste of the resurrection.
ARTHUR SCHOPENHAUER

Themes

WATER/EARTH Analysis and synthesis; wide-ranging mind; good memory; nervous and fretful; thoughtful; witty; analytical; perceptive;

kind; large-minded but good with detail; discerning but forgiving; an artist-scientist; a logical metaphysician; a quiet thinker; ironic; humorous; refined tastes; devoted servant.

Are you an artist who is impossible to pin down, or are you a down-to-earth realist? Do you want to take everything apart and put it under a microscope, or do you want to stand back and capture the grand design?

Your personality is a potentially very creative combination as it is a confrontation between intuition and reason, imagination and practical logic, the capacity for infinite understanding and for fastidiously precise judgements. You get an overall 'feel' for things – people or ideas – and then your fine analytical mind comes into play, putting your hunches to work in precise ways. The true essence of a person or situation speaks to your heart in a manner that defies scientific explanation. You then mould your behaviour in a modest, conscientious way that serves the emotional impression which has moved you.

When you get it together, you have natural organizational gifts. The broad brush-stroke and the fine line detail come equally easy to you, giving you an ability to hold the wider vision whilst attending to specifics. When you are able to combine your accurate sense of detail with your rich imagination, and your instinct for duty with your romantic, intuitive grasp of life's meaning, you can be a powerful force for good and an accurate barometer of soundness in people, policies and ideas.

The dilemma in you between your instinct to keep your feet on the ground and your desire simply to escape from life's pressures can be very strong. As the saying about Pisces goes, you cannot stand too much reality. This is due to your extreme sensitivity, and you need to be careful about what kind of atmospheres you live and work in. Crass and cruel traits in people can really get you down, yet you do sympathize with suffering, and want progress in *real* terms. You will happily work for the goals of improving social conditions, offering the principles and practices that restore health, helping lives become more sane and worth living.

The health of mind and body is often a primary interest. You know that you cannot have one without the other. Because you are a full-Moon personality, however, the interaction between your irrational, emotional nature and your instinct for orderly categorization of experience may at first be felt as difficult, and the two sides of you may seem irreconcilable. Your feelings and hunches may lead you in a direction you feel you must defend logically, and so you end up weaving intricate arguments that make your philosophy believable. If it makes sense to you, then it is alright. An individualist with a deep moral conviction about all you do, you are not, however, inflexible or dogmatic. Your views develop with experience, your outlook changes, your compassion deepens whilst your sense of duty remains intact.

A mystic can be defined as someone whose head is in Heaven and whose feet are on Earth. And that is a trick you manage with admirable ease, moving between the loftiest visions and their most down-to-earth and prosaic implementation. This combination of mysticism and matter-of-factness makes you one of those rare individuals who feels at home in almost any environment.

Relationships

The 'other' in your life is of immense importance to you, so much so that you may not want to admit that you need him or her as much as you do. Although your kindness and helpfulness is appreciated by many, living with you is not altogether easy. On the one hand you can be dreamy, devoted and caring, and on the other hand you can be cool, overly efficient and critical.

Although you are affectionate and sentimental rather than wildly passionate, your desire to drift off into romantic reverie can alarm your tidy, cerebral side. You try to defend yourself from the vulnerability of your feelings by slotting yourself into routines, by escaping behind a book or a garden patch. This can make you nervous and vacillating, unsure and unsettled with your lot in life.

You need intellectual rapport with your partner, and you thrive with a little encouragement, respect and trust. Your gentle adaptability, original brain and sense of humour make you a tremendously enjoyable person to know and love.

Your Greatest Strengths

Breadth of outlook; ability and willingness to look at any question from all angles; equal strengths of intuition and logic; kindness; forgiving nature; ironic sense of humour which helps you redeem the tragic side of life.

Your Greatest Weaknesses

Perfectionism; overly critical attitude to others; tendency to worry, feel unsettled and escape into fantasies or defensive addictions; proneness to confuse what you feel about something with what you rationally think you should do about it. In your combination, heart and mind can complement each other or clash.

Images for Integration

A mosaic picture of the universe, each piece perfect in itself ... Small events bring enormous consequences ... Faith and reason shake hands.

Famous Personalities

Douglas Adams (writer), Roberto Assagioli (psychologist), Alexander Graham Bell (physicist and inventor), Luther Burbank (geneticist), Peter Fonda (actor), Gabriel Garcia Marquez (writer), Charles Goren (contract-bridge master), Otto Hahn (research chemist), John Irving (writer), Karl Jaspers (psychiatrist and philosopher), Edward Kennedy (politician), Jack Kerouac (beatnik writer), Glenn Miller (band leader), Arthur Schopenhauer (philosopher), Gloria Vanderbilt (heiress, actress and painter), Irving Wallace (writer).

— **139** —

SUN PISCES ⟨ MOON LIBRA ♎

How do I love thee? Let me count the ways.
ELIZABETH BARRETT BROWNING

As life is action and passion, it is required of man that he should share the passion and action of his time, at peril of being judged not to have lived.
OLIVER WENDELL HOLMES JR.

Themes

WATER/AIR Sensitive and whimisical; intuitive; great insights; diplomatic; romantic; charming; gregarious; dependent; cagey; artistic; gentle and compliant; love of beauty and harmony; movement; easy-going; agreeable; trusting; gullible; Co-operative.

You have a conciliatory, tender, unworldly sort of personality, loving beauty and beautiful ideas as much as you abhor injustice and ugliness. You exude a wistful, intangible glamour, as if you were king or queen of the forest fairies incarnate, come to entice clumsy mortals to a place exquisitely serene and joyful. You are therefore essentially of an artistic temperament, very intuitive, ethereal, emotionally fragile, but opportunistic and resilient as well.

Terrifically sympathetic and agreeable, you are also receptive and understanding, romantic and sensuous, easy-going and somewhat self-sacrificing due to your very strong need for relationships. You love people, especially witty and fascinating people who stimulate you, and you really come alive at parties or in refined artistic or literary gatherings. Flirtatious and loquacious, you can be a warm, considerate, generous companion, and whether it is romantic or platonic, you will bring a touch of elegance and dignity to all your dealings with others.

A natural diplomat, you know how to get the best out of people. Sometimes you are not sure whether you are an intellectual or an artist, but you are one of those people who should always trust their inner hunches rather than dissect and analyse them to the point of confusion. Powerful feelings and intuitions can wash over you, and your need to express them is strong, be it through poetry, music, dance, theatre or social service.

Your mind is clear and balanced, you can see objectives and soar with ideas, and your instinct is to communicate your inner world effectively and eloquently. You need the input and encouragement of other people, and can work well with them. If, however, you try to intellectualize too much, you may vacillate and lose your confidence, thus halting the creative flow which is so essential for your wellbeing. At your heart of hearts you are deeply emotional, inspired by a profound reverential love for truth and an intuitive understanding of what is important in life.

You will want to combine intellect and feeling in whatever you do.

Your exceptional adaptability and sensitivity to group needs means you can work well as a group facilitator of some kind. But this personal talent is even stronger when it is balanced by a firm sense of self and healthy boundaries, which is something you may have to work on.

You have so much flowing flexibility and such a deep desire for social harmony that you can easily lose touch with your own needs and instinctive responses. You wince painfully if anyone looks at you cross-eyed; conflict is anathema to your emotional nature and throws you off-beam, as if it were a very tangible karate chop. When you can learn to deal effectively with self-doubt, your creativity will begin to flow.

The theatre is a natural environment for you, where you can express your many-sided, sensitive personality with flair and feeling. Likewise the caring professions may attract you, as people inspire you and you enjoy receiving insights from others. You are forever learning, open to the magic of life, and your innocence, elegance and vulnerability help you to create a world of beauty and delight.

Relationships

You are a real romantic and can enjoy the good life to the hilt. It is easy for you to become dependent on your loved one, and in order to keep the peace you may cling to a bad relationship for far too long, and this only eclipses your own creative power. Your underlying fear of confrontation is due to an even deeper fear of being rejected and alone, for you need others and you thrive when you are with someone who is earthy, grounded and stable.

Your Greatest Strengths

Intuition and imaginative faculties; charming, gracious and sensitive treatment of other people; refined, cultured, artistic approach to life; the ability to inspire others with your gentleness and graceful self-expression; your capacity for collaboration and joint projects.

Your Greatest Weaknesses

Holding unrealistic ideals by which you live and evaluate others; tendency to rationalize and believe what is most pleasant and expedient; proneness to indecision and overdependence on others.

Images for Integration

A theatrical-musical artist entertains his entourage of friends and fans ... Two lovers dream the same dream ... A team of writers create a masterpiece.

Famous Personalities

Elizabeth Barrett Browning (poet), Sir Richard Burton (explorer), Michael Caine (actor), Chopin (composer), Sandy Duncan (actress), George F. Handel (composer), Patty Hearst (kidnapped heiress), Quincy Jones (jazz musician), Rudolph Nureyev (dancer), Sidney Poitier (actor), Michael Redgrave (actor), Oliver Wendell Holmes Jnr (jurist).

— 140 —

SUN PISCES ✕ MOON SCORPIO ♏

It is the nature of a man as he grows older ... to protest against change, particularly change for the better.
JOHN STEINBECK

Love is a gift from God to man, obedience is a gift from master to man, and surrender is a gift from man to master.
MEHER BABA

Know how sublime a thing it is
To suffer and be strong.
HENRY WADSWORTH LONGFELLOW

Themes

WATER/WATER Emotional; intuitive; psychological insight; the agony and the ecstasy; passionate; complex; stubborn; rich imagination; strong in adversity; helpful; the will to expose exploitation and hardship; embraces the comic and tragic together; self-sacrifice v. self-control.

Truly, madly, deeply emotional – that is you. Overflowing with feeling, you are entirely subjective in approaching life and people. For better or for worse, your emotions, convictions and opinions rule you.

Enormously perceptive about people, motives and the vagaries of human nature, you could be drawn into detective work where your morbid fantasies can run riot. Likewise, you may find yourself in medical or scientific research where your intuitive hunches and deeply searching mind can come together to make healing discoveries for humankind. Or the world of psychology and alternative therapies may lure you into its fascinating realm of the underworld, for you are amazingly at home with the unconscious and all that is there, including madness. Private and brooding, but feeling like an open book, you are often like a crucible where the whole gamut of human emotions play themselves out.

Strongly intuitive, you are aware of various levels of interaction between and among people, and in any sort of gathering your quiet strength and intensity is felt by others. You can see through anyone, and at different times easily identify with the ecstatic, the funny, the depressed and the tragic in your friends and family. You have an instinctive understanding of people and can marshal much compassion for yourself and suffering humanity.

Nevertheless, you can be quite scathing when it comes to criticizing things you do not like or agree with. You can suddenly dig in your heels and become stubborn and cantankerous. This can develop into a negative tendency of jumping to emotionally charged conclusions, not realizing that rigid feelings and notions about issues prevent you from getting genuine new input and insight. And if these judgements are based on dark suspicions and fears, you will often end up needlessly sabotaging your own happiness.

Although you tune in sympathetically to people, you have difficulty in articulating your emotions, and can get terribly frustrated with feeling misunderstood. But once you have decided something is worth your effort you are blessed with fanatic dedication and perseverance. Hence you are fiercely loyal to your partner when you have found the right person, even though he or she may never completely fathom your private depths.

Your intellectual capacity is truly amazing when you get beyond your prejudices, and you could be interested in all manner of mysteries and miracles, including birth, death, reincarnation and the ancient wisdom traditions. In fact, to compensate for your tremendous emotional bias, you may swing into very heady areas, such as maths and computing, in order to keep a grip on life. You can appear to be laughing at yourself and taking things lightly when actually an awareness of the gravity of life and all its pain and injustices never leaves you. You prefer your own company much of the time; in silence you analyse and work things out for yourself.

Relationships

Just as your emotional nature is complex and at times unfathomable, so your relationships will tend to be intense, turbulent, and the focus of tremendous passion.

You have an enormous need for love and intimacy, and you can become quite dependent. There is a poignant vulnerability about you which makes others want to care for you, and their hearts go out to you. But equally you can be possessive, jealous and demanding, wanting nothing less than total and complete adoration from your loved one.

Not only is it no surprise to you but you actually expect love to involve pathos and suffering. Dramatic self-abandon versus total domination – no, you are not easy to live with, but you are exciting and unafraid of the truth about yourself that relationships will reveal to you.

Your Greatest Strengths

Acute perception and vivid imagination; tenacity, courage, and commitment in the face of adversity; desire and innate ability to understand great mysteries; ability to help and heal others who are in real despair.

Your Greatest Weaknesses

Tendency to rely too heavily on personal opinion; weakness for sensationalism; proneness to be unaware of persistent prejudices and irrational suspicions; negative self-absorption; tendency to manipulate in order to gain power.

Images for Integration

Longfellow's poem *The Secret of the Sea* ... Steinbeck's novel *The Grapes of Wrath*.

Famous Personalities

Prince Andrew (Duke of York), Meher Baba (Indian guru), Jim Backus (actor and comedian), Johnny Cash (singer), Cyrano de Bergerac (philosopher), Georges Dumas (psychologist), George Harrison (former Beatle), Hugh Johnson (wine connoisseur), David Livingstone (explorer), John Mills (producer and actor), David Niven (actor), Bernadette Peters (actress), John Steinbeck (writer), Elizabeth Taylor (actress), Henry Wadsworth Longfellow (poet).

— 141 —

SUN PISCES){ MOON SAGITTARIUS ⚹

The important thing is not to stop questioning.
ALBERT EINSTEIN

I am an atheist still, thank God.
LUIS BUÑUEL

My heart is warm with the friends I meet
and better friends I'll not be knowing
Yet there isn't a train I wouldn't take
No matter where it's going.
EDNA ST. VINCENT MILLAY

Themes

WATER/FIRE Philosophic mind; generous heart; far-ranging imagination; exuberant; adventurer; religious bent; ironic sense of humour; restless; seeker of truth; sensitive; affectionate; friendly; resilient; strong social awareness.

Are you a mystic or a philosopher? An artist or a scientist? Whatever you answer, the truth is that you have an inquiring mind and profound love of beauty – the beauty both of ideals and of the world.

You are a gentle, unobstrusive person, the soul of kindness and friendly helpfulness, whimsically optimistic and genuinely humble. Often you also seem to be not of this world, a sort of mischievous but benevolent angel whose imagination traverses the universe on a very large canvas, and using only grand symbols. Your mind is subtle and deep, sensing intricate relationships and boundless meaning, and you pursue avenues of thinking – often metaphysical, artistic or scientific – which may leave others behind but which will eventually influence people enormously.

Highly spiritual in essence, but tending to avoid organized religion in practice, you exude a deep confidence in yourself and in your calling, whatever it may be. You feel passionately about life, sensing equally its futility and its fertility, and this means you often bring a religious and almost reverential fervour to your endeavours and your manner of expression. Friends will be touched by your amazing ability to find value and meaning in the rejected and negative, and in your capacity to use such insights as the basis for forming new attitudes.

At times you are the self-confessed lone traveller, living in your own rich, imaginative inner world, sometimes soaring upwards with the truth of the cosmos, at other times down into the depths of despair. You are so sensitive and emotionally transparent that you find it almost impossible to armour yourself against the intrusion of the often horrendous events of the human community. You are called into action as you have to find some outlet for your passionate sense of social justice and responsibility.

So versatile and creative is this combination that you could go in many different directions: you may be the intuitive scientist trying to solve the riddle of the huge world; the priest or therapist traversing the heights and depths of the human psyche; the satirical writer who inveighs against all the various destructive schisms in society; or you could even be the restless drifter, the clown who, in the face of tragedy, knows that 'something will turn up'. Whatever you do, it is likely that a strange irony or conflict between beliefs and political ideologies will demand grappling with at some point in your life so that some sort of reconciliation is achieved.

Relationships

Emotionally you are immediate, open and giving, but very effusive and reluctant to be tied down. As long as you have a relationship that allows plenty of room for intellectual exploration and social exchange – preferably with people who inspire and stimulate you – you make an adoring, affectionate, devoted partner.

Exuding a most enticing mixture of humility and nobility, you are a generous judge of others' weaknesses and a real sucker for a sob story. Intimacy and companionship are important to you, but you get restless with an inner discontent – and you need your partner to understand this. You need periods of contemplative withdrawal so that you can reconnect with yourself, your beliefs, your passion and your optimism. Otherwise you may dissipate your energies in nervousness and spreading yourself too thin.

Your Greatest Strengths

Compassion; the breadth of your intellect and the depth of your enthusiasm; creative imagination; moral integrity; resilience; sense of humour; quiet ability to make everyone laugh and feel that you are their friend forever.

Your Greatest Weaknesses

Endearing naivety; tendency to emotionalize moral issues; misplaced enthusiams; grandiosity and self-deception; proneness to exaggeration, carelessness, and lack of concentration, and to be all things to all people. Try to pin yourself down to manageable-sized problems and tasks, keep your feet on the ground and in touch with important details, and you will find that your ideas have much more productive results.

Images for Integration

A black woman priest in the confessional hears a tale of woe from a white converted scientist, and they fall in love ... Einstein's Theory of Relativity.

Famous Personalities

Luis Buñuel (film director), Copernicus (astronomer), Billy Crystal (actor), Gabrielle D'Annunzio (poet and aviator), Albert Einstein (physicist), Jackie Gleason (actor), Victor Hugo (writer), Aniela Jaffe (Jungian therapist), Rupert Murdoch (newspaper magnate), Nijinsky (Russian dancer), Ishmael Reed (writer), Edna St. Vincent Millay (poet).

— 142 —

SUN PISCES ☓ MOON CAPRICORN ♑

Associate yourself with men of good quality if you esteem your own reputation; for 'tis better to be alone than in bad company.
GEORGE WASHINGTON

The only abnormality is the incapacity to love.
ANAIS NIN

But Lord! to see the absurd nature of Englishmen, that cannot forbear laughing and jeering at everything that looks strange.
SAMUEL PEPYS

Themes

WATER/EARTH Humane; helpful; charitable; serious and self-reflective; perceptive; cautious; discreetly ambitious; circumspect; pillar of strength; fount of compassion; philosophical humour; moral integrity; strategic; devoted; a reserved romantic; dutiful; deep sense of justice; dependable.

Do you identify with the down-and-outs but prefer to do so from a position of comfy security? Do you find yourself romantically pulled towards many people and different experiences, but then you feel the call of personal ambition which keeps you on the straight and even, devoted to family and those you can trust? Does the mystery of life and human love move you to fulfil personal reponsibilities and then go on to serve in the wider world?

You are a blend of gentle compassion and stoicism, of tenderness and taciturnity, of romance and the work ethic. Sometimes you are yielding, sometimes inflexible. Your quiet demeanour and reserve can be deceptive, for you have tremendous strength, initiative and self-respect which helps you get where you want to be.

Your sensitivity to the outer world and the people that fill it is acute; and depending on your particular interests, you will use your perceptions – about people's aims, needs, strengths and weaknesses – to achieve your goals and gain the recognition and respect you desire. In other words, you may be a successful business person, an enigmatic actor, a self-contained artist or an enthusiastic volunteer worker for the Salvation Army. In whatever role you choose, you use both imagination and logic, both feeling and shrewd calculation in creating the right scenario and asserting your gentle control.

Genuinely sympathetic and emotionally generous, you nevertheless possess an astute awareness of life's stark realities. Although your Piscean side wavers and is hesitant about taking on too much responsibility, your Capricorn side is fairly ambitious and really comes alive when you are getting your teeth into a challenging project. Hard times do not frighten you; in fact, they bring out both the romance and hardiness of your combination. Your values are of the intangible realm – love, relationship, respect, a sense of community – but you back them up with muscle power, and often real sweat and tears. Whatever it might be, you are willing to work with commitment to achieve your dream.

On the one hand you are a very matter-of-fact, practical person, and on the other a dreamy, tender-hearted romantic. Socially you can mix with a wide spectrum of people. You have a sense of the fragility and tragedy of life and can connect with others by feeling their plight. You feel for the underprivileged and those who suffer, but you prefer to show your compassion in a pragmatic way, helping others to help themselves.

You have a strong sense of yourself and can stick to your larger long-term purposes, but because you flow with what needs doing you make an excellent organizer and manager, able to harness the moods and energies of those around you productively. You are expressive in subtle but powerful ways and can be something of a practical visionary who is able to translate your own and other people's plans into achievable realities.

Relationships

Although sociable enough, you are really a private person who takes love and family duties very seriously. In a relationship you are warm, devoted, even romantic, although too much self-sufficiency can make you overly cautious, distant and a bit austere at times.

You come to know yourself and your needs early on, as well as just how much you will risk. Thus armed with self-knowledge, you seek out serious, secure relationships. Your emotional side thrives on intimacy, on shared sympathies, and self-sacrifice. But you have too much common sense to allow yourself to dissolve completely into the bliss of the moment if that would sabotage what is cooking on the backburner.

Although you are loving and adaptable, you want to know where you stand. You are sensitive, generous and protective of loved ones, and expect affection and respect in return. There may be a paternal quality about the way you form relationships which inspires others to lean on you, but you do not suffer fools gladly and you can adopt a puritanical manner when loved ones let you down. When you make a commitment, you intend to honour it, and the person who gets your loyalty and love knows he or she has a prize indeed.

Your Greatest Strengths

Genuine kindness; sensitivity to and understanding of human need; pragmatic and resourceful imagination; shrewd perception; quiet adaptability; abiding integrity; deep sense of duty.

Your Greatest Weaknesses

Lack of confidence; timidity; proneness to pessimism and worry; tendency to be secretive and defensive; a somewhat moralistic and judgemental approach to human relations.

Images for Integration

An old freighter chugs towards the port, bringing in the goods ... A famous actress leaves her estate to the Actors' Pension Fund.

Famous Personalities

Luigi Boccherini (Italian composer and cellist), William Cobbett (journalist and reform politician), Kenny Dalglish (footballer), Herb Elliot (athlete), Percival Lowell (astronomer), Prince Naruhito (Japanese Crown Prince), Anaïs Nin (writer), Samuel Pepys (diarist), Philip Roth (novelist), Walter Schirra (astronaut), Dinah Shore (entertainer and singer), Nina Simone (singer), George Washington (first American president).

— 143 —

Sun Pisces)(Moon Aquarius ≈

The humblest citizen of all the land, when clad in the armor of a righteous cause, is stronger than all the hosts of error.
WILLIAM JENNINGS BRYAN

Film is an art form of uniting, in peace, that family of man of which we are all part.
DAVID PUTNAM

Life will be richer and better for all of us if we will make a journey in truth along quiet pathways of philosophy.
MANLY PALMER HALL

Themes

WATER/AIR Mind and emotions; science fiction; humanitarian; receptive; friendly; charitable; moral certitude; missionary zeal; progressive thinker; servant of universal concerns; versatile; sociable; easy-going.

You are one of life's true humanitarians, an idealist through and through, often fundamentally out of step with the status quo and yet absolutely at one with the moral integrity of any issue. Somewhat aloof and elusive yet kind and considerate, you belong to the world, to your friends and to your causes. The secret and the mysterious fascinate you, but you want to *know*.

Beauty and truth will always dance and interweave through your life, and you may have artistic leanings. You seek alliances with people who share your same Utopian dreams, but whoever you meet will not stay a stranger for long as you are friendly, open and optimistic. Passionate convictions and moral certitude inspire your intellectual life and all your actions, and will involve you in various humane but probably unorthodox organizations.

Although you have a wide tolerance for all types of people, you come over strong when expressing and sometimes preaching your own views, and you may need to remind yourself that people will not always welcome your philosophical earnestness. But your idealism and sincerity are unmistakable and hence, despite occasional conversion tactics, you are usually loved and trusted.

Interested in people and what makes them tick, you easily get involved with and absorbed by others, yet always manage to remain one step removed. This makes you a good psychologist, counsellor or social worker, and you can relate emotionally whilst your brain is observing and adding it all up.

You are both intuitive and logical, a rare combination which can baffle others when they think they have got you pegged. One side of you is compassionate, artistic, impressionable; another side is detached and philosophical, broad-minded and unconventional, dedicated to scientific truth and its application for the common good.

You have a quirky sense of humour and can accept the odd and outrageous as the norm. Hence you pick up a bizarre mixture of friends, and truly enjoy each individual. You are a real character, the life of the party. But you are also a bit unfathomable and can hide a world of woe, so deeply do you feel about so many things, both personal and collective.

Relationships

With most people, and especially with your loved one, you are tender, devoted, considerate and understanding. You can tune into your partner easily, and it can seem that you take on his or her colouring and live your life according to his or her needs. In fact, however, there is a part of your soul that belongs only to yourself, and you will need time alone to explore your own thoughts and feelings and what you want to do with them.

You bring your humanitarian spirit, as well as your wit and wisdom, into your private life, and you will want to share your concerns with your partner in some way. Intellectual rapport is important, and so is the humour you share, which goes a long way in soothing and smoothing out problems. Emotionally you are loyal and honourable, but for you joy comes from many different things – music, art, philosophy and social involvement, with your ever-growing circle of friends.

Your Greatest Strengths

Positive, friendly feeling for humanity; ability to learn with both left and right sides of the brain; gentle but articulate and persuasive self-expression; wide acceptance of the whole gamut of society; moral authority and trustworthiness; genuine desire to leave the world better than when you found it.

Your Greatest Weakness

Emotional gullibility; need to push your moral concerns onto others; assumption that everyone feels as strongly as you do about whatever your current cause may be; allowing the woes of the world and a somewhat holier-than-thou attitude to get in the way of enjoying yourself.

Images for Integration

A musicologist plays the violin divinely as part of a demonstration of the theory of harmonics ... A boy scout swims five miles in a campaign to raise money for the peace movement.

Famous Personalities

George Abell (astronomer, writer and sceptic), Robert Altman (film director), Ursula Andress (actress), Balthus (painter), Harry Belafonte (singer), Jeremy Bentham (philosopher), Luitzen Brouwer (mathematician), William Jennings Bryan (poet), Glenn Close (actress), Prince Edward, Manly Palmer Hall (philosopher), James Russell Lowell (poet), Sam Peckinpah (film director), Baden Powell (founder of Scout movement), David Putnam (film producer), Joanne Woodward (actress).

SUN PISCES ♓ MOON PISCES ♓

I've seen every problem.
JENNIFER JONES

Joy is the voice of the escaped psyche.
ARTHUR GUIRDHAM

Themes

WATER/WATER Easy-going; emotionally receptive; unworldly; loving; shy; impressionable; perceptive; intuitive; idealistic; love of fantasy; generous; self-sacrificing; compassionate; romantic.

Are you going this way or that? Or rather, are you really going *your* way, or that of someone else who happened to be passing by, and was rather interesting, nice, mysterious, etc.? Do you silently commune with your inner muse, or drown your sorrows in self-absorbed introspection?

You are the most impressionable, receptive and romantic of all Sun–Moon combinations, and as a result you are very hard to pin down. You are also rather introverted and preoccupied with your inner world, which is very real to you although it does not always bear much resemblance to actuality. You are, in fact, quite a shy person, although you yearn to be truly understood, and normally respond warmly in happy social situations. Emotional sensitivity, compassion and the gift of piercing insight are among your greatest strengths, but you need to be careful as they can just as easily work against you.

Basically, your feelings have a sort of universal quality about them which can attract all and sundry to your open door. You can literally feel as much personal pain about the plight of famine-beleaguered farmers in China as you do about the stray cat or snoring wino in the street. Befriending and helping those in need is instinctive in you, and you can be enthusiastically, selflessly devoted to other people's projects, needs and concerns. You may express your altruism by working in the healing or caring professions, or on a more casual basis with your friends, family and community.

In the right mood you can create an atmosphere of warmth and conviviality, putting the stamp of unfussy enjoyment on everything you do. But you can be gullible and easily deceived too, as if there is something in you which is asking to be enchanted and whisked off into a romantic realm where princesses live in beautiful castles happily ever after. You sense somewhere within you the boundlessness and unity of all life, and, like a fish in the deep blue sea, you naturally want to swim around in it. You need to dream, to commune, to move, to go with the flow of your feelings.

Your shyness often makes you withdraw a bit from life in order to avoid demands from the outside world that you 'explain yourself' – something anathema to your very being. For who are you? You are many things and many people, but you are not easily defined. You do not relish a high profile or heavy burdens, but if you do carry public responsibilities you will serve with heart, mind and soul.

Some Sun–Moon Pisceans deal with their vulnerability by cutting themselves off completely from their feelings. If this applies to you, you will know how easy it is for you to disguise your fears with a joke or a penetrating insight. But some types go even further than that and become 'cold fish', actually polarizing into precise, analytical reason as a defence tactic.

You may be one of those unclassifiable characters whose distinction shines through a whole personality rather than being reflected in a list of worldly attainments. Your essence could be happy as a poet, actor, novelist, soldier, postman, baker, ironmonger, bookseller, socialist, saint or sinner (to name but a few). You may find that something magical happens inside when you are on stage, as you love the experience of communicating your feelings to others.

Relationships

You are the romantic's romantic, and you come to life when in love. For you, love is food for the soul. You are prone to living out a whole range of fantasies around your loved one whilst he or she is completely unaware of what you are doing. You will sacrifice everything for love, so just make sure your partner is worth it.

An earthy type will help you stay in touch with reality, and an airy type will struggle to bring you some objectivity. But do not deny yourself your dreams. Instead, try to find a creative outlet for them so your personal relationship can live, at least partially, in reality.

Your Greatest Strengths

Rich, colourful imagination; endless compassion and ability to identify with the whole spectrum of human joy and sorrow; receptivity and adaptability; humility and selflessness which allows you to put others first and work for the welfare of all.

Your Greatest Weaknesses

Intense subjectivity and sensitivity; proneness to think the world is out of step with you and to wallow in self-pity at the thought; tendency to sabotage your creativity by preferring the passive route of fantasy rather than exercising your will in the real world.

Image for Integration

Adrift at sea ... the stars and the ocean together create one world, no horizon ... the sunset beckons.

Famous Personalities

Paddy Ashdown (politician), Stephanie Beacham (actress), Enrico Caruso (opera singer), Mircea Eliade (psychologist and philosopher), Hans Eysenck (professor of psychology), Richard Garnett (librarian and writer), Arthur Guirdham (esoteric writer), Jennifer Jones (actress), Michaelangelo (artist), Maurice Ravel (composer), Nicolai Rimsky-Korsakov (composer), Bedřich Smetana (composer).

Part Three

FINDING YOUR SUN-MOON COMBINATION

FINDING YOUR SUN-MOON COMBINATION

This part of the book contains tables that will enable you to discover, quickly and easily, what your Sun and Moon signs are. All you need to know to be certain of your Sun sign and Moon sign is your day, month and year of birth. If, however, you find from the tables that the Sun or Moon changed sign during your birth day, you will also need to know your *time* of birth in Greenwich Mean Time – the standard clock time in use in Great Britain for which the tables are calculated.

If you were born at a time of the year when 'Summer Time' was in operation, which is usually late March to late October, you will need to *deduct one hour* from your birth time before using the tables. Table 3 on page 562 gives the precise dates and times each year when Summer Time began and ended in Great Britain from 1916 to 2000.

FINDING YOUR SUN SIGN

The Sun changes sign about every 30 days on about the 21st of each month. But the date of the change varies from sign to sign and *from year to year*. If you were born 'on the cusp' – on the first or last two or three days of a sign – it is important to check precisely which sign the Sun was in at your *time* of birth in your birth year.

Table 1 (beginning on page 474) gives the date and Greenwich Mean Time that the Sun changed, or will change, from one sign of the zodiac to the next for each year from 1920–2000. To find your Sun sign, locate the column giving your *year* of birth. Now look down until you find your *month* of birth. The *day* and *time* at which the Sun changed signs is given. If you were born even a minute before the time listed, then your Sun will be in the preceding sign. If you were born at or after the listed day and time, then your Sun is in the sign indicated.

For example, if you were born on 20th January 1970, you may wonder whether you are a Capricorn or an Aquarius. Turning to Table 1 under 1970 you will find the first entry reads 20JAN 11.24 AQ. This means that on 20th January the Sun entered Aquarius at 11.24 a.m. Thus if you were born at any time up until 11.23 a.m. on the morning of the 20th January your Sun is in Capricorn, but if you were born at 11.24 a.m. or later that day your Sun is in Aquarius.

FINDING YOUR MOON SIGN

The Moon changes sign about every two-and-a-half days. Table 2 (beginning on page 480) gives the date and time, in Greenwich Mean Time, that the Moon entered, or will enter, each sign from 1920–2000.

To find your own Moon sign, first turn to your *year* of birth, then to your *month* of birth and then to your birth *day*, if listed, or the nearest day of the month *before* your birthday. This will tell you which sign the Moon has entered before your birth. The following entry will tell you when the Moon next changed signs.

For example, if you were born on 20th January 1970 you will find under 1970, January, that the nearest entry is the 19th when the Moon entered the sign of Cancer at 8.14 p.m. The next entry is for 22nd January at 8.41 a.m. when the Moon changed signs and entered Leo. Thus if you were born at any time between 8.14 p.m. on 19th January 1970 to 8.41 a.m. on the 22nd January 1970, your Moon was in Cancer.

If you do not know your time of birth, then read the two possible combinations and see which is the most relevant to you.

BIRTHS OUTSIDE GREAT BRITAIN

If you were born outside Britain, and you were born close to the time that the Sun or Moon changed signs, you will need to convert your time of birth into Greenwich Mean Time before consulting the tables.

Table 4 (beginning on page 564) gives the normal time differences for most of the major countries of the world. If in doubt you should check with one of the firms that produces computer-generated charts such as Equinox, 78 Neal Street, Covent Garden, London WC2H 9PA.

Table 1

Finding Your Sun Sign

This table shows the time at which the Sun entered each of the zodiac from 1920–2000. The time is given in Greenwich Mean Time (GMT) using the 24-hour clock. For example, 22:29 is equivalent to 10.29 p.m., 13:20 to 1.20 p.m.

The abbreviations for the signs are:

AR = Aries	TA = Taurus	GE = Gemini
CA = Cancer	LE = Leo	VI = Virgo
LI = Libra	SC = Scorpio	SA = Sagittarius
CP = Capricorn	AQ = Aquarius	PI = Pisces

1920
21JAN 08:04 AQ
19FEB 22:29 PI
20MAR 21:59 AR
20APR 09:39 TA
21MAY 09:22 GE
21JUN 17:40 CA
23JUL 04:35 LE
23AUG 11:21 VI
23SEP 08:28 LI
23OCT 17:13 SC
22NOV 14:16 SA
22DEC 03:17 CP

1921
20JAN 13:55 AQ
19FEB 04:20 PI
21MAR 03:51 AR
20APR 15:32 TA
21MAY 15:16 GE
21JUN 23:36 CA
23JUL 10:30 LE
23AUG 17:15 VI
23SEP 14:20 LI
23OCT 23:02 SC
22NOV 20:04 SA
22DEC 09:07 CP

1922
20JAN 19:48 AQ
19FEB 10:16 PI
21MAR 09:48 AR
20APR 21:28 TA
21MAY 21:10 GE
22JUN 05:27 CA
23JUL 16:20 LE

23AUG 23:04 VI
23SEP 20:10 LI
24OCT 04:53 SC
23NOV 01:56 SA
22DEC 14:57 CP

1923
21JAN 01:35 AQ
19FEB 15:59 PI
21MAR 15:29 AR
21APR 03:05 TA
22MAY 02:45 GE
22JUN 11:03 CA
23JUL 22:01 LE
24AUG 04:52 VI
24SEP 02:04 LI
24OCT 10:51 SC
23NOV 07:54 SA
22DEC 20:53 CP

1924
21JAN 07:29 AQ
19FEB 21:51 PI
20MAR 21:20 AR
20APR 08:58 TA
21MAY 08:40 GE
21JUN 16:59 CA
23JUL 03:57 LE
23AUG 10:48 VI
23SEP 07:58 LI
23OCT 16:45 SC
22NOV 13:46 SA
22DEC 02:45 CP

1925
20JAN 13:20 AQ
19FEB 03:43 PI

21MAR 03:12 AR
20APR 14:51 TA
21MAY 14:33 GE
21JUN 22:50 CA
23JUL 09:45 LE
23AUG 16:33 VI
23SEP 13:44 LI
23OCT 22:32 SC
22NOV 19:36 SA
22DEC 08:37 CP

1926
20JAN 19:13 AQ
19FEB 09:35 PI
21MAR 09:01 AR
20APR 20:36 TA
21MAY 20:15 GE
22JUN 04:30 CA
23JUL 15:25 LE
23AUG 22:14 VI
23SEP 19:26 LI
24OCT 04:18 SC
23NOV 01:28 SA
22DEC 14:33 CP

1927
21JAN 01:12 AQ
19FEB 15:34 PI
21MAR 14:59 AR
21APR 02:32 TA
22MAY 02:08 GE
22JUN 10:22 CA
23JUL 21:17 LE
24AUG 04:06 VI
24SEP 01:17 LI
24OCT 10:07 SC
23NOV 07:14 SA

22DEC 20:19 CP

1928
21JAN 06:57 AQ
19FEB 21:19 PI
20MAR 20:44 AR
20APR 08:17 TA
21MAY 07:52 GE
21JUN 16:06 CA
23JUL 03:02 LE
23AUG 09:53 VI
23SEP 07:06 LI
23OCT 15:55 SC
22NOV 13:01 SA
22DEC 02:04 CP

1929
20JAN 12:42 AQ
19FEB 03:07 PI
21MAR 02:35 AR
20APR 14:10 TA
21MAY 13:48 GE
21JUN 22:01 CA
23JUL 08:54 LE
23AUG 15:41 VI
23SEP 12:52 LI
23OCT 21:42 SC
22NOV 18:48 SA
22DEC 07:53 CP

1930
20JAN 18:33 AQ
19FEB 08:59 PI
21MAR 08:29 AR
20APR 20:06 TA
21MAY 19:42 GE
22JUN 03:53 CA

23JUL	14:42	LE
23AUG	21:27	VI
23SEP	18:36	LI
24OCT	03:26	SC
23NOV	00:35	SA
22DEC	13:40	CP

1931

21JAN	00:18	AQ
19FEB	14:40	PI
21MAR	14:06	AR
21APR	01:40	TA
22MAY	01:15	GE
22JUN	09:28	CA
23JUL	20:21	LE
24AUG	03:10	VI
24SEP	00:24	LI
24OCT	09:16	SC
23NOV	06:25	SA
22DEC	19:30	CP

1932

21JAN	06:07	AQ
19FEB	20:29	PI
20MAR	19:54	AR
20APR	07:28	TA
21MAY	07:06	GE
21JUN	15:22	CA
23JUL	02:18	LE
23AUG	09:06	VI
23SEP	06:16	LI
23OCT	15:04	SC
22NOV	12:10	SA
22DEC	01:14	CP

1933

20JAN	11:53	AQ
19FEB	02:16	PI
21MAR	01:43	AR
20APR	13:18	TA
21MAY	12:57	GE
21JUN	21:12	CA
23JUL	08:06	LE
23AUG	14:52	VI
23SEP	12:01	LI
23OCT	20:48	SC
22NOV	17:54	SA
22DEC	06:58	CP

1934

20JAN	17:37	AQ
19FEB	08:02	PI
21MAR	07:28	AR
20APR	19:00	TA
21MAY	18:35	GE
22JUN	02:48	CA
23JUL	13:42	LE
23AUG	20:32	VI
23SEP	17:45	LI
24OCT	02:36	SC
22NOV	23:44	SA
22DEC	12:50	CP

1935

20JAN	23:29	AQ
19FEB	13:52	PI
21MAR	13:18	AR
21APR	00:50	TA
22MAY	00:25	GE
22JUN	08:38	CA
23JUL	19:33	LE
24AUG	02:24	VI
23SEP	23:38	LI
24OCT	08:29	SC
23NOV	05:35	SA
22DEC	18:37	CP

1936

21JAN	05:12	AQ
19FEB	19:33	PI
20MAR	18:58	AR
20APR	06:31	TA
21MAY	06:07	GE
21JUN	14:22	CA
23JUL	01:18	LE
23AUG	08:11	VI
23SEP	05:26	LI
23OCT	14:18	SC
22NOV	11:26	SA
22DEC	00:27	CP

1937

20JAN	11:01	AQ
19FEB	01:21	PI
21MAR	00:45	AR
20APR	12:19	TA
21MAY	11:57	GE
21JUN	20:12	CA
23JUL	07:07	LE
23AUG	13:58	VI
23SEP	11:13	LI
23OCT	20:06	SC
22NOV	17:17	SA
22DEC	06:22	CP

1938

20JAN	16:59	AQ
19FEB	07:20	PI
21MAR	06:43	AR
20APR	18:15	TA
21MAY	17:50	GE
22JUN	02:03	CA
23JUL	12:57	LE
23AUG	19:46	VI
23SEP	16:59	LI
24OCT	01:54	SC
22NOV	23:06	SA
22DEC	12:14	CP

1939

20JAN	22:51	AQ
19FEB	13:09	PI
21MAR	12:28	AR
20APR	23:55	TA
21MAY	23:27	GE
22JUN	07:39	CA
23JUL	18:37	LE
24AUG	01:31	VI
23SEP	22:50	LI
24OCT	07:46	SC
23NOV	04:59	SA
22DEC	18:06	CP

1940

21JAN	04:44	AQ
19FEB	19:04	PI
20MAR	18:24	AR
20APR	05:51	TA
21MAY	05:23	GE
21JUN	13:36	CA
23JUL	00:34	LE
23AUG	07:28	VI
23SEP	04:46	LI
23OCT	13:39	SC
22NOV	10:49	SA
21DEC	23:55	CP

1941

20JAN	10:33	AQ
19FEB	00:56	PI
21MAR	00:20	AR
20APR	11:50	TA
21MAY	11:23	GE
21JUN	19:33	CA
23JUL	06:26	LE
23AUG	13:17	VI
23SEP	10:33	LI
23OCT	19:27	SC
22NOV	16:38	SA
22DEC	05:45	CP

1942

20JAN	16:24	AQ
19FEB	06:47	PI
21MAR	06:11	AR
20APR	17:39	TA
21MAY	17:09	GE
22JUN	01:16	CA
23JUL	12:07	LE
23AUG	18:58	VI
23SEP	16:17	LI
24OCT	01:15	SC
22NOV	22:30	SA
22DEC	11:40	CP

1943

20JAN	22:19	AQ
19FEB	12:40	PI
21MAR	12:03	AR
20APR	23:31	TA
21MAY	23:03	GE
22JUN	07:12	CA
23JUL	18:04	LE
24AUG	00:55	VI
23SEP	22:12	LI
24OCT	07:08	SC
23NOV	04:22	SA
22DEC	17:29	CP

1944

21JAN	04:07	AQ
19FEB	18:27	PI
20MAR	17:48	AR
20APR	05:18	TA
21MAY	04:51	GE
21JUN	13:02	CA
22JUL	23:56	LE
23AUG	06:47	VI
23SEP	04:02	LI
23OCT	12:56	SC
22NOV	10:08	SA
21DEC	23:15	CP

1945

20JAN	09:54	AQ
19FEB	00:15	PI
20MAR	23:37	AR
20APR	11:07	TA
21MAY	10:40	GE
21JUN	18:52	CA
23JUL	05:45	LE
23AUG	12:35	VI
23SEP	09:50	LI
23OCT	18:43	SC
22NOV	15:55	SA
22DEC	05:04	CP

1946

20JAN	15:45	AQ
19FEB	06:08	PI
21MAR	05:33	AR
20APR	17:02	TA
21MAY	16:34	GE
22JUN	00:44	CA
23JUL	11:37	LE
23AUG	18:26	VI
23SEP	15:41	LI
24OCT	00:35	SC
22NOV	21:47	SA
22DEC	10:53	CP

1947

20JAN	21:32	AQ

19FEB	11:52	PI	20APR	21:48	TA	22JUN	04:31	CA	23AUG	21:44	VI
21MAR	11:13	AR	21MAY	21:15	GE	23JUL	15:25	LE	23SEP	19:09	LI
20APR	22:39	TA	22JUN	05:25	CA	23AUG	22:19	VI	24OCT	04:11	SC
21MAY	22:09	GE	23JUL	16:21	LE	23SEP	19:41	LI	23NOV	01:27	SA
22JUN	06:19	CA	23AUG	23:16	VI	24OCT	04:43	SC	22DEC	14:34	CP
23JUL	17:14	LE	23SEP	20:37	LI	23NOV	02:01	SA			
24AUG	00:09	VI	24OCT	05:36	SC	22DEC	15:11	CP	**1960**		
23SEP	21:29	LI	23NOV	02:51	SA				21JAN	01:10	AQ
24OCT	06:26	SC	22DEC	16:00	CP	**1956**			19FEB	15:26	PI
23NOV	03:38	SA				21JAN	01:49	AQ	20MAR	14:43	AR
22DEC	16:43	CP	**1952**			19FEB	16:05	PI	20APR	02:06	TA
			21JAN	02:38	AQ	20MAR	15:21	AR	21MAY	01:33	GE
1948			19FEB	16:57	PI	20APR	02:44	TA	21JUN	09:42	CA
21JAN	03:19	AQ	20MAR	16:14	AR	21MAY	02:12	GE	22JUL	20:38	LE
19FEB	17:37	PI	20APR	03:37	TA	21JUN	10:24	CA	23AUG	03:35	VI
20MAR	16:57	AR	21MAY	03:04	GE	22JUL	21:20	LE	23SEP	00:59	LI
20APR	04:25	TA	21JUN	11:12	CA	23AUG	04:15	VI	23OCT	10:02	SC
21MAY	03:57	GE	22JUL	22:08	LE	23SEP	01:35	LI	22NOV	07:19	SA
21JUN	12:11	CA	23AUG	05:03	VI	23OCT	10:34	SC	21DEC	20:26	CP
22JUL	23:08	LE	23SEP	02:24	LI	22NOV	07:50	SA			
23AUG	06:03	VI	23OCT	11:23	SC	21DEC	20:59	CP	**1961**		
23SEP	03:22	LI	22NOV	08:36	SA				20JAN	07:02	AQ
23OCT	12:18	SC	21DEC	21:44	CP	**1957**			18FEB	21:17	PI
22NOV	09:29	SA				20JAN	07:39	AQ	20MAR	20:32	AR
21DEC	22:34	CP	**1953**			18FEB	21:58	PI	20APR	07:55	TA
			20JAN	08:22	AQ	20MAR	21:16	AR	21MAY	07:22	GE
1949			18FEB	22:41	PI	20APR	08:41	TA	21JUN	15:30	CA
20JAN	09:09	AQ	20MAR	22:01	AR	21MAY	08:10	GE	23JUL	02:24	LE
18FEB	23:27	PI	20APR	09:26	TA	21JUN	16:20	CA	23AUG	09:19	VI
20MAR	22:48	AR	21MAY	08:53	GE	23JUL	03:15	LE	23SEP	06:43	LI
20APR	10:17	TA	21JUN	16:59	CA	23AUG	10:08	VI	23OCT	15:48	SC
21MAY	09:51	GE	23JUL	03:52	LE	23SEP	07:26	LI	22NOV	13:08	SA
21JUN	18:03	CA	23AUG	10:45	VI	23OCT	16:24	SC	22DEC	02:20	CP
23JUL	04:57	LE	23SEP	08:06	LI	22NOV	13:39	SA			
23AUG	11:48	VI	23OCT	17:06	SC	22DEC	02:49	CP	**1962**		
23SEP	09:06	LI	22NOV	14:22	SA				20JAN	12:58	AQ
23OCT	18:03	SC	22DEC	03:32	CP	**1958**			19FEB	03:15	PI
22NOV	15:16	SA				20JAN	13:29	AQ	21MAR	02:30	AR
22DEC	04:23	CP	**1954**			19FEB	03:49	PI	20APR	13:51	TA
			20JAN	14:11	AQ	21MAR	03:06	AR	21MAY	13:16	GE
1950			19FEB	04:32	PI	20APR	14:27	TA	21JUN	21:24	CA
20JAN	15:00	AQ	21MAR	03:53	AR	21MAY	13:51	GE	23JUL	08:18	LE
19FEB	05:18	PI	20APR	15:19	TA	21JUN	21:57	CA	23AUG	15:13	VI
21MAR	04:35	AR	21MAY	14:47	GE	23JUL	08:51	LE	23SEP	12:35	LI
20APR	15:59	TA	21JUN	22:54	CA	23AUG	15:46	VI	23OCT	21:40	SC
21MAY	15:27	GE	23JUL	09:45	LE	23SEP	13:09	LI	22NOV	19:02	SA
21JUN	23:36	CA	23AUG	16:36	VI	23OCT	22:12	SC	22DEC	08:15	CP
23JUL	10:30	LE	23SEP	13:55	LI	22NOV	19:29	SA			
23AUG	17:23	VI	23OCT	22:57	SC	22DEC	08:40	CP	**1963**		
23SEP	14:44	LI	22NOV	20:14	SA				20JAN	18:54	AQ
23OCT	23:45	SC	22DEC	09:25	CP	**1959**			19FEB	09:09	PI
22NOV	21:03	SA				20JAN	19:19	AQ	21MAR	08:20	AR
22DEC	10:14	CP	**1955**			19FEB	09:38	PI	20APR	19:36	TA
			20JAN	20:02	AQ	21MAR	08:55	AR	21MAY	18:58	GE
1951			19FEB	10:19	PI	20APR	20:17	TA	22JUN	03:04	CA
20JAN	20:52	AQ	21MAR	09:35	AR	21MAY	19:42	GE	23JUL	13:59	LE
19FEB	11:10	PI	20APR	20:58	TA	22JUN	03:50	CA	23AUG	20:58	VI
21MAR	10:26	AR	21MAY	20:24	GE	23JUL	14:45	LE	23SEP	18:24	LI

476

24OCT	03:29	SC
23NOV	00:50	SA
22DEC	14:02	CP

1964

21JAN	00:41	AQ
19FEB	14:58	PI
20MAR	14:10	AR
20APR	01:27	TA
21MAY	00:50	GE
21JUN	08:57	CA
22JUL	19:53	LE
23AUG	02:51	VI
23SEP	00:17	LI
23OCT	09:21	SC
22NOV	06:39	SA
21DEC	19:50	CP

1965

20JAN	06:29	AQ
18FEB	20:48	PI
20MAR	20:05	AR
20APR	07:26	TA
21MAY	06:50	GE
21JUN	14:56	CA
23JUL	01:48	LE
23AUG	08:43	VI
23SEP	06:06	LI
23OCT	15:10	SC
22NOV	12:29	SA
22DEC	01:41	CP

1966

20JAN	12:20	AQ
19FEB	02:38	PI
21MAR	01:53	AR
20APR	13:12	TA
21MAY	12:32	GE
21JUN	20:33	CA
23JUL	07:24	LE
23AUG	14:18	VI
23SEP	11:44	LI
23OCT	20:51	SC
22NOV	18:14	SA
22DEC	07:29	CP

1967

20JAN	18:08	AQ
19FEB	08:24	PI
21MAR	07:37	AR
20APR	18:55	TA
21MAY	18:18	GE
22JUN	02:23	CA
23JUL	13:16	LE
23AUG	20:12	VI
23SEP	17:38	LI
24OCT	02:44	SC
23NOV	00:05	SA
22DEC	13:17	CP

1968

20JAN	23:54	AQ
19FEB	14:09	PI
20MAR	13:22	AR
20APR	00:41	TA
21MAY	00:06	GE
21JUN	08:13	CA
22JUL	19:08	LE
23AUG	02:03	VI
22SEP	23:26	LI
23OCT	08:30	SC
22NOV	05:49	SA
21DEC	19:00	CP

1969

20JAN	05:39	AQ
18FEB	19:55	PI
20MAR	19:08	AR
20APR	06:27	TA
21MAY	05:50	GE
21JUN	13:55	CA
23JUL	00:48	LE
23AUG	07:44	VI
23SEP	05:07	LI
23OCT	14:11	SC
22NOV	11:31	SA
22DEC	00:44	CP

1970

20JAN	11:24	AQ
19FEB	01:42	PI
21MAR	00:57	AR
20APR	12:15	TA
21MAY	11:37	GE
21JUN	19:43	CA
23JUL	06:37	LE
23AUG	13:34	VI
23SEP	10:59	LI
23OCT	20:05	SC
22NOV	17:25	SA
22DEC	06:36	CP

1971

20JAN	17:13	AQ
19FEB	07:27	PI
21MAR	06:38	AR
20APR	17:54	TA
21MAY	17:15	GE
22JUN	01:20	CA
23JUL	12:15	LE
23AUG	19:15	VI
23SEP	16:45	LI
24OCT	01:53	SC
22NOV	23:15	SA
22DEC	12:24	CP

1972

20JAN	22:59	AQ
19FEB	13:12	PI
20MAR	12:22	AR
19APR	23:38	TA
20MAY	22:59	GE
21JUN	07:06	CA
22JUL	18:03	LE
23AUG	01:03	VI
22SEP	22:33	LI
23OCT	07:42	SC
22NOV	05:03	SA
21DEC	18:13	CP

1973

20JAN	04:48	AQ
18FEB	19:01	PI
20MAR	18:13	AR
20APR	05:30	TA
21MAY	04:54	GE
21JUN	13:01	CA
22JUL	23:55	LE
23AUG	06:54	VI
23SEP	04:21	LI
23OCT	13:30	SC
22NOV	10:54	SA
22DEC	00:08	CP

1974

20JAN	10:46	AQ
19FEB	00:59	PI
21MAR	00:07	AR
20APR	11:19	TA
21MAY	10:36	GE
21JUN	18:38	CA
23JUL	05:30	LE
23AUG	12:29	VI
23SEP	09:59	LI
23OCT	19:11	SC
22NOV	16:39	SA
22DEC	05:56	CP

1975

20JAN	16:37	AQ
19FEB	06:50	PI
21MAR	05:57	AR
20APR	17:07	TA
21MAY	16:24	GE
22JUN	00:26	CA
23JUL	11:22	LE
23AUG	18:24	VI
23SEP	15:55	LI
24OCT	01:06	SC
22NOV	22:31	SA
22DEC	11:46	CP

1976

20JAN	22:25	AQ
19FEB	12:40	PI
20MAR	11:50	AR
19APR	23:03	TA
20MAY	22:21	GE
21JUN	06:24	CA
22JUL	17:18	LE
23AUG	00:18	VI
22SEP	21:48	LI
23OCT	06:58	SC
22NOV	04:22	SA
21DEC	17:36	CP

1977

20JAN	04:15	AQ
18FEB	18:31	PI
20MAR	17:42	AR
20APR	04:57	TA
21MAY	04:14	GE
21JUN	12:14	CA
22JUL	23:04	LE
23AUG	06:00	VI
23SEP	03:30	LI
23OCT	12:41	SC
22NOV	10:07	SA
21DEC	23:24	CP

1978

20JAN	10:04	AQ
19FEB	00:21	PI
20MAR	23:34	AR
20APR	10:50	TA
21MAY	10:09	GE
21JUN	18:10	CA
23JUL	05:00	LE
23AUG	11:57	VI
23SEP	09:26	LI
23OCT	18:37	SC
22NOV	16:05	SA
22DEC	05:21	CP

1979

20JAN	15:59	AQ
19FEB	06:13	PI
21MAR	05:22	AR
20APR	16:35	TA
21MAY	15:54	GE
21JUN	23:56	CA
23JUL	10:49	LE
23AUG	17:47	VI
23SEP	15:17	LI
24OCT	00:28	SC
22NOV	21:55	SA
22DEC	11:10	CP

1980

20JAN	21:49	AQ
19FEB	12:02	PI
20MAR	11:10	AR

19APR	22:23	TA	21JUN	05:02	CA	22AUG	21:54	VI	23OCT	03:57	SC
20MAY	21:42	GE	22JUL	15:58	LE	22SEP	19:29	LI	22NOV	01:26	SA
21JUN	05:47	CA	22AUG	23:00	VI	23OCT	04:45	SC	21DEC	14:43	CP
22JUL	16:42	LE	22SEP	20:33	LI	22NOV	02:12	SA			
22AUG	23:41	VI	23OCT	05:46	SC	21DEC	15:28	CP	**1993**		
22SEP	21:09	LI	22NOV	03:11	SA				20JAN	01:23	AQ
23OCT	06:18	SC	21DEC	16:23	CP	**1989**			18FEB	15:35	PI
22NOV	03:42	SA				20JAN	02:07	AQ	20MAR	14:41	AR
21DEC	16:56	CP	**1985**			18FEB	16:21	PI	20APR	01:49	TA
			20JAN	02:58	AQ	20MAR	15:28	AR	21MAY	01:01	GE
1981			18FEB	17:08	PI	20APR	02:39	TA	21JUN	08:59	CA
20JAN	03:36	AQ	20MAR	16:14	AR	21MAY	01:53	GE	22JUL	19:51	LE
18FEB	17:52	PI	20APR	03:26	TA	21JUN	09:53	CA	23AUG	02:51	VI
20MAR	17:03	AR	21MAY	02:43	GE	22JUL	20:46	LE	23SEP	00:23	LI
20APR	04:19	TA	21JUN	10:44	CA	23AUG	03:46	VI	23OCT	09:37	SC
21MAY	03:39	GE	22JUL	21:37	LE	23SEP	01:20	LI	22NOV	07:07	SA
21JUN	11:45	CA	23AUG	04:36	VI	23OCT	10:35	SC	21DEC	20:26	CP
22JUL	22:40	LE	23SEP	02:08	LI	22NOV	08:05	SA			
23AUG	05:38	VI	23OCT	11:22	SC	21DEC	21:22	CP	**1994**		
23SEP	03:05	LI	22NOV	08:51	SA				20JAN	07:08	AQ
23OCT	12:13	SC	21DEC	22:08	CP	**1990**			18FEB	21:22	PI
22NOV	09:36	SA				20JAN	08:02	AQ	20MAR	20:28	AR
21DEC	22:51	CP	**1986**			18FEB	22:14	PI	20APR	07:36	TA
			20JAN	08:47	AQ	20MAR	21:19	AR	21MAY	06:48	GE
1982			18FEB	22:58	PI	20APR	08:26	TA	21JUN	14:48	CA
20JAN	09:31	AQ	20MAR	22:03	AR	21MAY	07:37	GE	23JUL	01:41	LE
18FEB	23:47	PI	20APR	09:12	TA	21JUN	15:33	CA	23AUG	08:44	VI
20MAR	22:56	AR	21MAY	08:28	GE	23JUL	02:22	LE	23SEP	06:19	LI
20APR	10:07	TA	21JUN	16:30	CA	23AUG	09:21	VI	23OCT	15:36	SC
21MAY	09:23	GE	23JUL	03:25	LE	23SEP	06:56	LI	22NOV	13:06	SA
21JUN	17:23	CA	23AUG	10:26	VI	23OCT	16:14	SC	22DEC	02:23	CP
23JUL	04:16	LE	23SEP	07:59	LI	22NOV	13:47	SA			
23AUG	11:15	VI	23OCT	17:14	SC	22DEC	03:07	CP	**1995**		
23SEP	08:47	LI	22NOV	14:45	SA				20JAN	13:01	AQ
23OCT	17:58	SC	22DEC	04:03	CP	**1991**			19FEB	03:11	PI
22NOV	15:24	SA				20JAN	13:47	AQ	21MAR	02:14	AR
22DEC	04:39	CP	**1987**			19FEB	03:59	PI	20APR	13:21	TA
			20JAN	14:41	AQ	21MAR	03:02	AR	21MAY	12:34	GE
1983			19FEB	04:50	PI	20APR	14:09	TA	21JUN	20:34	CA
20JAN	15:17	AQ	21MAR	03:52	AR	21MAY	13:20	GE	23JUL	07:30	LE
19FEB	05:31	PI	20APR	14:57	TA	21JUN	21:19	CA	23AUG	14:35	VI
21MAR	04:39	AR	21MAY	14:10	GE	23JUL	08:11	LE	23SEP	12:13	LI
20APR	15:50	TA	21JUN	22:11	CA	23AUG	15:13	VI	23OCT	21:32	SC
21MAY	15:06	GE	23JUL	09:06	LE	23SEP	12:48	LI	22NOV	19:02	SA
21JUN	23:09	CA	23AUG	16:10	VI	23OCT	22:05	SC	22DEC	08:17	CP
23JUL	10:04	LE	23SEP	13:45	LI	22NOV	19:36	SA			
23AUG	17:08	VI	23OCT	23:01	SC	22DEC	08:54	CP	**1996**		
23SEP	14:42	LI	22NOV	20:30	SA				20JAN	18:53	AQ
23OCT	23:54	SC	22DEC	09:46	CP	**1992**			19FEB	09:01	PI
22NOV	21:19	SA				20JAN	19:33	AQ	20MAR	08:03	AR
22DEC	10:30	CP	**1988**			19FEB	09:44	PI	19APR	19:10	TA
			20JAN	20:25	AQ	20MAR	08:48	AR	20MAY	18:23	GE
1984			19FEB	10:35	PI	19APR	19:57	TA	21JUN	02:24	CA
20JAN	21:05	AQ	20MAR	09:39	AR	20MAY	19:12	GE	22JUL	13:19	LE
19FEB	11:16	PI	19APR	20:45	TA	21JUN	03:14	CA	22AUG	20:23	VI
20MAR	10:24	AR	20MAY	19:57	GE	22JUL	14:09	LE	22SEP	18:00	LI
19APR	21:38	TA	21JUN	03:57	CA	22AUG	21:10	VI	23OCT	03:19	SC
20MAY	20:58	GE	22JUL	14:51	LE	22SEP	18:43	LI	22NOV	00:50	SA

21DEC	14:06	CP	18FEB	20:55	PI	21JUN	19:49	CA	23OCT	02:48	SC
			20MAR	19:55	AR	23JUL	06:44	LE	22NOV	00:20	SA
1997			20APR	06:57	TA	23AUG	13:51	VI	21DEC	13:38	CP
20JAN	00:43	AQ	21MAY	06:05	GE	23SEP	11:32	LI			
18FEB	14:52	PI	21JUN	14:02	CA	23OCT	20:53	SC			
20MAR	13:55	AR	23JUL	00:56	LE	22NOV	18:25	SA			
20APR	01:03	TA	23AUG	07:59	VI	22DEC	07:44	CP			
21MAY	00:18	GE	23SEP	05:37	LI						
21JUN	08:20	CA	23OCT	14:59	SC	**2000**					
22JUL	19:16	LE	22NOV	12:35	SA	20JAN	18:24	AQ			
23AUG	02:19	VI	22DEC	01:57	CP	19FEB	08:34	PI			
22SEP	23:56	LI				20MAR	07:36	AR			
23OCT	09:15	SC	**1999**			19APR	18:40	TA			
22NOV	06:48	SA	20JAN	12:38	AQ	20MAY	17:50	GE			
21DEC	20:07	CP	19FEB	02:47	PI	21JUN	01:48	CA			
			21MAR	01:46	AR	22JUL	12:43	LE			
1998			20APR	12:46	TA	22AUG	19:49	VI			
20JAN	06:46	AQ	21MAY	11:53	GE	22SEP	17:28	LI			

Table 2

Finding Your Moon Sign

The following table shows the time at which the Moon entered each sign of the zodiac from 1920–2000. The time is given in GMT using the 24-hour clock. For details of abbreviations used, see table 1, starting on page 474.

The Moon stays in each sign for about two-and-a-half days until the next entry which shows the day and time the Moon changes to the next sign. For example, if you were born on 14 May 1973, turn to 1973 on page 534. The month is given at the top of each column. The day is given on the far left; 01 is the first day of the month, and so on. Run your finger down the 'May' column until you are opposite the line numbered 14. There is no figure given for the 14th. Look at the previous day which does have a time given – the 12th – which shows that at 15:31 the Moon entered Libra. So the Moon on 14 May is still in Libra and remains there until the 15th at 1.10 a.m. when it enters Scorpio.

To take another example, if you were born on 4 August 1973 you will find 20:36SC at the relevant point in the table. This means that at 20:36 hours (8.36 p.m. GMT) the Moon entered Scorpio. So if you were born before 8.36 p.m. that day your Moon is in Libra. Born at 8.36 p.m. or later, and your Moon is in Scorpio.

1920

Day	January	February	March	April	May	June	July	August	September	October	November	December
01		07:54 CA	17:23 LE					19:18 PI				22:45 VI
02	22:13 GE			09:59 LI	01:38 SC				16:19 TA	02:32 GE	13:38 LE	
03		09:06 LE	20:40 VI			08:04 CP	02:30 AQ		20:57 GE			
04	22:19 CA			18:34 SC	12:59 SA			04:10 AR		05:29 CA	17:03 VI	03:50 LI
05		11:18 VI				20:38 AQ	13:37 PI					
06	22:30 LE		01:53 LI					10:56 TA		08:14 LE	22:23 LI	11:51 SC
07		16:19 LI		05:42 SA	01:39 CP		22:39 AR		00:03 CA			
08			10:10 SC			07:43 PI		15:15 GE		11:23 VI		22:09 SA
09	00:46 VI			18:25 CP	14:09 AQ				02:02 LE		05:49 SC	
10		01:13 SC	21:35 SA			15:57 AR	04:46 TA	17:11 CA		15:45 LI		
11	06:48 LI								03:55 VI		15:26 SA	09:59 CP
12		13:21 SA		06:32 AQ	00:32 PI	20:36 TA	07:40 GE	17:41 LE		22:14 SC		
13	16:57 SC		10:26 CP						07:11 LI			22:39 AQ
14				15:50 PI	07:23 AR	21:58 GE	08:03 CA	18:27 VI			03:03 CP	
15		02:14 CP	21:58 AQ						13:20 SC	07:30 SA		
16	05:43 SA			21:29 AR	10:35 TA	21:27 CA	07:32 LE	21:28 LI			15:44 AQ	11:04 PI
17		13:20 AQ							22:58 SA	19:16 CP		
18	18:33 CP		06:25 PI		11:13 GE	21:02 LE	08:12 VI					21:30 AR
19		21:39 PI		00:08 TA				04:13 SC			03:40 PI	
20			11:43 AR		11:01 CA	22:45 VI	12:02 LI		11:09 CP	07:52 AQ		
21	05:39 AQ			01:14 GE				14:45 SA			12:46 AR	04:22 TA
22		03:37 AR	14:58 TA		11:50 LE		20:03 SC		23:32 AQ	18:57 PI		
23	14:34 PI			02:22 CA		04:05 LI					18:03 TA	07:15 GE
24		08:06 TA	17:25 GE		15:11 VI			03:22 CP				
25	21:32 AR			04:49 LE		13:19 SC	07:31 SA		09:57 PI	02:53 AR	20:00 GE	07:13 CA
26		11:42 GE	20:01 CA		21:50 LI			15:36 AQ				
27				09:22 VI			20:22 CP		17:34 AR	07:34 TA	20:12 CA	06:16 LE
28	02:44 TA	14:41 CA	23:20 LE			01:15 SA						
29				16:19 LI	07:33 SC			01:55 PI	22:49 TA	09:59 GE	20:33 LE	06:37 VI
30	06:06 GE					14:06 CP	08:37 AQ					
31			03:48 VI		19:20 SA			10:03 AR		11:35 CA		10:06 LI

1921

	January	February	March	April	May	June	July	August	September	October	November	December
01	17:27 SC	10:04 SA			21:47 PI			03:18 CA	13:06 VI		16:08 SA	08:32 CP
02				01:22 AQ			15:23 GE					
03		22:14 CP	05:03 CP			01:03 TA		03:11 LE	13:05 LI	01:37 SC	23:38 CP	18:41 AQ
04	03:58 SA			13:28 PI	08:14 AR		16:56 CA					
05			17:45 AQ			05:17 GE		02:18 VI	15:23 SC	06:23 SA		
06	16:10 CP	10:59 AQ		23:31 AR	15:32 TA		16:34 LE				10:17 AQ	07:03 PI
07						06:46 CA		02:51 LI	21:20 SA	14:46 CP		
08		23:03 PI	05:43 PI		19:51 GE		16:27 VI				22:50 PI	19:37 AR
09	04:50 AQ			07:00 TA		07:19 LE		06:33 SC				
10			15:58 AR		22:19 CA		18:28 LI		06:58 CP	02:13 AQ		
11	17:10 PI	09:51 AR		12:16 GE		08:41 VI		13:59 SA			10:52 AR	05:46 TA
12							23:43 SC		19:01 AQ	14:51 PI		
13		18:44 TA	00:15 TA	15:59 CA	00:16 LE	12:10 LI					20:19 TA	12:08 GE
14	04:14 AR							00:30 CP				
15			06:29 GE	18:47 LE	02:51 VI	18:11 SC	08:05 SA		07:39 PI	02:34 AR		15:12 CA
16	12:40 TA	00:55 GE						12:42 AQ			02:40 GE	
17			10:37 CA	21:21 VI	06:46 LI		18:43 CP		19:29 AR	12:08 TA		16:35 LE
18	17:23 GE	03:58 CA				02:28 SA					06:41 CA	
19			12:52 LE		12:22 SC			01:20 PI		19:20 GE		18:02 VI
20	18:35 CA	04:34 LE		00:24 LI		12:39 CP	06:43 AQ		05:41 TA		09:33 LE	
21			14:08 VI		19:53 SA			13:30 AR				20:52 LI
22	17:45 LE	04:21 VI		04:53 SC			19:23 PI		13:41 GE	00:32 CA	12:17 VI	
23			15:49 LI			00:24 AQ						
24	17:04 VI	05:21 LI		11:45 SA	05:35 CP			00:07 TA	19:06 CA	04:08 LE	15:32 LI	01:32 SC
25			19:33 SC			13:03 PI	07:42 AR					
26	18:47 LI	09:28 SC		21:27 CP	17:17 AQ			07:58 GE	21:57 LE	06:40 VI	19:38 SC	08:01 SA
27							17:58 TA					
28		17:36 SA	02:33 SA			01:02 AR		12:17 CA	23:01 VI	08:49 LI		16:16 CP
29				09:26 AQ	05:51 PI						01:03 SA	
30	00:25 SC		12:58 CP			10:14 TA	00:37 GE	13:30 LE	23:41 LI	11:34 SC		
31					17:04 AR							02:31 AQ

1922

	January	February	March	April	May	June	July	August	September	October	November	December
01	14:44 PI	10:36 AR		20:29 GE	09:13 CA	22:48 VI	07:04 LI	20:35 SA	18:12 AQ	11:41 PI	07:05 AR	02:59 TA
02		22:41 TA	04:51 TA									
03	03:42 AR			03:46 CA	14:05 LE	01:43 LI	10:29 SC	03:22 CP		00:36 AR	19:40 TA	13:33 GE
04		07:42 GE							05:41 PI			
05	14:59 TA		14:48 GE		17:19 VI	04:42 SC	15:05 SA	12:19 AQ		13:20 TA		21:33 CA
06		12:30 CA		08:13 LE					18:29 AR		06:33 GE	
07			21:19 CA		19:21 LI	08:18 SA	21:13 CP	23:22 PI				
08	22:27 GE	13:39 LE		10:09 VI						00:45 GE	15:23 CA	03:32 LE
09			00:09 LE		21:00 SC	13:30 CP			07:24 TA			
10	01:47 CA	12:58 VI		10:36 LI			05:28 AQ	12:05 AR		09:52 CA	22:05 LE	08:09 VI
11			00:22 VI		23:32 SA	21:25 AQ			18:51 GE			
12	02:21 LE	12:34 LI		11:07 SC			16:16 PI	00:57 TA		16:01 LE		11:40 LI
13			23:44 LI								02:36 VI	
14	02:13 VI	14:23 SC		13:25 SA	04:25 CP	08:25 PI		11:42 GE	03:13 CA	19:04 VI		14:14 SC
15							04:59 AR				05:01 LI	
16	03:20 LI	19:32 SA	00:13 SC	19:01 CP	12:45 AQ	21:13 AR		18:40 CA	07:48 LE	19:43 LI		16:28 SA
17							17:28 TA				05:59 SC	
18	07:01 SC		03:34 SA					21:45 LE	09:08 VI	19:26 SC		19:35 CP
19		04:06 CP		04:27 AQ	00:21 PI	09:09 TA					06:53 SA	
20	13:33 SA		10:41 CP				03:10 GE	22:16 VI	08:43 LI	20:05 SA		
21				16:43 PI	13:13 AR	18:02 GE					09:32 CP	01:08 AQ
22	22:28 CP	15:13 AQ	21:18 AQ				08:56 CA	22:05 LI	08:27 SC	23:33 CP		
23						23:27 CA					15:36 AQ	10:14 PI
24				05:37 AR	00:46 TA		11:26 LE	23:02 SC	10:10 SA			
25	09:17 AQ	03:45 PI	09:55 PI							07:00 AQ		
26				17:08 TA	09:29 GE	02:28 LE	12:21 VI		15:15 CP		01:39 PI	22:22 AR
27	21:34 PI	16:41 AR						02:26 SA				
28			22:49 AR		15:27 CA	04:36 VI	13:27 LI					
29				02:20 GE				08:53 CP		18:07 PI	14:20 AR	11:12 TA
30			10:38 TA				15:59 SC		00:02 AQ			
31					19:34 LE							22:02 GE

1923

	January	February	March	April	May	June	July	August	September	October	November	December
01				19:26 SC	05:59 SA	21:03 AQ	13:28 PI	08:12 AR	16:50 GE	12:01 CA	05:01 LE	00:24 LI
02	05:40 CA	22:12 VI	08:41 VI					20:22 TA			12:07 VI	
03		23:38 LI	09:00 LI	19:34 SA	07:15 CP		23:51 AR		03:59 CA	21:15 LE		02:14 SC
04	10:34 LE			22:20 CP		04:42 PI					15:24 LI	
05					12:05 AQ			08:47 GE				01:57 SA
06	13:59 VI		09:16 SC		21:06 PI	16:02 AR	12:25 TA		11:54 LE	02:41 VI	15:37 SC	
07		01:37 SC						19:08 CA				01:31 CP
08	16:59 LI	04:58 SA	11:05 SA	04:49 AQ		04:57 TA			16:17 VI	04:36 LI	14:37 SA	
09					09:12 AR		00:37 GE					03:10 AQ
10	20:05 SC	10:07 CP	15:34 CP	14:51 PI			10:34 CA	02:19 LE	18:03 LI	04:26 SC	14:37 CP	
11					22:14 TA	17:03 GE						08:36 PI
12	23:34 SA		23:02 AQ					06:44 VI	18:47 SC	04:09 SA	17:39 AQ	
13		17:18 AQ		03:08 AR			17:54 LE					18:08 AR
14						03:10 CA		09:27 LI	20:06 SA	05:43 CP		
15	03:56 CP		09:08 PI	16:07 TA	10:27 GE						00:46 PI	
16		02:43 PI				11:12 LE	23:10 VI	11:38 SC	23:14 CP	10:29 AQ		06:22 TA
17	10:05 AQ	14:20 AR	21:06 AR		21:03 CA						11:25 AR	
18				04:33 GE		17:23 VI	03:05 LI	14:12 SA		18:42 PI		19:03 GE
19	18:57 PI								04:53 AQ		23:53 TA	
20			10:00 TA									
21				15:27 CA	05:41 LE	21:44 LI	06:08 SC	17:50 CP	13:03 PI	05:33 AR		
22	06:37 AR	03:15 TA	22:33 GE								12:32 GE	06:40 CA
23		15:32 GE		23:50 LE	11:55 VI		08:43 SA	23:04 AQ	23:23 AR	17:48 TA		
24	19:34 TA		09:05 CA			00:20 SC						16:40 LE
25					15:26 LI		11:33 CP				00:28 CA	
26		00:57 CA	16:13 LE	04:56 VI		01:46 SA		06:25 PI	11:22 TA	06:29 GE		
27	07:08 GE	06:30 LE		06:49 LI	16:35 SC		15:43 AQ				11:02 LE	00:51 VI
28			19:36 VI			03:19 CP		16:15 AR		18:40 CA		
29	15:20 CA			06:33 SC	16:37 SA		22:23 PI		00:06 GE		19:19 VI	06:51 LI
30			20:06 LI			06:44 AQ						
31	19:57 LE				17:27 CP			04:12 TA				

1924

Day	January	February	March	April	May	June	July	August	September	October	November	December
01	10:23 SC	21:03 CP				14:47 GE	09:28 CA		02:37 LI		00:39 CP	
02			07:11 AQ		20:38 TA			13:06 VI		15:54 SA		13:38 PI
03	11:48 SA	23:43 AQ		03:45 AR			21:11 LE		06:54 SC		02:53 AQ	
04			12:44 PI			03:26 CA		20:20 LI		18:03 CP		20:10 AR
05	12:22 CP			14:12 TA	08:48 GE				10:00 SA		07:34 PI	
06		04:12 PI	20:26 AR			15:29 LE	07:16 VI			21:20 AQ		
07	13:54 AQ				21:30 CA			01:24 SC	12:41 CP		14:39 AR	05:33 TA
08		11:36 AR		02:14 GE			14:55 LI					
09	18:14 PI		06:35 TA			01:41 VI		04:32 SA	15:33 AQ	02:07 PI	23:43 TA	16:52 GE
10		22:09 TA		14:53 CA	09:30 LE		19:37 SC					
11			18:44 GE			08:41 LI		06:20 CP	19:17 PI	08:31 AR		
12	02:22 AR				18:56 VI		21:32 SA				10:34 GE	05:21 CA
13		10:34 GE		02:15 LE		11:57 SC		07:52 AQ		16:50 TA		
14	13:48 TA		07:08 CA				21:49 CP		00:42 AR		22:56 CA	18:13 LE
15		22:34 CA		10:21 VI	00:28 LI	12:17 SA		10:28 PI				
16			17:32 LE				22:11 AQ		08:40 TA	03:23 GE		
17	02:27 GE			14:27 LI	02:10 SC	11:29 CP		15:32 AR			11:51 LE	06:07 VI
18		08:09 LE							19:24 GE	15:48 CA		
19	14:05 CA		00:27 VI	15:23 SC	01:34 SA	11:42 AQ	00:30 PI	23:54 TA			23:11 VI	15:15 LI
20		14:46 VI										
21	23:33 LE		04:00 LI	15:04 SA	00:49 CP	14:52 PI	06:12 AR		07:54 CA	04:21 LE		20:26 SC
22		18:57 LI						11:15 GE			06:52 LI	
23			05:27 SC	15:33 CP	02:05 AQ	21:56 AR	15:36 TA		19:52 LE	14:33 VI		21:55 SA
24	06:49 VI	21:47 SC						23:49 CA			10:18 SC	
25			06:29 SA	18:30 AQ	06:50 PI					20:49 LI		21:18 CP
26	12:14 LI					08:27 TA	03:36 GE		05:06 VI		10:38 SA	
27		00:16 SA	08:37 CP		15:16 AR			11:19 LE		23:27 SC		20:41 AQ
28	16:09 SC			00:39 PI		20:51 GE	16:12 CA		10:53 LI		09:58 CP	
29		03:12 CP	12:46 AQ					20:19 VI				22:05 PI
30	18:53 SA			09:39 AR	02:23 TA				13:59 SC	00:04 SA	10:25 AQ	
31			19:13 PI				03:39 LE					

1925

	January	February	March	April	May	June	July	August	September	October	November	December
01	02:57 AR		13:26 GE			12:30 LI	03:33 SC	17:47 CP		15:06 AR		
02		05:33 GE		22:32 LE	18:38 VI				04:02 PI		09:44 GE	03:18 CA
03	11:31 TA					18:21 SC	06:55 SA	17:41 AQ		18:20 TA		
04		18:10 CA	01:37 CA						05:02 AR		19:06 CA	15:13 LE
05	22:53 GE			09:55 VI	03:26 LI	20:33 SA	07:25 CP	17:23 PI				
06			14:22 LE						08:27 TA	00:35 GE		
07		06:49 LE		18:05 LI	08:22 SC	20:45 CP	06:50 AQ	18:46 AR			07:16 LE	04:14 VI
08	11:33 CA								15:39 GE	10:34 CA		
09		18:01 VI	01:24 VI	23:04 SC	10:27 SA	20:54 AQ	07:07 PI	23:24 TA			20:06 VI	15:53 LI
10										23:09 LE		
11	00:14 LE		09:44 LI		11:30 CP	22:40 PI	09:53 AR		02:35 CA			
12		03:06 LI		02:05 SA				07:56 GE			06:52 LI	00:04 SC
13	11:55 VI		15:38 SC		13:08 AQ		16:05 TA		15:30 LE	11:43 VI		
14		09:54 SC		04:32 CP		03:03 AR		19:39 CA			14:06 SC	04:24 SA
15	21:32 LI		19:52 SA		16:23 PI					21:57 LI		
16		14:28 SA		07:23 AQ		10:16 TA	01:37 GE		03:57 VI		18:13 SA	05:59 CP
17			23:07 CP		21:34 AR			08:41 LE				
18	04:11 SC	17:03 CP		11:02 PI		19:57 GE	13:32 CA		14:18 LI	05:12 SC	20:38 CP	06:36 AQ
19								21:13 VI				
20	07:33 SA	18:21 AQ	01:51 AQ	15:44 AR	04:41 TA				22:18 SC	10:11 SA	22:48 AQ	07:52 PI
21						07:36 CA	02:32 LE					
22	08:22 CP	19:37 PI	04:34 PI	21:59 TA	13:51 GE			08:06 LI		13:57 CP		10:57 AR
23						20:30 LE	15:17 VI		04:17 SA		01:38 PI	
24	08:09 AQ	22:21 AR	08:04 AR					16:45 SC		17:13 AQ		16:25 TA
25				06:33 GE	01:08 CA				08:37 CP		05:32 AR	
26	08:46 PI		13:34 TA			09:21 VI	02:30 LI	22:50 SA		20:15 PI		
27		04:03 TA		17:46 CA	13:59 LE				11:29 AQ		10:46 TA	00:18 GE
28	11:59 AR		22:07 GE			20:15 LI	10:57 SC			23:24 AR		
29								02:19 CP	13:19 PI		17:50 GE	10:26 CA
30	18:58 TA			06:37 LE	02:35 VI		15:56 SA					
31			09:42 CA					03:41 AQ		03:30 TA		22:26 LE

1926

	January	February	March	April	May	June	July	August	September	October	November	December
01			12:03 LI	12:08 SA	23:33 CP	11:53 PI	20:14 AR		01:48 CA			22:39 SC
02	11:27 VI	06:11 LI						11:25 GE	13:01 LE	07:49 VI	03:23 LI	
03		16:39 SC	22:28 SC	18:05 CP	03:32 AQ	14:45 AR	23:59 TA				14:38 SC	07:32 SA
04	23:45 LI							20:08 CA		20:29 LI		
05			06:40 SA	22:01 AQ	06:32 PI	18:28 TA	05:57 GE				23:51 SA	13:52 CP
06		00:02 SA										
07				00:04 PI	08:55 AR	23:43 GE	14:17 CA	07:12 LE		07:59 SC		
08	09:20 SC	03:49 CP	12:07 CP						14:23 LI		07:11 CP	18:22 AQ
09		04:37 AQ	14:40 AQ	01:03 AR	11:33 TA		00:51 LE	19:39 VI		17:54 SA	12:41 AQ	21:44 PI
10	15:02 SA					07:15 CA						
11		03:57 PI	15:04 PI	02:31 TA			13:08 VI		02:16 SC			
12	17:09 CP				15:46 GE	17:29 LE		08:26 LI	12:22 SA		16:22 PI	00:33 AR
13		03:47 AR	14:52 AR	06:20 GE	22:53 CA							
14	17:07 AQ						01:52 LI	20:17 SC			18:28 AR	03:24 TA
15			16:07 TA	13:54 CA		05:49 VI			19:37 CP			
16	16:48 PI	06:09 TA					13:08 SC			09:29 PI	19:54 TA	07:00 GE
17					09:20 LE	18:19 LI		05:40 SA	23:23 AQ			
18	18:03 AR	12:22 GE	20:42 GE							09:56 AR	22:11 GE	12:20 CA
19					21:55 VI		21:10 SA		00:07 PI			
20	22:15 TA			01:07 LE		04:40 SC		11:24 CP	23:20 AR	10:01 TA		20:17 LE
21		22:29 CA	05:30 CA	13:59 VI		11:35 SA					02:55 CA	
22					10:05 LI		01:28 CP	13:31 AQ	23:12 TA			
23	05:55 GE		17:35 LE							11:50 GE		
24		11:00 LE		01:52 LI		15:18 CP	02:48 AQ	13:15 PI			11:11 LE	07:02 VI
25	16:30 CA		06:36 VI		19:42 SC			12:30 AR		17:08 CA		19:31 LI
26		23:59 VI		11:19 SC		17:01 AQ	02:46 PI				22:36 VI	
27					02:14 SA			13:25 TA	08:35 CA			
28	04:53 LE		18:27 LI	18:19 SA		18:13 PI	03:14 AR			02:31 LE	11:14 LI	07:28 SC
29					06:24 CP			17:39 GE	19:10 LE			
30	17:50 VI									14:43 VI		
31			04:17 SC		09:19 AQ		05:47 TA					16:50 SA

1927

	January	February	March	April	May	June	July	August	September	October	November	December
01	22:52 CP			10:30 AR		09:50 CA	00:48 LE		00:35 SC		22:27 AQ	10:37 PI
02		13:07 PI	00:05 PI		20:53 GE			04:44 LI				
03				09:36 TA		15:37 LE	09:27 VI		13:10 SA	07:13 CP		14:20 AR
04	02:11 AQ	13:20 AR	23:19 AR		23:52 CA			17:16 SC			03:56 PI	
05				10:25 GE			20:48 LI		23:28 CP	15:07 AQ		15:46 TA
06	04:06 PI	14:50 TA	23:07 TA		06:39 LE	00:55 VI					05:53 AR	
07				14:43 CA				05:14 SA		18:51 PI		16:10 GE
08	06:00 AR	18:54 GE				12:49 LI	09:18 SC		05:50 AQ		05:37 TA	
09			01:29 GE	23:00 LE	17:03 VI			14:23 CP		19:15 AR		17:11 CA
10	08:56 TA						20:37 SA		08:16 PI		05:03 GE	
11		01:50 CA	07:30 CA			01:16 SC		19:45 AQ		18:18 TA		20:32 LE
12	13:30 GE			10:19 VI	05:27 LI				08:18 AR		06:15 CA	
13		11:11 LE	16:52 LE			12:16 SA	05:07 CP	22:04 PI		18:12 GE		
14	19:59 CA			22:54 LI	17:51 SC				08:03 TA		10:48 LE	03:26 VI
15		22:16 VI				20:52 CP	10:31 AQ	22:57 AR		20:50 CA		
16			04:23 VI						09:29 GE		19:14 VI	13:55 LI
17	04:31 LE			11:20 SC	04:58 SA		13:43 PI					
18		10:32 LI	16:49 LI			03:05 AQ		00:12 TA	13:49 CA	03:07 LE		
19	15:09 VI			22:49 SA	14:11 CP		15:57 AR				06:41 LI	02:32 SC
20		23:09 SC				07:25 PI		03:09 GE	21:13 LE	12:43 VI		
21			05:22 SC		21:16 AQ		18:24 TA				19:27 SC	14:59 SA
22	03:27 LI			08:35 CP		10:29 AR		08:19 CA				
23		10:35 SA	17:06 SA				21:46 GE		07:01 VI	00:27 LI		
24	15:55 SC			15:43 AQ	02:02 PI	12:54 TA		15:39 LE			07:54 SA	01:38 CP
25		18:56 CP							18:30 LI	13:08 SC		
26			02:39 CP	19:38 PI	04:38 AR	15:26 GE	02:31 CA				19:01 CP	09:54 AQ
27	02:22 SA	23:14 AQ						00:56 VI				
28			08:39 AQ	20:44 AR	05:51 TA	19:03 CA	09:01 LE		07:05 SC	01:48 SA		16:00 PI
29	09:13 CP							12:02 LI			04:07 AQ	
30			10:53 PI	20:29 TA	07:02 GE		17:42 VI		19:54 SA	13:23 CP		20:19 AR
31	12:22 AQ											

1928

Day	January	February	March	April	May	June	July	August	September	October	November	December
01	23:15 TA				03:37 LI		05:24 CP		17:26 AR	03:59 TA	14:41 CA	01:28 LE
02		11:22 CA	22:38 LE	11:54 VI		10:38 SA		05:35 PI				05:16 VI
03					15:38 SC		15:32 AQ		20:07 TA	05:10 GE	17:14 LE	12:52 LI
04	01:20 GE	15:53 LE		21:47 LI		22:59 CP		10:33 AR				
05			05:51 VI		04:32 SA							
06	03:28 CA	22:09 VI		09:28 SC			23:23 PI	14:18 TA	22:43 GE	07:22 CA	22:41 VI	12:52 LI
07			15:04 LI		17:09 CP	09:41 AQ						
08	06:53 LE			22:21 SA				17:22 GE	01:52 CA	11:18 LE	07:05 LI	23:46 SC
09		07:03 LI				17:54 PI	05:04 AR					
10	12:54 VI		02:31 SC					20:03 CA	05:50 LE	17:14 VI	17:53 SC	
11		18:41 SC		10:57 CP	11:35 PI	23:14 AR	08:49 TA					12:30 SA
12	22:18 LI		15:25 SA					22:57 LE				
13				21:07 AQ	15:30 AR				11:02 VI	01:14 LI	06:20 SA	01:30 CP
14		07:32 SA				01:46 TA	10:59 GE					
15	10:26 SC		03:34 CP		16:26 TA			03:08 VI	18:13 LI	11:28 SC	19:25 CP	13:36 AQ
16		18:54 CP		03:19 PI		02:24 GE	12:20 CA					
17	23:06 SA		12:32 AQ		15:57 GE			09:53 LI	04:05 SC	23:44 SA	07:40 AQ	23:49 PI
18				05:40 AR		02:35 CA	14:05 LE					
19		02:47 AQ	17:20 PI		15:58 CA			19:58 SC	16:23 SA			
20	09:49 CP			05:36 TA		04:02 LE	17:52 VI			12:50 CP	17:20 PI	07:16 AR
21		07:06 PI	18:54 AR		18:17 LE							
22	17:27 AQ			05:09 GE		08:27 VI	01:02 LI	08:29 SA	05:16 CP	00:33 AQ	23:15 AR	11:25 TA
23		09:09 AR	19:06 TA		00:07 VI							
24	22:24 PI			06:14 CA		16:42 LI	11:47 SC	20:59 CP	16:01 AQ	08:50 PI	01:31 TA	12:40 GE
25		10:42 TA	19:53 GE		09:36 LI							
26				10:12 LE					23:01 PI	13:05 AR		
27	01:48 AR	13:08 GE	22:41 CA			04:16 SC	00:35 SA	06:57 AQ			01:24 GE	12:16 CA
28				17:29 VI								
29	04:43 TA	17:04 CA			21:40 SC	17:13 SA	12:48 CP	13:30 PI	02:31 AR	14:17 TA	00:44 CA	12:07 LE
30												
31	07:47 GE		04:04 LE				22:34 AQ			14:11 GE		14:12 VI

1929

	January	February	March	April	May	June	July	August	September	October	November	December
01	20:08 LI						19:32 TA	08:16 CA	18:26 VI	06:10 LI		23:25 CP
02		01:59 SA	10:03 SA	07:03 CP	03:19 AQ	05:58 AR					04:47 SA	
03	06:11 SC						22:14 GE	08:11 LE	20:51 LI	11:40 SC		11:57 AQ
04		15:00 CP	22:55 CP	19:18 AQ	13:51 PI						15:57 CP	
05	18:51 SA									20:19 SA		
06		02:34 AQ	10:44 AQ	04:52 PI	20:51 AR	11:57 GE	22:21 CA	08:22 VI	02:20 SC		04:33 AQ	00:27 PI
07												
08	07:51 CP	11:42 PI	19:44 PI	10:58 AR	00:18 TA	11:35 CA	21:37 LE	10:55 LI	11:39 SA	07:50 CP	16:30 PI	
09												
10	19:33 AQ				01:22 GE	11:25 LE	22:10 VI	17:22 SC		20:26 AQ		17:50 TA
11		18:41 AR	01:52 AR	14:17 TA					23:45 CP		01:43 AR	
12	05:21 PI				01:44 CA	13:20 VI				07:40 PI		20:49 GE
13		00:02 TA	06:05 TA	16:13 GE			01:54 LI	03:44 SA	12:17 AQ		07:19 TA	
14	13:07 AR				03:03 LE	18:39 LI				16:02 AR		21:05 CA
15			09:24 GE	18:04 CA			09:45 SC	16:21 CP			09:53 GE	
16		04:02 GE			06:34 VI				23:07 PI	21:29 TA		20:35 LE
17	18:37 TA		12:24 CA	20:50 LE		03:33 SC	20:59 SA	04:50 AQ			10:53 CA	
18		06:46 CA			12:53 LI				07:31 AR			21:22 VI
19	21:44 GE		15:28 LE	01:05 VI		15:03 SA		15:46 PI		00:54 GE	11:58 LE	
20		08:41 LE			21:54 SC		09:47 CP		13:45 TA			01:03 LI
21										03:24 CA		
22	22:52 CA		19:05 VI	07:13 LI		03:45 CP	22:20 AQ	00:47 AR			14:32 VI	08:11 SC
23		10:59 VI			09:04 SA				18:24 GE	05:55 LE		
24	23:17 LE		00:12 LI	15:35 SC		16:24 AQ	09:39 PI	07:56 TA			19:23 LI	
25		15:15 LI			21:35 CP				21:52 CA	09:09 VI		18:11 SA
26			07:49 SC	02:16 SA		03:59 PI	19:13 AR	13:03 GE				
27	00:48 VI								00:28 LE	13:40 LI	02:40 SC	
28		22:54 SC	18:26 SA	14:44 CP	10:17 AQ	13:21 AR	02:26 TA	16:04 CA	02:52 VI		12:08 SA	05:56 CP
29	05:19 LI				21:37 PI					20:02 SC		
30												
31	13:58 SC						06:43 GE	17:26 LE				

1930

	January	February	March	April	May	June	July	August	September	October	November	December
01	18:30 AQ				13:54 CA		09:47 LI		20:35 CP	15:09 AQ		18:32 TA
02		00:23 AR				00:37 VI		04:25 SA			23:35 AR	
03			06:08 AR	03:43 GE	16:32 LE		14:56 SC		08:27 AQ	03:48 PI		01:32 GE
04	07:05 PI	09:49 TA				04:04 LI		14:35 CP			09:38 TA	
05			15:18 TA	08:12 CA	19:11 VI		22:50 SA		21:06 PI	15:53 AR		05:31 CA
06	18:28 AR	16:08 GE				09:30 SC					16:58 GE	
07				11:09 LE				02:26 AQ				07:53 LE
08		18:55 CA	22:16 GE			16:56 SA	08:50 CP		09:21 AR	02:15 TA	22:04 CA	
09	02:59 TA			13:11 VI	03:06 SC			15:02 PI				10:04 VI
10		18:59 LE	02:34 CA				20:23 AQ		20:18 TA	10:29 GE		
11	07:35 GE			15:17 LI	09:38 SA	02:21 CP		03:32 AR			01:45 LE	13:05 LI
12		18:14 VI	04:26 LE							16:29 CA		
13	08:35 CA			18:45 SC	18:39 CP	13:39 AQ	08:57 PI		05:01 GE		04:42 VI	17:20 SC
14		18:50 LI	04:54 VI					14:38 TA		20:19 LE		
15	07:37 LE			00:49 SA	06:04 AQ	02:13 PI	21:26 AR		10:43 CA		07:27 LI	22:55 SA
16		22:45 SC	05:44 LI					22:46 GE		22:25 VI		
17	06:56 VI			10:07 CP	18:34 PI	14:15 AR			13:18 LE		10:37 SC	
18			08:47 SC				07:54 TA			23:43 LI		06:12 CP
19	08:44 LI	06:49 SA		21:58 AQ	05:56 AR	23:35 TA		03:02 CA	13:45 VI		15:01 SA	
20			15:24 SA				14:39 GE					15:43 AQ
21	14:25 SC	18:13 CP						03:58 LE	13:43 LI	01:32 SC	21:43 CP	
22			01:40 CP	10:23 PI	14:16 TA	05:00 GE	17:22 CA					
23	23:57 SA							03:14 VI	15:07 SC	05:23 SA		03:35 PI
24		06:57 AQ	14:05 AQ	21:10 AR		06:57 CA	17:19 LE				07:23 AQ	
25					21:26 CA			02:58 LI	19:34 SA	12:27 CP		16:29 AR
26	11:54 CP	19:13 PI				07:06 LE	16:35 VI				19:33 PI	
27			02:23 PI	05:09 TA	22:45 LE			05:11 SC		22:54 AQ		
28						07:28 VI	17:18 LI		03:48 CP			03:51 TA
29	00:36 AQ		12:59 AR	10:27 GE				11:05 SA			08:06 AR	
30										11:23 PI		
31	12:59 PI		21:24 TA				21:06 SC					

1931

	January	February	March	April	May	June	July	August	September	October	November	December
01	11:35 GE	03:25 LE	14:25 LE	00:49 LI	11:26 SC	03:07 CP	18:56 AQ	01:10 AR	20:59 TA	15:03 GE	13:40 LE	00:16 VI
02	15:21 CA	02:57 VI	14:20 VI	00:51 SC	13:14 SA	10:23 AQ	05:10 PI	14:05 TA	08:43 GE	00:38 CA	18:08 VI	03:44 LI
03	16:33 LE	02:54 LI	13:32 LI	02:52 SA	17:35 CP	21:01 PI	17:40 AR		17:15 CA	06:50 LE	20:03 LI	05:43 SC
04	17:07 VI	05:04 SC	14:02 SC	08:21 CP	01:36 AQ	09:44 AR	06:14 TA	01:01 GE	21:48 LE	09:35 VI	20:21 SC	07:04 SA
05	18:49 LI	10:21 SA	17:30 SA	17:40 AQ	13:02 PI	21:55 TA	16:14 GE	08:10 CA	23:04 VI	09:50 LI	20:39 SA	09:18 CP
06	22:40 SC	18:39 CP	00:39 CP	05:49 PI	01:56 AR	07:22 GE	22:30 CA	11:31 LE	22:43 LI	09:17 SC	22:52 CP	14:10 AQ
07	04:50 SA	05:15 AQ	11:04 AQ	18:48 AR	13:54 TA	13:38 CA	01:41 LE	12:25 VI	22:41 SC	09:51 SA	04:40 AQ	22:51 PI
08	13:01 CP	17:23 PI	23:27 PI	06:50 TA	23:27 GE	17:37 LE	03:21 VI	12:45 LI	00:40 SA	13:18 CP	14:33 PI	10:50 AR
09	23:03 AQ		12:24 AR	16:56 GE	06:26 CA	20:33 VI	05:06 LI	14:11 SC	05:48 CP	20:39 AQ		23:46 TA
20	10:55 PI	06:21 AR	00:44 TA	00:42 CA	11:28 LE	23:23 LI	07:56 SC	17:47 SA	14:18 AQ	07:32 PI	03:09 AR	
21	23:55 AR	18:54 TA	11:19 GE	06:04 LE	15:07 VI	02:34 SC	12:19 SA	23:59 CP	01:28 PI	20:21 AR	16:00 TA	10:59 GE
22	12:10 TA	05:13 GE	19:04 CA	09:10 VI	17:51 LI	06:26 SA	18:23 CP	08:38 AQ	14:09 AR	09:12 TA		19:21 CA
26	21:19 GE	11:47 CA	23:29 LE	10:35 LI	20:08 SC	11:35 CP	02:25 AQ	19:28 PI	20:48 GE	20:48 GE	03:12 GE	01:16 LE
28					22:48 SA		12:46 PI		03:07 TA		12:09 CA	05:40 VI
29	02:10 CA		00:57 VI					07:56 AR		06:27 CA	19:06 LE	09:17 LI

1932

Day	January	February	March	April	May	June	July	August	September	October	November	December
01			07:06 CP		22:47 AR		00:07 CA	15:57 LE	08:31 LI	18:44 SC	04:55 CP	16:46 AQ
02	12:24 SC	01:39 CP		05:05 PI		06:32 GE						22:08 PI
03			13:59 AQ	16:54 AR	11:46 TA	17:21 CA	08:19 LE	21:15 VI	10:06 SC	19:03 SA	08:06 AQ	
04	15:16 SA	07:48 AQ										07:35 AR
05			23:15 PI		00:20 GE	02:15 LE	14:34 VI	00:56 LI	11:59 SA	21:01 CP	15:06 PI	
06	18:38 CP	16:15 PI										
07				05:44 TA		09:07 VI	19:13 LI	03:49 SC	15:12 CP	01:44 AQ	01:24 AR	19:41 TA
08			10:35 AR									
09	23:44 AQ	03:17 AR		18:28 GE			22:28 SC		20:17 AQ	09:27 PI	13:33 TA	
10			23:20 TA		20:46 LE	13:42 LI						
11	07:50 PI			05:47 CA			00:38 SA	09:38 CP	03:31 PI		02:13 GE	08:27 GE
12												
13	07:07 AR		12:03 GE	14:22 LE			02:35 CP	13:54 AQ	13:02 AR	07:24 TA	14:32 CA	20:29 CA
14		04:28 GE			03:13 VI	16:00 SC						
15	19:07 TA		22:47 CA	19:21 VI			05:44 AQ	20:14 PI	00:34 TA	20:02 GE		07:13 LE
16		14:03 CA			06:32 LI	16:46 SA					01:36 LE	
17				20:59 LI			11:34 PI					16:09 VI
18	08:02 GE	19:49 LE	05:56 LE		07:15 SC	17:31 CP		05:19 AR	13:14 GE	08:26 CA		
19				20:33 SC								22:32 LI
20		22:25 VI	09:19 VI		06:48 SA	20:12 AQ	20:52 AR	16:56 TA			10:09 VI	
21	04:22 CA			19:57 SA					01:13 CA	18:57 LE		01:53 SC
22		23:22 LI	09:56 LI		07:13 CP		08:54 TA				16:38 SC	
23	09:40 LE			21:15 CP		02:25 PI		05:34 GE	10:32 LE	02:03 VI		02:42 SA
24			09:35 SC		10:31 AQ		21:27 GE					
25	12:47 VI	00:20 SC				12:34 AR		16:51 CA		05:16 LI	15:58 SA	02:31 CP
26			10:07 SA	02:05 AQ					16:06 VI			
27	15:08 LI	02:39 SA			17:58 PI		08:08 CA			05:31 SC	15:16 CP	03:23 AQ
28			13:08 CP	10:56 PI		01:08 TA		01:03 LE	18:22 LI			
29	17:44 SC											
30					05:09 AR	13:35 GE		05:58 VI		04:41 SA		
31	21:07 SA		19:30 AQ		18:05 TA							07:16 PI

1933

Day	January	February	March	April	May	June	July	August	September	October	November	December
01	15:14 AR	10:40 TA		03:50 CA	23:07 LE	23:14 LI	10:57 SC	21:41 CP	06:59 AQ		13:53 TA	06:44 GE
02		23:05 GE								22:51 AR		18:52 CA
03	02:37 TA		07:17 GE	15:17 LE	08:41 VI		12:32 SA	22:22 AQ	09:44 PI		00:02 GE	
04		11:13 CA				02:25 SC						
05	15:20 GE		19:43 CA	23:33 VI	14:17 LI		12:16 CP		14:15 AR	06:18 TA	12:05 CA	07:48 LE
06		21:16 LE				02:32 SA		00:11 PI				
07					16:07 SC		12:06 AQ		21:35 TA	16:19 GE		19:59 VI
08	03:17 CA		06:18 LE	04:01 LI		01:33 CP		04:41 AR			00:58 LE	
09		04:43 VI			15:43 SA		14:02 PI					
10	13:27 LE		13:42 VI	05:32 SC		01:42 AQ		12:44 TA	08:01 GE	04:30 CA	12:24 VI	05:19 LI
11		09:59 LI			15:15 CP		19:31 AR					
12	21:41 VI		18:03 LI	05:52 SA		04:50 PI		23:57 GE	20:26 CA	17:02 LE	20:12 LI	10:27 SC
13		13:46 SC			16:46 AQ							
14			20:28 SC	06:54 CP		11:51 AR	04:49 TA				23:52 SC	11:49 SA
15	04:02 LI				21:34 PI			12:33 CA	08:31 LE	03:24 VI		
16		16:43 SA	22:19 SA	10:02 AQ		22:12 TA	16:44 GE				00:35 SA	11:09 CP
17	08:24 SC								18:14 VI	10:07 LI		
18		19:23 CP		15:54 PI	05:46 AR			00:23 LE			00:24 CP	10:37 AQ
19	10:54 SA		00:47 CP			10:26 GE	05:24 CA			13:27 SC		
20		22:29 AQ			16:27 TA			10:08 VI	00:51 LI		01:21 AQ	12:15 PI
21	12:18 CP		04:39 AQ	00:14 AR		23:06 CA	17:19 LE			14:54 SA		
22								17:30 LI	04:59 SC		04:50 PI	17:15 AR
23	13:57 AQ	02:56 PI	10:15 PI	10:31 TA	04:32 GE					16:13 CP		
24						11:17 LE	03:36 VI	22:45 SC	07:48 SA			
25	17:31 PI	09:42 AR	17:49 AR		17:12 CA					18:49 AQ	11:13 AR	01:42 TA
26				22:19 GE		22:01 VI	11:45 LI		10:23 CP			
27		19:20 TA						02:21 SA		23:18 PI	20:03 TA	12:43 GE
28			03:31 TA		05:33 LE		17:22 SC		13:27 AQ			
29	00:22 AR			10:59 CA		06:11 LI		04:52 CP				
30			15:13 GE		16:06 VI		20:27 SA		17:27 PI	05:41 AR		01:07 CA
31												

1934

	January	February	March	April	May	June	July	August	September	October	November	December
01					01:02 SA			13:26 TA				
02	13:56 LE	08:01 VI		13:35 SC		11:55 AQ	00:39 AR		15:40 CA	11:44 LE	08:36 VI	04:39 LI
03			00:02 LI		02:54 CP			21:49 GE				13:06 SC
04		17:59 LI		17:37 SA		14:06 PI	06:48 TA					
05	02:10 VI		06:59 SC		05:06 AQ			09:13 CA	04:32 LE	00:31 VI		17:52 SA
06		01:31 SC		20:46 CP		18:31 AR	15:56 GE				03:32 SC	
07	12:21 LI		11:58 SA		08:26 PI				17:16 VI	11:21 LI		20:09 CP
08		06:14 SA		23:43 AQ		01:17 TA	03:21 CA	22:08 LE			08:33 SA	
09	19:11 SC		15:22 CP		13:08 AR					19:32 SC		21:34 AQ
10		08:23 CP		02:53 PI			16:07 LE	10:59 VI	04:23 LI		11:56 CP	
11	22:18 SA		17:36 AQ		19:23 TA	10:14 GE				01:32 SA		
12				06:40 AR					13:20 SC		14:52 AQ	23:31 PI
13	22:37 CP	08:57 AQ	19:26 PI			21:14 CA		22:33 LI		06:04 CP		
14				11:56 TA	03:38 GE		05:07 VI		20:04 SA		17:56 PI	02:52 AR
15	21:56 AQ	09:27 PI	22:01 AR			09:53 LE		07:51 SC		09:32 AQ		
16				19:41 GE	14:17 CA		16:47 LI		00:36 CP		21:27 AR	07:57 TA
17	22:17 PI	11:39 AR				22:52 VI				12:09 PI		
18			02:46 TA					14:12 SA				14:59 GE
19				06:26 CA	02:55 LE				03:07 AQ	14:28 AR	01:47 TA	
20	01:27 AR	17:04 TA	10:52 GE			09:59 LI	01:31 SC	17:27 CP				00:11 CA
21				19:10 LE	15:36 VI				04:14 PI		07:48 GE	
22	08:26 TA	02:17 GE	22:13 CA			17:25 SC	06:28 SA	18:19 AQ		17:35 TA		
23									05:13 AR		16:26 CA	11:37 LE
24	18:54 GE	14:23 CA		07:20 VI	01:44 LI	20:49 SA	08:03 CP	18:08 PI				
25			11:02 LE						07:46 TA			
26		03:13 LE		16:33 LI	07:52 SC		07:44 AQ	18:44 AR			03:54 LE	00:32 VI
27	07:25 CA		22:44 VI						13:33 GE	07:47 CA		
28		14:46 VI		22:07 SC	10:29 SA	21:02 AQ	07:21 PI	21:55 TA			16:52 VI	12:59 LI
29	20:12 LE								23:14 CA	19:43 LE		
30			07:36 LI			21:38 PI	08:46 AR					22:42 SC
31					11:12 CP			04:55 GE				

1935

	January	February	March	April	May	June	July	August	September	October	November	December
01	04:27 SA	18:26 AQ	05:16 AQ		02:10 TA	20:43 CA	14:13 LE	09:07 VI	16:22 SC	08:41 SA		14:03 PI
02		17:47 PI	05:13 PI	15:32 AR	05:27 GE			21:55 LI			04:38 AQ	16:53 AR
03	06:44 CP	17:49 AR		16:19 TA						17:03 CP	08:20 PI	
04	07:04 AQ	20:22 TA	04:40 AR			06:19 LE	02:09 VI		02:48 SA			19:03 TA
05			05:43 TA					09:57 SC		22:21 AQ		
06				19:36 GE	11:50 CA	18:26 VI	14:53 LI		10:08 CP		09:54 AR	
07					21:55 LE			19:25 SA				21:37 GE
08	07:18 PI			02:49 CA					13:44 AQ	00:27 PI	10:29 TA	
09						07:00 LI	02:16 SC	01:10 CP				01:54 CA
10	09:03 AR	02:35 GE	10:11 GE						14:15 PI	00:21 AR	11:52 GE	
11	13:25 TA			13:53 LE	10:26 VI	17:36 SC	10:28 SA	03:21 AQ	13:21 AR	23:54 TA		09:07 LE
12		12:24 CA	18:52 CA								15:56 CA	
13					22:48 LI		15:03 CP	03:19 PI	13:11 TA	01:17 GE		19:33 VI
14	20:43 GE		06:49 LE	02:47 VI		00:58 SA					23:51 LE	
15		00:35 LE					16:53 AQ	02:55 AR	15:48 GE	06:21 CA		
16				15:01 LI	08:54 SC	05:22 CP						
17	06:37 CA	13:34 VI	19:52 VI				17:30 PI	04:08 TA	22:27 CA		11:11 VI	07:59 LI
18	18:27 LE				16:13 SA	07:56 AQ				15:35 LE		
19			08:08 LI	01:09 SC			18:33 AR	08:26 GE			23:53 LI	20:03 SC
20				09:06 SA	21:21 CP	09:56 PI						
21	07:20 VI	02:03 LI					21:21 TA		08:50 LE	03:44 VI		
22		13:05 SC	18:44 SC	15:13 CP	01:09 AQ	12:21 AR		16:17 CA			11:37 SC	05:44 SA
23	19:59 LI								21:18 VI	16:32 LI		
24		21:40 SA	03:23 SA	19:44 AQ		15:54 TA	02:42 GE				21:09 SA	12:27 CP
25					04:14 PI			03:01 LE				
26	06:47 SC				06:59 AR		10:44 CA		10:05 LI	04:15 SC		16:46 AQ
27		03:05 CP	09:48 CP	22:40 PI		21:06 GE		15:21 VI			04:28 CP	
28	14:11 SA						21:04 LE		22:06 SC	14:18 SA		19:42 PI
29			13:42 AQ		09:59 TA	04:26 CA					09:59 AQ	
30				00:27 AR				04:08 LI				
31	17:48 CP		15:15 PI		14:11 GE					22:32 CP		22:16 AR

1936

Day	January	February	March	April	May	June	July	August	September	October	November	December
01						14:11 SC	09:27 SA					
02		10:39 GE	22:25 CA		18:43 LI			09:26 AQ	22:43 AR	08:26 TA	20:00 CA	09:43 LE
03				00:08 VI			18:35 CP					
04	01:11 TA	16:58 CA				01:37 SA		12:36 PI	23:04 TA	08:37 GE		16:30 VI
05			07:20 LE	12:32 LI	07:17 SC						00:37 LE	
06	05:05 GE					11:03 CP	00:57 AQ	14:21 AR		11:29 CA		
07		01:26 LE	18:18 VI		18:54 SA				00:55 GE		08:59 VI	02:56 LI
08	10:29 CA			01:06 SC		18:18 AQ	05:11 PI	16:11 TA		17:46 LE		
09		11:48 VI							05:16 CA		20:15 LI	15:28 SC
10	18:02 LE		06:26 LI	13:03 SA	04:57 CP	23:28 PI	08:10 AR	19:11 GE				
11		23:45 LI							12:13 LE	03:02 VI		
12			19:04 SC	23:23 CP	12:47 AQ		10:46 TA	23:52 CA			08:52 SC	04:08 SA
13	04:05 VI					02:47 AR			21:20 VI	14:19 LI		
14		12:24 SC			17:52 PI		13:38 GE				21:33 SA	15:26 CP
15	16:10 LI		07:06 SA	06:49 AQ		04:49 TA		06:20 LE				
16		23:56 SA			20:14 AR		17:27 CA		08:13 LI	02:46 SC		
17			16:52 CP	10:38 PI		06:30 GE		14:45 VI			09:21 CP	00:43 AQ
18	04:38 SC				20:48 TA		22:57 LE		20:32 SC	15:37 SA		
19		08:22 CP	22:53 AQ	11:20 AR		09:09 CA					19:11 AQ	07:44 PI
20	15:11 SA				21:12 GE			01:18 LI				
21		12:47 AQ		10:37 TA		14:06 LE	06:54 VI		09:24 SA	03:37 CP		12:26 AR
22	22:19 CP		00:59 PI		23:20 CA			13:37 SC			02:05 PI	
23		13:56 PI		10:38 GE			17:31 LI		20:53 CP			15:05 TA
24			00:31 AR								05:37 AR	
25	02:02 AQ	13:35 AR	23:37 TA	13:23 CA	04:42 LE			02:10 SA		18:28 PI		16:24 GE
26						09:23 LI	05:55 SC		04:53 AQ		06:29 TA	
27	03:35 PI	13:51 TA		20:04 LE	13:48 VI			12:35 CP		20:10 AR		17:36 CA
28			00:31 GE				17:56 SA		08:39 PI		06:12 GE	
29	04:37 AR	16:30 GE						19:12 AQ		19:35 TA		20:14 LE
30			04:52 CA	06:23 VI	01:38 LI				09:10 AR		06:40 CA	
31	06:38 TA		13:04 LE				03:25 CP	22:05 PI		18:50 GE		

1937

	January	February	March	April	May	June	July	August	September	October	November	December
01	01:46 VI	07:11 SC	15:23 SC			08:57 PI		09:30 GE	21:21 LE	08:29 VI	07:49 SC	02:05 SA
02				00:17 CP	18:09 AQ	14:22 AR	00:35 TA					
03	10:56 LI					16:36 TA	02:16 GE	11:34 CA	01:34 VI	15:32 LI	19:46 SA	15:07 CP
04		19:59 SA	04:08 SA		01:57 PI	16:46 GE	02:54 CA					
05	22:59 SC			10:39 AQ	05:47 AR	16:32 CA	03:59 LE	13:35 LE	07:48 LI			
06			16:23 CP		06:32 TA	17:45 LE				00:56 SC	08:50 CP	03:40 AQ
07		07:34 CP		17:00 PI	05:56 GE	22:02 VI	07:16 VI	16:54 VI	16:59 SC			
08	11:43 SA			19:29 AR	06:00 CA					12:44 SA	21:18 AQ	14:22 PI
09		15:59 AQ	01:36 AQ		08:27 LE	06:09 LI	00:36 SC	22:58 LI				
10	22:54 CP		06:50 PI	19:40 TA					04:59 SA			21:55 AR
11		21:10 PI				17:31 SC	13:20 SA			01:47 CP	07:07 PI	
12									17:52 CP			
13	07:25 AQ		09:00 AR	19:34 GE				08:36 SC		13:37 AQ	12:59 AR	01:50 TA
14		00:12 AR	09:54 TA	21:02 CA	14:19 VI	06:25 SA	01:50 CP					
15	13:28 PI	02:35 TA						20:59 SA	04:52 AQ	22:03 PI	15:12 TA	02:43 GE
16			11:19 GE		23:35 LI	18:58 CP	12:20 AQ					
17	17:48 AR	05:23 GE		01:11 LE							15:10 GE	02:03 CA
18			14:25 CA					09:38 CP	12:19 PI	02:32 AR		
19	21:07 TA	09:05 CA	19:36 LE	08:16 VI		05:54 AQ					14:48 CA	01:49 LE
20								20:06 AQ	16:31 AR	04:09 TA		
21	23:54 GE	13:51 LE		17:51 LI	11:19 SC	14:36 PI	20:21 PI				15:55 LE	03:57 VI
22			02:44 VI			20:50 AR	02:16 AR	03:29 PI	18:49 TA	04:40 GE		
23												
24	02:39 CA	20:05 VI		05:21 SC	00:11 SA		06:32 TA	08:24 AR	20:46 GE	05:47 CA	19:56 VI	09:53 LI
25			11:47 LI			05:54 AQ						
26	06:08 LE			18:06 SA	12:54 CP			11:57 TA	23:24 CA	08:43 LE		19:45 SC
27		04:26 LI	22:51 SC			12:54 CP	02:16 AR				03:22 LI	
28	11:31 VI							15:01 GE		14:02 VI		08:12 SA
29						14:36 PI			03:14 LE		13:46 SC	
30	19:50 LI		11:33 SA	06:57 CP	00:13 AQ	20:50 AR	06:32 TA	18:03 CA		21:48 LI		
31												21:17 CP

1938

	January	February	March	April	May	June	July	August	September	October	November	December
01			09:13 PI		15:45 GE		12:24 VI		00:28 SA			
02		01:59 PI		04:43 TA		02:09 LE		06:50 SC			05:10 PI	00:02 AR
03	09:32 AQ		16:16 AR		16:51 CA		16:09 LI		12:29 CP	08:58 AQ		
04		09:55 AR		07:34 GE		04:21 VI		17:02 SA			14:35 AR	07:01 TA
05	20:07 PI		21:29 TA		18:42 LE		23:49 SC			20:28 PI		
06		15:58 TA		10:08 CA		09:35 LI			01:10 AQ		20:41 TA	10:19 GE
07								05:33 CP				
08	04:29 AR	20:08 GE	01:33 GE	13:05 LE		18:01 SC	10:46 SA		12:29 PI	05:23 AR		11:08 CA
09								18:15 AQ			00:03 GE	
10	10:06 TA	22:26 CA	04:46 CA	16:52 VI			23:22 CP		21:41 AR	11:43 TA		11:18 LE
11						04:58 SA					01:59 CA	
12	12:50 GE	23:33 LE	07:23 LE	22:02 LI	12:16 SC			05:45 PI		16:10 GE		12:38 VI
13						17:22 CP	12:05 AQ		04:55 TA		03:50 LE	
14	13:21 CA		10:06 VI		22:41 SA			15:34 AR		19:31 CA		16:28 LI
15		00:57 VI		05:21 SC			23:55 PI		10:23 GE		06:38 VI	
16	13:09 LE		14:09 LI			06:08 AQ		23:26 TA		22:19 LE		23:14 SC
17		04:28 LI		15:19 SA	10:51 CP				14:10 CA		11:04 LI	
18	14:12 VI		20:54 SC			18:03 PI	10:02 AR					
19		11:38 SC			23:38 AQ			04:52 GE	16:26 LE	01:09 VI	17:26 SC	
20	18:27 LI			03:31 CP			17:31 TA					
21		22:34 SA	07:01 SA			03:40 AR		07:40 CA	18:01 VI	04:43 LI		19:39 CP
22				16:11 AQ	11:09 PI		21:43 GE				01:57 SA	
23	02:55 SC		19:32 CP			09:50 TA		08:27 LE	20:19 LI	10:00 SC		
24		11:29 CP			19:36 AR		22:55 CA				12:38 CP	07:59 AQ
25	14:52 SA			02:53 PI		12:25 GE		08:43 VI		17:55 SA		
26		23:36 AQ	07:56 AQ				22:26 LE		00:56 SC			20:41 PI
27				10:09 AR	00:17 TA	12:27 CA		10:26 LI			00:59 AQ	
28	03:59 CP		17:51 PI				22:17 VI		09:02 SA	04:40 CP		
29				14:02 TA	01:52 GE	11:45 LE		15:26 SC			13:30 PI	08:14 AR
30	16:01 AQ								20:20 CP	17:09 AQ		
31			00:33 AR		01:53 CA		00:35 LI					16:48 TA

499

1939

	January	February	March	April	May	June	July	August	September	October	November	December
01		09:22 CA		04:39 VI		07:15 SA		04:42 PI			13:42 CA	
02	21:20 GE		19:30 LE		17:37 SC		09:54 AQ		10:47 TA	01:38 GE		02:23 VI
03		09:06 LE		05:49 LI		15:50 CP		17:22 AR			18:01 LE	
04	22:21 CA		19:16 VI		23:11 SA		22:18 PI		20:02 GE	08:17 CA		05:22 LI
05		08:02 VI		08:22 SC		02:40 AQ		04:47 TA			20:57 VI	
06	21:33 LE		19:25 LI		07:33 CP		10:50 AR		01:52 CA	12:10 LE		08:57 SC
07		08:29 LI		13:48 SA		15:05 PI		13:06 GE			23:03 LI	
08	21:09 VI		21:59 SC		18:41 AQ		21:27 TA		04:12 LE	13:46 VI		13:33 SA
09		12:22 SC		22:47 CP		03:11 AR		17:21 CA			01:14 SC	
10	23:11 LI		04:24 SA						04:10 VI	14:16 LI		19:52 CP
11		20:24 SA			07:09 PI	12:43 TA	04:21 GE	18:09 LE			04:41 SA	
12				10:34 AQ					03:39 LI	15:18 SC		
13	04:54 SC	07:42 CP	14:36 CP		18:40 AR	18:33 GE	07:16 CA	17:19 VI			10:42 CP	04:43 AQ
14				23:04 PI					04:44 SC	18:36 SA		
15	14:10 SA	20:22 AQ	03:02 AQ		03:28 TA	21:07 CA	07:30 LE	17:04 LI			20:01 AQ	16:15 PI
16				10:13 AR					09:02 SA			
17	01:43 CP	08:52 PI	15:32 PI			21:58 LE	07:07 VI	19:20 SC		01:22 CP		
18					09:07 GE				17:11 CP		08:01 PI	05:03 AR
19		20:24 AR		18:56 TA		22:56 VI	08:10 LI	01:14 SA		11:39 AQ		
20	14:15 AQ		02:41 AR		12:23 CA						20:36 AR	16:32 TA
21		06:19 TA		01:16 GE		01:30 LI	12:04 SC	10:34 CP	04:24 AQ			
22	02:51 PI		11:58 TA		14:34 LE					00:05 PI		
23				05:44 CA		06:25 SC	19:10 SA	22:09 AQ	16:59 PI		07:23 TA	00:37 GE
24	14:42 AR	13:47 GE	19:14 GE		16:51 VI					12:29 AR		
25				08:55 LE							15:09 GE	05:03 CA
26		18:07 CA			20:06 LI	13:39 SA	04:51 CP	10:42 PI	05:22 AR	23:10 TA		
27	00:30 TA		00:19 CA								20:11 CA	07:05 LE
28				11:27 VI		22:53 CP	16:15 AQ	23:14 AR	16:29 TA			
29	06:51 GE		03:14 LE		00:47 SC					07:32 GE	23:34 LE	
30				14:03 LI								08:29 VI
31												

1940

	January	February	March	April	May	June	July	August	September	October	November	December
01	10:44 LI	01:36 SA	15:02 CP	07:14 AQ	01:57 PI	10:43 TA	05:16 GE	01:20 LE	12:56 VI	23:12 SC	10:21 SA	03:12 AQ
02												
03	14:36 SC		01:07 AQ	19:12 PI	14:52 AR	20:49 GE	12:11 CA	02:50 VI	12:54 LI	23:54 SA	12:22 CP	11:35 PI
04		09:27 CP										
05	20:13 SA		13:07 PI				16:13 LE	03:49 LI	13:16 SC		18:03 AQ	23:26 AR
06		19:21 AQ		08:11 AR	03:12 TA	04:02 CA				03:29 CP		
07							18:45 VI	05:45 SC	15:36 SA			
08	03:30 CP		02:01 AR	20:39 TA	13:34 GE	09:01 LE				10:44 AQ	03:45 PI	12:28 TA
09		06:58 PI					21:07 LI	09:29 SA	20:46 CP			
10	12:42 AQ		14:45 TA		21:33 CA	12:41 VI				21:18 PI	16:13 AR	00:08 GE
11		19:49 AR		07:33 GE				15:15 CP				
12						15:44 LI	00:07 SC		04:52 AQ			
13	00:03 PI		01:53 GE	16:04 CA	03:23 LE			23:07 AQ		09:50 AR	05:13 TA	09:20 CA
14		08:36 TA				18:32 SC	04:04 SA		15:26 PI			
15	12:55 AR		09:58 CA	21:44 LE	07:18 VI					22:49 TA	17:01 GE	16:17 LE
16		19:10 GE				21:34 SA	09:17 CP	09:10 PI				
17			14:15 LE		09:41 LI				03:43 AR			21:35 VI
18	01:15 TA			00:34 VI			16:22 AQ	21:15 AR		10:59 GE	02:53 CA	
19		01:47 CA	15:20 VI		11:12 SC	01:44 CP			16:45 TA			
20	10:32 GE			01:23 LI						21:18 CA	10:39 LE	01:37 LI
21		04:20 LE	14:47 LI		13:00 SA	08:15 AQ	01:58 PI	10:17 TA				
22	15:35 CA			01:33 SC					05:05 GE		16:11 VI	04:30 SC
23		04:12 VI	14:33 SC		16:35 CP	17:55 PI	14:02 AR	22:13 GE		04:51 LE		
24	17:11 LE			02:48 SA					14:57 CA		19:25 LI	06:36 SA
25		03:29 LI	16:31 SA		23:19 AQ					09:10 VI		
26	17:13 VI			06:50 CP		06:13 AR	02:57 TA	06:54 CA	21:09 LE		20:45 SC	08:58 CP
27		04:14 SC	21:59 CP							10:37 LI		
28	17:43 LI			14:39 AQ	09:39 PI	18:52 TA	14:05 GE	11:31 LE	23:42 VI		21:18 SA	13:09 AQ
29		07:54 SA								10:25 SC		
30	20:18 SC				22:18 AR		21:33 CA		23:47 LI		22:50 CP	
31												

1941

	January	February	March	April	May	June	July	August	September	October	November	December
01	20:35 PI			08:07 GE	01:57 CA	00:38 VI	11:17 LI	22:50 SA	11:39 AQ	00:18 PI		21:59 GE
02		04:41 TA	12:23 TA								03:19 TA	
03	07:35 AR			19:44 CA	11:34 LE	05:17 LI	14:34 SC	01:17 CP	17:52 PI	09:38 AR		10:21 CA
04		17:09 GE	01:12 GE								15:52 GE	
05					18:06 VI	07:13 SC	16:14 SA	04:32 AQ		20:53 TA		
06	20:29 TA	02:57 CA	12:04 CA	04:26 LE					02:29 AR			21:43 LE
07					21:11 LI	07:24 SA	17:21 CP	09:51 PI			04:25 CA	
08	08:27 GE		19:19 LE	09:22 VI					13:33 TA	09:23 GE		07:13 VI
09		09:07 LE			21:33 SC	07:32 CP	19:36 AQ	18:13 AR			15:49 LE	
10				10:55 LI						21:53 CA		
11	17:33 CA	12:21 VI	22:52 VI		20:49 SA	09:42 AQ			02:06 GE			13:47 LI
12				10:32 SC			00:42 PI	05:32 TA			00:29 VI	
13	23:39 LE	14:08 LI	23:52 LI		21:04 CP	15:34 PI			14:10 CA	08:29 LE		16:52 SC
14				10:08 SA			09:34 AR	18:10 GE			05:22 LI	
15		15:53 SC	00:03 SC							15:36 VI		17:10 SA
16	03:45 VI			11:38 CP	00:15 AQ	01:31 AR	21:29 TA		23:36 LE		06:40 SC	
17			01:08 SA					05:38 CA				16:27 CP
18	06:59 LI	18:37 SA		16:31 AQ	07:34 PI	14:03 TA			05:29 VI	18:54 LI	05:54 SA	
19			04:25 CP				10:09 GE	14:16 LE				16:53 AQ
20	10:04 SC	22:54 CP			18:35 AR					19:26 SC	05:12 CP	
21			10:34 AQ	01:07 PI		02:44 GE	21:15 CA	19:53 VI	08:17 LI			20:32 PI
22	13:17 SA	05:02 AQ								19:01 SA	06:46 AQ	
23				12:35 AR	07:27 TA	13:51 CA		23:22 LI	09:23 SC			
24	17:01 CP		19:30 PI				05:48 LE			19:40 CP	12:09 PI	04:24 AR
25		13:18 PI			20:11 GE				10:24 SA			
26	22:06 AQ		06:39 AR	01:23 TA		22:55 LE	12:04 VI	01:49 SC		23:03 AQ	21:26 AR	15:43 TA
27		23:54 AR							12:44 CP			
28				14:12 GE	07:37 CA		16:41 LI	04:13 SA				
29	05:35 PI		19:14 TA			06:03 VI			17:17 AQ	05:52 PI	09:18 TA	04:27 GE
30					17:15 LE			07:18 CP				
31	16:02 AR						20:10 SC			15:39 AR		

502

1942

	January	February	March	April	May	June	July	August	September	October	November	December
01	16:42 CA		03:06 VI	19:55 SC	06:04 SA	15:59 AQ	03:46 PI	01:48 TA	20:40 GE	17:03 CA		18:55 LI
02		18:58 VI									01:19 VI	
03	03:33 LE		08:23 LI	21:05 SA	06:05 CP	19:14 PI	09:11 AR	12:54 GE				00:06 SC
04		01:18 LI							08:59 CA	05:36 LE	09:21 LI	
05	12:43 VI		11:50 SC	22:42 CP	07:56 AQ	02:11 AR	18:23 TA					01:34 SA
06		05:56 SC							21:15 LE	16:14 VI	13:27 SC	
07	19:49 LI		14:28 SA	01:57 AQ	12:44 PI	12:16 TA	06:11 GE	01:30 CA				01:07 CP
08		09:06 SA								23:33 LI	14:47 SA	
09			17:09 CP	07:20 PI	20:31 AR		18:52 CA	13:39 LE	07:31 VI			00:57 AQ
10		11:19 CP				00:12 GE					15:18 CP	
11	00:24 SC		20:31 AQ						15:06 LI	03:46 SC		02:56 PI
12		13:28 AQ				12:50 CA	07:08 LE	00:09 VI			16:48 AQ	
13	02:31 SA			14:49 AR	06:37 TA				20:19 SC	06:10 SA		08:05 AR
14						01:20 LE	18:08 VI	08:31 LI			20:28 PI	
15	03:07 CP	16:51 PI	01:09 PI	00:18 TA	18:15 GE				23:58 SA	08:13 CP		16:17 TA
16								14:38 SC				
17	03:52 AQ	22:47 AR	07:41 AR	11:36 GE	06:49 CA		03:02 LI			11:01 AQ	02:31 AR	
18						12:34 VI		18:35 SA	02:48 CP			02:46 GE
19	06:43 PI		16:39 TA		19:22 LE		09:02 SC			15:05 PI	10:38 TA	
20	13:08 AR	07:58 TA		00:10 CA		21:04 LI		20:47 CP	05:27 AQ			14:45 CA
21		19:48 GE	04:00 GE				11:58 SA			20:37 AR	20:35 GE	
22				12:22 LE	06:08 VI			22:08 AQ	08:34 PI			
23	23:19 TA		16:33 CA			01:50 SC	12:38 CP					03:35 LE
24		08:16 CA		22:03 VI	13:22 LI			23:55 PI	12:57 AR	03:52 TA	08:17 CA	
25						03:08 SA	12:37 AQ					16:10 VI
26	11:44 GE	19:06 LE	04:04 LE		16:32 SC			03:39 AR	19:34 TA	13:19 GE	21:09 LE	
27				03:51 LI		02:30 CP	13:49 PI					
28					16:39 SA							
29	00:04 CA		12:36 VI	05:59 SC		02:01 AQ		10:29 TA	05:05 GE	01:01 CA	09:29 VI	02:45 LI
30												
31	10:37 LE		17:37 LI		15:44 CP		17:56 AR			13:49 LE		

1943

	January	February	March	April	May	June	July	August	September	October	November	December
01	09:40 SC	23:16 CP	07:19 CP	18:27 PI	04:40 AR		17:13 CA		18:33 LI	10:05 SC		13:01 AQ
02						00:29 GE					03:37 CP	
03	12:34 SA	23:10 AQ	08:56 AQ	21:18 AR	09:57 TA			00:46 VI		17:03 SA		15:36 PI
04						10:45 CA	05:40 LE		04:20 SC		07:10 AQ	
05	12:35 CP	23:07 PI	09:54 PI		17:16 GE			12:51 LI		22:12 CP		18:59 AR
06				01:38 TA		23:03 LE	18:46 VI		11:39 SA		10:16 PI	
07	11:42 AQ		11:41 AR					22:40 SC				23:30 TA
08		00:59 AR		08:42 GE	03:17 CA				16:14 CP	01:40 AQ	13:10 AR	
09	12:03 PI		15:53 TA			12:04 VI	06:45 LI					
10		06:17 TA		19:03 CA	15:39 LE			05:08 SA	18:19 AQ	03:45 PI	16:32 TA	05:33 GE
11	15:21 AR		23:39 GE			23:23 LI	15:41 SC					
12		15:25 GE						08:09 CP	18:47 PI	05:12 AR	21:31 GE	13:47 CA
13	22:21 TA			07:40 LE	04:22 VI		20:37 SA					
14			10:51 CA			06:59 SC		08:36 AQ	19:09 AR	07:26 TA		
15		03:25 CA		19:59 VI	14:44 LI		22:07 CP				05:23 CA	00:37 LE
16	08:38 GE		23:42 LE			10:37 SA		08:07 PI	21:15 TA	12:06 GE		
17		16:19 LE			21:20 SC		21:46 AQ				16:28 LE	13:23 VI
18	20:53 CA			05:41 LI		11:30 CP		08:33 AR		20:28 CA		
19			11:43 VI				21:30 PI		02:42 GE			
20		04:21 VI		12:04 SC	00:34 SA	11:34 AQ		11:40 TA			05:22 VI	01:55 LI
21	09:44 LE		21:21 LI				23:08 AR		12:10 CA	08:12 LE		
22		14:30 LI		15:56 SA	02:00 CP	12:36 PI		18:35 GE			17:19 LI	11:46 SC
23	22:03 VI									21:10 VI		
24		22:25 SC	04:22 SC	18:40 CP	03:24 AQ	15:52 AR	03:53 TA		00:33 LE			17:44 SA
25								05:07 CA			02:10 SC	
26	08:48 LI		09:23 SA	21:22 AQ	05:58 PI	21:52 TA	12:04 GE		13:30 VI	08:38 LI		20:24 CP
27		03:59 SA						17:49 LE			07:35 SA	
28	16:51 SC		13:05 CP		10:16 AR		23:04 CA			17:15 SC		21:21 AQ
29				00:36 PI		06:27 GE			00:56 LI		10:43 CP	
30	21:35 SA		15:57 AQ		16:25 TA			06:47 VI		23:15 SA		22:17 PI
31							11:44 LE					

1944

Day	January	February	March	April	May	June	July	August	September	October	November	December
01	00:34 AR	17:17 GE	00:05 GE		23:05 VI			14:43 CP		14:30 AR		15:16 CA
02				02:55 LE			23:39 SA		04:14 PI		01:29 GE	
03	04:59 TA		08:38 CA			06:32 SC		17:11 AQ		13:46 TA		21:53 LE
04		02:40 CA		15:50 VI	11:40 LI				03:27 AR		05:04 CA	
05	11:45 GE		20:19 LE			14:28 SA	04:43 CP	17:35 PI		14:59 GE		
06		14:20 LE			22:18 SC				03:29 TA		12:44 LE	08:04 VI
07	20:48 CA			04:23 LI		19:42 CP	07:15 AQ	17:43 AR		19:57 CA		
08			09:19 VI						06:14 GE		23:59 VI	20:29 LI
09		03:08 VI		15:12 SC	06:27 SA	23:13 AQ	08:39 PI	19:19 TA				
10	07:58 LE		21:56 LI						12:47 CA	05:04 LE		
11		15:54 LI			12:33 CP		10:19 AR	23:38 GE			12:44 LI	08:43 SC
12	20:38 VI			00:03 SA		01:59 PI			22:51 LE	17:05 VI		
13			09:13 SC		17:10 AQ		13:16 TA					18:51 SA
14		03:24 SC		06:56 CP		04:41 AR		07:03 CA			00:48 SC	
15	09:29 LI		18:32 SA		20:35 PI		18:11 GE		11:01 VI	05:55 LI		
16		12:16 SA		11:46 AQ		07:52 TA		17:08 LE			11:02 SA	02:22 CP
17	20:28 SC				23:04 AR				23:48 LI	18:03 SC		
18		17:34 CP	01:14 CP	14:28 PI		12:11 GE	01:21 CA				19:21 CP	07:44 AQ
19								05:01 VI				
20	03:54 SA	19:28 AQ	04:56 AQ	15:36 AR	01:16 TA	18:28 CA	10:51 LE		12:11 SC	04:50 SA		11:39 PI
21								17:46 LI			01:48 AQ	
22	07:27 CP	19:09 PI	05:59 PI	16:29 TA	04:27 GE		22:25 VI		23:16 SA	13:49 CP		14:42 AR
23						03:25 LE					06:19 PI	
24	08:10 AQ	18:31 AR	05:42 AR	18:59 GE	10:04 CA			06:14 SC		20:20 AQ		17:24 TA
25						14:58 VI	11:08 LI		07:55 CP		08:57 AR	
26	07:48 PI	19:36 TA	06:01 TA		19:05 LE			16:52 SA		23:54 PI		20:26 GE
27				00:49 CA			23:17 SC		13:10 AQ		10:22 TA	
28	08:15 AR		08:58 GE			03:40 LI						
29				10:37 LE	06:59 VI			00:12 CP	14:58 PI	00:54 AR	11:55 GE	00:44 CA
30	11:07 TA		15:59 CA			15:11 SC	08:51 SA					
31					19:38 LI			03:44 AQ		00:46 TA		07:19 LE

1945

	January	February	March	April	May	June	July	August	September	October	November	December
01	16:50 VI			03:08 SA		15:25 PI	00:30 AR	11:23 GE		17:34 VI		
02			08:32 SC						03:19 LE		22:29 SC	17:30 SA
03		01:23 SC		13:52 CP	04:06 AQ	18:51 AR	03:05 TA	15:23 CA				
04	04:45 LI		20:45 SA						11:36 VI	04:17 LI		
05		12:57 SA		21:29 AQ	09:21 PI	20:23 TA	05:20 GE	20:52 LE			11:18 SA	05:24 CP
06	17:14 SC								21:49 LI	16:24 SC		
07		21:29 CP	06:38 CP		11:25 AR	21:15 GE	08:11 CA				23:35 CP	15:35 AQ
08				01:11 PI				04:24 VI				
09	03:56 SA		12:41 AQ		11:24 TA	23:02 CA	12:44 LE		09:48 SC	05:18 SA		23:21 PI
10		02:12 AQ		01:38 AR				14:21 LI			09:59 AQ	
11	11:28 CP		14:51 PI		11:12 GE		19:58 VI		22:38 SA	17:33 CP		
12		03:53 PI		00:40 TA		03:21 LE					17:05 PI	04:16 AR
13	15:57 AQ		14:33 AR		12:51 CA			02:25 SC				
14		04:13 AR		00:31 GE		11:08 VI	06:12 LI		10:12 CP	03:06 AQ	20:25 AR	06:30 TA
15	18:27 PI		13:55 TA		17:57 LE			14:56 SA				
16		05:06 TA		03:14 CA		22:07 LI	18:29 SC		18:20 AQ	08:34 PI	20:48 TA	07:03 GE
17	20:21 AR		15:05 GE									
18		08:02 GE		09:52 LE	02:57 VI			01:31 CP	22:19 PI	10:09 AR	20:03 GE	07:27 CA
19	22:48 TA		19:32 CA			10:36 SC	06:36 SA					
20		13:43 CA		20:03 VI	14:44 LI			08:33 AQ	23:11 AR	09:30 TA	20:14 CA	09:30 LE
21						22:27 SA	16:29 CP					
22	02:35 GE	21:59 LE	03:32 LE					12:06 PI	22:53 TA	08:50 GE	23:12 LE	14:43 VI
23				08:15 LI	03:21 SC		23:17 AQ					
24	08:06 CA		14:11 VI			08:14 CP		13:30 AR	23:31 GE	10:11 CA		23:45 LI
25		08:14 VI		20:53 SC	15:12 SA						05:59 VI	
26	15:33 LE					15:36 AQ	03:27 PI	14:34 TA		14:56 LE		
27		19:57 LI	02:15 LI						02:38 CA		16:18 LI	11:43 SC
28				08:57 SA		20:51 PI	06:08 AR	16:47 GE		23:13 VI		
29	01:09 VI		14:50 SC						08:47 LE			
30				19:41 CP	09:35 AQ		08:29 TA	20:59 CA			04:43 SC	00:33 SA
31	12:46 LI									10:08 LI		

1946

Day	January	February	March	April	May	June	July	August	September	October	November	December
01	12:12 CP	05:24 AQ		09:17 AR				12:05 LI			10:37 AQ	04:29 PI
02			20:25 PI		20:04 GE	06:29 CA	20:45 VI	21:23 SC	17:31 SA	14:30 CP	20:32 PI	12:05 AR
03	21:39 AQ	11:33 PI		09:57 TA								15:49 TA
04		15:38 AR	23:23 AR		20:23 CA	07:39 LE	03:21 LI		06:24 CP	02:28 AQ	02:28 AR	
05	04:48 PI			10:26 GE				09:36 SA				15:49 TA
06					23:05 LE	11:57 VI			17:42 AQ	11:10 PI	04:49 TA	
07		18:47 TA	01:08 TA	12:22 CA			13:42 SC	22:23 CP				16:30 GE
08	09:56 AR				04:57 VI	19:57 LI			01:46 PI	16:05 AR	05:07 GE	
09		21:45 GE	03:12 GE	16:38 LE			02:21 SA	09:24 AQ				15:50 CA
10	13:25 TA									18:21 TA	05:15 CA	
11			06:29 CA	23:20 VI	13:53 LI	07:05 SC	15:06 CP		06:49 AR			15:47 LE
12	15:42 GE	00:59 CA						17:41 PI		19:36 GE	06:53 LE	
13			11:15 LE		01:09 SC	19:51 SA			10:04 TA			18:09 VI
14	17:32 CA	04:51 LE		08:13 LI			02:17 AQ	23:37 AR		21:23 CA	11:05 VI	
15			17:33 VI			08:40 CP			12:46 GE			
16	20:03 LE	10:03 VI		19:03 SC	13:46 SA		11:15 PI	03:59 TA		00:35 LE	18:13 LI	00:08 LI
17						20:16 AQ			15:42 CA			
18		17:37 LI	01:41 LI	07:30 SA	02:43 CP		17:59 AR	07:23 GE		05:35 VI		09:44 SC
19	00:40 VI										03:59 SC	
20			12:05 SC			05:43 PI	22:35 TA			12:33 LI		21:49 SA
21	08:32 LI	04:06 SC		20:29 CP	14:32 AQ				23:38 VI		15:44 SA	
22						12:20 AR		12:38 LE				
23		16:42 SA	00:31 SA	07:57 AQ	23:39 PI		01:19 GE			21:41 SC	04:40 CP	10:50 CP
24	19:41 SC					15:56 TA		15:54 VI	05:40 LI			
25			13:18 CP				02:44 CA			09:04 SA		23:29 AQ
26		05:02 CP		15:55 PI	05:05 AR	17:07 GE			14:12 SC		17:30 AQ	
27	08:28 SA		23:51 AQ				03:58 LE	21:15 LI				
28		14:34 AQ		19:46 AR	07:04 TA	17:10 CA				22:00 CP		10:43 PI
29	20:19 CP								01:33 SA			
30			06:26 PI	20:32 TA	06:55 GE	17:48 LE	06:33 VI	05:49 SC				
31												19:31 AR

1947

Day	January	February	March	April	May	June	July	August	September	October	November	December
01	01:07 TA		20:59 CA		19:24 LI			07:50 AQ				
02		13:39 CA		08:31 VI		18:54 SA	13:03 CP		12:02 AR	02:16 TA	17:32 CA	02:30 LE
03	03:27 GE		22:59 LE					19:49 PI				
04		14:01 LE		12:40 LI	02:36 SC					07:44 GE	20:04 LE	04:23 VI
05	03:28 CA					06:52 CP	01:50 AQ					
06		14:42 VI	00:47 VI	18:57 SC				06:20 AR		11:48 CA	22:55 VI	08:14 LI
07	02:54 LE				12:09 SA		14:04 PI		02:18 GE			
08		17:39 LI	03:51 LI		23:55 CP			14:43 TA		14:42 LE		14:25 SC
09	03:45 VI			04:13 SA					06:13 CA		02:42 LI	
10			09:51 SC			07:48 PI	00:35 AR	20:17 GE		16:57 VI		22:50 SA
11	07:54 LI	00:28 SC		16:09 CP	12:41 AQ				08:04 LE		08:02 SC	
12			19:35 SA			17:35 AR	08:12 TA	22:50 CA		19:32 LI		
13	16:15 SC	11:16 SA							08:51 VI		15:34 SA	09:15 CP
14				04:51 AQ	00:20 PI	23:46 TA	12:17 GE	23:06 LE		23:46 SC		
15			08:01 CP						10:17 LI			21:16 AQ
16	04:03 SA	00:13 CP		15:47 PI	08:57 AR			22:49 VI			01:38 CP	
17			20:36 AQ			02:22 GE	13:14 CA		14:11 SC	06:53 SA		
18	17:11 CP	12:39 AQ		23:25 AR	13:52 TA		12:34 LE				13:46 AQ	09:59 PI
19						02:33 CA		00:04 LI	21:50 SA	17:14 CP		
20		22:58 PI	06:58 PI		15:52 GE		12:19 VI					21:37 AR
21	05:38 AQ			03:56 TA		02:07 LE		04:45 SC			02:17 PI	
22			14:23 AR		16:27 CA		14:33 LI		08:57 CP	05:39 AQ		
23	16:24 PI	06:58 AR		06:28 GE		03:01 VI		13:35 SA			12:54 AR	06:11 TA
24			19:29 TA		17:19 LE		20:41 SC		21:37 AQ	17:46 PI		
25		13:08 TA		08:23 CA		06:51 LI					20:06 TA	10:47 GE
26	01:11 AR		23:16 GE					01:31 CP				
27		17:47 GE		10:45 LE		14:17 SC	06:41 SA			03:32 AR	23:55 GE	12:03 CA
28								14:18 AQ				
29	07:46 TA		02:26 CA	14:16 VI	00:54 LI				18:58 AR	10:17 TA		11:42 LE
30						00:46 SA					01:31 CA	
31	11:53 GE		05:22 LE		08:42 SC			02:03 PI		14:36 GE		11:47 VI

1948

	January	February	March	April	May	June	July	August	September	October	November	December
01		02:28 SC	17:41 SA			15:55 AR	10:40 TA	07:21 CA	18:20 VI	04:30 LI	18:11 SA	
02	14:10 LI			23:19 AQ	19:44 PI							09:16 CP
03		10:26 SA					17:48 GE	08:13 LE	17:35 LI	04:59 SC	23:40 CP	
04	19:52 SC		03:51 CP			01:43 TA						17:32 AQ
05		21:30 CP		11:57 PI	07:28 AR		21:07 CA	07:32 VI	18:34 SC	07:56 SA		
06			16:14 AQ			08:06 GE					08:41 AQ	
07	04:41 SA			23:29 AR	16:48 TA		21:54 LE	07:29 LI	22:52 SA	14:32 CP		04:46 PI
08		09:59 AQ				11:29 CA					20:33 PI	
09	15:42 CP		04:53 PI		23:20 GE		22:04 VI	09:56 SC				17:30 AR
10		22:37 PI		08:59 TA		13:12 LE			06:57 CP	00:42 AQ		
11			16:34 AR				23:31 LI	15:49 SA			09:12 AR	
12	03:54 AQ			16:20 GE	03:38 CA	14:49 VI			17:59 AQ	13:03 PI		05:09 TA
13		10:37 AR									20:25 TA	
14	16:35 PI		02:41 TA	21:41 CA	06:39 LE	17:34 LI	03:28 SC	00:52 CP				13:45 GE
15		21:08 TA							06:27 PI	01:36 AR		
16			10:46 GE		09:15 VI	22:04 SC	10:11 SA	12:03 AQ			05:03 GE	19:01 CA
17	04:44 AR			01:16 LE					19:02 AR	12:54 TA		
18		04:57 GE	16:14 CA		12:08 LI		19:13 CP				11:12 CA	
19	14:42 TA			03:30 VI		04:29 SA		00:24 PI		22:15 GE		22:03 LE
20		09:10 CA	18:58 LE		15:56 SC				06:45 TA		15:33 LE	
21	21:02 GE			05:16 LI		12:51 CP	06:02 AQ	13:06 AR				00:19 VI
22		10:07 LE	19:42 VI		21:22 SA				16:40 GE	05:22 CA	18:49 VI	
23	23:24 CA			07:50 SC		23:15 AQ	18:13 PI					02:59 LI
24		09:22 VI	20:01 LI					01:04 TA	23:46 CA	10:10 LE	21:33 LI	
25	23:00 LE			12:32 SA	05:08 CP							
26		09:05 LI	21:49 SC			11:23 PI	06:58 AR	10:40 GE		12:54 VI		06:38 SC
27	21:57 VI			20:22 CP	15:31 AQ				03:35 LE		00:19 SC	
28		11:24 SC				23:56 AR	18:35 TA	16:34 CA		14:16 LI		11:29 SA
29	22:30 LI		02:47 SA						04:41 VI		03:52 SA	
30				07:17 AQ	03:46 PI							
31			11:34 CP				03:02 GE	18:41 LE		15:32 SC		17:47 CP

509

1949

	January	February	March	April	May	June	July	August	September	October	November	December
01	02:08 AQ	09:04 AR	15:35 AR	22:03 GE	12:44 CA	00:36 LE	13:22 LI	01:25 SA	12:05 CP	01:14 AQ	05:35 AR	01:22 TA
02	12:59 PI				19:11 LE	04:53 VI	16:22 SC	06:36 CP	19:37 AQ	11:20 PI	18:37 TA	13:29 GE
03		21:57 TA	04:33 TA		23:11 VI	07:58 LI	19:46 SA	13:34 AQ				
04				07:11 CA		10:14 SC		22:45 PI	05:26 PI	23:28 AR		23:32 CA
05			16:05 GE				00:03 CP				06:55 GE	
06	01:41 AR	08:40 GE		12:59 LE	01:07 LI	12:24 SA	06:09 AQ		17:14 AR	12:27 TA		
07							15:01 PI	10:20 AR			17:35 CA	07:28 LE
08	14:03 TA				01:53 SC	15:40 CP		23:18 TA				
09	23:31 GE			15:32 VI			02:43 AR		06:13 TA	01:02 GE		
10		15:22 CA	00:22 CA		02:57 SA	21:27 AQ	15:36 TA				02:00 LE	13:32 VI
11		18:01 LE	04:34 LE	15:48 LI				11:23 GE	18:47 GE	11:51 CA		
12					05:57 CP						07:43 VI	17:46 LI
13	04:57 CA	18:06 VI	05:24 VI	15:27 SC		06:39 PI	02:57 GE	20:16 CA		19:35 LE		
14			04:40 LI		12:19 AQ		10:52 CA		04:52 CA		10:36 LI	20:14 SC
15	07:07 LE	17:44 LI		16:23 SA			15:19 LE			23:42 VI		
16		18:53 SC	04:26 SC		22:27 PI	18:45 AR	17:36 VI		11:05 LE		11:19 SC	21:32 SA
17	07:52 VI			20:16 CP			19:20 LI	01:08 LE				
18			06:31 SA						13:34 VI	00:48 LI	11:16 SA	23:00 CP
19	09:03 LI	22:50 SA		03:59 AQ			21:44 SC	02:56 VI				
20						07:30 TA			13:41 LI	00:19 SC		
21	11:59 SC		12:05 CP	15:08 PI	11:03 AR			03:24 LI			12:20 LI	02:24 AQ
22		05:51 CP	21:10 AQ			18:20 GE			13:20 SC	00:08 SA		
23	17:09 SA	15:26 AQ			23:42 TA			04:19 SC			16:25 AQ	09:20 PI
24				04:01 AR					14:21 SA	02:11 CP		
25						02:01 CA		07:00 SA				20:05 AR
26	00:22 CP		08:50 PI	16:42 TA	10:27 GE				18:07 CP	07:51 AQ	00:35 PI	
27		02:54 PI				07:01 LE						
28	09:27 AQ		21:41 AR		18:39 CA					17:22 PI	12:18 AR	08:58 TA
29				03:49 GE		10:27 VI						
30	20:27 PI											21:13 GE
31			10:29 TA									

510

1950

Day	January	February	March	April	May	June	July	August	September	October	November	December
01		22:34 LE	08:30 LE						02:19 TA			21:53 VI
02	06:57 CA			00:41 LI				07:03 AR			05:38 LE	
03			12:24 VI		10:51 SA	23:18 AQ	13:52 PI		14:45 GE	10:59 CA		
04	13:58 LE	02:36 VI		00:36 SC				18:06 TA			14:21 VI	04:29 LI
05			13:59 LI		11:08 CP		22:25 AR			21:41 LE		
06	19:06 VI	05:19 LI		00:38 SA		04:57 PI			02:54 CA		19:10 LI	07:20 SC
07			14:55 SC		14:22 AQ			06:44 GE				
08	23:09 LI	07:50 SC		02:30 CP		14:44 AR	10:14 TA		12:35 LE	04:54 VI	20:29 SC	07:17 SA
09			16:38 SA		21:34 PI			18:27 CA				
10		10:51 SA		07:25 AQ			23:02 GE		18:55 VI	08:29 LI	19:51 SA	06:17 CP
11	02:28 SC		20:07 CP			03:13 TA						
12		14:45 CP		15:38 PI	08:18 AR			03:36 LE	22:28 LI	09:31 SC	19:25 CP	06:35 AQ
13	05:16 SA					16:06 GE	10:34 CA					
14		19:58 AQ	01:53 AQ		20:59 TA			10:03 VI		09:44 SA	21:15 AQ	10:11 PI
15	08:06 CP			02:31 AR			19:52 LE		00:27 SC			
16			09:59 PI			03:46 CA		14:31 LI		10:55 CP		17:59 AR
17	12:07 AQ	03:11 PI		14:59 TA	09:53 GE				02:13 SA		02:39 PI	
18			20:21 AR			13:38 LE	03:05 VI	17:50 SC		14:27 AQ		
19	18:41 PI	13:01 AR			21:51 CA				04:49 CP		11:40 AR	05:10 TA
20				03:54 GE		21:32 VI	08:34 LI	20:36 SA		20:53 PI		
21			08:32 TA						08:59 AQ		23:08 TA	17:49 GE
22	04:38 AR	01:12 TA		16:02 CA	08:07 LE		12:27 SC	23:24 CP				
23			21:28 GE			03:09 LI			15:09 PI	05:59 AR		
24	17:09 TA	14:03 GE			15:51 VI		14:56 SA				11:39 GE	06:18 CA
25				01:58 LE		06:19 SC		02:53 AQ	23:32 AR	17:03 TA		
26			09:17 CA		20:26 LI		16:40 CP					17:45 LE
27	05:44 GE	01:03 CA		08:31 VI		07:26 SA		08:02 PI			00:13 CA	
28			18:04 LE		22:01 SC		18:56 AQ		10:08 TA	05:23 GE		
29	15:51 CA			11:26 LI		07:48 CP		15:45 AR			12:02 LE	03:41 VI
30			23:01 VI		21:43 SA		23:19 PI		22:27 GE	18:04 CA		
31												11:21 LI

1951

	January	February	March	April	May	June	July	August	September	October	November	December
01		01:17 SA				02:33 TA		03:08 LE		18:24 SC	05:20 SA	15:45 AQ
02	15:59 SC		09:29 CP	22:45 PI	11:27 AR		08:28 CA		05:32 LI			
03		02:53 CP				14:03 GE		14:18 VI		21:49 SA	06:40 CP	18:08 PI
04	17:39 SA		12:11 AQ	05:16 AR	20:47 TA		21:01 LE		11:49 SC			
05		04:04 AQ				02:31 CA		23:34 LI		00:31 CP	08:43 AQ	23:18 AR
06			15:46 PI	13:53 TA	07:51 GE		08:37 VI		16:11 SA			
07	17:32 CP	06:29 PI				15:12 LE		06:24 SC		03:20 AQ	12:23 PI	07:05 TA
08			21:16 AR						19:07 CP			
09	17:36 AQ			00:41 GE	20:13 CA	02:47 VI	18:05 LI	10:31 SA		06:47 PI	17:53 AR	16:55 GE
10		11:43 AR							21:12 AQ			
11	19:56 PI		05:33 TA	13:05 CA	08:49 LE	11:31 LI	00:19 SC	12:18 CP			01:07 TA	
12		20:33 TA								11:20 AR		
13	02:05 AR		16:37 GE	01:18 LE	19:44 VI		03:03 SA	12:53 AQ	23:22 PI		10:15 GE	17:05 LE
14		08:18 GE				16:17 SC				17:37 TA		
15			05:07 CA				03:14 CP		02:48 AR		21:28 CA	
16	12:10 TA	20:52 CA		11:07 VI	03:05 LI	17:26 SA		13:53 PI		02:22 GE		05:52 VI
17			16:45 LE						08:42 TA			
18	00:36 GE	08:02 LE		17:13 LI	06:24 SC	16:38 CP	02:41 AQ	16:59 AR			10:13 LE	16:41 LI
19			01:39 VI							13:43 CA		
20	13:06 CA	16:43 VI		19:55 SC	06:44 SA	16:04 AQ	03:29 PI	23:27 TA	17:47 GE		22:36 VI	23:39 SC
21			07:21 LI							02:25 LE		
22				20:40 SA	06:08 CP	17:49 PI	07:22 AR	09:28 GE	05:34 CA		08:09 LI	02:27 SA
23	00:12 LE	23:01 LI								14:02 VI		
24			10:35 SC	21:20 CP		23:13 AR						
25	09:27 VI	03:31 SC			06:42 AQ		15:07 TA	21:44 CA	18:07 LE		13:32 SC	02:24 CP
26			12:40 SA							22:26 LI		
27	16:47 LI	06:49 SA		23:33 AQ	10:05 PI	08:17 TA	02:08 GE	10:10 LE	05:06 VI		15:20 SA	02:24 CP
28			14:51 CP									
29				04:14 PI		19:52 GE	14:43 CA	20:59 VI	13:09 LI	03:10 SC	15:22 CP	
30	22:04 SC				16:53 AR							01:36 AQ
31			18:02 AQ									

1952

	January	February	March	April	May	June	July	August	September	October	November	December
01	02:10 PI	19:51 TA		07:39 CA	04:13 LE		05:26 SC		09:03 AQ	19:35 AR	06:59 TA	03:08 CA
02			12:36 GE			12:26 LI		22:28 CP				
03	05:42 AR	04:55 GE		20:11 LE	16:58 VI		10:27 SA		08:59 PI	21:06 TA	11:02 GE	
04			23:40 CA			20:19 SC						13:23 LE
05	12:44 TA	16:44 CA					12:03 CP		08:57 AR			
06				08:41 VI	03:39 LI			22:05 PI		01:15 GE	18:12 CA	01:58 VI
07			12:30 LE			00:21 SA	11:55 AQ		10:48 TA		04:56 LE	
08	22:43 GE	05:36 LE		18:56 LI	10:49 SC			22:33 AR		09:16 CA		
09			00:52 VI			01:47 CP	11:59 PI		16:07 GE		17:47 VI	14:36 LI
10	10:34 CA			02:13 SC	14:50 SA					20:50 LE		
11		18:02 VI	11:17 LI			02:27 AQ	13:56 AR	01:46 TA				00:40 SC
12	23:19 LE			07:08 SA	17:09 CP				01:25 CA		05:57 LI	
13			19:21 SC			04:01 PI	18:45 TA	08:37 GE		09:51 VI		07:00 SA
14		05:00 LI		10:41 CP	19:14 AQ				13:39 LE		15:19 SC	
15	12:00 VI		01:16 SA			07:29 AR		18:53 CA				10:17 CP
16		13:45 SC		13:43 AQ	22:06 PI		02:37 GE		02:42 VI	21:44 LI	21:34 SA	
17	23:19 LI		05:19 CP			13:11 TA						12:02 AQ
18		19:43 SA		16:40 PI			13:05 CA	07:20 LE	14:41 LI		01:41 CP	
19			07:55 AQ		02:08 AR	21:03 GE				07:10 SC		13:46 PI
20	07:44 SC	22:50 CP		19:57 AR				20:23 VI			04:52 AQ	
21			09:39 PI		07:30 TA		01:20 LE		00:43 SC	14:12 SA		16:30 AR
22	12:22 SA	23:49 AQ				07:04 CA					07:55 PI	
23			11:34 AR	00:15 TA	14:38 GE		14:25 VI	08:42 LI	08:33 SA	19:29 CP		20:46 TA
24	13:39 CP	00:01 PI				19:02 LE					11:09 AR	
25			15:05 TA	06:41 GE				19:10 SC	14:06 CP	23:29 AQ		
26	13:07 AQ	01:12 AR			00:06 CA		02:55 LI				14:54 TA	02:48 GE
27				16:06 CA		08:06 VI			17:24 AQ	02:24 PI		
28	12:46 PI	05:01 TA			11:59 LE		13:05 SC	02:53 SA			19:53 GE	
29			21:36 GE			20:18 LI			18:53 PI	04:35 AR		
30	14:33 AR							07:24 CP				
31					00:57 VI		19:38 SA					10:54 CA

1953

Day	January	February	March	April	May	June	July	August	September	October	November	December
01	21:18 LE			05:20 SC		14:45 AQ	00:09 PI	10:57 TA	03:30 CA	18:54 LE		21:30 SC
02		05:32 LI	11:41 LI		03:55 CP						01:51 LI	
03		17:21 SC	23:31 SC	14:59 SA		18:12 PI	02:24 AR	15:11 GE	13:05 LE	06:41 VI		
04	09:42 VI										14:12 SC	08:09 SA
05				22:30 CP	09:13 AQ	21:01 AR	05:24 TA			19:29 LI		
06	22:37 LI							21:59 CA	00:47 VI			16:33 CP
07		09:20 SA	09:20 SA		12:47 PI	23:42 TA	09:43 GE				01:06 SA	
08	02:20 SA		16:11 CP	03:28 AQ				07:15 LE	13:28 LI	07:56 SC		22:59 AQ
09	09:44 SC	07:32 CP			14:49 AR						10:18 CP	
10				05:50 PI		03:03 GE	15:54 CA	18:33 VI		19:19 SA		
11	17:14 SA	09:17 AQ	19:38 AQ	06:19 AR	16:12 TA				02:06 SC		17:31 AQ	03:47 PI
12	20:55 CP					08:18 CA	00:28 LE					07:07 AR
13		08:58 PI	20:18 PI	06:31 TA	18:27 GE			07:08 LI	13:32 SA	04:51 CP	22:18 PI	
14		08:31 AR	19:39 AR			16:28 LE	11:28 VI					
15	21:57 AQ			08:27 GE	23:17 CA			19:44 SC	22:21 CP	11:34 AQ	00:36 AR	09:23 TA
16		09:51 TA	19:45 TA								01:16 TA	
17	22:07 PI					03:37 VI	00:03 LI			14:55 PI		11:28 GE
18	23:09 AR			13:53 CA	07:48 LE			06:31 SA	03:30 AQ		01:55 GE	
19		14:28 GE				16:17 LI	12:17 SC			15:27 AR		14:40 CA
20			22:35 GE	23:27 LE	19:32 VI			13:54 CP	05:06 PI		04:32 CA	
21							21:59 SA			14:47 TA		20:23 LE
22	02:21 TA	22:48 CA	05:29 CA		08:17 LI	03:58 SC		17:29 AQ	04:30 AR			
23				11:53 VI						15:05 GE	10:41 LE	
24	08:22 GE	10:06 LE	16:14 LE			12:48 SA	04:07 CP	18:12 PI	03:45 TA			05:24 VI
25	17:07 CA				19:33 SC					18:24 CA	20:41 VI	
26				00:41 LI		18:29 CP	07:03 AQ	17:46 AR	05:01 GE			17:11 LI
27		22:51 VI	05:04 VI		04:08 SA							
28				11:53 SC		21:52 AQ	08:08 PI	18:10 TA	09:57 CA	01:56 LE		
29	04:07 LE		17:52 LI		10:17 CP						09:05 LI	
30				20:53 SA			08:56 AR	21:06 GE		13:05 VI		
31	16:36 VI											05:43 SC

1954

	January	February	March	April	May	June	July	August	September	October	November	December
01	16:40 SA								22:48 SC	18:42 SA		
02		15:38 AQ	02:07 AQ	15:41 AR	01:43 TA	12:46 CA	02:17 LE					14:38 PI
03								03:14 LI			00:22 AQ	
04	00:46 CP	18:03 PI	04:32 PI	14:44 TA	01:07 GE	16:34 LE	08:57 VI			07:05 CP		19:35 AR
05								15:03 SC			07:34 PI	
06	06:10 AQ	19:14 AR	04:40 AR	14:41 GE	02:30 CA		18:54 LI		23:10 CP	16:46 AQ		21:23 TA
07						00:06 VI					10:42 AR	
08	09:44 PI	20:47 TA	04:33 TA	17:29 CA	07:29 LE			03:32 SA		22:17 PI		21:17 GE
09						10:59 LI	07:04 SC				10:49 TA	
10	12:27 AR	23:54 GE	06:07 GE		16:23 VI			14:20 CP		23:58 AR		21:07 CA
11				00:06 LE		23:31 SC	19:19 SA		11:56 PI		09:51 GE	
12	15:10 TA		10:38 CA					21:54 AQ		23:32 TA		22:49 LE
13				10:03 VI	04:04 LI				13:23 AR		09:59 CA	
14	18:29 GE	05:10 CA	18:18 LE			11:38 SA	05:40 CP			23:10 GE		
15				21:58 LI	16:42 SC			02:17 PI	13:45 TA		13:03 LE	03:54 VI
16	23:01 CA					22:06 CP	13:19 AQ					
17		22:01 VI	04:22 VI					04:38 AR	14:55 GE	00:49 CA	19:53 VI	12:52 LI
18				10:32 SC	04:54 SA		18:33 PI					
19	05:24 LE		15:58 LI			06:26 AQ		06:27 TA	18:13 CA	05:41 LE		
20		09:15 LI		22:55 SA	15:50 CP		22:07 AR				06:03 LI	00:43 SC
21	14:14 VI					12:37 PI		08:57 GE				
22		21:44 SC	04:26 SC						00:04 LE		18:14 SC	13:35 SA
23				10:12 CP	00:49 AQ	16:44 AR	00:53 TA	12:50 CA				
24	01:31 LI		16:56 SA						08:10 VI	00:12 LI		
25					07:09 PI	19:09 TA	03:31 GE	18:22 LE			07:02 SA	01:40 CP
26	14:04 SC								18:11 LI	12:11 SC		
27		19:58 CP	03:55 CP		10:32 AR	20:42 GE	06:42 CA				19:24 CP	12:01 AQ
28				00:22 PI				01:44 VI				
29	01:43 SA		11:38 AQ		11:34 TA	22:36 CA	11:11 LE		05:52 SC	00:59 SA		20:10 PI
30				02:09 AR				11:12 LI			06:19 AQ	
31	10:27 CP		15:17 PI		11:41 GE		17:50 VI			13:36 CP		

1955

	January	February	March	April	May	June	July	August	September	October	November	December
01	01:57 AR	14:03 GE		08:21 LE		20:54 SC	15:35 SA		15:23 PI	05:47 AR	19:23 GE	05:46 CA
02			22:40 CA					22:52 AQ				
03	05:25 TA	16:36 CA		14:32 VI	04:26 LI				21:24 AR	08:52 TA	20:11 CA	06:07 LE
04						09:24 SA	04:30 CP					
05	07:05 GE	19:28 LE	02:49 LE	22:34 LI	15:04 SC			08:04 PI		10:59 GE	22:20 LE	08:50 VI
06						22:21 CP	16:19 AQ		01:37 TA			
07	08:01 CA	23:43 VI	08:09 VI					14:59 AR		13:23 CA		14:49 LI
08				08:39 SC	03:19 SA				04:59 GE		02:36 VI	
09	09:41 LE					10:30 AQ	02:09 PI	20:03 TA		16:42 LE		
10		06:33 LI		20:42 SA	16:19 CP				08:01 CA		09:15 LI	00:00 SC
11	13:43 VI		15:20 LI			20:33 PI	09:33 AR	23:33 GE		21:11 VI		
12		16:39 SC	01:05 SC						11:03 LE		18:12 SC	11:34 SA
13	21:15 LI			09:41 CP	04:29 AQ		14:20 TA					
14			13:14 SA			03:25 AR		01:50 CA	14:34 VI	03:13 LI		
15		05:08 SA		21:20 AQ	13:53 PI	06:51 TA	16:43 GE				05:17 SA	00:24 CP
16	08:14 SC							03:34 LE	19:36 LI	11:23 SC		
17		17:35 CP	02:02 CP		19:21 AR		17:30 CA				17:59 CP	13:20 AQ
18	21:01 SA			05:28 PI		07:37 GE		05:58 VI		22:07 SA		
19			12:47 AQ		21:12 TA		18:03 LE		03:19 SC			
20		03:34 AQ		09:30 AR		07:15 CA		10:34 LI			06:59 AQ	01:02 PI
21	09:09 CP		19:45 PI		20:57 GE		20:06 VI		14:11 SA	10:52 CP		
22		10:10 PI		10:30 TA		07:36 LE		18:38 SC			18:11 PI	10:05 AR
23	18:59 AQ		23:09 AR		20:33 CA		01:16 LI			23:33 AQ		
24		14:06 AR		10:24 GE		10:26 VI			03:01 CP			15:33 TA
25					21:53 LE			06:04 SA			01:48 AR	
26	02:12 PI	16:46 TA	00:31 TA	11:09 CA			10:19 SC		15:07 AQ	09:38 PI		17:33 GE
27								18:57 CP			05:27 TA	
28	07:20 AR	19:24 GE	01:42 GE	14:09 LE			22:25 SA			15:47 AR		17:18 CA
29						03:05 SC			00:13 PI		06:11 GE	
30	11:07 TA		04:05 CA	19:58 VI	10:08 LI					18:30 TA		16:36 LE
31							11:19 CP	06:35 AQ				

1956

	January	February	March	April	May	June	July	August	September	October	November	December
01	17:31 VI							11:16 GE	23:14 LE	08:25 VI	22:25 SC	12:59 SA
02		13:33 SC		04:38 CP	01:28 AQ		22:26 TA					
03	21:45 LI		08:09 SA			07:05 AR		13:32 CA	23:20 VI	10:02 LI		22:36 CP
04				17:25 AQ	13:16 PI						04:56 SA	
05		00:13 SA	20:33 CP			13:22 TA	02:27 GE	13:27 LE		13:20 SC		
06	06:01 SC				22:05 AR				00:05 LI		14:24 CP	10:17 AQ
07		13:08 CP		04:38 PI		16:10 GE	03:20 CA	12:49 VI		19:47 SA		
08	17:33 SA		09:20 AQ						03:27 SC			22:57 PI
09				12:47 AR	03:24 TA	16:43 CA	02:43 LE	13:50 LI			02:19 AQ	
10		01:52 AQ	20:12 PI						10:47 SA	05:48 CP		
11	06:34 CP			18:03 TA	06:00 GE	16:46 LE	02:35 VI	18:20 SC			14:51 PI	10:38 AR
12		12:52 PI							21:46 CP	18:09 AQ		
13	19:19 AQ		04:27 AR	21:31 GE	07:21 CA	18:04 VI	04:54 LI					19:16 TA
14		21:49 AR						03:00 SA			01:37 AR	
15			10:33 TA		08:52 LE	21:59 LI	10:56 SC		10:28 AQ	06:25 PI		
16	06:47 PI			00:15 CA				14:48 CP			09:13 TA	00:07 GE
17		04:49 TA	15:12 GE		11:40 VI		20:38 SA		22:34 PI	16:35 AR		
18	23:11 TA			03:00 LE		05:03 SC					13:46 GE	01:52 CA
19		09:51 GE	18:48 CA		16:26 LI			03:38 AQ				
20				06:17 VI		14:55 SA	08:41 CP		08:47 AR	00:07 TA	16:18 CA	02:11 LE
21		12:51 CA	21:31 LE		23:27 SC			15:48 PI				
22				10:37 LI			21:29 AQ		17:01 TA	05:29 GE	18:11 LE	02:56 VI
23	03:06 GE	14:11 LE	23:53 VI			02:43 CP						
24				16:45 SC	08:47 SA			02:30 AR	23:25 GE	09:24 CA	20:32 VI	05:39 LI
25	04:20 CA	15:05 VI	02:59 LI			15:25 AQ	09:51 PI					
26					20:11 CP			11:24 TA		12:28 LE		11:09 SC
27	04:07 LE	17:20 LI		01:26 SA			20:54 AR		03:59 CA		00:11 LI	
28			08:19 SC			03:54 PI		17:59 GE		15:10 VI		19:20 SA
29	04:18 VI	22:45 SC		12:45 CP	08:52 AQ				06:49 LE		05:34 SC	
30			16:56 SA			14:43 AR	05:41 TA	21:51 CA		18:10 LI		
31	06:56 LI				21:09 PI							05:37 CP

517

1957

	January	February	March	April	May	June	July	August	September	October	November	December
01		12:21 PI		23:12 TA	13:47 GE	04:45 LE	13:24 VI	01:01 SC	21:05 CP	14:05 AQ	09:19 PI	
02	17:25 AQ		06:31 AR									05:56 AR
03		00:42 AR		07:31 GE	19:09 CA	06:59 VI	15:17 LI	06:47 SA			21:59 AR	
04	06:05 PI		17:21 TA						07:50 AQ	02:18 PI		17:48 TA
05		11:37 TA		13:38 CA	22:54 LE	09:46 LI	19:11 SC	15:23 CP			09:38 TA	
06	18:23 AR								20:04 PI	14:57 AR		
07			02:04 GE	17:25 LE	01:37 VI	13:41 SC					19:09 GE	03:01 GE
08		19:35 GE					01:21 SA	02:01 AQ				
09	04:27 TA		07:46 CA	19:13 VI	03:57 LI	19:10 SA			08:45 AR	02:48 TA		09:16 CA
10		23:39 CA					09:35 CP	14:02 PI			02:24 CA	
11	10:44 GE		10:12 LE	20:09 LI					20:58 TA	13:01 GE		13:24 LE
12		00:19 LE			06:48 SC	02:37 CP	19:43 AQ				07:36 LE	
13	13:06 CA		10:20 VI	21:45 SC				02:46 AR		20:54 CA		16:29 VI
14		23:17 VI			11:14 SA	12:24 AQ			07:27 GE		11:07 VI	
15	12:50 LE		09:59 LI				07:32 PI	15:01 TA				19:23 LI
16		22:50 LI		01:43 SA	18:14 CP				14:50 CA	01:59 LE	13:26 LI	
17						00:15 PI	20:14 AR					22:36 SC
18	12:04 VI		11:15 SC	09:08 CP					18:31 LE	04:24 VI	15:18 SC	
19		01:06 SC			04:13 AQ	12:46 AR						
20	12:55 LI		15:54 SA	19:54 AQ			07:58 TA		19:11 VI	05:03 LI	17:52 SA	02:31 SA
21		07:24 SA			16:21 PI	23:38 TA						
22	17:03 SC		00:34 CP				16:34 GE	08:51 LE	18:32 LI	05:31 SC	22:30 CP	07:47 CP
23		17:27 CP		08:23 PI	04:34 AR							
24						07:07 GE	21:06 CA	08:26 VI	18:40 SC	07:34 SA		15:18 AQ
25	00:53 SA		12:17 AQ	20:22 AR							06:16 AQ	
26		05:43 AQ			14:43 TA	11:01 CA	22:17 LE	07:41 LI	21:27 SA	12:42 CP		
27	11:33 CP		00:59 PI								17:16 PI	01:41 PI
28		18:25 PI		06:18 TA	21:47 GE	12:31 LE	21:59 VI	08:45 SC		21:33 AQ		
29	23:43 AQ		12:55 AR						03:59 CP			14:13 AR
30					02:06 CA		22:20 LI	13:07 SA				
31												02:38 TA

1958

	January	February	March	April	May	June	July	August	September	October	November	December
01	12:22 GE	04:41 CA		06:01 VI		02:53 SA		12:12 PI			08:09 CA	
02			18:27 LE		16:14 SC		19:45 AQ		19:24 TA	14:51 GE		
03	18:22 CA	07:38 LE		05:54 LI		05:22 CP		23:14 AR			17:03 LE	05:18 VI
04			19:15 VI		16:43 SA							
05	21:22 LE	08:11 VI		05:17 SC		10:33 AQ	03:57 PI		08:07 GE	02:01 CA	22:46 VI	09:31 LI
06			18:35 LI		19:21 CP			12:04 TA				
07	22:59 VI	08:23 LI		06:07 SA		19:24 PI	15:18 AR		18:23 CA	09:51 LE		11:29 SC
08			18:35 SC								01:16 LI	
09		10:03 SC		10:01 CP	01:29 AQ			00:16 GE		13:50 VI		12:02 SA
10	00:52 LI		20:57 SA			07:21 AR	04:09 TA		00:42 LE		01:30 SC	
11		14:11 SA		17:42 AQ	11:27 PI			09:25 CA		14:44 LI		12:47 CP
12	04:02 SC					20:13 TA	15:47 GE		03:20 VI		01:03 SA	
13		20:56 CP	02:37 CP		23:58 AR			14:44 LE		14:11 SC		15:38 AQ
14	08:49 SA			04:39 PI					03:45 LI		01:55 CP	
15			11:29 AQ			07:32 GE	00:15 CA	17:07 VI		14:09 SA		22:12 PI
16	15:13 CP	05:52 AQ		17:23 AR	12:50 TA				03:50 SC		05:53 AQ	
17			22:42 PI			16:04 CA	05:31 LE	18:17 LI		16:22 CP		
18	23:22 AQ	16:40 PI							05:16 SA		13:57 PI	08:46 AR
19				06:16 TA	00:15 GE	22:04 LE	08:42 VI	19:50 SC		22:04 AQ		
20			11:17 AR						09:13 CP			21:37 TA
21	09:42 PI	05:02 AR		18:03 GE	09:24 CA		11:12 LI	22:49 SA			01:29 AR	
22						02:22 VI			16:03 AQ	07:20 PI		
23	22:04 AR	18:05 TA	00:15 TA		16:15 LE		13:58 SC				14:31 TA	10:09 GE
24				03:47 CA		05:42 LI		03:39 CP		19:11 AR		
25			12:19 GE		21:00 VI		17:26 SA		01:33 PI			20:33 CA
26	10:57 TA	05:52 GE		10:44 LE		08:30 SC		10:28 AQ			03:01 GE	
27			21:53 CA		23:55 LI		21:54 CP		13:07 AR	08:08 TA		
28	21:48 GE	14:17 CA		14:41 VI		11:12 SA		19:25 PI			13:51 CA	04:33 LE
29										20:50 GE		
30			03:46 LE	16:07 LI	01:33 SC	14:33 CP	03:53 AQ		01:58 TA		22:41 LE	10:41 VI
31								06:35 AR				

1959

	January	February	March	April	May	June	July	August	September	October	November	December
01	15:22 LI		08:33 SA	22:42 AQ	11:59 PI			07:24 CA		22:09 LI		20:11 CP
02		03:11 SA				16:37 TA	12:06 GE		08:31 VI		10:02 SA	
03	18:43 SC		12:05 CP		22:19 AR			17:10 LE		23:55 SC		20:35 AQ
04		06:29 CP		06:24 PI					12:57 LI		10:05 CP	
05	20:56 SA		17:16 AQ			05:35 GE	00:04 CA					
06		10:40 AQ		16:33 AR	10:39 TA			00:30 VI	15:53 SC	00:55 SA	12:14 AQ	00:16 PI
07	22:50 CP					17:44 CA	10:09 LE					
08		16:50 PI	00:26 PI		23:34 GE			05:56 LI	18:21 SA	02:39 CP	17:35 PI	07:59 AR
09				04:32 TA			18:16 VI					
10	01:52 AQ		09:54 AR			04:20 LE		09:59 SC	21:05 CP	06:13 AQ		18:57 TA
11		01:55 AR		17:25 GE	11:57 CA						02:10 AR	
12	07:40 PI		21:37 TA			12:51 VI	00:27 LI	12:58 SA		12:06 PI		
13		13:48 TA			22:41 LE				00:44 AQ		13:04 TA	07:25 GE
14	17:09 AR			05:48 CA		18:43 LI	04:33 SC	15:19 CP		20:20 AR		
15		02:40 GE	10:31 GE						05:55 PI			20:01 CA
16				15:55 LE	06:38 VI	21:39 SC	06:42 SA	17:54 AQ			01:17 GE	
17	05:33 TA	13:51 CA	22:28 CA						13:17 AR	06:40 TA		
18				22:28 VI	11:07 LI	22:15 SA	07:42 CP	22:00 PI			13:57 CA	07:58 LE
19	18:16 GE								23:13 TA	18:40 GE		
20		21:39 LE	07:23 LE		12:25 SC	22:01 CP	09:05 AQ					18:30 VI
21				01:19 LI				04:52 AR			02:05 LE	
22	04:47 CA		12:28 VI		11:51 SA	23:00 AQ	12:41 PI		11:16 GE	07:23 CA		
23		02:06 VI		01:34 SC				14:59 TA			12:08 VI	02:29 LI
24	12:14 LE		14:27 LI		11:24 CP		19:54 AR		23:49 CA	19:04 LE		
25		04:29 LI		00:59 SA		03:09 PI					18:42 LI	07:01 SC
26	17:14 VI		14:54 SC		13:10 AQ			03:19 GE				
27		06:15 SC		01:33 CP		11:28 AR	06:44 TA		10:36 LE	03:49 VI	21:22 SC	08:16 SA
28	20:55 LI		15:31 SA		18:42 PI			15:34 CA				
29				04:56 AQ		23:11 TA	19:24 GE		18:04 VI	08:42 LI	21:12 SA	07:38 CP
30			17:49 CP									
31	00:06 SC				04:18 AR			01:33 LE		10:15 SC		07:15 AQ

1960

	January	February	March	April	May	June	July	August	September	October	November	December
01	09:19 PI	00:39 AR	18:18 TA			16:38 VI	08:47 LI	02:04 SA	12:35 AQ	22:15 PI	15:28 TA	07:00 GE
02	15:22 AR	09:16 TA		01:47 CA	21:59 LE		15:09 SC	03:26 CP	13:51 PI		23:44 GE	17:52 CA
03			05:08 GE			01:31 LI	17:43 SA	03:21 AQ		01:47 AR		
04	20:58 GE	20:58 GE		14:02 LE	08:59 VI	06:20 SC		03:42 PI	16:26 AR		10:26 CA	06:21 LE
05			17:37 CA				17:35 CP			07:10 TA		
06	01:23 TA			00:02 VI	16:30 LI	07:31 SA		06:21 AR	21:45 TA			19:14 VI
07		09:37 CA					16:44 AQ			15:17 GE	22:59 LE	
08	13:45 GE		05:25 LE	06:36 LI	20:07 SC	06:48 CP		12:36 TA				
09		21:08 LE					17:19 PI		06:32 GE			06:11 LI
10	02:23 CA			10:01 SC	20:55 SA	06:24 AQ				02:18 CA	11:24 VI	
11			14:48 VI				21:07 AR	22:30 GE				13:14 SC
12	13:59 LE	06:35 VI		11:37 SA	20:51 CP	08:18 PI			18:11 CA	14:55 LE		
13			21:20 LI								21:08 LI	16:07 SA
14	00:03 VI	13:56 LI		13:01 CP	21:52 AQ	13:43 AR	04:48 TA	10:44 CA	06:47 LE	02:40 VI		
15			01:37 SC									16:16 CP
16	08:14 LI			15:32 AQ	01:24 PI	22:33 TA	15:40 GE	23:18 LE	18:07 VI	11:32 LI	02:54 SC	
17		19:24 SC	04:38 SA									15:49 AQ
18	13:59 SC			19:56 PI	07:56 AR		04:09 CA			17:06 SC	05:17 SA	
19		23:12 SA	07:14 CP			09:46 GE		10:42 VI	02:58 LI			16:47 PI
20	17:03 SA			02:23 AR	17:00 TA		16:46 LE			20:16 SA	06:03 CP	
21			10:10 AQ			22:09 CA		20:10 LI	09:18 SC			20:34 AR
22	18:00 CP	01:40 CP		10:51 TA	03:55 GE					22:29 CP	07:05 AQ	
23			14:02 PI				04:32 VI		13:42 SA			03:30 TA
24	18:19 AQ	03:33 AQ			16:06 CA	10:51 LE		03:24 SC		00:58 AQ	09:50 PI	
25			19:30 AR	21:17 GE			14:34 LI		16:54 CP			13:02 GE
26	19:57 PI	06:04 PI			04:50 LE			08:19 SA		04:27 PI	14:51 AR	
27						22:53 VI			19:33 AQ			
28		10:37 AR	03:13 TA				21:55 SC	11:09 CP			21:59 TA	
29				09:23 CA						09:12 AR		
30												
31			13:32 GE									

1961

	January	February	March	April	May	June	July	August	September	October	November	December
01	00:22 CA		14:12 VI			17:45 AQ	02:53 PI	16:19 TA	05:52 GE		06:18 VI	03:08 LI
02	12:54 LE	07:48 VI								09:44 LE		
03		19:27 LI	01:21 LI	22:35 SA	08:40 CP	19:51 PI	05:13 AR	23:04 GE	15:00 CA		18:42 LI	13:30 SC
04										22:46 VI		
05						23:24 AR			03:01 LE		04:40 SC	20:25 SA
06	01:49 VI		10:24 SC	02:53 CP	11:24 AQ		10:02 TA	08:56 CA				
07		04:51 SC	17:04 SA	06:03 AQ	14:23 PI				16:06 VI	11:04 LI	11:51 SA	
08	13:31 LI					04:38 TA	17:28 GE	20:59 LE				00:31 CP
09		11:01 SA	21:19 CP	08:32 PI	17:56 AR					21:19 SC		
10	22:09 SC					11:41 GE		10:00 VI	04:34 LI		16:59 CP	03:12 AQ
11		13:51 CP	23:30 AQ	10:56 AR			03:13 CA					
12					22:25 TA			22:44 LI	15:24 SC		20:59 AQ	05:42 PI
13	02:41 SA	14:15 AQ		14:17 TA		20:50 CA	14:56 LE			05:21 SA		
14					04:35 GE				23:55 SA	11:24 CP		08:45 AR
15	03:41 CP	13:53 PI	00:27 PI					09:45 SC			00:19 PI	
16					13:17 CA							12:39 TA
17	02:56 AQ	14:41 AR	01:33 AR	19:55 GE		08:16 LE	03:54 VI		05:42 CP	15:37 AQ	03:11 AR	
18						21:12 VI	16:38 LI	17:44 SA		18:10 PI		17:48 GE
19	02:32 PI	18:22 TA	04:26 TA						08:43 AQ		06:04 TA	
20				04:50 CA	00:46 LE			22:08 CP		19:36 AR		00:50 CA
21	04:27 AR		10:32 GE			09:32 LI	03:05 SC		09:36 PI		09:59 GE	
22		01:52 GE		16:44 LE	13:39 VI			23:26 AQ		21:07 TA		10:26 LE
23	09:52 TA		20:22 CA			18:51 SC	09:43 SA	23:03 PI	09:40 AR		16:21 CA	
24		12:49 CA										
25	18:51 GE		08:48 LE	05:32 VI	01:18 LI		12:29 CP		10:42 TA	00:25 GE		22:30 VI
26						00:06 SA		22:49 AR			02:01 LE	
27		01:34 LE		16:35 LI	09:35 SC		12:42 AQ		14:32 GE			11:27 LI
28	06:23 CA		21:30 VI			02:00 CP				07:04 CA	14:25 VI	
29					14:11 SA		12:14 PI		22:20 CA			
30	19:05 LE			00:28 SC		02:18 AQ		00:37 TA		17:30 LE		
31			08:22 LI		16:20 CP		12:56 AR					22:43 SC

1962

	January	February	March	April	May	June	July	August	September	October	November	December
01		21:10 CP	06:38 CP	20:43 PI	06:13 AR	17:40 GE	06:19 CA		03:01 LI			14:26 AQ
02								07:58 VI			01:18 CP	
03	06:24 SA	22:57 AQ	09:52 AQ	20:42 AR	06:50 TA	21:57 CA	13:56 LE		15:46 SC	09:41 SA		19:54 PI
04								20:18 LI			09:02 AQ	
05	10:25 CP	22:53 PI	10:17 PI	20:26 TA	08:17 GE					19:36 CP		23:17 AR
06						05:23 LE	00:23 VI		03:26 SA		13:52 PI	
07	12:01 AQ	22:51 AR	09:32 AR	22:00 GE	12:28 CA			08:56 SC				
08						16:13 VI	12:48 LI		12:20 CP	02:22 AQ	15:45 AR	00:59 TA
09	12:54 PI		09:41 TA		20:35 LE			19:48 SA				
10		00:35 TA		03:13 CA					17:27 AQ	05:29 PI	15:45 TA	02:08 GE
11	14:34 AR		12:36 GE			04:52 LI	01:06 SC					
12		05:18 GE		12:36 LE	08:11 VI			03:18 CP	19:02 PI	05:41 AR	15:44 GE	04:22 CA
13	18:01 TA		19:26 CA			16:46 SC	11:01 SA					
14		13:20 CA			21:03 LI			07:08 AQ	18:33 AR	04:43 TA	17:49 CA	09:21 LE
15	23:42 GE			00:57 VI			17:32 CP					
16		00:04 LE	05:57 LE			02:04 SA		08:17 PI	18:01 TA	04:50 GE	23:41 LE	17:59 VI
17		12:27 VI		13:54 LI	08:44 SC		21:07 AQ					
18	07:40 CA		18:33 VI			08:30 CP		08:26 AR		08:05 CA		
19					18:03 SA		23:00 PI				09:34 VI	05:41 LI
20	17:50 LE			01:37 SC		12:49 AQ		09:21 TA		15:31 LE		
21			07:28 LI						00:26 CA		21:58 LI	18:18 SC
22	05:54 VI	01:22 LI		11:27 SA	01:09 CP	15:59 PI	00:34 AR	12:28 GE				
23			19:29 SC						09:07 LE	02:32 VI		
24	18:53 LI	13:37 SC		19:21 CP	06:31 AQ	18:43 AR	02:57 TA	18:34 CA			10:34 SC	05:33 SA
25									20:31 VI	15:14 LI		
26		23:46 SA	05:49 SA		10:30 PI	21:34 TA	06:57 GE				21:43 SA	14:19 CP
27	06:55 SC			01:09 AQ				03:30 LE				
28			13:46 CP		13:15 AR		13:01 CA		09:08 LI	03:49 SC		20:43 AQ
29	15:59 SA			04:41 PI		01:10 GE		14:36 VI			07:00 CP	
30			18:44 AQ		15:17 TA		21:21 LE		21:49 SC	15:20 SA		
31												01:21 PI

1963

	January	February	March	April	May	June	July	August	September	October	November	December
01			21:39 GE			00:09 LI					00:43 TA	
02	04:49 AR	16:03 GE		14:46 LE	06:13 VI			03:13 CP		13:49 AR	23:49 GE	10:45 CA
03						12:39 SC	08:12 SA		01:37 PI			
04	07:34 TA	20:40 CA	02:08 CA		17:43 LI			11:26 AQ		13:51 TA		12:20 LE
05				00:21 VI			19:04 CP		03:52 AR		00:08 CA	
06	10:15 GE		09:15 LE			01:01 SA		16:46 PI		13:59 GE		17:27 VI
07		03:06 LE		11:50 LI	06:16 SC				05:02 TA		03:24 LE	
08	13:42 CA		18:34 VI			12:07 CP	03:37 AQ	20:06 AR		16:01 CA		
09		11:36 VI			18:42 SA				06:46 GE		10:14 VI	02:22 LI
10	19:01 LE			00:14 SC		21:23 AQ	09:53 PI	22:38 TA		20:54 LE		
11		22:18 LI	05:36 LI						10:08 CA		20:08 LI	14:05 SC
12				12:48 SA	06:14 CP		14:16 AR					
13	03:07 VI		17:52 SC			04:21 PI		01:16 GE	15:30 LE	04:34 VI		
14		10:39 SC			15:52 AQ		17:15 TA				07:57 SC	02:54 SA
15	14:04 LI			00:27 CP		08:47 AR		04:40 CA	22:48 VI	14:24 LI		
16		22:58 SA	06:28 SA		22:33 PI		19:27 GE				20:40 SA	15:22 CP
17				09:34 AQ		10:55 TA		09:17 LE				
18	02:36 SC		17:35 CP				21:45 CA		07:59 LI	01:52 SC		
19		09:01 CP		14:54 PI	01:48 AR	11:44 GE		15:41 VI			09:23 CP	02:29 AQ
20	14:21 SA								19:10 SC	14:32 SA		
21		15:24 AQ	01:21 AQ	16:30 AR	02:22 TA	12:46 CA					20:52 AQ	11:29 PI
22	23:24 CP							00:26 LI				
23		18:18 PI	05:05 PI	15:51 TA	01:54 GE	15:44 LE	07:07 VI		07:50 SA	03:21 CP		17:41 AR
24								11:39 SC			05:33 PI	
25	05:15 AQ	19:05 AR	05:38 AR	15:07 GE	02:29 CA	21:56 VI	16:03 LI		20:15 CP	14:21 AQ		20:57 TA
26											10:25 AR	
27	08:36 PI	19:39 TA	04:57 TA	16:28 CA	05:59 LE			00:15 SA		21:37 PI		21:58 GE
28						07:41 LI	03:39 SC		06:03 AQ		11:49 TA	
29	10:44 AR		05:13 GE	21:26 LE	13:22 VI			11:57 CP				22:07 CA
30						19:48 SC	16:09 SA		11:47 PI	00:41 AR	11:15 GE	
31	12:55 TA		08:14 CA					20:37 AQ				23:10 LE

1964

	January	February	March	April	May	June	July	August	September	October	November	December
01		19:25 LI			05:43 CP	11:01 PI	00:53 AR		00:13 CA		00:25 LI	
02	02:48 VI		13:54 SC	09:42 SA				15:28 GE		12:43 VI		01:24 SA
03		05:13 SC		22:37 CP	18:07 AQ	18:03 AR	05:43 TA		02:37 LE		08:25 SC	
04	10:11 LI		01:47 SA					17:13 CA		17:45 LI		13:54 CP
05		17:35 SA		10:25 AQ	03:43 PI	21:20 TA	07:44 GE		05:13 VI		18:43 SA	
06	21:04 SC		14:36 CP					18:11 LE				02:58 AQ
07				18:47 PI	09:16 AR	21:51 GE	07:57 CA		09:20 LI	00:57 SC	07:06 CP	
08		06:11 CP						19:50 VI				15:00 PI
09			01:36 AQ	23:09 AR	11:09 TA	21:17 CA	08:01 LE		16:21 SC	11:03 SA		
10	09:49 SA	16:40 AQ						23:52 LI			20:08 AQ	
11			09:06 PI		11:02 GE	21:36 LE	09:44 VI			23:32 CP		00:13 AR
12	22:14 CP								02:48 SA			
13		00:09 PI	13:16 AR	00:37 TA	10:54 CA	00:28 VI	14:41 LI	07:32 SC			07:29 PI	05:33 TA
14									15:31 CP	12:15 AQ		
15	08:48 AQ	05:11 AR	15:31 TA	01:06 GE	12:32 LE	06:54 LI	23:32 SC	18:45 SA			15:11 AR	07:22 GE
16										22:33 PI		
17	17:04 PI	08:46 TA	17:26 GE	02:24 CA	17:03 VI	16:49 SC			03:48 AQ		18:58 TA	07:03 CA
18								07:39 CP				
19		11:49 GE	20:12 CA	05:40 LE			11:28 SA		13:22 PI	05:05 AR	19:59 GE	06:31 LE
20	23:11 AR							19:40 AQ				
21									19:44 AR	08:25 TA	20:04 CA	07:41 VI
22	03:24 TA	14:50 CA	00:15 LE	11:18 VI	00:42 LI	05:03 SA	00:27 CP					
23		18:11 LE						05:14 PI	23:46 TA	10:04 GE	20:59 LE	12:04 LI
24	06:05 GE		05:42 VI	19:09 LI	10:59 SC	18:02 CP	12:31 AQ					
25		22:30 VI						12:15 AR		11:38 CA		20:12 SC
26	07:52 CA		12:48 LI	05:02 SC	23:03 SA	06:22 AQ	22:36 PI		02:46 GE		00:03 VI	
27								17:24 TA		14:15 LE		
28	09:46 LE	04:46 LI	22:04 SC		12:00 CP	16:56 PI			05:40 CA		05:54 LI	07:21 SA
29				16:47 SA			06:26 AR	21:16 GE		18:26 VI		
30	13:09 VI								08:53 LE		14:31 SC	
31					00:32 AQ		12:01 TA					

1965

	January	February	March	April	May	June	July	August	September	October	November	December
01	20:07 CP			02:19 AR	20:27 GE	07:05 CA	17:12 VI	03:54 LI	23:59 SA	18:30 CP		23:23 AR
02		02:56 PI	09:38 PI								03:23 PI	
03				08:29 TA	22:39 CA	07:47 LE	19:43 LI	08:20 SC				
04	09:05 AQ	12:43 AR	18:45 AR						10:51 CP	06:49 AQ	14:22 AR	08:12 TA
05				12:56 GE		09:33 VI		16:49 SA				
06	21:07 PI	20:24 TA			00:50 LE		01:39 SC		23:34 AQ	19:15 PI	22:30 TA	13:28 GE
07			01:50 TA	16:25 CA		13:30 LI						
08					03:47 VI		10:54 SA	04:22 CP				15:58 CA
09	07:08 AR	01:36 GE	07:15 GE	19:24 LE		20:05 SC			11:57 PI	05:54 AR	03:54 GE	
10					08:04 LI		22:29 CP	17:09 AQ				17:09 LE
11	14:11 TA	04:14 CA	11:04 CA	22:15 VI					22:50 AR	14:17 TA	07:30 CA	
12					14:10 SC	05:11 SA						18:36 VI
13	17:48 GE	04:55 LE	13:24 LE				11:08 AQ	05:38 PI		20:40 GE	10:14 LE	
14				01:39 LI	22:32 SA	16:21 CP			07:57 TA			21:34 LI
15	18:35 CA	05:06 VI	14:56 VI				23:44 PI	16:57 AR			12:55 VI	
16				06:42 SC					15:07 GE	01:27 CA		
17	17:57 LE	06:46 LI	17:05 LI		09:21 CP	04:52 AQ					16:11 LI	02:40 SC
18				14:31 SA			11:13 AR	02:28 TA	20:01 CA	04:51 LE		
19	17:55 VI	11:46 SC	21:32 SC		21:51 AQ	17:29 PI					20:37 SC	10:01 SA
20							20:14 TA	09:21 GE	22:35 LE	07:13 VI		
21	20:28 LI	20:58 SA		01:24 CP								19:27 CP
22			05:37 SA		10:15 PI	04:29 AR		13:05 CA	23:30 VI	09:22 LI	02:57 SA	
23				14:05 AQ			01:49 GE					
24	03:02 SC	09:17 CP	17:07 CP		20:19 AR	12:16 TA		14:01 LE		12:32 SC	11:46 CP	06:44 AQ
25							03:54 CA		00:16 LI			
26	13:33 SA	22:14 AQ		02:03 PI		16:18 GE		13:36 VI		18:10 SA	23:03 AQ	19:18 PI
27			05:59 AQ		02:49 TA		03:38 LE		02:47 SC			
28				11:13 AR		17:20 CA		13:52 LI				
29	02:22 CP		17:32 PI		05:59 GE		02:55 VI		08:43 SA	03:06 CP	11:40 PI	07:40 AR
30				17:04 TA		16:59 LE		16:54 SC				
31	15:18 AQ									14:50 AQ		

1966

	January	February	March	April	May	June	July	August	September	October	November	December
01	17:47 TA		22:48 CA		19:31 LI		23:52 CP		22:27 AR	16:48 TA		
02		13:41 CA		10:32 VI		09:38 SA					17:43 CA	05:02 LE
03					21:24 SC			03:36 PI				
04	00:07 GE	14:14 LE	00:57 LE	10:40 LI		16:10 CP	09:15 AQ		10:59 TA	03:44 GE	23:36 LE	08:48 VI
05								16:14 AR				
06	02:41 CA	13:11 VI	00:37 VI	11:31 SC	00:52 SA		20:40 PI		21:53 GE	12:13 CA		11:43 LI
07			23:49 LI			01:21 AQ					03:10 VI	
08	02:50 LE	12:50 LI		14:54 SA	07:12 CP			04:37 TA		17:25 LE		14:18 SC
09						12:57 PI	09:16 AR		05:27 CA		04:54 LI	
10	02:35 VI	15:15 SC	00:48 SC	22:02 CP	16:51 AQ			14:38 GE		19:27 VI		17:14 SA
11							21:04 TA		09:01 LE		05:53 SC	
12	03:53 LI	21:34 SA	05:19 SA			01:27 AR		20:42 CA		19:29 LI		21:31 CP
13				08:42 AQ	04:55 PI				09:26 VI		07:36 SA	
14	08:08 SC		13:56 CP			12:30 TA	05:51 GE	22:50 LE		19:21 SC		
15		07:27 CP		21:13 PI	17:16 AR				08:33 LI		11:37 CP	04:20 AQ
16	15:40 SA					20:26 GE	10:44 CA	22:35 VI		20:59 SA		
17		19:27 AQ	01:35 AQ						08:34 SC		19:04 AQ	14:18 PI
18				09:27 AR	03:50 TA		12:27 LE	22:06 LI				
19	01:45 CP		14:19 PI			01:05 CA			11:21 SA	01:56 CP		
20		08:06 PI		20:01 TA	11:41 GE		12:47 VI	23:24 SC			05:54 PI	02:39 AR
21	13:27 AQ					03:29 LE			17:53 CP	10:41 AQ		
22		20:30 AR	02:33 AR		17:01 CA		13:38 LI				18:31 AR	15:07 TA
23				04:28 GE		05:08 VI		03:51 SA		22:21 PI		
24	01:59 PI		13:32 TA		20:37 LE		16:32 SC		03:48 AQ			
25		07:53 TA		10:49 CA		07:23 LI		11:37 CP			06:37 TA	01:14 GE
26	14:34 AR		22:41 GE		23:22 VI		22:05 SA		15:49 PI	11:04 AR		
27		17:03 GE		15:10 LE		11:04 SC		21:56 AQ			16:31 GE	07:58 CA
28										23:06 TA		
29	01:43 TA			17:50 VI	01:59 LI	16:31 SA	06:05 CP		04:30 AR		23:49 CA	11:58 LE
30								09:48 PI				
31	09:44 GE		09:13 LE		05:11 SC		16:02 AQ			09:28 GE		14:34 VI

1967

Day	January	February	March	April	May	June	July	August	September	October	November	December
01	17:04 LI	01:44 SC		00:11 CP		20:07 AR	16:43 TA		14:08 LE	03:39 VI	15:27 SC	02:10 SA
02			11:53 SA					22:32 CA				
03	20:17 SC	05:56 SA		07:50 AQ	00:47 PI				17:07 VI	04:35 LI	14:51 SA	02:25 CP
04			17:35 CP			09:04 TA	04:39 GE					
05		12:10 CP		18:30 PI	13:10 AR			04:26 LE	18:03 LI	04:15 SC	15:44 CP	04:57 AQ
06	00:28 SA					20:52 GE	13:48 CA					
07		20:17 AQ	02:04 AQ					07:36 VI	18:44 SC	04:32 SA	19:45 AQ	11:20 PI
08	05:54 CP			06:57 AR	02:09 TA		19:59 LE					
09			12:42 PI			06:18 CA		09:34 LI	20:40 SA	07:04 CP		21:44 AR
10	13:06 AQ	06:19 PI		19:56 TA	14:08 GE						03:43 PI	
11						13:20 LE	00:08 VI	11:44 SC		12:45 AQ		
12	22:44 PI	18:17 AR	00:54 AR						00:43 CP		14:59 AR	10:32 TA
13				08:15 GE	00:11 CA	18:24 VI	03:20 LI	14:53 SA		21:38 PI		
14			13:55 TA						07:09 AQ			23:19 GE
15	10:48 AR	07:19 TA		18:36 CA	07:49 LE	21:59 LI	06:17 SC	19:19 CP			03:53 TA	
16									15:53 PI	08:57 AR		
17	23:40 TA	19:16 GE	02:19 GE		12:53 VI		09:22 SA				16:41 GE	10:23 CA
18				01:54 LE		00:25 SC		01:18 AQ		21:41 TA		
19			12:10 CA		15:32 LI		12:59 CP		02:46 AR			19:21 LE
20	10:39 GE	03:49 CA		05:43 VI		02:20 SA		09:19 PI			04:14 CA	
21			18:04 LE		16:30 SC		17:59 AQ		15:20 TA	10:38 GE		
22	17:52 CA	08:05 LE		06:42 LI		04:46 CP		19:48 AR			13:48 LE	02:21 VI
23			20:08 VI		17:06 SA					22:28 CA		
24	21:21 LE	09:04 VI		06:19 SC		09:11 AQ	01:29 PI		04:21 GE		20:46 VI	07:27 LI
25			19:50 LI		18:58 CP			08:22 TA				
26	22:37 VI	08:44 LI		06:28 SA		16:49 PI	12:01 AR		15:45 CA	07:41 LE		10:36 SC
27			19:11 SC		23:44 AQ			21:08 GE			00:48 LI	
28		09:09 SC		08:55 CP					23:42 LE	13:20 VI		12:09 SA
29	23:33 LI		20:09 SA			03:53 AR	00:41 TA				02:13 SC	
30				14:58 AQ	08:18 PI			07:34 CA		15:32 LI		13:11 CP
31							13:01 GE					

1968

Day	January	February	March	April	May	June	July	August	September	October	November	December
01	15:24 AQ				01:50 CA		16:11 LI	02:12 SC	13:22 CP		16:51 AR	08:58 TA
02	20:36 PI	14:40 AR		06:41 GE		03:52 VI		05:11 SA	16:20 AQ	03:22 PI		21:06 GE
03			10:28 TA		12:54 LE	09:50 LI	20:21 SC	06:57 CP	20:28 PI	10:36 AR	03:01 TA	
04		02:15 TA	23:17 GE	19:13 CA	20:58 VI	12:31 SC	22:05 SA			20:07 TA	14:48 GE	09:44 CA
05	05:46 AR	15:09 GE		05:29 LE		12:43 SA	22:24 CP	08:37 AQ	02:50 AR			22:03 LE
06	18:03 TA		11:22 CA	12:04 VI	01:21 LI	12:06 CP	23:04 AQ	11:46 PI	12:07 TA	07:44 GE	03:26 CA	
07				15:01 LI	02:30 SC	12:47 AQ		17:53 AR	23:55 GE	20:23 CA	15:45 LE	09:00 VI
08		02:34 CA	20:28 LE	15:32 SC	01:54 SA		02:03 PI					17:09 LI
09		10:50 LE		15:23 SA	01:31 CP	16:43 PI	08:52 AR	03:36 TA	12:29 CA	08:08 LE	01:55 VI	21:32 SC
10	06:54 GE			16:23 CP		00:50 AR	19:30 TA	15:52 GE			08:27 LI	
11	17:54 CA			19:57 AQ	03:23 AQ				23:25 LE	16:59 VI	11:07 SC	22:28 SA
12		16:03 VI				12:25 TA		04:16 CA				
13	16:03 VI	19:22 LI		02:46 PI	08:54 PI		08:13 GE					21:33 CP
14			14:16 AQ			01:22 GE		14:41 LE				
15		22:00 SC	05:33 SC		18:15 AR				23:25 LE	22:05 LI	11:05 SA	20:59 AQ
16	02:09 LE	16:03 VI				13:43 CA		22:21 VI			10:20 CP	
17	08:11 VI		21:15 PI	00:23 TA	06:16 TA				07:16 VI		11:02 AQ	23:01 PI
18	08:11 VI			13:12 GE				03:45 LI	11:59 LI	00:06 SC		
19		19:22 LI			19:12 GE	00:31 LE						
20	12:48 LI						20:32 CA	07:38 SC	14:39 SC	00:33 SA		05:02 AR
21	16:28 SC	00:48 SA			07:43 CA							
22	19:24 SA	04:12 CP					06:56 LE	10:41 SA	16:31 SA	01:14 CP	14:52 PI	14:57 TA
23		08:37 AQ										
24	21:58 CP				18:53 LE	21:33 LI						
25		14:42 PI							18:45 CP	03:44 AQ	22:26 AR	03:12 GE
26				00:23 TA	19:12 GE		15:11 VI					
27		14:42 PI	06:32 AR									
28	01:07 AQ			00:23 TA	07:43 CA	00:31 LE	21:33 LI		22:12 AQ	08:55 PI		
29	01:07 AQ	23:14 AR	06:32 AR	13:12 GE	07:43 CA	09:27 VI				03:44 AQ	22:26 AR	
30	06:16 PI		17:55 TA	13:12 GE	07:43 CA	09:27 VI		10:41 SA	22:12 AQ	08:55 PI		14:57 TA
31	06:16 PI		17:55 TA		18:53 LE		21:33 LI	10:41 SA		08:55 PI		03:12 GE

1969

	January	February	March	April	May	June	July	August	September	October	November	December
01	15:54 CA	10:29 LE		20:04 LI	09:50 SC	21:07 CP	06:50 AQ	19:55 AR	19:24 GE		11:35 LE	08:14 VI
02			04:07 VI							14:53 CA		
03	03:55 LE	20:41 VI			11:19 SA		07:27 PI		06:57 CA			19:17 LI
04				00:23 SC		21:04 AQ		02:02 TA		03:26 LE	00:00 VI	
05		05:00 LI	11:34 LI		11:57 CP		11:17 AR		19:37 LE			02:31 SC
06	14:43 VI			02:58 SA		23:14 PI		11:49 GE			09:59 LI	
07		11:18 SC	16:57 SC		13:28 AQ					15:22 VI		05:43 SA
08	23:33 LI			05:05 CP		04:37 AR	18:54 TA		07:21 VI		16:18 SC	
09		15:23 SA	20:48 SA		17:04 PI			23:57 CA		00:49 LI		06:21 CP
10				07:46 AQ			05:31 GE				19:30 SA	
11	05:32 SC		23:41 CP		23:09 AR	13:07 TA		12:38 LE		07:19 SC		06:28 AQ
12		17:29 CP		11:41 PI			17:47 CA				21:09 CP	
13	08:19 SA					23:49 GE		00:33 VI	00:25 SC	11:33 SA		07:57 PI
14		18:31 AQ	02:10 AQ	17:13 AR	07:29 TA					14:35 CP	22:53 AQ	
15	08:39 CP					00:35 LE	06:29 LE		05:42 SA			11:56 AR
16		20:04 PI	05:04 PI		17:42 GE	11:53 CA		10:52 LI			01:53 PI	
17	08:17 AQ			00:43 TA					09:14 CP	17:21 AQ		18:35 TA
18		23:49 AR	09:27 AR			00:35 LE	18:42 VI	18:55 SC			06:33 AR	
19	09:21 PI			10:29 GE	05:31 CA				11:31 AQ	20:26 PI		
20		07:02 TA	16:20 TA			12:53 VI	05:20 LI				12:53 TA	03:28 GE
21	13:44 AR				18:13 LE			00:13 SA	13:22 PI	00:18 AR		
22		17:41 GE	02:12 GE	22:17 CA			13:04 SC				20:59 GE	14:08 CA
23	22:14 TA					23:03 LI		02:49 CP	15:56 AR	05:33 TA		
24			14:19 CA	10:52 LE	06:07 VI		17:11 SA					
25		06:11 CA				05:31 SC		03:36 AQ	20:29 TA		07:10 CA	02:21 LE
26	09:54 GE			21:57 VI	15:07 LI					13:01 GE		
27		18:12 LE	02:37 LE			07:59 SA	18:10 CP	04:03 PI			19:22 LE	15:20 VI
28	22:37 CA				20:05 SC				04:06 GE	23:13 CA		
29			12:54 VI	05:44 LI		07:45 CP	17:35 AQ	05:57 AR				
30					21:30 SA							03:19 LI
31							17:31 PI	10:50 TA				

530

1970

	January	February	March	April	May	June	July	August	September	October	November	December
01		01:50 SA						10:44 LE				
02	12:04 SC		12:54 CP		09:33 AR		17:22 CA		18:26 LI	11:36 SC	02:24 SA	18:45 AQ
03		04:22 CP		00:02 PI		02:10 GE		23:34 VI				
04	16:34 SA		14:35 AQ		13:05 TA		04:27 LE		05:55 SC	20:32 SA	08:33 CP	21:56 PI
05		04:19 AQ		01:33 AR		10:26 CA						
06			14:49 PI		18:17 GE			12:32 LI			13:11 AQ	
07	17:30 CP	03:37 PI		04:03 TA		21:17 LE	17:12 VI		14:59 SA	03:11 CP		01:04 AR
08			15:17 AR		02:17 CA			23:56 SC			16:33 PI	
09	16:48 AQ	04:17 AR		09:02 GE			06:03 LI		20:52 CP	07:26 AQ		04:25 TA
10			17:44 TA			10:03 VI						
11	16:37 PI	07:59 TA		17:33 CA	13:22 LE		16:41 SC	08:07 SA	23:34 AQ	09:30 PI	18:52 AR	08:34 GE
12			23:37 GE			22:29 LI						
13	18:48 AR	15:29 GE			02:11 VI		23:26 SA	12:25 CP	23:57 PI		20:50 TA	14:33 CA
14				05:16 LE		08:02 SC				10:12 AR		
15			09:19 CA		14:03 LI			13:31 AQ			23:49 GE	
16	00:20 TA	02:18 CA		18:07 VI		13:39 SA	02:19 CP		23:35 AR	10:59 TA		23:22 LE
17			21:40 LE		22:50 SC			13:02 PI			05:24 CA	
18	09:07 GE	14:54 LE		05:35 LI		16:05 CP	02:45 AQ		00:21 TA	13:43 GE		11:05 VI
19								12:51 AR			14:37 LE	
20	20:14 CA	03:42 VI	10:30 VI		04:12 SA		02:37 PI		04:02 GE			00:01 LI
21						17:01 AQ		14:47 TA		19:59 CA	02:50 VI	
22	08:41 LE		21:56 LI		07:13 CP		03:43 AR		11:41 CA			
23		15:30 LI		20:15 SA		18:12 PI					15:39 LI	11:27 SC
24	21:34 VI				09:26 AQ			20:04 GE				
25		01:23 SC	07:10 SC	00:27 CP		20:52 AR	07:19 TA		22:54 LE	18:58 VI	02:25 SC	19:28 SA
26					11:59 PI							
27	09:43 LI		14:07 SA	03:44 AQ		01:35 TA	13:54 GE	04:58 CA	11:54 VI			
28		08:38 SA			15:27 AR					07:38 LI	10:02 SA	00:02 CP
29	19:35 SC		19:00 CP				23:15 CA	16:38 LE				
30				06:38 PI		08:25 GE			00:34 LI	18:16 SC	15:05 CP	02:24 AQ
31			22:09 AQ		20:03 TA			05:36 VI				

1971

	January	February	March	April	May	June	July	August	September	October	November	December
01	04:08 PI	15:49 TA		16:51 CA	09:35 LE	17:27 LI	13:47 SC	08:50 SA	07:04 AQ	19:37 PI	05:56 TA	16:25 GE
02			03:01 GE									
03	06:27 AR	20:34 GE		02:06 LE	21:03 VI	05:36 SC	23:59 SA	16:32 CP	08:51 PI	19:41 AR	05:27 GE	17:51 CA
04			09:48 CA									
05	10:01 TA	04:07 CA		14:17 VI	09:59 LI	15:29 SA		20:47 AQ	08:44 AR	18:43 TA	07:15 CA	22:17 LE
06							07:04 CP					
07	15:09 GE	14:06 LE	19:56 LE			22:46 CP		22:34 PI	08:38 TA	18:54 GE	12:56 LE	
08				03:17 LI	22:03 SC		11:27 AQ					06:41 VI
09	22:09 CA		08:11 VI					23:27 AR	10:26 GE	22:11 CA	22:44 VI	
10		01:58 VI		15:28 SC	08:08 SA	04:04 AQ	14:15 PI					18:20 LI
11								00:56 TA	15:22 CA			
12	07:24 LE	14:51 LI	21:07 LI	02:03 SA	16:09 CP	08:02 PI	16:32 AR			05:31 LE	11:06 LI	07:02 SC
13								04:11 GE	23:38 LE			
14	18:57 VI	03:22 SC	09:32 SC		22:20 AQ	11:06 AR	19:10 TA			16:16 VI	23:50 SC	
15				10:38 CP				09:50 CA				18:38 SA
16			20:24 SA			13:39 TA	22:47 GE		10:29 VI			
17	07:53 LI	13:46 SA		16:46 AQ	02:40 PI			17:58 LE		04:47 LI	11:31 SA	04:08 CP
18						16:24 GE			22:47 LI			
19	20:04 SC	20:38 CP	04:37 CP	20:08 PI	05:12 AR		03:57 CA			17:31 SC	21:37 CP	
20						20:30 CA		04:19 VI				11:33 AQ
21		23:43 AQ	09:29 AQ	21:09 AR	06:32 TA		11:17 LE		11:33 SC			
22	05:16 SA					03:12 LE		16:23 LI		05:32 SA	05:53 AQ	17:10 PI
23		00:05 PI	11:08 PI	21:07 TA	08:02 GE		21:10 VI		23:43 SA			
24	10:33 CP					13:06 VI		05:09 SC		16:06 CP	11:48 PI	21:09 AR
25												
26	12:37 AQ	23:30 AR	10:46 AR	21:59 GE	11:26 CA		09:12 LI		09:53 CP		15:04 AR	23:45 TA
27						01:23 LI		16:57 SA		00:12 AQ		
28	13:02 PI	23:54 TA	10:16 TA	01:44 CA	18:16 LE		21:51 SC		16:39 AQ		16:08 TA	01:39 GE
29								01:54 CP		04:57 PI		
30	13:36 AR											
31			11:44 GE		04:48 VI					06:26 AR		04:02 CA

1972

	January	February	March	April	May	June	July	August	September	October	November	December
01	—	00:56 VI	18:59 LI	—	—	12:15 AQ	01:19 PI	14:58 TA	—	12:26 LE	—	—
02	08:23 LE	—	—	—	20:29 CP	—	—	—	02:11 CA	—	10:27 LI	03:42 SC
03	—	11:07 LI	—	02:28 SA	—	19:52 PI	06:23 AR	17:33 GE	—	19:31 VI	—	—
04	15:51 VI	—	07:00 SC	—	—	—	—	—	06:54 LE	—	21:46 SC	16:23 SA
05	—	23:18 SC	—	14:21 CP	06:35 AQ	—	09:26 TA	20:18 CA	—	—	—	—
06	—	—	19:37 SA	—	—	00:28 AR	—	—	13:16 VI	04:35 LI	—	—
07	02:34 LI	—	—	23:38 AQ	13:28 PI	—	11:05 GE	23:56 LE	—	—	10:16 SA	05:07 CP
08	—	11:38 SA	—	—	—	02:15 TA	—	—	21:37 LI	15:27 SC	—	—
09	15:04 SC	—	06:50 CP	—	16:35 AR	—	12:30 CA	—	—	—	23:11 CP	16:54 AQ
10	—	21:50 CP	—	04:58 PI	—	02:25 GE	—	05:23 VI	—	—	—	—
11	—	—	14:43 AQ	—	16:48 TA	—	15:05 LE	—	08:16 SC	03:52 SA	—	—
12	02:57 SA	—	—	06:32 AR	—	02:45 CA	—	13:28 LI	—	—	11:03 AQ	02:33 PI
13	—	04:37 AQ	18:40 PI	—	15:58 GE	—	20:16 VI	—	20:43 SA	16:44 CP	—	—
14	12:26 CP	—	—	05:55 TA	—	05:10 LE	—	—	—	—	19:57 PI	08:59 AR
15	—	08:12 PI	19:37 AR	—	16:17 CA	—	—	00:20 SC	—	—	—	—
16	19:04 AQ	—	—	05:17 GE	—	11:04 VI	04:49 LI	—	09:08 CP	03:51 AQ	—	11:59 TA
17	—	09:51 AR	19:28 TA	—	19:39 LE	—	—	12:50 SA	—	—	00:45 AR	—
18	23:28 PI	—	—	06:46 CA	—	20:39 LI	16:15 SC	—	19:04 AQ	11:12 PI	—	12:24 GE
19	—	11:12 TA	20:13 GE	—	—	—	—	—	—	—	01:54 TA	—
20	02:36 AR	—	—	11:47 LE	02:57 VI	—	—	00:39 CP	—	14:23 AR	—	11:57 CA
21	—	13:36 GE	23:26 CA	—	—	08:43 SC	04:47 SA	—	01:09 PI	—	01:06 GE	—
22	05:18 TA	—	—	20:25 VI	13:37 LI	—	—	09:44 AQ	—	14:38 TA	—	12:34 LE
23	—	17:52 CA	—	—	—	21:14 SA	16:11 CP	—	03:44 AR	—	00:31 CA	—
24	08:15 GE	—	05:46 LE	—	—	—	—	15:29 PI	—	14:03 GE	—	16:02 VI
25	—	—	—	07:35 LI	02:01 SC	—	—	—	04:28 TA	—	02:12 LE	—
26	12:02 CA	00:15 LE	14:48 VI	—	—	08:36 CP	01:08 AQ	18:40 AR	—	14:45 CA	—	23:22 LI
27	—	—	—	19:57 SC	14:33 SA	—	—	—	05:15 GE	—	07:24 VI	—
28	—	08:39 VI	—	—	—	18:03 AQ	07:29 PI	20:43 TA	—	18:15 LE	—	—
29	17:22 LE	—	01:42 LI	—	—	—	—	—	07:39 CA	—	16:15 LI	10:11 SC
30	—	—	—	08:31 SA	02:13 CP	—	11:51 AR	22:56 GE	—	—	—	—
31	—	—	13:49 SC	—	—	—	—	—	—	00:59 VI	—	22:52 SA

533

1973

	January	February	March	April	May	June	July	August	September	October	November	December
01		05:55 AQ	14:22 AQ				21:56 LE		05:18 SC			
02	11:31 CP			12:49 AR	01:02 TA	11:21 CA		13:12 LI			08:58 AQ	04:32 PI
03		14:22 PI	22:31 PI				23:32 VI		15:25 SA	12:03 CP		
04	22:48 AQ			14:59 TA	01:16 GE	11:49 LE		20:36 SC			20:26 PI	13:51 AR
05		20:29 AR										
06			03:37 AR	16:12 GE	01:35 CA	14:52 VI	04:24 LI		04:01 CP	00:49 AQ		19:09 TA
07	08:03 PI							07:37 SA			04:19 AR	
08		00:54 TA	06:51 TA	18:05 CA	03:36 LE	21:16 LI	13:06 SC		16:31 AQ	11:24 PI		20:59 GE
09	14:58 AR							20:30 CP			08:26 TA	
10		04:10 GE	09:32 GE	21:31 LE	08:13 VI					18:29 AR		20:53 CA
11	19:24 TA					06:53 SC	00:48 SA		02:41 PI		09:59 GE	
12		06:45 CA	12:30 CA		15:31 LI			08:53 AQ		22:36 TA		20:45 LE
13	21:41 GE			02:47 VI		18:44 SA	13:45 CP		09:56 AR		10:47 CA	
14		09:13 LE	16:08 LE					19:14 PI				22:21 VI
15	22:39 CA			09:50 LI	01:10 SC				14:59 TA	01:08 GE	12:20 LE	
16		12:32 VI	20:43 VI			07:37 CP	02:15 AQ					
17	23:40 LE			18:51 SC	12:42 SA			03:16 AR	18:48 GE	03:28 CA	15:42 VI	02:54 LI
18		17:59 LI				20:19 AQ	13:07 PI					
19			02:48 LI					09:15 TA	22:01 CA	06:25 LE	21:16 LI	10:44 SC
20	02:24 VI			06:02 SA	01:31 CP		21:44 AR					
21		02:35 SC	11:15 SC			07:29 PI		13:27 GE		10:19 VI		21:20 SA
22	08:17 LI			18:50 CP	14:18 AQ				00:56 LE		05:07 SC	
23		14:14 SA	22:26 SA			15:48 AR	03:41 TA	16:08 CA		15:29 LI		
24	17:53 SC								03:58 VI		15:11 SA	09:41 CP
25				07:22 AQ	01:06 PI	20:37 TA	06:59 GE	17:49 LE		22:29 SC		
26		03:04 CP	11:16 CP						08:01 LI			22:43 AQ
27	06:11 SA			17:10 PI	08:15 AR	22:18 GE	08:11 CA	19:33 VI			03:13 CP	
28			23:13 AQ						14:19 SC	07:58 SA		
29	18:54 CP			22:54 AR	11:28 TA	22:09 CA	08:30 LE	22:52 LI			16:17 AQ	11:10 PI
30									23:48 SA	19:57 CP		
31			07:55 PI		11:53 GE		09:35 VI					21:35 AR

1974

	January	February	March	April	May	June	July	August	September	October	November	December
01		16:54 GE		11:41 LE		11:10 SC	01:21 SA		01:29 PI		18:23 GE	06:22 CA
02	04:39 TA		02:59 CA		23:39 LI			06:46 AQ		04:40 TA		
03		19:06 CA		13:57 VI		19:21 SA	12:20 CP		12:58 AR		23:01 CA	08:32 LE
04	08:01 GE		04:49 LE					19:26 PI		12:01 GE		
05		19:11 LE		16:23 LI	04:43 SC				22:51 TA			10:40 VI
06	08:29 CA		05:34 VI			05:49 CP	00:42 AQ			17:30 CA	02:30 LE	
07		18:52 VI		20:25 SC	12:05 SA			07:15 AR				13:43 LI
08	07:42 LE		06:52 LI			18:03 AQ	13:26 PI		06:37 GE	21:03 LE	05:18 VI	
09		20:10 LI			22:15 CP			17:13 TA				18:14 SC
10	07:42 VI		10:40 SC	03:27 SA					11:40 CA	22:56 VI	07:59 LI	
11						06:44 PI	01:10 AR					
12	10:21 LI	00:58 SC	18:21 SA	13:56 CP	10:34 AQ			00:15 GE	13:55 LE		11:24 SC	00:35 SA
13						17:53 AR	10:21 TA			00:11 LI		
14	16:54 SC	10:02 SA			23:04 PI			03:49 CA	14:12 VI		16:39 SA	09:04 CP
15			05:42 CP	02:34 AQ			15:54 GE			02:23 SC		
16		22:17 CP				01:47 TA		04:27 LE	14:17 LI			19:48 AQ
17	03:12 SA		18:39 AQ	14:44 PI	09:20 AR		17:56 CA			07:14 SA	00:43 CP	
18						05:59 GE		03:43 VI	16:14 SC			
19	15:48 CP	11:22 AQ			16:11 TA		17:43 LE			15:44 CP	11:40 AQ	08:12 PI
20			06:33 PI	00:20 AR		07:21 CA		03:45 LI	21:46 SA			
21		23:16 PI			19:55 GE		17:10 VI					20:35 AR
22	04:51 AQ		16:02 AR	06:54 TA		07:30 LE		06:37 SC		03:20 AQ	00:12 PI	
23					21:46 CA		18:19 LI		07:22 CP			
24	17:01 PI	09:13 AR	23:10 TA	11:12 GE		08:11 VI		13:34 SA		15:57 PI	11:59 AR	06:45 TA
25					23:12 LE		22:46 SC		19:38 AQ			
26		17:11 TA		14:18 CA		10:57 LI					21:05 TA	13:16 GE
27	03:33 AR		04:33 GE					00:15 CP		03:14 AR		
28		23:10 GE		17:04 LE	01:25 VI	16:40 SC	07:00 SA		08:15 PI			16:16 CA
29	11:42 TA		08:40 CA					12:52 AQ		12:00 TA	02:58 GE	
30				20:01 VI	05:16 LI		18:11 CP		19:26 AR			17:05 LE
31												

1975

	January	February	March	April	May	June	July	August	September	October	November	December
01	17:33 VI		14:34 SC			01:32 PI						
02		05:53 SC		11:09 CP	05:34 AQ			04:02 GE	23:08 LE	10:04 VI	20:08 SC	07:33 SA
03	19:22 LI		19:06 SA			14:01 AR	09:55 TA					
04		12:10 SA		21:46 AQ	17:34 PI			10:17 CA	23:29 VI	09:39 LI	21:10 SA	10:58 CP
05	23:39 SC						18:59 GE					
06		21:42 CP	03:40 CP			01:19 TA		12:44 LE	22:38 LI	09:09 SC		17:12 AQ
07				10:17 PI							00:45 CP	
08	06:39 SA		15:10 AQ			09:50 GE	00:24 CA		22:46 SC	10:36 SA		
09		09:17 AQ		22:44 AR	17:03 TA						07:59 AQ	02:52 PI
10	15:58 CP					15:22 CA	02:50 LE	12:51 LI		15:29 CP		
11		21:46 PI	03:50 PI						01:41 SA		18:42 PI	15:07 AR
12				09:53 TA	01:45 GE	18:46 LE	03:55 VI	14:30 SC				
13	03:03 AQ		16:19 AR						08:12 CP	00:10 AQ		
14		10:23 AR			08:08 CA	21:11 VI	05:21 LI	18:59 SA			07:18 AR	03:40 TA
15	15:23 PI								17:51 AQ	11:40 PI		
16		22:10 TA	03:53 TA		12:39 LE	23:41 LI	08:23 SC				19:38 TA	14:13 GE
17				02:27 CA				02:25 CP				
18	04:04 AR		13:43 GE		15:46 VI		13:32 SA		05:32 PI	00:20 AR		21:49 CA
19		07:35 GE		07:14 LE		02:59 SC		12:10 AQ			06:15 GE	
20	15:22 TA		20:48 CA		18:06 LI		20:46 CP		18:07 AR	12:43 TA		
21		13:19 CA		09:43 VI		07:34 SA		23:33 PI			14:37 CA	02:53 LE
22	23:24 GE				20:26 SC					23:52 GE		
23		15:13 LE	00:31 LE	10:42 LI		13:56 CP	05:56 AQ		06:43 TA		20:48 LE	06:28 VI
24					23:52 SA			12:03 AR				
25	03:21 CA	14:37 VI	01:21 VI	11:40 SC		22:33 AQ	16:59 PI		18:13 GE	08:58 CA		09:27 LI
26											01:04 VI	
27	04:01 LE		00:51 LI	14:20 SA	05:31 CP			00:45 TA		15:20 LE		12:28 SC
28						09:33 PI	05:28 AR		03:07 CA		03:48 LI	
29	03:14 VI		01:08 SC		14:09 AQ			11:53 GE		18:47 VI		15:53 SA
30						22:03 AR	17:54 TA		08:21 LE		05:36 SC	
31	03:14 LI		04:10 SA					19:35 CA		19:55 LI		20:17 CP

1976

Day	January	February	March	April	May	June	July	August	September	October	November	December
01		19:47 PI		09:35 TA	04:05 GE	04:38 LE	15:47 VI	03:55 SC	16:29 CP	03:50 AQ		23:41 TA
02	02:34 AQ		14:22 AR								04:46 AR	
03		07:17 AR		22:16 GE	14:53 CA	10:21 VI	19:35 LI	07:03 SA	22:20 AQ	12:11 PI		12:39 GE
04	11:36 PI		03:18 TA								17:23 TA	
05												
06		20:13 TA		09:07 CA	23:09 LE	14:00 LI	22:34 SC	10:54 CP	06:12 PI	22:50 AR		00:22 CA
07	23:21 AR		15:56 GE								06:21 GE	
08		08:16 GE		16:37 LE	04:21 VI	15:59 SC	01:06 SA	15:57 AQ	16:19 AR	11:11 TA		10:13 LE
09	12:10 TA		01:59 CA								18:28 CA	
10		16:59 CA		20:16 VI	06:39 LI	17:07 SA	03:49 CP	23:01 PI	04:31 TA	00:14 GE		17:56 VI
11	23:19 GE		07:56 LE								04:37 LE	
12												
13		21:33 LE		20:54 LI	07:03 SC	18:46 CP	07:53 AQ	08:49 AR	17:33 GE	12:24 CA		23:14 LI
14	07:00 CA		09:59 VI								11:47 VI	
15		22:59 VI		20:14 SC	07:04 SA	22:31 AQ	14:36 PI	21:06 TA	05:07 CA	21:50 LE		02:02 SC
16	11:15 LE		09:45 LI								15:35 LI	
17		23:15 LI		20:15 SA	08:32 CP	05:43 PI	00:40 AR	09:55 GE	13:11 LE	03:25 VI		02:54 SA
18	13:25 VI		09:18 SC								16:32 SC	
19												
20		00:14 SC		22:44 CP	13:03 AQ	16:32 AR	13:11 TA	20:35 CA	17:16 VI	05:27 LI		03:12 CP
21	15:11 LI		10:34 SA								16:04 SA	
22		03:19 SA		04:48 AQ	21:27 PI	05:21 TA	01:41 GE	03:31 LE	18:28 LI	05:17 SC		04:48 AQ
23	17:49 SC		14:48 CP								16:04 CP	
24		08:54 CP		14:29 PI	09:07 AR	17:37 GE	11:40 CA	07:04 VI	18:34 SC	04:49 SA		09:36 PI
25	21:52 SA		22:19 AQ								18:30 AQ	
26												
27		16:48 AQ		02:38 AR	22:07 TA	03:29 CA	18:19 LE	08:41 LI	19:22 SA	05:56 CP		18:32 AR
28	03:25 CP		08:34 PI								00:47 PI	
29		02:41 PI		15:38 TA	10:22 GE	10:40 LE	22:24 VI	10:05 SC	22:14 CP	10:06 AQ		06:44 TA
30	10:34 AQ		20:37 AR								11:01 AR	
31					20:39 CA		01:14 LI	12:28 SA		17:54 PI		

1977

	January	February	March	April	May	June	July	August	September	October	November	December
01	19:44 GE			01:26 VI		02:54 SA		01:24 PI		20:34 GE		
02			09:25 LE		16:24 SC		12:57 AQ		00:52 TA			23:06 VI
03		00:12 LE		04:40 LI		02:07 CP		06:54 AR			05:03 LE	
04	07:13 CA		15:19 VI		15:59 SA		15:32 PI		12:27 GE	09:10 CA		
05		06:17 VI		05:40 SC		02:44 AQ		16:18 TA			15:17 VI	07:18 LI
06	16:21 LE		18:35 LI		15:54 CP		22:04 AR			20:58 LE		
07		10:36 LI		06:09 SA		06:36 PI			01:04 CA		21:51 LI	11:34 SC
08	23:23 VI		20:37 SC		17:59 AQ			04:29 GE				
09		14:04 SC		07:41 CP		14:35 AR	08:33 TA		12:15 LE	05:59 VI		12:22 SA
10			22:43 SA		23:29 PI			17:04 CA			00:42 SC	
11	04:48 LI	17:11 SA		11:24 AQ			21:15 GE		20:35 VI	11:29 LI		11:27 CP
12						01:57 TA					01:04 SA	
13	08:44 SC	20:14 CP	06:00 AQ	17:49 PI	08:30 AR			03:57 LE		14:11 SC		11:00 AQ
14						14:51 GE	09:50 CA		02:08 LI		00:51 CP	
15	11:18 SA	23:46 AQ	12:06 PI		20:05 TA			12:27 VI		15:27 SA		13:09 PI
16				02:52 AR			20:51 LE		05:46 SC		02:00 AQ	
17	13:02 CP		20:23 AR			03:29 CA		18:50 LI		16:51 CP		19:11 AR
18		04:46 PI		14:03 TA	08:51 GE				08:28 SA		05:59 PI	
19	15:12 AQ					14:53 LE	05:59 VI	23:36 SC		19:36 AQ		
20		12:23 AR	07:05 TA		21:36 CA				11:04 CP		13:14 AR	04:54 TA
21	19:31 PI			02:38 GE			13:10 LI					
22		23:07 TA	19:39 GE			00:29 VI		03:03 SA	14:12 AQ	00:27 PI	23:10 TA	16:51 GE
23				15:26 CA	09:14 LE		18:14 SC					
24	03:20 AR					07:35 LI		05:31 CP	18:30 PI	07:35 AR		
25		11:50 GE			18:31 VI		21:05 SA				10:48 GE	05:30 CA
26	14:42 TA			02:44 LE		11:42 SC		07:41 AQ		16:54 TA		
27			08:17 CA				22:15 CP		00:41 AR		23:20 CA	17:52 LE
28		00:02 CA		10:53 VI	00:28 LI	13:02 SA		10:47 PI				
29	03:38 GE		18:41 LE				23:05 AQ		09:22 TA	04:09 GE		
30				15:13 LI	02:57 SC	12:49 CP		16:11 AR			11:53 LE	05:14 VI
31	15:20 CA									16:40 CA		

1978

	January	February	March	April	May	June	July	August	September	October	November	December
01	14:32 LI		13:02 SA		09:00 PI		19:38 GE			14:18 LI		20:44 CP
02		07:14 SA				03:50 TA					10:03 SA	
03	20:36 SC		15:58 CP	00:06 AQ	14:27 AR		07:34 CA	02:10 LE		21:49 SC		21:36 AQ
04		08:50 CP				13:54 GE					12:40 CP	
05	23:04 SA		17:51 AQ	03:21 PI	21:52 TA		20:13 LE	14:29 VI		03:07 SA		23:37 PI
06		09:04 AQ									15:04 AQ	
07			19:46 PI	07:52 AR	07:18 GE	01:31 CA				06:53 CP		03:40 AR
08	22:55 CP						08:45 VI	01:30 LI			18:06 PI	
09		09:48 PI	23:09 AR	14:22 TA	18:42 CA	14:08 LE				09:43 AQ		09:51 TA
10	22:05 AQ						19:48 LI	10:11 SC				
11		12:57 AR		23:28 GE							22:12 AR	17:55 GE
12			05:19 TA		07:17 LE	02:36 VI	03:47 SC	15:43 SA	03:09 AQ	12:12 PI		
13	22:50 PI	19:51 TA						18:03 CP			03:35 TA	03:50 CA
14			14:49 GE	10:59 CA	19:16 VI	12:56 LI	07:50 SA		04:10 PI			
15	03:05 AR									15:06 AR	10:45 GE	15:37 LE
16		06:25 GE				19:29 SC	08:33 CP	18:15 AQ	05:50 AR			
17	11:30 TA		02:49 CA		04:25 LI					19:22 TA	20:17 CA	
18		18:57 CA					07:42 AQ	18:05 PI	09:43 TA			04:34 VI
19	23:07 GE		15:12 LE		09:40 SC	22:01 SA				02:06 GE		
20							07:27 PI	19:30 AR	16:56 GE		08:10 LE	16:40 LI
21		07:10 LE	01:49 VI	18:53 LI		21:52 CP				11:53 CA		
22	11:51 CA							00:06 TA			20:58 VI	
23		17:40 VI		23:40 SC	11:42 CP	21:08 AQ	09:47 AR		03:31 CA			01:32 SC
24	00:03 LE		09:41 LI					08:31 GE		00:05 LE		
25					12:10 AQ		15:51 TA		16:02 LE		08:07 LI	06:08 SA
26	10:57 VI	02:03 LI	15:01 SC	02:01 SA		21:57 PI				12:33 VI		
27					14:37 PI			19:59 CA			15:39 SC	07:16 CP
28	20:08 LI	08:28 SC	18:38 SA	03:28 CP			01:31 GE		04:12 VI			
29					19:52 AR					22:51 LI		06:54 AQ
30						09:21 TA		08:40 LE			19:23 SA	
31	03:04 SC		21:24 CP				13:29 CA			05:53 SC		

1979

	January	February	March	April	May	June	July	August	September	October	November	December
01	07:09 PI		07:09 TA		01:57 LE		19:09 LI		11:34 CP		10:09 AR	23:02 GE
02		22:03 TA		06:24 CA		22:41 VI		22:06 SA		00:24 PI		
03	09:42 AR		12:58 GE		14:41 VI		05:58 SC		13:59 AQ		11:16 TA	
04				17:58 LE				02:23 CP		00:29 AR		04:02 CA
05	15:18 TA	05:33 GE	22:35 CA			11:12 LI	12:56 SA		14:03 PI		13:25 GE	
06					02:47 LI			03:28 AQ		00:45 TA		12:10 LE
07	23:43 GE	16:06 CA		06:52 VI		21:05 SC	16:08 CP		13:29 AR		18:24 CA	
08			10:48 LE		12:10 SC			03:06 PI		03:07 GE		23:34 VI
09				18:45 LI			16:59 AQ		14:13 TA			
10	10:14 CA	04:26 LE	23:43 VI		18:25 SA	03:15 SA		03:10 AR		09:09 CA	03:15 LE	
11							17:23 PI		17:55 GE			12:30 LI
12	17:18 LE	17:18 VI		04:16 SC		06:24 CP		05:22 TA		19:12 LE	15:21 VI	
13			11:42 LI		22:26 CP		18:57 AR					
14	22:16 VI			11:18 SA		08:07 AQ		10:42 GE	01:28 CA			00:09 SC
15		05:38 LI	21:49 SC				22:43 TA			07:51 VI	04:17 LI	
16				16:23 CP	01:26 AQ	09:57 PI		19:18 CA	12:26 LE			08:37 SA
17	11:10 LI	16:13 SC					04:59 GE			20:45 LI	15:30 SC	
18			05:38 SA	20:02 AQ	04:19 PI	12:53 AR			01:15 VI			13:55 CP
19	23:41 SC	23:52 SA					13:41 CA	06:29 LE			23:57 SA	
20			10:56 CP	22:42 PI	07:31 AR	17:18 TA			14:11 LI	08:03 SC		17:12 AQ
21								19:12 VI				
22	09:51 SA	04:01 CP	13:52 AQ		11:21 TA	23:22 GE	00:31 LE		01:54 SC	17:10 SA	06:02 CP	19:50 PI
23				00:52 AR				08:14 LI				
24	16:09 CP	05:12 AQ	15:05 PI		16:28 GE		13:02 VI		11:36 SA		10:37 AQ	22:40 AR
25				03:28 TA		07:24 CA		20:12 SC		00:12 CP		
26	18:28 AQ	04:52 PI	15:48 AR		23:51 CA				18:40 CP		14:17 PI	
27				07:49 GE		17:47 LE	02:07 LI			05:17 AQ		02:08 TA
28	18:13 PI	04:54 AR	17:37 TA					05:39 SA			17:17 AR	
29				15:12 CA	10:08 LE		13:47 SC		22:49 AQ	08:29 PI		06:33 GE
30			22:09 GE			06:14 VI					19:55 TA	
31	18:11 AR											

1980

	January	February	March	April	May	June	July	August	September	October	November	December
01	12:30 CA	15:21 VI				19:30 AQ	05:49 PI	16:55 TA	01:50 GE		12:19 VI	07:13 LI
02	20:48 LE		10:40 LI	05:22 SC	22:22 SA				06:40 CA	19:58 LE		
03							08:47 AR	20:10 GE			00:31 LI	20:01 SC
04		04:04 LI	23:23 SC	16:35 SA	07:14 CP	00:10 PI			14:23 LE	06:20 VI		
05	07:49 VI						11:31 TA	01:12 CA			13:19 SC	07:58 SA
06		16:46 SC			14:04 AQ	03:24 AR				18:31 LI		
07							14:34 GE	08:23 LE	00:32 VI		01:26 SA	18:13 CP
08	20:38 LI		10:39 SA	01:43 CP	18:34 PI	05:30 TA						
09							18:45 CA	17:55 VI	12:23 LI	07:15 SC	12:16 CP	02:37 AQ
10		03:20 SA	19:03 CP	08:00 AQ	20:45 AR	07:23 GE						09:04 PI
11	08:55 SC			11:07 PI			01:03 LE	05:33 LI	01:07 SC	19:37 SA	21:11 AQ	
12		10:13 CP	23:46 AQ		21:25 TA	10:30 CA						13:22 AR
13	18:17 SA	13:20 AQ		11:40 AR			10:11 VI	18:16 SC	13:28 SA	06:37 CP		
14					22:08 GE	16:22 LE					03:22 PI	15:36 TA
15	23:51 CP	13:55 PI		11:11 TA			21:55 LI		23:45 CP	14:54 AQ		
16			01:11 PI		00:53 CA			06:09 SA			06:22 AR	16:39 GE
17				11:41 GE						19:32 PI		
18	02:25 AQ	13:43 AR	00:41 AR		07:15 LE	01:47 VI	10:34 SC	15:12 CP	06:30 AQ		06:51 TA	18:03 CA
19	03:33 PI			15:12 CA					09:27 PI	20:43 AR		
20		14:35 TA	00:13 TA		17:33 VI	13:55 LI	21:43 SA	20:33 AQ			06:28 GE	21:34 LE
21									09:37 AR	19:56 TA		
22	04:52 AR	17:58 GE	01:47 GE	22:53 LE	06:12 LI	02:27 SC		22:43 PI			07:19 CA	
23								23:11 AR	08:54 TA	19:18 GE		04:33 VI
24	07:32 TA		06:55 CA	10:13 VI		13:02 SA	05:46 CP	23:41 TA			11:23 LE	
25		00:35 CA							09:21 GE	21:00 CA		
26	12:12 GE		15:59 LE	23:10 LI	18:37 SC	20:47 CP	10:36 AQ				19:37 VI	15:05 LI
27		10:10 LE							12:47 CA			
28	19:03 CA						13:11 PI			02:39 LE		
29		21:53 VI	03:52 VI	11:35 SC	05:05 SA	02:04 AQ						03:37 SC
30												
31	04:09 LE		16:50 LI		13:15 CP		14:54 AR					

541

1981

	January	February	March	April	May	June	July	August	September	October	November	December
01	15:43 SA	10:37 CP		18:42 PI	06:58 AR	16:49 GE	02:58 CA	18:55 VI			12:46 CP	07:09 AQ
02									21:11 SC	17:00 SA		
03		17:55 AQ	03:51 AQ	20:26 AR	06:59 TA	16:39 CA	04:48 LE					17:16 PI
04	01:42 CP							02:24 LI			00:50 AQ	
05		22:21 PI	08:13 PI	20:05 TA	06:01 GE	18:43 LE	09:27 VI		09:24 SA	05:50 CP		23:49 AR
06	09:13 AQ							12:58 SC			09:52 PI	
07			09:49 AR	19:48 GE	06:18 CA		17:43 LI		21:49 CP	17:01 AQ		
08	14:42 PI	01:02 AR				00:26 VI					14:39 AR	02:32 TA
09			10:23 TA	21:34 CA	09:40 LE			01:23 SA				
10	18:44 AR	03:11 TA				09:56 LI	05:02 SC		07:59 AQ	00:33 PI	15:45 TA	02:31 GE
11			11:43 GE		16:56 VI			13:21 CP				
12	21:45 TA	05:52 GE		02:37 LE		21:55 SC	17:35 SA		14:35 PI	04:01 AR	15:00 GE	01:41 CA
13			15:06 CA					22:57 AQ				
14		09:43 CA		10:56 VI	03:25 LI				17:56 AR	04:43 TA	14:37 CA	02:09 LE
15	00:17 GE		21:03 LE			10:32 SA	05:19 CP					
16		15:11 LE		21:38 LI	15:38 SC			05:35 PI	19:30 TA	04:41 GE	16:33 LE	05:38 VI
17	03:08 CA					22:21 CP	15:02 AQ					
18		22:35 VI	05:20 VI					09:50 AR	20:59 GE	05:53 CA	21:54 VI	12:58 LI
19	07:21 LE			09:39 SC	04:15 SA		22:26 PI					
20			15:31 LI			08:36 AQ		12:44 TA	23:39 CA	09:35 LE		23:39 SC
21	14:03 VI	08:13 LI		22:16 SA	16:21 CP						06:34 LI	
22						16:44 PI	03:44 AR	15:19 GE		16:05 VI		
23	23:46 LI	19:55 SC	03:14 SC						04:08 LE		17:37 SC	12:11 SA
24				10:32 CP	03:01 AQ	22:18 AR	07:19 TA	18:17 CA				
25			15:51 SA						10:29 VI	00:57 LI		
26	11:49 SC	08:29 SA		20:58 AQ	11:06 PI		09:42 GE	22:10 LE			06:00 SA	00:59 CP
27						01:17 TA			18:41 LI	11:39 SC		
28		19:46 CP	03:53 CP		15:44 AR		11:41 CA				18:52 CP	12:54 AQ
29	00:12 SA			03:57 PI		02:22 GE		03:31 VI		23:49 SA		
30			13:16 AQ		17:10 TA		14:21 LE		04:54 SC			23:02 PI
31								11:03 LI				

1982

	January	February	March	April	May	June	July	August	September	October	November	December
01	06:34 AR	20:20 GE	01:50 GE	13:37 LE	23:45 VI	21:12 SC	14:26 SA	09:36 CP	16:11 PI	08:06 AR		10:58 CA
02											00:22 GE	
03	11:03 TA	22:18 CA	04:49 CA	18:19 VI				22:17 AQ		13:09 TA		11:27 LE
04					06:33 LI	08:32 SA	03:16 CP		00:24 AR		01:59 CA	
05	12:49 GE	23:50 LE	07:51 LE							16:39 GE		13:33 VI
06				00:27 LI	15:24 SC	21:13 CP	16:03 AQ	09:23 PI	06:27 TA		04:10 LE	
07	13:01 CA		11:28 VI							19:40 CA		18:11 LI
08		02:15 VI		08:33 SC				18:20 AR	10:58 GE		07:40 VI	
09	13:21 LE		16:35 LI		02:17 SA		03:35 PI			22:44 LE		
10		07:02 LI		19:07 SA					14:19 CA		12:46 LI	01:35 SC
11	15:37 VI				14:50 CP	21:45 PI	12:49 AR	01:00 TA				
12		15:16 SC	00:17 SC						16:46 LE	02:09 VI	19:43 SC	11:27 SA
13	21:17 LI			07:41 CP			18:59 TA	05:22 GE				
14			11:04 SA		03:45 AQ	06:21 AR			18:58 VI	06:23 LI		23:16 CP
15		02:46 SA					22:03 GE	07:41 CA			04:52 SA	
16	06:46 SC		23:47 CP		14:47 PI	11:07 TA			22:03 LI	12:21 SC		
17		15:37 CP					22:46 CA	08:41 LE			16:22 CP	12:12 AQ
18	19:01 SA			06:20 PI	22:05 AR	12:34 GE				21:03 SA		
19			11:53 AQ				22:36 LE	09:40 VI	03:32 SC			
20		03:15 AQ		12:24 AR		12:13 CA					05:21 AQ	00:56 PI
21	07:51 CP		21:01 PI		01:23 TA		23:20 VI	12:22 LI	12:30 SA	08:39 CP		
22		12:09 PI		14:59 TA		11:57 LE					17:43 PI	11:34 AR
23	19:26 AQ				01:55 GE			18:21 SC		21:36 AQ		
24		18:17 AR	02:37 AR	15:49 GE		13:36 VI	02:46 LI		00:31 CP			18:37 TA
25					01:39 CA						03:07 AR	
26	04:50 PI	22:32 TA	05:40 TA	16:44 CA		18:31 LI	09:59 SC	04:11 SA	13:22 AQ	09:13 PI		21:49 GE
27					02:27 LE						08:32 TA	
28	11:59 AR		07:44 GE	19:10 LE			20:48 SA	16:41 CP		17:26 AR		22:13 CA
29					05:43 VI	03:02 SC			00:19 PI		10:36 GE	
30	17:04 TA		10:10 CA							22:04 TA		21:34 LE
31					12:02 LI			05:23 AQ				

1983

	January	February	March	April	May	June	July	August	September	October	November	December
01	21:50 VI	09:47 LI	23:51 SC	16:21 SA	11:02 CP			07:37 TA		12:55 LE	23:31 LI	09:41 SC
02						19:42 PI			02:53 CA			
03		14:32 SC			23:09 AQ			14:43 GE		14:16 VI		14:56 SA
04	00:45 LI		07:15 SA	02:31 CP			00:06 TA		04:47 LE		01:53 SC	
05		23:29 SA				06:59 AR		18:09 CA		14:42 LI		22:29 CP
06	07:17 SC		18:30 CP	15:07 AQ	11:43 PI		05:42 GE		04:36 VI		06:09 SA	
07						15:05 TA		18:37 LE		16:06 SC		
08	17:14 SA	11:34 CP			22:16 AR		07:51 CA		04:14 LI		13:31 CP	08:40 AQ
09			07:31 AQ	03:31 PI		19:38 GE		17:49 VI		20:21 SA		
10		00:41 AQ					07:54 LE		05:50 SC			20:54 PI
11	05:26 CP		19:48 PI	13:37 AR	05:36 TA	21:33 CA		17:52 LI			00:11 AQ	
12		13:03 PI					07:43 VI		11:08 SA	04:30 CP		
13	18:26 AQ			20:59 TA	10:04 GE	22:22 LE		20:44 SC			12:41 PI	09:17 AR
14		23:47 AR	06:01 AR				09:10 LI		20:34 CP	15:59 AQ		
15					12:49 CA	23:38 VI						19:33 TA
16	07:02 PI		14:05 TA	02:15 GE			13:38 SC	03:34 SA			00:37 AR	
17		08:31 TA			15:02 LE				08:46 AQ	04:41 PI		
18	18:08 AR		20:20 GE	06:14 CA		02:37 LI	21:32 SA	14:00 CP			10:07 TA	02:24 GE
19		14:52 GE			17:37 VI				21:30 PI	16:19 AR		
20				09:27 LE		07:59 SC					16:46 GE	06:02 CA
21	02:37 TA	18:32 CA	00:52 CA		21:12 LI		08:11 CP	02:26 AQ				
22				12:12 VI		15:55 SA			09:10 AR	01:48 TA	21:11 CA	07:44 LE
23	07:41 GE	19:47 LE	03:43 LE				20:27 AQ	15:10 PI				
24				15:05 LI	02:18 SC				19:13 TA	09:11 GE		09:02 VI
25	09:29 CA	19:49 VI	05:18 VI			02:08 CP					00:20 LE	
26				19:05 SC	09:28 SA		09:12 PI	03:08 AR		14:48 CA		11:19 LI
27	09:10 LE	20:30 LI	06:49 LI			14:07 AQ			03:25 GE		03:02 VI	
28							21:21 AR	13:38 TA		18:51 LE		15:27 SC
29	08:35 VI		09:57 SC	01:29 SA	19:07 CP				09:25 CA		05:57 LI	
30						02:52 PI		21:49 GE		21:33 VI		21:44 SA
31					06:59 AQ							

1984

	January	February	March	April	May	June	July	August	September	October	November	December
01												
02	06:08 CP		17:29 PI	23:56 TA	16:02 GE	05:54 CA	19:28 VI	04:03 LI	16:30 SA	05:29 CP	07:50 PI	03:42 AR
03		11:22 PI										
04	16:31 AQ		06:07 AR		23:26 CA	10:19 LE	21:27 LI	06:04 SC	22:55 CP	14:04 AQ	20:20 AR	16:21 TA
05				10:05 GE								
06		00:03 AR	18:09 TA			13:28 VI		10:29 SA				
07	04:35 PI			17:59 CA	04:43 LE		00:29 SC		08:12 AQ	01:20 PI	08:53 TA	03:25 GE
08		12:05 TA				16:04 LI		17:24 CP				
09	17:15 AR		04:30 GE	23:02 LE	08:02 VI		05:03 SA		19:25 PI	13:51 AR	20:11 GE	11:57 CA
10		21:40 GE				18:49 SC						
11			11:49 CA	01:11 VI	09:54 LI		11:23 CP	02:25 AQ				18:09 LE
12	04:36 TA					22:27 SA			07:47 AR	02:28 TA	05:32 CA	
13	12:40 GE	03:21 CA	15:22 LE	01:29 LI	11:22 SC		19:41 AQ	13:13 PI			12:34 LE	22:36 VI
14						03:48 CP			20:33 TA	14:14 GE		
15		05:10 LE	15:47 VI	01:41 SC	13:50 SA			01:29 AR			17:08 VI	01:52 LI
16	16:48 CA					11:41 AQ	06:10 PI		08:26 GE	00:00 CA		
17	17:50 LE	04:32 VI	14:52 LI	03:44 SA	18:44 CP			14:14 TA			19:30 LI	04:27 SC
18						22:18 PI	18:26 AR		17:36 CA	06:41 LE		
19		03:40 LI	14:49 SC									
20	17:36 VI			09:11 CP	02:56 AQ			01:32 GE	22:49 LE	09:56 VI	20:31 SC	06:58 SA
21		04:45 SC	17:41 SA			10:40 AR	06:53 TA					
22	18:08 LI			18:28 AQ	14:09 PI			09:21 CA	00:19 VI	10:32 LI	21:34 SA	10:21 CP
23		09:23 SA				22:38 TA	17:11 GE		23:41 LI			
24	21:05 SC		00:36 CP					13:00 LE		10:08 SC	00:17 CP	15:47 AQ
25		17:50 CP		06:27 PI	02:40 AR		23:45 CA		23:04 SC			
26						08:04 GE		13:32 VI		10:44 SA		
27	03:13 SA		11:09 AQ	19:03 AR	14:13 TA						06:06 AQ	00:19 PI
28		05:02 AQ					02:42 LE	12:57 LI		14:05 CP		
29	12:13 CP		23:38 PI		23:23 GE						15:33 PI	
30				06:31 TA		17:31 LE	03:30 VI	13:23 SC	00:32 SA			11:50 AR
31	23:11 AQ		12:15 AR							21:14 AQ		

545

1985

	January	February	March	April	May	June	July	August	September	October	November	December
01	00:37 TA	05:59 CA	15:24 CA	10:26 VI	21:22 LI	07:33 SA	18:23 CP	12:33 PI	05:42 AR	00:36 TA	08:31 CA	00:59 LE
02												
03	12:01 GE	11:02 LE	21:28 LE	10:54 LI	21:17 SC	08:34 CP	21:36 AQ	21:42 AR	17:28 TA	13:37 GE	19:04 LE	09:15 VI
04												
05	20:18 CA	13:09 VI	23:43 VI	10:11 SC	20:56 SA	11:52 AQ						14:34 LI
06							03:41 PI	09:41 TA	06:28 GE	01:59 CA	02:18 VI	
07		14:11 LI	23:48 LI	10:18 SA	22:11 CP	18:47 PI						16:57 SC
08	01:28 LE						13:21 AR	22:31 GE	18:11 CA	11:34 LE	05:52 LI	
09		15:49 SC	23:48 SC	12:57 CP								17:14 SA
10	04:40 VI				02:38 AQ	05:25 AR				17:10 VI	06:31 SC	
11		19:09 SA		19:04 AQ			01:44 TA	09:29 CA	02:28 LE			17:00 CP
12	07:13 LI		01:30 SA		10:56 PI	18:12 TA				19:12 LI	05:53 SA	
13							14:23 GE	16:58 LE	06:53 VI			18:15 AQ
14	10:07 SC	00:28 CP	05:55 CP	04:31 PI	22:26 AR					19:13 SC	05:54 CP	
15						06:45 GE		21:16 VI	08:34 LI			22:50 PI
16	13:48 SA	07:37 AQ	13:11 AQ	16:18 AR			00:54 CA			19:05 SA	08:26 AQ	
17					11:24 TA	17:22 CA		23:44 LI	09:17 SC			
18	18:29 CP	16:38 PI	22:50 PI				08:25 LE			20:35 CP	14:43 PI	07:36 AR
19				05:13 TA					10:40 SA			
20					00:02 GE	01:32 LE	13:30 VI	01:52 SC				19:40 TA
21	00:39 AQ	03:43 AR	10:20 AR	18:01 GE					13:49 CP	00:55 AQ	00:43 AR	
22					11:05 CA	07:33 VI	17:11 LI	04:36 SA				
23	09:03 PI	16:27 TA	23:06 TA						19:12 AQ	08:28 PI	13:07 TA	08:45 GE
24				05:27 CA	19:54 LE	11:48 LI	20:17 SC	08:24 CP				
25	20:06 AR									18:48 AR		20:45 CA
26		05:11 GE	12:02 GE	14:11 LE		14:37 SC	23:13 SA	13:31 AQ	02:51 PI		02:08 GE	
27					02:06 VI							
28	08:54 TA		23:14 CA	19:25 VI		16:31 SA		20:25 PI	12:43 AR	06:59 TA	14:23 CA	06:45 LE
29					05:40 LI		02:22 CP					
30	21:01 GE									19:59 GE		14:44 VI
31			06:52 LE		07:07 SC		06:26 AQ					

1986

	January	February	March	April	May	June	July	August	September	October	November	December
01	20:46 LI					04:43 AR			01:09 LE		14:20 SC	02:08 SA
02		06:19 SC	14:52 SA		14:30 PI			06:04 CA		01:03 LI		
03		09:31 SA		03:12 AQ		15:45 TA	10:33 GE		10:06 VI		15:19 SA	01:29 CP
04			17:56 CP		23:01 AR			17:26 LE		04:36 SC		
05	00:45 SC	12:02 CP	21:43 AQ	09:04 PI			23:20 CA		16:34 LI		15:49 CP	01:23 AQ
06						04:27 GE				06:48 SA		
07	02:47 SA	14:35 AQ		17:12 AR	09:59 TA			02:44 VI	21:12 SC		17:29 AQ	03:49 PI
08						17:17 CA	10:56 LE			08:53 CP		
09	03:42 CP	18:33 PI	02:49 PI	03:36 TA	22:26 GE			10:05 LI			21:30 PI	09:50 AR
10							20:50 VI		00:41 SA			
11	05:01 AQ		10:04 AR			05:12 LE		15:36 SC		11:45 AQ		19:11 TA
12		01:21 AR		15:51 GE	11:18 CA				03:29 CP		04:15 AR	
13	08:39 PI		20:05 TA			15:19 VI	04:40 LI	19:18 SA		16:03 PI		
14		11:39 TA		04:42 CA	23:16 LE				06:07 AQ		13:25 TA	06:42 GE
15	16:03 AR					22:38 LI	09:58 SC	21:23 CP		22:13 AR		
16			08:23 GE	16:10 LE					09:27 PI			19:09 CA
17		00:18 GE			08:46 VI		12:34 SA	22:45 AQ			00:27 GE	
18	03:14 TA		21:05 CA			02:36 SC			14:33 AR	06:35 TA		07:44 LE
19		12:40 CA		00:24 VI	14:42 LI	03:35 SA	13:10 CP				12:46 CA	19:30 VI
20	16:13 GE							00:53 PI	22:26 TA	17:16 GE		
21		22:25 LE	07:38 LE	04:51 LI	17:03 SC		13:18 AQ				01:26 LE	
22						02:59 CP		05:28 AR				
23	04:15 CA		14:40 VI	06:16 SC	16:57 SA		14:59 PI		09:14 GE	05:38 CA		05:05 LI
24		04:58 VI				02:50 AQ		13:37 TA			12:46 VI	
25	13:48 LE		18:23 LI	06:17 SA	16:15 CP		20:03 AR		21:45 CA	18:03 LE		
26		09:07 LI				05:13 PI					20:59 LI	11:07 SC
27	20:52 VI		20:06 SC	06:42 CP	16:59 AQ		05:12 TA	00:59 GE	09:40 LE	04:21 VI		
28		12:06 SC				11:35 AR						13:20 SA
29			21:21 SA	09:06 AQ	20:54 PI		17:19 GE	13:40 CA	18:58 VI		01:13 SC	
30	02:10 LI					21:55 TA				11:05 LI		12:55 CP
31			23:26 CP									

1987

	January	February	March	April	May	June	July	August	September	October	November	December
01	11:54 AQ	02:09 AR	12:37 AR		07:39 CA	03:25 LE		01:09 SC	17:04 CP	01:52 AQ	13:40 AR	01:06 TA
02	12:36 PI	08:53 TA	18:12 TA	12:17 GE			09:55 LI				18:02 TA	
03				23:34 CA	20:07 LE	15:56 VI		06:47 SA	18:22 AQ	03:40 PI		08:14 GE
04	16:51 AR						18:03 SC					
05								08:51 CP	18:37 PI	05:35 AR		17:21 CA
06		19:23 GE	03:27 GE	12:04 LE	08:07 VI	02:25 LI	22:05 SA				00:16 GE	
07								08:37 AQ	19:35 AR	08:58 TA		
08	01:13 TA	07:55 CA	15:25 CA	23:28 VI	17:29 LI	09:07 SC	22:43 CP					04:41 LE
09								08:01 PI	22:58 TA	15:04 GE	09:10 CA	
10	12:39 GE	20:22 LE	03:55 LE			11:54 SA	21:49 AQ					17:31 VI
11				08:05 LI	23:09 SC			09:10 AR			20:45 LE	
12						12:05 CP	21:36 PI		05:55 GE	00:31 CA		
13	01:18 CA	07:27 VI	14:56 VI					13:39 TA			09:30 VI	05:40 LI
14				13:40 SC	01:41 SA	11:45 AQ			16:22 CA	12:34 LE		
15	13:45 LE	16:45 LI	23:34 LI				00:00 AR	21:59 GE			20:49 LI	14:41 SC
16				17:01 SA	02:37 CP	12:55 PI						
17							06:04 TA		04:50 LE	01:06 VI		19:33 SA
18	01:15 VI		05:57 SC	19:21 CP	03:43 AQ	16:56 AR		09:20 CA			04:47 SC	
19		00:05 SC	10:32 SA				15:33 GE		17:13 VI	11:50 LI		21:08 CP
20	11:10 LI	05:09 SA		21:46 AQ	06:25 PI			21:58 LE			09:17 SA	
21		07:57 CP	13:48 CP			00:09 TA	03:14 CA					21:20 AQ
22	18:31 SC			01:02 PI	11:23 AR				03:58 LI	19:42 SC	11:32 CP	
23						09:54 GE	15:50 LE	10:23 VI			13:13 AQ	22:10 PI
24	22:36 SA	09:08 AQ	16:18 AQ		18:39 TA				12:30 SC	00:58 SA		
25				05:41 AR		21:22 CA		21:36 LI				
26	23:43 CP	10:07 PI	18:46 PI				04:26 VI		18:49 SA	04:34 CP	15:40 PI	01:06 AR
27				12:07 TA	03:55 GE							
28	23:17 AQ		22:13 AR			09:52 LE	15:59 LI	06:49 SC		07:27 AQ	19:36 AR	06:37 TA
29				20:43 GE	14:59 CA				23:09 CP			
30	23:24 PI					22:35 VI				10:20 PI		14:29 GE
31			03:47 TA					13:24 SA				

1988

	January	February	March	April	May	June	July	August	September	October	November	December
01		18:06 LE		08:06 LI	01:39 SC		07:30 AQ	17:53 AR		22:39 CA		
02			13:06 VI						08:12 GE			
03	00:17 CA	06:54 VI		18:26 SC	08:52 SA	23:34 AQ	08:34 PI	20:24 TA			04:01 VI	00:56 LI
04									15:38 CA	08:32 LE		
05	11:48 LE		01:32 LI		13:54 CP		10:38 AR				17:04 LI	12:52 SC
06		19:36 LI		02:29 SA		02:01 PI		01:43 GE		21:02 VI		
07			12:28 SC		17:37 AQ		14:27 TA		02:15 LE			21:56 SA
08	00:35 VI			08:20 CP		05:05 AR		09:52 CA			04:46 SC	
09		06:42 SC	20:59 SA		20:39 PI		20:16 GE		14:48 VI	10:04 LI		
10	13:17 LI			12:10 AQ		09:03 TA		20:27 LE			14:06 SA	04:07 CP
11		14:36 SA			23:24 AR					21:58 SC		
12	23:39 SC		02:32 CP	14:24 PI		14:15 GE	04:08 CA		03:52 LI		21:13 CP	08:26 AQ
13		18:37 CP						08:46 VI				
14			05:08 AQ	15:47 AR	02:23 TA	21:19 CA	14:11 LE		16:07 SC	07:58 SA		11:53 PI
15	05:58 SA	19:26 AQ						21:52 LI			02:37 AQ	
16			05:42 PI	17:31 TA	06:32 GE					15:45 CP		15:03 AR
17	08:15 CP	18:44 PI				06:57 LE	02:17 VI		02:25 SA		06:34 PI	
18			05:45 AR	21:10 GE	13:06 CA			10:12 SC		21:05 AQ		18:11 TA
19	08:02 AQ	18:35 AR				19:03 VI	15:22 LI		09:45 CP		09:13 AR	
20			07:05 TA		22:52 LE			19:55 SA		23:59 PI		21:43 GE
21	07:27 PI	20:51 TA		04:05 CA					13:43 AQ		11:02 TA	
22			11:21 GE			07:57 LI	03:14 SC					
23	08:31 AR			14:35 LE	11:13 VI			01:49 CP	14:51 PI	00:59 AR	13:12 GE	02:35 CA
24		02:42 GE	19:27 CA			18:59 SC	11:43 SA					
25	12:37 TA				23:49 LI			04:05 AQ	14:30 AR	01:23 TA	17:19 CA	09:58 LE
26		12:12 CA		03:17 VI			16:08 CP					
27	20:03 GE		06:54 LE					04:01 PI	14:29 TA	02:56 GE		20:28 VI
28				15:38 LI			17:25 AQ				00:52 LE	
29		00:12 LE	19:49 VI			06:00 CP		03:29 AR	16:43 GE	07:28 CA		
30	06:12 CA						17:23 PI				11:59 VI	09:10 LI
31					16:57 SA			04:22 TA		16:03 LE		

549

1989

	January	February	March	April	May	June	July	August	September	October	November	December
01	21:35 SC		08:58 CP		11:51 AR	22:03 GE	09:19 CA	07:19 VI	01:48 LI	20:54 SC		17:42 AQ
02		23:30 CP		01:38 PI							02:46 CP	
03			13:37 AQ		11:55 TA	00:18 CA	14:38 LE	18:28 LI	14:24 SC	09:30 SA		00:48 PI
04	07:12 SA	02:51 AQ		01:52 AR							12:09 AQ	
05			14:59 PI		12:03 GE	05:29 LE	23:05 VI		02:51 SA	20:45 CP		05:12 AR
06	13:14 CP	03:52 PI		01:08 TA				07:05 SC			18:25 PI	
07			14:37 AR		14:20 CA	14:30 VI			13:14 CP	05:06 AQ		06:59 TA
08	16:31 AQ	04:18 AR		01:31 GE			10:30 LI	19:03 SA			21:08 AR	
09			14:26 TA		20:23 LE				20:02 AQ	09:37 PI		07:16 GE
10	18:31 PI	05:45 TA					23:09 SC				21:10 TA	
11			16:17 GE	04:58 CA		02:32 LI		04:17 CP	23:08 PI	10:41 AR		07:50 CA
12	20:36 AR	09:23 GE			06:31 VI						20:19 GE	
13			21:28 CA	12:31 LE		15:12 SC	10:31 SA	09:59 AQ	23:38 AR	09:53 TA		10:41 LE
14	23:36 TA	15:41 CA			19:08 LI						20:52 CA	
15				23:39 VI			19:01 CP	12:46 PI	23:23 TA	09:19 GE		17:19 VI
16						02:13 SA						
17	03:57 GE	00:33 LE		12:32 LI	07:48 SC		00:36 AQ	13:59 AR		11:09 CA	00:46 LE	
18						10:41 CP			00:16 GE			03:45 LI
19	09:57 CA	11:35 VI			18:52 SA		04:07 PI	15:11 TA		16:48 LE	08:55 VI	
20				01:14 SC		16:57 AQ			03:50 CA			16:18 SC
21	18:03 LE		06:24 LI		03:54 CP		06:41 AR				20:25 LI	
22		00:05 LI				21:36 PI		17:39 GE	10:44 LE	02:16 VI		
23			19:10 SC	12:39 SA	11:01 AQ		09:11 TA					04:37 SA
24	04:33 VI	12:57 SC						22:13 CA	20:33 VI	14:12 LI	09:13 SC	
25				22:16 CP		01:06 AR						
26	17:02 LI		06:54 SA		16:13 PI		12:15 GE				21:30 SA	15:11 CP
27						03:46 TA		05:11 LE		02:56 SC		
28		00:29 SA	16:26 CP	05:34 AQ			16:32 CA		08:16 LI		08:26 CP	
29	05:49 SC					06:09 GE		14:29 VI				23:38 AQ
30				10:04 PI	20:59 TA							
31	16:30 SA		22:46 AQ				22:41 LE			15:23 SA		

1990

	January	February	March	April	May	June	July	August	September	October	November	December
01	06:11 PI		01:43 TA	12:50 CA	00:09 LE	23:31 LI	18:02 SC		20:51 AQ	13:43 PI		16:23 GE
02		19:27 TA		17:51 LE	07:18 VI						05:32 TA	
03	10:57 AR		03:38 GE					02:08 CP		17:42 AR		15:28 CA
04		22:12 GE				11:22 SC	06:36 SA		04:06 PI		05:06 GE	
05	14:04 TA		07:03 CA	01:42 VI				12:19 AQ		19:06 TA		16:00 LE
06		01:27 CA			05:22 SC	00:00 SA			08:23 AR		05:07 CA	
07	16:02 GE		12:25 LE				18:40 CP	19:54 PI		19:47 GE		19:39 VI
08		05:52 LE		11:45 LI	17:56 SA	12:12 CP	05:07 AQ		10:56 TA		07:24 LE	
09	17:52 CA		19:48 VI							21:29 CA		
10		12:13 VI		23:18 SC		23:10 AQ		01:13 AR	13:05 GE		12:48 VI	03:01 LI
11	21:02 LE				06:21 CP		13:29 PI			01:16 LE		
12		21:10 LI	05:10 LI					04:55 TA	15:53 CA		21:09 LI	
13				11:48 SA	17:31 AQ	08:00 PI	19:36 AR			07:20 VI		13:28 SC
14	02:57 VI							07:42 GE	19:52 LE			
15		08:35 SC	16:25 SC			13:55 AR	23:29 TA				07:40 SC	01:44 SA
16	12:18 LI			00:15 CP	01:55 PI			10:13 CA		15:26 LI		
17		21:08 SA				16:43 TA			01:18 VI		19:40 SA	14:35 CP
18			04:56 SA		06:32 AR		01:32 GE	13:12 LE		01:24 SC		
19	00:16 SC			10:53 AQ		17:14 GE			08:34 LI			
20		08:30 CP			07:43 TA		02:44 CA	17:33 VI		13:10 SA	08:32 CP	02:59 AQ
21	12:44 SA		17:01 CP	17:57 PI		17:09 CA						
22		16:52 AQ		20:59 AR			04:29 LE				21:07 AQ	13:48 PI
23	23:28 CP				07:00 GE	18:25 LE		00:17 LI		02:03 CP		
24		21:50 PI	02:31 AQ	21:04 TA			08:18 VI		05:52 SA			21:45 AR
25					06:34 CA	22:42 VI		09:56 SC		14:14 AQ	07:32 PI	
26	07:26 AQ		08:09 PI	20:13 GE			15:19 LI		18:37 CP			
27		00:16 AR			08:29 LE			21:57 SA			14:06 AR	02:09 TA
28	12:51 PI		10:16 AR	20:40 CA						23:22 PI		
29						06:47 LI	01:39 SC		05:54 AQ		16:37 TA	03:26 GE
30	16:34 AR		10:27 TA		14:08 VI			10:23 CP				
31			10:43 GE				14:00 SA			04:14 AR		03:03 CA

1991

	January	February	March	April	May	June	July	August	September	October	November	December
01						23:42 AQ						
02	02:55 LE	20:02 LI	06:03 LI	07:59 SA	03:55 CP		17:51 PI	16:32 TA	03:02 GE	14:59 LE	04:12 LI	16:33 SC
03												
04	04:57 VI	04:01 SC	13:08 SC			11:37 PI	03:34 AR	20:54 GE	06:20 CA	17:45 VI	10:08 SC	01:33 SA
05				20:20 CP	16:51 AQ							
06	10:33 LI	15:23 SA	23:36 SA			20:26 AR	09:52 TA	22:47 CA	08:13 LE	21:01 LI	18:21 SA	12:41 CP
07												
08	19:59 SC			08:59 AQ	04:04 PI		12:42 GE	23:09 LE	09:36 VI	01:59 SC		
09		04:16 CP	12:14 CP			01:13 TA					05:16 CP	01:27 AQ
10				19:17 PI	11:35 AR		13:03 CA	23:35 VI	11:52 LI	09:58 SA		
11	08:06 SA	16:17 AQ	00:31 AQ			02:37 GE					18:07 AQ	14:20 PI
12					15:08 TA		12:35 LE		16:43 SC			
13	21:00 CP			01:49 AR		02:17 CA		01:52 LI		21:10 CP		
14		01:59 PI	10:11 PI		16:03 GE		13:11 VI				06:34 PI	01:07 AR
15				05:06 TA		02:11 LE		07:34 SC	01:15 SA			
16	09:05 AQ	09:12 AR	16:38 AR		16:15 CA		16:34 LI			10:04 AQ	16:08 AR	08:10 TA
17		14:25 TA	20:40 TA	06:41 GE		04:03 VI		17:11 SA	13:03 CP			
18	19:24 PI				17:31 LE		23:41 SC			21:53 PI	21:50 TA	11:21 GE
19				08:18 CA		09:01 LI						
20		18:11 GE	23:37 GE		21:01 VI			05:35 CP	01:57 AQ			
21	03:28 AR			11:05 LE		17:18 SC	10:17 SA		13:20 PI	06:34 AR	00:23 GE	11:55 CA
22	09:01 TA	20:56 CA						18:27 AQ				11:38 LE
23		23:13 LE	02:27 CA	15:30 VI	03:08 LI		22:56 CP		21:55 AR	11:56 TA	01:25 CA	
24						04:16 SA						12:24 VI
25	12:07 GE		05:44 LE	21:37 LI	11:42 SC			05:51 PI		15:09 GE	02:37 LE	
26						16:50 CP	11:50 AQ		03:59 TA			15:38 LI
27	13:23 CA		09:41 VI		22:21 SA			15:01 AR		17:37 CA	05:12 VI	
28		01:50 VI		05:35 SC			23:35 PI		08:26 GE			
29	14:04 LE		14:50 LI					21:59 TA		20:21 LE	09:47 LI	22:04 SC
30				15:42 SA	10:40 CP	05:48 AQ			11:59 CA			
31	15:44 VI		22:02 SC				09:20 AR			23:47 VI		

1992

	January	February	March	April	May	June	July	August	September	October	November	December
01	07:31 SA				19:09 TA		22:16 LE				12:43 AQ	09:23 PI
02		14:09 AQ		03:05 AR		11:58 CA		08:17 LI		17:30 CP		
03	19:10 CP		09:11 PI				22:38 VI		00:50 SA			21:49 AR
04				11:19 TA	00:28 GE	13:35 LE		11:16 SC			01:12 PI	
05		02:50 PI	20:07 AR						10:07 CP	04:53 AQ		
06	07:59 AQ			17:33 GE	04:10 CA		00:28 LI	17:57 SA			13:19 AR	08:17 TA
07		14:15 AR			07:07 LE				22:09 AQ	17:38 PI		
08	20:52 PI		05:06 TA	22:18 CA			04:54 SC				23:19 TA	15:37 GE
09		23:36 TA						04:00 CP				
10			12:04 GE		09:56 VI	23:27 SC	12:17 SA		10:57 PI	05:36 AR		20:06 CA
11	08:22 AR			01:46 LE				16:07 AQ			06:50 GE	
12		06:09 GE	16:50 CA		13:06 LI		22:15 CP		23:02 AR	15:48 TA		22:47 LE
13	17:00 TA			04:09 VI		06:29 SA					12:20 CA	
14		09:32 CA	19:21 LE		17:16 SC			04:51 PI				
15	21:55 GE			06:11 LI			10:03 AQ		09:47 TA	00:08 GE	16:24 LE	00:56 VI
16		10:16 LE			23:22 SA			17:12 AR				
17	23:26 CA			09:10 SC			22:44 PI		18:40 GE		19:29 VI	03:33 LI
18		09:47 VI	20:55 LI			03:19 AQ						
19	22:57 LE			14:41 SA	08:13 CP			04:10 TA		11:01 LE		07:19 SC
20		10:05 LI	23:20 SC			15:59 PI	11:08 AR		00:59 CA			
21	22:22 VI			23:41 CP	19:44 AQ			12:37 GE		13:28 VI		12:42 SA
22		13:11 SC					21:37 TA		04:19 LE		00:52 SC	
23	23:43 LI		05:13 SA			04:03 AR		17:37 CA		14:40 LI		20:04 CP
24		20:26 SA		11:39 AQ	08:25 PI				05:08 VI		05:01 SA	
25			15:09 CP			13:29 TA	04:45 GE	19:15 LE		16:05 SC		
26	04:33 SC				19:52 AR				04:56 LI		11:38 CP	05:43 AQ
27		07:33 CP		00:20 PI			08:09 CA	18:46 VI		19:29 SA		
28	13:20 SA		03:45 AQ						05:44 SC		21:19 AQ	17:29 PI
29		20:34 AQ		11:14 AR	04:16 TA	21:43 CA	08:40 LE	18:10 LI				
30			16:24 PI						09:34 SA	02:18 CP		
31	01:08 CP				09:19 GE		08:01 VI	19:38 SC				06:08 AR

1993

	January	February	March	April	May	June	July	August	September	October	November	December
01	17:31 TA	11:15 GE		14:22 LE	00:00 VI	10:23 SC	01:49 CP	16:36 AQ			10:13 GE	02:17 CA
02			02:17 CA						21:21 AR	16:14 TA		
03	01:42 GE	16:57 CA		16:11 VI	01:20 LI	13:01 SA	09:14 AQ				20:24 CA	09:33 LE
04			05:41 LE					02:43 PI				
05	06:11 CA	18:51 LE		15:55 LI	01:57 SC	17:26 CP	19:10 PI		10:10 TA	04:27 GE		14:44 VI
06			05:53 VI					14:39 AR			04:06 LE	
07	07:49 LE	18:29 VI		15:32 SC	03:34 SA				22:17 GE	14:42 CA		18:04 LI
08			04:47 LI			00:40 AQ	07:11 AR	03:22 TA			08:47 VI	
09	08:20 VI	17:59 LI		17:10 SA	07:51 CP					21:34 LE		20:05 SC
10			04:40 SC			10:57 PI	19:37 TA		07:37 CA		10:42 LI	
11	09:30 LI	19:24 SC		22:24 CP	15:44 AQ			14:47 GE				21:40 SA
12			07:34 SA			23:14 AR			12:52 LE	00:36 VI	10:59 SC	
13	12:42 SC						06:06 GE	22:47 CA				
14		00:08 SA	14:28 CP	07:36 AQ	02:51 PI	11:19 TA			14:20 VI	00:47 LI	11:21 SA	00:06 CP
15	18:31 SA						13:08 CA					
16		08:21 CP		19:33 PI	15:25 AR			02:44 LE	13:44 LI	00:01 SC	13:34 CP	04:51 AQ
17			00:52 AQ			21:12 GE	16:48 LE					
18	02:47 CP	19:06 AQ						03:41 VI	13:14 SC	00:23 SA	19:08 AQ	12:58 PI
19			13:11 PI	08:15 AR	03:17 TA		18:24 VI					
20	13:01 AQ					04:05 CA		03:36 LI	14:53 SA	03:42 CP		
21		07:12 PI		20:08 TA	13:08 GE		19:40 LI				04:28 PI	00:18 AR
22	00:48 PI		01:51 AR			08:26 LE		04:27 SC	19:54 CP	10:50 AQ		
23		19:50 AR			20:38 CA		22:01 SC				16:30 AR	13:04 TA
24	13:28 AR		13:59 TA	06:28 GE		11:18 VI		07:45 SA		21:18 PI		
25									04:19 AQ			00:46 GE
26	01:37 TA	08:11 TA		14:46 CA	02:03 LE	13:46 LI	02:13 SA	13:58 CP			05:14 TA	
27			00:48 GE						15:13 PI	09:39 AR		
28		18:52 GE		20:40 LE		16:38 SC	08:27 CP	22:41 AQ			16:47 GE	09:47 CA
29			09:15 CA							22:20 TA		
30					08:18 LI	20:29 SA			03:29 AR			
31								09:18 PI				15:59 LE

1994

	January	February	March	April	May	June	July	August	September	October	November	December
01	20:15 VI		14:43 SC		16:35 AQ			11:05 GE				
02		07:49 SC		03:38 CP		18:31 AR	14:24 TA		15:37 LE	06:40 VI	20:19 SC	07:13 SA
03	23:31 LI		16:54 SA		00:47 PI							
04		11:14 SA		09:46 AQ				22:22 CA		08:57 LI	19:46 SA	06:43 CP
05			21:25 CP			07:14 TA	03:13 GE					
06	02:29 SC	16:02 CP		18:51 PI	12:01 AR				22:57 LI	09:22 SC	20:01 CP	07:52 AQ
07						20:04 GE	14:18 CA					
08	05:34 SA	22:17 AQ	04:15 AQ					11:42 VI		09:47 SA	22:48 AQ	12:25 PI
09				06:09 AR	00:50 TA		22:43 LE		00:26 SC			
10	09:16 CP		13:10 PI			07:23 CA				11:44 CP		21:04 AR
11		06:23 PI		18:47 TA	13:44 GE				02:26 SA		05:04 PI	
12	14:25 AQ		23:59 AR			16:29 LE	04:48 VI	17:56 SC		16:09 AQ		
13		16:50 AR							05:45 CP		14:44 AR	08:56 TA
14	22:03 PI			07:48 GE	01:28 CA	23:17 VI	09:15 LI	20:54 SA		23:18 PI		
15			12:28 TA						10:42 AQ			21:59 GE
16		05:20 TA		19:41 CA	10:59 LE		12:35 SC				02:45 TA	
17	08:42 AR					03:48 LI		00:18 CP	17:31 PI	08:56 AR		
18		18:06 GE	01:29 GE		17:32 VI		15:09 SA				15:42 GE	10:25 CA
19	21:22 TA			04:45 LE		06:20 SC		04:34 AQ		20:35 TA		
20			12:54 CA		20:55 LI		17:31 CP		02:29 AR			21:13 LE
21		04:28 CA		09:59 VI		07:32 SA		10:28 PI			04:21 CA	
22	09:35 GE		20:39 LE		21:51 SC		20:39 AQ		13:47 TA	09:28 GE		
23		10:48 LE		11:41 LI		08:37 CP		18:55 AR			15:33 LE	06:01 VI
24	18:56 CA				21:43 SA					22:16 CA		
25		13:27 VI	00:14 VI	11:19 SC		11:10 AQ	01:57 PI		02:41 GE			12:28 LI
26		14:06 LI			22:17 CP			06:13 TA			00:09 VI	
27	00:39 LE		00:47 LI	10:49 SA			10:31 AR		15:12 CA	09:05 LE		16:18 SC
28								19:07 GE			05:22 LI	
29	03:39 VI		00:15 SC	12:05 CP	01:19 AQ					16:22 VI		17:46 SA
30						02:07 AR			00:56 LE		07:22 SC	
31	05:34 LI		00:42 SA		08:03 PI		22:13 TA	06:59 CA		19:46 LI		17:58 CP

1995

	January	February	March	April	May	June	July	August	September	October	November	December
01	18:39 AQ	08:05 PI		16:59 TA	11:53 GE	19:17 LE	11:36 VI	01:24 LI	16:57 SA	01:11 CP	13:18 PI	00:51 AR
02	21:49 PI	14:12 AR	23:30 AR					07:29 SC	19:45 CP	04:00 AQ	19:21 AR	09:40 TA
03				04:50 CA	00:45 CA	05:47 VI	19:56 LI	11:14 SA	21:48 AQ	07:36 PI		20:35 GE
04		00:08 TA	08:51 TA	17:40 CA	12:55 LE						03:35 TA	
05												
06	04:57 AR	12:44 GE	20:56 GE	05:16 LE	22:33 VI	13:14 LI	01:19 SC	12:52 CP	00:09 PI	12:42 AR	13:55 GE	08:45 CA
07	15:58 TA					17:04 SC	03:38 SA	13:28 AQ	04:15 AR	20:05 TA		21:25 LE
08												
09		01:17 CA	09:41 CA						04:15 AR		01:57 CA	
10	01:17 CA			13:39 VI	04:30 LI	17:50 SA	03:43 CP	14:46 PI	11:22 TA	06:10 GE		09:27 VI
11	04:57 GE	11:32 LE									14:38 LE	
12			20:29 LE									
13	17:20 CA			13:39 VI	06:54 SC	17:05 CP	03:21 AQ	18:41 AR	21:48 GE	18:20 CA		19:09 LI
14			03:55 VI			16:52 AQ	04:37 PI					
15	18:52 VI	18:52 VI		20:13 SC	06:59 SA			02:26 TA			02:03 VI	
16												
17	00:01 LI		08:18 LI			19:13 PI	09:23 AR	13:40 GE	10:16 CA	06:47 LE	10:18 LI	01:07 SC
18		03:55 SC	10:52 SC	20:52 SA	06:36 CP		18:21 TA					
19	11:40 VI	11:40 VI				01:29 AR			22:19 LE	17:12 VI	14:41 SC	03:13 SA
20	17:54 LI		12:57 SA	21:54 CP	07:40 AQ			02:24 CA				
21		17:54 LI	15:31 CP		11:40 PI	11:35 TA	06:24 GE		08:01 VI	00:16 LI	15:57 SA	02:46 CP
22	22:33 SC			00:38 AQ				14:13 LE	14:50 LI	04:07 SC	15:48 CP	01:52 AQ
23		22:33 SC	19:10 AQ	05:51 PI	19:13 AR	00:02 GE	19:17 CA	23:50 VI				
24									19:20 SC	05:57 SA	16:15 AQ	02:45 PI
25												
26	01:37 SA	01:37 SA		13:42 AR	05:46 TA	12:57 CA	07:07 LE		22:31 SA	07:15 CP	18:59 PI	07:06 AR
27	03:27 CP	03:27 CP	00:18 PI					07:15 LI				
28		17:16 PI		23:53 TA	18:07 GE		17:13 VI					
29						01:02 LE		12:51 SC		09:24 AQ		15:22 TA
30	05:03 AQ		07:26 AR		06:59 CA							
31												

1996

	January	February	March	April	May	June	July	August	September	October	November	December
01	02:30 GE		16:47 LE			01:43 SA			12:20 TA	04:02 GE		
02		09:46 LE		21:27 LI	12:43 SC		12:06 AQ	23:05 AR			09:16 LE	06:11 VI
03	14:56 CA					02:29 CP			19:09 GE	13:15 CA		
04		21:22 VI	04:13 VI		16:04 SA		12:07 PI				21:57 VI	18:24 LI
05				03:57 SC		02:45 AQ		03:33 TA				
06	03:31 LE		13:41 LI		17:54 CP		14:42 AR		05:30 CA	01:12 LE		
07		07:30 LI		08:21 SA		04:20 PI					09:29 LI	03:39 SC
08	15:29 VI		21:06 SC		19:39 AQ		20:43 TA	22:58 CA		13:49 VI		
09		15:35 SC		11:30 CP		08:24 AR			17:55 LE		18:02 SC	08:59 SA
10					22:29 PI							
11	01:55 LI	20:59 SA	02:33 SA	14:09 AQ		15:11 TA	05:52 GE		06:29 VI	01:00 LI	23:27 SA	11:15 CP
12								11:29 LE				
13	09:30 SC	23:30 CP	06:08 CP	16:59 PI	03:01 AR		17:08 CA		17:51 LI	09:46 SC		12:14 AQ
14						00:16 GE					02:44 CP	
15	13:25 SA		08:15 AQ	20:43 AR	09:25 TA			00:08 VI		16:07 SA		13:44 PI
16		00:00 AQ				11:08 CA	05:31 LE		03:20 SC		05:15 AQ	
17	14:07 CP		09:50 PI		17:48 GE			11:56 LI		20:38 CP		16:55 AR
18		00:10 PI		02:06 TA		23:21 LE	18:17 VI		10:30 SA		08:00 PI	
19	13:15 AQ		12:15 AR					21:51 SC		23:52 AQ		22:09 TA
20		01:58 AR		09:55 GE	04:17 CA				15:12 CP		11:34 AR	
21	13:02 PI		16:58 TA			12:07 VI	06:14 LI					
22		07:08 TA		20:25 CA	16:28 LE			04:48 SA	17:39 AQ	02:23 PI	16:12 TA	05:17 GE
23	15:37 AR					23:38 LI	15:43 SC					
24		16:14 GE	00:59 GE					08:22 CP	18:43 PI	04:51 AR	22:19 GE	14:14 CA
25	22:17 TA			08:45 LE	04:59 VI		21:24 SA					
26			12:06 CA			07:54 SC		09:10 AQ	19:46 AR	08:12 TA		
27		04:10 CA		20:49 VI	15:33 LI		23:18 CP				06:37 CA	01:09 LE
28	08:43 GE					12:02 SA		08:49 PI	22:24 TA	13:35 GE		
29			00:38 LE		22:30 SC		22:48 AQ				17:30 LE	13:46 VI
30	21:11 CA			06:27 LI		12:48 CP		09:15 AR		21:57 CA		
31			12:15 VI				22:01 PI					

557

1997

Day	January	February	March	April	May	June	July	August	September	October	November	December
01	02:33 LI	04:51 SA	12:01 SA	03:59 AQ	12:50 PI	00:39 TA	11:36 GE	10:27 LE	04:27 VI		04:27 SA	18:38 CP
02										11:58 SC		23:58 AQ
03	13:02 SC	08:44 CP	17:39 CP	05:43 PI	14:59 AR	04:55 GE	18:33 CA	22:15 VI	17:30 LI		12:31 CP	
04										22:43 SA	18:33 AQ	04:08 PI
05	19:28 SA	09:21 AQ	19:55 AQ	06:20 AR	17:04 TA	11:03 CA	03:45 LE		06:10 SC			
06								11:17 LI	16:55 SA	07:04 CP	22:35 PI	07:25 AR
07		08:34 PI	19:57 PI	07:21 TA	20:21 GE	19:59 LE	15:22 VI					
08	21:55 CP							23:50 SC	00:24 CP	12:29 AQ	00:44 AR	10:01 TA
09		08:30 AR	19:33 AR	10:28 GE								
10	21:59 AQ				02:13 CA	07:44 VI	04:21 LI	09:46 SA	04:10 AQ	14:59 PI	01:46 TA	12:36 GE
11		10:57 TA	20:38 TA	17:03 CA								
12					11:33 LE	20:36 LI	16:20 SC	15:43 CP	04:59 PI	15:25 AR	03:05 GE	16:25 CA
13	21:51 PI	16:54 GE										
14			00:49 GE	03:22 LE	23:44 VI	07:51 SC	01:03 SA	17:59 AQ	04:25 AR	15:16 TA	06:33 CA	22:58 LE
15	23:21 AR	02:13 CA										
16			08:51 CA	16:00 VI	12:28 LI	15:39 SA	05:46 CP	18:02 PI	04:21 TA	16:27 GE	13:38 LE	
17	16:54 TA	13:53 LE										08:59 VI
18			20:08 LE	04:37 LI	23:12 SC	20:02 CP	07:29 AQ	17:45 AR	06:38 GE	20:46 CA	00:33 VI	
19	03:40 GE	02:38 VI										
20			08:59 VI	15:20 SC	06:51 SA	22:21 AQ	08:00 PI	18:57 TA	06:38 GE	05:11 LE	13:29 LI	21:35 LI
21	10:53 CA	15:23 LI										
22			21:35 LI	23:33 SA	11:51 CP	00:09 PI	09:04 AR	22:56 GE	12:33 CA	17:00 VI	01:43 SC	10:07 SC
23	20:29 LE											
24		02:56 SC	08:42 SC	05:33 CP	15:20 AQ	02:39 AR	11:54 TA	06:10 CA	22:13 LE	06:05 LI	11:28 SA	20:08 SA
25												
26	07:51 VI			09:51 AQ	18:18 PI	06:24 TA	17:04 GE	16:19 LE	10:28 VI	18:16 SC		02:49 CP
27			17:40 SA									
28	20:27 LI				21:18 AR				23:33 LI			
29												06:59 AQ
30	20:48 SC		00:07 CP				00:38 CA					
31												

1998

	January	February	March	April	May	June	July	August	September	October	November	December
01												
02	09:56 PI	21:25 TA	05:01 TA	19:10 CA	09:49 LE	03:21 VI			02:23 CP		11:27 AR	21:30 GE
03	12:44 AR		07:15 GE			15:17 LI	11:46 SC	07:48 SA	09:21 AQ	23:24 PI	11:12 TA	21:28 CA
04		01:09 GE		02:36 LE	19:47 VI							
05	15:53 TA		12:27 CA			04:06 SC	23:24 SA	17:18 CP	12:48 PI	00:32 AR	10:11 GE	23:56 LE
06		06:58 CA		13:26 VI	08:19 LI				13:53 AR	23:58 TA		
07	19:42 GE		20:46 LE		21:10 SC	15:35 SA	08:28 CP	23:31 AQ	14:17 TA		10:39 CA	06:22 VI
08										23:44 GE		
09		14:57 LE		02:05 LI	08:48 SA	00:51 CP	14:52 AQ	03:04 PI	15:41 GE		14:33 LE	16:44 LI
10	00:43 CA		07:36 VI							01:48 CA		
11		01:10 VI		14:55 SC	18:40 CP	08:03 AQ	19:22 PI	05:11 AR	19:20 CA			05:17 SC
12	07:45 LE		19:59 LI							07:25 LE	22:38 VI	
13		13:18 LI		02:52 SA	02:31 AQ	13:32 PI	22:45 AR	07:05 TA	01:48 LE			17:47 SA
14	17:31 VI									16:32 VI	09:58 LI	
15			08:51 SC	13:05 CP	08:04 PI	17:23 AR	01:33 TA	09:46 GE	10:51 VI			04:55 CP
16		02:14 SC										
17	05:45 LI		20:56 SA	20:42 AQ	11:06 AR	19:47 TA	04:18 GE	13:56 CA	21:57 LI	04:02 LI	22:42 SC	14:17 AQ
18		13:56 SA										
19	18:35 SC		06:43 CP	01:07 PI	12:06 TA	21:26 GE	07:43 CA	20:01 LE	10:22 SC	16:37 SC	11:13 SA	21:45 PI
20		22:30 CP		02:31 AR								
21			13:02 AQ		12:25 GE	23:39 CA	12:49 LE		23:05 SA			03:04 AR
22	05:26 SA			02:09 TA				04:22 VI		05:17 SA	22:46 CP	06:05 TA
23		03:10 AQ	15:43 PI		13:58 CA		20:34 VI					
24	12:40 CP			01:56 GE		04:04 LE		15:02 LI	10:31 CP	17:05 CP		
25		04:42 PI	15:49 AR		18:38 LE						08:43 AQ	07:22 GE
26	16:27 AQ			03:57 CA		11:55 VI	07:15 LI		18:54 AQ			
27			15:07 TA					03:25 SC		02:45 AQ	16:14 PI	
28	18:09 PI	04:42 AR				23:06 LI	19:45 SC					
29			15:38 GE					15:55 SA		08:58 PI	20:34 AR	
30											21:52 TA	
31	19:21 AR											

1999

	January	February	March	April	May	June	July	August	September	October	November	December
01	08:16 CA		10:05 VI			02:06 CP		16:47 AR		13:32 CA		17:29 LI
02		01:37 VI		12:49 SC	07:36 SA				05:25 GE		04:07 VI	
03	10:31 LE		18:34 LI			13:37 AQ	04:35 PI	21:08 TA		17:14 LE		
04		09:55 LI			20:12 CP				08:10 CA		11:56 LI	03:36 SC
05	15:49 VI			01:08 SA		23:01 PI	11:22 AR	23:57 GE		22:40 VI		
06		21:06 SC	05:23 SC						11:29 LE		21:45 SC	15:28 SA
07				13:39 CP	07:40 AQ		15:22 TA					
08	00:53 LI		17:47 SA			05:09 AR		01:52 CA	15:57 VI	05:52 LI		
09		09:38 SA			16:16 PI		16:59 GE				09:15 SA	04:14 CP
10	12:48 SC			00:24 AQ		07:44 TA		03:55 LE	22:16 LI	15:01 SC		
11		21:10 CP	05:54 CP		20:54 AR		17:27 CA				22:00 CP	16:59 AQ
12				07:35 PI		07:49 GE		07:22 VI				
13	01:23 SA		15:32 AQ		21:57 TA		18:25 LE		07:09 SC	02:18 SA		
14		05:57 AQ		10:46 AR		07:14 CA	21:39 VI	13:25 LI			10:46 AQ	04:18 PI
15	12:29 CP		21:31 PI		21:08 GE				18:35 SA	15:03 CP		12:30 AR
16		11:40 PI		11:07 TA		08:07 LE		22:41 SC			21:21 PI	
17	21:12 AQ				20:40 CA		04:19 LI					16:45 TA
18		15:07 AR	00:13 AR	10:39 GE		12:12 VI			07:13 CP	03:17 AQ		
19					22:38 LE		14:30 SC	10:32 SA			03:58 AR	17:39 GE
20	03:41 PI	17:29 TA	01:09 TA	11:28 CA		20:10 LI			18:38 AQ	12:33 PI		
21								22:59 CP			06:26 TA	
22	08:26 AR	19:54 GE	02:05 GE	15:06 LE	04:16 VI		02:49 SA			17:42 AR		16:52 CA
23						07:18 SC			02:51 PI		06:14 GE	
24	11:53 TA	23:09 CA	04:33 CA	22:05 VI	13:29 LI		15:09 CP	09:49 AQ		19:26 TA		16:32 LE
25						19:51 SA			07:34 AR		05:29 CA	
26	14:30 GE		09:22 LE					17:49 PI		19:34 GE		18:34 VI
27		03:44 LE		07:47 LI	01:05 SC		01:55 AQ		09:51 TA		06:18 LE	
28	16:57 CA		16:35 VI			08:12 CP		23:09 AR		20:09 CA		
29				19:13 SC	13:37 SA		10:27 PI		11:21 GE		10:11 VI	00:15 LI
30	20:16 LE					19:20 AQ				22:47 LE		
31			01:50 LI					02:40 TA				09:37 SC

2000

	January	February	March	April	May	June	July	August	September	October	November	December
01	21:33 SA	17:10 CP		08:13 PI	00:55 AR	16:35 GE	03:11 CA	13:27 VI	05:56 SC	22:51 SA		03:24 PI
02			13:14 AQ								06:41 AQ	
03		05:31 AQ		15:23 AR	04:54 TA	16:31 CA	02:39 LE	15:32 LI	14:10 SA			14:19 AR
04	10:24 CP		23:31 PI							09:44 CP	19:13 PI	
05		16:02 PI		19:30 TA	06:24 GE	16:47 LE	03:20 VI	21:05 SC				21:28 TA
06	22:53 AQ								01:48 CP	22:34 AQ		
07			06:55 AR	21:59 GE	07:14 CA	18:58 VI	06:47 LI				05:03 AR	
08		00:18 AR						06:31 SA	14:46 AQ			00:52 GE
09	09:59 PI		12:02 TA		09:02 LE	23:59 LI	13:49 SC			10:37 PI	11:13 TA	
10		06:21 TA		00:16 CA				18:45 CP				01:50 CA
11	18:48 AR		15:46 GE		12:42 VI				02:35 PI	19:52 AR	14:28 GE	
12		10:23 GE		03:16 LE		07:56 SC	00:06 SA					02:10 LE
13			18:52 CA		18:28 LI			07:44 AQ	12:01 AR		16:22 CA	
14	00:38 TA	12:46 CA		07:19 VI		18:19 SA	12:28 CP			02:06 TA		03:31 VI
15			21:44 LE					19:42 PI	19:05 TA		18:20 LE	
16	03:25 GE	14:12 LE		12:36 LI	02:18 SC					06:19 GE		07:02 LI
17						06:27 CP	01:27 AQ				21:16 VI	
18	04:01 CA	15:54 VI	00:49 VI	19:36 SC	12:10 SA			05:45 AR	00:22 GE	09:38 CA		13:12 SC
19						19:26 AQ	13:45 PI					
20	03:59 LE	19:22 LI	04:57 LI					13:32 TA	04:16 CA	12:43 LE	01:36 LI	21:58 SA
21				04:59 SA	00:02 CP							
22	05:08 VI		11:17 SC			07:52 PI		18:55 GE	07:01 LE	15:54 VI	07:34 SC	
23		01:58 SC		16:48 CP	13:01 AQ		00:10 AR		09:03 VI			08:55 CP
24	09:10 LI		20:43 SA			17:56 AR	07:45 TA	21:59 CA			15:33 SA	
25		12:10 SA							11:23 LI	19:31 LI		21:27 AQ
26	17:02 SC			05:43 AQ	01:08 PI		12:03 GE	23:17 LE				
27			08:52 CP			00:20 TA				00:25 SC	01:58 CP	
28		00:45 CP		17:06 PI	10:08 AR		13:30 CA	23:55 VI	15:31 SC			10:28 PI
29	04:18 SA		21:35 AQ			03:00 GE				07:41 SA	14:27 AQ	
30							13:24 LE					
31					15:02 TA			01:33 LI		18:02 CP		

Table 3

British Summer Time

Date	Time	Subtract
21/05/1916	2:00	-1:00
1/10/1916	2:00	0:00
8/04/1917	2:00	-1:00
17/09/1917	2:00	0:00
24/03/1918	2:00	-1:00
30/09/1918	2:00	0:00
30/03/1919	2:00	-1:00
29/09/1919	2:00	0:00
28/03/1920	2:00	-1:00
25/10/1920	2:00	0:00
3/04/1921	2:00	-1:00
3/10/1921	2:00	0:00
26/03/1922	2:00	-1:00
8/10/1922	2:00	0:00
22/04/1923	2:00	-1:00
16/09/1923	2:00	0:00
13/04/1924	2:00	-1:00
21/09/1924	2:00	0:00
19/04/1925	2:00	-1:00
4/10/1925	2:00	0:00
18/04/1926	2:00	-1:00
3/10/1926	2:00	0:00
10/04/1927	2:00	-1:00
2/10/1927	2:00	0:00
22/04/1928	2:00	-1:00
7/10/1928	2:00	0:00
21/04/1929	2:00	-1:00
6/10/1929	2:00	0:00
13/04/1930	2:00	-1:00
5/10/1930	2:00	0:00
19/04/1931	2:00	-1:00
4/10/1931	2:00	0:00
17/04/1932	2:00	-1:00
2/10/1932	2:00	0:00
9/04/1933	2:00	-1:00
8/10/1933	2:00	0:00
22/04/1934	2:00	-1:00
7/10/1934	2:00	0:00
14/04/1935	2:00	-1:00
6/10/1935	2:00	0:00
19/04/1936	2:00	-1:00
4/10/1936	2:00	0:00
18/04/1937	2:00	-1:00
3/10/1937	2:00	0:00
10/04/1938	2:00	-1:00
2/10/1938	2:00	0:00
16/04/1939	2:00	-1:00
19/11/1939	2:00	0:00
25/02/1940	2:00	-1:00
4/05/1941	3:00	-2:00
10/08/1941	3:00	-1:00
5/04/1942	3:00	-2:00
9/08/1942	3:00	-1:00
4/04/1943	3:00	-2:00
15/08/1943	3:00	-1:00
2/04/1944	3:00	-2:00
17/09/1944	3:00	-1:00
2/04/1945	3:00	-2:00
15/07/1945	3:00	-1:00
7/10/1945	2:00	0:00
14/04/1946	2:00	-1:00
6/10/1946	2:00	0:00
16/03/1947	2:00	-1:00
13/04/1947	3:00	-2:00
10/08/1947	3:00	-1:00
2/11/1947	2:00	0:00
14/03/1948	2:00	-1:00
31/10/1948	2:00	0:00
3/04/1949	2:00	-1:00
30/10/1949	2:00	0:00
16/04/1950	2:00	-1:00
22/10/1950	2:00	0:00
15/04/1951	2:00	-1:00
21/10/1951	2:00	0.00
20/04/1952	2:00	-1:00
26/10/1952	2:00	0:00
19/04/1953	2:00	-1:00
4/10/1953	2:00	0:00
11/04/1954	2:00	-1:00
3/10/1954	2:00	0:00
17/04/1955	2:00	-1:00
2/10/1955	2:00	0:00
22/04/1956	2:00	-1:00
7/10/1956	2:00	0:00
14/04/1957	2:00	-1:00
6/10/1957	2:00	0:00
20/04/1958	2:00	-1:00
5/10/1958	2:00	0:00
19/04/1959	2:00	-1:00
4/10/1959	2:00	0:00
10/04/1960	2:00	-1:00
2/10/1960	2:00	0:00
26/03/1961	2:00	-1:00
29/10/1961	2:00	0:00
25/03/1962	2:00	-1:00
28/10/1962	2:00	0:00
31/03/1963	2:00	-1:00
27/10/1963	2:00	0:00
22/03/1964	2:00	-1:00
25/10/1964	2:00	0:00
21/03/1965	2:00	-1:00
24/10/1965	2:00	0:00
20/03/1966	2:00	-1:00
23/10/1966	2:00	0:00
19/03/1967	2:00	-1:00
29/10/1967	2:00	0:00
18/02/1968	2:00	-1:00

Continuous until

Date	Time	Subtract
31/10/1971	2:00	0:00
19/03/1972	2:00	-1:00
29/10/1972	2:00	0:00
18/03/1973	2:00	-1:00
28/10/1973	2:00	0:00
17/03/1974	2:00	-1:00
27/10/1974	2:00	0:00
16/03/1975	2:00	-1:00
26/10/1975	2:00	0:00
21/03/1976	2:00	-1:00
24/10/1976	2:00	0:00
20/03/1977	2:00	-1:00
23/10/1977	2:00	0:00
19/03/1978	2:00	-1:00
29/10/1978	2:00	0:00
18/03/1979	2:00	-1:00
28/10/1979	2:00	0:00
16/03/1980	2:00	-1:00
26/10/1980	2:00	0:00
29/03/1981	2:00	-1:00
25/10/1981	2:00	0:00
28/03/1982	2:00	-1:00
24/10/1982	2:00	0:00
27/03/1983	2:00	-1:00
23/10/1983	2:00	0:00
25/03/1984	2:00	-1:00
28/10/1984	2:00	0:00
31/03/1985	2:00	-1:00
27/10/1985	2:00	0:00
30/03/1986	2:00	-1:00
26/10/1986	2:00	0:00
29/03/1987	2:00	-1:00
25/10/1987	2:00	0:00
27/03/1988	2:00	-1:00
23/10/1988	2:00	0:00
26/03/1989	2:00	-1:00
29/10/1989	2:00	0:00
25/03/1990	2:00	-1:00
28/10/1990	2:00	0:00
31/03/1991	2:00	-1:00
27/10/1991	2:00	0:00
29/03/1992	2:00	-1:00
25/10/1992	2:00	0:00

FINDING YOUR SUN-MOON COMBINATION

28/03/1993	2:00	-1:00	31/03/1996	2:00	-1:00	28/03/1999	2:00	-1:00
24/10/1993	2:00	0:00	27/10/1996	2:00	0:00	24/10/1999	2:00	0:00
27/03/1994	2:00	-1:00	30/03/1997	2:00	-1:00	26/03/2000	2:00	-1:00
23/10/1994	2:00	0:00	26/10/1997	2:00	0:00	29/10/2000	2:00	0:00
29/03/1995	2:00	-1:00	29/03/1998	2:00	-1:00			
22/10/1995	2:00	0:00	25/10/1998	2:00	0:00			

Table 4

Time Zones Around the World

These are the *normal* amounts that clock time is ahead of (+) or behind
(–) Greenwich Mean Time (GMT). An asterisk (*) indicates that
Summer Time is used in the country. Some countries have more than
one time zone. For detailed information, check with a computer-
calculation company (see page 473) which has definitive information
for each country in each year.

If the time zone is ahead (+), *deduct* that number of hours to obtain
your GMT time of birth.

If the time zone is behind (–), then you should *add* that number of
hours to obtain your GMT time of birth.

For example, if you were born in Western Australia you will see that
it is given as +8 hours, indicating that it is normally 8 hours ahead of
GMT. Therefore *deduct* this number of hours from your birth time before
consulting the tables that enable you to find your Sun and Moon sign.

AFGHANISTAN	+4 hours	BARBADOS	–4 hours*
ALBANIA	+1 hour*	BELGIUM	+1 hour*
ALGERIA	+1 hour*	BELIZE	–6 hours*
ANDORRA	+1 hour	BENIN	+1 hour
ANGOLA	+1 hour	BERMUDA	–4 hours*
ANGUILLA	–4 hours	BHUTAN	+5.5 hours
ANTIGUA AND		BOLIVIA	–4 hours
BARBUDA	–4 hours	BOPHUTHATSWANA	+2 hours
ARGENTINA	–2 hours*	BOTSWANA	+2 hours
AUSTRALIA		BRAZIL	–2,–3,–4,
CAPITAL TERRITORY	+10 hours*		–5hours*
NEW SOUTH WALES	+10 hours*	BRUNEI	+8 hours
NORTHERN		BULGARIA	+2 hours*
TERRITORY	+9.5 hours*	BURKINA FASSO	GMT
QUEENSLAND	+10 hours*	BURMA	+6.5 hours
SOUTH AUSTRALIA	+9.5hours*	BURUNDI	+2 hours*
TASMANIA	+10 hours*	CAMBODIA	
VICTORIA	+10 hours*	(=KAMPUCHEA)	+7 hours
WESTERN		CAMEROON	+1 hour
AUSTRALIA	+8 hours*	CANADA	
AUSTRIA	+1 hour*	ALBERTA	–7 hours*
BAHAMAS	–5 hours*	BRITISH COLUMBIA	–8 hours*
BAHRAIN	+3 hours	MANITOBA	–6 hours*
BANGLADESH	+6 hours	NEW BRUNSWICK	–4 hours*

NEWFOUNDLAND	−4 hours*	GUADELOUPE	−4 hours
NOVA SCOTIA	−4 hours*	GUAM	+10 hours
ONTARIO	−5 hours*	GUATEMALA	−6 hours
PRINCE EDWARD ISLE	−4 hours*	GUINEA	GMT
QUEBEC	−5 hours*	GUINEA–BISSAU	GMT
SASKATCHEWAN	−7 hours*	GUYANA	−3 hours
YUKON	−8 hours*	HAITI	−5 hours
CAPE VERDE	+1 hour*	HONDURAS	−6 hours
CAYMAN ISLANDS	−5 hours*	HONG KONG	+8 hours*
CENTRAL AFRICAN		HUNGARY	+1 hour*
REPUBLIC	+1 hour*	ICELAND	GMT
CHAD	+1 hour*	INDIA	+5 hr 30m
CHILE	−6 hours*	INDONESIA	+9 hours*
CHINA	+8 hours*	IRAN	+3hrs 30m
CISKEI	+3 hours*	IRELAND	GMT*
COLOMBIA	−5 hours*	ISRAEL	+2 hours*
COMORES	+3 hours*	ITALY	+1 hour*
CONGO	+1 hour*	IVORY COAST	GMT
COOK ISLANDS	+10 hours*	JAMAICA	−5 hours*
COSTA RICA	−6 hours*	JAPAN	+8 hours
CUBA	−5 hours*	JORDAN	+2 hours
CYPRUS	+2 hours*	KAMPUCHEA	+7 hours
CZECHOSLOVAKIA	+1 hour*	KENYA	+3 hours
DENMARK	+1 hour*	KIRIBATI	
DJIBOUTI	+3 hours*	(GILBERT ISLANDS)	+10 hours
DOMINICA	−4 hours*	KOREA, NORTH	+9 hours
DOMINICAN REPUBLIC	−4 hours*	KOREA, SOUTH	+9 hours
EQUADOR	−5 hours*	KUWAIT	+3 hours
EGYPT	+2 hours*	LAOS	+7 hours
EL SALVADOR	−6 hours	LEBANON	+2 hours*
ENGLAND	GMT*	LESOTHO	+2 hours
EQUATORIAL GUINEA	+1 hour	LIBERIA	GMT
ETHIOPIA	+3 hours*	LIBYA	+1 hour*
FAROE ISLANDS	GMT	LIECHTENSTEIN	+1 hour*
FIJI	+12 hours*	LUXEMBOURG	+1 hour*
FINLAND	+2 hours*	MACAO	+8 hours
FRANCE	+1 hour*	MADAGASCAR	+3 hours
FRENCH GUIANA	−3 hours	MALAWI	+2 hours
FRENCH POLYNESIA	−10 hours	MALAYSIA	+8 hours
GABON	+1 hour*	MALI	GMT
GAMBIA	GMT	MALTA	+1 hour*
GERMANY	+1 hour*	MARTINIQUE	−4 hours
GHANA	GMT	MAURITANIA	GMT
GIBRALTAR	+1 hour*	MAURITIUS	+4 hours
GREECE	+2 hours*	MAYOTTE	+3 hours
GREENLAND	+1 hour*	MEXICO	zones −6, −7,
GRENADA	−4 hours		−8 hours*

MIDWAY ISLANDS	+11 hours	SOMALIA	+3 hours
MONACO	+1 hour*	SOUTH AFRICA	+2 hours
MONGOLIA	+9 hours	SPAIN	+1 hour*
MONTSERRAT	–4 hours	SRI LANKA	+5hrs 30m
MOROCCO	GMT	SUDAN	+2 hours
MOZAMBIQUE	+2 hours	SURINAM	–3 hours
NAMIBIA	+2 hours	SWAZILAND	+2 hours
NAURU		SWEDEN	+1 hour*
(PLEASANT ISLAND)	+12 hours	SWITZERLAND	+1 hour*
NEPAL	+5hr 30m	SYRIA	+2 hours*
NETHERLANDS	+1 hour*	TAIWAN	+8 hours*
NEW ZEALAND	+12 hours*	TANZANIA	+2 hours
NICARAGUA	–5 hours	THAILAND	+7 hours
NIGER	+1 hour	TOGO	GMT
NIGERIA	+1 hour	TONGA	+13 hours
NORWAY	+1 hour*	TRANSKEI	+2 hours
OMAN	+4 hours	TUNISIA	+1 hour*
PACIFIC ISLES		TURKEY	+3 hours*
TRUST TERR	+12 hours	UGANDA	+3 hours
PAKISTAN	+5 hours	UNITED ARAB	
PANAMA	–5 hours	EMIRATES	+4 hours
PAPUA NEW GUINEA	+10 hours	UNITED STATES	
PARAGUAY	–4 hours*	OF AMERICA	
PERU	–5 hours	EASTERN STANDARD	
PHILIPPINES	+8 hours	TIME	–5 hours*
PITCAIRN	–8hrs 30m	CENTRAL STANDARD	
POLAND	+1 hour*	TIME	–6 hours*
PORTUGAL	GMT*	MOUNTAIN	
PUERTO RICO	–4 hours	STANDARD TIME	–7 hours*
QATAR	+3 hours	PACIFIC STANDARD	
REUNION	+4 hours	TIME	–8 hours*
ROMANIA	+2 hours*	URUGUAY	–3 hours*
RUSSIA	zones +2,	VANUATU	+11 hours
	+3, +4, +5,	VENDA	+2 hours
	+6, +7, +9	VENEZUELA	–4 hours
RWANDA	+2 hours	VIETNAM	+7 hours
SANTA LUCIA	–4 hours	YEMEN,	
SAN MARINO	+1 hour*	NORTH & SOUTH	+3 hours
SAUDI ARABIA	+3 hours	FORMER YUGOSLAVIA	+1 hour*
SEYCHELLES	–4 hours	ZAIRE	+2 hours
SIERRA LEONE	GMT	ZAMBIA	+2 hours
SINGAPORE	+8 hours	ZIMBABWE	+2 hours
SOLOMON ISLANDS	+11 hours		

FOR YOUR FURTHER ASTROLOGICAL STUDY

The major address for astrological information is:

396 Caledonian Road,
London N1 1DN
Fax: 0171-700 6479

This is the home of The Urania Trust, the educational charity dedicated to promoting astrological education. Send a 6.5" x 9" stamped addressed envelope, or three international postal coupons, for a free copy of the latest *Astrology Yearbook* which gives information about astrology world-wide. The same address is the home of the Astrological Association of Great Britain which is open to astrologers at all levels. It produces the excellent bi-monthly *The Astrological Journal*. Also at this address is The Faculty of Astrological Studies, founded in 1948, which runs highly regarded correspondence courses, day courses and summer schools at all levels.

FURTHER READING

Campion, Nick. *The Practical Astrologer*, Cinnabar Books (1993).

Davison, Ronald. *Astrology*, Aurora Publishers (1993).

Fenton, Sasha. *Moon Signs*, Aquarian (1992).

Goodman, Linda. *Sun Signs*, Pan Books (1994).

Greene, Liz. *Astrology for Lovers*, Aquarian (1993).

Greene, Liz and Sasportas, Howard. *The Luminaries*, Weiser (1993).

Lewi, Grant. *Astrology for the Millions*, Llewellyn (1994).

Lewi, Grant. *Heaven Knows What*, Llewellyn (1994).

Orr, Marjorie. *Lovers' Guide*, Aquarian (1992).

Paul, Haydn. *Lord of the Light*, Element Books (1991).

Parker, Derek & Julia. *Parkers' Astrology*, Dorling Kindersley (1992).

Parker, Derek & Julia. *Sun & Moon Sign Library*, Dorling Kindersley (1992).